ADULT
DEVELOPMENT
AND AGING

A LIFE-SPAN PERSPECTIVE

ADULT DEVELOPMENT AND AGING

A LIFE-SPAN PERSPECTIVE

DAVID F. HULTSCH
FRANCINE DEUTSCH

The Pennsylvania State University

McGraw-Hill Book Company

New York St. Louis San Francisco Auckland Bogotá Hamburg
Johannesburg London Madrid Mexico Montreal New Delhi
Panama Paris São Paulo Singapore Sydney Tokyo Toronto

This book was set in Helvetica by Black Dot, Inc.
The editors were Patricia S. Nave, Janis M. Yates, and David Dunham;
the designer was Anne Canevari Green;
the production supervisor was Phil Galea.
The photo editor was Linda Gutierrez.
The drawings were done by Fine Line Illustrations, Inc.
R. R. Donnelley & Sons Company was printer and binder.

**ADULT DEVELOPMENT AND AGING
A LIFE-SPAN PERSPECTIVE**

1 2 3 4 5 6 7 8 9 0 DODO 8 9 8 7 6 5 4 3 2 1 0

See Acknowledgments on pages 409-415.
Copyrights included on this page by reference.

Library of Congress Cataloging in Publication Data

Hultsch, David F
    Adult development and aging.

    Bibliography: p.
    Includes indexes.
    1. Adulthood—Psychological aspects. 2. Aged—
Psychology. 3. Aging—Psychological aspects.
I. Deutsch, Francine, date   joint author.
II. Title. [DNLM: 1. Adult—Psychology. 2. Aged—
Psychology. 3. Aging. 4. Human development.
WT150 H917a]
BF724.5.H84   155.6   80-19013
ISBN 0-07-031156-0

To our parents and grandparents

David S. Hultsch	Arthur Deutsch
Lucille F. Hultsch	Dorace Deutsch
Elmer Y. Fries	Elaine Deutsch
Sarah G. Fries	Irving Deutsch
Olivia H. Warner	Bessie Asher
Stanley E. Warner	Fred Asher

from Dave and Fran with love

CONTENTS

PART II
BEHAVIORAL PROCESSES

PART III
THE LIFE COURSE

PREFACE

The last ten years have marked the reemergence and articulation of a view of development which has come to be known as the life-span developmental perspective. The objective of this text is to examine behavior development during adulthood and aging within the context of this perspective. This text is intended primarily for upper-division undergraduates in the behavioral sciences, particularly psychology and human development. The text should be accessible to students with a background in introductory psychology or human development. At the same time, it should provide the basis of study for students with more advanced backgrounds (e.g., courses in child development, adolescent development, etc.).

Point of View

Texts often present information in an encyclopedic manner. That is, they set forth the "facts." However, the facts available about any given topic are generally diverse and often conflicting. In our view, then, an understanding of a topic requires a framework within which the information may be integrated as well as the information itself. In this text, we will use the emerging life-span developmental perspective to integrate the theory and research related to adult development and aging. The life-span approach represents a conceptual orientation characterized by emphasis on:

1. *The description, explanation, and optimization of behavior:* the questions of what behaviors occur, why behaviors occur, and how to alter behaviors are considered equally important for understanding development.

2. *Multidirectional development:* processes of growth and decline occur at all points in the life cycle. Development, therefore, is not defined as a continuous process of growth, and aging is not defined as a continuous process of decline.

3. *The individual in context:* development is the result of interactions among multiple processes and events, including those related to age and to history. In order to understand development, we must look at the interaction between the individual and the contexts in which he or she lives (e.g., physical, familial, cultural, historical).

4. *Multiple theories and methods:* an adequate understanding of development cannot be obtained from any one theory or methodology, nor can it be obtained from a cataloging of empirical facts.

Organization

Individuals attempting to teach a course or write a text on adult development and aging immediately confront a difficult choice: should the material be organized by focusing on developmental processes or by examining the various stages of the adult life span? This choice is a difficult one, since there are positive features to both strategies. For example, a focus on processes allows one to appreciate the changes over time in the individual's biological, psychological, and social functioning. On the other hand, a focus on age stages allows one to understand the processes and life events which characterize particular portions of the adult life cycle: young adulthood, middle age, and old age.

In this text, we capitalize on the strengths of both approaches. Initially, we examine basic developmental processes which reflect the fundamental changes occurring during adulthood and aging. Subsequently, we examine the unique features of different portions of the adult life course which emerge as a consequence of the interaction between the basic processes and the larger social and historical context.

In our view, this organization follows logically from the life-span developmental perspective. The life-span perspective directs our attention to behavior-change processes. Thus, we first examine basic theoretical and empirical information related to these changes over the entire age range involved. However, the life-span view also emphasizes relations among processes and how these are influenced by normative and nonnormative events in the individual's context. In our view, this integration of the individual and context is best achieved by focusing on life transitions and life events. Thus, we turn our attention to the transitions and events associated with young adulthood, middle age, and old age. The book is organized as follows:

Part I, Conceptual Framework: In this part (Chapters 1 and 2), we describe the life-span developmental perspective and review the research methods used to investigate development. These chapters provide a framework within which the information on adult development and aging may be integrated and evaluated.

Part II, Behavioral Processes: In this part (Chapters 3 to 7), we examine changes in basic processes throughout adulthood. Biological, intellectual, learning and memory, personality, and social processes are considered.

Part III, The Life Course: Finally, in this part (Chapters 8 to 12) we examine the integration of processes, person, and context within a life-course perspective. Chapter 8 introduces the section by outlining a life-event and life-transition framework. Chapters 9 to 11 examine the transitions and events unique to young adulthood, middle age, and old age. Finally, Chapter 12 is devoted to death and dying—the final event in life.

Special Features

We have included a number of special features that will make the book more interesting and helpful to the student.

Chapter overviews.   Each chapter begins with a brief statement about its focus, a listing of the first- and second-order headings, and a list of issues to consider when reading the chapter. These overviews should orient the student to the chapters.

Chapter summaries.   Each chapter ends with a summary of the main points of the chapter. These summaries should aid the student in reviewing the chapter.

Boxed inserts.   Throughout the text, we have highlighted certain material by placing it in boxed inserts. These inserts are designed to accomplish various ends. Some are designed to provide an in-depth look at topics introduced in the text or to illustrate different techniques for measuring development. Others are "asides" designed to provide case examples or to illustrate interesting new ideas or controversies in the field.

Glossary.   A glossary of specialized terms that have been used in the text is provided at the end of the book.

References.   An extensive reference list at the end of the text permits the instructor and student to follow up topics of interest.

Instructor's manual.   A manual summarizing the main points of each chapter and including an extensive list of test questions, film suggestions, and other instructional aids is available to all instructors who adopt the text.

Acknowledgments

The journey from idea to published text is a long and arduous one. Many people helped us along the way and we wish to express our appreciation to them.

To our colleagues at Penn State and other institutions around the country who reviewed various drafts of the manuscript: Harry J. Berman, Sangamon State University; David Brodginsky, Rutgers University; Don C. Charles, Iowa State University; Vivian P. Clayton, Columbia University; Nancy W. Denney, University of Kansas; Diane Papalia Finlay, University of Wisconsin at Madison;

Margaret J. Gatz, University of Southern California; Gunhild O. Hagestad, Penn State University; Bert Hayslip, Jr., North Texas State University; Rita Heberer, Belleville Area College; Richard M. Lerner, Penn State University; Lynn S. Liben, Penn State University; Robert B. Mitchell, Penn State University; Rolf H. Monge, Syracuse University; Marion Perlmutter, University of Minnesota; Paul Roodin, State University of New York at Oswego; Ilene C. Siegler, Duke University Medical Center; Michael A. Smyer, Penn State University; Elizabeth J. Susman, Penn State University; and Edward W. Wickersham, Penn State University.

To our secretarial staff, Sally Barber, Joy Barger, Kathy Hooven, and Alice Saxion, who typed the many drafts of the manuscript, and especially to Barbara Huntley, who organized and double-checked everything.

To the anonymous individuals who talked with us about the events in their lives so that some of the ideas in the book could be illustrated by the experiences of real people.

To Linda Gutierrez, who researched and selected the photographs for the text.

To Jan Yates and David Dunham, our editors, and all of the staff at McGraw-Hill who turned our raw material into a finished product.

And finally, to our families and friends, and especially to Cindy, David, Debby, Amy, Carole, Joe, and Hedy (Talitha Dora), who provided their love and support.

To all of you, our warmest thanks.

David F. Hultsch
Francine Deutsch

ADULT DEVELOPMENT
AND AGING

A LIFE-SPAN PERSPECTIVE

CONCEPTUAL
FRAMEWORK

PART 1

A LIFE-SPAN DEVELOPMENTAL PERSPECTIVE

CHAPTER
OVERVIEW

How does one approach a complex topic such as adult development and aging? Many perspectives are possible, and several will be reviewed in this chapter. In particular, we will present the attributes of the life-span developmental ap-

proach, which constitutes the major conceptual framework for this book.
Introduction
A Scientific Perspective
    Models of human development
    Developmental issues

A Life-Span Developmental Perspective
    Defining a life-span developmental perspective
    Descriptive issues
    Explanatory issues
    Optimization and intervention issues
Conclusion

ISSUES
TO CONSIDER

What is the nature of scientific inquiry?
What general assumptions do the mechanistic, organismic, and contextual world views make about development?
How do the three world views differ in terms of their position on the nature-nurture issue?
What are the goals of develop-

mental research from the life-span developmental perspective?
What types of change does the life-span developmentalist focus on?
What are the major characteristics of the life-span developmental orientation?
Why does the life-span developmental perspective em-

phasize descriptive dimensions other than chronological age?
What major sources of influence on development are proposed by the life-span developmental perspective?
What features characterize the life-span developmentalist's approach to intervention?

INTRODUCTION

During adulthood we experience many events which give shape and substance to the life course. Consider how you would answer the following question: *What was the last major event in your life that, for better or worse, interrupted or changed your usual activities?*

How did adults of varying ages respond to this question? Consider the following excerpts from responses to it.

Pam, age 25

Getting married, of course, but really having our child. At the time, I felt very prepared, but looking back on it, I realize I wasn't prepared at all. Of course, I don't think it was a mistake. But there is so much more to parenting than you can ever learn from books or friends. You get tense, you get exhausted, and all your needs come last—the child always comes first. People tell you this before you have the baby, but you don't realize it until you are in the situation. Every three hours they eat, and every three hours or oftener, they have to be changed. You might have a week when you don't sleep because they are teething—it just physically wears you down. Jim has really helped a lot with this. Some men will sleep all night while the wife may be up every night for several months. But we are trying to split it up. One night, I'll get a full night's sleep, and the next night Jim will. That has really helped. I know if I'm just burdened one day with motherhood, I can depend on him to pick up and do the job. Once you make some of these adjustments, it makes parenting a little simpler. But we weren't really aware of how much time and adjustment Brian would take. It took having him to realize it.

Bob, age 30

That would have to be the trouble with the business. I sell and service air conditioners. I just opened the business about four years ago, and there were a lot of start-up costs. But just as I was beginning to get on my feet, this energy thing hit for real. Sales of air conditioners have really fallen off because of the cost of electricity. Even people who already have it aren't using it. I'll tell a customer that he needs a couple of hundred bucks worth of repairs on his central system, and he'll tell me that he'll do without it this summer. Between the drop in business and this crazy inflation, we're really getting squeezed. Besides the business loan, we owe a couple of thousand on our car. Then there's the usual credit card bills. On top of everything else our roof has started to leak, and it looks like the whole thing will have to be replaced. I'm not sure where we go from here. We've talked about trying to get another loan from the bank, but I don't know what we'll be able to get. I do know that if business doesn't pick up soon we're going to be in real trouble.

Frank, age 48

Well, that's easy. Four years ago, I was selling stocks in New York. Now I'm writing novels in central Pennsylvania. I was the great American success story—lots of money, two houses, two cars, the whole bit. But I just wasn't getting anything out of it. I was working too hard, and drinking too much. My marriage was falling apart, mostly because we never spent any time together. I still remember the day it all came to a head. I was sitting in the usual traffic jam on my way to the office when I said to myself, 'Why do I need all this crap?" I turned around, went home, and Carol and I talked about it all day. Of course, it all took a while—I think the whole thing scared us both. But after about a year and a half of discussion and planning, I quit my job and we moved out here. What a difference it's made. I mean I still work hard, but now I feel some satisfaction at the end of the day. Carol has gotten back into her painting, and our marriage has improved one hundred percent. One funny thing in all this has been the reaction of our old friends. They thought we were out of our minds. But one fellow comes to visit us every summer. I can tell he isn't happy, and that he wants to do the same kind of thing, but I'm not sure he will take the risk. And you know it is a risk. We weren't sure it would work. It has required a lot of adjustments. But we knew we had to do something, and for us this has worked.

Joan, age 42

My son getting married, and then having my granddaughter. This happened a little over two years ago. Paul was 18 then and Suzie was only 17. They were still in high school and Suzie got pregnant. That part was very difficult. My husband passed away quite a few years ago, so Paul and I were quite close. At first, I was so afraid this was going to ruin his life, I guess I handled it badly. I tried to convince him he was making a mistake, and there were several weeks of tears and arguments. The final straw came when I told Suzie's father about their plans. You see, they had asked me not to tell him—but I thought he had a right to know. That was a mistake. He beat her up and threw her out of the house. I felt so badly that I stopped arguing with the kids, and they moved in with me. Since then, Paul has finished high school and is working in a TV repair shop. He's taking courses part-time at the University too. And, of course, there's Amy. She just had her second birthday last week, and she's as cute as she can be. I guess it was hard on all of us, but when I look at that little girl I know it worked out for the best.

Max, age 62

Well, my heart attack, I guess. That certainly changed my activities, I used to work sixteen hours and smoke three packs of cigarettes a day. Now, I only work half days at the office, and no smoking. I guess it has been a change for the best. It was a pretty severe attack. I was in intensive care for three weeks, and it took almost six months before I could get around much. That was really frustrating. But I am beginning to get used to taking it slower. The doctor says if I go back to my old style I'll just do myself in. I still worry about the business though. My partner has been doing most of the work, and I know I am going to have to make some hard decisions soon. I guess I'm just not ready to retire yet.

Life events such as the birth of a child, changing a long-standing career, suffering a heart attack, or entering a new career late in life can be planned or unplanned, but, regardless, they all require adjustment. The timing and sequencing of life events are often important to successful adjustment.

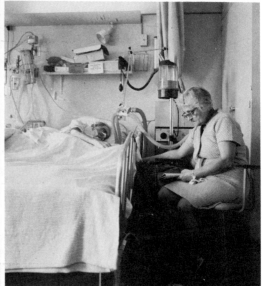

Alex Webb/Magnum

Michael Weisbrot

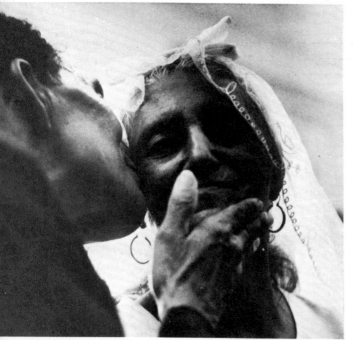

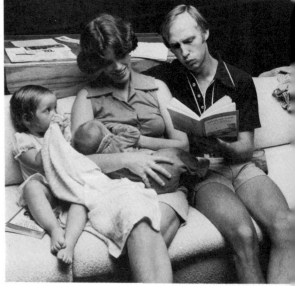

United Press International

Abigail Heyman/Magnum

Lydia, age 75

Well, about six years ago, I had been through some domestic problems. I had just gotten divorced. My first husband died, I had married again, and it didn't work out. It was a very unhappy time for me. After the divorce, I had taken a job, but I could only earn a certain amount of money before I lost my Social Security. So finally, I stopped work. Then, one Sunday morning I happened to pick up The New York Times *and saw an article about the Grey Panthers. One of the reporters at the* Times *had interviewed Maggie Kuhn, the founder. I hadn't heard of the Grey Panthers before that. I read this article and it hit me like a ton of bricks, and I said "This is exactly the way I feel. I would love to become involved in this movement." Everything that was said appealed to me. So I finally made arrangements through a mutual friend to meet Maggie. We had lunch together and we were friends from the beginning. That was six years ago. I have been working with the Grey Panthers ever since on the Media Watch Program. We monitor the media, particularly TV, and complain about the negative images of older people that they show. We have been working at it for four years and even the networks have told us we are responsible for some of the changes that have taken place. I feel I have a responsibility to do this because I am aware that older people are still valuable and are still able to be useful. Older people still have a lot to contribute to society. This work has been life to me because I was in a very depressed state before, and I don't know what I would have done. This was something that brought real life to me.*

We all experience various events during our lives. Indeed, adulthood and aging may be viewed as a series of transitions defined by such events. As you can see, different events were important to different people. Each event is like a snapshot which conveys some of the raw meaning of adult life. But in another sense, these snapshots are isolated personal experiences with little meaning outside of themselves. How can we use such information in order to understand the similarities and differences among adults. How can we place these snapshots into a sequence or film of adult life? No one sees events exactly as they are. We use different lenses in order to film the events of adult life. That is, we make certain assumptions and apply certain techniques of analysis in order to understand them. In this book, we will primarily use two sets of lenses.

First, we will attempt to understand adult development and aging from a scientific perspective, particularly that offered by the behavioral sciences such as psychology and sociology. The scientific perspective differs from a common-sense, religious, or mathematical perspective primarily because of its emphasis on the scientific method. The *scientific method* focuses on systematic, controlled, and objective investigation of relationships among objects and events. It suggests that in order to understand adult development and aging, we must somehow "get outside ourselves" so our subjective beliefs may be observed and tested against objective criteria.

Second, we will attempt to understand adult development and aging from a life-span developmental perspective. According to this perspective development is not a process of continuous growth nor is aging a process of continuous decline. Rather, processes of growth and decline are believed to occur at all points in the life cycle. In addition, the life-span developmental perspective focuses on interactions between the individual and the various contexts (familial, social, historical) in which he or she lives. Because of this emphasis, the life-span developmental approach draws information from many disciplines and stresses the usefulness of diverse theories and methods of investigation.

A SCIENTIFIC PERSPECTIVE

Scientists use a specific set of procedures to separate reality from myth. The fundamental task of scientists is to observe events in the world and to measure *variables* (characteristics of persons, objects, or events) objectively under particular conditions. Then scientists attempt to identify consistent relations among observations. Such regular, predictable relationships among variables are called *laws*. Finally, a *theory*—a set of statements consisting of defined and interrelated concepts integrating these laws—is developed. A theory serves to integrate knowledge and to guide further research.

Even though we can separate reality from myth by relying upon this *empirical* approach (objective observation) to knowledge and can detail what steps—observation, laws, and theory—are involved, a glance at the scientific literature shows that scientists do not agree about their observations, laws, and theories. This is the case primarily because scientists make different philosophical assumptions about the nature of the world. They consider facts to be abstractions they impose on nature through their use of specific assumptions. One way of thinking about these different assumptions is in terms of models (Lachman, 1960; Reese & Overton, 1970). How is a model defined?

A *model* is a representation of something. That is, a model does not describe reality, but represents reality *as if* it were thus and so. As such, a model functions as a metaphor. For example, consider a diagram of a stereo system. Such a diagram or model represents elements of the stereo system and depicts their interrelationships so the system can be assembled. The model is more or less useful to the extent that it serves as an effective guide for this task. Likewise, models of people serve as guides for the study of human development.

Since models are representations, they can differ in their degree of generality. Depicting the elements of a stereo system and their interrelationships, for example, represents the most specific type of model—a *scale model*. Theoretical models represent the next level of increasing generality. A useful *theoretical model* helps us to interpret, apply, and extend a theory by suggesting certain research questions (Reese & Overton, 1970). Theoretical models are developed within the context of broader models, sometimes termed *paradigms of science*. These are intended to represent large domains of knowledge such as an entire discipline (e.g., an area of study, such as psychology). Still broader models are termed *world views*. These are intended to represent all phenomena in the universe.

A model, regardless of its level of generality, can never be considered as true or false because it consists of untestable assumptions. Like scale models and theoretical models, paradigms of science and world views are evaluated according to their usefulness.

Models of Human Development

General representations of phenomena—world views and paradigms of science—constitute the basic assumptions within which scientists' work is rooted. Since developmentalists generate theories and research to explain human behavior from these two general levels of models, let us examine several major world views and their associated paradigms.

There are many potential world views and paradigms and many ways of classifying them (Pepper, 1942). However, three paradigms rooted in three corresponding world views appear to be particularly significant to the study of human development at the present time. As summarized in Table 1.1, these are the *reactive-organism*, *active-organism*, and *dialectical* paradigms rooted in the *mechanistic*, *organismic*, and *contextual* world views, respectively.

Mechanistic world view and reactive-organism paradigm The basic metaphor of the mechanistic world view is a machine. In this model, reality is represented as being composed of discrete parts located in time and space. Complex phenomena are ultimately reducible to these elementary parts and their relationships. In other words, the whole is equal to the sum of the parts. For the mechanist, movement of the parts depends on the application of forces outside the person which result in chainlike sequences of events.

Applied to the study of human development, the mechanistic world view yields a reactive model of development. The individual is seen as inherently at rest. Activity, and therefore change, is the result of external forces. Further, change is quantitative rather than qualitative. Complex activities such as emotions and problem solving are ultimately reducible to simple elements. As a consequence, there is no overall purpose to human activity—no end point or goal for behavior.

TABLE 1.1

WORLD VIEWS AND PARADIGMS OF SCIENCE RELEVANT TO
THE STUDY OF HUMAN DEVELOPMENT

World view	Mechanistic	Organismic	Contextual
Developmental paradigm	↓ Reactive organism	↓ Active organism	↓ Dialectical

Organismic world view and active-organism paradigm For some scientists, the universe is considered to be more like a biological organism than a machine. Reality is depicted as interrelated parts which constitute a complex organized system. The whole is always equal to more than the sum of the parts because complex phenomena are never reducible to elementary parts and their relationships. The parts of the organism only have meaning when they are considered in the context of the system of which they are a part. The organicist sees the universe as inherently active. Movement comes from within rather than from the application of external forces.

Applied to the study of human development, the organismic world view produces an active model of development. Individuals are considered to be dynamic. Development is explained by the individual's action on the environment. Moreover, change is considered to be qualitative rather than quantitative. Development is assumed to be directed toward some goal or end point.

Contextual world view and dialectical paradigm The basic metaphor of the contextual world view is the historic event. In this model, the essence of reality is represented as an ongoing, dynamic, and dramatic act or event. These events are composed of continually changing patterns. Like the organismic world view, contextualism emphasizes the interconnectedness of events. However, unlike the organismic model, it denies that the universe is directed toward some ideal form or goal. Rather, continuous change and novelty are seen as the basic nature of reality. Such continual change means that our understanding of the universe depends on when we look at it. Change is considered to be both quantitative and qualitative.

Applied to the study of human development, the contextual world view yields a dialectical model of development. From this perspective the individual is seen as continually changing. Activity is the result of reciprocal interactions between the changing individual and the changing context. This produces both quantitative and qualitative change. A single goal or end point of development is not assumed. Rather, multiple patterns of development are assumed as a function of the interaction between the changing individual and the changing context.

Developmental Issues

What is the impact of the mechanistic, organismic, and contextual world views and related paradigms on the study of human development? We may examine this question by asking a series of additional questions:

What changes?
What type of change occurs?
How is change explained?
Why does change occur?

Each of these questions involves a basic developmental issue, and each world view provides a different answer. Table 1.2 summarizes the developmental questions and how each is answered by the three world views. Let us examine the question "Why does change occur?" in the context of the *nature-nurture controversy* as an example of how the various world views differ from one another. This controversy revolves around the extent to which development is assumed to be a function of hereditary versus environmental influences. Most contemporary writers make the assumption that both *heredity* and *environment* are involved in development. However, the various world views make different assumptions about the relationship among these influences (Lerner, 1978).

The mechanistic world view assumes that heredity and environment are independent influences on behavior. The mechanist focuses on the question, "How much of each is involved in behavior?" From this perspective, one could suggest that intelligence is 80 percent heredity and 20 percent environment, or that personality is 40 percent heredity and 60 percent environment. Depending on the behavior involved, either heredity or environment may be predominant. In contrast, the organismic and contextual world views assume that the relationship between nature and nurture is *interactive*. That is, both nature and nurture must be fully present to produce development. Rather than the question "How much of each?" these world views ask the question "How?" That is, how do heredity and environment interact to produce development? While the organismic and contextual world views both take an interactive position, they differ in terms of the degree of interaction assumed. The organismic world view takes a *weak interaction position*. This position views nature as the basic influence, with nurture determining the rate or end point of development. The contextual world view takes a *strong interaction position* (Overton, 1973). This position views nature and nurture as completely interdependent. The same hereditary influences will lead to different outcomes within different environmental contexts, and the same environmental influences will lead to different outcomes in interaction with different hereditary influences.

Since each of the world views supplies different answers to the basic questions involved in the study of human development, which set of assumptions is correct? The answer is all of them and none of them. Because models represent the world rather than describe it, they cannot be proven true or false. In spite of this, many scientists spend time trying to show empirically that their perspective is correct while that of others is not supported. But to criticize one set of assumptions on the basis of a different set of assumptions is an unproductive exercise. Support for a model—"truth"—is relative to the particular perspective alone.

Implications of Models and Issues

What are the implications of the different assumptions derived from the various world views for the study of adult development and aging? Do they really make

TABLE 1.2

SUMMARY OF DEVELOPMENTAL ISSUES ACCORDING TO THE MECHANISTIC,
ORGANISMIC, AND CONTEXTUAL WORLD VIEWS

	Answers		
Question	Mechanistic World View	Organismic World View	Contextual World View
What changes?	Person represented as a machine; individual behaviors *added* to assess functioning of the whole. Focus on observable *behavior change* and on identifying factors that facilitate or interfere with behavior. No concern for optimum functioning (competence) that is directed toward an end state. Change may be *multidirectional*.	Person represented as a biological organism. Behaviors have meaning in relation to the whole system *(holism)*. Parts are *interactive*, and the whole is more than the sum of its parts. Focus on internal *structures*. Structures are functional when they serve an intended purpose, contribute to maintaining the whole, or have specific uses. Observable behavior used to infer structures and *structural change*. Interest in optimum functioning (competence) that is directed toward an end state. Change is *unidirectional*.	Person represented as an ongoing event. Behaviors are a part of a whole system *(holism)*. Behaviors have meaning only in relation to the entire system because parts are *interactive*. Focus on ways individuals interact in various environments over time (biological, social and physical). These interactions represent *transactional change*. Change may be *multidirectional*.
What type of change occurs?	Changes in behavior viewed as differences in degree *(quantitative change)*. Stage viewed as a sequence of quantitatively identical behaviors.	Changes in behavior viewed as differences in kind *(qualitative change)*. Stage viewed as an organized pattern of structural changes. Structural changes inferred from behavior rather than observed directly.	Changes in behavior viewed as differences in both degree *(quantitative change)* and kind *(qualitative change)*. Observed stages are different, depending on the *context*.
How is change explained?	Focus on establishing *cause-effect sequences*. Various mechanisms (reinforcement, punishment, extinction, etc.) determine quantitative change in behavior.	Focus on how behaviors are interrelated or *structured* and what *functions* are served by different structures.	Focus on identifying degree or kinds of *interactions* between organism and context. Products of the current and past context account for change. Change explained as the result of continual contradictions (asynchronies) within or between interactions.
Why does change occur?	Nature and nuture viewed as independent influences on behavior. Either nature or nuture may be predominant depending on the behavior involved.	Nature and nuture viewed as interactive but separate influences on behavior.	Influences viewed as totally interdependent. Nature and nuture viewed as interactive influences on behavior.

12

a difference? Indeed they do. As we have mentioned, facts are not naturally occurring events awaiting discovery. Rather, facts attain their meaning as they are interpreted within the context of a particular set of assumptions. Thus, the developmental issues generated by the various world views shape the theories that investigators use to interpret the facts derived from research. Furthermore, in shaping theories, the assumptions of the various world views shape the basic research questions used to uncover the facts in the first place. As a result, different theories arrive at different descriptions and explanations of the phenomena of adult development and aging. Each world view, then, has generated a "family" of theories (Reese & Overton, 1970). For example, the theories of Bijou and Baer (1961) and Bandura and Walters (1963) are consistent with the mechanistic world view; those of Erikson (1959), Piaget (1950), and Kohlberg (1969) are consistent with the organismic world view; and that of Riegel (1976) is consistent with the contextual world view. We will consider these different theoretical views in detail in later chapters.

A LIFE-SPAN DEVELOPMENTAL PERSPECTIVE

Where does this multitude of assumptions and theories leave us? Which approach is most useful? In our view, it is probably premature to accept any one approach at the present time. One set of assumptions and the theories they generate may be useful for understanding particular processes, while another set may be more useful for understanding others. The contrast among views, more than the view provided by any one set of assumptions and theories alone, will assist us in understanding adult development and aging.

However, such *pluralism* (use of many perspectives) alone can cause confusion. A framework is needed within which the multiple issues generated by a pluralistic set of models and theories can be integrated and applied to research questions. In our view, the *life-span developmental approach* provides such a framework. This approach is not a world view or a theory. Rather it is an orientation to the study of human development. We will see that supporters of this orientation hold much in common with the contextual world view (Baltes, Reese, & Lipsitt, 1980). However, they do not reject the usefulness of theory and research derived from the mechanistic and organismic world views. The life-span developmental perspective, then, supports the use of many perspectives. It provides a framework within which to integrate the diverse information currently available about human development. What are the characteristics of the life-span developmental approach?

Defining a Life-Span Developmental Perspective

A number of writers have attempted to articulate the characteristics of the life-span developmental approach (Baltes, 1973; Baltes, Reese, & Lipsitt, 1980;

THE LIFE-SPAN DEVELOPMENTAL APPROACH: OLD WINE IN A NEW BOTTLE

The life-span developmental approach has had a major impact on the field of developmental psychology within the last ten years. However, like other significant ideas, the approach is actually quite old, as illustrated by the following statement:

We mean by "development" all those changes which occur to constitute the life history of the individual. The infant does not merely start out from birth to become a school child or to attain voting age; his aim is far more complex than that. He sets out, from the moment of conception rather than from the moment of birth, and his goal is the production of an old man or woman; indeed, the ultimate goal of development is death.

Thus growth and decay are both developmental phenomena. The prenatal influences which prepare the way for an individual, and the enduring influences which he leaves behind him after his departure from life, should also be included in a study of his development. Perhaps the most important questions in the science of psychology, as well as in our general understanding of human affairs is, "How do people come to be what they are?" This, in the main, is the problem of developmental psychology. (Hollingworth, 1927, p. 2)

As you can see, this quotation is over fifty years old and is found in a text entitled *Mental Growth and Decline: A Survey of Developmental Psychology* written by H. L. Hollingworth. The life-span perspective, then, is not new.

Baltes (1979) recently has reviewed the history of the life-span perspective. His analysis suggests that it is grounded in three major works published in the eighteenth and nineteenth centuries—by Tetens in 1777, Carus in 1808, and Quetelet in 1835. In particular, Quetelet's volume entitled *A Treatise on Man and the Development of His Faculties* anticipates many current theoretical and methodological issues. With one exception (Sanford, 1902), Baltes (1979) notes that the life-span perspective lay dormant during the late nineteenth and early twentieth centuries, but it reappeared again in the 1920s and 1930s with the publication of three books, one by Hollingworth

in 1927, one by Bühler in 1933, and one by Pressey, Janney, and Kuhlen in 1939. In addition to emphasizing the basic concept of change over the entire life span, these texts are process-oriented and focus on many of the issues discussed in this chapter, such as multidirectional development, contextual influences, and social-evolutionary change.

What is the significance of the roots of the life-span perspective? Baltes (1979) points out that the significance goes beyond historical curiosity. "It indicates that the involvement of current life-span researchers in such themes as cohort effects, social change, and other macro-level features might be intrinsic to a life-span orientation rather than a reflection of the personal interest of the individual researchers" (p. 261). That is, the historical consistency and longevity suggest that these issues are central and significant ones.

While the writings of early proponents such as Hollingworth, and Pressey, Janney, and Kuhlen, laid the foundation for a life-span perspective, their work received limited recognition. In our view, the principal reason for this lack of interest on the part of other researchers is that the ideas of these life-span proponents were inconsistent with the predominant world views and paradigms of the time. Since the 1940s, however, and particularly during the last ten years, the life-span view has gained increasing recognition. For example, the volumes generated by a series of conferences at West Virginia University have explicitly presented a life-span perspective (Baltes & Schaie, 1973; Datan & Ginsberg, 1975; Datan & Reese, 1977; Goulet & Baltes, 1970; Nesselroade & Reese, 1973; Turner & Reese, 1980). The perspective increasingly has formed a framework for conceptualizing research, (e.g., Lerner & Ryff, 1978; Hultsch & Plemons, 1979). Finally, an increasing number of texts have used it as a framework (e.g., Baltes, Reese, & Nesselroade, 1977; Goldberg & Deutsch, 1977; Lerner & Spanier, 1980). It appears that within the current historical climate, the seeds of a life-span perspective may have fallen on fertile ground.

Baltes & Willis, 1977; Lerner & Ryff, 1978). A hallmark of this approach is the assumption that development occurs at all points along the life span from conception to death. This is an important assertion because traditional views of human development, consistent with the organismic world view, have emphasized maturation and growth during infancy, childhood, and adolescence; stability during adulthood; and degeneration and decline during old age. The emphasis on the pervasiveness of change throughout the life span, however, does not completely define the life-span developmental approach. More generally, the life-span developmental approach to the study of development is characterized by certain goals, concepts of change, and theoretical issues which typically have not been stressed in the various age-specific approaches.

Specifically, we may define the life-span developmental approach as follows: The life-span developmental approach is concerned with the description, explanation, and optimization of intraindividual changes in behavior, and interindividual differences in such changes in behavior, from conception to death (Huston-Stein & Baltes, 1976). Let us examine each of the components of this definition.

Description, explanation, and optimization   Life-span development-alists focus on three tasks: *description*, *explanation*, and *optimization* (Baltes, Reese, & Lipsitt, 1980; Huston-Stein & Baltes, 1976). The task of description involves the questions, "What is changing?" and "When is it changing?" The tasks of explanation and optimization involve the questions, "Why is something changing?" and "How can it be changed?" respectively.

Behavior-change processes   The target phenomena of the life-span developmental approach are *behavior-change processes*. Traditional age-change functions are seen as a special case of a more general set of behavior-change functions (Baltes & Willis, 1977). Since *age-change functions* only point out what behaviors are related to age, chronological age is viewed as a descriptive variable only. Life-span developmentalists may begin their research by asking the same question of different age groups in order to gain insights into the developmental processes involved at different age points. However, they will go beyond a comparison of age stages to an analysis of the processes involved in observed changes. Thus, the life-span approach does not require a comparative analysis of individuals at all points in the life span (Huston-Stein & Baltes, 1976; Lerner & Ryff, 1978).

Intraindividual change and interindividual differences   In focusing on the description, explanation, and optimization of behavior change across the life span, two phenomena—intraindividual change and interindividual differences—are of central interest to life-span developmentalists. Intraindividual change refers to change within an individual over time. Interindividual differences refer to differences between individuals at a given point in time.

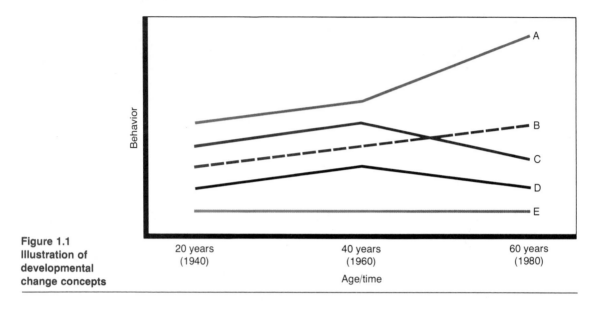

**Figure 1.1
Illustration of
developmental
change concepts**

From a life-span developmental perspective, it is vital to center both on intrainidividual change and on differences in such change between individuals (interindividual differences in intrainidividual change). These concepts are illustrated in Figure 1.1. This figure represents the scores of five hypothetical individuals (A to E) on a hypothetical behavior obtained at three points in time. The scores of four of the individuals (A to D) exhibit some change over the forty-year period. This change within individuals is what is meant by *intraindividual change (within-person change)*. One individual (E) does not exhibit such change. At each point in time, there are also differences in scores between individuals. For example, at time 1 (20 years of age), A scores higher than B, who scores higher than C, and so on. These differences between individuals are what we mean by *interindividual differences (between-person differences)*. Finally, the rate or direction of change may be different for various individuals. For example, from time 1 to time 2, the scores of persons A to D increase by the same amount. There are no differences in rate or direction of change. From time 2 to time 3, however, such differences exist. For example, the scores of individuals A and B continue to increase, while those of individuals C and D decrease. Similarly, the score of individual A increases more than that of B. These differential changes are what we mean by interindividual differences in intraindividual change (*between-person differences in within-person change*).

Now that we have defined a life-span developmental approach, let us examine several descriptive, explanatory, and optimization issues generated by this perspective.

Descriptive Issues

Multidirectional change   Traditional perspectives of change are based on a biological concept of development (Harris, 1957). In these traditional approaches, development is seen as unidirectional (moving in one direction only), irreversible, qualitative, goal-directed, and universal—characteristics which apply to the biological maturation of all organisms. Development ceases once *maturity* is reached (Freud, 1949; Piaget, 1972), and maturity is followed by stability and eventual decline as the organism ages (Hall, 1922). This traditional definition of development is consistent with the organismic world view.

From a life-span developmental perspective, however, such a biologically based definition of development is too narrow. Rather, development occurs at all points in the life span of the individual. Change is seen as *multidirectional* (Baltes, 1973; Baltes & Willis, 1977). That is, life-span development may be characterized by multiple patterns of change differing in terms of onset, direction, duration, and termination (Baltes, 1979; Baltes, Reese, & Lipsitt, 1980). In particular, a multidirectional perspective implies that behavior-change processes may show increments as well as decrements during the latter portion of the life cycle. This view is depicted in Figure 1.2 for several hypothetical behavior-change processes.

As a specific example of the multidirectionality of development, consider Horn's (1970, 1978) work on intelligence. Horn distinguishes between two types of intelligence, which exhibit different patterns of change during adulthood. He states, "Intelligence may thus both decrease and increase in adulthood; crystallized intelligence, if properly measured in samples of people who remain in the stream of acculturation, increases; fluid intelligence decreases" (Horn,

Figure 1.2
Illustration of hypothetical examples of multidirectional developmental change. Behavior-change processes differ in terms of their onset, directionality, duration, and termination over the course of the life cycle. *(Based on Baltes, 1979.)*

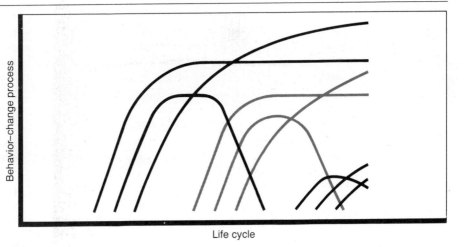

The many roles of Eleanor Roosevelt through her life span illustrate intraindividual change. From young to old, her family and societal (work) roles changed over her life span, while her impact maintained its effectiveness. (Culver Pictures)

1970, pp. 465–466). Examples of crystallized abilities, which increase during adulthood, include the ability to define words. Examples of fluid abilities, which do decline during adulthood, include the ability to visualize objects in space (See Chapter 4).

The concept of multidirectional development departs most sharply from traditional views because it suggests the potential for growth during adulthood and old age. We have just mentioned that abilities involving crystallized intelligence may increase with increasing chronological age during adulthood. Another example of the potential for growth during adulthood is provided by Butler's (1963) work on the life-review process. Butler proposes that older adults engage in a mental process of reviewing their life. This process is a response to the fact of impending death. It does not reflect mental deterioration or personality dysfunction. Rather, it can be a constructive process in which past experiences, particularly unresolved conflicts, are reviewed and reintegrated. Although the life review may lead to depression, guilt, and anxiety, depending on a number of factors, the process often leads to revised or expanded understanding. This understanding can give new meaning to life and mitigates the fear of death. Butler (1963) comments: "It seems likely that in the majority of elderly a substantial reorganization of the personality does occur. This may help to account for the evolution of such qualities as wisdom and serenity, long noted in some of the aged (p. 69)." Butler's description of the potential for significant personality growth in the very old illustrates our point that development occurs over the entire life span (See Chapter 6).

From a life-span developmental perspective, therefore, development is seen as involving multiple patterns of change for different behaviors and different individuals at different points in time. One result of such multidirectionality is that between-person differences tend to increase over the life span as within-person changes become increasingly divergent.

Descriptive continuity and discontinuity   An issue that is related to the direction and form of change concerns the question of whether change is continuous or discontinuous. *Descriptive continuity* occurs when behaviors at a later point in time may be described as increases or combinations of elements present at an earlier point in time. *Descriptive discontinuity* occurs when new or qualitatively different behaviors emerge at a later point in time.

For example, Costa and McCrae (1980) propose that personality may be described by three major dimensions: neuroticism, extraversion, and openness to experience. They indicate that these dimensions do not show qualitative change over time. That is, while there may be between-person differences in neuroticism, extraversion, and openness to experience, the nature of the dimensions and their relationships in a given individual do not change over the adult life cycle. This is a case of descriptive continuity.

Erikson (1959), on the other hand, theorizes that personality develops according to a fixed sequence of stages. Each of these stages is characterized by a crisis. The individual must accomplish certain developmental tasks during each stage in order to resolve the crisis, and thus, be able to meet the demands of later stages. The issues surrounding each crisis are unique. From this perspective, then, personality in young adulthood (focused on the development of intimacy) is qualitatively different from personality in midlife (focused on the development of generativity). This is a case of descriptive discontinuity.

A life-span perspective suggests that both types of description are useful. On the one hand, different types of description may be useful for different behavioral domains. That is, one behavioral domain may be best described as involving continuous change, and another may be best described as involving discontinuous change. On the other hand, the same behavioral domain may be best described in different ways at different points in the life span. For example, Reese (1976) has suggested that memory development may be qualitatively different during childhood, but vary quantitatively during adulthood.

Descriptive dimensions: chronological age, cohort, and life transitions In the previous sections, *chronological age* is referred to as a descriptive dimension along which behavior-change functions may be charted. However, from a life-span developmental perspective, chronological age is not necessarily the most useful descriptive variable available (Baltes, 1973; Baltes & Willis, 1977). Chronological age is only useful as a descriptive variable to the extent that within-person change patterns are homogenous enough to produce a high *correlation* between age and behavior change (Baltes & Willis, 1977). If large between-person differences in these patterns exist, then the use of chronological age as an organizing dimension is likely to be unproductive. Moreover, as we mentioned earlier, between-person differences in change tend to increase during adulthood as a function of the multidirectional nature of development. As a result, the life-span approach emphasizes the usefulness of examining several descriptive dimensions. In addition to chronological age, at least two other time-related variables—cohort and life transitions—appear to be useful.

Cohort may be defined by reference to year of birth (Schaie, 1965). Someone born in 1942, for example, is a member of the 1942 cohort. The specific range of time involved is arbitrary (it may be a month, a year, a decade, and so on). In other words, an individual is considered a member of a given cohort when born within a given range of time. Like age, cohort is a useful organizing variable to the extent to which between-person differences exhibit a high correlation with variables that change with time. Examples of potential cohort-related variables include historical changes in nutrition, health status, educational practices, and family structure (Baltes, Cornelius, & Nesselroade, 1979).

The usefulness of the cohort variable is demonstrated by research on intellectual development during adulthood (e.g., Schaie, 1979; see also Chapter 4). For example, Nesselroade, Schaie, and Baltes (1972) analyzed measures of several dimensions of intelligence obtained from members of eight birth cohorts (1866 to 1932) measured at two points in time (1956, 1963). Fifty-nine-year-olds measured in 1963 (1904 cohort) scored higher than fifty-nine-year-olds measured in 1956 (1897 cohort). The cohort differences reported were as large as, if not larger, than the age changes.

Life transitions may be defined by reference to life events such as marriage, birth of children, and retirement. While not all individuals experience these events, they are sufficiently widespread to serve as potentially useful organizing variables. For example, Lowenthal, Thurnher, and Chiriboga (1975) examined four life transitions defined by graduation from high school, marriage, the last child leaving home, and retirement. They found these significant events to be very useful as dimensions within which to investigate adult development. Such life events are referred to as normative life events.

Thus, from a life-span developmental perspective, chronological age is only one dimension along which behavior change functions may be charted. Other sequential variables such as cohort and life transitions may be equally useful.

Explanatory Issues

The changing individual in a changing world   Traditional views of development consistent with the organismic world view have emphasized the changing individual in a static world. In contrast, the life-span approach emphasizes a dynamic and interactive view of the relationship between the individual and the world (Lerner & Spanier, 1978).

How can this dynamic interaction between person and environment be explained? Baltes, Reese, and Lipsitt (1980) specify three major influence patterns that affect this relationship: (1) normative, age-graded influences, (2) normative, history-graded influences, and (3) nonnormative, life-event influences. *Normative, age-graded influences* consist of biological and environmental determinants that are correlated with chronological age. They are normative to the extent that their timing, duration, and clustering are similar for many individuals. Examples include maturational events such as changes in height, endocrine system function, and central nervous system function, and socialization events such as marriage, childbirth, and retirement. *Normative, history-graded influences* consist of biological and environmental determinants that are correlated with historical time. They are normative to the extent that they are experienced by most members of a cohort. In this sense, they tend to define the developmental context of a given cohort. Examples include historic events such as wars, epidemics, and periods of economic depression or prosperity, and sociocultural evolution such as changes in sex-role expectations, the educational system, and childrearing practices. Both age-graded and history-graded influences are related to time. The third system—*nonnormative, life-event influences*—cannot be directly related to time, since these events do not occur for all people, or even for most people. In addition, when nonnormative influences do exist, they are likely to differ significantly in terms of clustering, timing, and duration. Examples of nonnormative events are illness, divorce, promotion, and death of a spouse.

In general, the relationship among normative, age-graded influences, normative, history-graded influences, and nonnormative, life-event influences is dynamic and reciprocal. They are dynamic in that they are continually changing, and they are related reciprocally because each influence source has an effect on the other and, in turn, is affected by it.

A simplified example of the role of these multiple-influence systems on development is shown in Figure 1.3. This figure depicts the flow of three cohorts of individuals through time. The various life periods of each cohort occur at different points in historical time. Thus, each cohort is exposed to different normative, history-graded influences. Within this context, members of the cohort are exposed to normative, age-graded influences—the nature of which may vary from one cohort to another. Finally, members of the cohort are exposed to unique clusters of life events which vary in terms of their occurrence,

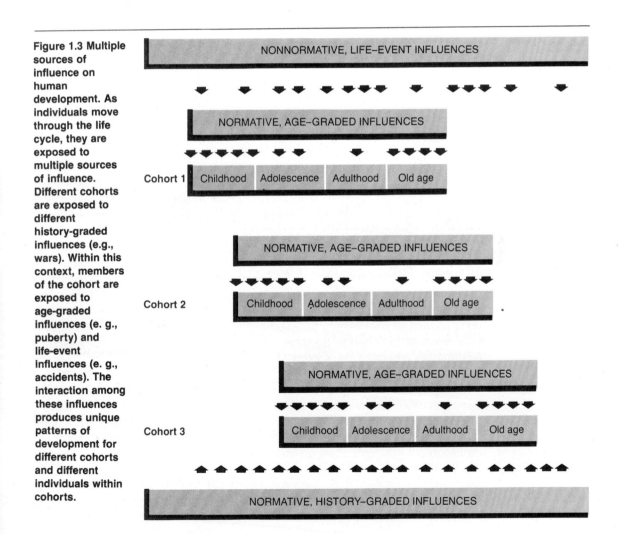

Figure 1.3 Multiple sources of influence on human development. As individuals move through the life cycle, they are exposed to multiple sources of influence. Different cohorts are exposed to different history-graded influences (e.g., wars). Within this context, members of the cohort are exposed to age-graded influences (e. g., puberty) and life-event influences (e. g., accidents). The interaction among these influences produces unique patterns of development for different cohorts and different individuals within cohorts.

timing, and duration for different individuals. The interaction among these multiple sources of influence produces different patterns of development for different cohorts and different individuals within cohorts.

Baltes, Reese, and Lipsitt (1980) have speculated that these three sources of influence exhibit different profiles over the life cycle. They suggest that normative, age-graded influences are particularly significant in childhood and again in old age, reflecting the importance, in those portions of the life cycle, of development based on maturation. Normative, history-graded influences are particularly significant during adolescence and young adulthood, reflecting the importance of the sociocultural context as the individual begins adult life. Finally, nonnormative, life-event influences are particularly significant during middle adulthood and old age, reflecting increasing between-person differences as individuals experience unique life events. Such a perspective accepts the idea that change is multidirectional.

Explanatory continuity and discontinuity The issue of continuous and discontinuous change is relevant to the task of explanation as well as the task of description (Huston-Stein & Baltes, 1976; Baltes & Willis, 1977). When the same sources of change account for behavior at different points in time, we have *explanatory continuity*. However, when different sources of change account for behavior at different points in time, *explanatory discontinuity* occurs. For example, Piaget (1950) emphasizes explanatory continuity. While different cognitive structures emerge at different points in the life span, these are explained by the same basic mechanisms. Kohlberg (1973), on the other hand, emphasizes explanatory discontinuity. He suggests that early moral development may be related to maturational variables but that later moral development may be related to experiential variables. Similar explanations of cognitive development have been suggested (Flavell, 1970).

A life-span perspective suggests that both types of explantion are useful. As we have seen, the life-span approach stresses the reciprocal interaction of multiple systems of influence. These processes result in multidirectional development and increasing between-person differences with increasing chronological age. Such a view suggests the likelihood of explanatory discontinuity as well as explanatory continuity. While a single explanatory mechanism may account for change in some behavioral domains, discontinuity among explanatory mechanisms is likely to be found in others.

Timing and patterning Current behavior may be related to events which have occurred in the past. Kagan and Moss (1962) report an interesting phenomenon which they call a "sleeper effect," which illustrates how past events may predict current behavior. As part of a longitudinal study of development from birth through young adulthood, Kagan and Moss found that maternal behaviors during early childhood were more predictive of adolescent and adult behavior than maternal behaviors during later childhood. For example, a critical maternal attitude during ages 0 to 3 predicted achievement in adult women, while such an attitude during ages 3 to 6 or 6 to 10 did not. It is

The Great Depression influenced several generations, but young adult males who had not achieved status in their careers and had family responsibilities felt the economic fallout the most. (United Press International Photo)

also true that events which affect history-graded variables may influence development even for individuals not in existence at the time of the event. For instance, the continuing depletion of the world's oil resources will likely cause widespread change within our culture, thus altering the developmental context of future generations.

Since development is considered a long-term phenomenon, the timing and sequencing of influences are also critical. This can be illustrated by the effects of life events on development. From a life-span developmental perspective, events do not have uniform meaning. When an event occurs in a person's life span is perhaps as important as whether the event occurs at all. For instance, think about the birth of a child. The impact of this event has a different meaning for a woman 26 years of age who is married and has a comfortable income than it does for a woman 16 years of age who is single and has few opportunities to obtain employment. Likewise, the death of a family member has a different impact for people at various points in their life spans.

Optimization and
Intervention Issues

Traditionally, interventionists have waited until a problem has appeared and then have tried to correct it (*remediation*), or reduce its intensity or duration (*rehabilitation*). Both of these strategies are important. However, the life-span developmental approach emphasizes the potential for growth throughout the life span. As a result, life-span developmentalists have promoted the usefulness of interventions focused on *prevention* and *enrichment* (Baltes & Danish, 1980; Lerner & Ryff, 1978). These refer to attempts to (1) reduce the likelihood that problems will occur, and (2) optimize the individual's knowledge, skills, and development. The likelihood of the former is often increased by achieving the latter.

Prevention and enrichment strategies are often educational in nature. For example, Danish and D'Augelli (1980) have described a life-development training program focused on the teaching of generic life skills such as goal assessment, decision making, risk taking, and planning self-development. These skills are assumed to be important resources for coping with such life events as retirement and divorce. Similarly, parent-effectiveness training is designed to teach adults how to be effective parents who are aware of and can respond to the developmental needs of their children (Guerney, 1977).

In considering which intervention strategies will lead to optimization it is necessary to recognize that intervention always involves value judgments. When should we intervene? How should we intervene? And for what purposes should we intervene? Whenever professionals develop and implement optimi-

Returning to or entering school for the first time, many middle-aged adults who receive support from others significant in their lives feel tremendous satisfaction. An increasing number of middle-aged women complete their higher educations successfully when they receive support, especially from their husbands. (United Press International Photo)

zation procedures, they must be aware of their own values and "guard against the tendency to decide what others should be like" (Vondracek & Urban, 1977, p. 418). People involved with intervention in the area of human development have become aware of the value conflict associated with decisions to intervene. Baltes and Danish (1980) offer an appropriate illustration of value conflict in their discussion of optimal aging in individuals:

In the medical sciences the criterion of lengthening life has a long tradition as a valuable general goal for intervention work aimed at optimization, both on the level of research and research application. Behavioral scientists have not yet agreed on a similar guiding principle. Life satisfaction measures come closest; however the assessment of life satisfaction in aging is at a preliminary stage . . . what is desirable, on a personal, professional, societal, and philosophical level? Moreover, length of life and life satisfaction do not always correlate well. This is particularly true for advanced age and situations of death and dying. (pp. 70–71)

Moreover, value conflict can occur at a societal level. For instance, allocating resources for preventive intervention with adults and the elderly may conflict with alternative types of programs for other target groups, such as infants and youth. Specialists must also be aware of the possibility that their well-intended efforts may be misguided attempts to impose their own standards on those they serve. They must examine their reasoning whenever they make a decision to intervene, at whatever level.

We have mentioned that the life-span developmental approach emphasizes multidirectional change produced by multiple influences. As a result, the life-span interventionist begins with the assumption that different methods of intervention will be required depending on the context. That is, the effects of a given intervention are likely to produce different results for different individuals. Lerner and Ryff (1978) conclude: "We must address the difficult issues of which behaviors, for which individuals, in which contexts, and in what time period are most likely to lead to optimal developmental outcomes. . . . In sum, there is no single yellow brick road to developmental optimization" (p. 14). Thus, the interventionist must examine an array of methods in order to determine which will be most useful in the particular context.

CONCLUSION

In our view, an adequate understanding of adult development and aging cannot be obtained by a cataloging of empirical "facts." Theory and research only have meaning as they are developed and interpreted within the context of a given framework. The life-span developmental perspective seeks to provide a framework within which the complex nature of human development may be studied. Throughout this text, we will attempt to use this approach to understand the phenomenon of adult development and aging.

CHAPTER SUMMARY

In this book, we will attempt to understand adult development and aging from two major perspectives: a scientific perspective and a life-span developmental perspective.

Scientists attempt to understand phenomena through the application of a specific set of procedures which constitute the scientific method. But scientists make different assumptions about the nature of the world. That is, science is relative rather than absolute. Facts are abstractions imposed on nature within the context of specific assumptions. These assumptions constitute different models or ways of representing the world. Three world views appear to be particularly significant for the study of human development.

The mechanistic world view represents the individual as a machine. This representation yields a reactive model of development. Within this view, the individual is seen as inherently at rest. Activity is the result of external forces which result in chainlike sequences of events. Development is explained by such forces. Change is viewed as quantitative rather then qualitative. Complex activities are ultimately reducible to simple elements.

The organismic world view represents the individual as a biological organism. This representation yields an active model of development. Within this view, individuals are considered to be dynamic. Development is explained by the individual's action on the environment. Further, development is considered to be qualitative rather than quantitative. Change is directed toward some ideal goal.

The contextual world view represents the individual as an ongoing event. This representation yields a dialectical model of development. Within this view, the individual is seen as continually changing. Activity is the result of reciprocal interactions between the individual and the context. This produces both quantitative and qualitative change. A single ideal goal is not assumed. Rather, multiple patterns of development are assumed as a function of the interaction between the changing individual and the changing context.

Each of these world views generates a specific set of answers to basic developmental questions, such as: "What changes?" "What type of change occurs?" "How is change explained?" "Why does change occur?" These differences are important because they shape the theory and research investigators use to examine the phenomena of adult development and aging.

Which of these assumptions is most useful for the study of adult development and aging? In one sense, all of them are potentially useful. However, a framework is required within which these different assumptions and theories can be integrated. The life-span developmental approach provides such a framework.

The life-span developmental approach is an orientation which is concerned with the description, explanation, and optimization of developmental processes over the human life course from conception to death. Several features characterize this approach: (1) Development occurs at all points in the life span. (2) Development is multidirectional—that is, it is characterized by multiple patterns of change differing in terms of onset, directionality, duration, and termination. (3) Development is characterized by both quantitative and qualitative change. (4) Developmental change may be charted along multiple time-related dimensions. Chronological age is one such dimension. Others include birth cohort and life transitions. (5) Development is produced by a dynamic interaction between the individual and the world. At least three sources of influence interact to produce developmental change: normative, age-graded influences, normative, history-graded influences, and nonnormative, life-event influences. (6) Different sources of change are likely to occur at different points in the life cycle. (7) The timing and patterning of different sources of influence are critical. (8) Life-span developmentalists promote the usefulness of interventions focused on prevention and enrichment rather than remediation and rehabilitation. (9) An optimization strategy presupposes a desirable state of affairs. Accordingly, particular attention must be devoted to value considerations in intervention. (10) Life-span developmentalists assume that multiple methods of intervention are required. The choice of which method to use depends on the context.

DEVELOPMENTAL RESEARCH METHODS

CHAPTER
OVERVIEW

In order to understand adult development and aging, researchers examine relationships among variables. In this chapter, we will examine methods which maximize accuracy and minimize inaccuracy in the discovery of such relationships. Both descriptive and explanatory developmental methods will be summarized.
Introduction
The Validity of Inferences

Internal validity
External validity
The relationship between internal and external validity
Internal and external validity in developmental research
Developmental Methods
Descriptive Methods
   Simple cross-sectional and longitudinal methods

Age differences versus age changes
   Threats to validity in simple descriptive methods
Explanatory Methods
   Experimental designs
   Nonexperimental designs
   Threats to validity in explanatory methods
Ethical Issues in Research
Conclusion

ISSUES TO CONSIDER

What are the purposes of research and research methods?
What is the significance of internal validity in research?
What is the significance of external validity in research?
What are the major potential threats to internal validity?
What are the major potential threats to external validity?

What are the two major descriptive developmental methods, and what are their major limitations?
What are sequential data-collection strategies, and how do they avoid the limitations of the simple designs?
How are experimental designs used to explain developmental processes?

What is the difference between true experimental and quasi-experimental designs?
What is the major limitation of an experimental approach?
What ethical considerations are important in research?

INTRODUCTION

Students sometimes find research methods mystifying. For example, one of us recalls a student complaining, after a lecture several years ago, "Why bother to describe all of this research stuff? Just tell us the way things are." Scientific research, of course, is simply a particular approach to discovering "the way things are."

The purpose of research is to examine relationships among variables (Kerlinger, 1973). It is the specification of such relationships that allows us to achieve the goals of description, explanation, and optimization described in Chapter 1. The difficulty is that relationships may be specified either accurately or inaccurately. As a result, our descriptions and explanations of phenomena may be valid or invalid, and our efforts at optimization may be effective or ineffective. How are we to maximize the accuracy and minimize the inaccuracy in our discovery of relationships among variables, and consequently, in our efforts at description, explanation, and optimization? By the application of research methods. The purpose of research methods is simply to reduce the degree of error in stating relations among variables. *Research methods constitute a set of "rules" and procedures to help us make valid inferences about phenomena.*

THE VALIDITY OF INFERENCES

Many types of errors are possible as we attempt to infer relations among variables. Two issues, however, are of particular concern: (1) the issue of whether an observed relationship is accurately identified and interpreted—the issue of *internal validity*, and (2) the issue of whether a relationship observed in one set of data may be observed in other sets of data which might have been observed but were not—the issue of *external validity*. Let us outline a hypothetical situation in order to provide a context within which to illustrate these two issues.

A researcher is contacted by the administrator of a small residential home for the aged. The administrator is concerned about the poor morale (e.g., feeling dissatisfied, unhappy, depressed) of the residents. Following a visit to the home, the researcher hypothesizes that the physical environment of the institution is not conducive to high morale (e.g., areas such as the lounge are arranged in ways that discourage social interaction; areas such as the residents' rooms are arranged in ways that offer little privacy; the rooms are drab, etc.). The researcher proposes, therefore, that a change in the physical environment of the home will result in an increase in morale among the residents. The administrator agrees to make the changes suggested and to assist in the study. The study is conducted as follows. Arrangements are made to send the residents to the homes of friends and relatives for one week while the institution is renovated. One week prior to the departure, each resident is asked to complete a questionnaire designed to measure morale. One week following the return to the newly renovated home, each resident is again asked to complete the question-

naire. A comparison of the first and second morale scores shows a dramatic increase in morale following the return of the residents to the renovated home. The researcher and administrator conclude that renovating the home led to an increase in morale. Are they right?

This hypothetical study attempts to examine the relationship between two variables—the characteristics of the physical environment and morale. It appears to suggest that a change in the former produces a change in the latter. However, this inference is subject to error. Let us examine the two major types of inferences involved.

Internal Validity

Internal validity refers to the adequacy with which relationships among variables are identified or interpreted (Campbell & Stanley, 1963; Cook & Campbell, 1975). Of particular concern is the establishment of accurate _causal relationships_, where the objective is to determine whether one set of events produced or caused another. The establishment of accurate causal relations is required for the explanation of phenomena.

Internal validity requires that there be no other plausible explanation for an outcome other than the presumed causal event. Internal validity is jeopardized when plausible alternative interpretations exist such that the outcome may not be due to the presumed causal event but to a third variable or variables. In our example, then, there should be no other explanation for the increase in morale other than the remodeling of the home. Is that the case? Are there any "third variable" explanations in our example? Yes. For instance, while the renovations were occurring, the residents visited the homes of friends and relatives. This change of location, and consequent opportunity to interact with others, may have caused the increase in morale rather than the change in the environment of the home. There is no way to determine which of these two plausible explanations (visiting friends and relatives versus renovation of the home) is accurate. One event has been confounded with the other. There are several classes of threats to internal validity. Some of these are summarized in Box 2.1.

External Validity

External validity refers to the adequacy with which relationships among variables may be generalized. In most cases, the observations made in a research study represent only some of a larger set of potential observations that might have been made but were not. Thus, observations are made on only some of a larger number of potential persons, potential settings, and potential times in history, using only some of a larger number of potential treatments and measuring instruments. External validity requires that relationships among variables remain consistent across these different potential data sets. External validity is jeopardized when interactions exist such that the observed relationship is modified by other variables. That is, there is a relationship between the variables, but only for certain types of people, or only in certain types of settings, or only at certain points in history, and so forth.

External validity assumes the existence of internal validity. If a relationship

In Depth   **BOX 2.1**
            POTENTIAL THREATS TO INTERNAL VALIDITY

It is possible to identify many threats to internal validity. For example, Cook and Campbell (1975) specify fourteen classes of threats. Several of these are summarized below. Each of these threats constitutes a potential class of rival explanations. In some cases, these rival explanations may be eliminated from consideration by including appropriate controls in the research design. In other cases, they cannot be eliminated from consideration, but their importance can be estimated.

History

This class of threats to internal validity consists of events external to the individual which are confounded with the presumed causal variable of interest to the researcher. Such events may operate over long periods of time (e.g., an economic depression during a long-term study) or short periods of time (e.g., a disruptive noise during a short-term study). If there is no way to distinguish the effects of such events from the effects of the researcher's deliberate manipulation, then these events become plausible rival explanations for the outcome of the study. In our hypothetical example above, for instance, it is impossible to determine whether the visit of the residents to the homes of family and friends or the researcher's manipulations of the physical environment of the nursing home caused the increase in morale. One way of controlling threats due to history is to examine equivalent sets of individuals both of which have been exposed to events constituting rival explanations, but only one of which has been exposed to the presumed causal event (e.g., multiple nursing homes are randomly divided into two groups. Residents of both groups visit the homes of friends and relatives, but only one group is exposed to the renovations of the nursing home).

Maturation

This class of threats to internal validity consists of events internal to the individual. Maturational effects are changes that would have occurred with the passage of time even in the absence of the presumed causal variable. Maturational effects include such things as fatigue, hunger, remission from illness, and so forth. For example, suppose we wish to examine the therapeutic effects of an exercise program on middle-aged men who have suffered a heart attack. Following several months of exercise therapy, the majority of the men have improved markedly. However, this outcome may simply reflect the normal recovery process rather than the impact of our exercise manipulation. One way of controlling threats due to maturation is to examine an equivalent set of individuals who have not experienced the presumed causal manipulation (e.g., patients are randomly divided into two groups—one group participates in the exercise program, the other does not).

Testing

This class of threats involves the effect that taking a test may have on a later testing. To the extent that such effects occur in designs which involve repeated testing, outcomes interpreted as due to the presumed cause may in fact be due to testing effects. Testing effects may reflect acquisition of the correct answers, changes in test-wiseness, test anxiety, and so forth. For example, suppose we were interested in determining the impact of a training program designed to increase older adults' knowledge of the metric system. We test their knowledge of the system, provide a training session designed to increase this knowledge, and then retest their knowledge of the system. Knowledge of the metric system increases from the first to the second testing. However, this increase may reflect a testing effect (e.g., test-wiseness) rather than the impact of our training program. One way of controlling threats due to testing is to compare an equivalent group of individuals who are tested, but not exposed to the treatment (e.g., individuals are randomly divided into two groups—one receives the training program the other does not. Both groups are tested twice).

Mortality

This class of threats consists of the loss of individuals from comparison groups as a result of events such as mobility, illness, and death. To the extent that groups being compared are affected differently by such events, the study is biased. For example, suppose we are interested in the role of instrumental skills (e.g., auto and household repair, financial management) in adjustment to widowhood. We devise a treatment designed to train such skills. The experimental group receives the training and the control group does not. Now suppose the incompetent members of the experimental group drop out because they are threatened by the content of the training. Such a loss is less likely to occur in the control group since they are not exposed to the training. Subsequent scores on the adjustment measure will tend to favor the experimental group, since only the more competent individuals remain. This difference reflects the impact of experimental mortality rather than the impact of the experimental manipulation. The impact of experimental mortality may be estimated statistically.

Selection

This class of threats consists of bias which results from the manner of selecting individuals in comparison groups. If differences between two or more groups exist prior to an experimental manipulation, differences in the variable of interest may be due to previous differences rather than to the manipulation. Selection effects typically operate when naturally existing groups are used as experimental subjects, exposed to different treatments, and then compared on some dependent variable. For example, suppose we are interested in comparing two different strategies for orienting middle-age students returning to the university. Two intact classes of such students are available. Method 1 is presented to one class and method 2 to the other class. Method 1 is superior. This effect may be a function of selection factors such that class 1 was superior to class 2 in the first place. Selection factors may be controlled by assigning subjects at random to treatments. If this is not possible, some estimate of selection factors may be obtained by pretesting groups on the dependent variable and other potential selection factors, and the results may then be taken into account statistically.

has not been accurately identified or interpreted, the question of whether it may be duplicated in other data sets is meaningless. Returning to our example, then, let us assume that the renovation of the home actually did cause an increase in morale among the residents. Will this relationship hold in studies involving different potential data sets, that is, how robust is this relationship? For example, there may be an interaction between the number of residents and the characteristics of the physical environment. Changes in the environment may affect morale in a small group of residents but not in a large group of residents. Thus, what was an effective manipulation in a small proprietary nursing home may not be effective in a large, state-operated nursing home.

As in the case of internal validity, there are many potential threats to external validity. It is important to recognize that the issue of external validity involves more than generalization across a sample of persons to a population of persons. Rather, as Baltes, Reese, and Nesselroade (1977) note, it "applies to inferences made from a sample of observations to a population of potential observations" (p. 51). Each observation represents a unique combination of person, setting, measurement, treatment, and historical time variables. These potential sources of interaction are summarized in Box 2.2.

The Relationship between Internal and External Validity

It is apparent that valid research requires both internal and external validity. Certainly, if a relationship is not accurately identified or interpreted, the

---

In Depth

BOX 2.2
POTENTIAL THREATS TO EXTERNAL VALIDITY

It is possible to specify many potential threats to external validity. Several of these are summarized below. Unlike many threats to internal validity, threats to external validity cannot be directly controlled. First, it is usually impossible to make all potential observations. The potential set is almost always larger than the subset we are able to observe. Second, it appears that interactions of the type which jeopardize external validity are widespread rather than limited (Cronbach, 1975; Gergen, 1973). This does not mean that external validity should be ignored. Rather, it suggests the need for examining relations within multiple persons, settings, and so forth to determine which of these variables interact with our variables of interest and which do not.

Persons
A particular relationship may be observed with one set of individuals but not with another. For example, a relationship between two variables may be observed in men but not in women.

Setting
A relationship may be observed in one setting but not in another. For example, a relationship between two variables may be found in the laboratory but not in the classroom.

Treatment
A relationship may be observed with a particular treatment but not with others. For example, one treatment designed to increase test anxiety may be effective while another treatment designed to manipulate this same variable may not.

Measures
A relationship may be observed with a particular measure or set of measures but not with others. For example, a relationship may be found between age and test anxiety using one measure of text anxiety but not be found if another measure of text anxiety is used.

Historical Time
A relationship may be observed at one point in historical time but not at another. For example, a relationship between age and cautiousness may exist during a period of economic depression but not during a period of economic growth.

In each of these cases, external validity is jeopardized because of the existence of an interaction between the two variables and a third variable. (Increased age is correlated with increased cautiousness, but only during periods of economic depression.) It should be noted that these five potential sources of interaction do not exhaust the list of potential threats to external validity. Rather, they constitute a set of classes of such threats.

inferences made are invalid. As a result, they will not aid in our tasks of description, explanation, and optimization. However, if a relationship is accurately identified and interpreted, but is restricted to the particular set of observations at hand, it may not be particularly useful. This is the case because research is typically directed at the description, explanation, and optimization of phenomena in general, rather than in a particular set of persons, in a particular setting, at a particular time, and so forth.

Unfortunately, an increase in internal validity often results in a decrease in external validity and vice versa. On the one hand, internal validity tends to be increased by the application of controls which are designed to eliminate all plausible explanations but the ones the investigator is interested in. This often results in highly limited and controlled situations which may threaten external validity. On the other hand, external validity tends to be increased by examining a wide variety of persons, settings, and so forth under conditions which closely approximate those occurring in the natural environment. Such a requirement may make it impossible to achieve the controls necessary for maximum internal validity because of practical or ethical considerations. Nevertheless, it is important for our research to achieve a balance between these two types of validity. While this may be difficult to accomplish in any one study, it should be the focus of a program of research.

Internal and External Validity in
Developmental Research

Two aspects of internal and external validity are of particular significance to developmental researchers (Baltes, Reese, & Nesselroade, 1977). First, many of the variables of concern to developmentalists (e.g., widowhood, health, age, socioeconomic status) are not amenable to manipulation or random assignment because of practical or ethical considerations. As a result, true experiments, the most effective strategy for controlling internal validity, are often not feasible. Second, many of the "threats" to internal and external validity summarized earlier are variables of primary concern to developmentalists—"their bread and butter variables" (Baltes, Reese, & Nesselroade, 1977, p. 46). For example, in the case of internal validity, threats due to history reflect events which constitute the long-term antecedents of developmental changes and differences. Similarly, in the case of external validity, threats due to changes in historical context reflect events which constitute the long-term antecedents of generational changes and differences. As Baltes, Reese, and Nesselroade (1977) point out, this state of affairs does not eliminate the need to attend to the issues of internal and external validity. For example, while a developmentalist's presumed causal variable may be an historical event, alternative historical explanations must still be ruled out. Thus, the issues of internal and external validity are fundamental to developmental research as well as to other types of research. In the following sections we will discuss the role of threats to internal and external validity in developmental research in more detail.

DEVELOPMENTAL METHODS

We may distinguish between two major types of developmental methods—*descriptive methods* and *explanatory methods*. Descriptive developmental methods focus on relationships among time-related variables (e.g., age, cohort, time of measurement) and variables of interest. The focus is on identifying and describing the relationships among within-person changes and between-person differences in such changes. Explanatory developmental methods focus on relationships among developmental antecedents. The focus is on the identification of the causes of within-person changes and between-person differences in such changes. This distinction between descriptive and explanatory developmental methods, while arbitrary, provides a way to organize our discussion that is consistent with the objectives of the life-span developmental approach (description, explanation, optimization) discussed in Chapter 1.

DESCRIPTIVE METHODS

Simple Cross-Sectional and Longitudinal Methods

There are two major descriptive developmental methods—the simple cross-sectional and simple longitudinal methods. In the *simple cross-sectional method*, individuals of different ages are observed on a single occasion at the same point in time. In the *simple longitudinal method*, the same individuals are observed at two or more points in time. Thus, a comparison is made of the same individuals at different ages. A third method—the *time-lag method*—is also relevant to developmental research. In this method, same-aged individuals are observed at different points in historical time. These basic strategies are illustrated in Figure 2.1.

Age Differences Versus Age Changes

Developmentalists are primarily interested in change. Within this context, it is important to note that the cross-sectional and longitudinal methods yield fundamentally different types of information. The cross-sectional method can only provide indirect evidence of change, while the longitudinal method provides direct evidence of change. The cross-sectional method involves *independent measures*; i.e., different persons are observed at different ages. As a result, this method only yields information on *age differences* (between-person differences). The longitudinal method involves *repeated measures*; i.e., the same persons are measured repeatedly at different times. As a result, this method yields information on *age changes* (within-person change and between-person differences in such change). Thus the longitudinal method is generally viewed as the more powerful method, since it permits direct examination of change.

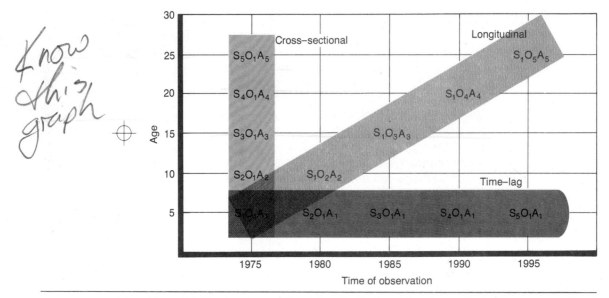

Know this graph

historical base

Figure 2.1 Simple cross-sectional, longitudinal, and time-lag methods. The cross-sectional method involves multiple samples (S_1–S_5) of different ages (A_1–A_5) at one point in time, each measured once (O_1). The longitudinal method involves following the same sample (S_1) through all ages (A_1–A_5), using repeated observations (O_1–O_5). The figure also illustrates the time-lag method (Schaie, 1965), which involves contrasting same-age (A_1) but different cohort samples (S_1–S_5), using one-shot observations (O_1) at different points in time. *(From Baltes, Reese, & Nesselroade, 1977.)*

Threats to Validity in Simple Descriptive Designs

All the simple descriptive designs described above (cross-sectional, longitudinal, time-lag) suffer from a number of difficulties involving threats to both internal and external validity. In the following sections we will briefly examine some of these problems and some of their potential controls.

History (cohort) effects   One issue which has received increasing attention by developmentalists has been the impact of history-graded influences on development (Baltes, Cornelius, & Nesselroade, 1979; Elder, 1975; Riley, 1976; Rosow, 1978; Ryder, 1965). Such effects are generally identified in terms of the cohort to which the individual belongs. The most general definition of cohort is "the aggregate of individuals (within some population definition) who experienced the same event within the same time interval" (Ryder, 1965, p. 845). Thus, one could talk of the 1942 birth cohort, the Depression cohort, the Vietnam war cohort, or the women's liberation cohort. Generally, cohort effects are seen as having a historical base or structure. Thus, it is meaningful to talk of the women's liberation cohort, but not the married women's cohort. Perhaps the

Elevating an awareness of women's needs and concerns was part of the discussion at the world conference of the International Women's Year, Mexico City, 1975, and has been a goal of the women's liberation cohort, whose full impact on society has not yet been studied. (United Nations)

most specific definition of cohort is *birth cohort* (Schaie, 1965). This provides a useful descriptive index. However, it is important to recognize that for cohort to serve an explanatory as well as a descriptive function, it must be linked to history-graded antecedents.

Methodologically, the possibility of effects related to history-graded influences raises a number of problems. In Chapter 1, we emphasized that the developmentalist is concerned with within-person change and between-person differences in such change. Consideration of the impact of history-graded influences, however, leads to a recognition that change can occur between cohorts as well as within a given cohort. More specifically, there are four potential components of variability:

1. *Within-cohort intraindividual change.* This refers to change within individuals in a given cohort. Such change is perhaps most reflective of normative, age-graded sources of influence. Such influences, you will recall, reflect both maturational events (e.g., puberty, menopause) and socializing events (e.g., marriage, retirement).

2. *Within-cohort interindividual differences in change.* This refers to differences in change between individuals in a given cohort. Such differences are perhaps most reflective of nonnormative, life-event sources of influence (e.g., illness, death of a family member, divorce). Nonnormative influences tend to produce divergence in behavior change.

3. *Between-cohort differences in intraindividual change* and

4. *Between-cohort differences in interindividual differences in intraindividual change.* The nature, sequence, level, rate, etc. of development and of interindividual differences may differ from one cohort to another. Such generational differences are perhaps most reflective of normative, history-graded sources of influence. It will be recalled that such influences provide the unique context for each cohort. They include historic events (e.g., war, economic depression) and sociocultural evolution (e.g., changes in education and health care). As a result, such influences produce divergence between cohorts. Developmental change and individual differences observed in succeeding cohorts may differ from that observed in earlier cohorts.

Recognition of these four components of variability alerts us to the limitations of the simple cross-sectional and longitudinal methods discussed earlier. In the case of the simple cross-sectional method, individuals of different ages are also members of different cohorts. Thus, to the extent that history-graded influences have produced between-cohort differences, the cross-sectional method lacks internal validity. Observed differences between the groups in the study that are presumably descriptive of age-graded sources of influence (age differences) may actually be descriptive of history-graded sources of influence (cohort differences).

In the case of the simple longitudinal method, this possible confounding of age with cohort is not present since all individuals are members of a single cohort. However, to the extent that history-graded influences have produced between-cohort differences, the longitudinal method lacks external validity. The simple longitudinal method examines only one cohort. The within-person change and between-person differences in change exhibited by this cohort may not be generalizable to other cohorts.

Thus, the simple developmental designs are susceptible to multiple threats to validity from history-graded effects. In order to examine these multiple types of variation, complex strategies which go beyond the simple cross-sectional and longitudinal methods are required. Several such complex descriptive strategies have been developed in recent years.

Sequential strategies   The limitations of the simple descriptive designs have been known for many years (Bell, 1953, 1954; Kuhlen, 1940, 1963). However, it was Schaie (1965) who devised a *General Developmental Model* designed to permit the separation of within- and between-cohort changes and differences. Schaie (1965) argued that behavior is a function of three components: The age of the individual, the cohort to which the individual belongs, and the time at which the measurement occurs. Schaie (1965) devised three data-collection and analysis strategies based on these three components. He proposed that the successive application of these strategies permits the unconfounding of the three components of behavior. Schaie also proposed that age changes reflect maturational factors, cohort differences reflect genetic and environmental factors, and time-of-measurement differences reflect factors involving cultural change. Thus, he argued that the General Developmental Model can be used to describe *and* explain developmental changes and differences.

Schaie's (1965) model represented a major methodological advance for developmental researchers. Others, however, took issue with the explanatory function of Schaie's approach (Baltes, 1968, Buss, 1973). In particular, Baltes took issue with Schaie's efforts at attaching explanatory significance to the components of his model (i.e., age = maturation, etc.). Resolving this controversy, Schaie and Baltes (1975) published a joint paper in which they distinguished between the descriptive and explanatory functions of the model. They agreed that, at the descriptive level, there are two basic data-collection strategies. They also agreed that, at the explanatory level, data collected via these strategies may be analyzed in many ways. Schaie's three data-analysis strategies represent one approach to explanation. In the present section, we will focus on the two descriptive data-collection strategies—cross-sectional and longitudinal sequences.

Cross-sectional and longitudinal sequences consist of sequences of either simple cross-sectional or longitudinal designs. The successive application of these strategies permits the descriptive analysis of behavior into its within- and between-cohort components. Figure 2.2 shows the contrast between the simple and sequential descriptive strategies. The top portion of the figure shows the simple cross-sectional and longitudinal designs described earlier. The bottom portion of the figure shows the two sequential strategies. *Cross-sectional sequences* involve successions of two or more cross-sectional studies completed at different times of measurement. *Longitudinal sequences* involve successions of two or more longitudinal studies begun at different times of measurement. The strategies differ in that cross-sectional sequences involve independent measures on different individuals, while longitudinal sequences involve repeated measures of the same individuals. In practice, one can apply both strategies simultaneously.

In any event, the application of sequential strategies permits the discrimination of within- and between-cohort sources of variance, thus increasing the validity of our descriptive efforts. The study described in Box 2.3 provides an example of the application of sequential strategies.

Selection effects The simple cross-sectional and longitudinal methods focus on the relationship between age and behavior. However, there may be other changes in the nature of the population selected for study, or differences in the composition of the samples drawn from this population. To the extent that these changes and differences are related to the dependent variable under study, the validity of the simple descriptive methods is jeopardized.

Selective survival effects represent a good example of this problem. As a given cohort ages it is reduced in size as individual members die. This process also differs over historical time. That is, the mortality curve changes from one cohort to another with changes in the prevelance of various diseases, the

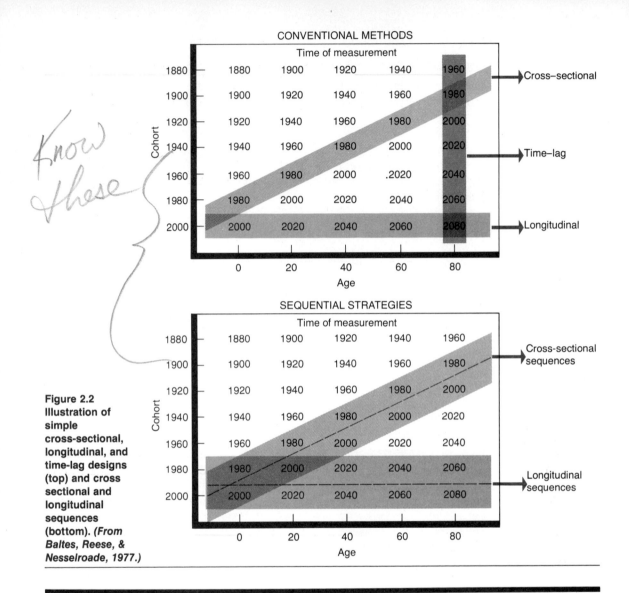

Figure 2.2
Illustration of
simple
cross-sectional,
longitudinal, and
time-lag designs
(top) and cross
sectional and
longitudinal
sequences
(bottom). *(From
Baltes, Reese, &
Nesselroade, 1977.)*

Know these

In Depth

BOX 2.3

An Example of a Sequential Design

The most extensive application of sequential methodology is Schaie's study of intelligence in adulthood. This study spans a period of fourteen years and has resulted in many analyses. However, for purposes of illustration, we will focus on the initial seven-year segment and on a particular analysis of these data (Nesselroade, Schaie, & Baltes, 1972). This analysis is based on seven-year longitudinal observations (from 1956 to 1963) of eight cohorts (average birth date from 1886 to 1932) ranging in age from 21 to 77 years of age. The basic design is shown in the figure opposite.

A total of 304 individuals were tested at both times of measurement on thirteen variables. These thirteen variables were reduced by statisti-

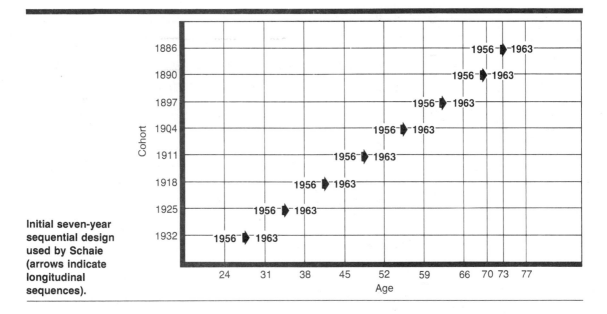

Initial seven-year sequential design used by Schaie (arrows indicate longitudinal sequences).

cal analysis to four composite variables. The figure below shows the outcome for Visualization—the ability to manipulate the images of spatial patterns into other arrangements (e.g., mentally rotate, trim, fold, or invert images of objects or parts of objects according to explicit directions). This figure contains the results of two "cross sections" (1956 and 1963) based on longitudinal sequences. Note that there is little longitudinal change over seven years for most age groups (dashed lines). The impact of cohort differences may be estimated by comparing same-aged persons measured in 1956 and 1963. For example, the boxed area of the figure shows the performance of 52-year-olds measured in 1956 and 1963 (cohort 1904 versus cohort 1911). Note the relatively large differences, in contrast to the age-related changes, which are minimal.

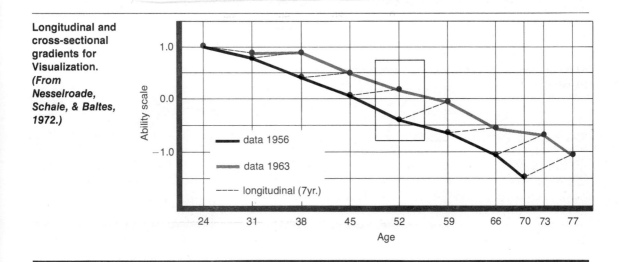

Longitudinal and cross-sectional gradients for Visualization. *(From Nesselroade, Schaie, & Baltes, 1972.)*

Life-long learning can be a very rewarding experience. Research has also shown that, on the average, more intelligent individuals live longer. (United Press International)

quality of health care, and so on. Such age- and cohort-related changes in survival may be related to behavior. Two hypothetical examples are shown in Figure 2.3. If survival correlates positively with behavior, as shown in the case of intelligence, then positive selection occurs. Individuals with low scores are lost, resulting in an increase in the average score. If survival correlates negatively with behavior, as in the case of smoking, then negative selection

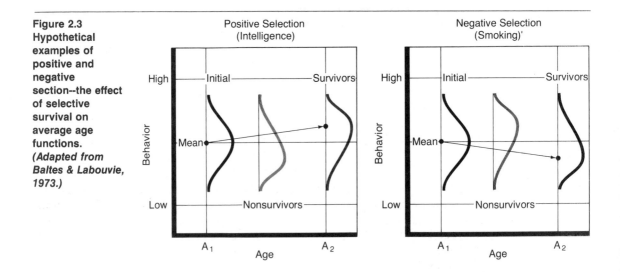

Figure 2.3 Hypothetical examples of positive and negative section--the effect of selective survival on average age functions. (*Adapted from Baltes & Labouvie, 1973.*)

occurs. Individuals with high scores are lost, resulting in a decrease in the average score. Recent evidence has suggested that such relationships between behavior and survival may be significant. For example, there appears to be positive selection in the case of intellectual behavior. That is, individuals who are more intelligent tend to survive longer (Baltes, Schaie, & Nardi, 1971; Riegel & Riegel, 1972). In such instances, the validity of the simple descriptive designs is threatened.

On the one hand, survival effects jeopardize the internal validity of the simple cross-sectional method. Thus, differences between the age groups may reflect age-related differences in survival rather than age-related differences in the behavior in question. On the other hand, survival effects jeopardize the external validity of the simple longitudinal method. Age-related changes in the behavior in question may vary for different cohorts as a function of the survival characteristics of the cohort.

In addition to survival, other selection variables may threaten the validity of the simple descriptive designs. For example, it is likely that there are age- and cohort-related differences on a number of variables such as educational level, health status, personality traits, and intellectual abilities. To the extent that these variables are related to the dependent variable under study, the validity of the simple designs is suspect. For example, consider the case of educational level and intellectual performance. We know that intelligence is related to education. We also know that older age/cohort groups, on the average, have had fewer years of education than younger age/cohort groups. In a cross-sectional study, then, is the poorer performance of the older adults related to age or to education? Internal validity is threatened. Similarly, in a longitudinal study, will changes observed in a cohort of poorly educated adults also be observed in a cohort of well-educated adults? In this case, external validity is threatened.

There is no simple solution to the problem of selection effects. One strategy which has been suggested is to equate the individuals involved on potential selection variables. This is a difficult strategy. For example, it assumes that the relevant selection variables are known. This may not be the case. It is generally agreed that the most effective procedure is to gather extensive information on the characteristics of the participants (Schaie, 1973). This information may then be used to describe the sample and to examine changes and differences in the dependent variable for different subgroups of individuals (e.g., males and females; survivors and nonsurvivors, etc.).

Experimental mortality In the previous section, we discussed mortality as one type of selection variable affecting the availability of individuals for study. Mortality may also be a factor once a sample has been selected and the research begun. More specifically, *experimental mortality* refers to the loss of individuals from the sample during the course of the research. Such loss may occur because of death or refusal to participate (e.g., because of boredom, anxiety, illness, etc.). Obviously, this problem is likely to be more prevalent in the case of the longitudinal method than the cross-sectional method, although it may occur in either case. To the extent that factors related to the loss of individuals from the sample are related to the dependent variable under study the validity of these simple designs is jeopardized.

As we have already noted, survival appears to be positively related to intellectual functioning. Several studies have demonstrated the impact of subject loss on longitudinal studies of intellectual ability (Baltes, Schaie, & Nardi, 1971; Riegel & Riegel, 1972). For example, Riegel and Riegel (1972) measured the intellectual abilities of adults ranging in age from 55 to 75 years in 1956 and 1962. A total of 380 individuals were originally tested in 1956. In 1962, 202 of these individuals were retested. An additional 62 had died, and 116 refused to be retested. The original scores of the entire group obtained in 1956 were then divided into three groups—retestees, nonsurvivors, and retest resistors. Examination of these original (1956) scores showed that nonsurvivors and retest resistors scored lower than persons who later agreed to be retested. In such cases, the internal validity of the simple longitudinal method is threatened. One cannot discriminate between age-related changes in intelligence and the effects of subject loss. Of course, there is no way to prevent experimental mortality. Such effects can be estimated and thus controlled, however, by discriminating between retestees and dropouts and plotting change separately for these groups as noted in the example above.

Testing effects Testing effects constitute a potential threat to the internal validity of simple longitudinal (repeated-measure) designs. When the same individuals are tested more than once, changes in performance may reflect exposure to the same stimulus materials rather than age-related changes in the attribute being measured. Considerable evidence has accumulated showing the importance of testing effects to a variety of attributes (learning, memory, intelligence, personality) over both short and long periods of time (Nesselroade & Baltes, 1974).

The magnitude of testing effects is illustrated by a recent study reported by Hofland, Willis, and Baltes (1978). These investigators conducted a short-term longitudinal study in which older individuals (average age 69.2 years) were retested repeatedly on two measures of intellectual ability over a four-week period. The mean percentage of correct solutions over the period for each of the ability measures is shown in Figure 2.4. These data show a dramatic improvement in performance. Further analyses of the results showed that with each succeeding retest, the individuals attempted or completed more items. Retest effects have been shown over periods as long as seven years (Schaie, 1973).

It is possible to modify the simple longitudinal (repeated-measure) design in order to control for testing effects. The simplest case is shown in Table 2.1. Individuals from a single cohort are divided at random into two groups. Group 1 is measured at time 1 and time 2, while group 2 is measured only at time 2. Comparison of the scores at time 2 provides an estimate of retest effects, since both groups are the same age but only group 1 has been tested before.

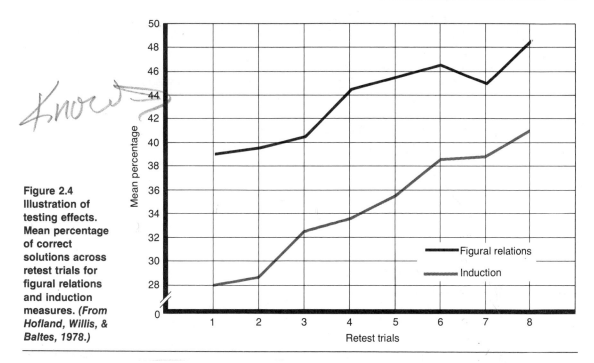

Know

Figure 2.4 Illustration of testing effects. Mean percentage of correct solutions across retest trials for figural relations and induction measures. *(From Hofland, Willis, & Baltes, 1978.)*

EXPLANATORY METHODS

Explanation involves the specification of causes (antecedents) of within-person change and between-person differences in such change. This requirement directs our attention, at least initially, to the issue of internal validity. That is, we must discriminate actual causes from potential causes which constitute plausible alternative explanations. This discrimination of actual from potential causes requires that we exert some form of control over the developmental process. Of course, direct control over all facets of development is impossible

Know

TABLE 2.1 MODIFICATION OF REPEATED MEASURES DESIGN TO CONTROL FOR TESTING EFFECTS		
Random Samples	**Time of Measurement**	
	Age 1	**Age 2**
Group 1	Time 1	Time 2
Group 2		Time 1

because of practical and ethical considerations. Accordingly, as Baltes and his colleagues (Baltes & Goulet, 1971; Baltes, Reese, & Nesselroade, 1977) have noted, explanatory methods involve an attempt to simulate the developmental process. Such *simulation strategies* involve the construction of a controlled artificial situation designed to represent or model the real situation. The necessity of creating such simulations directs our attention to the issue of external validity. That is, to what extent can information obtained from the artificial situation be generalized to the real situation?

There are many different simulation strategies. The most familiar of these is probably the laboratory experiment. Generally, these different simulation strategies may be divided into experimental and nonexperimental strategies. In the case of *experimental strategies* the independent (causal) variable is manipulated or controlled during the study. In the case of *nonexperimental strategies* the independent (causal) variable has occurred prior to the study.

Experimental Designs

An *experiment* may be defined as a set of procedures designed to assess the consequences of an experimenter-controlled or naturally occurring event (treatment) which intervenes in the lives of the respondents (Cook & Campbell, 1975). Experiments can be divided into two major categories depending on how the participants are assigned to treatments. Designs in which the participants are assigned to treatments in random fashion are called *true experiments*. Designs in which the participants are assigned to treatments in a nonrandom fashion are called *quasi experiments* (Campbell & Stanley, 1963; Cook & Campbell, 1975).

As we shall see, quasi experiments provide fewer controls over threats to

simulation strategies

experimental strategies

nonexperimental strategies

true experiment random

quasi experiment nonrandom

When individuals are assigned to treatments in a nonrandom fashion, the research design is called a quasi-experiment. (United Press International)

internal validity than true experiments. Both types of experiments (true or quasi) may be conducted in a variety of settings, including artificial settings such as the laboratory and naturalistic settings such as the workplace. There are numerous specific true and quasi-experimental designs. In the following sections, we will discuss only several examples in order to illustrate how these strategies may be applied to the study of development. For the sake of clarity we will restrict the number of *independent* (causal) and *dependent* (outcome) variables used. It should be noted, however, that most experiments involve the (simultaneous examination) of several independent and dependent variables. That is, they are *multivariate* in nature.

multivariate

True experiments   True experiments involve both a treatment event and the assignment of individuals to treatments in random fashion. *Randomization* involves the assignment of individuals of a group to subgroups in such a way that, for any given assignment to a subgroup, each member of the group has an equal probability of being chosen for that assignment. Several strategies, such as flipping a coin or consulting a table of random numbers, can be used to make such assignments. Random assignment of individuals to treatments is important because of its relationship to internal validity. It allows the investigator to assume that the treatment groups are approximately equal with respect to all variables except the one being manipulated. The larger the group the safer this assumption. Ideally, of course, if we knew all of the variables which affect the dependent variable and could control them, we would eliminate the necessity of random assignment. However, this is impossible. The alternative is to "spread out" the influence of these uncontrolled variables across the groups by means of random assignment. This allows us to assume that possible threats to internal validity are equally distributed across the treatment groups. Thus, the chances for internal validity are increased. True experiments constitute a common type of simulation in developmental research (Baltes & Goulet, 1971). Let us illustrate this approach by constructing a hypothetical example.

randomization

internal validity increased

Assume that we are interested in intellectual performance and that the descriptive data-collection strategies have shown that performance on this variable is inversely related to chronological age. That is, older adults perform more poorly than younger adults. Assume, further, that we hypothesize this difference may be a function of practice. This hypothesis suggests that younger adults perform better than older adults because they have had more recent test-taking experience (which may increase test-wiseness, decrease test anxiety, etc.). Accordingly, we design an experiment involving the manipulation of this presumed cause. Assume there are five age groups representing each decade from the twenties through the sixties. For each age group we form two subgroups by random assignment. Individuals in group 1 (experimental group) are given practice on tests similar to but different from the criterion test. Individuals in group 2 (control group) receive no practice. It is expected that this procedure will benefit the older adults more than the younger adults, since the former have less experience with tests than the latter. The design is diagramed in Figure 2.5, and the potential outcome is shown in Figure 2.6.

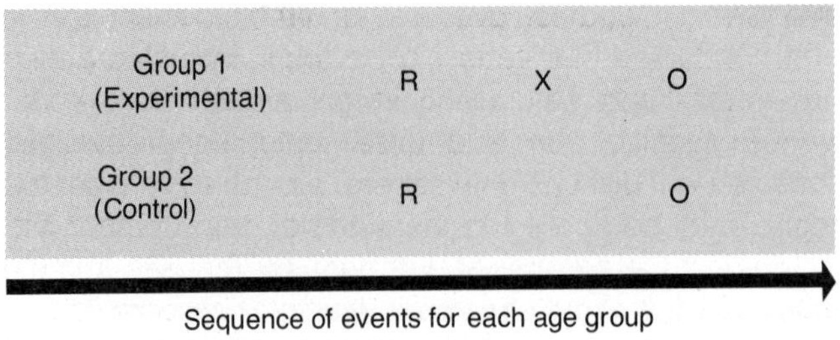

Group 1 (Experimental)	R	X	O
Group 2 (Control)	R		O

Sequence of events for each age group

Figure 2.5 Diagram of hypothetical true experimental design. (R = random assignment of individuals to groups; X = independent variable--practice on intelligence tests; O = dependent variable--criterion intelligence test.)

Note that in such a design, age differences per se are no longer of interest. Rather, the focus is on the interaction between age and the manipulated variable. That is, in our example, we are saying the age function for intellectual performance differs depending on the level of practice. Said another way, age differences are large when practice is lacking but nonexistent when it is present. Thus, age is no longer an independent variable as it is in the case of a simple cross-sectional method. Rather, it becomes part of the dependent variable. The focus is on how age functions are modified by other variables (Wohlwill, 1970). The modification of the age function is seen as a simulation of long-term developmental processes, and the manipulated variable is seen as the causal variable. Thus, it may be argued in our hypothetical example that older individuals perform more poorly because of lack of practice with tests.

Quasi experiments Quasi experiments involve a treatment but not the assignment of individuals to treatments in random fashion. The inability to assign individuals to treatments at random usually occurs because the individuals involved are members of intact, naturally occurring groups which

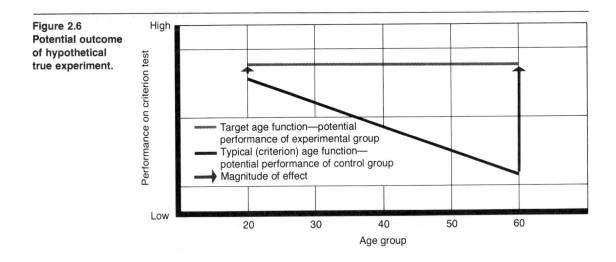

Figure 2.6 Potential outcome of hypothetical true experiment.

Performance on criterion test (High / Low)

- ‑‑‑‑ Target age function—potential performance of experimental group
- —— Typical (criterion) age function—potential performance of control group
- →→ Magnitude of effect

Age group (20, 30, 40, 50, 60)

cannot be modified for practical or ethical reasons. The inability to assign individuals to treatments in a random fashion weakens the internal validity of the design somewhat. We can no longer assume the groups are approximately equal with respect to all variables except the one being manipulated. There are several strategies which may be used to partially offset this weakness. In spite of these, the quasi-experimental designs are less powerful with respect to internal validity than true experiments. Nevertheless, the designs are valuable despite their limitations. In particular, true experiments are often not feasible in naturalistic settings because of practical or ethical considerations (e.g., it is often impractical to reassign individuals to classrooms at random, and it is unethical to expose individuals to highly stressful events at random). Many developmental questions are of this type. In such instances, quasi-experimental designs provide a useful strategy. Again, let us illustrate the approach by providing hypothetical examples.

Assume, as in our nursing-home example, that we are interested in the impact of the physical environment of nursing homes on the morale of the residents. It is hypothesized that certain changes (e.g., more privacy) will increase morale. However, since any physical modification affects the entire institution, the population of a single home cannot be divided at random. Similarly, individuals cannot be assigned at random to different institutions. Populations of homes for the aged occur as intact, naturally selected groups. Accordingly, we choose two institutions which are as similar as possible on a variety of characteristics thought to be relevant to morale (e.g., number of residents, health of residents). A measure of morale is obtained from the residents of both institutions (pretest). Physical modifications are then made to one of the homes chosen at random (treatment). The other institution remains unchanged. Finally, a measure of morale is again obtained from the residents of the two homes (posttest). The design and potential outcome are shown in Figures 2.7 and 2.8.

Note that this design is similar to the one outlined in Figure 2.5, except for the addition of a pretest measure and the absence of random assignment. The pretest is included because of this latter defect. The biggest threat to internal

Figure 2.7 Diagram of hypothetical quasi-experimental (pretest-posttest) design. (NR = nonrandom assignment of individuals to groups; X = independent variable--remodeling of home; O_1 = pretest--measure of morale; O_2 = posttest--measure of morale; dashed lines indicate intact groups.)

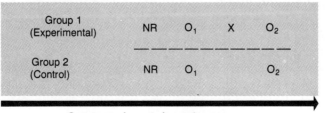

Sequence of events for each group

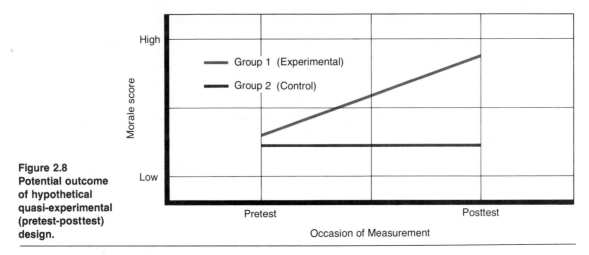

**Figure 2.8
Potential outcome
of hypothetical
quasi-experimental
(pretest-posttest)
design.**

validity in this design is selection. That is, the residents of the two homes may have differed in morale level even prior to the treatment. The more similar the selected groups are at the time of recruitment, and the more this similarity is confirmed by the pretest (as in our hypothetical results), the more confident we are that selection is not a factor. Figure 2.8 shows an idealized outcome in which there is little difference between the groups at the time of the pretest and a large difference following the treatment. Again, note that the interaction is the focus of the design. In this case, the interaction is between time of measurement (pretest-posttest) and the manipulated variable (physical rearrangement).

The quasi-experimental design just discussed emphasized a treatment under the direct control of the experimenter. However, quasi-experimental designs may also be used to investigate natural "treatments." For example certain life events such as illness, divorce, widowhood, or retirement are of interest to the developmentalist. Obviously, the experimenter cannot assign individuals at random to such treatments, nor can he or she even directly manipulate their occurrence. The experimenter, however, can manipulate observations made about the event to yield various quasi-experimental designs. An example is the time-series design. This involves the periodic measurement of an individual or group of individuals punctuated by a treatment event—either a natural event or an experimenter-controlled event. Assume we are interested in the impact the birth of a child has on the personality states of the mother. We are interested in anxiety, fatigue, and well-being. Accordingly we select a sample of pregnant women. Every day, beginning approximately one month prior to their delivery date, they complete a measure of personality state. At some point in this sequence, the baby is born. This is the "treatment." The women continue to complete the measure of personality state for two additional weeks following the birth of the child. The design is diagramed in Figure 2.9. In this design, the focus is on a change in trend for the different measures following the event. A hypothetical outcome is shown in Figure 2.10.

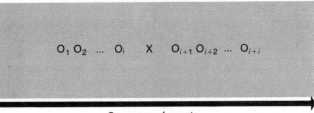

$$O_1 \ O_2 \ \ldots \ O_i \quad X \quad O_{i+1} \ O_{i+2} \ \ldots \ O_{i+i}$$

Sequence of events

Figure 2.9 Diagram of quasi-experimental (time-series) design . (X = independent variable--birth of a baby; $O_1 \ldots O_i +_i$ = dependent variable--repeated measurement of personality states).

The greatest threats to the internal validity in this design are history effects. For example, some event occurring more or less simultaneously with the birth of the child may have caused the changes in personality states. Internal validity is strengthened to the extent that many observations are obtained before and after the treatment and to the extent that different dependent variables show changes which coincide with theoretical predictions. An example of a change that coincided with theoretical predictions would be that anxiety and fatigue decrease, while well-being increases.

Nonexperimental Designs

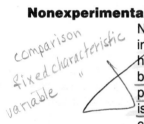

Nonexperimental research may be defined as a set of procedures in which the investigator does not have control over the presumed causal variable because it has already occurred or because it cannot be manipulated. In this instance, the basic strategy consists of the comparison of intact groups existing in the population. Comparison groups may be formed on the basis of fixed characteristics, such as sex and race. They may also be formed on the basis of variable characteristics or experiences, such as health status or educational level.

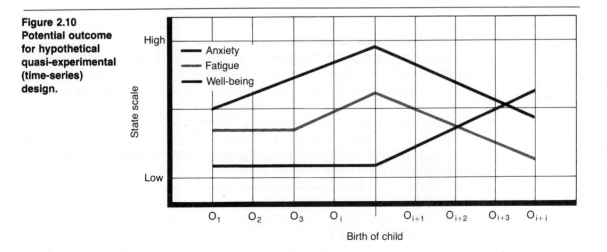

Figure 2.10 Potential outcome for hypothetical quasi-experimental (time-series) design.

These designs provide significant descriptive information. However, they may also be used for explanatory purposes. In this case, it is assumed that observations of fixed characteristics or experience variables will allow the investigator to simulate conditions that produce differences in behavior between individuals. However, the internal validity of these designs is quite weak. This results because of the lack of control over the independent variables and lack of random assignment of individuals to treatments. As a result, there are many potential rival explanations other than the event of interest. For example, assume that we are interested in the impact of divorce on the personal adjustment of young, middle-aged, and older women. For each of these age groups, we identify a sample of divorced and married women and measure their personal adjustment. This design lacks controls to safeguard internal validity. Thus, the divorced and married women may have differed on personal adjustment prior to the divorce (selection), or because of events other than the divorce (history), and so forth.

Why use such designs if their internal validity is so poor? In addition to the descriptive information they provide, these designs may be used for forming hypotheses. The information may then be tested using more rigorous experimental or statistical methods. Recent developments in statistical analysis labeled causal modeling techniques are proving productive in this regard (Jöreskog, 1979). *Causal modeling techniques*, such as structural equation analysis, permit causal inference within the framework of nonexperimental designs. A basic ingredient for the proper use of structural equation models is an explicit model of the network of causal relationships among the variables in question. Structural analysis involves the translation of these verbal hypotheses about causal relationships into precise mathematical statements. The equations are then solved, and it is possible to estimate how closely the observed data fit the causal hypotheses. Thus, nonexperimental designs may be used to generate hypotheses. Then, once a precise model is constructed, these hypotheses can be tested statistically.

Threats to Validity in Explanatory Designs

We have discussed a number of threats to the validity of the various explanatory designs reviewed above. Generally, the focus of concern in the case of explanatory designs has been on internal validity (Campbell & Stanley, 1963; Cook & Campbell, 1975). In recent years, however, increasing attention has been drawn to the issue of external validity in explanatory research (Bronfenbrenner, 1977; Hultsch & Hickey, 1978; Willems, 1973). We have noted that explanatory methods involve simulation to a greater or lesser degree. The usefulness of this strategy rests on the assumption that the differences and changes observed in the artificial situation are similar to, or identical to, the developmental changes occurring in the real world. This particular type of external validity has been labeled *ecological validity*. It refers to the individual's ecological environment or natural habitat.

The issue of ecological validity necessarily reflects many aspects of the research situation—physical surroundings, tasks, roles, and so forth. To the extent that individuals are asked to perform tasks or react to situations which are alien to their experience or values, the simulation may not be reflective of development in the natural environment. Further, note that experiences and values may differ as a function of age or cohort. Thus, what is ecologically valid for one group or at one point in time may not be valid for another group or at another point in time. For example, Sinnott (1975) administered both traditional and everyday forms of several Piagetian tasks to younger and older adults. Among the tasks were some designed to assess the capacity to consider all hypothetical possibilities. In the traditional tasks, the subjects were asked to form all possible pairs of six geometric shapes. The everyday tasks made the same reasoning demands within the context of familiar situations. For example:

You have six children who love to go camping. You have patience enough to take two children, but no more, with you on each trip. Each child wants a chance to camp with each of the other brothers and sisters sometime during the summer. How many trips would be necessary to give each child a chance to camp with every brother and sister if you take only two children each trip? How do you know? (Sinnott, 1975, p. 433)

While all groups did better with everyday problems than with traditional problems, the benefit of the former was greater for older adults than for younger adults. The performance of the younger adults increased by 10 percent while that of the older adults increased by 25 percent.

These concerns related to ecological validity do not mean that simulations, particularly those dissimilar from real life such as laboratory experiments, should not be used. First, simply doing research in the natural environment does not guarantee ecological validity. One can ask the wrong questions in the workplace as well as the laboratory. Second, simulations are essential for establishing causal relationships. This requires some intrusion into the system. However, the conclusions drawn from simulations must be validated by real-world observation and experiment. Both types of research are essential.

ETHICAL ISSUES IN RESEARCH

The previous sections of this chapter have focused on methods of research—techniques involved in the observation and manipulation of variables and the validity of these techniques. However, research also involves an interaction between people—the investigator and the participants.

In recent years, researchers, government officials, and the public have become increasingly concerned with the ethics of research. In particular, concern has been directed toward protecting the rights of the individuals who serve as the "subjects" of research. This concern has been formalized in a variety of ways. For example, the U.S. Department of Health and Human Services, a major source of funds for research, has developed a set of regulations which all recipients of federal research grants and contracts must follow. Similarly, many scientific societies such as the American Psychological Association have developed codes of ethics for the conduct of research. Many of the guidelines were developed because of past abuses. Medical research has been particularly subject to criticism in this area. However, abuses occur in behavioral research as well. Below is a list of ethically questionable practices.

1. Involving individuals in research without their knowledge or consent
2. Failure to inform participants about the true nature of the research
3. Misinforming participants about the true nature of the research
4. Coercing individuals to participate in research
5. Failure to honor promises or commitments to participants
6. Exposure of participants to physical or mental stress
7. Invading participants' privacy
8. Failure to maintain confidentiality of information received
9. Withholding benefits from participants in control groups

These problems may not arise because the investigator is evil or uncaring. Rather, the nature of the problems, variables, and people themselves may cause problems. For example, it may be very difficult to study a significant event such as the death of a spouse without exposing the individual to mental stress. Yet, knowledge of such an event is important both for its own value and for attempts to help individuals cope with such events. A critical issue, then, is the cost of research versus its benefits. All research has a cost, in other than monetary terms, to the individuals involved—time, stress, and so forth. Research may also produce benefits—knowledge. Obviously, benefits should exceed the cost. But ethical practice requires more than this. At some point, the cost may be too great no matter what the benefit. In other words, the end does not justify the means. It was just such an argument which permitted the Nazis to immerse concentration camp victims in frigid water until they died in order to determine how to better protect flyers who had to parachute into the North Sea.

Such extreme examples are relatively easy to judge as unethical. However, for most research on behavior there are no absolute answers. One justifiable approach appears to take the form of seeking the advice of others concerning the ethical acceptability of research. This may take place at two levels—internal consultation with colleagues and formal consultation with institutional committees set up for this purpose. The latter are required for research funded by the Department of Health and Human Services. However, none of these practices changes the fact that the ultimate responsibility for the ethical nature of the research rests with the investigator. One set of principles for coping with this important and difficult task is shown in Box 2.4. Several of these may be of particular significance for working with older adults (Reich, 1978). For example, research with older adults who are physically or cognitively impaired or who are institutionalized requires special care.

The following principles for ethical research are taken from the Manual of Ethical Principles published by the American Psychological Association (1973).

Principle 1 In planning a study the investigator has the personal responsibility to make a careful evaluation of its ethical acceptability, taking into account these Principles for research with human beings. To the extent that this appraisal, weighing scientific and humane values, suggests a deviation from any Principle, the investigator incurs an increasingly serious obligation to seek ethical advice and to observe more stringent safeguards to protect the rights of the human research participant. (p. 21)

Principle 2 Responsibility for the establishment and maintenance of acceptable ethical practice in research always remains with the individual investigator. The investigator is also responsible for the ethical treatment of research participants by collaborators, assistants, students, and employees, all of whom, however, incur parallel obligations. (p. 22)

Principle 3 Ethical practice requires the investigator to inform the participant of all features of the research that reasonably might be expected to influence willingness to participate, and to explain all other aspects of the research about which the participant inquires. Failure to make full disclosure gives added emphasis to the investigator's responsibility to protect the welfare and dignity of the research participant. (p. 29)

Principle 4 Openness and honesty are essential characteristics of the relationship between investigator and research participant. When the methodological requirements of a study necessitate concealment or deception, the investigator is required to ensure the participant's understanding of the reasons for this action and to restore the quality of the relationship with the investigator. (p. 29)

Principle 5 Ethical research practice requires the investigator to respect the individual's freedom to decline to participate in research or to discontinue participation at any time. The obliga-tion to protect this freedom requires special vigilance when the investigator is in a position of power over the participant. The decision to limit this freedom increases the investigator's responsibility to protect the participant's dignity and welfare. (p. 42)

Principle 6 Ethically acceptable research begins with the establishment of a clear and fair agreement between the investigator and the research participant that clarifies the responsibilities of each. The investigator has the obligation to honor all promises and commitments included in that agreement. (p. 54)

Principle 7 The ethical investigator protects participants from physical and mental discomfort, harm and danger. If the risk of such consequences exists, the investigator is required to inform the participant of that fact, secure consent before proceeding, and take all possible measures to minimize distress. A research procedure may not be used if it is likely to cause serious and lasting harm to participants. (p. 61)

Principle 8 After the data are collected, ethical practice requires the investigator to provide the participant with a full clarification of the nature of the study and to remove any misconceptions that may have arisen. Where scientific or humane values justify delaying or withholding information, the investigator acquires a special responsibility to assure that there are no damaging consequences for the participant. (p. 77)

Principle 9 Where research procedures may result in undesirable consequences for the participant, the investigator has the responsibility to detect and remove or correct these consequences including, where relevant, long-term aftereffects. (p. 83)

Principle 10 Information obtained about the research participants during the course of an investigation is confidential. When the possibility exists that others may obtain access to such information, ethical research practice requires that this possibility, together with the plans for protecting confidentiality, be explained to the participants as a part of the procedure for obtaining informed consent. (p. 89)

CONCLUSION

An understanding of adult development and aging has multiple values—including scientific and practical. The information we gain through research shapes our attitudes, beliefs, behaviors, and social policies about this portion of the life cycle. In one sense, then, erroneous information can be worse than a lack of information. In this chapter, we have attempted to point out some of the pitfalls that are possible as we attempt to understand adulthood and aging. As you read the remainder of the book, keep these pitfalls in mind. In the long-term pursuit of understanding a critical, analytic mind is a fundamental requirement.

CHAPTER SUMMARY

The purpose of research is to examine relationships among variables. But such relationships may be specified either accurately or inaccurately. The purpose of research methods is to maximize accuracy and minimize inaccuracy in our discovery of relationships among variables.

Many types of errors are possible as we attempt to infer relations among variables, but two areas of concern are particularly important. One concern focuses on the issue of whether an observed relationship is accurately identified or interpreted. This is the issue of internal validity. Internal validity requires that there is no other viable explanation for an outcome other than the presumed causal event. Internal validity is jeopardized when plausible alternative interpretations exist. Multiple threats to internal validity exist, including those related to history, maturation, testing, mortality, and selection. Another concern focuses on the issue of whether a relationship observed in one set of data may be observed in another set of data. This is the issue of external validity. External validity requires that relationships among variables not be limited to the data set being observed. It should be possible to generalize the relationships across potential data sets (e.g., different persons, settings, treatments, measures, times of measurement). External validity is jeopardized when interactions exist such that the relationship is modified by the status of other variables. In particular, a relationship may exist only for certain types of people, certain types of settings, or at certain points in history. Valid research requires both internal and external validity. However, increases in one sometimes cause decreases in the other.

There are two major types of developmental methods. Descriptive developmental methods focus on relationships among time-related variables (e.g., age) and other variables. Explanatory developmental methods focus on relationships among developmental antecedents.

There are two major descriptive developmental methods—the simple cross-sectional and simple longitudinal methods. In the simple cross-sectional method, individuals of different ages are observed on a single occasion at the same point in time. In the simple longitudinal method, the same individuals are observed at two or more points in time. These two methods yield different types of information. In the cross-sectional method, different persons are observed at different ages. As a result, the method only yields information on age differences. In the longitudinal method, the same persons are measured repeatedly at different times. As a result, the method yields information on age changes.

The simple descriptive designs suffer from a number of difficulties in drawing inferences from them. One major difficulty stems from the potential impact of history-graded influences on development. In the case of the simple cross-sectional method, individuals of different ages are also members of different cohorts. As a result, differences between the groups may actually be descriptive of cohort differences rather than age differences. In the case of the simple longitudinal method, only one cohort is examined. Changes exhibited by this one cohort may not be generalizable to other cohorts. These limitations may be partially overcome by the application of two types of sequential data-collection strategies. Cross-sectional sequences involve successions of two or more cross-sectional studies completed at different times of measurement. Longitudinal sequences involve successions of two or more longitudinal studies begun at different times of measurement.

Explanatory developmental methods attempt to simulate the developmental process. This involves the construction of a controlled and time-compressed situation designed to represent the real situation. Experimental strategies represent the most common simulation strategy. For experimental strategies, the independent or causal variable is manipulated or controlled during the study. Designs in which participants are assigned to treatments in random fashion are called true experiments. Designs in which participants are assigned to treatments in nonrandom fashion are called quasi experiments. In both instances, the focus is on the interaction between age and the manipulated variable. The modification of the age relationship is seen as a simulation of long-term developmental processes, and the manipulated variable is seen as the causal variable. The usefulness of experimental strategies depends on their ecological validity. That is, the strategy rests on the assumption that the differences and changes observed in the artificial situation are similar to, or identical to, the developmental changes occurring in the real world.

Finally, research involves an interaction between people—the investigator and the participants. As such, ethical considerations in this relationship must be given serious consideration. A number of codes of ethics and related procedures have been developed for this purpose.

PART 2

BEHAVIORAL PROCESSES

3

BIOLOGICAL PROCESSES

INTRODUCTION

At age 25, a white male in the United States can expect to live an additional 47 years. By age 45, this figure has been reduced to about 29 years, and by age 85 it is only about 6 years. This reduced probability of survival is accompanied by a host of physical changes, for example, wrinkled skin, poorer vision and hearing, less muscle strength, reduced cardiac and lung capacity, and loss of brain weight. What causes these changes? Can they be slowed or reversed? How are they related to behavior? Can the human life span be lengthened? In this chapter we will explore some potential answers to these questions.

A BIOLOGICAL DEFINITION OF AGING

Generally, biologists define aging as a set of deleterious changes which decrease the probability of the individual's survival (Comfort, 1964; Strehler, 1962). These changes are typically viewed as inevitable, irreversible, unidirectional, and universal. That is, biological aging is seen as an inevitable internal process rather than as a result of external conditions or events.

Regardless of which theory of aging—genetic cellular, nongenetic cellular, and/or physiological—is supported, biological aging is an internal process. (Mimi Forsyth/Monkmeyer)

cohort life table—longitudinal (follows a single cohort)

current life table—cross sectional (actual population at a given time)

Some idea of the scope of these changes in the population as a whole may be gained by examining life tables which summarize mortality rates. There are two types of life tables. The *cohort life table* provides a longitudinal perspective. It follows the mortality experience of a single cohort. For example, mortality rates for all persons born in 1900 are plotted until no one from this group remains alive. The *current life table* provides a cross-sectional perspective. It considers the age-specific mortality rates for an actual population at a given time. For example, the current life table for 1976 tabulates the mortality rates for individuals of different ages in 1976. The current life table is more practical to construct than the cohort life table and is the method used by the National Center for Health Statistics. Figure 3.1 shows two indices from the 1976 U.S. Life Tables for men and women (U.S. Department of Health, Education, and Welfare, 1978). These data illustrate rather dramatically the effects of aging on the population in general and its differential effects on men and women in particular.

BIOLOGICAL THEORIES OF AGING

What causes the decreasing survival potential revealed in the mortality data of Figure 3.1? Why does the human life span appear to have an upper limit, as summarized in Box 3.1? There are a number of biological theories which focus

Figure 3.1a Number of individuals surviving. Shows the number of persons, starting with a cohort of 100,000 live births, who survive to the exact age marking the beginning of the age interval. For example, of 100,000 female babies born alive, 98,631 will complete the first year of life and enter the second; 97,868 will reach age 20; and 65,138 will reach age 75. (From U.S. Department of Health, Education, and Welfare, 1978.)

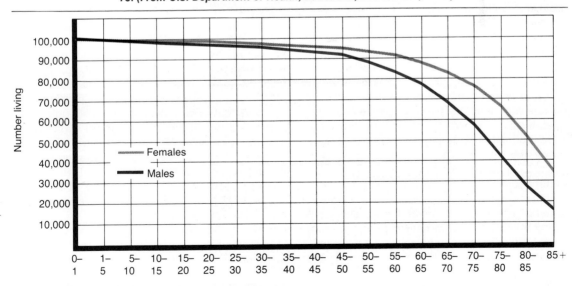

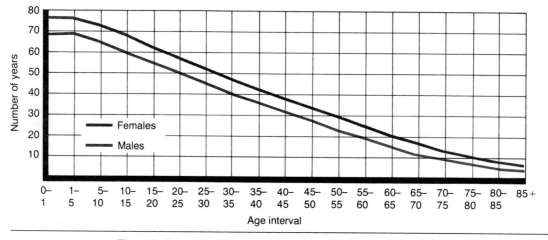

Figure 3.1*b* Average years of life remaining, age interval. For example, at age 20 a woman can expect to live an additional 58.2 years, and at age 80 she can expect to live an additional 8.7 years. *(From U.S. Department of Health, Education, and Welfare, 1978.)*

In Depth

BOX 3.1
DID METHUSELAH REALLY LIVE 969 YEARS?

The purported longevity of Methuselah is undoubtedly a myth. But how long can human beings live? In examining this question it is important to distinguish between *life expectancy* and *maximum life span*. Life expectancy refers to the average length of life. Maximum life span refers to the extreme upper limit of human life.

Life expectancy fluctuates dramatically as a function of nutrition, disease, sanitation, health care, and other environmental factors. For example, it is estimated that the average life expectancy at birth in ancient Rome was as low as 22 years. Estimates place the life-expectancy figure during the Middle Ages in the 30- to 35-year range. This figure changed little during the sixteenth and seventeenth centuries, and increased only to around 40 by the middle of the nineteenth century. The greatest gains have been made during this century, with life expectancy at birth in the United States increasing from 47.3 years in 1900 to 72.8 years in 1976. Note, however, that

increases in life expectancy at maturity and beyond are much smaller. For example, in 1900, average life expectancy at age 20 in the United States was 42.8 years. By 1976 it had increased to only 47.3 years (U.S. Department of Health, Education, and Welfare, 1978). The dramatic increase in life expectancy at birth is largely a function of health-related advances which, in particular, have led to a reduction of infant mortality. As a result, a greater proportion of all persons are living longer. For example, in 1900 only 40.9 percent of the cohort born 65 years earlier were still alive; in 1976, 75.1 percent were still alive. However, there is little evidence to suggest that the maximum life span of human beings has changed. This has been estimated at between 110 and 120 years.

A few years ago there were a number of reports in the popular press of extraordinary longevity in several parts of the world. These included the Republic of Georgia in the U.S.S.R., the Vilcabamba valley in Ecuador, and the province of Hunza in Kashmir. These areas were supposed to contain far more persons over the age of 100 than one would expect. For example, while about 3 centenarians per 100,000 population would be normal, regions in the Caucasus mountain area of the U.S.S.R. report about 400 centenarians per 100,000 population. In these areas, reports of persons aged 100 to 120 are common, and reports of persons aged 120 to 170 are not unusual.

While these claims make "good press," a careful examination of the evidence suggests they are unfounded (Medvedev, 1974). Generally, the documentation is very poor. There was no birth registration, and few of the very old are able to produce reliable documents of other types (e.g., military, marriage, education). Usually, the reports have been substantiated by recall of significant past events and by interviews with other residents of the village. Medvedev (1974) notes that social rather than biological factors may account for the phenomenon. For example, in these regions older persons receive a great deal of honor and respect. Centenarians often hold special positions in the community and engage in special activities (e.g., leaders of local celebrations). Such positive valuing of the extremely old may result in exaggerations of chronological age. There may also be more practical reasons involved, as Medvedev relates:

The famous man from Yakutia who was found to be 130 years old received especially great publicity because he lived in the place with the most terrible climate. . . . When publicity about him became all-national and a large article with a picture of this outstanding man was published in the central government newspaper, Isvestia, the puzzle was quickly solved. A letter was received from a group of Ukrainian villagers who recognized this centenarian as a fellow villager who deserted from the army during the First World War and forged documents or used his father's (most usual method of falsification) to escape remobilization. It was found this man was really only 78 years old. (1974, p. 387)

Thus all indications point to an upper limit on the human life span of about 110 to 120 years. However, some writers speculate that this limit may be exceeded in the not-too-distant future as researchers discover the basic mechanisms of the aging process (Medvedev, 1975). Such a breakthrough, however, would probably raise a host of ethical issues. What problems do you foresee?

on these questions. Each of these theories has had some success in explaining a portion of the aging phenomenon, but none of them has achieved general acceptance.

All modern biological theories of aging have a genetic basis (Shock, 1977a). It is assumed that the life span of a species is ultimately determined by a program built into the *genes* of the species. Thus the human has a maximum life span of about 115 years, the horse 62 years, the cat 28 years, and the mouse only 3.5 years.

Support for the genetic basis of aging comes from Hayflick's (1965) work which shows that certain cells of the body, grown under culture conditions (in vitro), are able to divide only a limited number of times. Previous to this discovery, it had been thought that cells could divide indefinitely under culture conditions. However, Hayflick found that fibroblast cells (connective tissue cells which normally divide) taken from human embryonic tissue undergo only about fifty doublings before cell division ceases. Further, the older the individual from whom the cell samples are obtained, the fewer doublings the cells will undergo. However, the cells of a very elderly individual will still divide, suggesting that people rarely live out their potential life span. Hayflick's work, then, suggests that the aging of the organism may be programmed into the genetic code of the cell.

While it is clear that aging has a genetic basis, the various biological theories may be divided into three major groups for the purposes of our discussion: genetic cellular theories, nongenetic cellular theories, and physiological theories (Shock, 1977a). Let us briefly examine some examples from each of these groups.

Genetic Cellular Theories

damage to genetic information involved in formation of cellular proteins

These theories suggest that aging results from damage to the genetic information involved in the formation of cellular proteins. The information stored in the genetic code is determined by the structure of a complex molecule known as *deoxyribonucleic acid* (*DNA*). DNA controls the formation of essential proteins required by the cell. However, the information from the DNA must be transcribed and transferred to another location in the cell where the actual assembly of the proteins occurs. A second molecule, *ribonucleic acid* (*RNA*), performs this function. Several theorists have argued that the breakdown of these basic genetic mechanisms causes aging.

DNA damage theories Sinex (1974), for instance, has suggested that mutations damage the DNA at a faster rate than it can be repaired. This process continues until the cell dies. Such damage to the DNA would be particularly deleterious to nondividing cells such as nerve and muscle cells. Similarly, Curtis (1966) has suggested that cells undergo mutations, most of which are deleterious. His work was based on experiments with rats and mice which showed that the incidence of abnormal chromosomes increased markedly after exposure to radiation and progressively with age. Nevertheless, calculations suggest that the rate at which mutations occur in the absence of radiation is too small to account for the overall age changes observed.

Hahn – faulty transcription of RNA from the DNA

Strehler

Error theories According to these theories, aging is the result of errors involved in the transmission of information from the DNA to the final protein product (Medvedev, 1964). Unlike DNA molecules, which are highly stable, RNA molecules are formed continuously. Therefore, Hahn (1970) has suggested that aging results from faulty transcription of the RNA from the DNA. Similarly, Orgel (1963) has suggested that the faulty selection of amino acids by enzymes is a key factor in cell death. Although the initial frequency of errors may be low, they would increase over time. Eventually, this accumulation of errors would result in an *error catastrophe* and cell death. Strehler (1978) has proposed that the loss of sequential multiple copies of the same genetic information is critical. A particularly important group of genes that are present in multiple copies are those responsible for the production of the RNA required for protein synthesis. Strehler and his colleagues have found that the number of copies of these genes in the tissues of both dogs and humans decreases with age. Such a loss would result in increased error, and eventually, cell death.

Nongenetic Cellular Theories

These theories focus on changes that take place in the cellular proteins after they have been formed.

Accumulation theories   These theories suggest that aging results from the accumulation of deleterious substances in the cells of the organism. Almost 100 years ago, investigators discovered that old cells universally contained dark-colored inclusions called *lipofuscin.* These waste pigments or cellular "garbage" have been shown to increase at a constant rate with time. The accumulation of lipofuscin is particularly prevelant in cells which do not undergo division, such as nerve and muscle cells, especially cardiac muscle cells. It has been argued that the presence of this insoluble waste material interferes with cellular metabolism and ultimately may result in cell death (Carpenter, 1965). There is limited evidence to suggest the mechanism by which this impairment may occur. Recently, however, it has been shown that the amount of RNA in nerve cells decreases in direct proportion to the increase in the lipofuscin content of the cells (Mann & Yates: reported in Strehler, 1978). Additional evidence isolating the exact nature of the toxic substances involved and demonstrating how the presence of lipofuscin impairs cellular functioning is required. Nevertheless, as Strehler (1978) points out, it is probably impossible to clutter up as much as 75 percent of a cell's interior with lipofuscin without interfering with its functioning.

Cross-linkage theory   According to the cross-linkage theory, *cross-linkages* or bonds develop with the passage of time either between components of the same molecule or between molecules. Bjorksten (1968) suggested that cross-linking leads to progressive biochemical failure and represents a primary cause of aging. Most of the work on this theory has involved the study of extracellular proteins such as elastin and collagen. It has been well established that these proteins, which surround the blood vessels and cells, slowly cross-link with age. It has been proposed that such changes may have far-reaching effects on the functioning of cells—e.g., they may lead to severe oxygen deficiency. Bjorksten (1968) has suggested that similar changes may occur in intracellular proteins such as the DNA molecules. Indeed, cross-linking of DNA has been observed in both culture tissue (in vitro) and living tissue (in vivo). To the extent that cross-linkage of the DNA molecules occurs in the cells with increasing age, a mechanism for explaining cell failure may be available.

Free-radical theory   This theory is related to cross-linkage theory, and may be viewed as one way in which cross-links are produced. *Free radicals* are unstable chemical compounds which react with other molecules in their vicinity.

[handwritten margin notes: Harman antioxidants]

As a result of these reactions, cells may be altered in structure and function. Again, alteration of key proteins (e.g., DNA) could result in eventual cell death (Harman, 1968). Free radicals are generated by common substances such as various foods and tobacco smoke. The formation of free radicals is accelerated by radiation and inhibited by antioxidants. Harman has presented evidence suggesting that mice fed antioxidants show an increased average life span. As a result, various antioxidant dietary supplements such as vitamin E have been proposed as a means of combatting damage to free radicals. However, tests of these claims remain inconclusive.

Physiological Theories

These theories suggest that aging results from the failure of some physiological coordinating system, such as the immunological or endocrine system, to properly integrate bodily functions.

[handwritten margin note: antibodies/cells]

Immunological theories The immune system protects the body against invading microorganisms and mutant cells (e.g., cancer cells) in the body. Two mechanisms are involved. First, the immune system generates antibodies which react with the proteins of foreign organisms. Second, it forms cells which engulf and digest foreign cells. Deleterious changes occur in this system with age. For example, the production of antibodies peaks in adolescence and thereafter declines with age. The immune system may also lose its ability to recognize mutated cells. For example, the great increase in cancer in older adults is probably related to failures in the immune system. Further, Walford (1969) has noted that there is an increase with age in *autoimmunity*, in which the body, in effect, attacks itself. This may result from a failure of the immune system to recognize normal cells as normal or from errors in antibody formation, so that the antibodies react to normal cells as well as foreign ones. This theory is supported by findings which indicate increase of autoimmune antibodies in the blood with increasing age (Walford, 1969).

[handwritten margin note: autoimmunity]

[handwritten margin notes: pancreas/diabetes, Finch, hormones]

Neuroendocrine theories There is considerable evidence to show that the endocrine system declines in its function with age. For example, with increasing age, the pancreas fails to quickly release sufficient insulin when blood sugar rises. Related to this is the fact that the incidence of adult-onset diabetes increases with age, becoming particularly prevalent in the elderly. Similarly, age-related changes occur in the gonads, adrenals, and other sites of hormone production. None of the site-specific changes noted above appear to account for aging. However, Finch (1976) has suggested that aging may be controlled in similar fashion to developmental events such as puberty and menopause. In particular, he has suggested that cellular aging is regulated by hormonal events. The hormonal changes of aging are controlled by the brain, particularly the pituitary gland and the hypothalmus. Finch argues that aging pacemakers in these control centers initiate a cascade of neurological and hormonal events which regulate the aging process.

Integration of Theories

While each of these theories focuses on a different aspect of the aging process, the theories are not necessarily incompatible. Strehler (1978), for instance, suggests the following integration.

1. The primary event in aging is the loss of the ability of the cell to divide. This event is programmed in the genetic code of the cell.
2. After cell division has stopped, the cell is particularly susceptible to environmental damage. Further, the degree to which the cell can repair itself depends on other genes. A key defect that accumulates is the loss of some of the copies of a group of genes responsible for protein synthesis.
3. Decreased RNA results in an increased accumulation of damaged enzymes and lipofuscin, which impairs cell function.
4. Decreased normal functioning at the cellular level results in decreased integration among the physiological systems of the body. Ultimately, the systems break down and the individual dies.

BIOLOGY-BEHAVIOR INTERACTIONS

We have briefly reviewed some of the molecular, cellular, and physiological changes that may be responsible for the aging process. These changes affect virtually all major systems of the human body: skeletal, muscle, skin, pulmonary, cardiovascular, neural, endocrine, reproductive, gastrointestinal, and excretory. But what relationship do these changes have to behavior—the basic focus of our inquiry in this text? In the following sections, we will illustrate several biology-behavior interactions of varying types. Of course, such interactions are extensive. Our intent is to be illustrative rather than exhaustive.

In examining these interactions, several things should be kept in mind. First, while the changes associated with biological aging are inevitable and universal, they do not affect all systems equally. Figure 3.2 shows the wide variation in amount of decline which occurs in several indices with age. Second, while biological aging may be inevitable and universal, it is not unmodifiable. Interventions such as hormone therapy and physical exercise can modify its effects.

In addition to the fact that biological change is differential and modifiable, there is evidence to suggest that biological functioning affects behavioral functioning only at certain points. Birren (1963) suggested that behavioral functions are affected only when biological functions reach some critical or limiting level. In an intensive study of forty-seven elderly men, Birren divided the individuals, who had initially been selected for their good health, into two groups. About half had measurable evidence of minor disease (e.g., varicose veins) or no evidence of disease at all. About half evidenced incipient disease processes of a potentially serious nature. In the first group, only five of the correlations between measures of biological functioning and behavioral func-

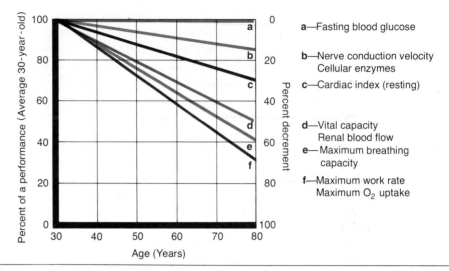

Figure 3.2 Age decrements in physiological functions in males. Mean values for 20- to 35-year-old subjects are taken as 100 per cent. Decrements shown are schematic linear projectives--large individual differences occur: *(a)* fasting blood glucose; *(b)* nerve conduction velocity and cellular enzymes; *(c)* resting cardiac index; *(d)* vital capacity and renal blood flow; *(e)* maximum breathing capacity; and *(f)* maximum work rate and maximum oxygen uptake. *(From Shock, 1972.)*

tioning were significant. In the less healthy group, twenty-six of these correlations were significant. These results caused Birren to suggest a *discontinuity hypothesis*. That is, only when certain limits are reached—for example, as a result of disease—does the linkage of biology and behavior become noticeable. Other studies have reported similar findings (Lieberman, 1975).

From this perspective, then, biological functioning sets a lower limit on behavior. Below a certain level biological variables become critical. Above a certain level other variables become critical. Of course, the location of this lower limit will vary with the biological and behavioral processes in question. The work of Birren and his colleagues (1963) suggests that relatively low levels of biological impairment may prove to be very significant for behavioral performance.

In the following sections, we will illustrate several biology-behavior interactions in order to illustrate the linkage between these domains. Note that such interactions may be of several types (e.g., biology influences behavior; behavior influences biology). We will attempt to illustrate some of these possibilities in our examples.

The Eye and Visual Perception

Surveys of the incidence of blindness and visual acuity show that both of these difficulties are associated with increasing chronological age. For example, the prevalence of *legal blindness* (corrected distance vision of 20/200 or worse in the better eye, or a visual field limited to 20 degrees in its greatest diameter) increases from less than 100 cases per 100,000 for individuals under age 21 to more than 1400 cases per 100,000 for individuals over age 69 (National Society for the Prevention of Blindness, 1966). Similarly, the incidence of poor *visual acuity* also increases with chronological age (Anderson & Palmore, 1974; U.S. National Health Survey, 1968). Figure 3.3 shows the corrected visual acuity in the better eye for 213 participants in the Duke Longitudinal Study aged 60 to 90 years (Anderson & Palmore, 1974). Visual acuity of 20/50 or worse indicates impairment sufficient to limit activities such as reading and driving. These data show that while 57 percent of those aged 60 to 69 had optimal visual acuity, only 27 percent of those aged 70 to 79, and only 14 percent of these aged 80 and over, functioned at this level. Anderson and Palmore (1974) also reported that *cataracts* (opacities of the lens that obstruct light waves) were present in 9 percent of those aged 60 to 69, 18 percent of those aged 70 to 79, and 36 percent of those aged 80 and over. What causes the increasing visual impairment associated with age?

Structural changes in the eye   The visual problems summarized above reflect the impact of two sets of age-related changes in the eye (Fozard, Wolf, Bell, McFarland, & Podolsky, 1977).

The first set of structural changes becomes evident in the thirties and forties. These changes affect the *transmissiveness* (the amount of light reaching the eye) and *accommodative power* (the ability to focus and maintain an image on the retina) of the eye. Several factors reduce the amount of light reaching the retina. These include decreased pupil size and increased clouding and yellowing of the lens (Fozard et al., 1977). As a result of these changes, middle-aged and older adults require more illumination than younger adults in order to maintain the same degree of visual discrimination. At the same time,

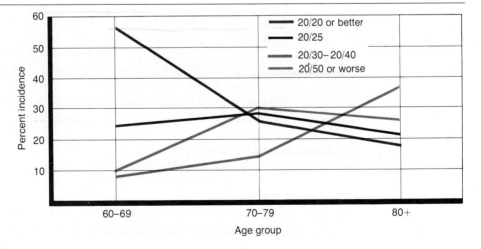

Figure 3.3
Corrected best distance vision in the better eye. *(Based on Anderson & Palmore, 1974, Table 2-7, p. 27.)*

the increasing opacity of the lens results in an increased susceptibility to glare (Wolf, 1960). In addition to reducing the amount of light, the yellowing of the lens reduces the sensitivity of the eye to the blue-violet end of the spectrum. As a result, reds and yellows are discriminated better than blues and violets. By old age, color sensitivity over the entire spectrum declines markedly (Gilbert, 1957).

During the thirties and forties the lens also becomes thicker and less elastic. As a result, it cannot change shape as readily. This impairs the ability of the eye to focus and maintain an image on the retina. In particular, it becomes difficult for middle-aged and older adults to view close objects clearly (*presbyopia*). This can result in the need for bifocals. The sharpest decline in accommodation occurs between 40 and 59 years of age (Brückner, 1967).

The second set of structural changes becomes evident in the fifties and sixties. These changes affect the retina itself. They appear to be primarily the result of vascular insufficiencies which result in reduced blood supply to the retina and, consequently, metabolic deficiencies and cell loss (Fozard et al., 1977). One result of these changes is a decrease in the size of the visual field and an increase in the size of the blind spot. The retina also becomes less sensitive to low levels of illumination. For example, *dark adaptation* (the ability to adjust vision when moving from high to low levels of illumination) varies with age. The time required to adapt increases, and the final level of functioning decreases, particularly for elderly adults (Domey, McFarland, & Chadwick, 1960).

Visual perception These structural changes in the eye have a significant impact on adult behavior in a variety of contexts (Fozard et al., 1977; Fozard & Popkin, 1978). For example, we noted that older adults are less sensitive to light at low levels of illumination. Many tasks, such as driving at twilight or night, require partial dark adaptation. This involves crossing over from rod to cone vision and vice versa. Research suggests that under such conditions the decrease in acuity is much greater for older adults than for younger adults (Richards, 1966). Similarly, abrupt changes of illumination can cause difficulty for older adults. In particular, accidental falls may be related to such changes. Archea (reported in Fozard & Popkin, 1978) found that most falls occur on the step at the top of the landing. Fozard and Popkin (1978) note: "In many houses, the stairway between the first and second floors is located at the end of the hall. As people walk toward the end of the hall, they typically look into windows that permit a great deal of light to enter. They then turn 90° to start down the "dark" stairs—precisely the situation in which Archea has found most falls to occur" (p. 979).

Even at middle levels of illumination, older adults require more illumination than younger adults. For example, a study by Hughes (reported in Fozard and Popkin, 1978) examined the effect of illumination level on the work performance of younger (19 to 27 years) and middle-aged (46 to 57 years) office workers. The task involved a search for 10 target numbers printed on sheets containing a total of 420 numbers. Each worker performed several searches under three

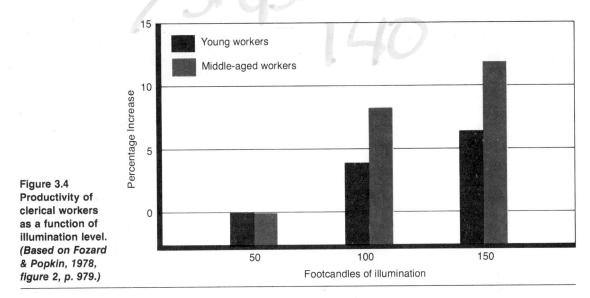

Figure 3.4 Productivity of clerical workers as a function of illumination level. (Based on Fozard & Popkin, 1978, figure 2, p. 979.)

levels of illumination. The results are diagramed in Figure 3.4. This figure shows that increased levels of illumination resulted in greater efficiency for both younger and middle-aged workers. However, the middle-aged workers benefited more from the increase than the younger workers.

Finally, using an intriguing approach, Pastalan, Mautz, and Merrill (1973) have attempted to simulate the effects of structural changes in the eye, such as opacities and yellowing of the lens. These investigators took photographs of various scenes with normal and with coated camera lenses. The coatings on the lens were designed to simulate the scenes as they would appear to the eyes of a person in the late seventies or early eighties. Figure 3.5 shows the same scene photographed through the normal and coated lenses. The coated lens simulates an acuity level of approximately 20/40. These photographs provide a dramatic illustration of the difficulties faced by many older adults.

Our brief review suggests that the structural changes which occur in the eye with increasing age have marked behavioral significance. The research also suggests that many of the visual problems of older adults may be helped through appropriate environmental design. Fozard and Popkin (1978), for instance, suggest that increased local lighting of work areas, steps, and ramps and increased contrast in visual information displays would compensate for many visual problems of the elderly.

The Central Nervous System and Speed of Response

There is relatively clear evidence which indicates that, with advancing age, individuals show a tendency toward increasing slowness of response (Welford, 1958; 1977). This is a gradual change occurring across the entire life span. It

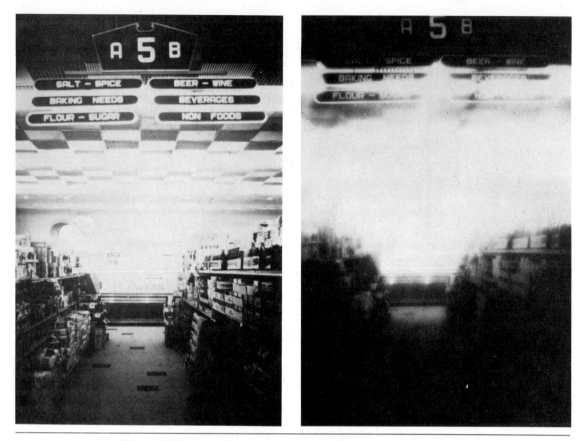

Figure 3.5 Photographic simulation of a scene as seen by a modal person in the late seventies or early eighties is shown in the right-hand member of the pair. This simulation illustrates the increased susceptibility to glare by the elderly. The prints were made from color slides prepared by Dr. Leon Pastalan. *(From Fozard et al., 1977.)*

shows up in a variety of so-called speeded tasks. *Speeded tasks* are those where errors would be unlikely if the individual had an unlimited amount of time to complete the tasks. Typically, they involve relatively simple responses such as pushing buttons, sorting items, crossing out items, and so forth. The objective, of course, is to complete the task as rapidly as possible. Several brief examples will suffice.

Reaction-time (*RT*) tasks involve a measure of the time elapsing between the appearance of a signal and the beginning of a responding movement. Reaction time is usually viewed as a function of the central nervous system. It involves perceptual abilities and decision-making processes. Reaction-time tasks vary in complexity. For example, *simple RT tasks* involve only one signal and one response (e.g., pushing a button when a light goes on). *Disjunctive RT tasks* involve multiple signals and/or responses (e.g., pushing the right-hand button when the red light goes on and the left-hand button when the green light goes on, or pushing the button only when the red light goes on). Hodgkins (1962) examined simple RT performance (subject released a key when a signal light was lit) in over 400 females aged 6 to 84 years. Hodgkins found that mean speed increased with age until the late teens, remained constant until the mid-twenties, and then declined steadily throughout the remainder of the age range. The degree of change in reaction time was 25 percent between the twenties and the sixties and 43 percent between the twenties and seventies. The slowing seen with age in simple RT tasks is magnified in the case of disjunctive RT tasks (Griew, 1958) or tasks requiring the subject to remember previous signals and responses (Kay, 1954).

Slowing is also seen with sorting tasks. Botwinick, Robbin, and Brinley (1960) asked younger and older persons to sort seventy-one ordinary playing cards (excluding face cards) into slots in a sorting bin. They were asked to sort the cards by matching the number of the card to the number of a stimulus card located above the bin. When no match was possible, the card was to be placed in the last slot. Five levels of difficulty were created by varying the number of stimulus cards involved: 1, 3, 5, 7, or 9. The results indicated that the older adults were slower than the younger adults and that this difference increased as the complexity of the task increased.

A third type of speeded task involves copying simple materials or performing various canceling operations. For example, Botwinick and Storandt (1974) asked individuals ranging in age from the twenties through the seventies to copy rows of numbers and to "cancel" rows of ¼-inch horizontal lines by drawing a vertical line through them. The results showed a steady decline with age in the speed of carrying out these tasks for both men and women.

As we have implied, the slowing of behavior with age appears in a wide range of tasks. Indeed, it appears to be a general characteristic of older adults. That is, younger adults appear to be fast or slow depending on the characteristics of the task and situation, e.g., familiarity, motivation. Older adults, however, seem to have a characteristic or general slowing of behavior independent of task and situation (Birren, Riegel, & Morrison, 1962). This general slowing does not appear to be primarily a function of *peripheral nervous system* factors (e.g., sensory acuity, Botwinick, 1971; speed of peripheral nerve conduction, Birren & Botwinick, 1955; speed of movement once a response is initiated, Botwinick & Thompson, 1966). Rather, it appears to reflect a basic change in the way the *central nervous system* processes information (Birren, 1974).

Brain electrical activity and the slowing of behavior   Considerable evidence has accumulated to link changes in brain electrical activity to the slowing of behavior (Marsh & Thompson, 1977; Woodruff, 1979). The *electroencephalogram* (*EEG*) represents a record of the brain's electrical activity. It is obtained by attaching electrodes to the scalp and amplifying the resulting electrical activity many times. The human EEG displays continuous rhythmic activity—differing wavelike patterns varying in frequency and amplitude. There are four basic patterns, each of which is associated with different behavioral

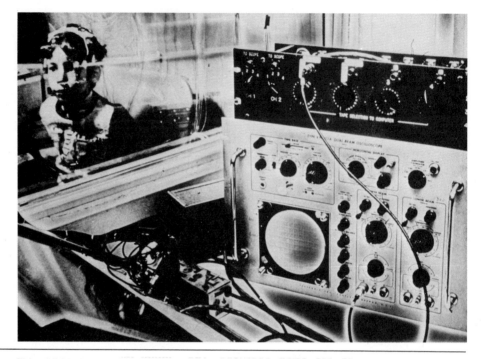

This child is being tested for brain function by an electrical recording technique called the *quantitative electrophysiological battery* (QB). Patients taking the QB wear a set of electrodes that is wired to a computer terminal. They are then exposed to a carefully designed series of stimuli, including light flashes, clicks, and taps. As various combinations of stimuli are presented, the computer records about thirty aspects of electrical activity at close to sixty brain sites. The resulting pattern is called an EEG. A number of brain problems produce readily detectable departures from normal patterns. (Psychology Today)

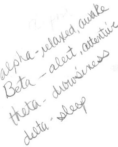

alpha - relaxed, awake
Beta - alert, attentive
Theta - drowsiness
delta - sleep

states. The dominant rhythm is the *alpha*, with a frequency of 8 to 13 cycles per second (cps). It is associated with a relaxed, awake state. *Beta* rhythm is faster (18 to 30 cps) and is associated with an attentive, alert state. *Theta* (5 to 7 cps) and *delta* (0.5 to 4 cps) are slow frequencies associated with drowsiness and sleep, respectively.

The bulk of the work on aging has focused on the alpha rhythm. Generally, this research has suggested a slowing of *alpha frequency* with increasing age (Busse & Obrist, 1963; Obrist, 1954; 1963). Most of these studies also show a decrease in the time older adults produce alpha, which has been labeled a decrease in *alpha abundance*. This research indicates that alpha frequency reaches its maximum of between 10 and 11 cps during adolescence and begins to gradually slow after the age of 25 to 30. The average frequency decreases to about 9 cps by the sixties and to 8 to 8.5 cps after age 80. This slowing has been confirmed in longitudinal data as well (Obrist, Henry, & Justiss, 1961; Wang & Busse, 1969).

Declines exhibited by an older adult such as memory loss are often explained by the statement "Oh, X is getting senile." The use of the term senility has become very imprecise. What exactly does it refer to? Butler and Lewis (1977) note that the lay term senility actually refers to two chronic brain syndromes—*senile psychosis* (sometimes called senile dementia or senile brain disease) and *psychosis associated with cerebral arteriosclerosis*.

These chronic diseases are *organic brain disorders* which are mental conditions associated with the impairment of brain functioning. According to Butler and Lewis (1977), organic brain syndromes are characterized by five features: the impairment of comprehension, memory, judgment, orientation, and shallow affect (emotion). The damage associated with *chronic brain syndromes* is irreversible. It should be distinguished from that associated with *acute brain syndromes*, which is reversible. The two types of syndromes are often confused. The characteristics of the chronic brain syndromes associated with "senility" may be described as follows (Butler & Lewis, 1977):

Senile psychosis This refers to chronic disorders associated with the degeneration of the brain cells themselves. The age of onset generally falls between 60 and 90 years of age, with the average being 75 years. As a result of the relatively late age of onset, the disease occurs more frequently in women than in men. The disease is characterized by gradual and progressive deterioration in physical, mental, and emotional functioning. Early symptoms may include decline in personal care, lack of interest and apathy, loss of inhibitions, and errors in judgment. As the disease progresses, the traditional impairment of mental functioning associated with organic brain syndromes (e.g., memory and comprehension) becomes more evident. The person may exhibit sleeplessness and restlessness, and may wander away from home. Paranoid tendencies may also become manifested. Little is known about the causes of senile brain disease, although multiple mechanisms, including genetic, immunological, and stress factors, have been suggested. The steady and progressive course of the disease eventually results in death.

Psychosis associated with cerebral arteriosclerosis In contrast to senile psychoses, which show steady decline, arteriosclerotic psychoses result in uneven decline. The syndrome is associated with vascular damage caused by arteriosclerotic diseases. It occurs earlier in life than senile brain disease. The age of onset ranges from 50 to 70 years, with the average being 66 years. Arteriosclerotic psychoses occur more frequently in men than women. Early symptoms of the disease include dizziness, headaches, and decreased vigor. In over half the cases, the onset occurs suddenly as an attack of confusion. The progress of the disease reflects an up-and-down pattern. For example, the person's memory may be impaired one minute and intact the next. There is great diversity in the course of the illness from person to person. Physical impairment is often greater than intellectual impairment, although the latter can be great after massive or repeated strokes or heart attacks. Death usually occurs from cerebrovascular accidents, myocardial infarction, or pneumonia.

It is important to note that while these syndromes have an organic base, their onset and course may be significantly affected by social and environmental factors. Further, since the symptoms are largely behavioral, misdiagnosis occurs easily. What is often labeled an organic brain syndrome may actually be a wholly behavioral reaction (e.g., depression) to stressful life events or environmental circumstances. Finally, these diseases are not untreatable. Both mental and physical functioning can be improved even though the biological damage is irreversible. With adequate services and assistance, many individuals would be able to remain in their own homes throughout most of the course of the illness.

The exact mechanisms involved in the slowing of the EEG with age remain somewhat unclear. However, the most powerful explanation associates it with central nervous system pathology (Obrist, 1972). Basically, it is proposed that reduced cerebral blood flow and consequent hypoxia (reduced oxygen) results in neuronal loss. The initial reduction of cerebral blood flow appears to be related to arteriosclerotic deposits or other vascular problems. Comparisons of matched samples with and without arteriosclerotic diseases typically yield differences in cerebral blood flow as well as alpha frequency (Dastar, Lane, Hansen, Kety, Butler, Perlin, & Sokoloff, 1963; Obrist & Bissell, 1955). While evidence for a disease-related explanation of alpha slowing is strong, other basic aging mechanisms may be involved as well. There is also evidence to suggest that slowing occurs in essentially disease-free older adults (Obrist, 1963).

The slowing of alpha with age has also been related to the slowing of behavior with age. Woodruff (1979) notes that two basic hypotheses have been proposed. The more general hypothesis is based on general theories of activation and arousal. These theories suggest that if the central nervous system of older adults is less responsive, then older adults should show slower EEG rhythms as well as slower behavior as a result. In this case, slowing is actually a result of reduced cortical excitability—alpha is merely an index of this state. Reduced excitability could be a result of disease processes or other fundamental changes in brain physiology. Surwillo (1968) has suggested a more specific hypothesis in which he proposes that alpha constitutes a kind of internal biological clock. In this case, the slowing of alpha is seen as causally linked to the slowing of behavior rather than as an index of reduced central nervous system excitability.

Both of these hypotheses, however, suggest that the slowing of alpha should be related to the slowing of behavior. This appears to be the case. For example, Surwillo (1963) reported a correlation of .72 between average reaction time and average alpha period (inverse of alpha frequency) for 100 individuals whose ages ranged from 28 to 99 years. In spite of this, there is little support for the hypothesis that slowing of behavior is a direct result of the slowing of alpha.

In a study designed to examine this issue Woodruff (1975) used biofeedback techniques to manipulate alpha. Woodruff trained 10 younger and 10 older adults to increase the abundance of alpha activity at their modal level, and at frequencies above and below their modal level. At each of these levels, Woodruff tested the individual's reaction time once the appropriate criterion of alpha production had been reached. Comparisons with control subjects indicated that biofeedback itself did not affect reaction time. Further, reaction times were faster for 9 of 10 older subjects and 7 of 10 younger subjects when they were producing fast brain waves than when they were producing slow brain waves. The group means are shown in Table 3.1. Thus, Woodruff's data suggest that a shift in brain-wave frequency is related to a shift in reaction time. However, correlations between brain-wave frequency and reaction time within persons were relatively small. As a result, Woodruff's data do not support

---

TABLE 3.1
MEAN REACTION TIME (MILLISECONDS) FOR
YOUNGER AND OLDER ADULTS UNDER THREE
LEVELS OF ALPHA FREQUENCY

	Reaction time	
Biofeedback Conditions (alpha frequency)	Younger (18–29 yr)	Older (60–81 yr)
Fast	207.4	259.4
Moderate	211.9	280.0
Slow	214.8	285.4

Source: Adapted from Woodruff, 1975.

Surwillo's hypothesis that the slowing of alpha causes the slowing of behavior. Rather, she suggests that the arousal hypothesis is the simplest explanation. Increased alpha production was accomplished through arousal of the subject's central nervous system, and faster reaction times resulted.

The older adult's central nervous system appears to be in a state of underarousal compared to that of younger adults, possibly as a result of vascular pathology. As a result, older individuals have slower modal brain-wave frequencies and these are associated with slower mean reaction times.

Cardiovascular disease and the slowing of behavior. The relationship between central nervous function and the slowing of behavior is also apparent as the link between health status and behavior is examined (Birren & Spieth, 1962; Spieth, 1965).

For example, Spieth (1965) examined speeded performance among young and middle-aged men who had mild to moderate degrees of cardiovascular disease. The subjects of Spieth's inquiry were present or former air pilots and air-traffic controllers ranging in age from 35 to 59 years. The research was done in connection with a physical examination for renewal of medical certification to fly or control air traffic. The individuals were classified into five health-status groups: (I) healthy, (II) mild to moderate congenital or rheumatic heart defects; (III) arteriosclerotic or coronary disease without *hypertension* (high blood pressure); (IV) essential hypertension or cardiovascular disease with hypertension; and (V) history of cerebrovascular disease or old cerebrovascular accident. These groups reflect a continuum of disease severity from mild to moderately severe. Note, however, that these men were not acutely ill. Essentially, they were under no restriction of ordinary activity.

The men were administered a battery of speeded tasks including simple and complex RT tasks. An interesting feature of Spieth's study is that one may assume that such tasks were not highly unfamiliar to the subjects because of their experience as pilots and air-traffic controllers. The tasks, then, were probably relatively high in ecological validity for these individuals.

Spieth's results indicate that speed of performance declined in a relatively linear fashion with increasing degrees of cardiovascular impairment. This effect occurred on all tasks, although it was greater on complex compared with simple tasks. Spieth's study, then, suggests that individuals suffering even mild to moderate levels of cardiovascular impairment perform more poorly than healthy individuals.

Thus, there appears to be an important link between biological functioning, particularly central nervous functioning, and the slowing of behavior with age. Other variables are important as well. For example, it has been demonstrated that older persons can increase their speed of response with practice (Hoyer, Labouvie, & Baltes, 1973). Similarly, it has been demonstrated that older adults appear to be more cautious, exhibiting a tendency to compensate for a loss of speed by increased accuracy (Welford, 1958; Rabbitt & Birren, 1967). These factors, however, seem only to explain a portion of the slowing (Welford, 1977). Fundamentally, the slowing of behavior with age appears to be a function of a basic change in the speed of central nervous system functioning. This type of interaction suggests a rather direct link between biology and behavior. That is, changes in the physiology of the central nervous system produce pervasive changes in the timing of behavior.

Personality and Cardiovascular Disease

The incidence of cardiovascular disease is related to many factors, including diet, smoking, obesity, and psychosocial variables. In the case of the psychosocial variables, linkages have been found between cardiovascular disease and both personality and situational stress. Often these two sets of factors are interrelated. Of particular interest, however, has been the work of Rosenman and Friedman, who have described a behavior pattern associated with high coronary risk (Friedman & Rosenman, 1974; Rosenman, 1974; Rosenman & Friedman, 1971). This behavior pattern has been labeled *Type A behavior pattern*. It is contrasted with *Type B behavior pattern*, which is associated with low coronary risk. In contrast to the interactions considered in the previous sections in which biology affected behavior, this research provides an example of the influence of behavior on biology.

The Type A behavior pattern   As described in Box 3.3, the Type A pattern is characterized by a number of behavioral tendencies, including excessive competitiveness, acceleration of the pace of ordinary activities, impatience with the rate at which most events take place, thinking about or doing several things simultaneously, hostility, and feelings of struggling against time and the environment. The converse of the Type A pattern is characterized by the relative absence of these behavioral tendencies. It is important to note that these are patterns, rather than true typologies. Rosenman and Friedman report that only about 10 percent of their subjects had fully-developed Type A or B behavior. It is also important to note that these behavior patterns are not context-free personality traits. Rather, they appear when a predisposed

Discovery

BOX 3.3

ARE YOU A TYPE A OR TYPE B?

Classification of individuals into Type A and Type B behavior patterns has been based on a structured interview, a battery of perceptual motor tasks, and self-report questionnaires. Friedman and Rosenman (1974) define the patterns as follows.

You possess Type A behavior pattern if:

1 You explosively accent key words when you speak; you utter the last words of your sentences more rapidly than the opening words.
2 You always move, walk, and eat rapidly.
3 You are often impatient with how slowly things happen; you attempt to finish the sentences of persons speaking to you before they can. You become furious when other cars on the road hold you back; you find it anguishing to wait in line.
4 You do or think about two or more things at once. You worry about work on your day off; you think about unrelated topics when someone else is talking.
5 You prefer to talk about topics that interest you; you only pretend to listen to other people's topics.
6 You feel vaguely guilty when you relax.
7 You don't see the most important, interesting, or lovely things you come into contact with.
8 You're preoccupied with *getting* things worth having rather than becoming things worth *being*.
9 You always feel a sense of time urgency.
10 You feel hostile toward and challenged by other Type A individuals.
11 You have habitual gestures or tics—e.g., fist clenching, jaw clenching, tooth grinding—that suggest an inner struggle.
12 You are afraid to stop hurrying because you think that's what makes you successful.
13 You evaluate your own and others' activities by translating them into numbers.

You possess Type B behavior pattern if:

1 You are free of all the Type A habits and traits.
2 You feel no general hostility and you display competitiveness only when it is demanded by the situation.
3 You play to relax rather than to prove yourself.
4 You can relax without guilt and work calmly.

How do you classify yourself? Remember that the definition of the Type A given here represents "full-blown" Type A behavior in all its manifestations. Many individuals exhibit some but not all of these characteristics. These patterns are a matter of degree.

individual encounters situations that bring them into play. Finally, it is important to note that these behavior patterns are not correlated with intelligence, occupational category, socioeconomic status, and other indices of "success." Thus, a bank president may be either a Type B or a Type A, and, conversely, a janitor may be a Type A or a Type B.

Type A behavior and cardiovascular disease There have been numerous studies of the linkage between Type A behavior and coronary disease. A primary investigation, however, was a prospective study of over 3500 men aged 39 to 59 begun in 1960 (Rosenman, Friedman, Straus, Jenkins, Zyzanski, Wurm, & Kositcheck, 1970; Rosenman, Friedman, Straus, Wurm, Jenkins, Messinger, Kositcheck, Hahn, & Werthessen, 1966; Rosenman,

Friedman, Straus, Wurm, Kositcheck, Hahn, & Werthessen, 1964). These men were free from coronary disease when the initial measures of behavior pattern and physiological indices were obtained. Follow-up evaluations were completed at the end of 2½, 4½, and 8½ years.

The data indicated that coronary heart disease was much more prevalent among Type A men than among Type B men. The figures from the 4½-year follow-up (Rosenman et al., 1970) are shown in Table 3.2. It can be seen that 71.5 percent of the 30- to 49-year-old men who developed coronary heart disease were Type A while only 28.5 percent were Type B. In cases where coronary heart disease was not present 46.8 percent were Type A and 53.2 percent were Type B. The figures for the older age group are similar. Type A men also show chemical changes associated with coronary heart disease prior to the onset of clinical signs, including elevated serum cholesterol and triglicerides, accelerated blood coagulation, and increased daytime excretion of catecholamines.

Rosenman and Friedman's data also indicate that coronary heart disease was predicted by other risk factors, such as smoking, diabetes, high blood pressure, and high blood cholesterol levels. Indeed, many of the men showing Type A behavior also had high levels of these risk factors. However, statistical control of these other risk factors did not eliminate the impact of Type A behavior in young and middle-aged adult men. Even with these factors controlled, Type A men were almost three times as likely to develop coronary heart disease as Type B men. However, the older the individual, the more other risk factors begin to play a role. In other words, the link between Type A behavior and coronary heart disease is particularly significant for those in their thirties and forties.

Thus, Rosenman and Friedman's research indicates that the biochemical abnormalities associated with coronary heart disease and the incidence of coronary heart disease are substantially higher in individuals exhibiting Type A behavior than in individuals exhibiting Type B behavior. Of course, these data are still correlational in nature. Research with animals, however, has provided additional evidence that Type A behavior is causally related to coronary heart disease. In these studies, aggressive behavior was induced in rats by producing lesions in the hypothalmus. Such experimentally altered animals were more

TABLE 3.2

RELATIONSHIP OF TYPE A AND B BEHAVIOR PATTERN TO
CORONARY HEART DISEASE (CHD) IN TWO AGE GROUPS OF MEN

Behavior Pattern	30–49 years		50–59 years	
	CHD Present, %	CHD Absent, %	CHD Present, %	CHD Absent, %
Type A	71.5	46.8	70.0	56.3
Type B	28.5	53.2	30.0	43.7

Source: From Rosenman et al., 1970.

CARDIOVASCULAR DISEASE: THE NUMBER ONE KILLER

Diseases of the cardiovascular system represent the major causes of death in the United States. The data summarized in the accompanying table show that in 1977, for instance, diseases of the heart were the leading cause of death, accounting for 37.8 percent of all deaths. When one adds cerebrovascular and arteriosclerotic diseases, almost 50 percent of all deaths are related to the cardiovascular system. What are some of the causes of these deaths?

Arteriosclerosis literally means "hardening of the arteries." More accurately, it refers to a group of processes which have in common thickening and loss of elasticity of the arterial walls (Kohn, 1977). Prominent among these is *atherosclerosis,* a term often used interchangeably with arteriosclerosis. In atherosclerosis, arterial lesions develop, and fat, cholesterol, and collagen accumulate at the site of these injuries. With time, the lesions become raised and begin to close off the space (lumen) inside the vessel. Such raised lesions are called plaques. The plaques, consisting mostly of collagen, become increasingly scar-like. Eventually, they may ulcerate or hemorrhage or lead to the formation of blood clots in the artery. Artery damage may be present for years without causing any noticeable symptoms. However, as the interior diameter of the vessel is decreased or the wall of the vessel loses its elasticity, a variety of problems may occur, including coronary heart disease. In this case, the degenerative changes of the artery wall related to coronary artery disease reduce the volume of blood supplied to the heart muscle and increase the possibility of the formation of blood clots.

These conditions may lead to several results. *Angina pectoris* is characterized by agonizing pain felt in the region of the heart, left shoulder, and arm. It occurs when the heart muscle suffers from a lack of oxygen due to an inadequate blood supply. The pain of angina pectoris often occurs when the individual is under significant physical or emotional stress. The pain, however, rarely lasts for more than a few minutes once the stress that brought it on is reduced.

A *myocardial infarction* is an area of dead tissue in the heart muscle. It occurs because the

DEATH RATES FOR 15 LEADING
CAUSES OF DEATH:
UNITED STATES, 1977

Rank	Cause of Death	Death rate, per 100,000 Population	Percent of Total Deaths
	All causes	878.1	100.0
1	Diseases of heart	332.3	37.8
2	Malignant neoplasms, including neoplasms of lymphatic and hematopoietic tissues	178.7	20.4
3	Cerebrovascular diseases	84.1	9.6
4	Accidents	47.7	5.4
	Motor vehicle accidents	22.9	
	All other accidents	24.8	
5	Influenza and pneumonia	23.7	2.7
6	Diabetes mellitus	15.2	1.7
7	Cirrhosis of liver	14.3	1.6
8	Arteriosclerosis	13.3	1.5
9	Suicide	13.3	1.5
10	Certain causes of mortality in early infancy	10.8	1.2
11	Bronchitis, emphysema, and asthma	10.3	1.2
12	Homicide	9.2	1.0
13	Congenital anomalies	6.0	0.7
14	Nephritis and nephrosis	3.9	0.4
15	Septicemia	3.3	0.4
	All other causes	112.0	12.8

Source: U.S. Department of Health, Education, and Welfare, 1979.

While facilities such as this intensive care unit save many lives, diseases of the cardiovascular system represent the leading causes of death in the United States today. (Bruce Roberts/Photo Researchers)

muscle tissue has been deprived of oxygen for too long a period of time. In most cases this occurs because of the formation of a blood clot or *thrombus* in the coronary artery which has blocked the blood supply. Depending on the size and location of the infarction the individual may die or recover with varying degrees of impairment.

The degeneration of the cardiovascular system increases with age, and incipient signs of atherosclerosis are common in adolescents and young adults (Kohn, 1977). Risk factors associated with cardiovascular disease, in addition to Type A behavior, include smoking, elevated serum lipids, excess body weight, diabetes mellitus, hypertension, and prolonged hemodialysis.

likely to develop coronary heart disease than control animals. Friedman and Rosenman (1974) conclude: "There is extraordinarily good scientific evidence on hand to indicate that Type A Behavior Pattern is the major cause of premature coronary artery disease in this country" (p. 266).

Physical Exercise and Physiological Vigor

Research on the effects of physical exercise provides another significant example of the influence of behavior on biological functioning. It is well known that a regular regime of physical exercise produces significant improvements in the physiological functioning of young adults. The training effects of exercise include an increase in work capacity, maximum oxygen uptake, and muscle tone, and a decrease in heart rate, blood pressure, and body fat. However, in order to obtain such training effects, the exercise must be lengthy enough and severe enough to produce sufficient physiological stress. A short walk to the corner drugstore or a game of shuffleboard will not produce a training effect.

Benefits come largely from regular *aerobic exercises* which demand oxygen, such as running, jogging, brisk walking, swimming, bicycling, and the like (Cooper, 1968; deVries, 1975).

Training effects in middle-aged and older adults   The older adult has lost part of the capacity to respond to physiological stress as a result of both aging and disease processes. Consequently, until recently it was questioned whether middle-aged and older adults could benefit from physical exercise. However, research during the last decade has demonstrated the beneficial effects of exercise well into old age. For example, deVries (1970) observed a significant training effect in men aged 51 to 87 who participated in a vigorous exercise program. The program consisted of calisthenics, running and walking, and either stretching exercises or swimming. The men were tested initially and after six, eighteen, and forty-two weeks of participation. The most significant findings were related to oxygen-transport capacity. Vital capacity increased by 19.6 percent, and oxygen pulse and minute ventilation at 90 percent of maximum heart rate increased by 29.4 percent and 35.2 percent, respectively. Significant improvements in percentage of body fat, physical work capacity, and blood pressure were also observed. The findings for several indices are shown in Figure 3.6. These effects were observed regardless of the participants' age or history of physical activity in young adulthood. Similar training effects have been observed in women aged 52 to 79 (Adams & deVries, 1973). Stamford (1972) has even demonstrated training effects for elderly patients at a state

With a history of physical exercise, older adults can engage in and enjoy physically active lives. (Abram G. Schoenfeld/Photo Researchers)

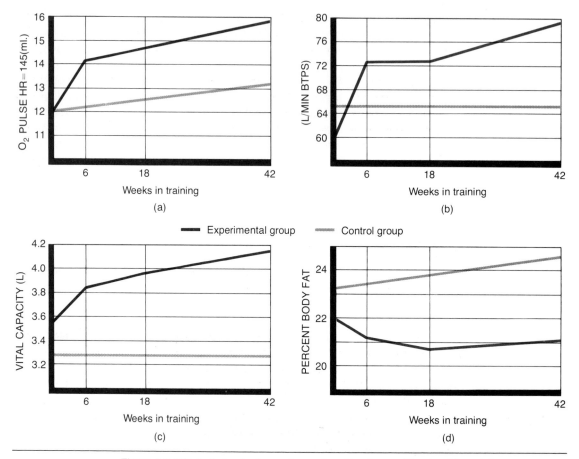

Figure 3.6 Effect of physical exercise on functional capacities in older adults. *(a)* maximal oxygen pulse; *(b)* minute ventilation; *(c)* vital capacity; *(d)* percentage of body fat.

institution following a light exercise program 12 weeks in length. These studies suggest that <u>physical exercise can significantly improve the physical vigor of middle-aged and older adults as well as younger adults.</u>

The impact of physical exercise on physical functioning suggests that this variable should be related to longevity. Indeed, people who are physically active do tend to live longer than those who are not physically active (Shock, 1977b; Woodruff, 1977). Unfortunately, such data are usually confounded by many other variables (e.g., physically active individuals also smoke less). Nevertheless, the evidence relating physical exercise to longevity is suggestive, and the evidence relating it to increased functional capacity is clear.

Prescribing exercise in adulthood Observation of the number of joggers along the road suggests that interest and participation in physical exercise are on the increase. Strenuous physical exercise, however, should be undertaken cautiously, especially in middle and old age, since activity which overstresses the system is dangerous. Current research, therefore, has begun to focus on the question, "How much is enough?" (deVries, 1971; Sidney & Shephard, 1978). In this regard, data collected by deVries (1975) suggest that for all but highly conditioned elderly men, 30 to 60 minutes of vigorous walking which raises the heart rate to 100 to 120 beats per minute is sufficient to bring about some improvement in cardiovascular functioning. It has been consistently suggested, however, that individuals undergo a physical examination by a physician and an evaluation by an exercise physiologist before undertaking any exercise program (Cooper, 1968; deVries, 1975; Woodruff, 1977).

The Reproductive System and Sexual Behavior

As people age, a variety of changes occur in their reproductive system. However, it is clear that the impact of these changes on sexual behavior is mediated by both sociocultural attitudes and expectations and the individual's past behavior. The interaction between biology and behavior in the area of sexuality is quite complex.

Changes in the female.   During a period lasting about 15 or 20 years, from about age 45 to 60, referred to as the *climacteric,* the body makes the transition from being able to reproduce to not being able to reproduce. The climacteric is highlighted by a decline in ovarian functioning with many associated biological changes in other tissues and systems as well. One particular event in this process—*menopause* or the cessation of menstruation—typically occurs during a two-year period at around age 47. A normal menopause, however, can occur between the ages of 36 and 60.

The major biological change during the climacteric is the aging of the ovaries, during which time they may become less able to respond to two hormones produced by the pituitary glands—follicle-stimulating hormone (FSH) and luteinizing hormone (LH). These are known as the gonadotropic hormones. There is also a decline in the output of the two major products of the ovaries: eggs (ova) and the sex hormones—*estrogens* and *progestogens* (Specifically, the ovaries become progressively less responsive to the stimulating effects of FSH and LH, with a resulting decrease in follicle development, sex hormone secretion, and release of eggs (ovulation).) The decline in estrogens and progestogens results in inadequate uterine stimulation, excess secretion of FSH and LH, and, consequently, the end of menstruation.

Several changes take place in sexual organs because of the decline in estrogens, including thinning of the vaginal epithelium, decreased vaginal lubrication, decreased vaginal size, increased incidence of vaginitis, and increased intensity of uterine contractions during orgasm. All these changes may cause pain during intercourse, and thus result in the avoidance of sexual intercourse. However, the decline in estrogens does not change the female's sexual desire, interest, or ability to reach orgasm. Moreover, it seems that these

The type of relationship shared over the years determines in large measure how older couples interact. (Ginger Chih/Peter Arnold, Inc.)

changes are related to the lack of sexual activity. According to Masters and Johnson (1966), women who maintained a pattern of regular intercourse once or twice a week did not complain of difficulties during intercourse when they were experiencing menopause. But those who had intercourse infrequently (once a month or less) or who did not masturbate regularly reported difficulties. The continuation of sexual activity over the life span, therefore, depends on the frequency and regularity of past activity.

Physical symptoms such as "hot flashes," headaches, dizziness, heart palpitations, and joint pains may also occur due to the decline in estrogens. Only about 10 percent of all women describe severe distress during menopause, but as many as 50 percent suffer some uncomfortable symptoms (McKinlay & Jeffreys, 1974). In general, a woman's attitude about menopause may influence her sexuality in later years. Some women feel, for instance, that menopause marks the end of their sexual life (Rubin, 1966). Perhaps these women use menopause as an excuse to stop engaging in an activity that they never really enjoyed but thought that they should pretend to enjoy. For other women, however, menopause is sexually liberating because it means that sexual intercourse and pregnancy are no longer related (Hyde, 1979).

Changes in the male   Although males do not experience menopause, they do experience age-related changes in the reproductive system. For example, there is a gradual decline in sperm production, although viable sperm are produced by the oldest of men. Similarly, androgen (testosterone) levels gradually decrease. In addition, erection occurs more slowly; the seminal fluid becomes thinner and its volume decreases; the force of the ejaculation decreases; after ejaculation, the erection is lost more rapidly; and it takes longer to achieve another erection following ejaculation. Any or all of these changes can cause the male to believe he is losing his sexual abilities. However, there is no time in a man's life when he completely loses his sexual ability as a result of aging per se. Indeed, as men age they have better control over ejaculations. Thus they are able to prolong coitus, and, as a result, are often considered better sexual partners (Hyde, 1979; Masters & Johnson, 1966).

Sexual behavior   What changes in sexual behavior occur with age? What biological, psychological, and social factors affect these changes?

Pfeiffer, Verwoerdt, and Davis (1974) report the results of a cross-sectional analysis of 502 men and women from 46 to 71 years of age. Information on sexual interest, enjoyment of sexual relations, frequency of sexual relations, and reasons for changes in frequency of sexual relations was collected as part of a self-administered questionnaire concerning medical history. Data summarizing current level of sexual interest and current frequency of sexual intercourse as a function of sex and age are shown in Tables 3.3 and 3.4. Two aspects of these data are of particular interest. First, dramatic sex differences are evident. Men reported greater sexual interest and activity than women. Second, older adults reported less current sexual interest and activity than younger adults. However, it is also clear that sex was still a significant factor in the lives of the majority of the respondents. Only 6 percent of the men and 33 percent of the women indicated they were no longer interested in sex. Only 12 percent of the men and 44 percent of the women indicated they no longer had sexual relations. Interestingly, the 66- to 71-year-old group actually reported slightly higher levels of sexual involvement than the 61- to 65-year-old group. Pfeiffer et al. (1974) suggest that this finding may reflect the impact of positive selection. These data are cross-sectional, and, therefore, reflect age differences rather than age changes. Pfeiffer and his colleagues have also reported data based on a 10-year longitudinal examination of 254 men and women initially 60 to 94 years of age (Pfeiffer, Verwoerdt, & Wang, 1968; Verwoerdt, Pfeiffer, & Wang, 1969). Analyses of these data generally confirm the influence of age and sex on sexual behavior. However, while the cross-sectional data showed a gradual decline in sexual interest and activity, the longitudinal data showed multiple patterns of change in these indices, including increases and stability as well as decline. For example, approximately 20 percent of the men showed increases in sexual interest and activity with increasing age.

This research, then, suggests that sexual behavior exhibits multiple patterns of change with increasing age. What variables affect these patterns of

TABLE 3.3
CURRENT LEVEL OF SEXUAL INTEREST (PERCENTAGE)

Age Group	Number	None	Mild	Moderate	Strong
Men					
46–50	43	0	9	63	28
51–55	41	0	19	71	10
56–60	61	5	26	57	12
61–65	54	11	37	48	4
66–71	62	10	32	48	10
Total	261	6	26	56	12
Women					
46–50	43	7	23	61	9
51–55	41	20	24	51	5
56–60	48	31	25	44	0
61–65	43	51	37	12	0
66–71	54	50	26	22	2
Total	229	33	27	37	3

Source: From Pfeiffer, Verwoerdt, and Davis, 1974.

TABLE 3.4
CURRENT FREQUENCY OF SEXUAL INTERCOURSE (PERCENTAGE)

Age Group	Number	None	Once a Month	Once a Week	2–3 Times a Week	More Than 3 Times a Week
Men						
46–50	43	0	5	62	26	7
51–55	41	5	29	49	17	0
56–60	61	7	38	44	11	0
61–65	54	20	43	30	7	0
66–71	62	24	48	26	2	0
Total	261	12	34	41	12	1
Women						
46–50	43	14	26	39	21	0
51–55	41	20	41	32	5	2
56–60	48	42	27	25	4	2
61–65	44	61	29	5	5	0
66–71	55	73	16	11	0	0
Total	231	44	27	22	6	1

Source: From Pfeiffer, Verwoerdt, and Davis, 1974.

change? Using data collected from the 502 middle-aged and older adults mentioned previously, Pfeiffer and Davis (1974) examined the impact of a number of biological, psychological, and social variables on sexual activity. The results of these analyses suggest that continued sexual activity among older adults is particularly dependent on previous sexual behavior and experience. For men, past sexual interest, enjoyment, and frequency all appear to be important. For women, past sexual enjoyment appears to be particularly important.

In addition to past experience, several other factors appear to be significant. The availability of a socially sanctioned and sexually capable partner is predictive of sexual interest and activity for women. Thus, marital status is a significant determinant of sexual activity for women. Indeed, the overwhelming majority of women over age 60 said they stopped having sexual intercourse because their husbands lost interest in sexual relations, lost the ability to have an erection, became ill, or died. Much of the decline in sexual interest and activity among women, therefore, may reflect a protective response. For men, health status appears to be particularly significant. Subjective assessments of health status predicted sexual interest and enjoyment. Objective assessments of health status predicted frequency of sexual relations. These results suggest that multiple factors in addition to age influence sexual behavior during middle age and old age. For men, past sexual experience (interest, enjoyment, and frequency) and subjective and objective health status are particularly significant. For women, past sexual enjoyment and marital status are particularly significant.

The participants in the studies summarized above were white, middle- and upper-middle-class, nonmetropolitan residents of North Carolina. Similar results may not be obtained with other racial, socioeconomic, or residential groups. Further, similar results may not be obtained for other cohorts. Nevertheless, despite these limitations, these studies suggest that sexuality remains an important component of behavior into old age. The impact of biological change in the reproductive system is mediated by a number of factors, particularly past sexual experience.

CONCLUSION

There is no general agreement about the fundamental cause or causes of biological aging. Many of the theoretical views we have summarized show promise. However, it is likely that these various ideas will have to be integrated since there is no real reason why we should expect there to be a single cause of aging.

Regardless of the antecedents of biological aging, it is clear that this process has an impact on behavior. Behavior also has an impact on biological functioning, both directly and indirectly. For example, structural changes in the eye with increasing age have a direct effect on visual perception. Similarly, research on the central nervous system and the slowing of behavior with age suggests that biological changes produce pervasive changes in behavior. The slowing of behavior with age appears to be largely a function of a basic change in the speed of central nervous system processing brought about by changes in brain physiology. Research in other areas suggests that behavior directly affects biology. The work of Rosenman and Friedman suggests that personality patterns are a significant factor in the etiology of cardiovascular disease. Research on physical exercise and development has clearly shown that this activity affects the functional capacity of adults, including middle-aged and older adults. Finally, research on sexuality has shown that the impact of the biological changes associated with aging may be mediated by behavioral and cultural factors.

CHAPTER SUMMARY

Biologists define aging as a set of deleterious changes which decrease the probability of the individual's survival. A number of biological theories have been developed to account for these changes. Generally, all these theories have a genetic base. That is, it is assumed that the life span of the species is ultimately determined by a program built into the genes of the species. Within this general context, however, the various biological theories of aging may be divided into three major groups.

Genetic cellular theories suggest that aging results from damage to the genetic information involved in the formation of cellular proteins. Within this group of theories, emphasis has been placed on damage to DNA (DNA damage theories) and on errors involved in the transmission of information from DNA by RNA (error theories).

Nongenetic cellular theories focus on changes that take place in the cellular proteins after they have been formed. Within this group of theories, emphasis has been placed on the accumulation of deleterious substances in the cells (accumulation theories) and damage to the cell proteins caused by the formation of cross-linkages or other reactions (cross-linkage and free-radical theory).

Finally, physiological theories suggest that aging results from the failure of some physiological coordinating system to properly integrate bodily functions. Within this group of theories, emphasis has been placed on the failure of the immune system (immunological theories) and on the failure of the endocrine system (neuroendocrine theories).

These molecular, cellular, and physiological changes affect all major systems of the human body. They also affect behavioral functioning. It appears, however, that biological functioning affects behavioral functioning only at certain points. In particular, it has been suggested that behavioral functioning is affected only when biological functioning reaches some critical or limiting level. The interaction between biology and behavior may be illustrated by several examples.

There are two sets of age-related structural changes in the eye. The first set becomes evident in the thirties and forties, and affects the transmissiveness and accommodative power of the eye. The second set becomes evident in the fifties and sixties, and affects the retina. Both of the sets of age-related changes alter visual perception. Visual acuity decreases with increasing age, and older adults are more sensitive to glare and less sensitive to color and low levels of illumination. Performance on many tasks such as reading and driving is impaired by these changes.

The speed of the central nervous system decreases with increasing age. This conclusion has been based primarily on an examination of brain electrial activity measured by electroencephalogram (EEG) recordings. The alpha rhythm of the EEG, for example, reaches its maximum frequency in adolescence and begins to gradually slow after young adulthood. This slowing may be related to disease processes (particularly vascular disease) as well as to basic aging processes. The older adult's central nervous system, then, appears to be in a state of underarousal compared to that of younger adults. This slowing of central nervous system functioning appears to account for a large part of the pervasive slowdown observed among older adults on a wide range of tasks (e.g., reaction time).

Loss of visual perception and slowing of behavior are illustrations of the impact of biology on behavior. However, behavior also has an impact on biology. For example, the incidence of cardiovascular disease has been related to many factors, including psychosocial variables. Researchers have identified a high-coronary-risk behavior pattern which has been labeled Type A. The Type A pattern is characterized by a number of behavioral tendencies, including excessive competitiveness, acceleration of the pace of ordinary activities, impatience with the rate at which most events take place, thinking about or doing several things simultaneously, hostility, and feelings of struggling against time and the environment. The converse of the Type A pattern (Type B) is characterized by the relative absence of these behavioral tendencies. Research has shown that coronary heart disease is much more prevalent among Type A men than among Type B men.

With increasing chronological age there is a gradual loss of physiological vigor (oxygen uptake, muscle tone, etc.). Recent research has demonstrated that regular physical exercise produces significant improvements in physiological vigor, even for elderly adults.

Both men and women experience deleterious biological changes in the reproductive system with increasing age. At the same time, age-related changes in sexual behavior (interest, enjoyment, frequency) are also observed. Multiple patterns of change, reflecting stability and increases as well as declines, are seen. These changes in sexual behavior do not appear to be the direct result of biological change. Rather, the impact of biological change is mediated by a number of other variables. For men, past sexual experience and health status are particularly significant. For women past sexual enjoyment and marital status are particularly significant. In general sexuality remains an important component of behavior well into old age.

4

INTELLECTUAL PROCESSES

CHAPTER
OVERVIEW

The prevailing cultural stereotype suggests that intelligence declines with increasing age during adulthood. This chapter examines the adequacy of this view by reviewing several major approaches to intellectual development in adulthood. Biological, learning, and social influences on intellectual change are also examined.

Introduction
Psychometric Approaches
   Primary mental abilities
   Fluid and crystallized intelligence
Piagetian Approach
   Basic processes of intellectual functioning
   Piagetian research with adults and the aged
   Competence versus per-

formance and Piagetian tasks
Contextual Approach
   Age versus cohort
   Biological antecedents
   Learning antecedents
   Socioenvironmental antecedents
Conclusion

ISSUES TO CONSIDER

What are the methodological problems which have plagued research on intellectual development during adulthood?

What do the terms fluid intelligence and crystallized intelligence refer to?

How do fluid and crystallized abilities change over the adult life span?

What are the major characteristics of thought within each stage of Piaget's theory of cognitive development?

How does Piaget's theory characterize intellectual development during adulthood?

What adult age differences are observed on Piagetian tasks of cognitive functioning, and how may these be interpreted?

What role do cohort effects play in adult age differences in intellectual performance?

How do biological and health variables affect intellectual

functioning during adulthood and old age?

In what ways, and to what extent, are adult intellectual abilities subject to modification through the process of learning?

How do social and cultural factors influence intellectual performance during the adult years?

INTRODUCTION

What happens to intellectual processes during adulthood and old age? Do certain abilities decline or improve with old age and why? What conclusions about the development of intellectual processes have been supported by early researchers and what viewpoint prevails currently?

Early theorists and researchers maintained that universal decline in intelligence during adulthood is a function of intrinsic, biologically based aging processes. Wechsler (1958), for example, portrays a bleak picture stating that "nearly all studies . . . have shown that most human abilities . . . decline progressively after reaching a peak somewhere between ages 18 and 25" (p. 135).

This early descriptive work, however, suffers from a number of methodological problems. First, most of this research was based on measures of intelligence which were developed without a theoretical framework. The most widely used instrument—the Wechsler Adult Intelligence Scale (WAIS)—consists of eleven subtests. Six subtests deal with verbal content and five subtests focus on perceptual motor performance. The test produces three scores: a verbal score, a performance score, and a full-scale (composite) score. Considerable research demonstrates that older adults show more decline on performance scores than on verbal scores. However, it is difficult to attach meaning to these results in the absence of a theoretical framework. Second, much of the early work was based on either cross-sectional or longitudinal data-collection strategies. As we examined in Chapter 2, these strategies have significant limitations because of their confounding with cohort, time of measurement, selective survival, and other variables. Indeed, because of these difficulties, early cross-sectional and longitudinal results tend to display somewhat dissimilar pictures of intellectual decline with age. Cross-sectional results reflect earlier and steeper declines, and longitudinal strategies point to later and less steep declines. Such differing results are not surprising given the different problems of validity involved in both data-collection strategies. For example, in the case of the cross-sectional strategy, differences may be magnified because of the presence of cohort differences favoring later-born cohorts. With the longitudinal strategy, decline may be underestimated because of selective survival effects. That is, those who are less able drop out or die while those who are more able remain to be tested. In any event, despite these difficulties, early descriptive research firmly established the conclusion that intelligence declines with increasing chronological age during adulthood.

Does intelligence decline with increasing age? Although extensive research has been conducted during the roughly 20 years since Wechsler answered "yes" to this question, there actually is no definitive answer. Researchers have not come closer to a precise yes or no response. Rather, we have witnessed increasing controversy over the timing, extent, and sources of intellectual change during adulthood. For example, Baltes and Schaie (1974) have concluded that "general intellectual decline in old age is largely a myth" (p. 35). In contrast, Botwinick (1977) has concluded that "decline in intellectual ability is

Intelligence does change during adulthood, although debates abound as to the type of change, the direction of change, the extent of change, and the sources that account for the change. (Sybil Shelton/Monkmeyer)

clearly part of the aging picture" (p. 580). These disagreements reflect differing sets of assumptions, which result in varying theoretical and methodological approaches to the phenomenon. In the following sections, we will review three approaches to research on intelligence—the psychometric approach, the Piagetian approach, and the contextual approach.

PSYCHOMETRIC APPROACHES

One major attempt to define and understand intellectual development has involved examining the interrelationships of various tests purported to measure intelligence. The *psychometric* approach to intelligence focuses on consequences or responses, in contrast to the experimental work which will be reviewed in the next chapter, which focuses on an examination of antecedent (stimulus) and process (internal-event) variables. In psychometric approaches, the emphasis is on defining the domain of intellectual behaviors by specifying the interrelationships of different measures (responses) thought to characterize intelligence. Less emphasis is placed on the antecedent and process components, although some research and theory has attempted to link them.

Primary Mental Abilities

How is intelligence measured? Many tests have been developed to assess intelligence. Amazingly, these measures tend to correlate positively, although not highly, with one another. That is, relative to other people, an individual scoring high on a test of, say, arithmetic ability will tend to score high on a test

In Depth

BOX 4.1

IS AGE KINDER TO THE INITIALLY MORE ABLE?

This question was asked by Owens (1959) and summarizes the focus of an intriguing set of research. Owens states that some intellectual decrement occurs with increasing age. However, do individuals with higher levels of ability show less decline than individuals with lower levels of ability? As you might expect, there is no simple answer to this question. Some studies have found evidence to support the hypothesis (Bayley & Oden, 1955; Riegel, Riegel, & Meyer, 1967). Others have found that groups of various ability show similar rates of decline (Eisdorfer, 1962; Eichorn, 1973). Some have cautioned that ability-related changes may represent statistical artifacts (Baltes, Nesselroade, Schaie, & Labouvie, 1972).

Blum and Jarvik (1974) reviewed the literature and summarized the results of a longitudinal study on this issue. In this study, a group of older men tested originally in 1947 (average age 64 years) were retested in 1967 (average age 84 years). The results indicated that the initially more able (as estimated by vocabulary score)

declined less than the initially less able on a battery of eight intellectual abilities. When the men were classified on the basis of level of education rather than level of ability, the better-educated individuals showed less decline.

This study suggests that those who are initially bright and well educated do not decline as much in later life as those who are initially less bright and less well educated. It should be noted that Blum and Jarvik's sample was relatively old. Studies examining this issue with younger samples do not tend to find this result. Thus the advantage of being initially more able may appear relatively late in life.

Finally, Blum and Jarvik (1974) propose that the relationship between higher ability and less decline may reflect greater cognitive activity and consequent maintenance of performance by brighter and better-educated individuals. They conclude that providing continuing educational opportunities during adulthood might help reverse age-related declines in abilities in later life.

of, say, vocabulary ability even though the tests appear to be measuring different things. In addition, performance on measures of intelligence tends to correlate positively with commonsense indices (e.g., scholastic achievement) of intellectual ability. Such relationships led early investigators to postulate the existence of a *general intelligence* that would be reflected on performance on all cognitive tasks (Spearman, 1927).

Nevertheless, modern theories of intelligence clearly have suggested that it is more useful to conceptualize this domain as containing multiple abilities. As a consequence, investigators have attempted to find dimensions that describe what is common to various tests. These results suggest that the bulk of individual differences found among many ability tests may be accounted for by a relatively small number of factors reflecting *primary mental abilities*. Estimates of the number of such ability factors range from 7 to 120, although most investigators tend to focus on the lower end of this range.

Finding common dimensions to various tests of intelligence requires the application of *factor-analytic techniques* and has yielded several major theoretical formulations of intelligence (Cattell, 1971; Guilford, 1967; Horn,

1970, 1978; Thurstone & Thurstone, 1941; Vernon, 1961). However, few of these theorists have incorporated any developmental variables into their theories. An exception has been the work of Cattell (1963), later refined by Horn (1970, 1978). As a result, the theoretical effort of Cattell and Horn has become the major psychometric approach within which adult intelligence has been examined.

Cattell

Fluid and Crystallized Intelligence

Horn

Horn (1978) has argued that a reduction of the multitude of intelligence tests to a specific number of primary mental abilities is too complex a task at this stage of our thinking. An alternative strategy is to examine what is common to the primary abilities by applying the same statistical techniques to these factors as originally was applied to the individual tests. Such analyses generate a set of *second-order abilities*. Within this framework, the work of Cattell and Horn suggests that the intelligence domain may be described by two basic factors: *fluid intelligence* and *crystallized intelligence*.

second-order abilities

Defining fluid and crystallized intelligence
According to Horn (1978), both fluid and crystallized intelligence involve behaviors characteristic of the essence of human intelligence: perceiving relationships, abstracting, reasoning, forming concepts, and solving problems. However, they reflect different processes of acquisition, are influenced by different antecedents, are reflected in different measures, and show different patterns of change over the course of adulthood. Let us examine these differences.

On the one hand, fluid intelligence reflects incidental learning processes—the degree to which the individual has developed unique qualities of thinking independent of culturally based content. Crystallized intelligence, on the other hand, reflects intentional learning processes—the degree to which the individual has been acculturated, that is, has incorporated the knowledge and skills of the culture into thinking and actions.

As one would expect, given this distinction between incidental and intentional processes of acquisition, fluid and crystallized intelligence are indexed by different types of tests. No single measure of fluid or crystallized intelligence exists because each of these abilities is a conglomerate of several abilities indexed by many measures (Horn, 1978). Thus, any given test may reflect both abilities, although some tests are relatively pure measures of one or the other. Regardless, fluid intelligence tends to be indexed by tests which minimize the role of cultural knowledge, while crystallized intelligence tends to be indexed by tests which maximize the role of such knowledge. Turn to the sample items illustrated in Table 4.1 and see how well you fare. Relatively little cultural knowledge, other than basic terms and relationships, is required to answer the fluid items. But considerable knowledge about the culture in which you live must have been acquired in order to answer the crystallized items.

Developmental patterns and sources of influence   Horn's theoretical model describing the development of fluid and crystallized intelligence over the life span and the major sources of influence on this development are shown in Figure 4.1. As indicated in this figure, the theory postulates that fluid intelligence declines during adulthood after a peak in early adulthood, while crystallized intelligence increases throughout adulthood.

TABLE 4.1
SAMPLE TEST ITEMS MARKING FLUID AND CRYSTALLIZED INTELLIGENCE

Secondary Ability	Primary Ability	Test Item
Fluid	Induction	Each problem has five groups of letters with four letters in each group. Four of the groups of letters are alike in some way. You are to find the rule that makes these four groups alike. The fifth group is different from them and will not fit the rule.[a]
		1. NOPQ DEFL ABCD HIJK UVWX
		2. NLIK PLIK QLIK THIK VLIK
		3. VEBT XGDV ZIFX KXVH MZXJ
Fluid	Visualization	Below is a geometric figure. Beneath the figure are several problems. Each problem consists of a row of five shaded pieces. Your task is to decide which of the five shaded pieces will make the complete figure when put together. Any number of shaded pieces from two to five may be used to make the complete figure. Each piece may be turned around to any position but it cannot be turned over.[b]

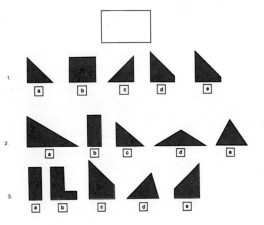

TABLE 4.1 *(Continued)*

SAMPLE TEST ITEMS MARKING FLUID AND CRYSTALLIZED INTELLIGENCE

Secondary Ability	Primary Ability	Test Item
Crystallized	Verbal meaning	Choose one of the four words in the right-hand box which has the same meaning as the word in the left-hand box.[c]

1.	bizarre	market odd	conventional imaginative
2.	pecuniary	involving money trifling	esthetic unusual
3.	germane	microbe relevant	contagious different

Crystallized	Mechanical knowledge	Complete each of the statements by selecting the correct alternative or answer.[d]

1. The process of heating two pieces of heavy metal so hot that they will fuse (melt together) is known as:

    riveting   welding
    soldering   forging

2. A paint sprayer functions in exactly the same way as a:

    centrifugal water pump
    carbon dioxide fire extinguisher
    perfume atomizer
    vacuum cleaner

3. The tool used to rotate a cylindrical object such as a water pipe is a:

    Stillson wrench   box end wrench
    open end wrench   socket wrench

Answers: *Induction*—(1) DEFL (2) THIK (3) VEBT; *visualization*—(1) a, c, d, e (2) a, d, e (3) b, c, e; *verbal meaning*—(1) odd (2) involving money (3) relevant; *mechanical knowledge*—(1) welding (2) perfume atomizer (3) Stillson wrench.

[a]Letter Sets Test, I-1; Educational Testing Service, 1962, 1976.

[b]Form Board Test, VZ-1; Educational Testing Service, 1962, 1976.

[c]Vocabulary Test, V-5; Educational Testing Service, 1962, 1976.

[d]Mechanical Information Test, MK-2; Educational Testing Service, 1962 (test no longer in print).

Source: Adapted from Ekstrom, French, Harman, and Derman, 1976; French, Ekstrom, and Price, 1963.

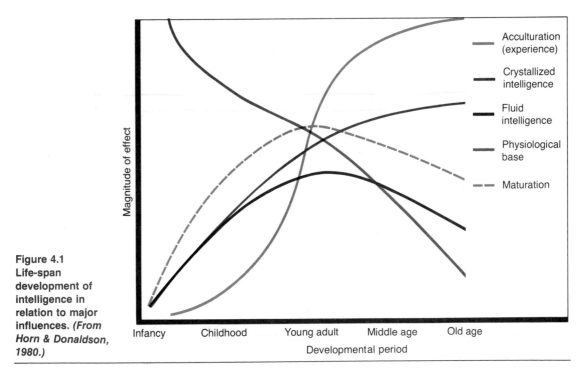

Figure 4.1 Life-span development of intelligence in relation to major influences. *(From Horn & Donaldson, 1980.)*

We have noted that incidental learning produces fluid intelligence. According to Horn and Donaldson (1980), incidental learning processes are particularly influenced by physiological and neurological functioning. As indicated in Figure 4.1, the physiological base deteriorates from birth through death as a result of negative maturational processes, injury, and illness. For example, in late adulthood there is considerable evidence of such deterioration indexed by loss of brain weight, reduction of cerebral blood flow and oxygen consumption, and increase in inert waste products in the neurons. Positive maturational influences are significant during early life but decrease in later life. These positive maturational influences mask the loss of the physiological base during childhood and adolescence, resulting in gains in fluid intelligence. Following biological maturity, however, the effects of physiological loss become more apparent and fluid intelligence declines.

Although physiological functioning is a major source of influence on fluid intelligence, it is not "built in." Rather, Horn (1978) emphasizes that fluid abilities are gained through incidental learning processes. Such learning processes appear to be supported by a relatively fixed neurological base (Horn & Donaldson, 1980). This means that once the neurological base is damaged the skill is lost. In contrast, with learning processes which support crystallized intelligence, damage of one part of the neurological base may not result in loss of the skill, since other parts of the neurological base support the skill.

While the decline of fluid intelligence during adulthood is primarily physiologically based, other factors may contribute as well. For example, as the individual acquires culturally based mnemonics, algorithms, and procedures for solving problems (crystallized intelligence), the basic incidental learning skills of fluid intelligence may be used less and less. Thus part of the decline in fluid abilities may reflect a lack of usage of the incidental learning processes on which it is based (Horn & Donaldson, 1980).

We have noted that acculturation produces crystallized intelligence. As shown in Figure 4.1, the experiences which produce such acculturation accumulate over the life span. The individual, then, continues to learn about the culture, and much of what is learned is not forgotten. As a result, information is added to the system. This information also may be restructured as it is organized and related in different ways. Skills may be more finely tuned through practice. These processes occur throughout adult life, although in different contexts such as the family, school, and work. As a result, it is hypothesized that crystallized intelligence increases during adulthood.

Research has tended to confirm the predictions of Horn's (1970, 1978) theory. For example, Horn and Cattell (1966, 1967) examined age differences in fluid and crystallized tests as well as tests which combined these two factors (omnibus measures). Their results are displayed in Figure 4.2. Fluid intelligence decreases steadily from adolescence through middle age and crystallized intelligence increases, and omnibus measures show few age-related differences because the two factors cancel each other out.

From empiricism to theory   Horn's (1970, 1978) theory is particularly useful since it moves the field from a strictly empirical level to a theoretical level. Previous research had demonstrated that abilities involving verbal performance

Horn
omnibus
measures

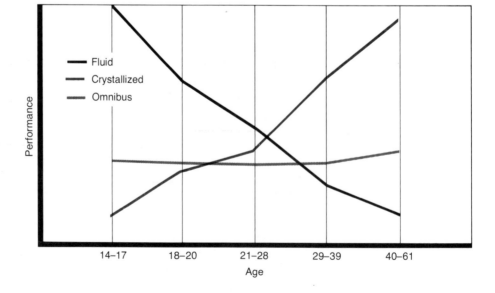

Figure 4.2 Fluid and crystallized intelligence as a function of age. (*Adapted from Horn, 1970.*)

Fluid
Crystallized
Omnibus

Performance

14–17   18–20   21–28   29–39   40–61

Age

(e.g., vocabulary, information) tend to increase while those involving perceptual-motor performance (e.g., incomplete pictures, block design) tend to decrease with increasing age during adulthood (Botwinick, 1967; Wechsler, 1958). Horn's theory is critically important because it provides a rationale for this finding.

In addition to providing a framework for organizing existing data, such a theory also provides a mechanism for future investigation. For instance, in addition to fluid and crystallized intelligence, Horn (1978) has identified several other second-order abilities involving visual, auditory, and memory functions. These second-order abilities are seen as processes which support fluid and crystallized intelligence in a hierarchical manner. Horn's model, therefore, will enable researchers to examine the interface between intellectual abilities and learning and memory processes. As a result, research on intellectual development increasingly will focus on antecedent and process variables as well as consequents.

PIAGETIAN APPROACH

Basic Processes of Intellectual Functioning

Another major approach concerned with the development of intellectual thought is based on the work of Piaget (Piaget, 1950, 1951, 1952, 1968; Flavell, 1963; Gruber & Vonèche, 1977). This approach is consistent with the organismic model. For these researchers, intellectual functioning is considered to be a special form of adaptation through activity. This activity serves to generate *cognitive structures*—ways of organizing knowledge that are constructed through interaction with the environment. These structures, comprised of *schemes* (singular, *scheme*) are modes of action which are inferred from behavioral content. A scheme, for instance, in early life may be a sensorimotor action such as grasping. As the child gets older, schemes may be used on the level of thought as well—for example, in applying classification schemes to sort objects into light and heavy.

How do individuals make intellectual progress? Schemes are modified by organization and adaptation, two *functional invariants* that exist throughout development. *Organization* refers to a person's ability to arrange cognitive activity into a system of interrelated elements. For example, the ability to organize knowledge into hierarchical classes—dogs fit into a category in the class of mammals, which is one category in the class of animals—occurs at about 7 to 11 years of age. *Adaptation* refers to a person's ability to alter cognitive structures to fit the environment. Two complimentary processes—assimilation and accommodation—explain the way in which adaptation occurs, and, hence, the manner in which schemes are altered. *Assimilation* means that individuals understand experience by applying their existing schemes. That is, a child uses repetition, generalization, and differentiation to stabilize, consolidate, and extend the domain of application. For example, infants may respond with one scheme, such as vision. With maturation and experience, by repeating, differentiating, and generalizing, they begin to combine schemes, such as vision and hearing. Simultaneously, the individual's cognitive structures are modified through the process of *accommodation* to the extent that existing structures are inadequate to understand experience. A child may use one grasping scheme for a rattle, but will need to modify this scheme when presented with a differently shaped object. Modification of a scheme is a gradual process. Adaptation, therefore, actually reflects an equilibrium between assimilation and accommodation.

Description of behaviors of each stage   With development, Piaget proposes that individuals' structural abilities change, enabling them to use increasingly complex structures to understand the environment. This change in intellectual development occurs in a four-stage sequence. Table 4.2 summarizes the behavioral characteristics associated with each stage.

TABLE 4.2
SUMMARY OF PIAGET'S STAGES OF INTELLECTUAL DEVELOPMENT

Sensorimotor stage (0–2 years)

Reflex actions or the use of ready-made schemes. Primary circular reactions—actions centered on the body and are repeated; schemes coordinated (e.g., reaching and grasping). Secondary circular reactions—actions centered on environmental consequences (e.g., shakes rattle to hear noise); actions are intentional; environment perceived as child's actions on it (egocentric); secondary circular reactions are coordinated. Tertiary circular reactions—experimentation with new features of objects and events; schemes dominated neither by actions centered on the body nor by the environment; tertiary circular reactions are coordinated. Transition period to preoperational thought: a greater sophistication in using schemes which allow experimentation (e.g., sitting in a box saying "choo-choo"; standing on something to reach an object).

Preoperational stage (2–7 years)

Occurrence of symbolic functioning. Child used signifiers (words, images, etc.) to differentiate them from significants (internalized representations of earlier experiences to which words or images refer); relates to own behavior, and no other behavior seen as different from own (egocentric); begins to develop sense of time, space, causality. Transition period to concrete operational thought: faster cognitive activity; thought becomes less static; child not as overwhelmed by perceptual experiences.

Concrete operational stage (7–11 years)

Child performs mental operations and can reverse them (e.g., addition and subtraction, multiplication and division); understands heirarchical nature of class relations; develops understanding of logical and infralogical groupings; overcomes problems of preoperational period; trial-and-error approach to problem solving. Transition period to formal operational thought: cognitive activity begins to occur in the absence of concrete objects; less trial-and-error solution seeking.

Formal operational stage (11+ years)

Adolescent capable of hypothetical (e.g., if . . . then thinking), counterfactual, and abstract thought; truth value determined by logic rather than concrete experience.

Source: This table is based on material from Gruber and Vonèche (1977); Flavell (1963); and Piaget and Inhelder (1969).

Characteristics attributed to stages   The concept of stage is basic to Piaget's theory of intellectual functioning. What characteristics are attributed to it? A major characteristic attributed to stages is that qualitatively distinct stages emerge in development in an unchanging and constant order, but the age at which a stage occurs may vary. The environment, or more generally the culture, is responsible for altering the age at which a particular behavior occurs. A second feature of stages concerns the structures themselves: The structural properties that define a stage form an integrated whole. A final characteristic of stages is that each one is marked by an initial period of preparation and final period of achievement. During the preparation period, structures which define the stage are forming and becoming organized. Thus, a range of lesser structural stability to greater structural stability may be apparent.

environment

verbal stimulus
concrete event
solve problem

Methodological procedures   Three types of procedures are used to assess a person's level of functioning so structures can be inferred from behavior: (1) a verbal stimulus is presented, and the individual produces a response; (2) while witnessing a concrete event, the individual is interviewed with questions and probes to determine why a response was given; and (3) a task is set up so the person is required to solve a problem. Within this framework, numerous tasks have been developed to assess operations of individuals.

To illustrate the type of procedure used, we will describe one of Piaget's tasks used to assess conservation abilities. For example, a person is presented with two identical objects (e.g., balls of clay) and asked: "Do they both have the same amount of clay or does one have more?" When the person has admitted

Piagetian tasks require manipulating—in this case, books and blocks—and answering questions about stimulus properties. (Sybil Shelton/Monkmeyer)

that they have equal amounts of clay, the shape of one of the objects is altered (e.g., one of the balls is shaped into a sausage). The person is then asked: "Do they still have the same amount of clay or does one have more?" *Conservation* is demonstrated when the person indicates that the objects still contain the same amount of substance regardless of the change in form. When conservation—whether of number, weight, volume, etc.—is achieved, a person is no longer confused by irrelevant perceptual cues (see Figure 4.3). Many *operations*, for example, conservation, classification, and seriation, are considered to be achieved during the stage of *concrete operations*. The same or similar tasks used with children are used to assess the operational abilities of adults.

Piagetian Research with Adults and the Aged

It may be inferred from our brief description of Piaget's stages that classical Piagetian theory focuses on childhood and adolescence. Once *formal operations* are achieved, qualitative change is assumed to cease. Piaget and Inhelder (1969) state: "Finally, after the age of eleven or twelve, nascent formal thought restructures the concrete operations by subordinating them to new structures *whose development will continue throughout adolescence and all of later life*" (pp. 152–153, italics added).

More recently, Piaget (1972) has suggested that while all normal individuals attain formal operations, if not between 11 and 14 years of age at least between 15 and 20 years of age, they do so in different areas according to their aptitudes and occupational specializations. For example, a carpenter may be capable of *hypothetical thought* (e.g., dissociating variables, performing combinational analyses, reasoning with propositions involving negations and reciprocities) in the context of constructing a house, but not in the context of traditional Piagetian tasks which are based on logical-mathematical concepts. Similarly, a theoretical physicist may be capable of formal reasoning with logical-mathematical tasks, but perform at a concrete level when attempting to construct a shed to keep garden tools in. Thus, according to Piaget (1972), an individual's lack of knowledge in a particular context, or inability to use previously acquired knowledge, will hinder the application of formal operations and result in the application of concrete operations to the problem.

Thus, Piaget (1972) suggests that all individuals progress through a series of stages of cognitive thought culminating in the ability to perform formal operations attained some time during adolescence. This stage of formal operations will be applied or used differently by individuals according to their particular aptitudes or experiences, but no new qualitative changes during the adult years are proposed. Other theorists (e.g., Riegel, 1973; Arlin, 1975) have proposed the existence of a fifth stage, noting that formal operational thought is confined to finding solutions to problems—the generation and evaluation of all possible combinations of hypotheses. Arlin (1975), for example, proposes a "problem-finding" stage focused on the discovery of new problems and ideas.

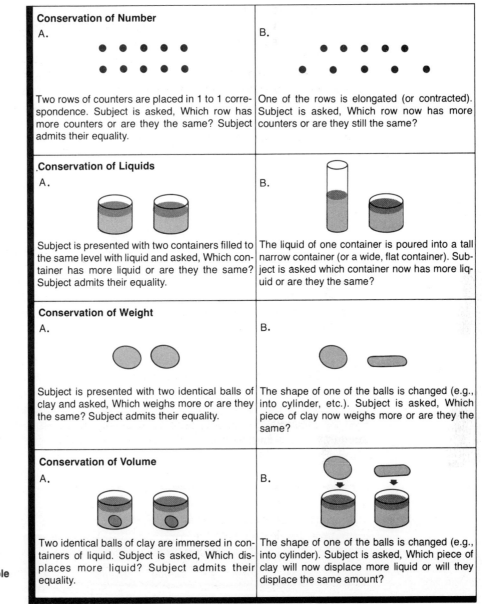

Conservation of Number

A.

B.

Two rows of counters are placed in 1 to 1 correspondence. Subject is asked, Which row has more counters or are they the same? Subject admits their equality.

One of the rows is elongated (or contracted). Subject is asked, Which row now has more counters or are they still the same?

Conservation of Liquids

A.

B.

Subject is presented with two containers filled to the same level with liquid and asked, Which container has more liquid or are they the same? Subject admits their equality.

The liquid of one container is poured into a tall narrow container (or a wide, flat container). Subject is asked which container now has more liquid or are they the same?

Conservation of Weight

A.

B.

Subject is presented with two identical balls of clay and asked, Which weighs more or are they the same? Subject admits their equality.

The shape of one of the balls is changed (e.g., into cylinder, etc.). Subject is asked, Which piece of clay now weighs more or are they the same?

Conservation of Volume

A.

B.

Two identical balls of clay are immersed in containers of liquid. Subject is asked, Which displaces more liquid? Subject admits their equality.

The shape of one of the balls is changed (e.g., into cylinder). Subject is asked, Which piece of clay will now displace more liquid or will they displace the same amount?

Figure 4.3 Sample conservation tasks.

Nevertheless, evidence for a fifth stage is limited at this time, and traditional Piagetian theory suggests that adult intelligence is characterized by stability. However, recently a number of researchers applying Piaget's theory to the latter portion of the life span have found evidence of age-related differences on a variety of Piagetian tasks (see Denney, 1974c; Hooper & Sheehan, 1977; and Papalia & Bielby, 1974 for review). We will examine several of these differences in the following sections.

Conservation abilities   Several studies have investigated conservation abilities in adults and the elderly and generally have revealed that older adults do more poorly on such tasks than adolescents or young adults. For example, Papalia (1972) investigated conservation of number, substance, weight, and volume in individuals ranging in age from 6 to 82 years. Her results are shown in Table 4.3.

With the exception of the 55- to 64-year-old group, performance tends to decrease with increasing chronological age during adulthood. Further, the elderly adults performed best on those conservation abilities which appear earlier during childhood (number, substance), and worst on those which appear later in childhood (weight, volume). This led Papalia (1972) to conclude that there is "a regression with age to less complex modes of responding" (p. 240). She speculated that this regression is a function of increasing neurological decrement with increasing age. Other studies have supported Papalia's (1972) basic conclusion that older adults frequently exhibit poorer performance on the various conservation tasks than younger adults (Papalia, Kennedy, & Sheehan, 1973; Papalia, Salverson, & True, 1973; Rubin, Attewell, Tierney, & Tumulo, 1973).

Classification abilities   A number of studies have also investigated classificatory behavior on a variety of tasks. These studies have generally shown poorer performance on the part of elderly adults as compared with younger adults (Denney, 1974c). For example, several studies have examined adult age differences on *free-classification tasks* in which individuals are asked

TABLE 4.3
PERCENTAGE OF INDIVIDUALS PASSING
EACH TASK AT EACH AGE LEVEL

Age Level	Conservation Task			
	Number	Substance	Weight	Volume
6–7	75	56	38	6
11–13	100	69	50	12
18–19	100	100	100	50
30–54	100	88	82	38
55–64	100	100	94	75
65 +	100	62	50	6

Source: Adapted from Papalia, 1972.

to group stimuli that are alike or that go together in some way. Many of these studies have noted that younger and older adults employ different classification criteria (Denney, 1974a, 1974b; Denney & Lennon, 1972). Younger adults tend to classify items on the basis of perceptual or conceptual similarity—that is, common attributes shared by all items. Thus, a pick and a shovel may be classified together because they both have handles or because they are both tools. Elderly adults tend to classify items on the basis of their functional interrelationships as defined by past experience or the testing situation. A shovel and a wheelbarrow, therefore, may be classified together because the shovel is used to put dirt into the wheelbarrow. Such functional classification is also characteristic of young children, leading some investigators to suggest the possibility of a structural regression during later life. However, Denney (1974c) suggested that the use of complementary criteria "constitutes a more natural way of organizing one's experience" (p. 49), and is not necessarily a structural regression caused by neurological degeneration.

Formal operational abilities   There have been relatively few studies of older adults' capacity to engage in the hypothetical thought characteristic of formal operations. Those which have been done suggest that older adults perform more poorly on such tasks than younger adults. For example, Tomlinson-Keasey (1972) presented sixth-grade girls, young adult, and middle-aged women with a series of formal operational tasks (e.g., pendulum, balance, and flexibility problems). In the case of the sixth-grade girls, 32 percent of the girls' responses were at the formal level, with 4 percent at the most advanced stage. The percentages for the young adult and middle-aged women were 67 and 23 percent, and 54 and 17 percent, respectively. Thus, the middle-aged women did not perform as well as the young women. Other studies using elderly adults show even more pronounced age differences (Clayton & Overton, 1976). Still other investigations examining different aspects of formal reasoning (e.g., volume conservation, combinatorial reasoning) support the conclusion that there are age-related differences on these tasks (Papalia, 1972).

However, the use of formal operations appears to depend heavily on the particular problem and the individual's past experience. Several recent studies have used everyday as well as traditional forms of formal operational problems (Sinnott, 1975; Sinnott & Guttmann, 1978). These studies suggest that adults solve everyday problems more easily than traditional problems. Further, the advantage provided by the use of everyday materials appears to be greater for older adults than for younger adults. For example, Sinnott (1975) found the performance of her younger adults increased by 10 percent with familiar materials while that of her older adults increased by 25 percent. At a more general level, however, adults of all ages often perform poorly on formal operational problems whether their content is familiar or not. For instance, Capon and Kuhn (1979) found that few adult female shoppers were able to use a proportional reasoning strategy in order to determine which of two sizes of a common item sold in the supermarket was the better buy. In general, research suggests that the use of formal operations is far from universal among adults and appears to depend heavily on experience.

Competence versus Performance and Piagetian Tasks

As summarized in our brief review, there appears to be strong evidence to suggest that older adults do not perform as well as younger adults on a variety of Piagetian tasks. How is this fact to be interpreted? Two interpretations have dominated the literature.

Competence refers to the formal, logical representation of cognitive structures. Thus, the older adult's poorer performance may reflect a loss of cognitive structures necessary for logical thought (Hooper, Fitzgerald, & Papalia, 1971; Papalia, 1972; Rubin, Attewell, Tierney, & Tumulo, 1973). Generally, it has been assumed that this loss is a result of inevitable neurological degeneration accompanying the aging process. Further, since competencies appearing late in childhood are lost first and competencies appearing early in childhood are lost later, it has been suggested that the deficit in adulthood reflects a structural regression reversing the order of development in childhood.

Performance refers to processes by which available competence is assessed and applied in real situations. Thus, the older adult's poorer performance may reflect a number of task or situational factors which interfere with performance even though the underlying structural competence required is unimpaired. Such factors may include "lack of familiarity with the testing situation, irrelevance of the tasks, a constricting life space, disuse of relevant skills or strategies, memory limitations, and preferential modes of thinking" (Hornblum & Overton, 1976, pp. 68–69).

In many respects it is impossible to evaluate these two interpretations at the present time. For example, to date, all the studies examining adult performance on Piagetian tasks have employed a cross-sectional data-collection strategy. Adequate evaluation of the structural-regression hypothesis requires the application of longitudinal or sequential data-collection strategies in order to examine change rather than differences (see Chapter 2). Thus, at the present time the competence interpretation is not supported by experimental evidence. Evidence relevant to the performance interpretation is also limited, since most investigators have simply compared the performance of different age groups under standard conditions. One alternative is to expose individuals to short-term training experiences. Improvements following training are assumed to reflect changes in performance factors (e.g., attention, strategy use), rather than changes in underlying competence (Bearison, 1974). In a study of this type, Hornblum and Overton (1976) were able to improve older adults' performance on several conservation tasks simply by providing verbal feedback on the accuracy of their responses during training. However, few studies of this type are available to illustrate the extent of training possible.

CONTEXTUAL APPROACH

The research reviewed in the last two sections emphasizes both gains and losses in intellectual functioning during adulthood. Gains are seen in abilities which reflect acculturation—measures of crystallized intelligence. Losses are seen in abilities which reflect incidental learning—measures of fluid intelligence and Piagetian operations. These latter abilities, as we discussed, are thought to be particularly affected by the degeneration of the physiological base with aging. Thus, research derived from both psychometric theory and Piagetian theory suggests that some intellectual functions remain stable or increase, but others decline as a necessary consequence of the aging process.

Other researchers, however, have argued that aging does not necessarily imply inevitable, irreversible, and universal decrement—even in the case of fluid abilities (Baltes & Labouvie, 1973; Labouvie-Vief, 1977; Schaie, 1970, 1974, 1979). Although these researchers do not deny the reality of decrement in cognitive functioning in many elderly people, they suggest that the past view of intellectual decrement is too pessimistic. Rather, the emphasis is on the relative *plasticity* and period-specific nature of intellectual performance.

Thus, a contextual approach places heavy emphasis on the contextual determinants of intellectual functioning. Unquestionably, age-related performance differences do occur. However, from a contextual perspective, it is questionable whether such functions represent irreversible and universal age changes. On the one hand, there is emphasis on the potential for change.

The routine cognitive performance of older individuals as they function in psychological research settings may be an extremely poor indicator of what they can do, and this competence-performance gap may be decreased by relatively benign interventions. It therefore appears that there may be a good deal more plasticity to intelligence in old age than has been acknowledged thus far. (Labouvie-Vief, 1977, p. 245)

On the other hand, there is emphasis on the role of context, particularly the historical context within which individuals experience events.

It is in the nature of cohort effects and historical change that the data presented are restricted to the culture and generations studied. Cultural change over the last decade has been rapid. Accordingly, the relative deprivation of the current elderly and the relative contributions of cohort effects may be particularly pronounced at this point in historical time. (Barton, Plemons, Willis, & Baltes, 1975, p. 235)

Thus, the contextual perspective does not so much propose a different definition or theory of intelligence as it focuses on a different set of antecedents and methods.

Controversy

BOX 4.2

THE INTELLIGENCE WAR

In a recent series of articles in the *American Psychologist*, John Horn and Gary Donaldson (Horn & Donaldson, 1976; 1977) and Paul Baltes and Warner Schaie (Baltes & Schaie, 1976; Schaie & Baltes, 1977) exchanged their views on the course of intellectual development during adulthood. Considerable disagreement was expressed over the extent and significance of intellectual decline during the latter part of the life cycle.

Horn and Donaldson critized both the theoretical conception and data-collection and analysis strategies of Baltes and Schaie. They concluded: "It is thus premature and incorrect to infer on the basis of existing evidence that there is no notable maturational decline in intellectual abilities in adulthood and that the major portion of such change as might be indicated represents only differences between the environments of persons of different generations" (Horn & Donaldson, 1976, p. 707).

In their replies, Baltes and Schaie argued that Horn and Donaldson misinterpreted both their theoretical and methodological efforts. They concluded: "It seems fair to conclude that research on intelligence in adulthood and old age has pointed to large interindividual differences, multidimensionality, multidirectionality, and the import of generational differences.... We see these findings as suggesting much more plasticity in adult development than what has traditionally been assumed" (Baltes & Schaie, 1976, p. 721).

The somewhat heated debate between these researchers illustrates the degree of controversy surrounding the issue of intellectual decline in adulthood. In our view, despite their sharply expressed differences, Horn and Donaldson on the one hand, and Baltes and Schaie on the other, are not that far apart. Both appear to agree that intellectual decline does occur during adulthood, particularly late in life. However, both also appear to agree that adult intellectual functioning is modifiable, and that different individuals exhibit different patterns of development. Nevertheless, the data on intellectual change during the adult years are open to many interpretations, and it is likely that this topic will continue to be a source of lively controversy.

Age versus Cohort

At the heart of the disagreement over intellectual change during adulthood is the issue of whether the observed differences reflect age-related change or cohort-related differences. From Chapter 2, you may recall that the cross-sectional and longitudinal data-collection strategies typically used in developmental investigations have a number of limitations. In particular, the cross-sectional strategy confounds age with cohort, and the longitudinal strategy confounds age with time of measurement. To the extent that history-graded or life-event sources of variance are antecedents of the behavior in question, these designs will provide an erroneous description of the developmental functions involved. Differences documented by the cross-sectional strategy may reflect age-related changes or the impact of differential experiences on different birth cohorts. Changes documented by the longitudinal strategy may reflect true age-related changes or the impact of events occurring at a given point in historical time which affect individuals of all ages. Some resolution of this dilemma is possible, however. We mentioned, for example, that Schaie

(1965, 1973) and Baltes (1968) proposed strategies involving the simultaneous and sequential application of cross-sectional and longitudinal strategies in order to partially unconfound age and historical-evolutionary effects.

A number of studies are now available which support the view that history-graded sources of variance contribute substantially to adult differences in intellectual performance (Nesselroade, Schaie, & Baltes, 1972; Schaie & Labouvie-Vief, 1974; Schaie, Labouvie, & Buech, 1973; Schaie & Parham, 1977; Schaie & Strother, 1968). These reports are based on a large sample of individuals first tested in 1956 and retested in 1963 and 1970. In addition, new independent samples of individuals were tested in 1963 and 1970 in order to control for retesting and sample attrition effects. Using this data set, the various investigators examined several arrangements of the data in order to investigate different issues. However, we will use a fraction of these data to illustrate several central themes. Figure 4.4, for example, contains the results of an analysis on one primary mental ability reported by Schaie and Labouvie-Vief (1974). In this figure, the cross-sectional gradients (top right) support the traditional finding of age-related decline. Note the general downward trend

Figure 4.4 Cross-sectional and longitudinal age gradients for verbal meaning. *(Adapted from Schaie & Labouvie-Vief, 1974.)*

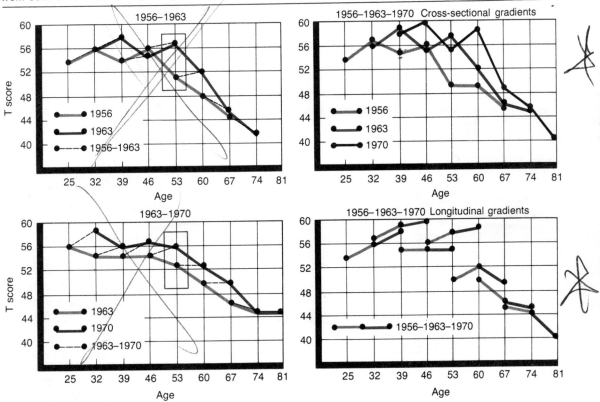

occurring after a peak in early adulthood. Notice also that the peak tends to occur later with later times of measurement (1956; 1963; 1970). Thus, availability of three cross-sectional gradients obtained at different points in time hint at the role of historical variables such as increased education.

When the same data are plotted in terms of 7- and 14-year longitudinal gradients (bottom right), a different picture emerges. Here increments are observed for the younger groups (aged 25, 46, or 53 years at first testing), while genuine decrements appear to occur no earlier than age 60.

Figure 4.4 also shows the combined cross-sectional and longitudinal gradients for 1956–1963 (top left) and 1963–1970 (bottom left). In addition to repeating the information in the right-hand portion of the figure, these gradients allow comparison of same-aged individuals who were born at different points in time. For example, the boxed areas of the figure compare individuals who are all 53 years of age but who were born at different points in time. Note the large differences. Figure 4.5 represents a more comprehensive example of such a comparison. This figure estimates cohort differences in composite measures of intelligence and educational aptitude for individuals 53 years of age born during different periods of history from 1899 to 1931. Clearly, substantial differences are associated with the cohort variable. These illustrations are confirmed in much more detail by other analyses (Schaie & Labouvie-Vief, 1974).

In general, these results suggest the need to consider the role of historical-evolutionary change in intellectual functioning. For the most part, cohort differences are larger than age changes, particularly in individuals younger than 65. Most of young adulthood, middle age, and early old age is characterized by stability or increases in intellectual performance. Decline, however, does occur relatively late in life (Schaie & Parham, 1977). This is illustrated by the figures in Table 4.4, which show the age at which a reliable decrement over a seven-year period appears. The difference in the repeated-

Figure 4.5 Cohort gradients for the composite measures of intellectual ability and educational aptitude. *(From Schaie & Labouvie-Vief, 1974.)*

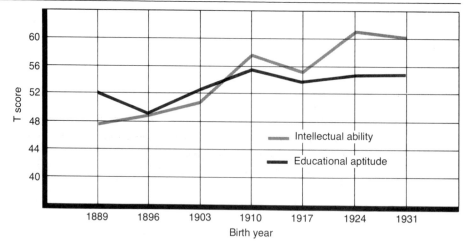

TABLE 4.4

AGES AT WHICH RELIABLE DECREMENT
OVER A SEVEN-YEAR PERIOD IS FIRST SHOWN

Variable	Age	
	Repeated Measurement	Independent Random Samples
Verbal meaning		74
Space	74	67
Reasoning	74	
Number	74	60
Word fluency	53	39
Intellectual aptitude	67	67
Educational aptitude	74	74
Motor cognitive rigidity		
Personality-perceptual rigidity	74	
Psychomotor speed	67	67

Source: From Schaie and Parham, 1977.

measurement study and that using independent random samples reflects the positive bias of repeated measures due to sample attrition. With the exception of word fluency, most measures do not demonstrate a reliable decrement until the late sixties or middle seventies.

These data point out the importance of the role of the environmental-historical context in which individuals develop. However, since cohort, like age, is a descriptive variable (see Chapter 1), identifying it as an important variable does not explain how it operates. Cohort reflects the operation of history-graded antecedents which differentially affect groups of individuals born at different points in time. Thus, for cohort, as for age, the task is to identify these antecedents. Several sets of influences which may be useful in delineating a life-span perspective on adult intelligence will be examined in the next sections.

Biological Antecedents

In Chapter 3, we summarized some of the degenerative biological changes which occur during adulthood. The scope of these changes suggests the plausibility of Horn's (1970, 1978) view that the decline of intellectual abilities, particularly fluid abilities, is due to the degeneration of the physiological base, especially as it affects central nervous system functioning. However, it is important to determine whether declines in intelligence are the result of pathologically based processes related to stress or disease or of genetically based aging processes unrelated to pathology (Jarvik & Cohen, 1973). Although such a distinction is complex and can be made only tentatively, it is,

The bulk of the research on intellectual change we have discussed so far deals with quantitative change. That is, the focus has been on increments and decrements of an ability rather than on a change in the nature of an ability. Even Piaget's theory, which proposes qualitative changes during childhood and adolescence, suggests that no new qualitative development occurs during adulthood, although some extensions of Piaget's theory propose regressive qualitative change. However, is it possible that qualitative changes in intelligence occur during adulthood? Do middle-aged and older adults think differently from younger adults rather than less quickly, efficiently, or accurately? Schaie (1977) recently has speculated about the possibility of such qualitative stages in adult intelligence. He suggests the following.

Acquisitive: childhood and adolescence Schaie suggests that during childhood and adolescence the focus is on the acquisition of information and the development of problem-solving skills required by the culture. It is this stage which we typically measure with our various intellectual measures. Schaie proposes that this stage ends during adolescence and is superseded by other stages with different goals requiring different skills.

Achieving: young adulthood During the acquisitive stage, the individual has operated, to a greater or lesser degree, within a protected environment. The achievement of adult status, however, typically signals a change in environmental conditions. In particular, the individual is less likely to be shielded from the consequences of problem-solving failures. As a result, according to Schaie, the goal is no longer acquisition of information but the achievement of competence. Thus, cognitive functioning and social functioning begin to merge to a greater extent than in previous stages. Schaie suggests that cognitive functioning is likely to be more effective in tasks that have "role-related achievement potential"— that is, those tasks related to the enterprises to which the individual has become committed.

Less efficient performance would be expected on problem-solving measures which are task-specific.

Responsible: middle age The next stage occurs during middle age, when the individual has achieved competence and role independence and now assumes responsibility for others. Schaie suggests that the responsible stage, extending from the late thirties to the early sixties, requires a pattern of problem solving which focuses on the consequences of problem solutions for one's family and significant others. Particularly in the thirties and forties, some individuals also develop what Neugarten (1969) termed "executive abilities." These are similar to the abilities that Schaie associates with the responsible stage, but involve the assumption of responsibility for larger social systems beyond the familial system— units of a corporation, government, university, and so forth.

Reintegrative: old age All these stages involve the integration of intellectual abilities at higher levels of role complexity. According to Schaie, during the final, reintegrative stage, the emphasis is on simplification. This does not mean the individual stops being intellectually involved. Rather, the emphasis is on attention to cognitive demands that are meaningful within the life of the individual. This stage "completes the transition from the 'what should I know,' through the 'how should I use what I know,' to the 'why should I know' phase of life" (p. 135). As a result, cognitive processes are mediated by motivational and attitudinal factors to a much larger degree than at any other stage.

To the extent that Schaie's (1977) characterization of stages proves to have merit, it is quite clear that new measurement techniques will be required. In essence, many of the adult age differences shown by current measures may reflect the fact that we are measuring abilities which are not central to the skills of middle-aged or older adults. The development of such new measurement techniques will be a major task but a significant one.

however, important. For example, from an optimization perspective, declines related to disease processes are more likely to be amenable to intervention than those which are related to the process of aging per se.

Within this context, evidence at the present time suggests that intellectual decline is not uniformly distributed in the population. Linkages between biological functioning and intellectual performances are observed primarily in populations with pathology such as cardiovascular disease. For example, in a now-classical study, Birren, Butler, Greenhouse, Sokoloff, and Yarrow (1963) examined the relationship of health and psychological functioning in a group of community-dwelling men. Individuals were classified into two groups on the basis of health status. Group I consisted of individuals with measurable evidence of trivial disease (e.g., partial deafness, varicose veins) or without any measurable evidence of disease at all. Group II consisted of individuals with measurable evidence of potentially serious disease (e.g., arteriosclerosis). However, these "unhealthy" individuals were not acutely ill. That is, they showed only incipient signs of disease. Symptoms were not present at the behavioral level, and the existence of the disease was unlikely to be detected by other than a rigorous medical examination. Nevertheless, in spite of the incipient nature of the disease involved, there were significant functional differences between groups I and II. In particular, cerebral blood flow was approximately 16 percent lower in group II than in group I. Cerebral oxygen consumption also tended to be lower. These differences were accounted for by the individuals in group II who showed incipient signs of arteriosclerosis. Thus, groups I and II differed in terms of degree of pathology.

These groups also displayed significant differences in cognitive performance. Group I subjects scored higher than group II subjects on a battery of twenty-three tests of cognitive functioning. In particular, performance on the verbal measures of the Wechsler Adult Intelligence Scale (WAIS) was significantly related to health status: "healthy" group I individuals scored higher than "unhealthy" group II individuals. The scores of group I elderly were likewise higher than those of a group of younger adults. The scores of group II elderly were equivalent to those of the younger adults. This led the authors to suggest that late-life illness such as that exhibited by group II resulted in a loss of ability. Finally, the correlations between physiological and cognitive indices were more numerous and higher for group II than group I. As we mentioned in Chapter 3, this latter result led Birren and his colleagues to formulate a discontinuity hypothesis concerning the relationship between biological functioning and cognitive functioning. That is, it appears that intellectual functioning is built on a biological base. When the biological base is intact, there is little relationship between biology and intelligence. However, when the biological base is damaged by illness or injury, a new set of relationships between biology and intellectual functioning emerges.

More recent studies, reviewed by Eisdorfer and Wilkie (1977), of the relationship of health to cognitive functioning have confirmed and expanded the findings of Birren and his colleagues.

Brain function   A large number of studies have shown a significant relationship between indices of central nervous system pathology (electroencephalogram, blood flow, oxygen consumption) and intellectual impairment, with greater degrees of pathology related to poorer intellectual performance (Obrist, Busse, Eisdorfer, & Kleemeier, 1962; Wang, 1973; Wang, Obrist, & Busse, 1970). This relationship is seen both in institutionalized elderly with various brain disorders and in community-dwelling elderly with incipient signs of disease.

Cardiovascular disease   Spieth (1965) found that airline pilots and air-traffic controllers with cardiovascular disease did not perform as well as healthy individuals on a battery of cognitive tasks, including subtests of the WAIS. Again these individuals were not critically ill and were capable of normal activity. However, the more severe levels of disease were associated with greater cognitive impairment.

Hypertension   High blood pressure is related to decrements in intellectual functions. Wilkie and Eisdorfer (1971) found that individuals with high blood pressure showed significant intellectual decline over a ten-year period, while those with normal or slightly elevated blood pressure showed little change or increases.

Terminal drop   The significance of the relationship between biological functioning and intellectual functioning is underscored by an interesting set of research which has examined the relationship between intellectual decline and death (Jarvik & Falek, 1963; Kleemeier, 1962; Lieberman, 1965; Riegel & Riegel, 1972). Individuals' intellectual performance shows a marked decline several years prior to death. This phenomenon has been labeled *terminal drop* (Kleemeier, 1962). Since the incidence of mortality increases with age, an apparent decrement in intelligence is produced as larger and larger numbers of persons exhibit terminal drop. (See Chapter 2 for a discussion of the impact of terminal drop on the validity of longitudinal descriptions of change.)

While the terminal-drop phenomenon is easily interpretable as a consequence of biological deterioration, it is important to realize that sociocultural factors may be involved as well—e.g., nutritional and health care conditions. Thus, it is conceivable that the relationship between death and intellectual decline may be cohort-specific.

Learning Antecedents

Since learning processes may be viewed as the antecedents or building blocks of intellectual abilities, one strategy for examining the role of learning processes in intellectual functioning is to determine whether intellectual performance can be modified by manipulating variables such as practice and strategies. Underlying this approach is the assumption that age-related performance declines may not reflect biologically based decline but rather experientially

Receiving feedback about the accuracy of one's responses is likely to improve test performance. (United Press International)

based variables such as lack of practice or use of inappropriate strategies. A variety of intervention approaches have been applied in an attempt to modify the intellectual and problem-solving performance of older adults. These include such strategies as feedback, modeling, and strategy instruction (Denney, 1979).

Feedback   Several investigators have examined the effect of *feedback*—knowledge of the accuracy of one's response—on intellectual performance. For example, Hornblum and Overton (1976) focused on the effect of feedback on conservation performance. An area-conservation (surfaces) task was used for training. Individuals in the experimental group were provided with feedback contingent upon the correctness of their responses ("Yes, that's right, let's go on" versus "No, that's not right; there is [is not] the same amount of space remaining on the board"). Individuals in the control group received the same problems but were not given feedback. Following training, the participants received six posttests examining both area and volume conservation. Exposure to feedback increased conservation on posttests. These effects were apparent on tasks that were both near (similar) and far (dissimilar) to the training task. This suggests that training activated existing operational structures.

   Other studies have provided evidence of the importance of feedback, although in some instances this variable has been combined with other training (Sanders, Sterns, Smith, & Sanders, 1975; Schultz & Hoyer, 1976).

Modeling   Denney and Denney (1974) used a *modeling* strategy to improve the performance of older adults on a concept-identification task. The task is similar to the game "twenty questions." The person is presented with a picture of a number of objects. The object of the task is to identify the object the experimenter is thinking of by asking questions that can be answered "yes" or "no." Younger adults tend to ask questions which exclude whole groups of items at a time (e.g., "Is it in the right half?") and, thus, solve the problem quickly. In contrast, older adults tend to ask questions that eliminate only one item at a time (e.g., "Is it the house?"), and, thus, solve the problem more slowly (Denney & Denney, 1973). In the training study, the investigators were able to improve the performance of older adults by exposure to another person (model) using more efficient techniques. These included simply asking questions which eliminated more than one item at a time and asking such questions plus verbalizing the underlying strategy. Both techniques were effective in reducing the number of questions the elderly had to ask before solving the problem.

Other studies have also shown positive effects of modeling on problem-solving performance (Denney, 1974a; Labouvie-Vief & Gonda, 1976; Meichenbaum, 1974).

Strategy instruction   Several researchers have attempted to improve older adults' concept-identification and problem-solving performance by verbally instructing them to use particular strategies. For example, Sanders, Sterns, Smith, and Sanders (1975) presented older adults with a concept-identification task under four different conditions: reinforced training, training, practice, and control. In the training conditions, participants were presented with a programmed learning sequence beginning with simple problems without irrelevant dimensions and working up to more complex problems with irrelevant dimensions. They were given strategy hints, memory cue cards, and verbal feedback after each response. In the reinforced training condition, tokens for correct responses were given as well. In the practice condition, participants were given the same problems, but were not given strategies, hints, or other training aids. Finally, in the control condition, participants were given only the pretest and posttest. Both training conditions led to improved performance compared with practice alone and the control condition. This research suggests that direct training can improve older adults' performance on problem-solving tasks. Other studies confirm this finding (Sanders, Sanders, Maye, & Sielski, 1976). However, some techniques do not appear to facilitate improved performance (Heglin, 1956; Young, 1966). It appears that the usefulness of strategy instruction depends greatly on the particular task and training technique used.

New directions   Thus, several different training strategies have emphasized the relative modifiability of intellectual performance in adulthood. Learning, particularly the acquisition or sharpening of higher-order skills, seems to play a key role in intellectual development. However, with some exceptions, the research we have examined suffers from a number of deficiencies. The training is limited in scope and duration. Typically, training is provided on a specific task during a single session. Further, the effects of training are usually measured immediately following training but not at later points in time. As a result, it is not possible to assess the durability of the training effect. Also, no attempt is made to determine whether the training transfers to tasks similar to but different from the trained task. Finally, no attempt is made to relate the training program to any existing theories of learning or intelligence.

As an illustration of the type of research that is required, let us examine a recent study by Plemons, Willis, and Baltes (1978). These investigators attempted to examine the degree to which fluid intelligence can be modified in older adults (fluid abilities, you will recall, tend to show normative decline with increasing chronological age). The experimental group participated in an eight-session training program designed to facilitate understanding of the relational rules found in measures of figural relations—a primary ability reflective of fluid intelligence. The control group did not receive any training. The performance of these two groups was then compared on posttests administered at three points in time following training—after one week, after one month, and after six months. Four tests varying in their similarity to the training materials were used. One would expect significant training effects for tests similar to the training materials but insignificant training effects for tests dissimilar to the training materials.

The results are shown in Figure 4.6. In the case of the most direct measure (near-near transfer) of training, the group receiving training outperforms the group not receiving training (top left panel). This effect was present even after six months. In the case of the less direct measure (near transfer) of fluid intelligence, immediate but not persistent training effects are obtained (top right panel). Finally, in the case of measures dissimilar to the training items (far and far-far transfer), no training effects are obtained (bottom panels). Consequently, training may have a relatively long-term impact on intellectual performance, at least in the case of measures with a high degree of similarity to those involved in training.

Overall, the results of various training studies point to the importance of learning processes in intellectual development, and suggest the performance of older adults may be relatively plastic.

Socioenvironmental Antecedents

In the previous sections, we have emphasized sets of antecedents which are centered specifically *in* the aging individual, for example, biological processes and learning processes. However, from a life-span perspective, the socioenvironmental context surrounding the individual may be a powerful source of antecedents that affect intellectual change during adulthood as well. Increasingly, researchers have begun to emphasize the role of these contingencies on the competence of adults (Baltes & Labouvie, 1973; Labouvie-Vief, 1977; Lawton & Nahemow, 1973).

Generally, it may be argued that the latter part of the life span, particularly the postretirement portion, is characterized by environmental contingencies which discourage the development of social and intellectual competence

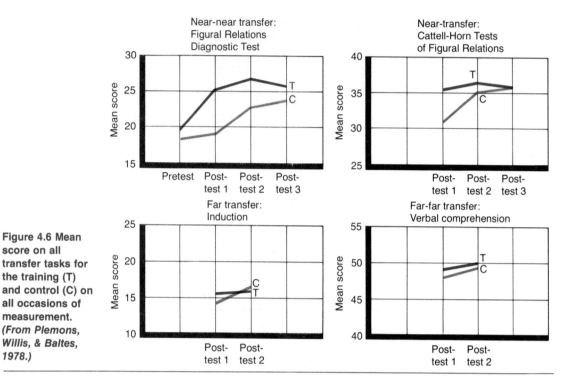

Figure 4.6 Mean score on all transfer tasks for the training (T) and control (C) on all occasions of measurement. *(From Plemons, Willis, & Baltes, 1978.)*

(Kuypers & Bengtson, 1973; Labouvie-Vief, 1977). For example, young adulthood and middle age are marked by relatively well-defined roles and expectations, but this is, generally, less true in old age (Bengtson, 1973; Rosow, 1974). If anything, the role is one of a "sick" person, and the expectations are of increasing dependence and incompetence. Further, it has been suggested that such expectations lead to a withdrawal of appropriate reinforcers for competent behavior. As a result, the process becomes one of a self-fulfilling prophecy in which the older individual expects to and, therefore, does become less competent. In some settings, loss of competency actually results from reinforcement of incompetent behavior (e.g., patients in nursing homes having self-care functions performed for them).

Kuypers and Bengtson (1973) suggest several ways in which the social environment can interact with self-concept and competence of the older individual to create a negative spiral of breakdown (a *social-breakdown model*). Essentially, this involves: (1) a socially vulnerable position in which the individual is dependent on external sources of self-labeling; (2) negative social labeling of the group of which the individual is a part, e.g., as "incompetent"; (3) the socialization of the group into a dependent role, which results in the individual's learning "skills" appropriate to this role and allowing previous skills to atrophy; and (4) the individual's identification and self-labeling as "sick," "inadequate," etc. Many of the performance-related problems of older adults in

Some professions such as the arts encourage competent, creative individuals to continue with their work during old age. (Alex Webb/Magnum)

cognitive testing situations, such as anxiety and lack of confidence (see Chapter 5), may be related to such factors.

CONCLUSION

We have reviewed several different approaches to intellectual functioning in adulthood. Each of these paints a somewhat different picture of intellectual growth and decline. The theories involving fluid versus crystallized intelligence and extensions of Piaget's theory tend to paint a somewhat pessimistic picture, while a life-span contextual view is more optimistic. Nevertheless, in our opinion, all these contemporary perspectives suggest that the stereotypic view of general and universal decline in intellectual functioning is unwarranted.

Significant evidence has accumulated to support the life-span concepts of multidimensionality and multidirectionality in intellectual functioning. Within this context, we are becoming increasingly sensitive to such variables as cohort effects that are produced by shifts in educational experience or performance effects that are produced by stress or fatigue. This is not to suggest that the elderly do not perform more poorly than they did when they were young, or than do today's youth, on some measures under some conditions. It does suggest, however, that such declines may not be the inevitable result of aging per se.

Our task, then, remains to specify the variables which do function as antecedents to intellectual change—whether they are age-graded, history-graded, or nonnormative in nature. We have reviewed the beginnings of research required to determine this and have seen initial, but compelling, evidence that many variables, e.g., health status, experience and training, and social values, may influence intellectual development.

We also must be increasingly concerned with whether we are measuring adult intelligence in an ecologically meaningful manner. Increasingly, it has been suggested that current measures may be appropriate predictors of adaptation to the educational events of childhood and adolescence but not to the life events of adulthood. As we come to understand these events better, our conceptions of adult intelligence are likely to change.

CHAPTER SUMMARY

Early research suggested that adult intelligence exhibits universal decline. However, this work suffered from a number of theoretical and methodological limitations. Recent research may be viewed within the context of three traditions. Psychometric approaches attempt to define intellectual development by examining the interrelationships of various tests designed to measure intelligence. This work has suggested that intelligence may be conceptualized as containing multiple abilities. While several theories have been developed within this framework, that of Cattell and Horn has proved the most useful in viewing adult intelligence. According to these investigators, fluid intelligence, which is measured by tests that minimize the role of cultural knowledge, reflects the degree to which the individual has developed unique ways of thinking through incidental learning. Crystallized intelligence, which is measured by tests that maximize the role of cultural knowledge, reflects the degree to which the individual has been acculturated through intentional learning. Research shows that fluid abilities tend to decrease while crystallized abilities tend to increase over the adult life span.

Piaget proposes that cognitive development progresses through a sequence of four stages. According to this view, the final stage—formal operational thought—is reached during adolescence. Adult intelligence, therefore, is characterized by stability. In spite of this, research has found evidence of age-related differences on a variety of Piagetian tasks. Older adults generally have been found to perform more poorly than younger adults on tasks reflective of both concrete operational thought (conservation, classification) and formal operational thought. Some researchers have suggested that these results reflect structural regression resulting from neurological degeneration. Others have suggested that older adults' poorer performance may reflect situational factors such as lack of motivation or lack of practice.

Research growing out of a contextual approach emphasizes the relative plasticity and cohort-specific nature of intellectual functioning. Using sequential data-collection strategies researchers have demonstrated that historical-evolutionary sources of variance contribute substantially to age differences in intellectual performance. For the most part, cohort-related differences are larger than age-related changes prior to age 65. Most of young adulthood, middle age, and old age is characterized by stability or increases in intellectual performance. Decline, however, does occur late in life.

A variety of antecedents appear to influence intellectual development. Decline appears to be closely linked to pathology, particularly cardiovascular disease. Intellectual performance also shows a marked decline, labeled terminal drop, several years prior to death. The importance of learning antecedents for intellectual development is demonstrated by research which has modified the intellectual and problem-solving performance of older adults. These studies have shown that various techniques such as feedback, modeling, and strategy instruction are effective in improving the performance of older adults. Finally, it is important to recognize that the socioenvironmental context may influence adults' cognitive functioning. It has been suggested that our culture tends to discourage the competence of older adults, thus leading to a self-fulfilling prophecy in which the older adult expects to and becomes less competent. Future research is required to specify the influences on adult intelligence in further detail.

5

LEARNING AND MEMORY PROCESSES

CHAPTER
OVERVIEW

Learning and remembering new information appear to become increasingly difficult during adulthood. This chapter examines theory and research on this problem derived from several approaches. Attention is focused on the extent to which the learning and memory performance of adults can be improved.

ISSUES
TO CONSIDER

How do the associative, information-processing, and contextual approaches differ in terms of their general conclusions on adult learning and memory performance?

How does the pacing of tasks affect adult learning performance?
How do noncognitive factors such as motivation influence adult learning?

What are the characteristics of the three memory stores proposed by the information-processing model?
Why might an older adult have difficulty remembering a

long list of items but not a short list of items?

What appears to be the primary source of difficulty for the adult: encoding or retrieval?

What techniques could be used to facilitate the learning of middle-aged and older adults?

What types of memory tasks, if any, do older adults do well on?

To what extent do cohort effects play a significant role in age-related differences in learning and memory performance?

How does the issue of ecological validity limit the conclusions of laboratory research on adult learning and memory?

INTRODUCTION

What happens to the ability to learn and remember new information with increasing age? Many people believe that learning and memory abilities, after a peak in early adulthood, decline with increasing age. The following joke illustrates this attitude.

An old man skillfully defeated a group of much younger men at a gymnasium in a variety of athletic sports, including swimming, running, and weight lifting. "You must be at least 70 years old," said one of the young men admiringly, "yet you beat us at every sport we tried. Are you that good at everything?"

"Not at all," said the old man. "I'm not what I used to be. For instance, when I went to bed last night I had intercourse with my wife. When I woke up this morning I also had intercourse with her. Then I got out of bed to take a shower and when I returned I had intercourse once again. You see, my memory is bad. (Richman, 1977, p. 211)

The conclusion that age-related deficits in learning and memory processes are characteristic of adults also is reflected in the scientific community. For example, Arenberg (1977) in a paper entitled "Memory and Learning Do Decline Late in Life" concludes that while age-related decrements in these processes are not inevitable, they are substantial and normative. Arenberg suggests that to deny the existence of this pattern of decline is to engage in wishful thinking.

Are age-related deficits in learning and memory processes characteristic of adults? As in the case of research on intelligence, a definitive answer to this question is difficult to supply. This problem reflects not only the complexity of the processes involved but also the fact that there are several research traditions based on different sets of assumptions (see Chapter 1). Accordingly, three relatively distinct approaches to learning and memory in adulthood—the associative, information-processing, and contextual approaches—will be examined in this chapter. We will point out how each approach differs in the emphasis received over historical time, in the way learning and memory are defined, and in conclusions drawn concerning the relationship among age, learning, and memory in adulthood. In this sense, then, there are at least three answers to our original question, "What happens to the ability to learn and remember new information with increasing age?"

ASSOCIATIVE APPROACHES

Defining Associative Approaches to Learning and Memory

Associative approaches are rooted in the assumption that all learning and memory are based on the association of ideas or events which occur together in time. This view, originating in classical times, was elaborated in the seventeenth century by the British associationist philosophers Hobbes and Locke. Current associative theories of learning and memory reflect this basic assumption.

From an associative perspective, learning involves the formation of *stimulus-response (S-R) bonds*, and the contents of memory are defined by such associations. The act of remembering involves emitting previously acquired responses under appropriate stimulus conditions. Changes in learning and memory are seen as quantitative rather than qualitative. Acquisition may occur as a function of increases in the number of S-R associations or as a function of strengthening existing associations through processes such as repetition. Forgetting is a function of the loss or weakening of associative bonds through processes such as *decay* or *interference*. Associative approaches to learning and memory are consistent with the mechanistic model (See Chapter 1).

Associative approaches and adult learning and memory

Associative views dominated work on adult learning and memory until the late 1950s (Jerome, 1959; Kay, 1959). By and large, the research derived from this framework has provided a relatively pessimistic perspective about the learning and memory capacities of middle-aged and older adults. For example, some researchers (Cameron, 1943; Welford, 1958) found that the aged are more susceptible to interference than younger individuals. The antecedents of interference effects generally were thought to stem from biological degeneration of the aging organism. Thus, associative approaches tend to project the view that aging involves irreversible decrements in learning and memory performance in which the principal antecedents are biological.

Experimental procedures for measuring adult learning and memory

Investigators following an associative approach have generated numerous tasks for studying learning and memory. Two procedures in particular—paired-associate and serial learning—have been used extensively. What is involved in each of these tasks?

In a *paired-associate* learning task, the individual learns to associate pairs of items, typically unrelated words, such that the individual can provide the second word of the pair when presented with the first word of the pair. A list of

Depending upon how the task is presented and the length of time given to older adults, their performance can be similar to that of younger adults. (Irene Bayer/Monkmeyer)

TABLE 5.1
SAMPLE PAIRED-ASSOCIATE LIST

List Words	Component	Phase	Interval
Arrow	S	Test	Anticipation
ARROW-STORM	S–R	Study	Inspection
Iron	S	Test	Anticipation
IRON-HARP	S–R	Study	Inspection
Pipe	S	Test	Anticipation
PIPE-WHALE	S–R	Study	Inspection
Toast	S	Test	Anticipation
TOAST-CHAIR	S–R	Study	Inspection
Oven	S	Test	Anticipation
OVEN-TREE	S–R	Study	Inspection

such pairs usually are presented for learning. The sample list shown in Table 5.1 depicts the *anticipation method* of presentation. In this method, first the stimulus (S) word is presented, and then the stimulus-response (S-R) word pair is presented. Each of the components is presented, usually visually, for a brief interval of several seconds until the entire list has been seen. As noted in the table, presentation of the stimulus-response pair constitutes a study phase of the task. Thus, following the first trial when the pairs of words are seen for the first time, the individual's job is to provide the response word of each pair when the stimulus word is presented alone (test phase). Following this, presentation of the stimulus-response pair provides feedback to the individual on the accuracy of the response and gives the individual an opportunity to study the pair again (study phase). The time span of the test phase is labeled the *anticipation interval*, while the time span of the study phase is labeled the *inspection interval*.

Usually, paired-associate lists are repeated several times, although the pairs often are shown in a different order on each trial. Several performance measures, such as the number of trials to a specific criterion (e.g., one perfect recall of the list) or the number of errors per trial, are obtained.

In a *serial learning task* a list of single items is used, and the individual's job is to learn the list in the exact order in which it is presented. That is, the words are presented one at a time and the individual is to respond by naming the next word on the list before it is presented. Thus, the focus is on associating each word with the next word in the list rather than on associating pairs of words, as in the paired-associate task.

Pacing

It has been mentioned that the paired-associate and serial learning procedures of the associative approach are rapidly paced. In addition, the slowing of behavior has been viewed by some as a major characteristic of the aging process (See Chapter 3). Thus, it is logical that investigators interested in the learning and memory of adults have examined the pacing of the task as a major independent variable.

What effect does the pacing of a task have on adults? Reviews of research on this variable indicate that the acquisition of younger adults is superior to that of older adults and that the faster the pace of the task the greater the age differences (Arenberg & Robertson-Tchabo, 1977; Witte, 1975).

For example, in an initial and now classical study, Canestrari (1963) presented younger (17 to 35 years) and older (60 to 69 years) individuals with three paired-associate tasks, each of which was presented at a different rate: 1.5 seconds, 3.0 seconds, and self-paced. Canestrari's (1963) findings are shown in Figure 5.1. Fewer errors occurred for both age groups at the slower (3.0-second) pace. However, the older learners benefited more from the slowing of the pace of the task than the younger learners. When the individuals were allowed to regulate the pace of the task themselves (self-paced), the older learners exhibited a further improvement in performance while the younger learners did not. An analysis of the time taken during the self-paced condition showed that the older learners took more time than the younger learners. This extra time tended to be taken during the test phase rather than during the study phase of the task. Canestrari also found that the differences between the age groups were accounted for by *errors of omission* rather than *errors of commission*. In other words, the higher error rates of the older learners occurred because they did not provide a response during the test phase rather than because they provided an incorrect response.

Since Canestrari (1963) varied both the anticipation and inspection intervals simultaneously, he could not determine whether older learners require additional time to provide a response, to study the pair, or both. In order to investigate this question, Monge and Hultsch (1971) varied both intervals independently. Each interval could be 2.2, 4.4, or 6.6 seconds in length. Young

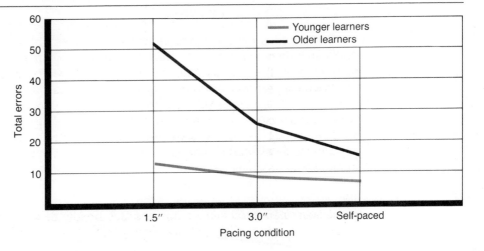

Figure 5.1 Mean total errors to criterion as a function of age group and pacing condition. *(Based on Canestrari, 1963, Table 2, p. 166.)*

and middle-aged men learned a paired-associate list under each one of the nine possible combinations of anticipation and inspection intervals. The results indicated that middle-aged learners benefited from both longer anticipation and inspection intervals but young learners benefited only from longer inspection intervals. Therefore, longer inspection intervals benefit both age groups equally, while longer anticipation intervals benefit the middle-aged but not the young.

The Canestrari (1963) and Monge and Hultsch (1971) studies illustrate several aspects of the age-pacing issue consistently reported in the literature. These may be summarized as follows:

1. Generally, the paired-associate acquisition of younger adults is superior to that of older adults, and the faster the pace of the task the greater the age differences (Arenberg, 1965, 1967b; Canestrari, 1963, 1968; Hulicka, Sterns, & Grossman, 1967; Monge & Hultsch, 1971). Similar results are obtained with serial learning procedures (Eisdorfer, 1965; Eisdorfer, Axelrod, & Wilkie, 1963).

2. The age-pace effect is a function of the anticipation interval rather than the inspection interval. Longer inspection intervals benefit younger and older learners equally (Hulicka, Sterns, & Grossman, 1967; Kinsbourne & Berryhill, 1972; Monge & Hultsch, 1971). Longer anticipation intervals benefit older learners more than younger learners (Arenberg, 1965, 1967b; Monge & Hultsch, 1971).

3. Age differences in errors reflect a larger incidence of errors of omission on the part of older learners as compared with younger learners. There are no age differences in errors of commission (Canestrari, 1963; Eisdorfer, 1965; Eisdorfer, Axelrod, & Wilkie, 1963).

4. No matter how much time is provided, elderly learners rarely perform as well as younger learners (Arenberg, 1967b; Canestrari, 1963). An exception to this conclusion is the Monge and Hultsch (1971) study which compared young and middle-aged learners. In this case, no age differences were observed at the slower paces.

These points describe the role of the pacing variable in paired-associate and serial learning tasks. However, a question remains concerning the explanation of the effects of this variable. The following sections focus on this question.

Cognitive versus Noncognitive Processes in Adult Learning

A major issue which has emerged from the verbal learning research we have been reviewing focuses on the question of whether the observed age-related deficits in acquisition are related to cognitive or noncognitive processes (Botwinick, 1967). In other words, is the older adult's difficulty related to learning processes (e.g., inefficiency in forming S-R bonds) or to noncognitive factors such as personality traits or states which are relevant to the learning situation (e.g., greater cautiousness or anxiety).

For example, some researchers (e.g., Canestrari, 1963) suggested that the poorer performance of the older learners was simply the result of the fact that there was an insufficient amount of time to make a response rather than the result of a learning disability. This conclusion was based largely on the fact that the age differences were linked to the length of the anticipation interval and to the greater number of omission errors on the part of the older learners. This explanation proved to be an oversimplification.

Arenberg (1965), in a direct test of the time-to-respond hypothesis, alternated self-paced test trials with paced test trials. The rationale was as follows: If the older learner's problem is solely a function of insufficient time to

---

Update

BOX 5.1
MEMORY COMPLAINTS: ABILITY OR AFFECT?

Memory dysfunction is one of the most prominent stereotypes associated with aging. In fact, memory problems are one of the most frequently cited complaints reported by older adults. Yet there is evidence to suggest that the memory complaints of older adults may be related to degree of affect, particularly depression, rather than degree of ability.

In a study focused on this issue, individuals with varying degrees of depression and brain dysfunction were compared on memory complaints and on actual memory performance (Kahn, Zarit, Hilbert, & Niedereche, 1975). The sample of 153 adults aged 50 to 91 (average 65.1 years) was classified into two groups according to the presence or absence of signs of brain dysfunction. Measures of depression, memory complaint, and memory performance were then obtained from all individuals.

It was discovered that within the group without signs of brain dysfunction, those who were more depressed had a greater number of memory complaints than those who were less depressed. Their actual memory performance, however, did not differ. Furthermore, individuals with normal brain function had as many memory complaints as those with altered brain function even though the latter group had far greater difficulty on the

actual memory tasks. This work suggests that memory complaints among the elderly may be related, at least in part, to depression and other affective states rather than to changes in memory ability.

Memory complaints among adults may be related in part to depression rather than actual memory loss. (Michael Weisbrot)

respond, then there should be age differences in performance on the experimenter-paced test trials but not on the self-paced test trials. However, Arenberg (1965) found that the older adults performed more poorly than the younger adults on both types of test trials. These results do not rule out potential noncognitive explanations, such as cautiousness or anxiety. However, they do suggest that time per se is not an adequate explanation. An analysis of omission and commission errors, then, cannot provide a definitive answer to the learning question. What is required is an examination of the underlying cognitive and noncognitive processes involved in performing the task.

Noncognitive Processes, Task Performance, and Adult Learning and Memory

Cautiousness or response reluctance   A recurring noncognitive explanation for age-related differences in acquisition has focused on the presumed cautiousness of older adults (Botwinick, 1967). Thus, it has been suggested that the poorer performance of older adults relative to younger adults, particularly as reflected by omission errors, is a function of their reluctance to venture a response unless they are absolutely certain of its accuracy. While this is a plausible explanation, it has not been widely investigated. In part, this lack of research may reflect the existence of theoretical and methodological confusion surrounding the construct of cautiousness (Okun, 1976). Nevertheless, several studies have examined the idea.

One approach has been to require the learner to give a response. If the poorer performance of older learners reflects their tendency to withhold correct responses because they are not certain of their accuracy, then requiring a response should reduce observed age differences. However, the studies using this procedure have found no evidence of reduced age differences (Witte & Freund, 1976). Similarly, Taub (1967) found that the performance of older adults was not improved by instructions encouraging them to guess. A recent study by Okun, Siegler, and George (1978) used a different approach. These investigators obtained measures of risk taking as well as learning performance from younger and older individuals and then examined the relationships among these measures. While there were methodological problems with this study, there was some evidence to suggest that the relationship between age and errors of commission was partially accounted for by age-related differences in cautiousness.

Overall, then, while the cautiousness hypothesis is plausible, there is only limited support for it. However, since only a small number of studies have directly examined it, the issue remains open.

Physiological arousal and anxiety   Another noncognitive explanation of age-related deficits in learning is based on the hypothesis that older adults are more aroused or anxious in learning situations than younger adults and, as a consequence, perform more poorly. Two sets of studies have examined this hypothesis. The first set of studies has focused on the *arousal* construct assessed by physiological measures. The second set of studies has dealt with the *anxiety* construct assessed by self-report measures.

Physiological arousal   Eisdorfer (1968) and his colleagues have investigated the role of physiological arousal in age differences in learning performance. This work is based on a general theoretical formulation which characterizes the relationship between arousal and performance as an inverted U-shaped curve. That is, an optimum level of arousal for performance is proposed. Up to this point, increases in arousal will be accompanied by increments in performance. Beyond this point, increases in arousal will be accompanied by decrements in performance.

Eisdorfer (1968) proposed that older adults are characterized by overarousal in the learning situation rather than underarousal. He investigated this hypothesis in several studies using serial learning tasks and a physiological measure of arousal. The latter consisted of the level of free fatty acid in the blood stream—an index of autonomic nervous system activity in response to stress.

An initial study (Powell, Eisdorfer, and Bogdonoff, 1964) revealed substantial age differences in arousal during a serial learning task, with older individuals showing higher levels than younger individuals. In particular, while the free fatty acid level of the younger age group plateaued during the learning task and declined following it, that of the older group increased throughout the task, reaching a peak approximately fifteen minutes following it. Thus, older adults, rather than being less involved in the task than the younger individuals, were more involved and under greater stress.

This study suggests that older learners exhibit higher levels of autonomic arousal, but it does not establish a cause-effect linkage between arousal and learning performance. Such a linkage requires demonstrating that the manipulation of arousal levels affects learning performance. In an attempt to provide such evidence, Eisdorfer, Nowlin, and Wilkie (1970) varied arousal by administrating the drug Propranolol, which blocks end-organ autonomic activity. A group of older men received either Propranolol or a *placebo* (a substance having no physiological effect) during the learning task. An analysis of the free fatty acid levels of the two groups showed that following administration of the drug and the placebo, the arousal level of the drug group decreased while that of the placebo group increased. Furthermore, the drug group made significantly fewer errors than the placebo group. Thus, these data provide evidence of a causal relationship between arousal and learning performance. Unfortunately, no younger individuals were tested in this study. As a result, the question of whether age differences in performance are a function of a greater arousal on the part of the older learners is not definitively answered by these data.

Studies of physiological arousal and learning performance are complicated by several problems. For example, techniques such as drawing blood samples are themselves stressful and, thus, confound arousal produced by the learning task with arousal generated by the measurement technique itself (Troyer,

Eisdorfer, Bogdonoff, & Wilkie, 1967). Further, the use of a single measure of arousal makes the data less useful because it appears that there are multiple arousal responses, and these may exhibit different rates of age-related change (Elias & Elias, 1977). Nevertheless, the research reviewed in this section suggests the possibility that part of the performance deficit exhibited by older learners may be related to <u>overarousal</u>.

Anxiety   A second set of studies has examined the role of stress in learning performance by measuring self-reported anxiety. Indirect support for the hypothesis that anxiety has a negative effect on learning performance in older individuals is suggested by studies indicating that supportive instructions, which presumably reduce anxiety, facilitate the performance of older adults to a greater extent than that of younger adults (e.g., Lair & Moon, 1972). However, these studies did not include an independent measure of anxiety. As a result there is no way of determining the impact of the instructional conditions on age-related anxiety levels. However, Whitbourne (1976) used a separate measure of anxiety and found that older men were more anxious than younger men following a sentence memory task. Moreover, there was a negative relationship between text anxiety and memory performance; high anxiety scores were associated with low memory scores.

Additional evidence on the role of anxiety in the cognitive performance of adults comes from informal observations of older individuals in the research context. These observations suggest that older adults are more likely to refuse to participate in research than younger adults and, if they do, are more likely to

Anxiety in novel learning or testing situations is postulated to be a major factor in the poorer performance of older adults. (Michael Weisbrot)

withdraw prior to completion of the task. In the experimental setting, statements about declining abilities, dislike of tests, and fear of failure are frequently obtained from older adults but rarely obtained from younger adults. These informal data reinforce the conclusion that older adults find such experimental settings more stressful than younger adults. Thus, researchers studying physiological arousal and anxiety states suggest the possibility that these states may account for part of the cognitive performance deficit typically observed with increasing adult age.

Cognitive Processes, Task Performance, and Adult Learning and Memory

Analysis of the paired-associate task suggests that two stages are involved in the learning process (Underwood & Shultz, 1960). First, there is a *response learning stage* during which the responses are identified and made available for recall. Second, there is an *associative stage* during which the stimuli and responses are linked and recalled together.

Response learning To our knowledge, only one study specifically has focused on the response learning stage. In this study, Witte and Freund (1976) investigated the paired-associate learning of younger and older adults as a function of three methods. In two conditions (multiple-choice method and associative matching), the responses were available during the test trials and the learner simply had to choose the correct response from among the alternatives or match the correct response with the correct stimulus. In these conditions only the associative stage of learning should be involved. In the third condition (recall), the responses were not available on the test trials. In this condition, both the response learning and associative stage should be involved. Thus, if the locus of the age-related deficit in learning is in the response learning stage, age differences should be reduced under the multiple-choice and matching methods compared to the recall method. Witte and Freund (1976) found the matching and multiple-choice methods facilitated the performance of both age groups. However, the availability of the responses did not facilitate the performance of the older learners to a greater extent than that of the younger learners. While this study does not provide any direct support for age-related differences in the response learning phase, it is probably premature to completely reject this hypothesis.

Mediational strategies There is more evidence for age-related deficits in the associative stage. A major mechanism by which individuals form associations between stimulus and response is the process of *mediation*. This process has been conceptualized as the formation of a covert response which forms a link between stimulus and response. These links may consist of verbal responses, visual images, or other covert responses. Thus, it is assumed that the overt stimulus (S) produces a covert response or mediator (r). The covert stimulus consequences (s) of this mediating response then produce the overt response (R). Schematically, the process may be represented as follows:

$$S \rightarrow r - s \rightarrow R$$

For example, the pair FLOWER-MEADOW may be linked by visualizing a field of flowers. Alternatively, the pair may be linked by the concept "nature." Mediational responses involve active processing on the part of the learner.

There is considerable evidence suggesting that older adults do not use mediators as extensively or as efficiently as younger adults. Several studies have requested younger and older learners to specify the strategies they used to learn items (Erber, 1976; Hulicka & Grossman, 1967; Rowe & Schnore, 1971). These studies indicate that younger learners are more likely to use mediational strategies spontaneously than older learners. Several investigators also reported that when mediators are used, older learners prefer verbal mediators to visual ones, while the reverse is true for younger learners (Hulicka, Sterns, & Grossman, 1967; Rowe & Schnore, 1971).

If older adults do not use mediators as extensively or effectively as younger adults, then instructions to use mediational strategies should benefit older learners more than younger learners. This appears to be the case (Hulicka & Grossman, 1967; Hulicka, Sterns, & Grossman, 1967; Treat and Reese, 1976). The use of mediators supplied by the experimenter also appears to benefit older learners (Canestrari, 1968), although experimenter-supplied mediators may not be as effective as self-generated mediators. While mediational instructions typically have reduced observed age-related differences in paired-associate learning performance, they have generally not eliminated such differences, since older learners require more time to develop and apply mediators (Treat & Reese, 1976).

These studies suggest, then, that older learners do not spontaneously use mediational strategies, particularly strategies based on imagery, as frequently or efficiently as younger learners. However, when instructed to use mediators, or when mediators are supplied by the experimenter, older learners are able to use these devices and performance improves. In spite of this, their performance only rarely equals that of younger learners.

If we assume that there are characteristic differences in the learning strategies used by younger and older adults, these differences must still be explained. To date, little research has been done on the potential antecedents of such strategy differences. Two rather global hypotheses contrasting physiological and experiential antecedents have been offered (Witte, 1975). First, it has been suggested that physiological degeneration of the central nervous system with increasing age may impair the spontaneous application of such higher-order learning strategies. Second, it has been suggested that such strategies are likely to reach their optimum development in formal learning situations such as school. As a result, the higher-order learning strategies of older individuals may be inefficient because of disuse. Alternatively, the educational experience of older cohorts may have deemphasized the use of such strategies. There is weak evidence related to both of these hypotheses. For example, Rust (1965) reported differences in the use of mediational strategies between individuals with and without symptoms of arteriosclerosis. Gladis (1964) found that presenting multiple paired-associate tasks, which presumably would provide practice in higher-order skills, improved the performance of middle-aged learners to a greater extent than that of young learners. Overall, however, the antecedents of these age differences remain to be demonstrated.

Transfer and Interference in Adult Learning and Memory

Transfer of training—the effect of learning one task on the learning or retention of another task—is a major concern in associative approaches to learning and memory. If learning the first task facilitates learning the second task, then transfer is positive. If learning the first task interferes with learning the second task, then transfer is negative. Transfer may occur specifically or nonspecifically. *Specific transfer effects* are dependent on the similarity between tasks, such as the degree to which the words of two lists are synonymous. *Nonspecific transfer effects* are the result of more general factors, such as warm-up or learning to learn. One major hypothesis derived from this framework has been the suggestion that older adults may be more susceptible to interference than younger adults (Welford, 1958).

Established verbal habits One approach to investigating the role of interference in adult learning has been to examine the effect of established verbal habits on the learning process by varying the associative strength of the word pairs to be learned. When one word frequently elicits another in a free-association task, the pair is said to have *high associative strength*; when one word infrequently elicits another in such a task, the pair is said to have *low associative strength*. Such free associations presumably reflect the individual's established verbal habits. For example, the pair DARK-LIGHT has high associative strength, while the pair DARK-FAST has low associative strength.

If the associative habits of older adults are more established than those of younger adults, it follows that age-related differences should be minimized with lists that are high in associative strength. This appears to be the case (Botwinick & Storandt, 1974; Kausler & Lair, 1966). In the most comprehensive of these studies, Botwinick and Storandt (1974) presented adults ranging in age from 21 to 80 years with three paired-associate lists which varied in terms of their associative strength and difficulty. The low-difficulty list consisted of high-associative-strength word pairs such as OCEAN-WATER; the moderate-difficulty list consisted of low-associative-strength word pairs such as BOOK-HAIR; and the high-difficulty list consisted of consonant-word pairs such as FP-WAGON. Botwinick and Storandt (1974) found no age-related performance differences on the easy list but marked age-related differences in performance on the moderate and difficult lists.

If the performance of older adults is facilitated by lists which are consistent with preestablished verbal habits, it follows that lists which are constructed specifically to conflict with these habits should interfere with their performance. In an attempt to test this hypothesis, Lair, Moon, and Kausler (1969) compared middle-aged and older individuals on lists which were high and low in response competition. The low-competition list consisted of pairs of relatively low associative strength. The high-competition list consisted of high-associative-strength word pairs such as BLOSSOM-FLOWER and HOT-COLD. However, instead of being paired together these words were re-paired so that for each stimulus word its highly associated response was present in the list but paired with another word (e.g., BLOSSOM-COLD; HOT-FLOWER). Such a list should produce a great deal of interference with prior verbal habits. Differences between the age groups were much larger for the high-competition list than for the low-competition list. This supported the interference hypothesis. The older adults were more susceptible to the effects of response competition, as would be expected when strongly reinforced verbal habits competed with the formation of new associations.

Laboratory paradigms   Another approach to studying the effects of transfer and interference has been to rely on associations established in the laboratory. Such a procedure is potentially more precise than assessing established verbal habits. For example, if an association is established between two items a-b (e.g., RADIO-SWEET), then the learning of a new association a-c (e.g., RADIO-PEPPER) tends to interfere with the retention of the original pair (a-b).

A number of studies have examined adult age differences in interference using paradigms of this type. With some exceptions (Gladis & Braun, 1958), these studies have supported the hypothesis that older adults are more susceptible to interference effects than younger adults (Arenberg, 1967a; Cameron, 1943; Wimer & Wigdor, 1958). Unfortunately, all these studies suffer from design problems which make it impossible to evaluate their usefulness in supporting this conclusion (Goulet, 1972). In particular, interference in such paradigms depends on the degree of learning of the original task. Since this almost always differs as a function of age, the interference hypothesis has not been adequately demonstrated by laboratory paradigms.

Age versus Cohort

Virtually all the studies reviewed thus far have been based on the cross-sectional data-collection strategy. As we saw in Chapter 2, this data-collection strategy confounds age and cohort effects. In the absence of appropriate data-collection strategies it is not possible to describe these results as age-related changes. There is only one source of data which allows us to address age-related changes. These data are from the Baltimore longitudinal study of men reported by Arenberg and Robertson-Tschabo (1977). Analysis of their data led these investigators to conclude that learning performance actually does decline with increasing age, particularly after 60 years of age. However, additional data based on the sequential data-collection strategies discussed in Chapter 2 are required to resolve this question.

INFORMATION-PROCESSING APPROACHES

Defining Information-Processing Approaches to Learning and Memory

Information-processing approaches to learning and memory, pioneered by Broadbent (1958), are based on the principles underlying modern computers. For example, the computer contains an input unit which enters the information into the computer, a working unit which holds information being actively processed, and a core unit which stores information for later use. Incorporating these principles, information-processing approaches to learning and memory are based on the concepts of storage structures and control operations. A generalized model is outlined in Figure 5.2. Typically, three *storage structures* are proposed: a sensory store, a short-term store (primary memory), and a long-term store (secondary memory). Information is retrieved from one store and entered into the next by *control operations* such as attention, elaboration, and organization which transform the information involved.

Sensory, short-term, and long-term stores   Stimuli are received and registered in the visual and auditory sensory stores. Sensory memory is part of the peripheral sensory system, and items are represented as literal, visual, or auditory copies. These representations persist only for a brief time, decaying in the absence of further processing. Information is retrieved from the sensory

Figure 5.2 A generalized information-processing model of learning and memory.

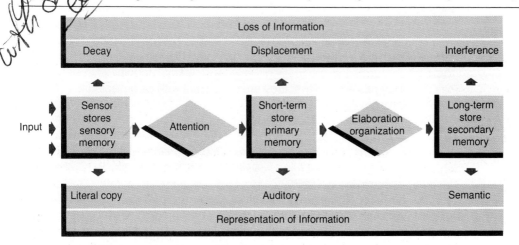

stores by attending to it, whereupon it is entered into the short-term store. Here items are coded in auditory or other physical fashion. The capacity of the short-term store is limited to about five units, with information being lost principally by displacement. The duration of primary memory from the short-term store can be extended by rehearsal, or the material can be transferred to long-term storage by processing the items in terms of their semantic content (meaning). Retrieval from the long-term store is dependent on the development of a retrieval plan based on elaboration or organization of the information. The long-term store has unlimited capacity, and the duration of secondary memory is lengthy, if not permanent.

Since the division of memory into three components is one of convenience, we are not implying that items are placed into one of three separate memory systems as a secretary might place a letter into one of three separate files. Instead, there is a continuing elaboration of the memory trace from its initial perceptual processing to its integration into the individual's knowledge structure. This point was emphasized by Waugh and Norman (1965), who argued that the definition of the various stages of memory should be linked to processes rather than retention intervals. This is important because Waugh and Norman showed that long-term memory processes (e.g., elaboration) mediate performance, in part, even in tasks where the retention interval is extremely short. To avoid confusion, they suggested relabeling short-term and long-term memory as *primary memory* and *secondary memory*, respectively. This terminology will be used in the following sections.

Control processes   Within information-processing approaches, the control processes which transfer material from one storage structure to another produce qualitative changes in the material. While some of these processes appear to be automatic, others are clearly under the control of the individual. Thus, unlike the associative approach outlined previously, information-processing approaches assume that the individual actively transforms the material and that what is learned and recalled is largely a function of these transformations. That is, what is learned and remembered is not a set of stimulus-response associations, but a totality—the organization of which is imposed by the individual through the various processing mechanisms. Therefore, information-processing views are clearly "cognitive" in nature, and Reese (1973) has argued that they are consistent with an organismic world view (See Chapter 1).

Information-processing approaches and adult learning and memory   Information-processing views have dominated work on adult learning and memory from the early 1960s until the present (Craik, 1977). Research based on these approaches has suggested that age differences in sensory and primary memory are minimal. However, when the material to be learned and remembered exceeds the capacity of primary memory, large age differences are observed, thereby implicating difficulties in acquisition or retrieval in secondary memory. Information-processing views of learning and memory have emphasized active processing on the part of the individual, and have suggested age-related decrements in such processing. However, in contrast to associative approaches, they have stressed the fact that these decrements can be modified by manipulation of variables, that is, changing the organization of the material, instructions, and the like. Thus, although information-processing approaches tend to project a model of age-related changes in learning/memory performance based on decrements, they also suggest that these decrements can be compensated for.

Sensory Memory

As summarized above, *sensory memory* is a part of the peripheral sensory system. Research on adult age differences in this system is very limited. Although several studies have suggested the possibility of age-related decrements in visual sensory memory (Schonfield & Wenger, 1975; Walsh, 1975), these appear of limited significance to overall age differences in memory performance (Craik, 1977).

Primary Memory

As we noted earlier, primary memory is a temporary maintenance system for conscious processing. As such, it serves an important control function for both storage and retrieval from the permanent maintenance system of secondary memory.

One relatively pure measure of *primary memory* is derived from the *free-recall task*. In free recall, the individual is presented with a series of items during an input phase and is asked to recall as many of the items as possible in any order during an output phase. Presentation of the items may be simultaneous or successive, but it is usually successive. There may be just one input and one output phase, or several input and output phases may be combined in an alternating or other type of sequence. Single words are usually the items of concern, although other types of material such as syllables, letters, or geometric figures are used. What is "free" about free recall is the order in which the individual may recall items.

Typically, one outcome of the free-recall procedure is that the last few items of the list are recalled first. This *recency effect* is considered to be a measure of primary memory. Both Craik (1968b) and Raymond (1971) report finding no age-related differences in recency using this task. These authors concluded that primary memory processing does not decline with increasing age.

Primary memory also may be assessed by tasks involving the *immediate memory span*. The immediate memory span is defined as the longest string of items (digits, letters, words) that can be immediately reproduced in the order of presentation. This task probably involves both primary and secondary memory components. That is, the average immediate memory span is about five items for words and seven items for digits. The capacity of primary memory, however, is estimated to be smaller than this. Thus, immediate-memory-span tasks reflect a small secondary memory component as well as a large primary memory component.

If primary memory does not decline with age, then one would expect little decrement with immediate-memory-span tasks. This appears to be the case. For example, several studies have found no age-related decrements on memory-span tasks involving digits (Craik, 1968a; Drachman & Leavitt, 1972; Talland, 1968). Other studies have found slight decrements (Botwinick & Storandt, 1974). This slight decline probably is related to the secondary memory component of the task. While age-related differences in performance are not observed on the usual memory-span task, this is not so when the task is modified to require division of attention or reorganization of the material (Craik, 1977; Talland, 1968). In this case, older adults find the task more difficult than younger adults.

Although the capacity of primary memory does not decline with increasing adult age, there is some evidence to suggest that the rate at which information can be retrieved does decline. Anders, Fozard, and Lillyquist (1972) used an approach devised by Sternberg (1966). In this procedure the individual is presented with a set of items. Immediately following presentation of the set, a single item is presented, and the individual's task is to decide as quickly as possible whether this test item was a member of the original set. Sternberg found that the larger the set of items, the longer individuals took to decide whether the test item was a member of it. He suggested that measures derived from what he called this "decision latency" could be used as an index of the rate at which the individual is able to search the contents of primary memory. Anders and his colleagues applied this paradigm to individuals from three different age groups. Their results indicated that the speed of search through the contents of primary memory declined with age, with younger individuals being substantially faster than either middle-aged or older individuals.

Earlier we noted that material is lost from primary memory through interference from incoming items. Are older individuals more susceptible to such interference? The answer to this question appears to be no (Craik, 1977). Wickelgren (1975), for example, compared the retention of children, young adults, and elderly adults over intervals ranging from two minutes to two hours. A continuous-recognition procedure was used in which the individual is shown a word and must decide whether or not it has been presented before. A total of 3120 words was presented during the experiment, with "old" words appearing at various intervals following their initial presentation. Presumably, interference increases as the delay (number of intervening items) between the first and second presentation of the word increases. Thus, if older adults are more susceptible to interference in short-term-retention tasks, there should have been increasing performance differences between the groups as the delay interval increased. However, Wickelgren (1975) found identical forgetting rates for all three age groups over the two-hour period. Other studies, using different approaches, have found no evidence that older adults are more susceptible to the effects of interference (Craik, 1971; Talland, 1968).

The research reviewed in this section suggests that age differences in primary memory are minimal (Craik, 1977). Although there is evidence that the rate of search through the contents of primary memory decreases with age, the overall capacity of this system appears to be unaffected by age. Furthermore, there is little evidence to suggest that older adults are more susceptible to interference effects in primary memory than younger adults.

Secondary Memory

Secondary memory is a permanent maintenance system characterized by semantic content. If sensory and primary memory processes are only minimally related to age, then observed age-related differences in performance should be connected with secondary memory components.

Elaboration and organization　We have noted that retrieval from primary memory and entry into secondary memory require _elaboration_ and _organization_ of the material. For example, it has been suggested that memory depends on the individual's perceptual and cognitive analysis of the material: the more elaborate the analysis, the better the acquisition and retention of the material (Craik & Lockhart, 1972). More elaborate or deeper levels of processing are those involving semantic analyses. Thus, it is possible to define a progression from relatively unelaborated or shallow levels of processing (e.g., physical characteristics of stimuli) to relatively elaborated or deeper levels of processing (e.g., semantic, or meaning, characteristics of stimuli).

The role of elaboration in memory may be illustrated by an experiment conducted by Craik and Tulving (1975). Individuals were presented with a word list and asked to perform three orienting tasks involving different levels of analysis. They found that both recall and recognition of the words increased as the levels of processing increased. The generation of a rich, elaborate code for the items to be remembered, therefore, is central to secondary memory. The most effective encoding, however, is not restricted to a single item. Rather, the items to be remembered are organized into higher-order units. The formation of such units has been labeled "chunking" (Miller, 1956). Chunks are based largely on the principles of grouping and relating. The importance of organizational processes in secondary memory is illustrated by a series of studies completed by Mandler (1967). Mandler asked individuals to sort large sets of unrelated words into categories of their own choosing prior to free recall. Following this, free recall of the words was requested. The findings revealed a strong relationship between the number of categories used during sorting and the number of words recalled during free recall. The greater number of categories (chunks) the individual made, the better the recall.

Compared to younger adults, older adults are deficient in terms of the elaborative and organizational processes of secondary memory (Craik, 1977; Hultsch, 1969; 1971). That is, older adults do not spontaneously use organizational strategies as extensively as younger adults, or if they do, they use them less effectively. However, when various organizational strategies are built into the situation, the performance of older adults improves significantly. The following two studies illustrate these conclusions.

Eysenck (1974) conducted a study in which he applied the orienting task procedure described earlier. Individuals performed one of four orienting tasks:

(1) counting the numbers of letters in each word; (2) finding a word that rhymed with each word; (3) finding a suitable modifying adjective for each word; and (4) forming an image of each word. These conditions were presumed to reflect a continuum from shallow to deep processing. In addition, in a fifth condition, the individuals were instructed to learn the words. All groups subsequently were asked to recall the words. Eysenck (1974) found that the differences between the younger and older individuals were greatest when the orienting task required deeper processing of the material. These results led Eysenck (1974) to suggest that older individuals exhibited a "processing deficit" at deeper semantic levels.

Hultsch (1971) used Mandler's (1967) procedure (summarized earlier) in which individuals are asked to categorize words to a criterion of two identical sorts prior to free recall. Individuals from three age groups performed the task. In order to determine the impact of organizational processes on recall, Hultsch manipulated experimentally the opportunity to organize the words. Half of the individuals at each age level were instructed to sort the words into from two to seven categories. The other half of the individuals were not allowed to physically sort the words into categories. The "nonsorting" individuals inspected the words one at a time. They were given the same number of input trials prior to recall as a randomly assigned "sorting" partner. The results of this study are summarized in Figure 5.3. The middle-aged and older individuals exhibited less of a recall deficit under conditions that maximized the possibility for meaningful organization.

These studies examined age-related differences in elaborative and organizational processes of secondary memory by manipulating conditions (e.g., instructions) presumed to influence these processes. It is also possible to measure organizational behavior itself, and several indices have been developed which measure the amount of organization in the individual's recall (Bousfield & Bousfield, 1966; Tulving, 1962). These measures are based on the extent to which the individual recalls pairs of words in the same order on

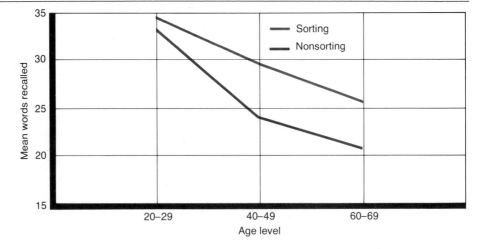

Figure 5.3 Mean number of words correctly recalled as a function of age and sorting condition. *(From Hultsch, 1971.)*

successive trials in spite of the fact the words are presented in a different order each time. Tulving (1962) has suggested that these pairings represent the formation of an organized unit by the learner. The tendency to recall words together as a unit increases systematically over trials and is correlated with the amount of correct recall. The results of these studies are consistent with our previous conclusions. The data, appropriately computed, show significant age-related differences in amount of organization in recall (Hultsch, 1974).

This sample of studies suggests that older adults are less effective or efficient at elaborating or organizing items to be remembered, although this deficit can be reduced by various manipulations which facilitate these processes. Studies other than those already mentioned are consistent with this conclusion (Earhard, 1977; Laurence & Trotter, 1971; Perlmutter, 1978).

Encoding versus storage versus retrieval The studies reviewed above suggest that there are age-related decrements in the elaborative and organizational processes of secondary memory. The question remains whether the problem reflects difficulty involving *encoding* (formation of a code at the time of input), *storage* (retention of this code until the time of output), or *retrieval* (utilization of the code at the time of output).

Of these processes, there is little evidence to support the hypotheses that age-related differences are the result of faulty code retention. Presumably such forgetting is a function of interference processes, and the available research provides little evidence for age differences in susceptibility to interference in secondary memory (Hultsch & Craig, 1976; Smith, 1974, 1975). This suggests that the locus of the difficulty is in the original encoding of the material or the utilization of this code at the time of retrieval. Before we discuss age-related research on these issues, these processes will be reviewed in more detail.

Since retrieval presupposes encoding, a retrieval cue will be effective only when the material has been organized appropriately at the time of encoding (Tulving & Thompson, 1973). Hence, the effectiveness of a retrieval plan depends on the context in which the word was encoded. Once something has entered secondary memory, it is unclear whether it is ever forgotten. However, information may be irretrievable. This can be illustrated by presenting a word list only once and following the presentation with multiple recall trials. That is, the individual only has one opportunity for encoding, but multiple opportunities for retrieval. Studies using this approach show that even though individuals may fail to recall a word on the first retrieval attempt, the word may be recalled on later retrieval attempts (Tulving, 1967). This suggests that the item was in memory but unavailable. There are at least two components to retrieval (Tulving & Pearlstone, 1966). One has to do with the accessibility of the higher-order units which constitute the retrieval plan; the other has to do with the retrieval of specific items within these higher-order units. In other words, the retrieval plan may be inaccessible, or, even if it is available, it may be ineffective in locating specific items. With these points in mind, let us consider the encoding versus retrieval issue in adult memory.

Recall versus recognition One approach to comparing encoding and retrieval processes has been to compare *recall* and *recognition*. In a now-classical study, Schonfield and Robertson (1966) compared the recall and recognition performance of individuals ranging in age from 20 to 75 years. As shown in Figure 5.4 there were systematic age-related declines in recall scores but not in recognition scores. Other studies have found similar results, although in some cases decrements in recognition scores as well as recall scores have been reported. The decrements in the recognition scores were related to the difficulty of the recognition task (Kausler, Kleim, & Overcast, 1975). These results led Schonfield and Robertson (1966), as well as other investigators, to conclude that the memory deficit of older individuals primarily reflects a retrieval problem rather than an encoding or storage problem.

More recent evidence (Smith, 1980) suggests that age differences in recall and recognition performance may be explained on the basis of encoding strategy. It has been shown, for instance, that while recall is particularly dependent on the grouping and relating of items (organization), recognition is particularly dependent on discriminating items one from another (elaboration). In this sense, retrieval plans are more important for recall than for recognition. Smith (1980) has reported that younger individuals spontaneously tend to use organizational strategies. Therefore, on a recall task where organizational strategies are primary, younger individuals perform better than older individuals. However, on a recognition task where elaborational strategies are primary, the organizationally based strategies of the younger individuals are not as effective. As a result, age-related differences in performance typically are reduced. Older individuals tend to use elaborative strategies spontaneously, but there is evidence of a processing deficit in this strategy as well. That is, conditions that facilitate elaborative strategies do not improve the performance of older individuals to the same extent that they improve the performance of younger individuals (Eysenck, 1974; Mason 1979). Therefore, the recent work

Figure 5.4 Recall and recognition scores as a function of age. (Based on Schonfield & Robertson, 1966, table 3, p. 231.)

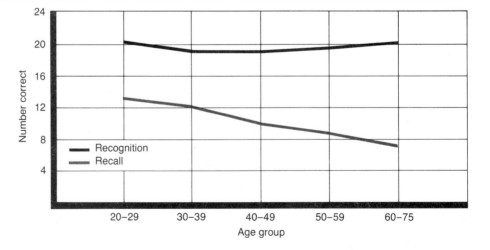

of Smith and his colleagues (Smith, 1980) suggests that age-related differences in recall and recognition tasks are a function of differential encoding strategies.

Cued versus noncued recall A second procedure for discriminating encoding and retrieval processes is to compare *cued recall* and *noncued recall*. If the older adult's problem is retrieval, then the presence of retrieval cues (e.g., category names) at the time of recall should reduce age differences. Several studies have shown this to be the case (Laurence, 1967; Hultsch, 1975). Others have not (Drachman & Leavitt, 1972). The difference appears to be a result of the fact that the former studies used semantic retrieval cues (e.g., category names) and the latter used structural cues (e.g., first letter of the word). That is, it is unlikely that structural cues will be effective if the items have been encoded on the basis of other features. Smith (1977) attempted to resolve this discrepancy by presenting both structural cues (first letter of the word) and semantic cues (category names). These cues were presented at time of output only and also at both time of input and time of recall. Smith (1977) found that the structural cues were ineffective in reducing age-related performance differences while the semantic cues eliminated them. In addition, cues were only effective when presented at both input and output rather than output alone. This study again supports the hypothesis that older individuals do not process the items as deeply as younger individuals. Providing a semantic cue at the time of input facilitated the elaboration of the item, and thus, performance.

The findings summarized in the preceding sections suggest that the age-related deficits in secondary memory observed under multiple testing conditions are due to the same basic cause—namely, a failure to engage in deep semantic elaborational and organizational processing of the material (Craik, 1977; Smith, 1980).

A CONTEXTUAL APPROACH

Defining a Contextual Approach to Learning and Memory

In 1932, Bartlett published a book entitled *Remembering* in which he described a series of experiments on the retention of meaningful text materials. For example, in one study, participants attempted to recall an unusual Indian folktale on several occasions over a period of months. Bartlett reported that there was a high proportion of inaccuracy in the participants' recall and that they appeared to be unaware of the extent of this inaccuracy. Further, the inaccuracy resulted not only from omission and condensation but also from transformation and elaboration of the original material. These elaborations appeared to be efforts to recast the unusual tale used into a form compatible with the participants' cultural knowledge and social conventions. These results led Bartlett (1932) to suggest that we form schemata or concepts of the world based on past experience. During learning, new information is integrated with existing schemata. When the material to be remembered conflicts with existing

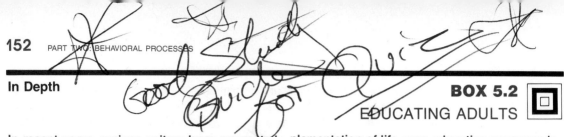

In Depth

BOX 5.2

EDUCATING ADULTS

In recent years, various writers have suggested that education should be reconceptualized as a continuous, life-long process (Agruso, 1978; Birren & Woodruff, 1973). The facts that we are in a time of rapid cultural change, and that increasing numbers of adults reach old age and have increasing amounts of leisure time, underscore the importance of such proposals. Of course, the implementation of life-span education programs involves many philosophical, economic, and technical considerations. From a purely technical standpoint, however, available research on adult learning and memory provides a number of suggestions for structuring educational interventions for adults. Some of these are summarized below.

EDUCATIONAL INTERVENTIONS FOR ADULTS

Component	Intervention Strategy
Pacing	Allow individuals to set their own pace, if possible. Tasks or methods involving significant time pressure are likely to be difficult for adults.
Arousal anxiety	Some degree of arousal is necessary for learning. However, older adults may become too aroused or anxious in a learning situation. Allow individuals an opportunity to become familiar with the situation. Minimize the role of competition and evaluation.
Fatigue	Some tasks may produce considerable mental or physical fatigue—a problem which is likely to particularly affect older adults. Shorten the instruction sessions, or provide frequent rest breaks.
Difficulty	Many tasks are quite complex. Arrange materials from the simple to the complex in order to build individuals' confidence and skills.
Errors	Structure the task so errors are avoided and do not have to be unlearned.
Practice	Provide an opportunity for practice on similar but different tasks. Such practice helps to develop generalizable higher-order skills.
Feedback	Provide information on the adequacy of previous responses.
Cues	Materials should be presented to compensate for the potential sensory problems of older adults. Direct attention toward the relevant aspects of the task. Reduce the level of irrelevant information to a minimum.
Organization	Learning and remembering often require that information be grouped or related in some way. Instruct individuals in the use of various mnemonic techniques (mental images, verbal associations, etc.) which may be used to elaborate or organize the material.
Relevance/experience	People learn and remember what is important to them. Attempt to make the task relevant to individuals' concerns. Performance is likely to be facilitated to the extent that the individuals are able to integrate the new information with known information.

schemata, as in the case of the unusual folktale used by Bartlett, recall is distorted. Thus, memory is viewed as an active process involving reconstruction and elaboration of the original information.

Bartlett's work was published almost fifty years ago, but it was essentially ignored for many years. Recently, however, many of the issues raised by Bartlett have reemerged as researchers have begun to formulate a contextual approach to learning and memory (Bransford, McCarrell, Franks, & Nitsch, 1977; Jenkins, 1974; Meacham, 1977). Such an approach yields a different conceptualization of learning and memory than either the associative or information-processing views. The contextual approach, for example, does not view learning and memory as involving associative bonds between stimuli and responses or storage structures and control processes. Rather, it focuses on the nature of the events the individual experiences. What is learned and remembered depends on the total context of the situation. The physical, psychological, and social context in which the event was experienced, the knowledge, abilities, and characteristics the individual brings to the context, the situation in which we ask for evidence of remembering, etc., are all important. This perspective, then, views learning and memory as a by-product of the *transaction* between individual and context. Learning and memory are not seen as isolated processes. Rather, the emphasis is on the interaction of the various perceptual, inferential, linguistic, problem-solving, personality, and social processes that contribute to individuals' understanding of events. In addition, memory is not seen as a static process. Rather, remembering is a reconstruction of past events. This depends, in large measure, on the degree to which the material has been related to what the individual already knows during acquisition. In addition, recall depends on events that occur after the acquisition of the information. Thus, the individual continually constructs and reconstructs events as the context changes. Finally, because memory processes do not represent isolated behaviors, the contextual approach does not focus on circumscribed tasks of limited meaning. Rather, the emphasis is on tasks high in ecological validity, tasks which are meaningful to the individual and which relate to the individual's everyday life.

Meaning and context in learning and memory Much of the work within the contextual framework has focused on knowledge actualization, and comprehension of meaningful sentence and text materials.

Knowledge actualization (Lachman & Lachman, 1980) involves memory for real-world knowledge. This encompasses an enormous range of information, such as the location of the nearest gas station, the name of the starting quarterback of the Pittsburgh Steelers, the knowledge that it is important to maintain a balanced diet, and the fact that gold has greatly increased in value over the last several years. Some of the information is salient to one's daily life and some of it is not. However, all of it was acquired during a lifetime of formal education or everyday experience. In other words, it was not acquired for the express purpose of remembering it in the laboratory.

The comprehension of meaningful sentence or text material involves abstracting and organizing information from the text and integrating this information with what one already knows (Kintsch & van Dijk, 1978). This processing occurs at multiple levels, including the *graphemic* (letters), *phone-*

mic (sounds), *lexical* (words), and *semantic* (meaning). Each of these analyses leave traces in memory. Normally, however, a reader or listener is concerned primarily with the meaning of the text. Therefore, memory for the semantic level is likely to be stronger than memory for other levels. As a result, the knowledge one gains from processing the text goes beyond what is shown in verbatim recall or recognition. Memory for the meaning or gist of the material is likely to be far more complete and longer-lasting than memory for the specific wording or other surface properties of the material.

Meaning and context in adult learning and memory

Encouragement of the application of a contextual approach to the study of adult learning and memory is relatively recent (Hultsch & Pentz, 1980; Meacham, 1977). To date, only a handful of studies have examined adult knowledge actualization and memory for meaningful sentence and text materials. Nevertheless, an interesting pattern appears to be emerging within this limited work—age-related differences in performance appear to be less prevalent than previously suggested.

Knowledge Actualization

We have mentioned that knowledge actualization involves memory for accumulated knowledge about the world which has been acquired through education and other real-world experience. Studies examining such memory have found either no age differences (Lachman, Lachman & Thronesbery, 1979) or age differences favoring older adults (Botwinick & Storandt, 1974, 1980; Perlmutter, 1978). For example, Lachman, Lachman, and Thronesbery (1979) asked young (19 to 22 years), middle-aged (44 to 53 years), and elderly (65 to 74 years) adults to respond to 190 questions covering such topics as famous people, news events, history, geography, the Bible, literature, sports, mythology, and general information (e.g., "What was the former name of Muhammad Ali?" "What is the capital of Cambodia?"). No evidence of age differences in retrieval of world knowledge was found in this study. The elderly group actually answered more questions correctly than the younger groups, although the differences were not statistically significant.

Dated information was purposely omitted from the Lachman, Lachman, and Thronesbery (1979) study. However, as one might expect, there are cohort differences in world knowledge. For example, Botwinick and Storandt (1980) examined recall and recognition of historical and entertainment facts from each of seven decades—1910 through 1970 (e.g., "What was the name of the plane in which Lindberg flew the Atlantic?" "Who was 'the Sweater Girl?'" "What was the name of the first man to set foot on the moon?"). Subjects from each decade from the twenties through the seventies performed the task. With the exception of those in their seventies, the older adults (forties, fifties, sixties) recalled and recognized more information than the younger adults (twenties, thirties), although the differences were not large. But to some extent, knowledge actualization was cohort-specific. Items from earlier decades were recalled less well by most subjects. However, older adults recalled material from earlier decades better than younger adults. The reverse was true for material from recent decades.

In general then, it appears that older adults are able to recall factual information as well as or better than younger adults, although some of this information is cohort-specific. Older adults also appear to have accurate knowledge of their own memory processes—knowledge which has been labeled *metamemory*. For example, Perlmutter (1978) found no age differences on measures of memory knowledge (e.g., "Is it easier to remember visual things than verbal things?"), memory strategy use (e.g., "How often do you write reminder notes?"), and memory monitoring (e.g., prediction of the number of items that would be recalled following various memory tasks).

Comprehension and Memory for Sentences and Text

Only a few studies have examined adult age differences in comprehension and memory for sentence and text materials. Several of these have required verbatim recall. The typical finding in these instances is that older adults recall fewer words than younger adults. But what about the retention of the meaning or gist of the material as opposed to the exact wording of the material?

A study by Walsh and Baldwin (1977) suggests that older adults may integrate and retain the meaning of sentences as well as younger adults. These investigators used a task devised by Bransford and Franks (1971) in which individuals are presented with a set of sentences, each of which represents a partial meaning of a complete idea. For example, the sentence "The tall tree in the front yard shaded the man who was smoking his pipe" involves four separate ideas. These ideas may be expressed in four sentences as follows:

"The tree was tall."
"The tree was in the front yard."
"The tree shaded the man."
"The man was smoking his pipe."

These one-idea sentences can be combined into longer sentences as well. Examples of two-idea and three-idea sentences would be, respectively,

"The tree shaded the man who was smoking his pipe."
"The tree in the front yard shaded the man who was smoking his pipe."

During the first part of the task, the participants were shown enough of the possible one-, two-, and three-idea sentences to expose them to all four components of the complete idea. Four such complete ideas were used. Following this, a recognition set of sentences was presented, and the individuals were asked to judge whether they had heard each sentence before and asked how confident they were of this judgment. This recognition set contained repetitions of the sentences actually seen (*old*), sentences that were consistent with the idea sets but which had not been seen (*new*), and sentences which were unrelated to the idea sets (*noncase*). Generally, participants were certain they had heard the complex sentences that described all four events. In fact, they had never heard a sentence describing all four events, or even a sentence that long. Nevertheless, the more idea units a sentence contained, the more likely it was to be recognized as having been seen before. That is, fours were recognized more often than threes, which were recognized more often than twos, which were, in turn, recognized more often than ones. Further, these judgments were almost the same for both old and new sentences. Thus, whether the sentence occurred or not had little influence on its rating as long as it was consistent with the idea. Noncase sentences—those inconsistent with the idea sets (e.g., "The tree in the front yard shaded the old car")—were not recognized. Clearly, the individuals did not remember words or sentences but formed a precise, unified representation of the meaning of each idea set. Furthermore, both age groups retained equally precise representation of the total ideas involved.

Could this absence of age-related differences in sentence integration be attributed to a unique sample of older individuals? To test this possibility, Walsh and Baldwin (1977) asked the participants to complete a digit-span and a free-recall task. The data from these tasks were consistent with the conclusions elaborated in the section on information-processing approaches: no age differences were observed in primary memory (digit-span task and the recency portion of free-recall task). However, the older participants recalled only 55 percent as many words as the younger participants on the secondary memory component of the free-recall task. Thus, age-related differences were evident on the free-recall task but not on the linguistic-abstraction task. This study suggests that the nature of semantic memory under these conditions is similar for younger and older individuals: both age groups remember the meaning of the sentence as distinct from its wording.

CONCLUSION

We have reviewed three different approaches to learning and memory in adulthood. All three approaches suggest that age-related decrements in these processes are possible. However, the emphasis on decline varies, with associative approaches reflecting the most pessimistic view and a contextual approach reflecting the most optimistic view.

This discrepancy may be related, in part, to the ecological validity of the tasks and settings used in the research. Ecological validity, you will recall, refers to the extent to which the tasks and setting are meaningful to an individual and are consistent with that individual's everyday experience. It appears that many tasks typically used to measure learning and memory are relatively low in ecological validity.

The potential importance of ecological validity is illustrated by an ingenious study conducted by Bahrick, Bahrick, and Wittlinger (1975), who tested individuals of different ages for memory of the names and faces of high school classmates. While there was a decline in both recall and recognition perform-

Thirty-five years after graduation, individuals can still identify about 90 percent of the names and faces of the members of their class. (F. B. Grunzweig/Photo Researchers)

ance as a function of time since graduation (and, therefore, increasing age), a substantial amount of information was retained. Individuals were able to identify about 90 percent of the names and faces of the members of their class at the time of graduation. This information was retained virtually unimpaired for at least thirty-five years, declining only to about 75 percent after forty-eight years. Recall measures declined more, although this decline is largely attributable to the forgetting of names of classmates who had been known only vaguely. From this perspective, much of the demonstrated age-related decline in memory performance may simply reflect experimental artifact.

While this is an attractive perspective, it is probably an oversimplification. On the one hand, many laboratory tasks probably reflect a reasonable degree of ecological validity. For example, remembering lists of numbers and words probably taps processes necessary for remembering telephone numbers and shopping lists. On the other hand, age-related differences do occur on tasks which appear to be relatively ecologically valid, such as comprehending and remembering short news articles (Dixon, Simon, Nowak, & Hultsch, 1980).

Perlmutter (1980) suggests that this apparent difficulty may be resolved if a distinction is drawn between the process and knowledge requirements of memory tasks. Perlmutter argues that basic memory mechanisms (e.g., encoding, retrieval) may decline with age. However the individual's store of information about the world increases with age. This allows older adults to perform tasks requiring such knowledge as well as or better than younger adults in spite of less-effective memory mechanisms. As one elderly acquaintance stated: "I know a lot if you ask me the right questions." Such a view emphasizes the importance of context. An accurate portrayal of changes in learning and memory during adulthood will require further examination of a broad range of individuals, tasks, and settings.

CHAPTER SUMMARY

It has generally been concluded that learning and memory processes decline with increasing age during adulthood. However, different theoretical approaches paint different pictures of this decline. Recent research may be reviewed within the context of three traditions.

Associative approaches define learning as the formation of stimulus-response bonds, and view forgetting as a process that involves the weakening or loss of such bonds. Research within this tradition has devoted considerable attention to the influence of the pacing of the task on adult learning and memory. Generally, the performance of older adults is impaired more by rapid pacing than the performance of younger adults. The poorer performance of older adults on associative tasks, particularly those which are rapidly paced, has been attributed to both cognitive and noncognitive factors. On the one hand it has been suggested that older adults are more cautious, aroused, or anxious in the learning situation, and that these noncognitive factors inhibit adequate performance. There is some support for these suggestions, particularly the hypothesis that arousal or anxiety negatively affects performance. On the other hand, it has been suggested that older adults' cognitive processing may be ineffective. In particular, it has been shown that older adults do not use mediators as extensively or as efficiently as younger adults. Similarly, older adults appear to be more susceptible to interference from previously acquired stimulus-response bonds.

Information-processing approaches propose that memory involves multiple storage structures and control processes. Typically three storage structures (sensory, primary, secondary) are proposed. Information is retrieved from one store and entered into the next by various control processes (attention, elaboration, organization) which transform the information involved. Research suggests that there are relatively few age-related differences within the temporary sensory or primary memory systems. Large age differences, however, occur within the secondary memory system. Secondary memory depends on the elaboration and organization of the information in terms of its semantic or meaning content. Compared with younger adults, older adults appear to be deficient in these processes. The older adults' difficulty, then, appears to involve primarily the encoding of the material rather than the processes of storing or retrieving it for later use.

A contextual approach to learning and memory suggests that what is learned and remembered depends on the total context of the event. Learning and memory are a by-product of the transaction between the individual and the context. Learning involves the integration of new events with past experience and remembering involves a reconstruction of past events. Much of the work within

this tradition has focused on memory for real-world knowledge and on comprehension and memory for meaningful sentence and text materials. To date, few
studies have examined adult age differences in such processing. What research is
available, however, suggests that age difference on some of these tasks may not
be large. Studies examining memory for world knowledge have generally found
that older adults retrieve such information as well as or better than younger
adults. Similarly, older adults appear to have accurate knowledge about their own
memory processes. Within some contexts older adults appear to integrate and
retain the meaning of sets of sentences as well as younger adults.

PERSONALITY PROCESSES

ISSUES
TO CONSIDER

How do various theorists explain personality development?

What three crises, according to Erikson, occur during adulthood?

Why is it difficult to determine whether adult personality is characterized by continuity or change?

Why are unidimensional cross-sectional studies of personality difficult to interpret?

What changes in adult personality are suggested by the Chicago studies?

What changes in adult personality are suggested by the Berkeley studies?

What changes in adult personality are suggested by the Normative Aging Study?

What conclusions on adult personality are suggested by recent sequential studies?

How does life-course analysis apply to the study of adult personality?

INTRODUCTION

Generally, personality refers to some set of relatively enduring characteristics of the individual. However, there is considerable disagreement among researchers about how to measure, describe, and explain such characteristics. Indeed, in her recent review, Neugarten (1977) concludes that the disarray in the general field of personality is reflected in research on adult personality. She states: "The empirical work appearing over the last 20 years in the area of personality and aging has not only been sparse, but it has been marked by methodological flaws and conceptual impoverishment" (p. 644).

Within this context, researchers examining adult personality have attended to one central issue—whether adult personality is characterized by continuity or by change. Therefore, in this chapter, we will focus on this central issue. First, however, we will briefly consider theories of personality in order to place the study of adult personality in a conceptual context.

THEORIES OF PERSONALITY

How are people's needs and drives included in theories of personality? Do people alter their needs and drives over time? Consider the perspective of a 20-year-old male, who reminisces:

When I was in sixth grade, all I did was play basketball and trade baseball cards—girls were funny things in skirts and panties, and they couldn't play basketball worth a damn. But when I was in ninth grade, creation played its abominable joke, and girls became relevant. I dropped baseball cards, and substituted skin. I haven't been the same since. (van den Daele, 1975, p. 82)

Likewise, what effects do environments have on personalities? How do theories of personality include environmental impacts? A 31-year-old male reflects on his military experience after graduating cum laude in literature:

I slept for 3 hours, maybe 4 hours a night. I was harassed, harangued, and humiliated by turns. I was praised for endurance, toughness, leadership, and all the manly virtues. I forgot my Dante and Virgil, I got in line. . . . (van den Daele, 1975, p. 82)

Theories of personality vary in terms of the relative emphasis placed on these two influences on personality.

On the one hand, orthodox *psychoanalytic theory* emphasizes the role of internal factors in personality. Freud (1949) hypothesized that life is governed by a psychic energy termed *libido*. Individuals are born with a finite amount of libido; however, its location within the body changes over time. That is, rather than being distributed evenly, libido is concentrated in specific body areas at different points in the life span. Such a concentration of energy leads to an excessive amount of tension, which may be released by applying stimulation to the bodily area where the libido is centered. Appropriate stimulation results in reduction of tension or in gratification. According to Freud, there is a universal, biologically based sequence of libido progression which yields five stages of psychosexual development. Although experience may determine whether appropriate stimulation occurs, it does not alter the libido or its sequence of changes.

On the other hand, *social-learning theories* emphasize the role of external factors in personality. Although the specific positions vary, these theorists believe that personality characteristics are learned as a response to, or in interaction with, the environmental context (Bandura & Walters, 1963; Brim, 1968; Mischel, 1973). For example, Bandura and Walters (1963) theorize that by observing others' behavior, an individual can acquire new responses that were not previously present. Such changes occur even though there is no direct reinforcement to the person. Seeing the consequences of the behavior to the person who serves as the model can affect the observer's behavior independently of any direct reinforcement. Personality, then, is learned through interaction with the environment at multiple levels (e.g., family, friends, society).

Still another group of theories emphasize the role of both internal and external factors in personality (Bühler, 1959; Erikson, 1959, 1963; Peck & Havighurst, 1960). Sometimes called *ego theories*, these views have their roots in the orthodox psychoanalytic perspective of Freud. Freud suggested that an innate structure of the personality—the *id*—is the center of the libido. The function of the id is solely to obtain pleasure. In addition to the id (and the *superego*), Freud specified another structure of the personality—the *ego*. The function of the ego is to adapt to reality. The ego organizes processes such as perception, cognition, and interpersonal behavior which permit it to adapt to reality. While Freud recognized the significance of all three structures of personality (id, ego, superego), he emphasized the role of the id and its internal processes. In contrast, ego theorists have emphasized the role of the ego in personality.

For example, according to Erikson (1959, 1963), personality is determined both by an inner maturational "ground plan" and by the external demands of society. For Erikson, ego development involves a sequence of eight psychosocial stages. These stages are biologically based and constitute a fixed, *universal sequence*. Within each stage, however, a particular capability of the ego must be developed if individuals are to adapt to the demands placed on them by society at that point in the life span. If the capability is not developed within the allotted time, that aspect of the ego will be impaired. Each stage, then, constitutes a crisis— either the individual will attain and sense the development of the appropriate capability, or will not attain and will not sense the development of the appropriate capability. Erikson's first five stages concern childhood and adolescence. His last three stages, however, concern young adulthood, adulthood, and old age.

In young adulthood, the crisis is between developing a sense of *intimacy* versus a sense of *isolation*. Intimacy requires the sharing of all aspects of the self (e.g., feelings, ideas, goals) without fearing the loss of one's identity.

Interest in the welfare of the younger generation reflects Erikson's concept of generativity. (Jan Lukas/Photo Researchers)

Moreover, the individual must be receptive to these things from the partner. If individuals cannot share and be shared, then they will feel a sense of isolation.

In adulthood the crisis is between developing a sense of *generativity* versus a sense of *stagnation*. Generativity requires that the individual contribute to the maintenance and perpetuation of society. One can be generative by creating products associated with the maintenance of society (e.g., goods and services), or by producing, rearing, and socializing children in order to perpetuate society. If the individual is unable to create products for the maintenance or perpetuation of society, then a sense of stagnation results.

In old age, the crisis is between developing a sense of ego *integrity* versus a sense of *despair*. In this stage, individuals realize that they are reaching the end of life. If they have successfully progressed through the previous stages of development, they will face old age with enthusiasm; they will feel that a full and complete life has been led. If not, they will feel a sense of despair; they will feel that their life has been wasted.

Erikson proposes that the degree to which a sense of intimacy, generativity, and integrity are successfully achieved depends on whether a person has developed a strong sense of *identity*. With a strong sense of self, an individual is more likely to enter into adult roles in the family and community that reflect a mixture of adult freedom and responsibility. An individual's personality pattern therefore represents an identity that stabilizes during adolescence and young adulthood and determines the way in which ego crises will be experienced and dealt with in later life. Box 6.1 illustrates some of these ideas.

Profile

BOX 6.1
THE DEVELOPMENT OF A PERSONALITY

One of the case studies in R. W. White's (1961) longitudinal study of personality development illustrates the importance of stabilizing one's identity and shows how a strong sense of self can be operative in the resolution of adult ego crises.

As a result of his blue-collar parents' pressure, Joseph Kidd attended a major university to study medicine. He felt caught in the situation and was confused about his values. The values of his childhood neighborhood emphasized easy money and exploitation and did not include a press for upward mobility. He found he lacked a strong commitment to getting a college education and even to becoming a physician. While in college, Kidd was unable to study effectively. He was fearful of others, driven by emotions, and uncertain about himself. He often tried to act like other people. He frequently would act childishly to gain attention and his orientation toward females was idealized and nonphysical. Kidd's relationships with family and friends declined. He flunked out of college and got a job.

In his job his role was clearly defined. He was able to evaluate his performance, and his sense of self became stronger. Kidd began to assert himself. He became more autonomous as he became more involved in decision making in his job. His parents reduced their control and became more accepting. This contributed to a more positive self-image. He began incorporating affection into his relationships. After being promoted, he realized that he was competent and began to define his life by his occupation.

Kidd entered the military. He found the first year enjoyable because his role as a private during World War II was clearly defined. Several senior officers commended his performance, and he was appointed in charge of 80 men. But he discovered that he disliked issuing commands or administering discipline. He began to have negative feelings toward himself again. He felt like a failure.

Returning home after four years in the service, Kidd found that his father's once-prosperous flower shop had begun to decline. With his mother's encouragement, he took over the family business. This effort reflected his most successful attempt at exerting an influence over his environment.

Between the ages of 19 and 29, Kidd moved toward an increasing sense of stability of his identity. He started to be aware of his feelings and intentions and discovered areas where he could be effective. As the flower shop became more successful, Kidd branched out with his interests. He found pleasure in leisure activities. Finally, he left home and took a position with a large industrial firm. He progressed well in his role and began dating seriously. He married and had four children.

The next decade marked his strong involvement in his occupation and his movement into leadership roles in the community. He was elected for three terms on the city council. Although his emotional investment in family life and in his roles as husband and father was never that strong, he behaved in socially expected ways. At midlife Joseph Kidd had a stable sense of self, he was able to maintain a level of intimacy with others, and he was able to be concerned for others. He showed a sense of generativity rather than a sense of stagnation.

Another group of ego theorists have developed personality theories with a slightly different emphasis. Like Erikson, these individuals support a stage sequence of personality development, but they focus on specific events or issues that are considered to produce change in personality during adulthood.

For example, Benedek (1950, 1970) focuses on the events of parenthood and the climacterium in women in relationship to personality changes. Peck (1968), a key figure of this group, posits stages during middle and old age that revolve around central physical or social issues. Peck (1968) feels people confront the following four issues during middle age:

1. Socializing versus sexualizing in human relationships—the climacteric is a time to view men and women as companions, not as sex objects.
2. Valuing wisdom versus physical powers—with aspects of physical decline imminent, individuals should change from a focus on physical prowess to a focus on mental capabilities.
3. Mental flexibility versus mental rigidity—individuals should use new experiences for developing new ways to perceive, think, and behave and not rely upon old ways.
4. Cathectic flexibility versus cathectic impoverishment—during the time when love objects are removed (e.g., children leave home, a spouse or parent dies, a home is sold, a job is left) emotions should be reinvested in other people and activities.

Peck (1968) feels three additional issues are confronted as old age approaches:

5. Ego differentiation versus work-role preoccupation—during a time of role change or role loss people should not dwell on their work roles for defining their self-worth. Rather they should allow themselves to explore new roles and feel a sense of self that goes beyond the work role.
6. Body transcendence versus body preoccupation—a sense of well-being should come from satisfying relationships and activities, not health; thus individuals should try not to mope or complain about physical difficulties.
7. Ego transcendence versus ego preoccupation—individuals must realize death is inevitable; then energy can be directed toward others, which produces feelings of self-satisfaction.

Still other ego theorists spoke about different aspects of personality change with age. (Bühler) (1935, 1959), for instance, discussed that the personality changes over the life span because motivation changes. She felt that motivation affects the ways in which goals are reached and how new goals are structured.

CONTINUITY AND CHANGE OF PERSONALITY

As we have seen, different theories of personality place varying degrees of emphasis on the importance of internal and external variables in personality development. None of these theories, however, has achieved general acceptance. Indeed, in many instances, support for them is quite weak. Nevertheless, it is possible to use these theories as initial frameworks for describing the phenomena associated with personality development. For example, Erikson's

Erikson's

theory suggests that personality development across the life span should be characterized by both continuity and change. In fact, rather than examining the relative importance of internal and external variables, the first task of the developmentalist is to examine whether or not there are systematic changes in personality over the life span. This is a difficult task regardless of what theoretical position is assumed.

It is a difficult task, in part, because the majority of the studies which have been conducted in this area have relied on either the simple cross-sectional or simple longitudinal data-collection strategies. From Chapter 2, you may recall that these data-collection strategies have a number of limitations. In particular, the cross-sectional strategy confounds age with cohort, and the longitudinal strategy confounds age with time of measurement. Differences documented by the cross-sectional strategy may reflect age-related changes or the impact of differential experience on different birth cohorts. Changes documented by the longitudinal strategy may reflect true age-related changes or the impact of events occurring at a given point in historical time which affect individuals of all ages. With these points in mind, let us examine the evidence for continuity and change in adult personality.

Cross-Sectional Studies

Unidimensional studies Literally hundreds of cross-sectional studies examining age differences on a single dimension of personality have been published. The focus of these studies is diverse. For example, researchers have studied aspects of cognitive development such as *egocentrism* (Looft, 1972) and aspects of social development such as achievement (Veroff, Atkinson, Feld, & Gurin, 1960). They also have investigated personal styles such as cautiousness (Botwinick, 1966), *rigidity* (Botwinick, 1967), and creativity (Kogan, 1973). Still others have examined individuals' self-perceptions of many areas (e.g., happiness, morale, hope, life satisfaction, dreams, and attitudes toward aging).

The results of these studies have been mixed. Some researchers have reported significant age differences, while others have not. An exception has been the characteristic of *introversion*. In this case, multiple studies support the conclusion that introversion is greater among older adults than among younger adults (Neugarten, 1977).

The inconsistent findings generated by these unidimensional studies appear to be largely a function of methodological problems. In addition to the confounding of age and cohort mentioned earlier, these studies suffer from a number of deficiencies (Neugarten, 1977):

1. Their internal validity is threatened by history effects: events such as marriage, illness, and retirement, rather than age, may influence personality change.
2. Their internal validity is also threatened by selection effects: age groups have generally varied both within and between studies on factors such as education and health and socioeconomic status.

3. Their external validity is threatened by the use of measures of uncertain meaning for older adults.

These difficulties, as well as others, make the results of the various unidimensional studies very difficult to interpret.

Multidimensional studies   Other cross-sectional studies have attempted to examine age-related differences on multiple rather than single dimensions of personality. This approach is illustrated by the work of Neugarten and her colleagues at the University of Chicago (Neugarten & Associates, 1964). The Chicago group conducted a sequence of interrelated cross-sectional studies over a ten-year period. Relatively large samples of healthy adults between the ages of 40 and 80, residing in the metropolitan area of Kansas City during the 1950s, participated in these studies. While these studies suffer from many of the methodological problems outlined previously, they do examine patterns of age differences for multiple indices of personality. Generally, these studies found evidence both for continuity and for change of adult personality. On the one hand, personality structure was stable. Four personality types—integrated, defended, passive-dependent, and unintegrated—emerged among respondents regardless of age. Similarly, characteristics dealing with the *socioadaptational* aspects of personality (e.g., goal-directed behavior, coping styles, life satisfaction) were not age-related. For example, Neugarten and her colleagues found no relationship between age and a measure of life satisfaction considered to reflect adaptative adjustment to aging. It seems, therefore, that the ways a healthy adult interacts with the environment are rather stable, even though roles and statuses may alter. Neugarten (1964) points out:

In a sense, the self becomes institutionalized with the passage of time. Not only do certain personality processes become stabilized and provide continuity, but the individual builds around him a network of social relationships which he comes to depend on for emotional support and responsiveness and which maintain him in many subtle ways . . . as individuals age, they become increasingly like themselves . . . the personality structure stands more clearly revealed in an old than in a younger person (p. 198).

On the other hand, Neugarten and her colleagues found marked age differences in the *intrapsychic* dimensions of personality (e.g., active versus passive mastery, inner versus outer orientation). For example, there were age differences in the perception of the self in relation to the environment. Forty-year-olds felt in charge of their environment, viewed the self as a source of energy, and felt positive about risk taking. Sixty-year-olds, however, saw the environment as threatening and even dangerous, and the self as passive and accommodating (Neugarten, 1964; Neugarten & Datan, 1973). This change was described as a movement from *active mastery* to *passive mastery*. Figure 6.1 shows these differences for the Kansas City sample. Gutmann (1964) has reported similar age-related differences in other cultures.

' Know

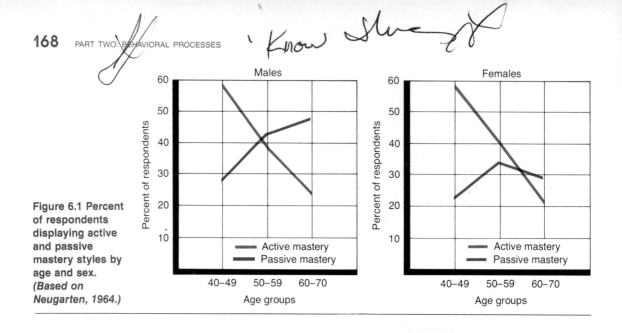

Figure 6.1 Percent of respondents displaying active and passive mastery styles by age and sex. (*Based on Neugarten, 1964.*)

Similarly, there appears to be an increased preoccupation with inner life among older adults. They engaged in greater introspection and self-reflection than younger adults, and showed a general movement from an outer-world to an inner-world orientation. Rosen and Neugarten point out that ". . . the older person tends to respond to inner rather than outer stimuli, to withdraw emotional investments, to give up self-assertiveness, and to avoid rather than embrace challenges" (1964, p. 99). This change was described as an increased *interiority* of the personality.

Along with the increase in passive mastery and interiority, Neugarten and her colleagues noted a sex difference among the older portion of their sample: "[W]omen, as they age, seem to become more tolerant of their own aggressive, egocentric impulses; while men, as they age [seem to become more tolerant] of their own nurturant and affiliative impulses" (Neugarten & Gutmann, 1958, p. 89). This shift in sex-role perceptions occurred only for the older people in the sample. (Perhaps this perception reflects the actual decreased authority older men experience with retirement and the increased authority older women experience with widowhood.) Or, with decreased concern with social norms, the elderly may be reflecting more upon the less apparent and less socially sanctioned aspects of their sex-role behavior, which might account for the differences in their perspective compared with the perspective of younger adults.

In summary, then, these studies point out that there are age-related differences in the intrapsychic aspects of personality. It is difficult to determine the reasons for these differences. Increased difficulty in dealing with the environment may reflect physiological or cognitive changes (see Chapters 3, 4, and 5), and decreased concern with the environment may reflect changes in social roles or life-event experiences (see Chapters 7 and 8).

Longitudinal Studies

Cross-sectional studies, of course, yield information on age (or cohort) differences rather than age changes. As a result, they only provide an indirect answer to the question of continuity versus change. Longitudinal studies, on the other hand, focus directly on this question. However, longitudinal studies are constrained by methodological problems as well (e.g., internal validity is threatened by factors such as experimental mortality and testing effects; external validity is threatened by factors such as cultural change).

A significant number of studies have collected information on adult personality. Some of these have been restricted to the early adult years (e.g., Kagan & Moss, 1962), or to limited sets of personality characteristics (e.g., Kelly, 1955). Others, however, have covered significant spans of time and have included multiple measures of personality. In particular, we will examine two sets of studies, one conducted at the University of California at Berkeley and one at the Veterans Administration in Boston.

Berkeley studies During the late 1920s and early 1930s, three longitudinal studies were begun at The University of California at Berkeley: The Berkeley Guidance Study, the Berkeley Growth Study, and the Oakland Growth Study. Each of these studies involved regular assessments during childhood and several follow-up assessments during adulthood. In addition, the parents of these children were studied—once when they were about 30 years of age and again when they were about 70 years of age.

The initial data emerging from these studies identified the young adult personalities as stable. The males represented five personality types, and the females represented six personality types (Block, 1971). However, as new data on the same individuals were analyzed, focusing on personality *traits* rather than types, evidence of change in personality began to emerge (Haan, 1976; Haan & Day, 1974). Two major types of personality change were studied—ordered transpositions and experiential change. *Ordered transpositions* were defined as changes in degree of characteristics, but not in relative position within the group (e.g., Sue is more dependable than Joan in young adulthood; both become more dependable over time so that Sue is still more dependable than Joan in middle age). *Experiential changes* were defined as changes in both degree of a characteristic and relative position within the group (e.g., Sue is more insightful than Joan in young adulthood; both become more insightful over time so that Joan is now more insightful than Sue in middle age). These two types of change were contrasted with lack of change, which was labeled "unaltered sameness" (Haan, 1976).

A summary of the results of a variety of personality assessments of the Berkeley subjects during middle age is presented in Table 6.1. There is evidence for both continuity and change. As shown in Table 6.1 (characteristics reflecting information processing and interpersonal relations tend to change, while those reflecting socialization and self-presentation tend to remain stable.) Haan (1976) summarizes these changes by saying, "[T]he life span seems

Know Alin (handwritten)

TABLE 6.1

**ITEMS CLASSIFIED ACCORDING TO VARIOUS
DEVELOPMENTAL PATTERNS**

Unaltered Sameness	Ordered Transposition	Experiential Change
Information processing		
Verbally fluent	−Brittle ego defenses*	−Self-defensive
	+Philosophically concerned*	−Extrapunitive
		+Evaluates motivations
		−Fantasizing
		+Insightful
		−Projective
Interpersonal reactions		
Socially poised	−Gregarious	−Bothered by demands
Assertive		+Straightforward
Aloof		(mixed) interest
		in the opposite
		sex
Socialization		
Fastidious	+Dependable	−Feels guilty
Undercontrolled		
Overcontrolled		
Sex-type behavior		
Rebellious		
Rushes limits		
Self-presentation		
Rapid tempo		
Arouses liking		
Basic hostility		
Satisfied with self		
Physically attractive		
Cheerful		
Self-dramatizing		
Talkative		
Self-defeating		

*The plus (+) indicates that means over time generally increased; the minus (−) that they decreased.

Source: From Haan, 1976.

---

typified by movement toward greater comfort, candor, and an objective sense of self that now characterizes these now forty- and fifty-year old people" (p. 64).

In addition, 142 parents of the Berkeley subjects were assessed twice—initially when they were in their thirties and again when they were in their seventies (Maas & Kuypers, 1974). The major tool was an interview schedule divided into twelve sections or "arenas" of living. The questions dealt with home, neighborhood, work, retirement and leisure activities, parenting, grandparenting, brothers and sisters (family of origin), marriage, friendships, formal organizational memberships which included church and various political roles, health, death, and perspectives on past life or "life review." Several other instruments, including self-report diaries, were also used. Using the information obtained from the interviews, Maas and Kuypers examined different patterns of life-style and personality among these adults. Let us examine each of these patterns in turn.

In the case of life-styles, Maas and Kuypers distinguished ten clusters—six for the mothers and four for the fathers. Four of the clusters for the mothers are summarized in Table 6.2 and illustrated in Box 6.2. Several of these groups showed changes from young adulthood to old age.

At the age of thirty, work-centered mothers expressed dissatisfaction with their economic and marital situations, but as they aged, relief from these distresses occurred. "With the loss of their spouses in their middle years (their fifties, on the average), these women ventured into a totally new and apparently highly gratifying style of life, centered on their employment, independence from marital ties, adequate economic rewards, and a circle of new friends" (Maas & Kuypers, 1974, p. 118).

The group-centered mothers, also, showed a more psychologically compatible and satisfying life in later years than they had in earlier years. They stated that in old age they were more fully involved in extrafamilial activities and formal organizations than during their thirties because they were "freed from parental and, in some cases, a wife's responsibilities" (Maas & Kuypers, 1974, p. 123).

The uncentered mothers were happy and healthy at age thirty, but had lost their health and physical stamina by age seventy. In fact, these mothers had the lowest economic status of all the aging mothers. They were strongly focused on family and home during their thirties, but with age came losses—of husband and home. At seventy they showed little interest in activities or roles such as that of grandparent.

The disabled-disengaged mothers showed both continuities and discontinuities over their adult lives. A preoccupation with illness persisted, and their parenting style showed little change. They also showed increased withdrawal from society.

Finally, the husband-centered and visiting mothers showed few changes in life-style over the period.

In general, then, the women in this study evidenced quite a lot of change in life-styles, with the most dramatic changes occurring for the work-centered mothers. For the fathers in the Berkeley Study, in contrast, continuity was more characteristic.

It is as though the trajectory for our fathers' ways of living were established early in their adult lives. . . . Unwell disengaged fathers were also both unwell and relatively disengaged in their early adult years. . . . The family centered

Don't know

TABLE 6.2
LIFE-STYLE COMPONENTS FOR FOUR FEMALE LIFE-STYLE CLUSTERS

	Husband-Centered	Work-Centered	Uncentered	Disabled-Disengaged
Home and visiting	Low involvement as guest	Visits others weekly More visiting than in forties	High involvement as guest Visits others more than once a month	Low involvement as hostess Low involvement as guest
Work and leisure	A few interests pursued alone Satisfied economically	Works part- or full-time High involvement and satisfaction with work Many leisure interests	A few interests pursued with others Not satisfied economically	A few interests pursued alone A moderate number pursued with others
Marriage	High involvement as spouse Closer than average relationship	Not presently married	Not presently married	Open, communicating, close marriage High involvement as spouse Sees marriage as having changed for better
Parenting	Very satisfied with children Does not see children often	Very satisfied with children's visits	Sees children often	Mixed satisfaction and dissatisfaction Little expression of affect
Grandparenting	Low involvement as grandparent		Sees grandchildren often	Low involvement Mixed satisfaction and dissatisfaction
Friendship				Has less meaning than in forties
Clubs	Low involvement and low satisfaction	Low involvement	Low involvement and low satisfaction	Low involvement
Health		Very satisfied	Not satisfied	Has seen a doctor and been hospitalized in the last year Not satisfied
Death	Talks of death with relative ease		Talks of death with difficulty	Talks of death with difficulty

Source: Based on Mass & Kuypers, 1974.

fathers manifest more family centeredness in old age than they had in early adulthood, with no evidence of going off course in their life-long focus on family. (Maas & Kuypers, 1974, p. 130)

Maas and Kuypers distinguished seven personality groupings—four for the

Profile

BOX 6.2

FEMALE LIFE STYLES

From the interviews conducted by Maas and Kuypers (1974) we gain insight into the several life-styles they described.

Husband-Centered

Monday [late July] *Got up at 8 o'clock and after breakfast did some washing and other household chores. We had lunch at about 1 o'clock. My husband is working on his new garden shed which is almost finished, while I did some kibbitzing. While my husband took a nap I wrote several letters, went over our bank statement and relaxed and read for a while. Later on my husband and I talked about future plans for the nursery. After 5 o'clock we sat on the deck and had a highball and watched various birds, squirrels, and rabbits perform. Weather a beautiful 80°. At 6 o'clock watched the evening news on TV for an hour and at seven had dinner. After dinner we both read until about 11 o'clock and went to bed.*

Tuesday *Got up at 7:30 and after breakfast was busy all morning with various things and at 11 o'clock went to Palo Alto. On the way I stopped at the house of some people whom I met recently, and who have lived here and grown up around here all their lives, very interesting to hear about their lives. Both are in their late sixties. Did shopping and talked to many people and made an appointment with the dentist. Arrived home about 2:30 p.m. My husband had taken his nap and was working on the garden shed again. At 4 o'clock we had tea and I told my husband all the people I had met and what we talked about, etc. In the evening we watched TV together, channel 9 for a while. After that we read until 11 o'clock. (p. 50)*

Work-Centered

Monday *Very warm today. My boss returned this morning. I took the accumulated mail into his office. He stood up and shook my hand. Figured and paid the premium on Workmen's Compensation for the month. Figured and paid the payroll taxes to the federal government. This must now* *be done twice a month until the end of the quarter, at which time wages must be reported individually to both the state and federal governments. Also filled out the form for the State Board of Equalization which accompanies our check for transportation taxes on the highway hauling. This is in addition to the taxes paid quarterly on all gross trucking revenue. These have to be watched carefully to avoid paying penalties. In addition I must make quarterly and annual reports to both the I.C.C. and P.U.C. The annual reports must be notarized and I am completely responsible for them. My duties involve license fees; use tax on trucks, tractors, and trailers; insurance of many kinds; the various benefit and pension plans for the four unions represented here; and, of course, all accounting necessary to a business of this kind. Stopped on my way home to have my watch checked. It needed cleaning. Went in to see my neighbor for a few minutes and then home for the evening. Listened to the news broadcast for a while. Wanted to water the yard before it became too dark. As I was watering the front, Mrs. Johnson, who lives across the street on the corner, came over to chat for a little while. She is very nice but works too hard.*

Tuesday *A funny thing happened to me on my way to work this morning—at least it was unusual. A man on the Third Street bus insisted on my taking his seat. When he reached Garvey Street, the light was against us and the bus driver let me off so that I could catch the #42 which was about to cross Ninth Street. Some of the drivers will not do this as it is not the regular stop. It then means a wait of another ten minutes or longer. These buses break down constantly. But this morning, a girl from the office who drives from Novato each day gave me a lift the rest of the way. I think I am the only one in the office who does not drive to work. Took the Shattuck Avenue bus to Berkeley from the Terminal about 4:30 p.m. It detoured at Derby Street going west to Sacramento Street, north to Virginia Street, and then back to Shattuck*

Avenue, to avoid downtown Berkeley. I stopped off at the cleaners to leave my blue coat and go to the drug store to leave some film and buy some ice cream. I again boarded the F Bus, transferring at Solano Avenue and the Alameda. And so to home. A short time later, Lucy phoned. She said that she had been trying to get me for some time. We talked for a while, then I fed Caramel and made myself a peanut butter sandwich and a sundae with the ice cream. Then I took some of the ice cream to my next door neighbor, also a banana. I didn't stay, however. Usual TV, music exercises before retiring. (pp. 65–66)

Uncentered

Thursday Up at 6:15. Read Bible. Breakfast 7:30. Listened to Through the Bible 8–8:30. Husband and I had devotions together. 9 walked down to Aunt Sue's. Started water for her on yard. Walked home. Packed suitcase. Cleaned. Prepared lunch. Straightened up kitchen, watered yard, took shower about 2:30. Left for Livermore at 3:30. Had dinner with daughter and family. The four of us left for church where memorial service was held for husband's sister. After service visited with friends—good to see them. Back to daughter's about 10. Bed at 11.

Friday Up at 6. Ate breakfast with daughter and grandson. Cleaned up room, repacked suitcase, went to son's store about 10. Stopped at drug store. We then went to see our auditor at his office. Went to friend's house about eleven. Gave us some plants. Stopped at Safeway. Had lunch with businessman from San Francisco at restaurant in Hayward. Wasn't able to lead my B.S.F. class today as we stayed overnight in Livermore. Left restaurant at 1:15. Went to doctor's office where stitches were removed from husband's surgery. While he was at doctor's went to friend's house for a few minutes. Picked husband up—came home. I am still driving as he can't wear his glasses yet. Home about 3:30. Stopped at Aunt Sue's about 4. Brother-in-law and his wife came for a few minutes. Worked in yard until time for dinner preparations. Went for a walk first with my husband. Worked in yard—mostly weeding. Came in at 9. Writing this now and then to bed. Haven't had time this week to make the dress I hope to cut out and sew. Nor have I had time to finish sweater—nor do my handcraft work, which is for fun. (p. 61)

Disabled-Disengaged

Monday Spent most of the morning getting prices on moving console cabinet to home of son in Menlo Park. [Afternoon] Movers called for and picked up cabinet. Cleaned the wall and floor afterward. One bookcase sent with cabinet. Filed books in cartons, remaining bookcases. (Evening: no entry)

Tuesday Up early and left for Menlo Park to see last of bookcase and console cabinet. Left after 11 a.m. and went to San Francisco; lunch in SF, looked for bookcase replacements in SF and Oakland; tired out, left for home without making decision. [Afternoon] Home from shopping, nap. [Evening] TV and bed.

Wednesday Shifting furniture, sorting books. [Afternoon] Nap, visit from son and daughter-in-law. [Evening] Dinner. 7:15–9:15 p.m. CCS meeting, acted as discussion leader at California Conservation Society meeting. (p. 70)

mothers and three for the fathers. These groupings and their associated characteristics are shown in Table 6.3.

In this case, the fathers, but not the mothers, tended to show changes in personality patterns from young adulthood to old age. The conservative-ordering fathers changed the most. As young adults, these fathers were shy, distant, withdrawn, and conflicted. They reported numerous marital problems.

At seventy, marital problems were not considered important, and these men became conventional and controlling. Some changes also occurred for active-competent fathers. When they were in their thirties, they were exploitive, irritable, tense, and nervous. As older adults, they were direct, capable, charming, and conforming. They spent much of their leisure time alone, yet they were highly involved in the role of friend.

Thus, in the case of life-style patterns, continuity between young adulthood and old age was more apparent among the fathers than among the mothers. In the case of personality patterns, continuity between young adulthood and old age was more apparent among the mothers than among the fathers. Maas and Kuyper's (1974) results, then, emphasize both continuity and change, as well as sex differences, in life-style and personality patterns. They conclude:

Most clearly, however, the majority of lives in this study run contrary to the popular and literary myth of inescapable decline in old age. Whether one considers the women or the men, and whether one examines their psychologi-

Maas + Kuyper's (1974)

Some researchers feel that personality characteristics, such as extraversion and openness to change, that are evident in old age were present earlier in the life span. (Brody/Editorial Photocolor Archives)

Don't worry

TABLE 6.3

PERSONALITY GROUPS AND PERSONALITY CHARACTERISTICS*

Data Source	Area	Measure
Interview ratings	Intellectual functioning	Estimated intellectual capacity
		Mental alertness
		Mental speed
		Accuracy of thinking
		Use of language
	Presentation of self	Personal appearance
		Energy output
		Freshness
		Restlessness
		Talkativeness
		Excitability
		Self-assurance
		Criticalness
		Openmindedness
		Frankness
	Relation to child	Critical
		Interest
	Mood	Cheerfulness
		Worry
		Satisfaction with lot
		Self-esteem
		LSR
Questionnaire	Perception	Locus of control
		Locus of evaluation
Test	Intelligence	Full-scale IQ
		Verbal IQ
		Performance IQ
	Total number of parents	

*All entries in columns indicate significant difference of .05 or below between identified group and all remaining parents of the same sex, with the exception of the WAIS IQ scores, where no significant differences were observed.

†First number is mean full-scale score; second number is standard deviation.

Source: From Maas and Kuypers, 1974, Table 25, pp. 150–151.

Mothers' Groups				Fathers' Groups		
Person-oriented	Fearful-ordering	Autono-mous	Anxious-asserting	Person-oriented	Active-competent	Conservative-ordering
Higher	Lower					
Alert	Remote					
Active	Sluggish					
Accurate	Inaccurate		Inaccurate			
	Halting					
Positive						
	Sluggish					
Fresh	Worn					
			Restless			Placid
	Mute		Talkative			Mute
	Apathetic		Excitable			
Self-assured	Not assured		Not assured			
			Critical			
Open		Closed				Closed
	Covers thought					Covers thought
			Critical	Not critical		
High	High	Indif-ferent	Indiffer-ent			
Cheerful	Depressed					Depressed
Little worry	Worrisome		Worrisome			
High	Dissatis-fied		Dissatis-fied			
High	Low	High				
High	Low		Low			
Internal	External					
(117;11.9)†	(112;8)	(116;11.3)	(118;12.8)	(129;10.6)	(127;23.2)	(130;10.2)
43	11	7	8	13	9	12

cal capacities and orientations or their styles of living, most of these aging parents give no evidence of traveling a downhill course. By far most of these parents in their old age are involved in rewarding and diversely patterned lives. Most of them manifest high levels of coping capacities. And for those small proportions in our study whose personalities and life-styles seem problematic, it is not merely old age that has ushered in the dissatisfactions and the suffering. In early adulthood these men and women were in various ways at odds with others and themselves or too constricted in their involvements. Old age merely continues for them what earlier years have launched. Finally, even when young adulthood is too narrowly lived or painfully overburdened, the later years may offer new opportunities. Different ways of living may be developed as our social environments change with time—and as we change them. In this study we have found repeated evidence that old age can provide a second and better chance at life. (p. 215)

Normative aging study   This interdisciplinary longitudinal study, which is being conducted at the Veterans Administration Outpatient Clinic in Boston, involves a sample of approximately 2000 men, ranging in age from the twenties through the eighties. Psychological measures have included global assessments of intelligence, personality, values, and attitudes, and laboratory-based assessments of perception, decision making, and memory. Much of the information on personality from this study has been reported by Costa and his colleagues (e.g., Costa & McCrae, 1976, 1977, 1978).

Costa and McCrae (1980) propose that personality may be described by three broad dimensions: Neuroticism, Extraversion, and Openness to Experience. Each of these dimensions represents a cluster of traits—generalized dispositions to think, feel, and behave in certain ways. Costa and McCrae suggest that each dimension reflects six traits:

Neuroticism—Anxiety, Hostility, Depression, Self-consciousness, Impulsiveness, Vulnerability

Extraversion—Attachment, Gregariousness, Assertiveness, Activity, Excitement seeking, Positive Emotions

Openness to Experience—Openness to Fantasy, Esthetics, Feelings, Actions, Ideas, Values

These characteristics predict a wide variety of attitudes, feelings, and behaviors (Costa & McCrae, 1977, 1978, 1980; Nuttal & Costa, 1975; McCrae, Bartone, & Costa, 1976). For example, men high on Neuroticism were more likely to drink and smoke, have more health problems and complaints, have sexual difficulties, be separated or divorced, and feel unhappy and dissatisfied with life. Men high on Extraversion were more likely to select jobs where dealing with people was more central than the task. Thus, they preferred occupations such as social work, advertising, and law. Introverts selected professions that were task-oriented (e.g., architect). Men high on Openness to Experience were more likely to have higher theoretical and aesthetic values and lower religious and economic values. The lives of these men were also more eventful—for example, they were more likely to quit a job, be demoted, or change careers.

Longitudinal analyses of the traits associated with Neuroticism, Extraversion, and Openness to Experience suggest that adult personality is characterized by continuity rather than change. Costa and McCrae (1980) report continuity in mean scores, correlation coefficients, and relationships to other variables. Ten-year retest correlations, for example, ranged from .58 to .69 for traits reflecting Neuroticism, from .70 to .84 for traits reflecting Extraversion, and from .44 to .63 for traits reflecting Openness to Experience.

Other evidence corroborates this view of stability in personality across the life span. For instance, Skolnick (1966) reported 20-year stability coefficients ranging from .21 to .34 for Thematic Apperception Test (TAT) measures of power, affiliation, aggression, and achievement. Similarly, Britton and Britton (1972) reported correlations ranging from .21 to .52 for seventeen men and .27 to .53 for twenty-nine women on multiple characteristics such as happiness, self-confidence, and interpersonal acceptance over nine years.

Sequential Studies

Sequential data-collection strategies, as you will recall, consist of sequences of cross-sectional and/or longitudinal studies. Sequential strategies permit the separation of age- and cohort-related effects—a separation which is essential if the question of continuity versus change in adult personality is to be answered. Only a few sequential studies focused on personality have been completed to date. Generally, these studies have suggested that adult personality is characterized more by continuity than by change (Douglas & Arenberg, 1978; Siegler, George, & Okun, 1979; Schaie & Parham, 1974; Woodruff & Birren, 1972).

Siegler, George, and Okun (1979), for instance, administered the Cattell 16 Personality Factor test to 331 men and women. Twelve two-year birth cohorts ranging in age from 46 to 69 years of age at the first time of measurement participated in the study. They were assessed four times over an eight-year period between 1968 and 1976. Siegler and her colleagues found that the strongest effects were related to sex. Females were less reserved and more submissive, tender-minded, naive, and tense than males. With the exception of Factor B, which is a measure of intelligence, few reliable age changes or cohort differences were evident.

In another recent sequential study, Douglas and Arenberg (1978) found evidence for age changes and cohort differences on the Guilford-Zimmerman Temperament Survey. The participants in this study were 915 men aged 17 to 98 years of age. Seven-year longitudinal data were available for 336 of the participants.

The Guilford-Zimmerman Temperament Survey provides an assessment of ten traits: General Activity (pace of activity), Restraint (emotional maturity), Ascendance (social assertiveness), Sociability (gregariousness), Emotional

Stability (optimism), Objectivity (realistic outlook), Friendliness (agreeableness), Thoughtfulness (reflectiveness, introspection), Personal Relations (tolerance and cooperativeness), and Masculinity ("masculine" interests).

The data were analyzed using conventional cross-sectional and longitudinal as well as sequential arrangements designed to distinguish among age changes, cultural changes, and cohort differences (Schaie, 1965). Longitudinal changes were found on five scales, but only two of these were interpreted as age-related changes. Masculine interests (Masculinity) declined over the entire age range. Preference for rapidly paced activity (General Activity) declined with increasing age after the forties. Differences on three other scales were interpreted as cultural change effects. The tendency toward reflective and introspective thinking (Thoughtfulness), tolerance and cooperativeness with other people (Personal Relations), and agreeableness and thoughtfulness toward other people (Friendliness) declined during the period. Finally, differences on two other scales were interpreted as cohort effects. Earlier-born men were more serious-minded, persevering, and responsible (Restraint) and less socially assertive (Ascendance) than later-born men. The data are summarized in Table 6.4.

Douglas and Arenberg's (1978) findings contradict many of those from previous studies. For example, cross-sectional studies have suggested a movement from active to passive mastery and from an outer-world to an inner-world orientation with increasing age. In the present study, however, two traits that may be related to these characteristics (Thoughtfulness and Ascendance) showed cohort differences rather than age changes. Although the various measures involved may not be equivalent, Douglas and Arenberg's results suggest the need for caution in interpreting earlier studies.

TABLE 6.4
SUMMARY OF AGE-RELATED CHANGES,
CULTURE-RELATED CHANGES, AND COHORT-RELATED
DIFFERENCES IN PERSONALITY

Personality Trait	Source		
	Age-Related	Culture-Related	Cohort-Related
General activity	Declined		
Masculinity	Declined		
Thoughtfulness		Decreased	
Personal relations		Decreased	
Friendliness		Decreased	
Restraint			Decreased
Ascendance			Decreased

Source: Based on Douglas and Arenberg, 1978.

Life-Course Analysis

Research examining the issue of continuity versus change in adult personality has obviously produced mixed results. Evidence for both continuity and change exists. However, much of the research is plagued by difficult methodological problems. Within this context, the evidence for age-related continuity appears to be stronger than the evidence for age-related change. The few sequential analyses currently available suggest that sex and cohort differences are more significant than age changes. What does such a conclusion imply? Costa and McCrae (1980) suggest:

The personologist interested in continuity or change should, we believe, reformulate goals. Instead of looking for the mechanisms by which personality changes with age, we should look for the means by which stability is maintained. Are traits genetically determined and therefore as stable as genetic influences? Do individuals choose or create environments which sustain the behavior that characterizes them? Are we locked into our nature by the network of social expectations around us? Do early childhood influences continue to operate beyond the reach of corrective experiences?—and within any one of these perspectives—genetic, behavioral, social role, or psychoanalytic—by what mechanisms are we enabled to assimilate the changing experiences of a lifetime to our own nature? How do we cope, or adapt, or defend so as to preserve our essential characteristics unchanged in the face of all the vicissitudes of adulthood and old age. These are questions for the student of personality and aging. (p. 27)

In this context, Elder (1975, 1977b) has suggested the need for a *life-course analysis* of personality. This approach focuses on the examination of age- and sex-differentiated life patterns in relation to the historical context in which they are embedded. In particular, attention is directed toward an examination of the occurrence, duration, and timing of events within the life course, and the role of personality in adapting to these events. In Chapters 8 through 12, we will examine the role of life events and transitions in shaping the life course.

CONCLUSION

The study of personality during the last half of the life span appears to be more complex than during the first half. Accumulated physical, psychological, and social factors interact with historical and cultural factors to yield a complex pattern of influences on personality. Consequently, we agree with Neugarten (1977), who recognizes that:

[W]e are culture-bound and history-bound in the very ways we approach our field of study and in the conclusions we draw. Just as new paradigms are likely to appear in the field of personality, so new perspectives can be anticipated

with regard to the nature of aging, for increased longevity, changing rhythms of the life cycle, and other social biological realities will come to characterize the society in which we live. (p. 644)

She continues by saying that ". . . whether or not an Einstein appears within the field of personality, we will have changing views of aging over the next few decades, and these will themselves influence our views of the aging personality" (p. 644).

CHAPTER SUMMARY

There is considerable confusion in the field over the definition and measurement of personality. This is reflected in the various theories of personality. For example, orthodox psychoanalytic theory emphasizes the role of internal factors in personality. Social-learning theories emphasize the role of external factors in personality. Ego theories emphasize the role of both internal and external factors in personality. Within this last group, Erikson's theory is particularly significant. For Erikson, personality development involves a universal sequence of eight psychosocial stages. Within each stage, a particular capability of the ego must be developed if individuals are to adapt to the demands placed on them by society. This causes a series of crises in personality development. Erikson proposes that these ego crises occur during adulthood in the following sequence: (1) intimacy versus isolation; (2) generativity versus stagnation, and (3) integrity versus despair. He maintains that individuals are more likely to enter into adult roles in the family and community that reflect a mixture of freedom and responsibility when they have a strong sense of self. The integrated adult personality has a stable sense of self that interacts with strivings toward intimacy, generativity, and integrity.

Regardless of which theory one supports, the first task of developmentalists is to examine whether or not there are systematic changes in personality over the life span. This is a difficult task because the majority of the studies which have been conducted have relied on simple cross-sectional or longitudinal data-collection strategies. Differences documented by the cross-sectional strategy may reflect age-related changes or cohort differences. Changes documented by the longitudinal strategy may reflect true age-related changes or may be a reflection of cultural changes.

Partly as a result of these difficulties, inconsistent results have been reported by the various studies. Neugarten and her colleagues, for example, in multidimensional cross-sectional studies, found continuity in the structure and socioadaptational aspects of personality. However, they found age differences in the intrapsychic aspects of personality. Older adults were characterized by passive rather than active mastery, and by an inner-world orientation rather than an outer-world orientation.

The Berkeley longitudinal studies also report evidence for both continuity and change, as well as for sex differences in life-style and personality patterns. In the case of life-style patterns, continuity between young adulthood and old age was more apparent among men than women. In the case of personality patterns, continuity between young adulthood and old age was more apparent among the mothers than among the fathers. Analyses based on the Normative Aging Study data, however, show little evidence of age-related change on any aspects of personality.

Finally, recent sequential studies have suggested that personality is characterized more by continuity than by change. Sex and cohort differences appear to be more significant than age changes.

These results suggest the need for a life-course analysis which focuses on the examination of age- and sex-differentiated life patterns in relation to the historical context. Attention should be devoted to an examination of life events and to the role of personality in adapting to these events.

7

SOCIAL PROCESSES

CHAPTER
OVERVIEW

Individuals develop within a social context, or culture. In this chapter we will examine the cohort and age-status systems of this social context. Role change, marital satisfaction, occupational satisfaction, and life satisfaction are also considered.

Introduction
Social Aspects of the Aging Process
  Age and cohorts
  Age and individuals
  Intergenerational relations
Adult Socialization and Satisfaction
  Life events

Status and role change
Preparation for social roles
Marital satisfaction
Occupational satisfaction
Life satisfaction
Conclusion

ISSUES
TO CONSIDER

Why is it important to study adult socialization within a cultural context?

What are the differences between the macro and micro levels of analysis for studying adult socialization?

What are the differences in the aging process at the cohort level and at the individual level?

In what ways can adulthood, middle age, and old age be differentiated?

How are intergenerational relations studied?

How can societal and familial interactions be portrayed?

How does Rosow conceptualize status and role change over the life span?

What factors affect marital satisfaction over the life span?

What factors affect occupational satisfaction over the life span?

What factors affect life satisfaction over the life span?

INTRODUCTION

Among the Comanche brothers, it is a practice, under certain circumstances, to lend their wives to each other for sexual purposes, and certain Eskimo groups characteristically offer their wives for the night to a visitor, practices that Americans and many others would look upon as highly immoral. . . . Among the Toda of South India to thumb one's nose at another person is a sign of respect; in Western Europe and the United States, to do so is a gesture that expresses defiance and disrespect. (Chinoy, 1967, p. 91)

The different customs cited in the quotation reflect what is known as cultural diversity. Yet in a world full of such cultural diversity many uniformities exist. According to Murdock (1945), cultural uniformities include "age-grading, athletic sports, bodily adornment, calendar, cleanliness training, community organization, working, cooperative labor, cosmology, courtship, dancing . . . [and so forth]" (p. 124). What, then, is culture?

 Culture may be defined as a legacy or heritage comprising the knowledge, beliefs, values, assumptions, patterns of behavior, and material items that have, in a given society, demonstrated effectiveness in dealing with the world. Despite its importance, culture is such an all-pervasive part of our environment and development that we often take it for granted. The key for developing a sensitivity to culture is to study social processes, that is, how changing patterns of learned behavior are shared by and transmitted among members of society. A major way in which individuals learn what behaviors are expected of them is through the cultural attitudes that are supported and shared among generations. One example of a cultural attitude that varies from place to place involves how people regard the aging process. A recent study (Bengston, Dowd, Smith, & Inkeles, 1975) suggests that young men in developed nations are less likely to look forward to old age than men from less-developed nations. The men in the study were also assessed on the degree to which they were "modern," the basis for classification being exposure to occupations that provide modernizing experiences. The data showed that individual modernity was not related to negative attitudes toward aging. Thus, at a societal level, negative cultural attitudes toward aging exist. Such negative attitudes often are perpetuated by myths that are supported culturally. A myth is a "recurring theme or character type that appeals to the consciousness of a people by embodying its cultural ideals or by giving expression to deep, commonly felt emotions" (Morris, 1975, p. 869). At the heart of all myths is some reality that has been widely accepted by members of society at some point and has become part of the socialization process.

Socialization refers to the process by which individuals, over the course of their lives, acquire ways to perform new roles. How do they learn which procedures and agencies will facilitate their opportunities? How do they learn which roles will bring rewards and which roles are considered undesirable? And how do people adjust to changing roles and role loss? As the socialization process operates, individuals in various age relationships (e.g., adult and child)

The family serves as the major vehicle for sharing cultural attitudes between generations. (United Nations; Bruce Roberts/Photo Researchers)

learn from each other. In our attempt to understand how the socialization process occurs for individuals of varying ages, we need to be aware how age is stratified in a society and how societal changes and social and nonsocial events affect age strata. *Age strata* alter as society changes, and thus represent the basic core of social organization, molding sociocultural life both at a specific point in time and over generations (Sorokin, 1968). Thus, we will examine adult socialization at two levels of analysis—the macro level, that of aging cohorts, and the micro level, that of aging individuals. In doing so, the reciprocal nature of socialization within and between younger and older individuals and cohorts will be examined.

SOCIAL ASPECTS OF THE AGING PROCESS

The process of aging is not simply an individual process. It involves a dynamic interaction between individuals and society. More specifically, the movement within and between two major societal structures—cohorts and roles—defines the social aging process. People within a cohort die, and new cohorts emerge. People move from one role to another over the course of their lives. A person

In Depth

BOX 7.1
BELIEFS AND ATTITUDES ABOUT AGING

Our beliefs and attitudes toward aging are evidenced in many aspects by our culture. Consider some of the following examples.

Philosophers
From the ancient philosophers (e.g., Plato, Aristotle, and Seneca), to the medieval (e.g., Bacon, Acquinas, and Machiavelli), to the modern (e.g., Locke, Rousseau, Kant, and Darwin), to the contemporary (e.g., James, Camus, Sartre, and de Beauvoir) writers have discussed ideal and actual aging. Using the available literature of these four time periods, Svobada (1977) analyzes how four thematic dimensions (definition of senescence, psyche of the elderly, powers of the elderly, and the position of the elderly) were handled. Within each of the major time periods, attitudes and beliefs about aging were riddled with contradiction and ambivalence.

Seneca, for instance, declared that old age "is a natural and good time" when there is "no falling away." Aristotle maintained that "old age is a time when the body loses heat" which makes the body "dry out" so "the skin of the eye becomes thicker" and "hair grows coarser." However, Aristotle felt the mind is immutable and unaffected by aging. In contrast, Lucretius felt that the "mastering might of time" causes the mind to halt.

Such contradiction and ambivalence persisted over the centuries. Like Aristotle, Acquinas and Hegel maintained that the body may falter but the mind remains strong, with the "spirit peaking in judgment and maturing during old age." Machiavelli advised that as a consequence of a worn-out body "love is revolting to the old" and should be left to the young. Schopenhauer and Sartre deplored the "dreariness of old age," declaring it a "boring experience" when one is a "stranger in another time."

Children's literature
Children's books contribute to the formation of attitudes about aging. Recently, concern has been expressed about how the elderly are depicted in this literature (e.g., Ansello, 1977a, 1977b). Analyzing almost 700 circulating children's picture books of older characters for behavioral and trait correlates, Ansello (1977a) found that ageism prevailed and a limited view of development was evident. Older characters were portrayed as peripheral to the plot, physically declining, and habitual. The emergent stereotype was of a person who is unimaginative, unexciting, dependent, and not self-disclosing. In general, old age was painted as a boring, dull time when people have limited abilities and behavioral capacities.

Television
With television's high level of usage, it may be one of the most potent vehicles for conveying beliefs and attitudes about aging. Although the number of old people portrayed on television approximates their relative number in society, older people are underrepresented in prime-time shows. Regardless of when shows are aired, the elderly are not represented accurately in terms of sex, marital status, and jobs. The portrait of the older person is essentially an "unportrait," meaning they are depicted unidimensionally and negatively as unhealthy, unstylish, and uninteresting. It is lamentable that television does not present the elderly possessing experience, wisdom, and skills as well as emotional depth.

may be located within a particular cohort, and identified as playing a particular kind of role, at any age. The concepts of cohort and of roles are descriptively meaningful for studying the socialization process.

Age and Cohorts

An individual's cohort is made up of those who were born during the same time interval as that individual and hence will age together (Riley, 1976).

Cohort flow   At any given point in time, it is possible to describe the age strata in a population as a composite of several cohorts. The process of *cohort flow* reflects what happens to different cohorts over their life course: their formation, their modification through migration, and their reduction and eventual dissolution through death of their members (Riley, 1976).

Each cohort begins with a given size, which, except for additions from immigration, is the maximum size it will ever attain. Over the life course of the cohort individual members die until the entire cohort is destroyed. A cohort also starts with a given membership which has certain characteristics and dispositions. Some of these are quite stable (e.g., sex and race). However, the composition of the cohort changes over time even with respect to the stable characteristics. For example, women outlive men and whites outlive blacks (Riley, 1976).

Cohort differences and succession   Cohorts also differ markedly from one another in various respects. For example, Easterlin (reported in Collins, 1979) notes that a cohort's size exerts powerful societal leverage that affects cohort members' job opportunities and procreation desires. In large cohorts, competition for jobs is intense, and a subjective feeling that "times are tough" may curtail the process of family formation. In smaller cohorts, however, fewer people compete for jobs. People feel optimistic about their opportunities, and this stimulates the family-formation process, producing an increase in the birth rate for that cohort. Accordingly, Easterlin feels members of small, "shortage" cohorts have an easier situation not only when entering the job market but also when they are older.

The *pattern* of differences involved in the succession of cohorts may also be significant. Easterlin suggests that a small cohort following a large one benefits continually as members of the two cohorts age. The smaller group fills the slots (e.g., in education and business) that were made by the larger cohort. Basing his analysis upon an examination of birth-rate patterns, Easterlin theorizes that a self-generating mechanism produces cylic swings in birth-rate pattern and hence cohort structure. Examination of the birth rates of twenty to twenty-five years ago suggests that during the 1980s we will witness a growing scarcity of younger adults, a scarcity even greater than that which occurred in the 1940s and 1950s. Easterlin speculates that this will result in an increase in birth rate and a decrease in divorce and suicide rates.

Age and Individuals

Age grades   All societies divide their members into groups according to age. For the most part, three age classes or *age grades* exist: children, adults, and the aged (Eisenstadt, 1956). But some societies support as many as six age grades: infants, children, adolescents, adults, the middle-aged, and the aged (Prins, 1953). The position that a person holds in an age grade reflects that individual's social age.

In nonindustrial societies the passage to adulthood is clearly marked by physical maturation. When physical maturity is reached, *rites de passage*, ranging from primitive rites (such as bodily mutilation) to social ceremonies (such as religious blessings), are performed. This results in a child or group of children emerging with adult status (Muus, 1975). In Western societies, however, such rites have become rituals, lacking in social meaning. For instance, bar mitzvahs (religious ceremonies for 13-year-old Jewish boys) are still practiced, but they no longer signify adulthood.

As a culture increases in technological and symbolic complexity, the acquisition of skills required for becoming an adult is prolonged. In our society, adulthood legally begins when individuals can marry without parental permission (age 18, typically), vote (age 18), enlist in the armed forces (age 18), and assume full responsibility for legal contracts (age 21). The exact age for many legally related activities is not as precise. For instance, an individual must be 17 years old to see an X-rated movie, but pays adult prices at age 12. The hallmark of adulthood is a capacity for economic independence which usually occurs along with beginning a career and/or getting married. Adults are expected to be responsible, competent, and know about, as well as participate in, the human sexual experience. However, our society does not provide systematic guidelines that permit members to move smoothly into adult status.

Once adult status is achieved there are specific social tasks to be accomplished. Honigmann (1959) identified the basic tasks of adulthood as ". . . selecting and learning to live with a mate; rearing children; organizing his [her] nuclear family, perhaps within a larger extended family; executing occupational roles in satisfactory fashion; assuming some share of administrative responsibility . . . [and] helping to enforce social pressures" (pp. 582–583). The accomplishment of all or some of these basic tasks accords an adult status. To the extent that an adult accomplishes these tasks better than other members of reference groups, the individual obtains a higher status. As tasks such as rearing children are completed, or as proficiency in a task increases—for example, an individual might be asked to assist others in maintenance of the social system—young adults are considered middle-aged.

Old age is defined in a temporal way; that is, the aged are those who have lived many years. Often people are considered old when they retire from gainful employment. With the Social Security Act, our federal government sanctioned certain ages as the time to begin collecting a pension. Some people may fall in between when the government views them as too young for Social Security, but employers define them as too old to retain their positions.

Age-status system   According to Neugarten and Hagestad (1976), people of varying ages are given certain social roles. These social roles reflect an underlying age-grade and age-status system within which age norms provide social control. A "mental map" of the life cycle is created whereby people anticipate that particular events will occur at particular times. In essence, people have built-in social clocks that mirror cultural norms and tell them whether their behavior is age-appropriate—whether it is on time or off time.

Analyzing the age-status system is one way to look at social organization. Societal norms dictate age-appropriate behavior, and people are socialized according to these norms. This creates predictable, age-related patterns of behavior and social interaction.

Riley, Johnson, and Foner (1972) reported that as each cohort moves from one age grade to another (e.g., young adulthood to middle age), specific roles are assigned and behaviors expected of each role are acquired. Moreover, Neugarten, Moore, and Lowe (1968) indicated that people do indeed anticipate what behaviors are associated with what ages. For example, middle-aged respondents said "middle age is when you become mellow" and "old age is when you take things easy and let others do the worrying" (Neugarten & Hagestad, 1976, p. 44). Even though perceptions differed a bit according to sex, social class, and age, consensus about age grades was evident. Individuals are

assignment of roles

* Neugarten

Controversy

BOX 7.2
AGEISM AND SOCIETAL FACTORS

Several studies have described various forms of discriminatory inequality between age groups in our youth-oriented culture (Palmore & Whittington, 1970). In 1969, Butler called this inequality *ageism*, and, at the White House Conference on Aging in 1971, ageism was condemned.

Many people, however, maintain that older adults still are not given meaningful societal roles and are not considered valued members of society (Butler, 1974; Kalish, 1975). Rosow (1976) contends that we are witnessing an increasing struggle for age rights as a result of rising economic costs, decreasing energy resources, and an increase in the numbers of adults, primarily the aged. Even the elderly, who view themselves slightly more positively than other age groups view them, feel that being old is less desirable than being young (Colette-Pratt, 1976). A negative attitude toward the elderly is apparent by the time people reach adolescence (Hickey & Kalish, 1968).

Other investigators, however, paint a more positive picture of the situation of the elderly. Neugarten and Hagestad (1976) feel that increased consciousness about the elderly's plight is leading to a decrease in ageism. In addition, economic preferences are being conferred on the elderly, which is viewed as an improvement in status. They cautiously admit, though, that such a trend could be reversed with continued inflation and economic stagnation.

Update

BOX 7.3

THE DOUBLE-JEOPARDY HYPOTHESIS

What does it mean to be an elderly member of a racial minority in contemporary society? One perspective suggests that the minority aged suffer from a situation involving a kind of *double jeopardy*. That is, the impact of race discrimination and the impact of age discrimination combine to make the relative status of such groups weaker than that of other groups, the members of which are of like age but are not minorities. Another perspective suggests that advancing age acts to "level" racial diferences that were present during middle life.

Dowd and Bengtson (1978) tested these two hypotheses by examining the variables of health,

income, life satisfaction, and social participation (reported interaction with family, kin, neighbors and friends) in a sample of over 1200 middle-aged and older blacks, Mexican Americans, and whites in Los Angeles county. Differences among the three groups were particularly apparent in the areas of income and self-assessed health, which offered support for the double-jeopardy hypothesis. However, life satisfaction and social participation declined among all groups, supporting the "age-as-leveler" hypothesis. In some areas, then, minority aged do appear to be victims of double jeopardy, while in other areas they are not.

---

also aware of the social norms for timing of certain events. Neugarten and Hagestad (1976) report that individuals can state whether or not they were early, late, or on time with events such as marriage or entering the job market (e.g., "I married early," or "I had a late start because of the Depression") (p. 44). They conclude: "From a societal perspective, then, the age norm system does not only provide mechanisms for allocating new recruits to major social roles; it also creates an ordered predictable life course, it creates timetables, it sets boundaries for acceptable behavior at successive life stages" (p. 45).

Intergenerational Relations

A major concern of social theorists is how the generations interact. What is the role of generational succession in the aging process? Two general approaches to the generational concept have been used by investigators. Those using the cohort perspective emphasize the characteristics of different birth cohorts or age strata. Those using the lineage perspective emphasize continuities and discontinuities in socialization resulting from intergenerational transmission processes (Bengtson & Cutler, 1976).

Cohort perspective   The various generations differ from one another in many ways, for example, in kind and degree of social and political alienation. Three basic hypotheses have been proposed to account for generational differences in social and political alienation: (1) maturation, (2) generation, and (3) period effects.

Maturational interpretations propose that alienation is related to life-cycle stage. Alienation among youth (e.g., Seeman, 1959) has been found to relate to perceived powerlessness. Alienation among the elderly (e.g., Martin, Bengtson, & Acock, 1973) has been found to relate to losses in status, abilities, and resources. Thus, although alienation occurs among both young people and the elderly in our society, the reasons for that alienation seem to be different for different age groups. (Miller, Brown, & Raine, 1973).

A generational interpretation of alienation is based on evidence showing substantial discontinuities between birth cohorts. Certain labels (e.g., "lost generation" or "beat generation") are used to represent members of a cohort throughout their lives, not just during an age period. For instance, Keniston (1968) portrayed student activists of the sixties as an alienated *generation* rather than as alienated *youth* per se. These feelings of alienation were said to persist among the members of the cohort over their life span. In contrast, Bengtson (1970) reviewed several "generational gap" studies and found that the supposed gap between the young and the old reflects differences in maturational level and life-stage responsibilities rather than cohort differences. Others (e.g., Friedenberg, 1969; Slater, 1970), still maintain that there is a considerable gap between parents and youth, but they feel that the youth will mature with the passage of time.

Finally, a period interpretation maintains that societal events (e.g., political assassinations, the Vietnam war, Watergate) account for alienation. For example, an analysis of the period from 1952 to 1968 showed that similar trends in political alienation existed for the population as a whole, regardless of age, sex, income, or educational level (House & Mason, 1975).

Which of the various explanations of alienation—maturational, generational, or historical—is most viable? Cutler and Bengtson (1974) used a cohort analysis to analyze three measures of political alienation during the period 1952 to 1968. They examined maturational, generational, and period effects. Their data showed that fluctuations in political alienation affected most people in a similar manner. All groups, except those people born between 1916 and 1923, felt that political alienation between 1952 and 1960 decreased and that there was a significant increase in alienation between 1960 and 1968. However, all groups reported that political alienation was higher in 1968 than in 1952. Cutler and Bengtson concluded that the period effect, that is, the impact of history, is the most viable means of accounting for these alienation data.

Lineage perspective   A lineage perspective focuses on what is transmitted among the generations. Specifically, it focuses on what is exchanged between the young and the old in terms of knowledge and skills, power and responsibility, and caregiving of dependent members. According to Bengtson and Cutler (1976), three questions stand out in lineage generational analysis.

What perceptions do older people have of cross-generational relationships— both within the family and the broader society? What is the nature and extent of interaction between aged individuals and their families—patterns of help or exchange, contact, and affection? How much consensus—and how much conflict—exists between older parents and their middle aged children or grandchildren? (p. 144)

Bengtson and Cutler (1976) identify five key points concerning socialization and lineage. First, the nature of intergenerational family relations alters over time. Interactional patterns and patterns of affection also change, as do patterns involving power, responsibility, and concern over one another's welfare (Bengtson & Black, 1973). Second, American families perceive high solidarity among members. Third, elders feel they receive slightly more affection than other family members, while younger family members feel they receive more goods and services than older members. Fourth, although the study of attitudes and values is complex, it is doubtful that the generation gap, whether assessed in terms of cohorts or lineage, exists. There appears to be more consensus among and between generations than differences. Fifth, many elements of the historical period need to be included in investigations of intergenerational relations. Thus, the socialization process in adulthood can be studied as one of transmission and interaction between family members, and between families and society.

ADULT SOCIALIZATION AND SATISFACTION

Once adult status is achieved, healthy adults play out their lives striving for satisfaction or fulfillment in the roles they occupy. Specifically, we will focus on status and role changes as the individual moves from young adulthood through middle age and old age. We will use three psychosocial dimensions—marital satisfaction, occupational satisfaction, and life satisfaction—to illustrate how roles and role changes occur over the life course and to examine how the life course is perceived by individuals. Before beginning the discussion of specific roles, however, it is important to recognize the influence that life events—both social and nonsocial—may have on individuals and cohorts.

Life Events

Social events range from those involving a certain legal status (e.g., entrance into the military, marriage, divorce, voting) to those in which personal negotiation is the most critical factor (e.g., promotion or demotion). Although we often assume that only social events (e.g., marriage, divorce) will influence adult socialization, nonsocial events, for example biological events (e.g., illness) and environmental events (e.g., famine), also may modify the age structures and roles of one or more cohorts. For example, at the macro level, the flow of young people into the work force could be decelerated by a protracted period of education (social process) or by a disease which is fatal to that age group (nonsocial process). As we mentioned before, changes in rate of cohort flow modify the social structure in ways that affect not only the specific cohort but also the age-graded system as a whole (Waring, 1975).

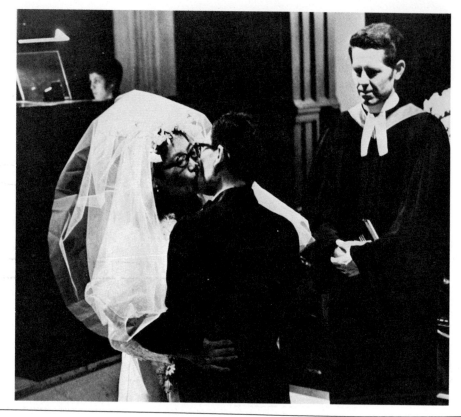

Marriage is considered to be a major positive life event, but it usually results in a significant change in the life pattern of a couple. (Bruce Anspach/Editorial Photocolor Archives)

Status and Role Change

What happens to people's roles in adulthood? How does status change with certain roles? According to Rosow (1976), "[S]tatus is treated as a position in a social structure and role [is] the pattern of activity intrinsic to that position" (p. 458). From this conceptual framework Rosow (1976) describes a typology of four role categories—Institutional, Tenuous, Informal, and Nonrole—in which status and role can vary independently. These categories may be described as follows:

Institutional: Institutional roles are those in which normative expectations are associated with definite positions or attributes; men, women, professionals, manual workers, parents, children, Catholics, Jews, public officials, etc. They are statuses with roles.

Tenuous: The Tenuous role type refers to statuses without roles. There are two subtypes—titular and amorphous. Titular positions include honorific (e.g., Nobel Laureate) and nominal (e.g., token-promotion) types. The former constitute social promotions; the honor is symbolic, and no specific role activities beyond the most superficial are associated with the position. The latter constitute social demotions, in which role functions are significantly limited. Amorphous positions include de facto types, in which objective circumstances prevent the individual from performing a role (e.g., chronically unemployed), and role-attrition types, in which role responsibilities dwindle away or are lost (the elderly who have experienced the reduction or loss of institutional positions in the family, labor force, etc.).

Informal: Informal roles encompass a wide range of roles, for example, heroes, villains, playboys, tough guys, blackmailers, prima donnas, gossips. These are roles without statuses.

Nonrole. The term *nonrole* refers to the absence of roles and statuses. This type simply permits the classification of idiosyncratic behavior and, for all practical purposes, is unimportant.

Rosow (1976) contends that the three role types exhibit different patterns of change over the life span, as shown in Figure 7.1. Institutional roles increase through midlife, and then decrease sharply during old age. Tenuous roles are relatively numerous during childhood and relatively few during adulthood, and they reach their highest point during old age. Finally, informal roles increase until adulthood, then level off. The relative imbalance between institutional roles and tenuous roles in old age (shaded portion of Figure 7.1) suggests that this portion of the life span becomes increasingly nonnormative. According to Rosow (1976), this has several consequences:

First, the loss of roles excludes the aged from significant social participation and devalues them. It deprives them of vital functions that underlie their sense of worth, their self-conceptions and self-esteem. . . . Second, old age is the first stage of life with systematic status loss for an entire cohort. . . . Third, persons in our society are not socialized to the fate of aging. . . . Fourth, because society does not specify an aged role, the lives of the elderly are

Figure 7.1 Relative importance of role types in the life span. (From Rosow, 1976.)

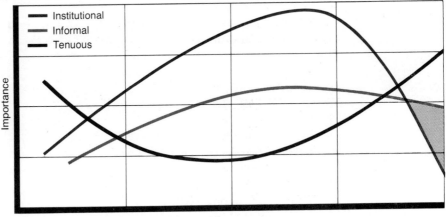

Legend:
— Institutional
— Informal
— Tenuous

Importance (y-axis)

Life span (x-axis)

socially unstructured. . . . Finally, role loss deprives people of their social identity. (pp. 466–467)

Rosow's taxonomy, therefore, provides a broad perspective within which the timing and ordering of various socializing events during adulthood may be considered.

Preparation for Social Roles

An awareness of when events typically occur and how events are typically sequenced is necessary to understand socialization in adulthood. The normal sequence and rhythm of events in adult life is called the *social clock* (Neugarten & Datan, 1974). If adults go through their lives following this social clock, they are better able to predict their life courses and anticipate the new roles they will assume. Off-phase or off-time events, such as a parent dying when a child is an adolescent, often are crisis events.

Since there is a considerable degree of choice in our society, people's timetables for different events, such as those related to family life or to occupation, are varied. Despite this variation some normative patterns emerge for cohorts. For example, Table 7.1 shows that while wide variations among individuals occur, the median age at which various events occur has remained relatively stable over time. However, normative patterns vary as a function of sex, class, and other group characteristics. Olsen (1969) obtained life histories of people aged 50 to 70 residing in a Midwestern city during the mid-1950s. He reported a relationship between social class, age, and life events. For both sexes, the higher the social class, the higher the median age at which the following events occurred: finished formal education, left parental home,

TABLE 7.1

MEDIAN AGE OF WHITE EVER-MARRIED MOTHERS AT SELECTED STAGES OF THE FAMILY LIFE-CYCLE*

Subject	Years of Birth of Mothers			
	1900–1909	1910–1919	1920–1929	1930–1939
First marriage	21.1	21.5	20.7	19.9
Birth of first child	23.0	23.7	22.9	21.5
Birth of last child	31.0	31.9	31.2	29.2–30.2†
First marriage of last child	52.3	53.2	52.5	50.5–51.5
Marriage ended by death (usually of husband)	63.7	64.4	64.7	64.8
Average number of children born	2.98	2.94	3.21	3.22†

*The corresponding ages for husbands are about 3 years older.
†Projected completed fertility.
Source: From Norton, 1974.

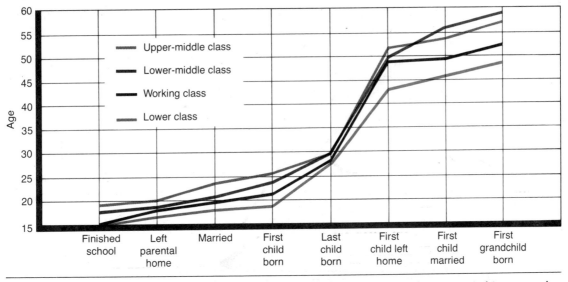

Figure 7.2 Median ages at which women of different social classes reacted to successive events in the family cycle. *(From Olsen, 1969.)*

married, first child born, last child born, first child married, and first grandchild born. Figure 7.2 indicates the social-class differences for women in the sequencing and ordering of these events. The patterns are similar for men.

How do changing roles and the timing and ordering of role events over the life-cycle affect individuals' satisfaction?

Marital Satisfaction

If marital and family roles are not assumed according to the prescribed age-norm system, dissatisfaction can result. For example, Nydegger (1973) has demonstrated that middle-class women who married at either too young or too old an age, in their own opinion, were more apt to be dissatisfied with their lives when their children were launched than were women who married between 20 and 30 years of age. On the other hand, being off time can be beneficial for men. Men who were early fathers felt strains that influenced their role performance negatively. Late fathers (older than 40), however, were more comfortable with their role as fathers and were more effective than either early or on-time men. Nydegger suggests that if parenthood and the demands of building a career did not coincide, then men would be more effective fathers. Perhaps if certain roles are delayed, some kinds of role strain and overloads can be avoided.

Marital satisfaction in general is associated with the length of time spent in dual roles of husband/father and wife/mother and with the events associated with particular stages of the family life-cycle. Duvall (1971) proposed a model for marriage and family structure that has four major periods—the newlywed marriage, the parental marriage, the middle-age marriage, and the retirement marriage. Accompanying role changes are associated with each family period. These periods can be further divided into eight stages:

Stage 1: Beginning families—no children; 0 to 5 years of marriage
Stage 2: Childbearing families—oldest child less than 3 years of age
Stage 3: Families with preschoolers—oldest child between 3 and 6 years of age
Stage 4: Families with school-age children—oldest child between 6 and 13 years of age
Stage 5: Families with teenagers—oldest child from 13 to 21 years of age
Stage 6: Launching families—from first child leaving to last child leaving
Stage 7: Families in middle years—last child leaving to retirement of first spouse
Stage 8: Aging families—retirement of first spouse to death of one spouse

Each stage is accompanied by certain tasks and goals. For instance, the beginning family must establish an independent home, while the parental family must change roles and relationships to accommodate the children.

What happens to marital satisfaction as a family moves through these stages? In a longitudinal study that considered the first 20 years of marriage (stage 1 to the end of stage 5), Pineo (1961) reported that marital satisfaction declined after stage 1, hitting its low point during stage 5, a stage at which couples reported having more parental responsibility and changing roles, such as parent, worker, citizen, friend, than at any earlier stage. Couples in stage 5 appeared to experience role strain. Marital satisfaction, however, seemed to recover after the children left home, but it never returned to the level it reached during stage 1. Other data, however, suggest that the happiest couples are those with empty nests (Rollins & Feldman, 1970; Miller, 1976).

A few studies have used a macro level of analysis. Bart (1972) found that the middle-aged women of today married early, gave birth to more children than mothers from younger cohorts, moved to the suburbs or grew up there, and tried a life of full-time "super-mom." This woman wanted to create a perfect home and raise perfect children. However, when "perfect" children leave a family whose orientation is that of a mother who is overinvolved, the resulting change in maternal role can cause severe depression. This is especially true after the launching of the youngest child. The intensity of pressure accompanying such a role change is reflected by the increased divorce rates between 1970 and 1974 for all women, but especially for women about age 40 (Bernard, 1975). The increase for women over 40 is also high: between 1960 and 1969 divorce rates for women aged 40 to 49 increased by more than 40 percent (Krishnan & Kayami, 1974).

However, the launching of the last child and the subsequent empty-nest situation may not be a negative experience for most women. When leisure time is shared jointly, marital satisfaction increases (Hagestad, 1980). Also, in a longitudinal study, Livson (1974) reported two different types of middle-aged, middle-class married women—the *traditionals* and the *independents*. The traditional women found continued satisfaction in interpersonal relationships after the children left home. This probably was a result of jointly shared activities with one's spouse. In contrast, the profile for middle-aged independent women showed that they were never suited to domestic roles. During marital career stages 3 and 4, they reported feeling out of touch with any intellectual or creative potential they thought they had. But by the age of 50 these women found new ways to express their earlier ambitions and desires. Thus, for middle-class married women who consider themselves to be independent, middle age can provide an opportunity to alter conventional roles in a positive way (Livson, 1977).

For stage 7 and stage 8 families, the affective aspects of the marital relationship are perceived as most rewarding. The areas most often cited as rewarding were companionship and marital expression of "true" feelings. Moreover, more than 90 percent of these couples described their relationship as "very happy" or "happy," and half stated that their marriage had improved with time. Different values and life philosophies as well as lack of mutual interests were the problems most often identified. Table 7.2 shows the most rewarding

TABLE 7.2

PERCEPTIONS OF OLDER HUSBANDS AND WIVES CONCERNING THE MOST TROUBLESOME AND MOST REWARDING ASPECTS OF MARRIAGE RELATIONSHIPS DURING THE LATER YEARS

	Percent
Rewarding aspects	
Companionship	18.4
Mutual expression of true feelings	17.8
Economic security	16.2
Being needed by mate	12.0
Affectionate relationship with mate	11.2
Sharing of common interests	9.3
Having physical needs cared for	7.6
Standing in the community	7.0
Troublesome aspects	
Different values and life philosophies	13.8
Lack of mutual interests	12.5
Mutual inability to express true feelings	8.6
Unsatisfactory affectional relationships	8.5
Frequent disagreements	8.5
Lack of companionship	7.7
Other	8.5
Nothing troublesome	36.2

Source: From Stinnett, Carter, & Montgomery, 1972.

and the most troublesome aspects of marriage as reported by older married people in a study conducted by Stinnett, Carter, and Montgomery (1972). Since the study was cross-sectional, it is difficult to determine whether these interpersonal factors were perceived as critically important throughout the marriage or whether they are characteristic of the relationship after the children were launched and one spouse had retired.

There are several plausible explanations for these trends in marital satisfaction over the life course. First, divorced couples are no longer in the married groups being assessed. Because of this attrition process, the percentage of happy individuals might be expected to increase. Second, the role strain of younger couples should subside as some roles are given up during middle and later life and others are altered. Finally, considerable cross-sectional, longitudinal, and even cross-cultural evidence shows that women display more instrumental and assertive behaviors in their marriage during later life, whereas men recognize and accept their affiliative and emotional needs in later life (Gutmann, 1977).

Update

BOX 7.4
ALTERNATIVE LIFE-STYLES

Singleness
In the United States between 1970 and 1975, the percentage of 20- to 24-year-old unmarried females increased from 28 to 40 percent. Although Glick (1977) feels that part of this increase reflects the postponement of marriage, an estimated 6 to 7 percent of these women will never marry.

Why would people want to remain single? Several factors—including changing sex-role expectations, particularly for women; decreased cultural emphasis on childbearing; and the availability of special facilities and services (e.g., housing, newspapers and magazines, entertainment spots)—have probably contributed to the growth of this life-style. Evidence suggests that single women of all ages are happier than single men (Campbell, 1975) and that they have lower rates of depression and neurosis than married women (Bernard, 1972). Moreover, Gubrium (1975) found that single elderly people represent a distinct type, one that is different from other old people. In a study based upon interview data, he

reported that the social world of single old people is relatively isolated, but not perceived as lonely. In fact, they viewed their state of singleness as just an extension of their past.

Cohabitation: The Arrangement
The college years seem to be the time when members of a particular cohort experiment with cohabitation. In a typical arrangement a couple shares expenses and living arrangements, and engages in sexual activity. According to Skolnick (1973), the tension between commitment and freedom helps explain the advantages and disadvantages of such an alternative life-style. Most couples cohabit because they feel this arrangement will lead to greater emotional maturity and help them acquire ways to live with and relate to others (Stinnett & Walters, 1977). In a recent study (Stafford, Backman, & Debora, 1977), married and cohabiting couples were compared. Data indicated that the same conflicts over the division of labor and role behavior exist for both types of couples, but cohabiting men do help with laundry

and dishes more often than married men and cohabiting women do more home repair and gardening than married women.

Dual-Career Couples

The advantages of a dual-career marriage are financial and personal. Although these marriages can be characterized by pride, companionship, role sharing, and feelings of self-expression and growth for women, they also have unique strains. As the wife assumes a full-time career and the husband develops relationships with the children, time limitations and an increase in responsibilities may produce "role overload." There appears to be an optimal way to balance demands at home with the demands of careers, but there is often a problem in reaching this balance. The difficulty seems to lie with timing, or "role cycling." When one partner must spend more time in career behavior, the other must spend more time in home activities. However, at some point someone's "give" has to become "take" in order to minimize stress and feelings of being taken advantage of (Rapoport & Rapoport, 1971). With changes that affect work patterns, such as a reduction in the hours and/or days of a work week, better child-care services (Deutsch, in press), and more efficient transportation, the dual-career marital pattern of marriage should increase. Moreover, with increasing financial stress caused by inflation and the rising cost of energy, this alternative life-style may become a necessity.

Communes

In 1969 there were only 500 communes in the United States. From 1975 to 1977, there were approximately 3000. Membership usually consists of middle- or upper-class adults between the ages of 20 and 28 (Stinnett & Walters, 1977). A shared ideology is present, although communes exhibit diversity in structure and functioning. Members want to create the intimacy of an extended family, while striving for spiritual rebirth, personal growth, a "natural life," and greater freedom (Zablocki, 1971).

Homosexual Marriage

Since the obligations and responsibilities of partners in a homosexual marriage are neither institutionalized nor legally defined, these relationships are often unstable. Many homosexuals, however, do wish to develop marriages whether or not legally sanctioned and do not wish to change their sexual orientation. With psychologists and psychiatrists no longer regarding homosexuality as a mental illness, homosexuality has become much more visible in the 1970s than it was in the 1950s. Hunt (1974), however, reported that homosexual behavior has not increased since the time of the Kinsey report.

Occupational Satisfaction

The occupational role provides an identity for an individual that is both social and personal. A person's career is an organized path that traverses time and space. An individual's occupational role and career occupy much time and energy during adulthood and for the majority of people end, voluntarily or not, with retirement.

Retirement is a phenomenon of modern industrial society. Previous socioeconomic systems in man's history have had varying numbers of older people, but none has ever had the number of or proportion of aged that obtains in the industrialized societies of present day. More important, the older people of previous societies were not retired persons; *there was no retirement role. (Donahue, Orbach, & Pollak, 1960, p. 336)*

The life-cycle of one's work, therefore, is from occupational role to retirement role.

What promotes satisfaction with a work role? Recently, a new cultural attitude seems to be prevalent. This attitude conveys the sentiment that an adult is not only entitled to a job but is entitled to a job that is really liked. Kanter (1978) expressed this view when she pointed out that there is ". . . a growing concern for jobs as a source of meaning in life, including the expectation that they provide for psychological fulfillment as well as quality of life outside the job" (pp. 3–4).

Basically, occupational satisfaction results when the fit between individual interests and abilities and job characteristics is a good one. Thus, the factors related to occupational satisfaction often deal with adjustments that are specific to the person and job (Healy, 1973; Quinn, Staines, & McCullough, 1974). These factors can include: (1) familiarity with the occupation as a result of earlier experience (e.g., Rauner, 1962), (2) similarity between an individual's characteristics and the characteristics of the environment (e.g., Holland, 1973), (3) good occupational role models (e.g., Bell, 1970), (4) challenging but not threatening job requirements and expectations, (5) reduced concern with prestige, (6) match between personal values and expressed work values, and (7) the socialization context of the work environment (e.g., Henry, Sims, & Spray, 1971).

People work for different reasons; for example, money, status, prestige, service, companionship, satisfaction (Terkel, 1972), and occupational satisfaction or dissatisfaction often depends upon the fit between a person's reasons for working and the characteristics of the work situation. An individual's perception of work, and the associated reasons for working, are determined largely by previous work experiences and occupational aspirations.

A complicated matching process between people and occupations goes on all the time. Employers want the people who best can fill positions and people want the positions that are best for them. Thus, despite obvious persistent job discrimination connected with race, sex, age, etc., people who have aspiration, preparation, and ability tend to occupy jobs that produce the highest levels of satisfaction (Terkel, 1972).

With the focus of occupational satisfaction on matching person and position, two different types of work groups emerge. The first group of people derive little satisfaction from the work process itself, either in terms of accomplishments or feelings of self-fulfillment, but gain satisfaction from the direct status benefits related to salary. These people feel that work is a necessary evil, one that must be engaged in in order to do what one wants. The end of a work day marks the end of any work-related concerns. Satisfaction with activities (e.g., family and friends) outside of work is quite high; it is related to occupational satisfaction in that work provides the means to engage in those activities. The second group of people have a strong work orientation. For these people a major source of satisfaction comes from the process of work and the related accomplishments. Through work, they feel useful, they enjoy opportunities for self-expression, they enjoy the companionship of coworkers, and they derive a sense of status and self-esteem from their accomplishments on the job. Moreover, work-related concerns are continued during evenings and on weekends. The satisfaction from leisure activities is low seemingly because the satisfaction from occupation is so high (e.g., Friedman & Havighurst, 1954; Havighurst, 1957; Meltzer, 1963).

Both orientations—money-related and work-satisfaction-related—exist across all fields of work, although there is a higher proportion of work-oriented white collar individuals. Blue-collar workers tend to be more dissatisfied with their jobs than white-collar workers. There are many explanations for this. Blue-collar workers often have fewer opportunities for interesting and varied tasks, and working conditions are often poor (Herzberg, 1966). The group of people who feel the most dissatisfied with work are those who perceive that they are being discriminated against (Blood & Hulin, 1967). For instance, many women report feelings of dissatisfaction related to discrimination. These women feel that single women and men can concentrate more on their occupations because they do not have to expend energy on other roles. On the other hand, many women who occupy multiple roles—e.g., wife and mother—perform

---

Controversy

BOX 7.5

SEXISM

1. Starting salaries for women who graduated from college in 1970 were 3 to 10 percent lower than for men in the same fields (Ritzer, 1977).
2. Annual earnings for females were about 40 percent of the median annual earnings for males, and the inequity is growing worse (Blau, 1975).
3. Women are underrepresented in professional ranks (Ritzer, 1977).
4. Women face role strains in trying to achieve a balance among familial and work roles (Hackman, 1977).
5. Society does not tolerate a "nonworking" father (Fasteau, 1974).

While sex discrimination continues to be a problem, it is clear that sex roles are changing within our society. (Bjorn Enstrom/Photo Researchers)

equally as well as do single people in their occupational roles (e.g., Falk, 1966; Kreps, 1976).

Related to the above is the issue of whether or not opportunities have been provided at all. In fact, a lack of opportunity is related more to overall rate of unemployment than either personal dissatisfaction or employer dissatisfaction. Moreover, this lack of work opportunity interacts with a history of a lack of opportunities for certain groups in particular, producing a situation of extreme concern. For instance, among high school dropouts unemployment rates ranged from less than 5 percent for whites to greater than 20 percent for blacks during the late 1960s. In contrast, unemployment rates during the same time period for college graduates were between 1 and 4 percent. Despite fluctuations in unemployment rates, they are higher for minority groups than for whites, for women than men, and for younger age groups than older. Unemployment is highest for black men and women and lowest for white men. (U.S. Department of Health, Education, and Welfare, 1976).

Life Satisfaction

Most investigators feel that life satisfaction contributes to "good" mental health, and much theory and research has been generated in this area. In this section we will examine a few of the many perspectives and consider the evidence related to them.

Disengagement versus activity According to Cumming and Henry (1961), there is a reduction in life activities and ego energy in later life. Through the process of social withdrawal (connected with societal reactions related to a person's inclusion or exclusion from social life) and psychological withdrawal (connected with a person's own thoughts and feelings), there is a severing and altering of ties between a person and others in society that Cumming and Henry referred to as *disengagement.* The disengagement model emphasizes the synchrony of timing of social and individual changes. Thus, as society reduces activities, there is a concomitant reduction in role involvement. According to Cumming and Henry, it is this reduction of interaction with the environment that maintains an individual's sense of life-satisfaction.

A majority of researchers (e.g., Maddox, 1964) have argued against disengagement and have pointed out that when age is held constant, there are substantial variations in the indicators of social and psychological disengagement displayed. Essentially, individuals who do disengage display different patterns and rates of disengagement. Furthermore, investigations indicate that engagement (activity and involvement) can lead to life satisfaction. In a classic study of successful aging, Neugarten, Havighurst, and Tobin (1968) described eight patterns (see Table 7.3). The older people in the study, who had different life-styles and personalities, had different degrees of life satisfaction. Recent data indicate that if an individual has been active, involved, and satisfied throughout life and if the environment continues to provide opportunities for similar involvement, then life satisfaction results in old age (Neugarten & Hagestad, 1976). This perspective suggests that psychological well-being is a

TABLE 7.3

PERSONALITY TYPE IN RELATION TO ACTIVITY AND LIFE SATISFACTION

Personality Type	Role Activity Type	Life Satisfaction
Integrated	Reorganizers: competent, engaged, and involved; substitutes new activities for old	High
	Focused: integrated personality, medium levels of activity, centered in one or two role areas	High
	Disengaged: low levels of activity and role involvement, voluntarily reduces role commitment, high self-esteem	High
Armored-defended	Holding on: holds on to midlife roles and activities; when successful, maintains adequate levels of life satisfaction	High
	Constricted: low to medium involvement in few areas; constricted role activity; preoccupied with losses and deficits	High to medium
Passive-dependent	Succor-seeking: medium activity level; maintains adequate levels of life satisfaction when strong dependency needs fulfilled	Medium
	Apathetic: low role activity; passive and apathetic	Medium to low
Unintegrated	Disorganized: deteriorated cognitive processes; poor emotional control	Low

Source: Based on Neugarten, Havighurst, & Tobin, 1968, Table 1, p. 174.

function of the degree to which an individual can maintain patterns of activity and involvement throughout life. This model suggests that the overall relationship between social and personal systems need not change with the passage of time, and that when roles are taken away (e.g., retirement, loss of a spouse) successful adaptation is measured by an ability to compensate (e.g., increase activity in other areas).

Social-breakdown syndrome Another perspective relevant to life satisfaction deals with the premise that negative psychological functioning will result when a person has a poor sense of self, does not have the skills to deal with self and environment, and receives negative feedback from the outside world. Kuypers and Bengtson (1973) summarize a seven-stage formulation of the development of what they called the *social-breakdown syndrome.* The steps include: (1) an individual susceptibility, (2) dependence on external labels, (3) the labeling of individuals by society as incompetent, (4) assuming a dependent

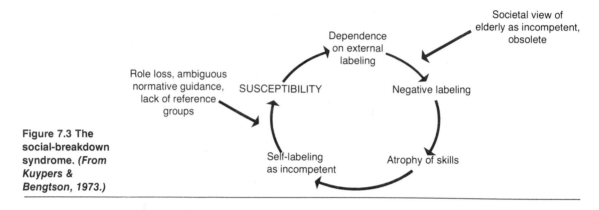

Figure 7.3 The social-breakdown syndrome. *(From Kuypers & Bengtson, 1973.)*

role, (5) acquiring "skills" that fit in with the dependent role, (6) atrophy of previous social skills, and (7) identifying and labeling self as inadequate ("sick"). These steps are graphically presented in Figure 7.3.

According to Kuypers and Bengtson (1973), the social-breakdown syndrome can be prevented by reorganizing the social system and providing individuals with opportunities to feel competent in old age. Figure 7.4 presents their proposed model which attempts to reverse the social-breakdown syndrome.

Figure 7.4 Reversing the social-breakdown syndrome. *(From Kuypers & Bengtson, 1973.)*

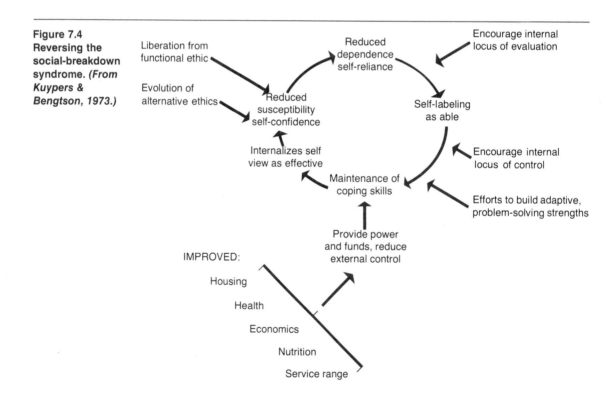

Health and life satisfaction Regardless of which one of the three perspectives discussed—disengagement, activity, or social breakdown—is supported, empirical evidence has found that relationships do exist between life satisfaction and health, activity, income, and education. The more satisfied individuals are healthier and more socially active and have more income and education. But the question remains, "How do these variables interact?"

In a study conducted by Palmore and Luikart (1974), 502 people aged 46 to 71 were assessed. Findings were that: (1) health was viewed as most valuable in contributing to life satisfaction; (2) participating in organizational activity was the next most important factor that contributed to life satisfaction, especially among the middle-aged; (3) believing that one has control over one's destiny (internal locus of control) was the third important factor predicting life satisfaction; (4) having a confidant, status at work, employment, and social activity were associated with satisfaction for men; (5) income and education contributed to satisfaction for the younger middle-aged (ages 46 to 59); (6) age, sex, total social contacts, career, marital status, and intelligence did not predict life satisfaction for any group. These data suggest that by improving health and finding ways to increase social activity, individuals can increase their satisfaction with their lives.

Maintaining one's health and activity level also seem to be critical factors, affecting life satisfaction cross-culturally. Even in Japan, which is a culture where older adults are more valued than in the United States, the same two important variables—health and activity—emerge (See Box 7.6).

In Depth **BOX 7.6**

THE HONORABLE ELDERS AND LIFE SATISFACTION

In a recent analysis, Palmore (1975) examined the status of the elderly in Japan—a culture which has traditionally respected the elderly. Palmore's report is based on surveys conducted by the Japanese Census Bureau, the Ministry of Health and Welfare, the Prime Minister's Office, and the Tokyo Metropolitan Government involving approximately 2000 persons.

Palmore suggests that the greater integration of Japanese aged into their society accounts in part for their relatively high levels of life satisfaction. Some of his findings are summarized below.

Health and Medical Care
The area most often selected as important for life satisfaction in the future by aged Japanese (75 percent) is health. Although figures for average life expectancy and the proportion of the elderly that are institutionalized are similar to those for the aged in other countries, subjective reports revealed that poor health increased with age. The Japanese elderly receive medical care free or at minimal cost. They stated that good health could be maintained by a good diet, engaging in exercise, keeping a routine, avoiding overexertion, and working at a job that is not considered too hard.

Family and Living Arrangements
The aged in Japan are more integrated into their families than the aged in other industrialized countries. More than 75 percent live with their children, and very few single aged live alone.

Financial necessity or a housing shortage did not account for this difference. People preferred this living arrangement and felt it contributed to life satisfaction. The majority of those who maintain separate households from children live less than 30 minutes travel time away. Also, fifty percent of the sample said they visit their children at least once a week.

Work and Retirement

About twice as many Japanese men continue to work past the typical age for retirement (62 to 70 years) as men in other industrialized nations. Two traditions seem to account for this phenomenon—respect for the aged and a feeling that it is one's duty to work. This finding needs to be interpreted cautiously, however, because in Japan more of the elderly are self-employed, work in family businesses, or are farmers. This suggests that they can regulate aspects of their own lives, including retirement, a great deal. Those who stop working do so voluntarily and usually for health reasons—a reason preferred by workers in the United States as well.

Income and Support

There is an increasing movement toward establishing pension plans that will provide support for the elderly of Japan. However, as compared with pension support in other countries, Japanese pension support is minimal. In fact, the Japanese elderly refer to it as "pocket money." Japan, in fact, spends less on social security benefits per person for those over 65 years of age than any other industrialized nation. Most Japanese with parents also stated they would provide financial support for parents if needed. Palmore (1975) concludes that as the pension system matures, benefits should improve.

Respect for the Elders

Many traditional practices are evidence of the respect that exists for the elders of Japan. For instance, honorific language is used in referring to the elders, best seats are freely relinquished, elders are served first, cooking caters to the tastes of elders, elders participate in family rituals (e.g., birthday and holidays), and all people bow to elders. Moreover, the person who turns 65 is given an elaborate celebration by the family. Respect for elders, however, varies, depending on several factors. It occurs more in rural areas than in urban, more in traditional households than in modern, and more among the middle-aged than among younger persons. Thus, patterns of respect appear to be changing with successive cohorts.

Activities and Satisfaction

Since more time is spent working—at a job or at home—Japanese elders have less leisure time. Fifty percent of the elders stated that they had hobbies such as travel, music, and gardening. Social activities include visiting neighbors and attending elders' club activities. Job-related activities were satisfying for men, whereas women derived satisfaction from family activities. In general, Japanese elders show a trend toward increasing life satisfaction with increasing age.

Conclusions

The elders of Japan appear to be more integrated into their society than the aged of other countries. Palmore (1975) proposes that respect and integration go hand in hand. That is, in order to integrate the elderly into our society and increase their status, we must change our entire attitude toward aging and the aged to one of respect.

CONCLUSION

Aging is a societal process as well as an individual process. As cohorts follow one another, they both respond to social change and at the same time contribute to it. For example, successive cohorts have experienced significant changes in the participation of women in the labor force, and these changes, in turn, have produced changes in family relationships and childrearing practices. This dynamic relationship between individuals and society suggests that the aging process is continually changing. Growing old in the United States in the 1980s is not the same as growing old in the United States in the 1880s. Neither of these is the same as growing older in Japan or Nigeria. Your own aging, then, is likely to differ in significant ways from our present understanding of the process. (An understanding of adult development and aging requires a continuing examination of the interaction between the changing life course of individuals and the changing structure of societies.)

CHAPTER SUMMARY

culture

To understand the process of socialization, it must be placed within a cultural context. Culture is that part of our heritage comprising the knowledge, beliefs, values, assumptions, patterns of behavior, and material items that have demonstrated effectiveness, over time, in dealing with the world. A sensitivity to culture is necessary for understanding how changing patterns of learned behavior are shared and transmitted among members of society. Attitudes toward aging are a part of the cultural heritage of a given society. Negative attitudes toward aging are associated with more modern, compared with less modern, nations.

Adult socialization can be examined from two different levels of analysis—the macro level, involving examination of aging cohorts, and the micro level, involving the examination of aging individuals. Such an analysis shows the reciprocal nature of socialization, with older and younger cohorts and older and younger individuals learning from each other. Examination of concepts relating to age and cohorts and age and individuals, such as cohort flow and succession, age grading, and the age-status system, suggest that aging is a societal as well as an individual process. Individuals' development is influenced by their position in the age structure and the related age-status system of the society in which they live. The presence of multiple age grades may produce intergenerational conflict. However, it appears that there is more consensus and continuity between generations than there is discord and discontinuity.

Socialization in adulthood can be analyzed in terms of three psychosocial dimensions—marital satisfaction, occupational satisfaction, and life satisfaction. Within these dimensions, roles and role changes, and how the life course is perceived by individuals, differ from cohort to cohort.

Rosow

Rosow's conceptual framework for studying status and role change describes four role categories—Institutional, Tenuous, Informal, and Nonrole. Rosow contends that institutional role types increase over the life span and decrease during old age. Tenuous roles are relatively numerous in childhood and adolescence, decrease in adulthood, and reach their highest point in old age. Rosow's taxonomy provides a life-span perspective about role and status change and serves as a means for judging the impact of the timing and ordering of events during adult socialization.

People's timetables for assuming different roles show that individual and cohort differences exist. For example, in the area of marital satisfaction, Nydegger found that marrying off time was not beneficial for middle-class women, but was for men. Some data suggest that older men may be more effective fathers because role strains and overloads are reduced. Data also show that marital satisfaction depends upon role status and upon what stage of the family life-cycle a couple is in. Marital satisfaction seems to decline over time, especially during the stage of rearing adolescents. After children leave home, it recovers but never to its original level.

At the macro level, data suggest that middle-aged women who marry early and finish childrearing early suffer negative reactions to the role change they undergo when their children leave home. However, depending upon women's personalities, life-satisfaction continues. For the independent personality, ending the period of childrearing can be marked by an opportunity to alter conventional roles.

Despite differences in personalities, and some evidence of negative trends affecting life satisfaction with age, most older couples were happy and felt that their relationship had improved over time. In terms of occupation, satisfaction is achieved when jobs are perceived as being meaningful and as psychologically fulfilling.

Data indicate that life satisfaction contributes to "good" mental health in our culture and cross-culturally. Three possible ways of looking at the aging process as it relates to life satisfaction involve disengagement versus activity, the social-breakdown syndrome, and health. Although disengagement may occur for some older people voluntarily, people prefer maintaining patterns of activity throughout their lives, thus enhancing their feelings about life satisfaction. Negative psychological effects occur when people have a poor sense of self, cannot deal with the environment, and receive negative feedback. Seven factors can lead to the syndrome of social breakdown: (1) individual susceptibility, (2) dependence on external labels, (3) the labeling of a person as incompetent by society, (4) assuming a dependent role, (5) learning "skills" for a dependent role, (6) loss of previous social skills, and (7) identifying self as inadequate. According to Kuypers and Bengtson, this syndrome can be prevented if the social system is reorganized so that people feel competent in old age.

Finally, data suggest that the healthy are more satisfied with life, more socially active, and have more income and education. Health and activity, are the two key variables for feeling satisfied with life. It seems that once adult status is achieved, healthy adults continue to be active in their striving for satisfaction and fulfillment in their roles.

PART 3

THE LIFE COURSE

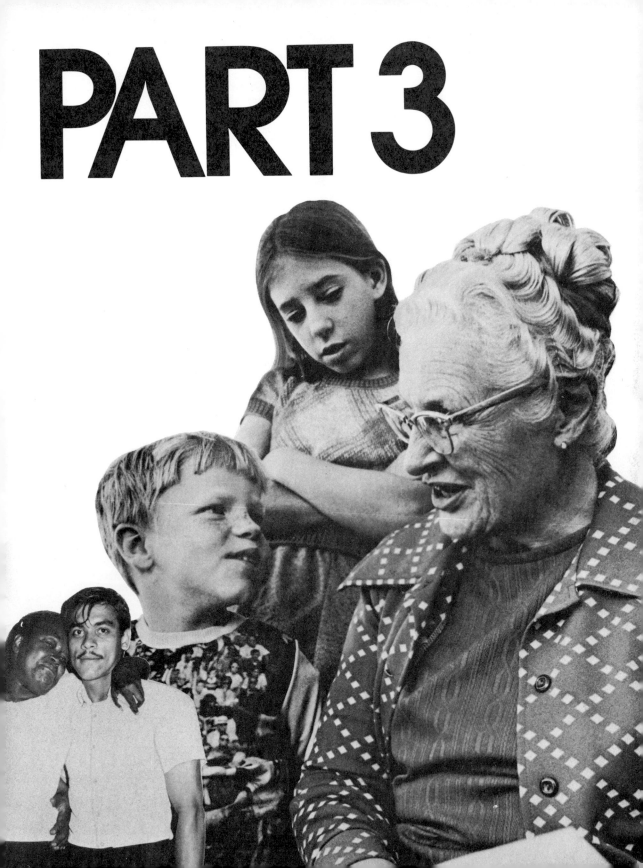

PART 3

8

LIFE EVENTS
AND LIFE TRANSITIONS

CHAPTER
OVERVIEW

Our lives are punctuated by transitions defined by life events. In this chapter we will examine the role of life events in the life course. Adaptation to different types and sequences of life events will be considered.

Introduction
A Life-Event Framework
   Types of life events
   The timing, sequencing, and

clustering of life events
   Is there a universal sequence of life events?
   Exposure to life events
Adapting to Life Events
Conclusion

☞ ISSUES ☜
TO CONSIDER

How may a life-event framework be used to understand development?

What general types of life events may be identified?

How are the timing and sequencing of life events important for development?

What does Levinson propose as a universal sequence of periods in the adult male life cycle?

What age and sex differences occur in exposure to and content of life events?

What cohort differences occur in exposure to and content of life events?

What factors mediate adaptation to life events?

What general steps characterize the adaptation process?

INTRODUCTION

In the chapters of the previous section, we have focused on basic developmental processes (biological, intellectual, learning and memory, personality, social) involved in behavior change. An understanding of these processes is fundamental to our descriptive, explanatory, and optimization efforts. However, a focus on basic processes alone leads to a fragmented view of adult development. The life-span developmental perspective draws our attention to additional issues. How do the basic processes interact with one another? How do they interact with the larger familial, social, cultural, and historical contexts in which the individual lives? How can we obtain an integrated view of the individual's development over the life course? These are difficult questions to answer. However, recent work within both psychology and sociology on life events and transitions provides one way of approaching them (Datan & Ginsberg, 1975; Lowenthal, Thurnher, & Chiriboga, 1975; Riley, 1979). In this chapter, then, we will examine the role of life events and transitions in life course development. This chapter also provides an introduction to Chapters 9, 10, 11 and 12 where major life events and transitions associated with young adulthood, middle age, and old age are considered.

A LIFE-EVENT FRAMEWORK

Our lives are punctuated by transitions defined by various life events. Riegel (1975), for instance, found that individuals recalling both their personal and cultural pasts focused on periods of transition, defined by critical events, rather than on periods of stability. A representation of the distribution of such events and transitions during adulthood is shown in Table 8.1. Such a listing of life events and transitions by itself is simply descriptive. However, when life events are viewed as important antecedents of behavior change during adulthood, a potentially powerful explanatory framework is generated (Hultsch & Plemons, 1979).

The framework includes four main elements, which are illustrated in Figure 8.1: a set of antecedent life-event stressors, a set of mediating factors, a social-psychological adaptation process, and consequent adaptive or maladaptive responses. Within this framework, all life events are viewed as potential stressors to the extent that they require a change in the individual's customary patterns of behavior. This means that events which are typically thought of as positive (e.g., marriage, being promoted at work), as well as events which are typically thought of as negative (e.g., death of a spouse, being fired from work), are potentially stressful. Mediating factors include both internal resources (e.g., physical health, intellectual abilities) and external resources (e.g., income, social support from others). Social-psychological adaptation involves the application of coping strategies and resultant changes in behavior. This process may lead to either functional or dysfunctional outcomes.

The stress or crisis of life events does not reside within the event or within the individual. Rather the crisis arises from an interaction between the individual and the situation—an *asynchrony* between change within the individual and

TABLE 8.1

LEVELS AND EVENTS IN ADULT LIFE

Level, years	Males		Females		Sudden changes
	Gradual changes				
	Psychosocial	Biophysical	Psychosocial	Biophysical	
I (20-25)	College/first job Marriage First child		First job/college Marriage	First child	
II (25-30)	Second job Other children Children in preschool		Loss of job Children in Preschool	Other children	
III (30-35)	Move Promotion Children in school		Move Without job Children in school		
IV (35-50)	Second home Promotion Departure of children	Departure of children	Second home Second career Departure of children	Departure of children	
V (50-65)	Unemployment Isolation Grandfather Head of kin	Incapacitation	Unemployment Grandmother Head of kin	Menopause	Loss of job Loss of parents Loss of friends Illness
VI (65+)	Deprivation	Sensory-motor deficiencies		Widowhood Incapacitation	Retirement Loss of partner Death

Source: From Riegel, 1975.

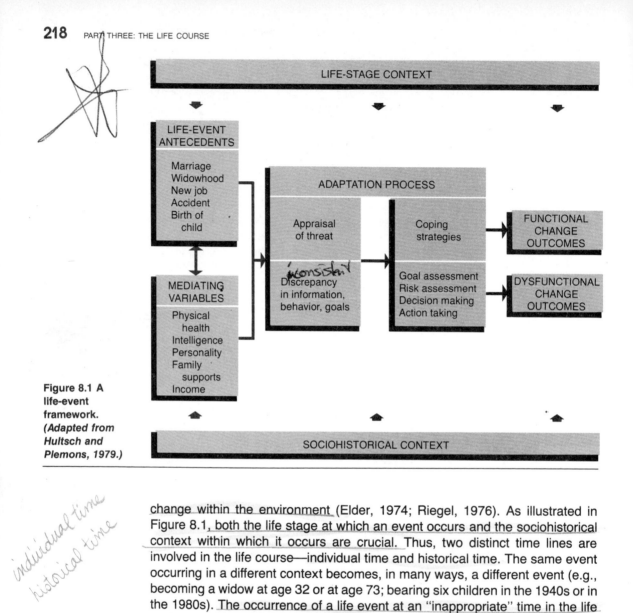

Figure 8.1 A
life-event
framework.
*(Adapted from
Hultsch and
Plemons, 1979.)*

change within the environment (Elder, 1974; Riegel, 1976). As illustrated in Figure 8.1, both the life stage at which an event occurs and the sociohistorical context within which it occurs are crucial. Thus, two distinct time lines are involved in the life course—individual time and historical time. The same event occurring in a different context becomes, in many ways, a different event (e.g., becoming a widow at age 32 or at age 73; bearing six children in the 1940s or in the 1980s). The occurrence of a life event at an "inappropriate" time in the life cycle or history is likely to create more asynchrony.

Thus, development may be characterized as adaptation to a series of crises, asynchronies, or transitions defined by life events. Such a perspective is useful since it forces us to focus on the interface between the individual and his or her world.

Types of Life Events

In the broadest sense, an event is a noteworthy occurrence. But what is a "significant," "stressful," or "critical" *life event*? Some investigators have restricted their definition of life events to "personal catastrophies" such as life-threatening illnesses (Hudgens, 1974). However, a more common approach has been to include a wide array of events "whose advent is either indicative of, or requires a significant change in, the ongoing life pattern of the individual" (Holmes & Masuda, 1974, p. 46). Such events may occur in a variety of domains, including school (started school, changed schools, graduated from school, failed at school), work (changed jobs, was promoted, was laid off or fired, retired), love and marriage (engaged, married, separated or divorced, spouse died), children (became pregnant, first child born, had an abortion, child died), residence (remodeled home, moved to a better residence, moved to a worse residence, lost home through a disaster), finances (took out a mortgage, gained a substantial increase in income, suffered a substantial loss in income, went on welfare), social activities (took a vacation, acquired a pet, broke up with a friend, close friend died), and health (became physically ill, was injured, health improved). Note that some of these events are "negative" in the sense that they are typically socially undesired, and some of them are socially desired and hence "positive." In either case, they require adaptation and change on the part of the individual experiencing them.

From a life-span developmental perspective, life events may be grouped into one of three major classes: normative, age-graded events; normative, history-graded events; and nonnormative events.

Normative, age-graded events Normative, age-graded events consist of biological and environmental events that are correlated with chronological age. Their occurrence depends in part on biological capacity and/or social norms. As a result, their timing, duration, and clustering tend to be similar for many individuals. Examples of normative, age-graded events include marriage, birth of a child, menopause, and retirement. These events primarily affect the individual experiencing them and secondarily affect the individual's significant others. Normative, age-graded events constitute a social clock for the adult life cycle.

Normative, history-graded events Normative, history-graded events consist of cultural events that are correlated with historical time. They are normative to the extent that they are experienced by most members of a cohort. Examples of normative, history-graded events include wars, political upheavals, mass migrations or immigrations, and economic prosperity or depression. These events play a primary role in defining the developmental context of a particular birth cohort. Further, to the extent that they affect cultural change, they continue to exert their influence on later cohorts.

Nonnormative events When life events are related weakly both to measures connected with the individual's life stage and to those connected with historical time, they are called nonnormative events. Such events are relatively idiosyncratic in terms of occurrence or timing during the life cycle or are limited to a relatively small proportion of the total population. Examples of nonnormative events include accidents, illnesses, divorce, floods, droughts, and limited occupational layoffs.

Discovery

BOX 8.1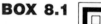
THE MEASUREMENT OF LIFE EVENTS

How do life events differ from one another? Intuitively, we know that events such as the death of a spouse, changing schools, getting a promotion, and acquiring a pet are different in many ways. One major experimental approach to this problem has been to measure the amount of stress or behavioral change associated with different events (Dohrenwend, Krasnoff, Askenasy, & Dohrenwend, 1978; Holmes & Rahe, 1967). Generally, researchers have done this by asking people to rate lists of life events compiled by the investigator. The widely used Social Readjustment Rating Scale developed by Holmes and Rahe (1967) to measure the stress of life events is illustrative of this approach. In their procedure, a designated target stimulus is given an assigned value, and judges are asked to rate the stimuli in relation to this target. Holmes and Rahe designated the event of marriage as the target and assigned it a value of 500. Individuals were then asked to provide judgments about the amount of readjustment required for each of the other events on the list in relation to marriage. The average rating (divided by 10) was then used to index the stressfulness of events reported by other individuals. The events on Holmes and Rahe's list and their average Life Change Unit scores are shown below. How many of these events have you, or others you know, experienced recently? Would you rank the events the same way?

SOCIAL READJUSTMENT RATING SCALE

Rank	Life event	Mean value
1	Death of spouse	100
2	Divorce	73
3	Marital separation	65
4	Jail term	63
5	Death of close family member	63
6	Personal injury or illness	53
7	Marriage	50
8	Fired at work	47
9	Marital reconciliation	45
10	Retirement	45
11	Change in health of family member	44
12	Pregnancy	40
13	Sex difficulties	39
14	Gain of new family member	39
15	Business readjustment	39
16	Change in financial state	38
17	Death of close friend	37
18	Change to different line of work	36
19	Change in number of arguments with spouse	35
20	Mortgage over $10,000	31
21	Foreclosure of mortgage or loan	30
22	Change in responsibilities at work	29
23	Son or daughter leaving home	29
24	Trouble with in-laws	29
25	Outstanding personal achievement	28
26	Wife begin or stop work	26
27	Begin or end school	26
28	Change in living condition	25
29	Revision of personal habits	24
30	Trouble with boss	23
31	Change in work hours or conditions	20
32	Change in residence	20
33	Change in schools	20
34	Change in recreation	19
35	Change in church activities	19
36	Change in social activities	18
37	Mortgage or loan less than $10,000	17
38	Change in sleeping habits	16
39	Change in number of family get-togethers	15
40	Change in eating habits	15
41	Vacation	13
42	Christmas	12
43	Minor violations of the law	11

Source: From Holmes & Rahe, 1967.

The Timing, Sequencing, and Clustering of Life Events

The life-span developmental perspective emphasizes multidirectional changes as a result of the patterned interaction of many antecedents. This implies a sensitivity to the timing and sequencing of events over the life span. Thus, from this perspective, events do not have uniform meaning. When an event occurs is perhaps as important as whether it occurs at all. Elder's (1974) work on the impact of the Great Depression on men who experienced this event at different times in the life cycle is an example of this point. In the case of middle-class men, Elder reports that younger men were more negatively affected by the Depression than older men. Individuals who experienced the Depression as young men were just beginning their work careers, while the older men had already established them. Over the years, men who had experienced the Depression at an early age showed a much higher rate of career instability and disadvantage than men who experienced the Depression at a later age. Elder notes that this pattern was reversed in the case of lower-class men. In this group, the Depression had a more negative impact on men who were older at its onset than on men who were younger, reflecting a historical pattern of age discrimination in unskilled occupations.

In Depth

BOX 8.2

THE GREAT DEPRESSION—A HISTORY-GRADED EVENT

The Great Depression was a major historical event. Some historians, for example, see it as a watershed in the evolution of American society. How did people adapt to this event, and what impact did it have on their lives? Elder (1974) has examined this question through a reanalysis of longitudinal data collected as part of the Oakland Growth Study. This project, originally designed to investigate the physical, intellectual, and social development of boys and girls, was begun in 1931. The children were initially selected from the fifth and sixth grades of elementary schools in Oakland, California. The children and their families were studied intensively from 1932 to 1939 and were retested as adults in 1953–1954, 1957–1958, and 1964. The children were preadolescents and adolescents during the Depression decade and graduated from high school just before World War II.

Elder's (1974) reanalysis of these data illustrates the tremendous impact of a major cultural event. In part, the impact of the Depression was determined by the degree of economic loss suffered by the family. Contrary to popular assumption, economic hardship in the Depression was not a pervasive experience. While unemployment approached one-third of the work force in 1933, evidence suggests that the Depression decade was not a time of great economic deprivation for at least half the population. Status losses were common among the middle classes, but severe physical hardships were concentrated among the rural and urban poor. Thus, Elder (1974) divided his Oakland families into deprived and relatively nondeprived groups on the basis of amount of income lost between 1929 and 1934. The average loss of the deprived group was three to four times that of the relatively nondeprived group.

In adapting to the economic losses of the Depression, families often moved from a state of crisis to disorganization, to partial recovery through new modes of action, to eventual stabilization. Strategies used, particularly by deprived

The economics of a society often trigger changes that create cultural events, such as unemployment, which affects younger and older cohorts and minority groups more than others. (Andrew Sacks/Editorial Photocolor Archives)

families, included having the mother work, taking in boarders, getting money from relatives, and obtaining public assistance. Public assistance, however, represented a strategy of last resort, and was often used only following prolonged unemployment. Employment of the mother, while not socially acceptable, was more common. This strategy, as well as taking in boarders, resulted in striking changes in the division of labor within the family. In particular, these strategies increased the power of the mother and decreased the power, prestige, and emotional significance of the father as perceived by the children. In addition, they shifted increasing responsibilities in the household economy to the children. Girls were most often involved in household tasks (food preparation, laundry, making clothing), while boys were most often involved in part-time jobs (newspaper carrier, store clerk, delivery boy). This downward extension of adultlike experience had considerable effect on the children's maturity. For example, deprivation and its associated familial adaptations were related to interest in becoming an adult, industriousness, financial responsibility, and an interest in persons outside of the family. These values affected later life

events. For example, boys from deprived families made firmer vocational commitments in late adolescence than boys from nondeprived families. In adulthood, they were more likely to have followed the occupation which they preferred in adolescence, entered their career at an earlier age, and developed a more orderly career. In middle age, men from deprived families did not differ from men from nondeprived families in commitment to work. However, work had a different meaning to the deprived men. They were more likely to prefer job security and a modest income to the risk of obtaining a higher income. They also expressed more dissatisfaction with their incomes and working conditions.

Elder reports many other influences of this cultural event. Even from this sample, however, it is clear that the Depression produced significant changes in family structure, behavior, and values, some of which were significant many years later. Interestingly, some of the adaptations connected with the Great Depression (e.g., working women and increased adultlike experience for children) may be increasing within the present historical context as a result of the severe inflation the economy has been experiencing.

The timing of history-graded and nonnormative events is largely idiosyncratic. However, the timing of age-graded events is defined, in part, by age norms. According to theory, age norms specify appropriate times for certain life events such as leaving the family home, achieving economic independence, marrying, bearing children, retiring, and so forth (Neugarten & Datan, 1973; Neugarten & Hagestad, 1976). As individuals move through the life cycle, a system of positive and negative sanctions makes them aware of whether they are early, on time, or late with respect to the norms for these events. Again, from a life-span developmental perspective it is not only the presence or absence of an event that is crucial, but also its timing. For example, Lowenthal, Thurnher, and Chiriboga (1975) report that the failure of an expected event to occur was particularly stressful in the later stages of life. Middle-aged men, for instance, indicated that being off time with respect to promotions or salary increases was a major reason for a reduction in their life satisfaction. Similarly, Bourque and Back (1977) note that events such as the departure of children and retirement are perceived by respondents as most disruptive if they occur at a nonnormative age. The departure of children from the home is least traumatic during the fifties; retirement is worst if it happens during the early sixties, which is just prior to the normative age. Being off time is not always negative. Nydegger (1973), for instance, found that late fathers were more comfortable and effective in their

(handwritten margin notes: Neugarten + Datan; Bourque + Back)

Older fathers appear to be better fathers. (Fujihira/Monkmeyer)

role as fathers than either early or on-time fathers. By delaying this event, these men avoided a conflict between the demands of parenting and the demands of establishing an early career.

Even when events occur within the limits of their normative age range, their temporal order (sequence) can be critical. Hogan (1978), for example, examined the effects of different orders of three life events experienced by men in young adulthood—completion of education, first job, and first marriage—on later marital stability. In the normative ordering of these events, a man first finishes his formal schooling, next becomes financially independent through employment at a full-time job, and finally marries (Hogan, 1978). Other events, however, particularly military service and the achievement of advanced levels of education, may disrupt the sequence. Hogan's analyses indicate that the nonnormative ordering of these events substantially increased the likelihood that the first marriage would end in a separation or divorce.

Another consideration with respect to the timing of events concerns the clustering of events. Events may be particularly difficult to deal with when they occur close together. There is considerable support for this notion. Holmes and Masuda (1974) asked physicians to provide an account of their life-event experiences and major health changes for the previous 10 years. Reported life events were assigned their values from the Social Readjustment Rating Scale, and the Life Change Unit Scores of the life events were then plotted year by year along with the major health changes. The results indicated that the vast majority of health changes were associated with a clustering of life events whose values summed to at least 150 Life Change Units per year. Further, the more severe the life crisis, the greater the risk of an associated health change. Table 8.2 shows that as the Life Change Unit score increased, so did the percentage of illness associated with the crisis. Of the mild life crises, 37

TABLE 8.2
RELATIONSHIP OF LIFE CRISIS MAGNITUDE TO PERCENTAGE OF LIFE CRISES ASSOCIATED WITH HEALTH CHANGES

	Number of life crises		Total number of life crises	Life crises associated with health changes, %
	Associated with health changes	Not associated with health changes		
Mild life crises (150–199 LCU)	13	22	35	37
Moderate life crises (200-299 LCU)	29	28	57	51
Major life crises (300+ LCU)	30	8	38	79
Total	72*	58	130	55

*Same life crises were associated with more than one health change.
Source: From Holmes & Masuda, 1974.

percent had an associated health change. This figure increases to 51 percent for moderate life crises, and to 79 percent for major life crises.

Similarly, in a developmental study, Palmore and his colleagues (Palmore, Cleveland, Nowlin, Ramm, & Siegler, 1979) note that many adults adapted quite well to the occurrence of a given event such as retirement, widowhood, departure of the last child from home, and illness. However, the simultaneous or consecutive occurrence of two or more such life events produced more serious problems of adaptation.

Finally, it is important to note that the issue of the pattern of events extends beyond a single individual. That is, it is not just the pattern of events within a single life cycle that is important, but how these events interact with events in the life cycles of significant others. Elder (1977a) stresses this point in relation to the family. In this context, for example, scheduling problems often arise. For instance, the events of early career establishment may conflict with the events of bearing and rearing children.

Is there a Universal Sequence of Life Events?

Obviously, not everyone experiences the same life events in the same order. But is there an underlying structure to adult life within which life events have their impact? Several theorists have suggested that this is the case (Bühler, 1962; Erikson, 1963; Levinson, 1978). For example Bühler (1962) identified three broad sets of events—biological, biographical, and psychological—which wax and wane over the life span. She proposed a set of ten transitions which occur over the course of the life cycle. Similarly, Erikson (1963) proposed a sequence of eight stages which shape the structure of the life cycle (see Chapter 6). More recently, Levinson (1978) and his colleagues have proposed a sequence of five eras and related periods which span the male adult life cycle.

Levinson's theory is based on a biographical study of forty men. The men ranged in age from 35 to 45 years of age at the start of the study. They were drawn from four occupational groups: hourly workers, executives, academic biologists, and novelists. Each man was seen from five to ten times over a period of ten to twenty months for a total of ten to twenty hours. A follow-up interview was conducted two years later. In addition to this primary sample, Levinson also examined the lives of approximately 100 other men as depicted in autobiographies.

Levinson focused on constructing the universal sequences which underlie the unique and diverse individual biographies of the subjects. Five eras within the life span were identified, each of roughly twenty-five years' duration. These are not stages of biological, psychological, or social development, but represent a life-cycle macrostructure. The eras are (1) preadulthood, age 0 to 22; (2) early adulthood, age 17 to 45; (3) middle adulthood, age 40 to 65; (4) late adulthood, age 60 to 85; and (5) late late adulthood, age 80+. The evolution of these eras is structured by a series of developmental periods and transitions. The primary task of the stable periods is to build a life structure. This involves making certain crucial choices and striving to attain particular goals. Stable periods ordinarily last six to eight years. The primary task of the transition periods is to terminate the existing life structure and initiate a new one. This involves a reappraisal of the current structure, exploration of new possibilities for change, and a movement toward crucial choices that will provide the basis for a new life structure. Transition periods ordinarily last four to five years. To date, Levinson's research has focused on the periods within early adulthood and middle adulthood. Within these eras, Levinson has identified eight periods; these are shown in Figure 8.2.

Early adult transition   This transition ordinarily begins at age 17 or 18 and extends until age 22 or 23. The early adult transition represents a developmen-

Figure 8.2 Eras and developmental periods in early and middle adulthood. *(From Levinson, 1978.)*

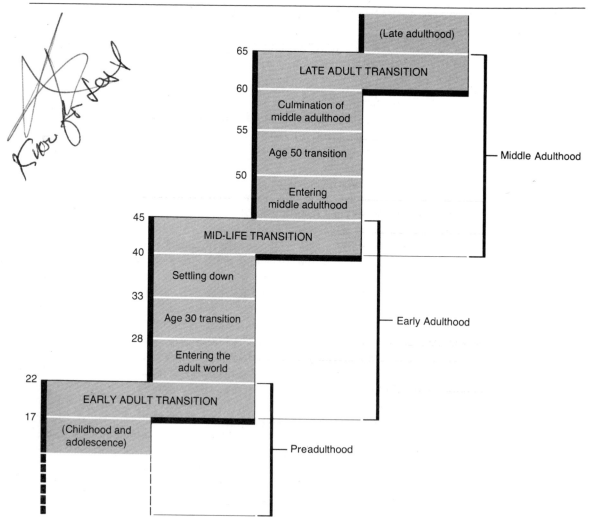

tal link between preadulthood and early adulthood. It involves two major tasks. The first task is to terminate the adolescent life structure. This involves modifying relationships with the family and other persons, groups, and institutions significant to the preadult world. The second task is to make a preliminary step into the adult world. This involves making initial explorations and choices for adult living. Major life events within this transition may include graduation from high school, moving out of the family home, entering college, and graduation from college. "In this period a young man is on the boundary between adolescence and adulthood. The transition ends when he gets beyond the boundary and begins to create a life within the adult world" (Levinson, 1978, p. 57).

Entering the adult world　This period begins in the early twenties and ends in the late twenties. The focus of the period is on exploration and provisional commitment to adult roles and responsibilities. The young male adult faces two tasks, which, according to Levinson, are antithetical. On the one hand, he must explore alternative possibilities for adult living—keeping his options open and avoiding strong commitments. On the other hand, he must create a stable life structure—becoming responsible and "making something" of himself. Levinson notes: "Finding a balance between these tasks is not an easy matter. If the first predominates, life has an extremely transient, rootless quality. If the second predominates, there is the danger of committing oneself prematurely to a structure without sufficient exploration of alternatives" (p. 58). Examples of life events which are often crucial during this period include occupational choice, first job, marriage, and the birth of children.

Age-thirty transition　The age range from 28 to 33 years represents a transition period between entering the adult world and the next period. This transition period provides an opportunity to modify the provisional adult life structure created earlier. As Levinson notes, adult life is becoming more serious: "A voice within the self says: 'If I am to change my life—if there are things in it I want to modify or exclude, or things missing I want to add—I must now make a start, for soon it will be too late'" (p. 58). Levinson argues that the life structure is always different at the end of this transition than it was at the beginning, although the changes made vary from man to man. Some men have a relatively smooth transition, building directly on the past. The focus is on adjustment and enrichment. However, Levinson notes that for most men a moderate to severe crisis is common. Life events such as divorce and occupational change are frequent during this period. Levinson concludes:

The shift from the end of the Age Thirty Transition to the start of the next period is one of the crucial steps in adult development. At this time a man may make important new choices, or he may reaffirm old choices. If these choices are congruent with his dreams, talents and external possibilities, they provide the basis for a relatively satisfactory life structure. If the choices are poorly made and the new structure is seriously flawed, he will pay a heavy price in the next period. (p. 59)

Settling down   This period begins in the early thirties and extends until about age forty. As implied in the name, this period emphasizes stability and security. The individual makes deeper commitments to his occupation, family, or whatever enterprises are significant to him. In addition, there is an emphasis on what Levinson calls "making it." This involves long-range planning toward specific goals within the context of a timetable for their achievement—an effort which Levinson labels a personal enterprise. Until the early 30s, the young man is a novice adult. During the settling-down period, his task is to become a full-fledged adult. Levinson uses the metaphor of a ladder to characterize this period. "At the start of this period, a man is on the bottom rung of his ladder and is entering a world in which he is a *junior member*. His aims are to advance in the enterprise, to climb the ladder and become a *senior member* in that world. His sense of well-being during this period depends strongly on his own and others' evaluation of his progress toward these goals" (p. 60). Levinson notes that most of his subjects fix on a key life event such as a promotion or a new job as representative of ultimate affirmation or devaluation by society.

During the last years of the settling-down period, there is a distinctive phase which Levinson has designated as "becoming one's own man." This phase ordinarily occurs at age 36 to 40. The major task of this phase is to achieve a greater measure of independence and authority in connection with the goals of the various enterprises. Levinson notes that a man often becomes sensitive about anything that interferes with these aims.

Midlife transition   This transition spans a period of from four to six years, reaching a peak in the early forties. The midlife transition represents a developmental link between early adulthood and middle adulthood and is part of both eras. It represents a beginning and ending, a meeting of past and future. The transition may be relatively smooth, but is more likely to involve considerable turmoil. However, this outcome is not entirely dependent on a man's previous success or failure in achieving goals. "It becomes important to ask: 'What have I done with my life? What do I really get from and give to my wife, children, friends, work, community—and self? What is it I truly want for myself and others?'" (p. 60). The creation of a life structure in early adulthood involved a commitment to some goals and a rejection of others. No one life structure can permit the expression of all aspects of the self. A task of the midlife transition is to work on and partially resolve the discrepancy between what is and what might be. According to Levinson, the midlife transition is not prompted by any one life event or series of events. Rather, multiple processes and events are involved, including the reality and experience of bodily decline, changing relations among the various generations, and the evolution of career and other enterprises.

Entering middle adulthood   As the midlife transition ends, there is a new period of stability. A new life structure emerges which provides the basis for moving into middle adulthood. This period begins at about age 45 and extends until about age 50. Sometimes the start of this new life structure is marked by a

After evaluating his life, this long-standing executive quit his job and bought a boat to sail and . . . (Seattle Post-Intelligencer, March 13, 1977)

significant life event—a change in job or occupation, divorce or love affair, or a move to a new community. In other instances, the changes are more subtle. As was the case following the age-thirty transition, the life structure that emerges following the midlife transition is crucial for the individual's adjustment.

Some men have suffered such irreparable defeats in childhood or early adulthood, and have been so little able to work on the tasks of their Mid-Life Transition, that they lack the inner and outer resources for creating a minimally adequate structure. They face a middle adulthood of constriction and decline. Other men form a life structure that is reasonably viable in the world but poorly connected to the self. Although they do their bit for themselves and others, their lives are lacking in inner excitement and meaning. Still other men have started a middle adulthood that will have its own special satisfactions and fulfillments. For these men, middle adulthood is often the fullest and most creative season in the life cycle. (pp. 61–62)

Subsequent periods "Entering Middle Adulthood" is the last specific period for which Levinson has data because of the current age of the men in his sample. However, he has projected a tentative view of subsequent periods during middle adulthood. He proposes that an age-fifty transition, which is analogous to the age-thirty transition, occurs between age 50 and 55. In this period, a man can modify the life structure formed in the mid-forties. A stable period, which is analogous to the settling-down period, occurs between age 55 and 60. This period is the culmination of middle adulthood. Finally, between age 60 and 65, a late adult transition ends the period of middle adulthood and provides a basis for living in late adulthood.

Thus, Levinson proposes that male adult development consists of a universal sequence of periods. Within this context, he does not focus on life events per se. For Levinson, examination of events such as marriage, divorce, birth of a child, and retirement can only yield diverse biographies. "Life as it evolves" must be examined by specifying an individual's life structure, which involves three components:

1. The individual's sociocultural world, including social structures (family social class and occupation and political affiliation), and historic events such as war, economic depression, and prosperity
2. The individual's participation in this world, including both specific roles, such as husband, friend, worker, and parent, and the life events related to those roles, such as marriage, birth of a child, promotion, and retirement
3. Aspects of the self including fantasies, moral values, talents and skills, moods, and so forth

Levinson, then, views life events as part of an organized whole rather than as discrete elements. It is this whole, and the universal sequence it forms, that is crucial. Is Levinson correct? Is there a universal sequence of adult male development? As he acknowledges, it is too early to answer this question. Levinson's sample of men is small. Certainly, an alternative sequence may be found for women. Nevertheless, Levinson's theory provides a provocative view of adult development which highlights the importance of life events during adulthood.

Exposure to Life Events

How frequently do individuals experience life events? What kinds of life events do they experience? We would expect to find both age and sex differences in exposure to and content of life events because of different normative expectations. Similarly, we would expect to find cohort differences in exposure to and content of life events because of cultural change. Let us examine these differences.

Age and sex differences in exposure to life events   Information on the issue of age and sex differences in exposure to life events is available from Lowenthal, Thurnher, and Chiriboga's (1975) study of individuals at four stages of life (high school seniors, young newlyweds, middle-aged parents, and older adults about to retire). These investigators found that, generally, young persons (high school seniors and young newlyweds) reported more exposure to life events than older persons (middle-aged parents, adults about to retire). However, the two younger groups tended to report more positive stresses, while the two older groups tended to report more negative stresses. Age and sex differences were apparent in the nature of the stressful events as well (see Table 8.3). The major cause of stress in the younger stages was education. This was followed by stresses related to dating and marriage. Stresses related to dating and marriage and changes in residence were more significant for women, while stresses related to leisure activities and the military were more significant for men. Differences between the sexes were more dramatic for the

TABLE 8.3

SOURCES OF STRESS OVER THE PAST TEN YEARS

Source of stress	Younger			Older		
	Men	Women	Total	Men	Women	Total
Education	71*	80	76	2	9	6
Residential	33	40	36	9	4	6
Dating and Marriage	33	50	40	2	12	8
Friends	27	44	35	13	5	9
Family	24	36	30	13	26	20
Marriage	18	28	23	9	12	11
Health	10	22	16	13	38	27
Work	22	14	18	45	21	32
Leisure activities	35	12	23	6	2	4
Military	27	2	14	0	4	2
Death	14	12	13	18	19	19
Finances	6	4	5	18	11	14

*Percentage of respondents indicating area as a source of stress.
Source: Adapted from Lowenthal, Thurnher, & Chiriboga, 1975.

older respondents. Indeed, there was no overall "major" source of stress for these groups. The most salient source of stress for men was work, while the most salient sources of stress for women were health and the family. In part, these differences are a function of the fact that older women appear to be stressed by events occurring to others, particularly their children. Events connected with their children's schooling (child dropped out of school), marriage (child separated or divorced), and occupation (child changed jobs) were significant stressors. These appeared to be particularly important for middle-aged women.

Longitudinal data based on five- and seven-year follow-up interviews extend these findings by focusing on changes in stress (Chiriboga, 1978). Overall, it was shown that the number of events associated with negative stresses increased more for middle-aged and older adults than for the two younger groups. More specifically, high school seniors and newlyweds showed little change in family stress, while the two older groups—especially the middle-aged—showed increases in negative stresses in this area. Middle-aged men and women showed the greatest increase in positive stresses, while the older age group showed the greatest decrease. Most of these changes were in the area of marriage. Middle-aged men and women showed the largest increases, while older and newlywed men and women showed a decline on this dimension. These data suggest that middle age is a time of dramatic change, reflecting changes in both positive and negative components of stress. Later

TABLE 8.4
STRESS TYPOLOGY

Exposure to stress	Perception of Stress	
	High	Low
High	Overwhelmed	Challenged
Low	Self-defeated	Lucky

Source: Adapted from Lowenthal, Thurnher, & Chiriboga, 1975.

life, however, tends to be associated with an increasing amount of negative stress.

However, the mere occurrence of an event is not the entire story. How a person interprets the event is critical. Thus, what one person may experience as a catastrophe, another person may experience as a challange. Lowenthal and her colleagues used the distinction between exposure to stress (self-reported incidence of life events) and perceived stress (preoccupation with themes of loss, stress, and deprivation in a life-history interview) to identify four types of people (see Table 8.4).

Within this framework, "overwhelmed" people were exposed to frequent or severe stress and perceived their lives as highly stressful. "Challenged" people, although they were also exposed to frequent or severe stress, did not perceive their lives as stressful. The "lucky" were exposed to infrequent or mild stress and perceived their lives as relatively unstressful. On the other hand, "self-defeating" people, who were similarly exposed to infrequent or mild stresses, perceived their lives as highly stressful.

The distribution of these types by age and sex is shown in Table 8.5. Examination of the extreme right-hand column of this table indicates that more than 50 percent of the total sample were preoccupied with stress (overwhelmed or self-defeating), suggesting difficulty adapting to life events. The distribution of the four types was quite similar across the four age groups. Within each age group, however, there were dramatic differences between men and women, and, with respect to these differences, the two younger and the two older groups resembled one another. For example, among the highly stressed young, men were more likely to be overwhelmed than women. But among the highly stressed old, women were more likely to be overwhelmed than men. These data suggest that older women may have fewer resources than men to deal with high levels of stress. Whether this represents a developmental effect or a cohort effect is unknown at this point. Thus, the data reviewed in this section suggest that there are both age and sex differences in life-event experiences. The sex differences, however, may be more significant than the age differences.

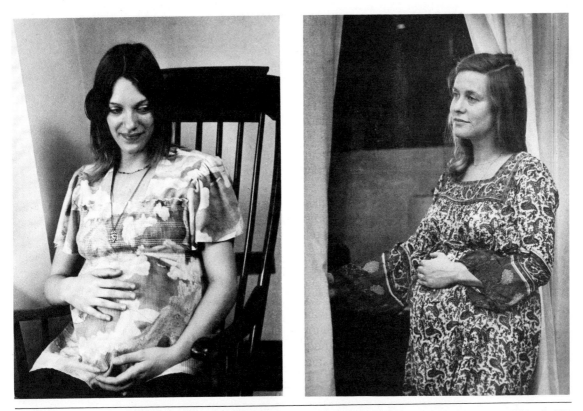

Having a baby is a significant life event, but the timing of that event in the individual's life span is particularly critical. (Erika/Photo Researchers; Erika Stone/Peter Arnold)

TABLE 8.5
STRESS TYPE BY STAGE AND SEX (PERCENTAGES)

Stress type	Younger Men	Younger Women	Older Men	Older Women	Combined Men	Combined Women	Total
Considerable presumed stress							
Challenged	16	21	30	7	23	14	19
Overwhelmed	36	27	21	40	28	34	31
Light presumed stress							
Lucky	32	21	31	32	32	26	29
Self-defeating	16	31	18	21	17	26	21
Total	100	100	100	100	100	100	100

Note: Columns grouped under "Age group" — "Younger", "Older", and "Younger and older combined" (each with Men/Women), plus Total.

Source: Adapted from Lowenthal, Thurnher, & Chiriboga, 1975.

Cohort differences in exposure to life events Of course, different cohorts are exposed to different history-graded events. Individuals born in 1920, for example, experienced World War II while those born in 1960 did not. However, there are also cohort differences in exposure to and timing of age-graded events. These differences reflect cultural changes (e.g., industrialization, urbanization) and their accompanying demographic, technological, political, and economic developments.

For example, Uhlenberg (1979) has constructed a profile of the characteristics of three birth cohorts: 1870–1874, 1900–1904, and 1930–34. The 1870 cohort reached age 65 in the early 1940s; the 1900 cohort reached this age in the early 1970s; and the 1930 cohort will not reach it until the turn of the century. Uniform changes in the characteristics and experiences of these three cohorts are evident, as summarized in Table 8.6. This sample of data suggests the following:

1. With changing policies on immigration, successive cohorts are composed of fewer foreign-born individuals.
2. With industrialization, a decreasing proportion of individuals are living in a rural environment, and an increasing proportion are living in an urban environment.
3. With changing economic patterns, a decreasing proportion of the male work force are in farming occupations, and an increased proportion are in white-collar occupations.
4. With changing marital patterns, a decreasing proportion of women are remaining single and an increasing proportion are experiencing divorce.
5. With the decline in childlessness between the second and third cohorts, a decreasing proportion of women are entering old age childless.
6. With increasing sex differences in survival (and the tendency in our culture for women to marry men older than themselves), an increasing proportion of women are experiencing widowhood.
7. With changing economic patterns, an increasing proportion of men are experiencing retirement from the work force.

Thus, Uhlenberg's data suggest that demographic and cultural changes since 1870 have significantly altered the life-event experiences of adults born just a generation apart.

Differences between cohorts are also seen in the timing of specific life events. For example, until recently, successive cohorts have exhibited a decrease in age at first marriage, birth of first child, and birth of last child. In the last few years, however, there has been an increase in age at first marriage, along with a decline in the number of children born (Neugarten & Hagestad, 1976). Similarly, entry into the labor force has been increasingly delayed, and exit from the labor force has been increasingly accelerated for successive cohorts of men. The participation of women in the work force has also changed markedly. During the period 1950 to 1970, the proportion of middle-aged

TABLE 8.6

CHARACTERISTICS OF THREE COHORTS DURING ADULTHOOD AND OLD AGE

Cohort characteristics	Cohort		
	1870	1900	1930
During adulthood			
Size when aged 25–29, in thousands	6,529	9,834	10,804
Percent foreign-born when aged 25–29	17	11	3
Percent rural when aged 25–29	47	37	28
Percent distribution of males by occupation when aged 35–39			
White-collar	NA	31	44
Blue-collar (nonfarm)	NA	52	53
Farm	NA	17	3
Marital status of females			
Percent never married by age 50	10	8	5
Percent divorced by age 40-44 (of those ever-married)	NA	1	21
Percent distribution of females by children ever born			
0	23	28	13
1–3	36	51	52
4+	41	21	35
During old age			
Size when aged 65–69, in thousands	3,807	6,992	9,023
Percent of initial cohort surviving to age 65			
Males	37	50	63
Females	42	62	77
Percent foreign-born when aged 65–69	21	13	7
Sex ratio when aged 65-69	99	81	80
Average no. of years of life remaining at age 65			
Males	11.7	13.7	?
Females	12.8	17.1	?
Percent of males in labor force when age 65–69	69	42	25
Ratio of age groups 70+/65–69, when age 65–69	1.4	1.8	2.4

Source: Adapted from Uhlenberg, 1979.

women in the work force doubled. During recent years, an increasing proportion of young mothers have remained in the work force (Neugarten & Hagestad, 1976).

There are also differences between cohorts in sequences of life events. For

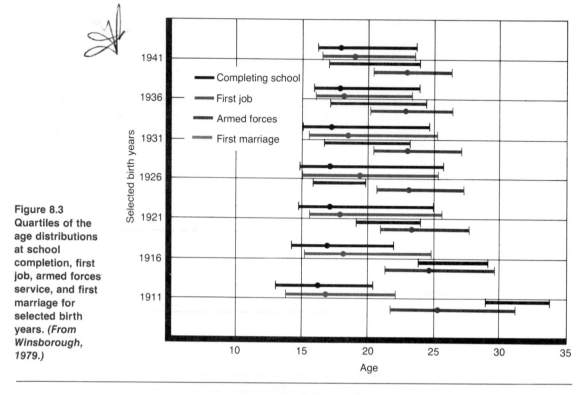

**Figure 8.3
Quartiles of the
age distributions
at school
completion, first
job, armed forces
service, and first
marriage for
selected birth
years. *(From
Winsborough,
1979.)***

example, in spite of the fact that entrance into the labor force has been increasingly delayed for successive cohorts, the entire transition from school-boy to married adult has occurred more rapidly for recent cohorts (Winsborough, 1979). In this study, four events were examined: (1) completing high school; (2) taking a first full-time job; (3) entrance to and exit from the armed forces, and (4) entrance into first marriage. Figure 8.3 shows the time taken to complete these events for selected male cohorts. The top line for each birth year reflects duration of the school exit process. The line begins when 25 percent of the cohort had completed school, moves through the median age (indicated by the point on the line), and terminates when 75 percent of the cohort had completed school. In similar fashion, the second line reflects the duration of the first job transition; the third line, duration of military service; and the fourth line, duration of the first marriage transition. The entire process of moving over the four life events took approximately eighteen years for the early cohorts and less than 10 years for the recent cohorts.

Cohort differences in the timing of life events have also resulted in changes in the age grading of the life cycle. Generally, the number of age grades has increased. Adolescence, for example, did not acquire its current status as a stage of the life cycle until late in the nineteenth century. As entry into the work force became increasingly delayed by higher education, a new stage of the life cycle labeled "youth" was proposed (Keniston, 1970). Similarly, as children were born and left home earlier in the life of the parent, attention began to be focused on middle age as a stage in the life cycle. Finally, as longevity increased, and particularly as the retirement age decreased, a distinction was drawn between the "young-old" and the "old-old" (Neugarten & Hagestad, 1976). The former group, mainly 55 to 75 years of age, consists of individuals who are relatively healthy and economically secure but relatively free of occupational and familial responsibilities. Thus, the data reviewed in this section indicate that life-event experiences have changed significantly over historical time.

ADAPTING TO LIFE EVENTS

In addition to the nature of the events themselves, there are two general factors that must be considered in order to understand how individuals adapt to life events. The first general factor consists of a variety of characteristics of the individual and the environment that mediate the impact of life events. These characteristics define the resources that will facilitate, and the deficits that will interfere with, the individual's adaptation to the demands of an event. These resources and deficits set the limits of the adaptational process. They are the tools the individual has to work with. The second general factor consists of the adaptation process itself. This process involves behaviors such as analyzing the problem, searching for solutions, evaluating the costs and benefits of alternative solutions, and acting to accomplish certain ends. In effect, these behaviors represent what people actually do when confronted with a life event. Let us briefly examine each of these factors.

Mediating Variables

Many different variables function as mediators of life events, including biological, psychological, social, and physical characteristics of the individual and the environment. We will not attempt to specify all these potentially relevant mediators, but instead will discuss a sample of them. Within this context, three general points are important:

1. There are large between-person differences with respect to these variables, both within and between cohorts.
2. Generally, the better the individual's resources, the better he or she is able to adapt to life events (Palmore, Cleveland, Nowlin, Ramm, & Siegler, 1979). However, it is also important to examine the relative distribution of resources and deficits (Lowenthal & Chiriboga, 1973).
3. The impact of resources and deficits varies over the life span (Lieberman, 1975; Lowenthal & Chiriboga, 1973). That is, what is a resource at one point in the life span may be irrelevant or may be a deficit at another point in the life span. The reverse is also true. Further, the balance of resources to deficits may have a different significance at different phases of the life cycle. Within this framework, let us briefly examine three sets of mediating variables.

Biological and intellectual variables   It may be argued that biological and intellectual resources set a floor or lower limit on adaptation (Lieberman, 1975). That is, they are necessary but not sufficient for adaptation. For example, adaptation requires a certain expenditure of biological energy dependent on physical health. It is reasonable, then, to suppose that the physical capacities of the individual impose some limits on the ability to adapt.

Similarly, the intellectual capacities of the individual impose some limits on adaptational capacity. Various cognitive abilities (the ability to attend to, encode, store, and retrieve information; crystallized abilities reflective of knowledge of the culture; fluid abilities reflective of the perception of relationships in novel situations) are all probably required in order to appraise threat accurately and to select and implement coping strategies effectively. To the extent that the individual cannot perform these intellectual tasks, adaptation will be impaired.

There is evidence to support the role of biological and intellectual capacities in setting lower limits. Lieberman (1975), for instance, examined the adaptation of elderly adults to radical changes in their environment (e.g., institutionalization). The results of these studies suggested that those who were physically and cognitively impaired could not adapt. In one study, for example, physical and cognitive characteristics accounted for 73 percent of the variance predicting breakdown. However, while inadequate physical and intellectual resources appear to predict breakdown, the reverse is not true. Adequate resources do not necessarily predict successful adaptation. Thus, biological and intellectual resources set lower limits. Below these limits the individual cannot mobilize the basic resources necessary for successful adaptation. Above these limits other psychological and social variables appear to be critical.

Personal and social variables   The individual's personality is an important mediator of life events. For example, as we noted in Chapter 6, Costa and McCrae (1980) have identified three broad domains of adult personality: neuroticism, extraversion, and openness to experience. In examining the role of these domains in relation to life events, Costa and McCrae found that virtually all events over which individuals had any control were related to personality.

Other findings stress that the role personality plays in mediating the individual's response to life events varies over the life cycle. For example, Lieberman (1975) reported that such traditionally positive characteristics as ego strength and impulse control were not predictive of adaptation in older adults experiencing radical change. Indeed, Lieberman found that those elderly who were aggressive, narcissistic, demanding, and irritating were those individuals who were most likely to survive the crisis. Thus, traditional views of psychological health were not applicable to older adults in this setting. Lieberman concludes: "A certain amount of magical thinking and perceiving oneself as the center of the universe, with a pugnacious stance toward the world—even a highly suspicious one—seemed more likely to insure homeostasis in the face of a severe crisis" (pp. 155–156)

The impact of life events is also mediated by social factors such as socioeconomic status, income, and interpersonal support systems including family and friends. For example, supportive interpersonal relationships may serve as resources for the individual to the degree to which they provide physical, psychological, or financial support (Adams & Lindemann, 1974). The availability of these resources is likely to vary over the life cycle. For example, supportive frameworks and interpersonal relationships frequently decrease with increasing age. Older individuals tend to belong to fewer groups, to have fewer friends, and to see their friends less often (Rosow, 1973). However, there is also evidence to suggest that interpersonal relationships among older adults are more likely to be complex and subtle (Lowenthal, Thurnher, & Chiriboga, 1975). In this sense, older adults may get more out of the relationships they do have. Among men in particular, interpersonal resources increasingly seem to serve as buffers against stressful events (Lowenthal, Thurnher, & Chiriboga, 1975). While the presence of a social network is often a resource for older adults, its absence may not be a deficit, at least for some individuals. For example, life-long isolation is not necessarily associated with maladaptation in later life (Lowenthal, Thurnher, & Chiriboga, 1975). The life-long isolate does not suffer from age-linked losses of social networks because he or she never had social ties. However, a pattern of marginal social relationships appears to be associated with poor adaptation at all points in the life cycle. Thus, again we see that whether a characteristic is a resource or a deficit depends on one's stage in the life cycle.

Past experience and anticipatory socialization An individual's past behavior tends to be the best predictor of his or her future behavior. Responses to life events, then, are likely to depend, in part, on the individual's past experience with similar events (Lawton & Nahemow, 1973; Lieberman, 1975). Generally, it may be argued that successful adaptation in the past enhances the ability of the individual to cope with future events. Past experience may modify both affective responses to the event (e.g., reducing anxiety) as well as the strategies used in coping with the event (e.g., goal setting and decision making). Persons *know* they can deal with this type of event. Of course, for past experience to be effective the individual must be able to recognize the similarity between past and current events. In this regard, events which on the surface appear quite different probably require the application of similar analytic, problem-solving, and decision-making processes. This suggests the possibility of the development of generic life development and life-crisis skills which may be taught to individuals (Danish & D'Augelli, 1980).

One might expect that older adults are able to use their past experience resource to a greater extent than younger adults. Indeed, there is some evidence to suggest that this resource is used by older adults and may underlie, at least partially, the finding that older adults reported fewer stresses than younger adults (Lowenthal, Thurnher, & Chiriboga, 1975). However, past experience may also be a deficit to the extent that the individual has been unable to cope with previous events. A history of past failure may lead the individual to perceive life events as overwhelming and to attempt to "avoid" them (Levinson, 1978; Lowenthal, Thurnher, & Chiriboga, 1975).

Many life events can be anticipated. Thus, many of the behaviors necessary for successful adaptation to such events may be learned through *anticipatory socialization*—a process of learning the attitudes, values, beliefs, activities, etc., that are typically associated with a role one will occupy in the future or a situation one will face. Such learning may occur through a variety of mechanisms, including formal instruction, observation, modeling, and imitation. Anticipatory socialization for an event may serve as a resource to the extent that it decreases the ambiguity of the situation and increases the responses available to the individual (Albrecht & Gift, 1975). There appears to be less anticipatory socialization for events which are seen as involving defeats or losses. In addition, with respect to different points in the life span, there is evidence that there is less anticipatory socialization for events associated with aging than for events at other points in the life span (Rosow, 1973). Such anticipatory socialization requires an orientation toward the future on the part of the individual. In this regard, positive assessments of the future, as well as introspective abilities, appear to be significant resources for older adults (Lieberman, 1975; Lowenthal, Thurnher, & Chiriboga, 1975).

The resource-deficit balance   In addition to resources, individuals also have deficits, which are not necessarily the absence of or the opposite of resources. The importance of the relative balance between resources and deficits is illustrated by Lowenthal, Thurnher, and Chiriboga's study of four life stages. These investigators measured both resources (e.g., trust, empathy, hopefulness, openness to change, physical health) and deficits (e.g., anxiety, depression, hostility, feelings of inferiority, self-criticism). Respondents were then ranked in the top, middle, or bottom third on their summed resource and deficit scores. This produced a nine-cell typology (i.e., high resources–high deficits to low resources–low deficits). Lowenthal and her colleagues found that resources and deficits were not simply opposite ends of the same continuum. While 36 percent of the individuals fell into convergent categories (i.e., high resources–low deficits; low resources–high deficits), 46 percent fell into clearly divergent categories (i.e., high resources–high deficits; intermediate resources–high deficits).

Comparison of the nine groups on measures of happiness also reveals the importance of the interaction between resources and deficits, as well as the age-specific nature of adaptation. For the entire sample, the happiest people were at the extremes (high resources–high deficits and low resources–low deficits) and in one intermediate group (intermediate resources–low deficits). The least happy groups were low resource–high deficit, intermediate resource–high deficit, and intermediate resource–intermediate deficit. Developmentally, however, the pattern varied. Among the high school seniors, the happiest individuals were those with high resources and high deficits. However, the advantage of such complexity decreases over the life span. That is, the happiest newlyweds were those who had high resources and low deficits. Among middle-aged respondents, the happiest individuals were those with intermediate resources and low deficits. Finally, among the older adults, the happiest individuals were those with low resources and low deficits.

Thus, the pattern appears to be one of movement from psychological complexity to psychological simplicity. Examination of differences among the groups on other variables supports this description. On the one hand, those high on both resources and deficits reported more life events and turning points in their lives, experienced and perceived more stress in their lives, and engaged in a broader range of activities than other groups. On the other hand, those low on both resources and deficits reported fewer life events and turning points in their lives, had few recent positive *or* negative emotional experiences, projected minimally into the future, and displayed little complexity in their goals for the next few years. The characteristics of the complex, therefore, resemble the

Environmental occurrences, such as earthquakes, can have devastating and lasting effects. (United Press International)

cultural stereotype of the young, while the characteristics of the simple resemble the cultural stereotype of the old. Lowenthal and her colleagues suggest that the convergence of optimum balance style and cultural stereotypes may not be coincidental.

The Adaptative Process

What do people actually do when confronted with a life event? In actuality they may engage in many different behaviors. However, these behaviors are part of an overall *adaptation process*, which is characterized by several general steps. Box 8.3 provides an example of behaviors involved in adapting to divorce.

In Depth

BOX 8.3

DIVORCE—A NONNORMATIVE EVENT

Divorce was relatively uncommon in the United States during the first half of the twentieth century. However, in recent years, particularly since the early sixties, divorce rates have escalated dramatically. They more than doubled from 1960 to 1977, and it is estimated that about half of all marriages involving young Americans will end in divorce (Glick & Norton, 1976). In spite of the fact that there is considerable evidence to suggest that divorce is a disruptive event, there have been few attempts to examine the adjustment process involved (Chiriboga, 1977; Hetherington, Cox, & Cox, 1979; Spanier & Casto, 1979). A recent study by Spanier and Casto (1979) is illustrative of an attempt to examine this issue. Their analyses were based on interviews of adults aged 21 to 65 who had been separated or divorced during the two years preceding the interview. Spanier and Casto found that two related adjustments are involved in the process of separation or divorce. The first involves the adjustment to the dissolution of the marriage (e.g., working out property settlements and custody arrangements; informing and dealing with family and friends; and coping with feelings about the self and spouse, such as love, hate, guilt, self-esteem, and self-confidence). The second involves the adjustment to the process of creating a new life-style (e.g., finding a new place to live, making economic adjustments, adjusting to single parenthood, finding new friends, and resuming dating). Several examples of these adjustments are given below.

Dependent children were often a source of significant adjustment problems. Many parents attempted to minimize the negative effects of the separation on the children. One father said:

We wanted there to be as little disruption as possible for the kids. Because both of the kids were loved very much by both of us and because of our agreement to share custody, I feel they suffered only minimally . . . now they don't have to compete with the other parent for attention and they don't have to live with constant quarreling. (p. 216)

In a minority of cases, however, the children were used to punish the other spouse or to obtain a better settlement. Once a separation or divorce had occurred, the parent receiving principal custody was faced with the task of performing multiple roles alone. Parents often felt trapped.

I hate feeling totally responsible for the kids. They're mine completely. At least when I was married, I could mentally not feel responsible at times. . . . It gets lonely with the kids in bed by 8:00. It's an ambiguous role. [I want to go out but] I don't want the kids to be stuck with a babysitter three or four nights a week. (p. 223)

Nevertheless, most parents were glad to have custody of the children. Those who did not have custody viewed their loss as a serious deprivation.

Spanier and Casto also note that all of their respondents reported emotional problems as a result of the separation or divorce. The severity of these problems appeared to be significantly related to the degree to which the event was anticipated and the degree of attachment to the former spouse that remained. A sudden and unexpected separation often caused extreme reactions. A husband commented:

I was at first extremely distraught. I think that I was in a suicidal state for a while. I contemplated suicide at one time. After this period I just kind of went into a state of shock that lasted [a couple of months]. After that I just felt hurt that all of it had happened. (p. 218)

Similarly, a continued feeling of attachment was often a major cause of emotional problems. A young woman put it this way:

I still think about him. Knowing that he won't come home for dinner is sad. Dinner is the hardest time. We still talk and I wonder how he's doing. . . . [There are other] memories like him cooking breakfast on Sunday mornings. And the family at home at Christmas. It's hard seeing his car downtown and thinking about he and I apart. (p. 219)

Spanier and Casto also found that individuals who developed new social relationships, including new heterosexual social relationships, had fewer adjustment problems than indivduals who did not. For example, only 7 percent of those who were dating regularly, living with someone of the opposite sex, or remarried were having serious adjustment problems. In contrast, 45 percent of those with little or no heterosexual activity were having serious adjustment problems. The following comment was typical:

Getting involved with a woman has helped me to realize I can now communicate intimately and establish a relationship with someone. This has been very helpful. It's made the adjustment much easier. (p. 225)

Other factors predictive of adjustment included economic status and health status.

Spanier and Casto conclude that the adjustment to separation and divorce is more related to the process of creating a new life-style than to the process of dissolving the old one. This finding stresses the importance of mediating factors, such as personality traits, social competence, and economic resources, in coping with divorce.

Once an event occurs (or is anticipated) the individual assesses it with respect to its significance or degree of threat. The ability of the individual to make this assessment depends upon a certain level of adequacy in cognitive functioning. As noted previously, cognitive abilities appear to create a lower limit in this regard (Lieberman, 1975). That is, if cognitive functioning is below a certain level, the individual is unable to conduct an appraisal of the event sufficient to determine the degree of threat posed. Above this particular level of adequacy, however, increasing cognitive ability is not correlated with increased ability to carry out the appraisal process.

The degree to which the situation or event is assessed as threatening or stressful depends upon both event and mediating factors. As discussed previously, these will vary depending upon the type of life event, its historical and sociocultural context, the previous life history of the individual, and the point in the individual's life cycle at which the life event occurs. Regardless of these differences, the appraisal process is seen as being similar for all individuals. This process revolves around the degree of dissonance (Festinger, 1957; Lazarus, 1966) or incongruity (Moss, 1973) experienced by the individual as a result of the occurrence of the life event. One way of thinking about this process is to envision the life event as presenting the individual with certain information or requirements which either have not been previously encountered or which are in conflict with the individual's current information, values, goals, or behavior.

The outcomes of this initial appraisal of the event range from no threat or stress perceived to intense threat or stress perceived. If no stress is perceived, the individual is essentially unaffected by the life event. If the event is appraised as threatening or stressful, the individual begins to seek some means of resolving the conflict.

The first phase of the individual's attempts to recreate congruity with the environment involves the selection of particular *coping strategies*. As we have mentioned, the sequences of previous events and the individual's mastery of these will have resulted in an established repertoire of coping strategies and decision-making tendencies. Thus, one can expect between-person differences in the strategies available and in the selection of strategies.

Selection of coping strategies will also be influenced by the constraints perceived in the immediate context. For example, direct action or manipulation of the environment may be a feasible alternative under some circumstances and not under others. Circumstances under which action tendencies are less likely would be either conditions in which their expression would expose the individual to threat from a different source or those in which direct action would have little or no value. Examples of the latter type of situation are severe injury, terminal illness, and death of a loved one. Here the individual is relatively helpless in the sense that there is little opportunity for direct action on the environment. Although such events may occur at any point in the individual's life span, there is a prevalence of such events later in the life cycle. Older adults also tend to be under more constrictions in terms of decreased financial resources, decreased status, and decreased options for alternative support networks and employment opportunities (Rosow, 1973). This suggests that the use of psychological coping strategies will tend to increase over the adult life span, while the use of direct-action coping strategies will tend to decrease. Guttmann (1978), in a study of adult decision making in relation to life events, did find that action takers tended to be younger than non-action takers. In particular, individuals 80 years of age and over tended to take limited action or no action. Those with higher incomes and more education were also more likely to be action takers.

Another important determinant of strategy selection is the degree of perceived threat. There is some evidence that a high degree of threat leads to a decrease in variability of response and an increase in stereotyped behavior (Lazarus, 1966). Thus, when the degree of threat is intense, one might expect the selection of typical defensive maneuvers such as avoidance and denial.

Such strategies may be partly successful in that they prevent the individual from becoming involved in problems too complex to handle. However, long-term use of such strategies tends to be maladaptive in that the behavioral and psychological flexibility of the individual becomes impaired. Some events simply cannot be avoided. In his studies of institutionalization, for instance, Lieberman (1975) reports that those who did not deny the threat and were able to engage in appraisal and resolution processes consistent with the threat fared better than those who either denied the effect of the threat or refused to acknowledge it.

Following the initial selection of coping strategies, attempts to cope with the situation using these strategies are undertaken. A variety of outcomes of this process are possible. The individual may find the initial selection of strategies to be adequate to cope with the events. In that case, the chosen coping behavior of the individual tends to remain stable. A second possibility is that the individual may find his or her usual strategies of coping inadequate or, at the most, marginally adequate. In that case, a phase of exploration may begin, involving searching for new solutions, seeking out and evaluating new information, and reappraising current assumptions and life goals. This explorative phase is a highly unstable period. It is often accompanied by confusion, frustration, disruption of usual behavioral and psychological processes, and a general increase in susceptibility to pathology (Moss, 1973).

The outcomes of the adaptation process depend, to a great extent, on the individual's balance of resources and deficits. With a high ratio of resources to deficits, the individual may be open to new ways of coping, and be able to mobilize the energy to undertake whatever learning of new behaviors and reorganization of current psychological structures is necessary. For the individual who possesses a low ratio of resources to deficits, however, the outcome is more likely to involve physical or psychological dysfunction. This type of individual can become so preoccupied with defending the self against the perceived threat that he or she cannot be open and responsive to the environment and, is thus, unable to find new solutions. The resulting state of perpetual defensiveness, nonresolution, and instability renders such a person particularly susceptible to the development of physical or psychological dysfunction.

CONCLUSION

Many things happen to us as adults. We may experience marriage, childbirth, parenthood, divorce, remarriage, promotion, retirement, economic prosperity, war, accident, or illness. We will all experience death. A life-event framework allows us to examine these events as significant antecedents of development. From a life-span developmental perspective, this approach is particularly useful because it directs our attention to the interaction between the individual and the larger context in which he or she lives. In the remaining chapters of the book, we will examine the major life events and transitions which occur during young adulthood, middle age, and old age.

CHAPTER SUMMARY

Individuals experience many transitions during the life course, which can be defined by various life events. These events may be viewed as antecedents of developmental change. Within this framework, life events are seen as potential sources of stress. Through a social-psychological adaptation process, these events may lead to functional or dysfunctional outcomes. The impact of events is mediated by both internal and external resources. Thus, development may be characterized as adaptation to a series of crises precipitated by life events.

Life events may be defined as occurrences that result in a change in the ongoing life pattern of the individual. Events may be age-graded (marriage, retirement), history-graded (war, economic depression), or nonnormative (divorce, illness).

From a life-span developmental perspective, the timing, sequencing, and clustering of life events are important. The timing of age-graded events is defined in part by age norms. As individuals move through the life cycle, they may be on time or off time with respect to various events. Similarly, individuals may experience different sequences or clusters of life events. All these factors appear to affect the way in which life events are experienced.

Several theorists have suggested that there is an underlying structure to adult life. In particular, Levinson has proposed a universal sequence of periods and transitions in the development of men within which life events have their impact. The primary task of the stable periods is to build a life structure by making certain choices and striving to attain certain goals. The primary tasks of the transition periods are to terminate the existing life structure and initiate a new one by reappraising the old choices and goals and moving toward new ones. As a result of this sequence of periods and transitions, different life events may be important at different points in the life cycle.

There are both age and sex differences in exposure to and content of life events. Generally, younger adults report more exposure to life events than older persons. Further, younger adults experience more positive stresses, while older adults experience more negative stresses. Sex differences appear to be even more significant than age differences. In particular, older women appear to have fewer resources than men for dealing with high levels of stress.

There are also cohort differences in exposure to and content of life events produced by cultural changes. These include differences in the frequency of events (e.g., divorce) and in the timing of events (e.g., more rapid exit from the labor force).

In addition to the nature of life events themselves, there are two factors which determine how individuals adapt to life events. The first consists of the characteristics of the individual and environment that mediate the impact of events. These include biological (e.g, health), psychological (e.g., personality), social (e.g., family support), and experiential (e.g, anticipatory socialization) variables. The second consists of the social-psychological adaptation process itself. This includes a sequence of behaviors that involves appraisal of the threat and selection, application, and modification of coping strategies.

32 pgg.

9

YOUNG ADULTHOOD

CHAPTER
OVERVIEW

During young adulthood strong societal norms push individuals toward the development of commitments. In this chapter we will examine three areas of commitment—moral, interpersonal, and mastery or competence. Specific life events— college, marriage, parenthood, work, and divorce—will be discussed as arenas for the development and dissolution of commitments. The role of mediating variables in these events will also be considered.

ISSUES
TO CONSIDER

What does it mean to be committed?

How can commitment be conceptualized and defined?

In what ways can moral reasoning be examined developmentally?

What are the differences between Kohlberg's old and new theory of the development of moral reasoning?

How does the college experience influence moral reasoning?

What factors contribute to the development of interpersonal commitment?

What are the characteristics, functions, and problems of dating?

How are mates selected?

What types of marriages exist, and what factors contribute to a successful marriage?

Why do couples want children?

What is involved in mothering and fathering?

What are current divorce trends?

In what ways and to what extent are people affected by divorce?

INTRODUCTION

Throughout this book, we have discussed specific theories that deal with particular processes. However, many of these theories do not give us insight into the interaction between the individual and society. Lowenthal (1977) proposes that we can look at the interplay between the individual and the social context as the individual moves through successive periods in life by examining the individual's commitments. According to Lowenthal, the most basic commitment is one to "physical, economic, and psychosocial survival, a *sine qua non* for all other commitments" (p. 118). She feels that an individual must have a commitment not just to self-preservation but also to developing a personal sense of dignity and self-worth. Lowenthal suggests that three areas of commitment—moral, interpersonal, and mastery or competence—are particularly significant during young adulthood.

Lowenthal maintains that commitment should be studied in three ways: (1) to identify factors associated with the nature of and changes in commitments, (2) to assess what happens when frustration is experienced while striving for commitments, and (3) to measure how fulfillment and frustration with commitments are handled. Conceptually then, commitments are viewed from a contextual model in which the individual is in a dynamic relationship with the social context. This conceptualization allows us to show how the process areas examined earlier (cognitive, personality, etc.) serve as mediators in the development of commitments and related life events in young adulthood. These mediators account for different levels of commitment and changes in commitments. The mediating process determines what level of frustration is experienced as well as what coping or adaptive strategies will be used to achieve a balance between frustration and fulfillment of commitments.

In this chapter, we will consider the moral, interpersonal, and competence commitments of young adulthood. Specific associated life events—college, marriage, parenthood, and work—will be discussed because they serve as arenas for becoming committed. The nonnormative event of divorce will also be examined to illustrate how frustrations are coped with and how continued attempts in fulfilling commitments are made.

THE CONCEPT OF COMMITMENT

Commitment represents an underlying theme of young adulthood because individuals have been socialized to establish commitments at this period in their lives. A commitment can concern an object alone, (for example, job, wife, or children.) Commitment can also involve a process—an affirmatory experience through which an individual continuously defines his or her identity and involvement in the world. Perry (1970) feels that commitments refer to affirmations "in all the plurality of the relativisitic world—truths, relationships, purposes, activities, and cares, in all their contexts—one affirms what is one's own. As ongoing activities, commitments require the courage of responsibility, and presuppose an acceptance of human limits, including the limit or reason."

(p. 135). For this affirmatory process to occur, individuals must be aware of and cognitively able to consider which commitments are desirable. Individuals must value the end state they are striving for. They must also feel emotional about a commitment. And, finally, they must continue to engage in behavior that will actualize the commitment. Whether individuals decide to continue to work toward commitment to a relationship, to a job, or to moral principles, the important crosscultural features of the process of making and actualizing commitments involve how individuals value the way they think, feel, and act. Hence, a person's sense of self is a critical factor in establishing and maintaining commitments.

Commitments are sometimes sought sequentially. More often, however, they are sought simultaneously, such as in attempting to reach a level of intimacy with a significant other while also striving for commitment to a career. Individuals must balance energies and time in dealing with the relative importance of multiple commitments. A simple analogy may be helpful here. Most parents believe they love each of their children equally, in an absolute, unqualified, committed manner. Yet, under certain circumstances, a parent may show preference for one child over others. Commitments are, in a sense, like the children loved so dearly. They are typically regarded as absolutes, yet they are competing with each other in terms of relative importance.

MORAL COMMITMENT

Developing moral commitment involves increasingly understanding the rules of one's society and, often, behaving in ways consistent with these rules. However, any society can establish any particular *behavior* as moral (e.g., the murder of Jews in Nazi Germany). Thus, behavior alone cannot be an unequivocal measure of morality.

Stages of Moral Reasoning

Kohlberg (1963) is interested not only in what moral responses people make in situations, but also in the reasoning that leads people to a particular response. To assess moral reasoning, he devised a series of stories, each presenting imaginary moral dilemmas. These dilemmas present a conflict that involves the need for choosing between two culturally unacceptable alternatives. The following story is an example.

In Europe, a woman was near death from a special kind of cancer. There was one drug that the doctors thought might save her. It was a form of radium that a druggist in the same town had recently discovered. The drug was expensive to make, but the druggist was charging 10 times what the drug cost him to make. He paid $200 for the radium and charged $2000 for a small dose of the drug. The sick woman's husband, Heinz, went to everyone he knew to borrow money, but he could only get together $1000, which is half of what it cost. He told the druggist that his wife was dying and asked him to sell it cheaper or let *him pay later. But the druggist said: "No, I discovered the drug and I'm going to make money from it." So Heinz got desperate and broke into the man's store to steal the drug for his wife. Should the husband have done that? (Kohlberg, 1963, pp. 18-19)*

In assessing peoples' reactions to the dilemma, the response itself is irrelevant. The reasoning used to resolve the conflict is critical. On the basis of peoples' answers to the questions posed at the end of the stories, respondents were classified as being at various stages, representing various levels of moral reasoning. These levels form a stage theory of developing moral commitment based upon an organismic model.

Originally Kohlberg's six stages were divided into three levels, with two stages associated wtih each level. Recently, he and his collaborators (Colby, 1978; Colby, Kohlberg, & Gibbs, 1980) have redefined the theory and redesigned the coding of responses to the dilemmas. We will consider both the old and new version for several reasons. First, it represents an illustration of the dynamic, changing nature of scientific inquiry. Second, few data have been collected on the new version, and many of the empirical findings are related to the old one. Third, the old version gives more elaborate descriptions of the stages than the new version.

There are no age limits associated with the levels of moral development proposed by Kohlberg. Many of the stages pertain to adult development. It is assumed that the second stage of moral reasoning occurs some time during Piaget's preoperational period of cognitive development, specifically between 2 and 6 years of age. The subsequent stages of moral reasoning are contingent upon formal operational thinking (Kohlberg, 1973). Thus, for Western cultures they are associated with adolescence and adulthood.

Stages of Moral Reasoning

Kohlberg's original levels and stages in the development of moral reasoning are presented in Table 9.1. In the present version of the theory (Colby, 1978; Colby, Kohlberg, & Gibbs, 1980; Kohlberg, 1976, 1978) the definitions of the first five stages have been altered and the last stage has been deleted. These newly conceptualized stages are presented in Table 9.2. The developmental trend, cutting across all stages, is toward increasing the scope of people's interactions in society. These interactions move from a level at which an individual wants to be perceived as "good" by others to an institutional level, and reflect an increasing ability to handle abstractions (e.g., from a simple conception of rightness versus wrongness to the idea of a contract between self and society).

Longitudinal data were collected by Kohlberg and his associates (Colby, Kohlberg, & Gibbs, 1980) on a group of adult males who were in childhood and adolescence when first tested. Findings from this sample support the idea of a stage sequence for moral development. The data show that movement from

---

TABLE 9.1
KOHLBERG'S ORIGINAL STAGES OF MORAL REASONING

Level 1: preconventional moral reasoning

Moral reasoning involves the influence of physical and external events and objects. Societal standards are not used as a means for making decisions about moral rightness or wrongness.

Stage 1: Obedience and punishment orientation   An act is considered wrong or right when it does or does not receive punishment. Powerful authority figures play a key role because they have the power to punish.

Stage 2: Naively egotistic orientation   The needs of a person are considered in determining the rightness or wrongness of an act. If a person steals to get food because of being very hungry, the act of stealing is thought of as morally right.

Level 2: conventional moral reasoning

An act is viewed as moral when it agrees with the established order of society. A person's thinking, therefore, reflects acting as others expect.

Stage 3: Good-person orientation   A person wants to be seen as "good." Stereotyped societal roles are used as prescriptions for winning the approval of others and being labeled a good person. Acts are judged as moral when they help others or lead to the approval of others.

Stage 4: Authority and social-order-maintenance orientation   The rules and institutions of society are seen as ends in themselves rather than as a way of earning approval. Acts are considered moral when they maintain rules of society and allow institutions to continue functioning. At this stage a person may start to think about what *society* must do to behave morally. As these considerations continue to develop, a person will move into the next level of moral reasoning.

Level 3: postconventional moral reasoning

Rules of institutions and society are no longer thought of as ends in themselves. These rules are considered to be relative, subjective, and arbitrary.

Stage 5: Contractual legalistic orientation   A person sees the implicit reciprocal contract between self and society. Thus, conforming to rules will provide certain protections to the individual.

Stage 6: Conscience, or principle orientation   A person sees the arbitrary features of contracts with society. Thus, the individual's conscience, in essence, determines whether an act is moral. The individual identifies universal principles of morality that transcend societal rules.

Source: Based on Kohlberg, 1963.

one stage to the next is gradual, and so a person often exhibits more than one kind of reasoning at a time. Figure 9.1 indicates the percentage of each kind of reasoning at each different age level for men who continued in the study. Although different kinds of reasoning occur at different ages, stage 1 and 2 reasoning predominated in childhood, stage 2 and 3 in adolescence, and stage 3 and 4 in young adulthood. Note that stage 5 reasoning does not show a substantial increase until the mid-twenties, suggesting that the development of higher levels of moral reasoning is an adult phenomenon. When average moral maturity scores derived from people's responses to the dilemma interviews are

TABLE 9.2
KOHLBERG'S REDEFINED STAGES OF MORAL REASONING

Level I: preconventional

Stage 1: Heteronomous morality Interests and viewpoints of others not recognized. Person's perspective is egocentric. Actions are still considered physically, not psychologically, as with the earlier stage 1 description.

Stage 2: Individualism, instrumental purpose, and exchange A person is viewed as having interests to pursue, and people may have conflicts over opposing views. Thus, awareness of people having concrete individualistic perspectives exists.

Level II: conventional

Stage 3: Mutual interpersonal expectations, relationships, and interpersonal conformity A person is considered in relation to others. There is awareness of shared feelings, agreements, and expectations. The golden rule is supported. A generalized perspective of morality does not exist.

Stage 4: Social system and conscience Areas of interpersonal motives and agreement are separated from societal viewpoints. The system is supported in terms of rules and roles.

Level III: postconventional, or principled

Stage 5: Social contract or utility and individual rights Individual and societal perspectives are integrated by formal mechanisms (contracts, due process, etc.). Both moral and legal points of view are considered. These are seen to be often in conflict and difficult to integrate.

Source: Based on Kohlberg, 1976.

Figure 9.1 Mean percentage of reasoning at each stage for each age group. *(From Colby, Kohlberg, & Gibbs, 1980.)*

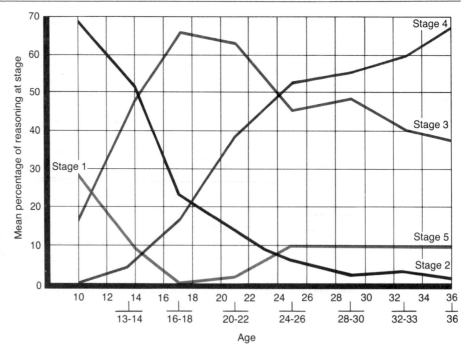

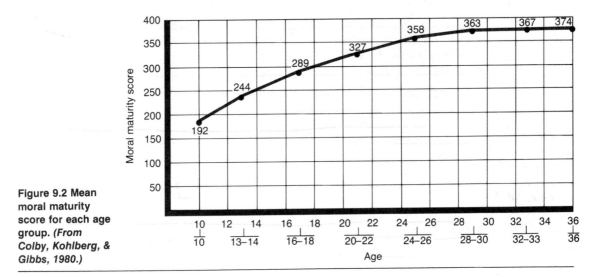

Figure 9.2 Mean moral maturity score for each age group. (From Colby, Kohlberg, & Gibbs, 1980.)

plotted, as in Figure 9.2, the curve shows a continuous, smooth increase with age.

Mediating Processes

Many factors have been reported to mediate moral reasoning. We will illustrate the mediating influence of cognition, personality, and socialization.

Cognition Considerable data show that people who function at more advanced levels of moral reasoning are also functioning at the level of formal operations (Faust & Arbuthnot, 1978; Walker & Richards, 1979). Moreover, experiencing a cognitive conflict between knowledge associated with two different stages is associated with changes in moral reasoning. Turiel (1969) suggests that people who are between stages rather than at a particular stage may be more receptive to the positive effects of cognitive conflict in facilitating advanced moral reasoning. He says that "[such] stage mixture serves to facilitate the perceptions of contradictions making the individual more suscepti- ble to disequilibrium and consequently more likely to progress developmentally" (p. 130).

There is some support for the notion that cognitive conflict accounts for increased advanced-level moral reasoning among young adults. Lazarowitz, Stephen, and Friedman (1976) showed that college students were positively influenced by exposure to reasoning above their own level in a laboratory situation. However, when young adults were at lower levels of moral reasoning (stages 1 and 2), their reasoning was not changed by reasoning different from their own. In fact, when a more advanced reason was given (e.g., a stage 3 reason was given to a stage 2 person), reactions were negative. This may be because cognitive conflict only operates to increase the level of moral reasoning in some cases, because different people have different emotional reactions to moral statements, or because not all people go through a stagelike progression. Any of these positions remains possible at this time.

It is also possible that other variables cause the cognitive conflict which in turn influences moral reasoning. In a study of college students (Arbuthnot, 1975), an immediate and delayed increase in moral-reasoning scores resulted when role playing was used in a moral-dilemma situation against an opponent who used reasoning that was one stage above the subject's initial assessed stage. Role playing at a higher moral level than one's own may enhance moral reasoning because it produces cognitive conflict.

[handwritten margin note: Role play may ↑ moral reasoning because it produces a cognitive conflict.]

Personality   Aspects of personality development also relate to moral reasoning. Loevinger (1966; Loevinger & Wessler, 1970) proposes a model of ego development that describes a stage involving feelings of autonomy, coping with conflict, and toleration of differences that is comparable to postconventional moral reasoning. In this model, people who are conforming and conscientious seem to correspond with people who show stage 3 and stage 4 moral reasoning.

Socialization   The possible implications of socialization research for studies on moral development are extensive. Since Kohlberg's longitudinal study is the only one, thus far, that assesses moral reasoning in adults, greater research efforts are needed to understand the development of moral reasoning and explain individual differences. Perhaps certain cohorts are more advanced in moral reasoning because of a particular patterning of their life events. Perhaps specific settings foster the development of moral reasoning.

Research indicates that most American adults are at stage 4 in their moral reasoning (Turiel, 1969). Some groups, however, reason at more advanced levels, e.g., today's adolescents and young adults who have experienced certain familial and social settings (Haan, 1978; Haan, Smith, & Block, 1968).

Over a two-year period, Rest (1975) conducted a longitudinal study of young adults (aged 16 to 20 years), assessing them twice on moral reasoning and moral attitudes as well as other measures that might be correlated with moral reasoning. Both younger and older groups showed increases in moral reasoning scores which were correlated with changes in socially sanctioned attitudes. The younger group shifted from preconventional to conventional thought. The high school graduates who went to college changed twice as much in principled reasoning as did noncollege people. It appears, then, that there is something in the college milieu that facilitates moral reasoning.

Perhaps specific aspects of behavior in particular contexts foster moral reasoning. In an extensive study of male and female college students and in-training Peace Corps volunteers, Haan, Smith, and Block (1968) reported that young adults who scored highest on Kohlberg's moral-dilemma measure were also most actively involved in political and social activities and were more likely to have had interruptions in their college careers. The men of this group portrayed the "ideal" male as perceptive, empathic, and altruistic. The women of this group portrayed the ideal woman as rebellious and free.

Young adults reasoning at a conventional level were not likely to engage in political and social activities or interrupt their college careers. They felt that the ideal person, regardless of sex, possesses self-control and social skills. Men and women perceived the ideal person of their own sex traditionally. For instance, the ideal male was characterized as practical, sociable, and orderly rather than curious, rebellious, or individualistic.

Those people at the preconventional level of reasoning experienced interruptions in their college careers and showed a strong sex difference in political and social activities. Men belonged to fewer organizations than those reasoning at higher moral levels, but participated at an intense level. The women in this group were the greatest joiners, but participated the least compared with women in the other two groups. Men and women perceived the ideal person of their own sex as rejecting interpersonal obligations and as stubborn and aloof.

Obviously, then, an individual's level of moral reasoning is related to different attitudes, personality, and behavior. However, the question still remains, "What makes certain environments such as college a facilitator for moral reasoning for some people and not for others?" To put it another way, "Why is there such variability in moral reasoning among young adults in college?"

Different family histories could be one answer to these questions. Young adult college students who were at different levels of moral reasoning reported different family interactions. A key finding for both men and women was that conflict with the same-gender parent was related strongly to advanced levels of moral reasoning. However, intense family conflict (especially for men and with fathers) was associated with thinking at a preconventional level. When little to no family conflict was reported, individuals were at a conventional level of thinking (Haan, Smith, & Block, 1968). Again, the idea of cognitive conflict emerges. Perhaps cognitive conflict—one way to enhance advanced-level moral reasoning—is socialized in family contexts. Since the college environment is one which is conducive to cognitive conflict, we will consider the event of college as a possible arena for developing moral commitment.

College

Perry (1970) studied the responses of about 500 students (aged 17 to 22) enrolled in a single college during the years 1954 to 1963. These students answered a checklist of educational views and were interviewed. The results led Perry to propose a scheme of intellectual and ethical development consisting of nine positions which reflect movement toward realizing moral commitment as an ongoing, unfolding activity through which life-style is expressed. Since male-female differences were not evident, the scheme applies to the entire group of young adults. The following reflects the nature of intellectual and ethical development in a college environment:

Position 1: The world is viewed in polar terms of we-right-good versus others-wrong-bad. Right answers exist in the absolute.

Position 2: Diversity of opinion and uncertainty are thought of as the result of guidelines given by poorly qualified authorities or as an exercise designed so that individuals can learn for themselves.

Position 3: Diversity and uncertainty are considered legitimate but temporary because authorities have not found the answers. Standards are puzzling.

Position 4: Uncertainty and diversity are legitimate, and people are entitled to their opinions. Relativistic reasoning within a context is discovered.

Position 5: All knowledge and values are viewed as relativistic within contexts.

Position 6: Orientation to relativism occurs through a simple form of personal commitment.

Position 7: A commitment is made in an area.

Position 8: Implications of a commitment are explored along with issues of responsibility.

Position 9: Identity is affirmed through commitment, the balancing of commitments, and the realization of multiple responsibilities.

Perry also feels that many undergraduate students experience conditions of delay, deflection, or regression. Students may exploit the opportunities for detachment which are offered in positions 4 and 5. This is referred to as temporizing. Thus, responsibility may be denied through passivity or through alienation that is used opportunistically. Or students may retreat, using the dualistic, absolutist positions 2 or 3. Finally, there are numerous reasons why some students may delay their advancement to a higher level of commitment, or escape advancement altogether.

Perry contends that the way in which students develop commitments is related to their styles of life and areas of concern. The areas of concern include decisions regarding major field, career, religion, tastes, morality, politics, finances, social concerns, friendship, and marriage. The stylistic aspects of commitment reflect a balancing of external and internal decisions. External balances involve decisions about time spent on studies and extracurricular activities, number and intensity of friendships, amount of altruistic social service, degree of specialization versus breadth, etc. The internal striving for equilibrium involves inner acceptances, affirmations, or commitments. These include:

1. Action and contemplation: "I've come to learn when to say something to myself, well, now enough of this mulling and doubting, let's do something" (p. 38).

2. Permanence and flexibility: "I used to think I had to finish anything I started or I'd be a quitter; now I see it's a nice point when to stop something that may be unprofitable and put the effort in more hopeful directions" (p. 38).

3. Control and openness: "It's good to have a plan, but if you insist on following it without a change ever . . ." (pp. 38–49).

4. Intensity and perspective: "That's the trick, I guess, you have to have detachment, or you get lost, you can't see yourself and your relation to what you're doing, and yet if you stay detached you never learn from total involvement, you never live . . ." (p. 39).

Thus, Perry maintains that a "liberal education" goes beyond the content of courses and provides opportunities for development toward moral commitment.

INTERPERSONAL COMMITMENT

In youth you find out what you care to do and who you care to be—even in changing roles. In young adulthood you learn whom you care to be with—at

Developing a relationship involves openness, honesty, and expressiveness by both individuals. (Bernstein/Editorial Photocolor Archives)

work and in private life, not only exchanging intimacies, but sharing intimacy. (Erikson, 1974, p. 124)

As younger adults make decisions about ways to focus their lives, they seek to establish intimacy rather than isolation (Erikson, 1974). Many interpersonal decisions are made by individuals in this age grade about whom to date and whether or not to marry, and, if the decision is to marry, about who should become a marital partner.

Toward Interpersonal Intimacy

What does it mean to be committed to another individual? An interpersonally committed person is pledged to a relationship. A mature, intimate, committed relationship is rooted in love that does not diminish a person's independent identity, but reinforces it.

According to Erikson (1963), a strong sense of self is necessary in order to achieve intimacy. A weak identity actually can prevent an individual from establishing a close relationship. As identities alter over the life span, one or both adults may experience periods of a weak identity. This may make it difficult to maintain the relationship. The reason most often cited for the association of a weak identity and poor interpersonal commitment is that numerous demands are placed on one person for fulfilling the needs of the other. The person with a weak sense of self needs a great deal of praise and can be threatened by the strengths of the other individual. Although the strong person may enjoy this position of personal security, communication problems usually develop.

Erikson (1959, 1963) also acknowledges that during young adulthood an individual is supposed to help contribute to the perpetuation of society. This is usually accomplished by young adults who create an interpersonal relationship, socially sanction it with marriage, and allow reproduction to occur. The psychosocial pressure for individuals during this stage of life is to form a close, stable interpersonal relationship. If stability is lacking, there is little assurance that children will be socialized appropriately; hence the perpetuation role will not be served properly. Although it is possible to bear children outside of marriage, these children, for Erikson, are not in a context that is likely to maximize societally approved socialization.

Erikson argues that to successfully maintain a close and stable relationship, each person must give of himself or herself totally. All aspects of a person, such as ideas, goals, dreams, feelings, and values, must be shared unconditionally with the other person, who, in turn, must reciprocate. Each individual should no longer focus on self, but rather should be more interested in meeting the needs of the other and deriving satisfaction from meeting those needs. The relationship will be maintained to the extent that such mutual interchange is attained. When a person cannot share or be shared, a sense of isolation will be felt which will erode the relationship.

As we discussed previously, Erikson proposed that development occurs in a series of stages, each of which is characterized by a crisis, for example, between a sense of identify versus role confusion (late adolescence) and

Discovery

BOX 9.1

PERSPECTIVES ON LOVE

Question What were your expectations of love before and after marriage or cohabitation?

Husband (*age 88*): After my first wife died (we were married 43 years), I remarried 2 years later. I knew my present wife for 25 years so I knew what I was in for. With my age, I feel that sex still is an important part of love, but it is not everything. There was no serious difference. My two wives were home economics majors and make a nice home. I have had no sacrifices with my new wife. She is unselfish and liberal. I have learned a lot from her. With her, I have a much richer life. Our social life increased because she has many friends. She is a good companion. Loving one another enhances my capacity to love other people. She has helped me prepare for older age. There is no selfishness in our marriage and this means there is love.

Wife (*age 67*): I worked for 38 years before getting married. Before marriage I experienced filial love or love of friends and agape love or love of the unlovable, without it being returned, but I had not experienced eros or erotic love. Since my marriage I feel fulfilled and loved. We have very good companionship and there is more sex than I anticipated. As a single woman, I was not invited to many places, but now I have plunged into having lots of couples as friends. It has been very pleasant; I feel fulfilled. I want to help others and there is no need for return. My family has broad-ened because my husband had one child from his first marriage and now I have that family as part of my own. In general, my husband does more of some things and I do more of others, but they balance and we have security and companionship. This is love.

Young woman cohabiting: Before I moved in with_____, I knew I loved him. We were realistic. I did not love him all the time; in fact, sometimes I hated the things he did and I told him. Maybe I just grew up, but it was love. I needed to be with him. Together we have security and now I don't have to be around him all the time. I think our communication is what is terrific. We talk and exchange thoughts and feelings. I have learned so much about myself.

Young man married: After being married 4 years, love as such is not as conscious as it was before marriage and yet a strong intimate relationship is there. I don't think about whether I love her anymore, I just know it. Love, for me, is commitment.

Middle-aged married woman: After many broken engagements (that I initiated), I have become realistic about love. We love each other. We have security and trust. But since the kids, their demands come first and ours later. Love is really a meshing of two lives together, a give and take.

Source: From Deutsch & Goldberg, 1974

between intimacy and isolation (young adulthood). Constantinople (1969) devised a study to see whether supporting data for Erikson's stages of development could be found. More than 900 male and female college students, freshman through seniors, were assessed in 1965, and subgroups were reassessed in 1966 and 1967. A sixty-item test, designed to reflect the way in which each positive and negative aspect of a stage crisis was resolved, was developed. High scores on positive dimensions (e.g., identity, industry) and low scores on negative areas (e.g., diffusion, inferiority) would indicate successful resolution of a stage crisis. Constantinople found that across all groups, scores on the positive areas increased over time while those on the negative decreased. There was more successful resolution of stage crises among males and females having higher college standing and more among seniors than freshman. These findings are interesting because they suggest that aspects of socialization, (in this case the college experience,) may mediate in the development of the ability to make interpersonal commitment. Moreover, stage resolution for intimacy versus isolation was not very evident for younger college students, which is (consistent with Erikson's position) Follow-up data showed consistent increases in the successful resolution of the crisis between identity and role confusion from freshman to senior years across subjects and from one year to the next within subject groups. Thus, perhaps college students who have just resolved their identities are also just beginning to deal with intimacy issues. When other changes in scores occurred, however, they did not always reflect the process Erikson proposes and often were explained by cohort and time-of-measurement effects. Constantinople's data, then, provide partial support for the stagelike character of ego development offered by Erikson and raise interesting thoughts about the interaction of commitments and contexts (e.g., college).

Dating and Courtship

Although many older people date, it is viewed as "an activity characteristic of adolescents and young adults" (Winch, 1971, p. 259) because it assists individuals in being emancipated from families of origin. What are the characteristics, functions, and problems of dating?

Characteristics of dating   As long ago as the 1930s, Waller (1937) assessed dating among college students at the Pennsylvania State University. He found that students perceived dating as a recreational activity in which campus leadership, money, a car, and good clothes are the most important characteristics. In serious courtship, however, personality features are considered important. These aspects of dating were assessed as a dimension of the "Rating Dating Complex" in terms of points scored with a date. However, other researchers (e.g., Gorer, 1964) maintained that dating is a positive competitive game in which "the ideal date is one in which both partners are so popular, so skilled, and so self-assured that the result is a draw" (p. 114).

Most people feel that the distinctions between casual dating and a serious relationship are not clear. DeLora (1963) proposed, for instance, that dating is best viewed as a continuum from "casual" to "engaged", this is depicted in Table 9.3.

Functions of dating   Dating can function as a recreational or socializing activity, it can serve as a means to achieve status and it can be a way to select a mate. Although many people contemplate marriage at some point during dating, not all people progress along the dating continuum. Also, not all dates serve a particular function. In a retrospective study, for instance, Hicks (1970) reported that among married couples at the Pennsylvania State University different forms of dating were perceived as serving different

TABLE 9.3
TYPES OF DATING

Casual	Steady	Going Steady	Preengaged	Engaged
Goals				
Getting acquainted	Entertainment; enjoyment	Companionship	Trial engagement	Getting ready for marriage
Norms				
Interpersonal; Uninvolved; Rational	Individualistic; free; No commitment	Personalized; Monogamous; Intimate; Emotional	Personalized; Monogamous; Intimate; Emotional; Future-oriented	Personalized; Monogamous; Intimate; Emotional; Future-oriented; Rational plans

Source: Adapted from De Lora, 1963.

functions. Only casual or steady dating was considered fun and recreational. On the other hand, "going steady" served a socializing function: those informally engaged were planning for the future, and couples formally engaged were busy making wedding plans.

Dating, indeed, serves as a means of socializing and, therefore, is a way for individuals to discover whether they are fun to be with, overly emotional, too serious, and so on. As Winch (1971) states: "The opportunity to associate with those of the opposite gender gives a person the chance to try his own personality and to discover things about the personalities of others" (p. 351).

Mate selection is a primary function of dating. Although our system of mate selection is flexible, it is also competitive. Many complex rules, strategies, and goals are followed. For example, it is often considered a social norm for men to move a relationship toward sexual intimacy before making a final decision on selecting a mate. For women, on the other hand, the goal is to move the relationship toward commitment.

Since dating can serve varied functions for different people, how do couples maintain their interest? According to Waller (1938), who created the expression "the principle of least interest," the person who is least interested in continuing a dating relationship is in the power position, meaning in a position to dominate or perhaps exploit the other person. Given the possibility of such an imbalance, Hill, who revised Waller's book (1951), grimly addressed the consequences:

Once the relationship has become exploitative, the likelihood that it can progress through other stages is probably decreased . . . the prolongation of some of these unbalanced, least-interest dominated relationships produces some very unsatisfactory marriages. . . . A further consequence of the principle is that one who has suffered exploitation in one affair may try to be the exploiter in the next. (p. 191)

Problems of dating Insincerity and superficiality in dating are serious problems in our society, and attitudes fostered by dating may lead to difficulties in marital relations, too. Perhaps the lack of sincerity in dating results from its multiple functions. How can we demand, on the one hand, that dating be fun and recreational, and, on the other hand, expect it to be a serious process leading to mate selection.

An interview study of people dating and selecting a mate for the second time, revealed that all people felt that "on round two" they were much clearer about what kind of person they wanted and what behaviors were expected (Westhoff, 1975). Specifically, they wanted to develop a sincere, committed relationship. As one college administrator recalls:

My first marriage was an automatic act, the thing I was supposed to do after graduation from college, something expected of me at that point. . . . Nobody made me remotely aware of all the preparation and skills. . . . I had to face most of these important things just winging it. . . . (p. 11)

Since a high proportion of parents attempt to influence dating behavior with tactics such as persuasion or threats, balancing what an individual wants to do with parental approval is often difficult (Bates, 1942; Sussman, 1953). Seeking approval from peers can also present difficulties for individuals who do not have certain prerequisites. Elder (1969), for instance, found that females' physical attractiveness is an important determinant of males' reactions to females and is an initial determinant of their liking them. Also, for college females, there is a strong positive relationship between the frequency of dating and feelings of self-esteem. Being asked for a date can contribute to a good self-concept, and a good self-concept can make an individual appealing to date (Klemer, 1971).

Mate Selection

Models of mate selection Of the findings dealing with mate selection in our culture, the clearest is that people marry people who are similar to themselves. When partners are similar on some social and psychological dimensions, the marriage is called a *homogamous* one. Today a great majority of marriages are between people of the same racial origin who have similar educational and socioeconomic backgrounds (Melville, 1977).

Thus, it seems not to be the case that opposites attract. Researchers have not been able to support the theory of *heterogamy* in mate selection (e.g., Bowerman & Day, 1956). Young adults, however, were not aware of their complementary behaviors or traits, and they stated that these were not relevant for mate selection.

Among the most important aspects of likes being attracted to likes are:

1. As a result of similar attitudes and values, people from the same social class marry.

2. People are likely to meet when they live near each other (residential propinquity), which occurs for people with the same social background.
3. Marriage partners are similar in ways related to particular racial and ethnic backgrounds because a great proportion of people of the same racial and ethnic origins marry (ethnic endogamy).
4. Parental, familial, and peer pressures promote social homogamy.
5. Marriage is likely to occur between people of the same social class because educational opportunities are more available to the middle and upper social strata.

Although homogamy predominates in terms of characteristics such as race, religion, age, education, and location of residence, people who marry do differ on such factors as personality, attitudes, and needs.

Premarital sexual behavior In a cross-sequential study conducted from 1958 to 1968, Christensen and Gregg (1970) compared data among three groups: (1) Danish college students, (2) a conservative group of Mormon college students, and (3) a Midwestern college population. During the ten-year period attitudes and behavior about premarital sex became more liberal, especially for women, even though males continued to be more liberal than females. Among the Danish population, increasing similarity between male and female premarital sexual behavior and attitudes was evidenced. Moreover, this intersexual convergence was apparent in that more than 95 percent of men and women reported having had a premarital sexual experience. Both American samples reported approving of premarital intercourse. Females in the American samples reported a threefold increase in premarital sexual intercourse over the ten-year period. However, Americans seem to be maintaining a traditional view about sexual behavior prior to marriage. That is, premarital sexual behavior is said to occur only in the context of intimacy and love. Therefore, many young adults experience sex within a committed relationship. Nevertheless, attitudes still reflect a double standard. It is still more acceptable for males to have casual sexual experiences than it is for females (Kaats & Davis, 1970). However, casual sex for females meets greater approval in the 1970s than it did in the 1960s (Kaats & Davis, 1970). Despite some changing attitudes and behavior, it appears that we are not witnessing a revolution in premarital sexual behavior, but rather an evolution.

Marriage

Types of marriage After intensive interview sessions with 437 upper-middle-class married couples, Cuber and Harroff (1965) identified five types of marriages:

1. *Conflict-habituated:* Arguing, bickering, nagging, or fighting prevail, but are

Controversy

BOX 9.2
MARRIAGE CONTRACT

A marriage contract can serve as one way for a couple to clarify and reconcile individual and shared assumptions, goals, and values. It explicitly states the rules and expectations for living together (Harshbarger & Bogdanoff, 1972; Harshbarger, 1974, 1976). Some possible issues to be included and questions to be addressed in a marriage contract are as follows:

1. Issue: family planning
   a. Do we want to have children? If yes, answer b to d.
   b. Should we adopt or have our own?
   c. How many children and how should they be spaced?
   d. Do we support birth control? If yes, answer e.
   e. What methods of birth control should be used?

2. Issue: childrearing
   a. How would physical responsibilities for children be allocated?
   b. What type of parent-child interaction would be supported?
      Type of physical contact?
      Kind of discipline?
      Amount of time spent?
      Use of child-care facilities?
   c. What kind, if any, of religious education is desired?
   d. What are our feelings about sex education?

3. Issue: place of residence
   a. Who and what will determine where we live (for example, either set of parents, our occupations)?
   b. What kind of geographical locale is preferred?
   c. What type of home is desired?
   d. What kind of neighborhood is preferred?
   e. What kinds of physical arrangements are desired in the home (for example, sleeping arrangements, recreational space)?

4. Issue: family income
   a. Who will work?
   b. How much time should either or both spend working (part-time versus full-time)?
   c. How will the income be allocated?
      Joint or separate checking accounts?
      Joint or separate savings accounts?
   d. Who will manage financial matters?
      Giving allowances?
      Paying bills?
   e. Who will decide about major and/or minor expenditures?

5. Issue: household tasks
   a. What division of labor is preferred (for example, should tasks be divided equally, shared, rotated periodically)?
   b. If we cannot manage all household tasks, then what should be done (for example, should we reduce the amount of time spent working outside the home, or should we hire help)?

6. Issue: choice of life-style
   a. How do we feel about open or closed marriages, friendships with members of the opposite sex, separate vacations, and so on?
   b. What things do we value (for example, getting ahead, raising a family, meeting different people)?
   c. Should we live as a nuclear family or not? If not, how should we live (for example, as a group, commune, extended family)?
   d. What are our attitudes about sex?
      How important is sex in our lives?
      Do we support sexual monogamy?
   e. How important is disclosing feelings to each other?
      Should we maintain open communication in all areas?
      Should we objectively criticize each other when we become annoyed over a behavior?
   f. What should we do if the relationship is not working?
      Do we support divorce?
      Do we support family or marriage counseling?

Source: From Goldberg and Deutsch, 1977.

viewed by the couple as acceptable behaviors, which may even provide stability.

2. *Devitalized:* Although the couple is bored or disenchanted with the marriage, they believe that they still have love for each other.

3. *Passive-congenial:* Conflict is always minimized; marriage is considered a convenient arrangement, with partners not being involved with each other.

4. *Vital:* Partners are highly and actively involved with each other in all aspects of family life.

5. *Total:* There is a profound, intense involvement with each other. Involvement is so complete that the couple may be perceived as isolated and neurotic.

Marital sexual behavior Hunt (1974) measured sexual activity and pleasure in marriage with numerous questionnaires. He reported substantial differences from the findings of the Kinsey reports (Kinsey, Pomeroy, & Martin, 1948, 1953). Specifically, for instance, Hunt found increases in the frequency of sexual intercourse, frequency of female orgasm during sexual activity, and the number of married people who feel sex is "pleasurable." With more information about sex available today, accessibility to contraceptives, and emphasis on sexual therapy (Masters & Johnson, 1966, 1970), sexual activity in marriage appears to play a major role for younger cohorts. These trends seem to reflect a change in cultural attitudes compared with those in evidence twenty-five years ago. They will also be instrumental in producing continuing cultural change.

Parenthood

In our culture individuals are socialized to believe that after marriage the role of parent should be assumed. Parenting is seen as normal and natural. Further, Americans believe that since proper parenting is normal and natural, it is not possible for "good" parents to have "bad" children. Parents are expected to provide appropriate experiences for their children. They are also expected to have confidence in their judgments, feelings, and behavior toward their children.

These attitudes can create problems for adults who are experiencing the life event of parenthood, particularly for the first time. For instance, 50 to 80 percent of new parents reported that the birth of their first child was a moderate to severe crisis (Dyer, 1963; LeMasters, 1957). But recent evidence (e.g., Hobbs & Cole, 1976) suggests that the birth of the first child is viewed as "moderately stressful" by parents who also reported that many rewards were experienced with the advent of their new role.

There also appears to be a sex difference in how individuals experience parenthood. Women who had borne their first child reported that the postpartum period was characterized by emotional stress and negative mood changes. Men, on the other hand, did not report such changes (Leifer, 1977).

There are many reasons that these data are contradictory. First, in earlier studies interviews rather than questionnaires were employed to obtain data. These interviews reflect higher crisis scores compared with the questionnaires. Hobbs and Cole (1976) expressed concern about the low return rates (less than

50 percent) for the questionnaires in their study. Second, reasons for having children could influence the way in which parenthood is regarded. Was the child conceived because the couple loves children? Did the couple want to remove the pressure of parents desirous of being grandparents? Did they desire a replacement for themselves, want to make a statement expressing their love for each other, or want to have someone take care of them in old age? Moreover, was the child planned or not? Third, differences in socioeconomic status could explain the equivocal findings. Russell (1974) found that middle-class couples stated that fewer rewards are accrued from parenting than did working-class couples. But middle-class parents read more books on childrearing than lower-class parents, and these books, though helpful, are often used as a standard by which parents judge themselves. As a result, middle-class couples who are parents for the first time may be more anxious than lower-class couples. This anxiety could contribute to their crisis perspective about parenthood.

In addition, since the husband-wife relationship is valued more by middle-class couples than lower-class couples, the birth of the first child could be more disruptive. For example, the amount of time spouses interact by talking with one another is reduced by as much as 50 percent after their first child arrives.

Other sources of stress for middle-class American parents have been delineated by Rossi (1968):

1. *Cultural pressure:* Society sanctions commitment to parenthood as an event that is normal in an adult's life course. Hence, for couples not wanting children, feelings of "are we abnormal?" must be dealt with.
2. *Inception:* Becoming a parent may not be planned or may not be planned well.
3. *Irrevocability:* The parental role is irrevocable. Almost any other decision relating to life events can be changed or reversed, but parenthood cannot.
4. *Preparation:* Individuals are not formally trained to be parents. It is assumed that because people have been children and interacted with care givers they will know what to do with their children. The assumption is that parenthood is natural, normal, and right.
5. *Guidance:* There is no recipe for determining what are the best reasons for having a child or which childrearing practices will produce competent, mentally healthy adults.

Thus, we can conclude that, for many reasons, parenthood is a crisis for some young adults while for others it represents a positive transition to a newly acquired role. Regardless of whether parenthood is perceived as crisis or transition, as stressful or rewarding, men and women experience parenthood differently.

Mothering The decision about whether to be or not to be a mother is a difficult one for many young women in our culture. Many social sanctions exist

Parenthood represents an irreversible role that can make achieving other desired roles more difficult. (United Press International)

pressuring women to make a commitment to motherhood. Many women have been socialized to believe that they will naturally love their child and will be able to nurture him or her properly. This view of the supposed norm is derived from the notion that something exists known as the "maternal instinct"; that is, there is a natural, normal fit between women and motherhood.

The concept of maternal instinct was widely expressed in the psychoanalytic and ethological writings of the 1950s and 1960s. Bowlby (1969), for instance, portrayed the mother-child relationship as intimate, loving, dedicated, and natural: "What is believed to be essential for mental health is that an infant and young child should experience a warm, intimate, and continuous relationship with his mother (or permanent mother-substitute—one person who steadily mother's him) in which both find satisfaction and enjoyment" (Bowlby, 1972, p. 13). Although the mother's constant presence was thought to be critical for satisfactory child development, parenting goals were not explicitly advanced. Rather, Bowlby (1972) developed a deprivation thesis, which suggested that an impoverished child becomes a socially incapable adult and depriving parent. However, many developmentalists (e.g., Hoffman, 1974; Rutter, 1974) have turned away from hypotheses supporting the notion of a maternal instinct and from investigations of maternal deprivation. Rutter (1974) states:

That "bad" care of children in early life can have "bad" effects, both short-term and long-term, can be accepted as proven. What is now needed is a more precise delineation of the different aspects of "badness" together with an analysis of their separate effects of the reasons why children differ in their response. (p. 128)

Just as we have moved from supporting the idea that only mothers can parent so too have we recognized that some women may not want to have children or may not want to be the sole caregiver. College women who stated positive attitudes toward feminism, for instance, were more likely not to want to bear or rear children than women who held negative opinions about the women's liberation movement (Loff, 1973). Moreover, investigations of children reared in day-care centers demonstrate no significant differences on many developmental indications (cognition, language, attachment, etc.) between children who received day care and those who were reared entirely at home (Caldwell, Wright, Honig, & Tannenbaum, 1970; Kearsley, Zelazo, Kagan, & Hartmann, 1975). Other researchers (e.g., Hoffman, 1974) have shown that maternal employment has no negative effects on children's development (see Chapter 10).

Fathering   It has traditionally been believed that fathers are important in the childrearing context. However, studies have concentrated on the effects of their absence, and the effects—positive or negative—of their presence have received little research attention. In fact, Mother's Day has been a part of our federal government's recognized calendar since 1914, but it was only in 1972 that American federal law assigned a special day to fathers.

On addressing the undesirable consequences of father absence, particularly to boys, many researchers (e.g., Lynn, 1974) accept the correlational evidence between father absence and juvenile delinquency, despite the controversy about the reasons for the relationship. Delinquency in boys could result from a masculine protest against feminine domination, from inadequate childrearing supervision, from the lack of a male model, and from the resulting loss of family cohesion. The assumption underlying this type of research has been that if a man is a good provider he is a good father. Thus, the research has been narrowly confined to the extreme situation of complete father absence either because of occupational necessities or because of emergencies such as wars.

According to Farrell (1974), men need to redefine their role in the family so they can become involved in childrearing and channel their energies in roles leading to increased fulfillment. Fathers of newborns were observed to be "engrossed" in their infants and stated that they were bonded, absorbed, and preoccupied with their child in a way that did not differ from mothers (Greenberg & Morris, 1974). In fact, the only finding (Parke & O'Leary, 1975) that differentiates mothers' and fathers' behavior toward the first newborn child was the fact that fathers smiled less frequently than mothers.

Men, in general, have the capacity for parenting just as women do, but their family roles often are limited because of the nature of their work roles (Pleck,

Many men enjoy being fathers, and they should be given opportunities for interacting with their children. (Christa Armstrong/Photo Researchers)

1975). Evidence also suggests that men who find themselves in a single-father situation through desertion or divorce, or who are catapulted into a strong parenting role by unemployment, particularly when wives are employed, feel unaccepted, left out, and inadequate (Pleck, 1975).

It seems that fathering needs to be revitalized. Why? Women are demanding it. It is a role that could happen to the best of men. Children need it. And men not only *can* parent, but want to learn more about it (Levine, 1976).

Adoption   Often parenting, whether we refer to mothering or fathering, is thought of as a role for biological parents. But adults can become parents through adoption as well. Just as couples have different reasons for having children, so they give a variety of reasons for adopting children. About one-half of all adoptions in America and Britain are adoptions by step-parents and other relatives. Infertility in one or both parents is another major reason for adopting (Group for the Advancement of Psychiatry, 1973).

Becoming a parent by adoption when infertility is the reason usually involves ambivalent feelings. The infertile person must change his or her self-image from that of a person who is fertile to that of one who is not, which can lead to lower self-esteem (Group for the Advancement of Psychiatry, 1973). Adoptive parents also often have intensified feelings of wanting to be successful parents, which can lead to feelings of failure if the child shows constant concern about the biological parents. This problem, however, varies "depending on the age at which children are adopted and the age at which children are told" (Group for the Advancement of Psychiatry, 1973, p. 85). A consistently recurring problem, then, for both child and parents involves the reconciliation of the conflict involving the discrepancy between the biological and social parentage of the child.

Whether a couple decides to have a child or to adopt a child, the role of parenting should not be undertaken in order to "save" a marriage. In fact, if a child is introduced into a family for this purpose, the likelihood of exacerbating already-existing problems increases dramatically (Rapoport, Rapoport, & Strelitz, 1977).

Divorce

Law and divorce   With a couple's desires to find an intimate, committed relationship can come the realization that the marriage is not working and that it needs to be dissolved. However, the law has been traditionally unwilling to make divorce easy. For years, court proceedings supported the idea that guilt must be assigned to one partner or another, with punitive actions being taken against the marital partner most responsible for the "breakup" of the marriage and social entitlements accorded to the "injured" partner and withheld from the guilty one. After the Matrimonial Causes Act of 1937, the number of divorces granted increased dramatically, and after the Divorce Reform Act of 1969 and the Matrimonial Proceedings Act of 1970, the bases on which a divorce could be

In Depth

BOX 9.3

VOLUNTARY CHILDLESSNESS: A REVERSIBLE DECISION

Why do married people decide not to have children or adopt children? If the onset of parenting would conflict with expending major energy in one's career, some people delay parenting or postpone it permanently. Even if the possible conflict between family and occupational involvement is not a factor, some people do not see a personal developmental potential for themselves in parenthood. Others have expressed that they do not wish to be affiliated with a cohort based upon their children's ages.

For women, age is a critical factor, since it affects fertility. For women who choose a career first, then family, the likelihood of achieving the second goal may be difficult after the age of thirty. If a woman who is over thirty wants to be a mother as well as maintain a career, she may be well advised to reconsider her options periodically. Obviously some women take this factor into account, as illustrated by the remarks of a voluntarily childless woman:

We re-examine the situation from time to time, as I don't think it's something you can just decide for good. I don't think it can be, especially for a woman, because time runs out and then you find you can't have children whether you want them or not. (Read, 1974, p. 30)

Regardless of the reasons for remaining childless (temporarily or permanently), voluntary childlessness seems to be becoming more legitimate than in the past, as evidenced by the influence of organizations (e.g., NOW).

An example of the thought processes involved in deciding whether to have or not to have children are the opinions of a husband obtained five years apart.

Age 30. Deciding not to have children was a critical event for us. I think the first reason for us even before I started graduate school was that it made sense to spend our money other ways. Children are very expensive and we just didn't want the expense of a child when we couldn't afford it so well. I think the major reason, the one that I feel is my most important reason, is that I just didn't feel ready, I just didn't feel mature enough and I still don't, and I think that if and when we decide to have children it will be when I really feel competent to handle the task and kind of can keep the whole thing low-key enough so that I don't overly interfere with the child's development. I'm thirty so it shouldn't be an issue, but I just don't think that having a child is something you should rush into and I've seen too many parents who get overly wrapped up in their child and I think you hamper the child's development and I'd rather—I think pretty clearly Cindy and I would rather attend to our own development than be currently burdened with a baby.

Age 35. Well, I'm so excited I can't begin to tell you. Cindy and I decided to have a child. We were ready. I wanted to be a father. I finished with school and Cindy was making a pretty good income. We both were going to keep working and share with the baby. Cindy's pregnancy was most enjoyable for me. I enjoyed experiencing how her moods changed and even her appetite. Feeling our child move was very exciting. It was a big baby boy—over nine pounds: healthy and happy. I think he looks like Cindy's side of the family. She says he has my personality. Well, I feel like an old man now. I'm 35 years old and by the time my child is 15, I will be 50. But, if I keep in shape, we should be able to do a lot of things together. You know something. I'm glad we never took permanent action about not having children. Being a father is a marvelous experience.

Source: Authors' files.

obtained were broadened. The rights of children were given no major role until the provisions of the Children's Act in 1975 required child representation and expeditious court proceedings. Although statutes involving divorce and custody are becoming more enlightened, Mead (1971) points out the need for attitude changes about divorce.

If we could rephrase divorce as a necessary component of relationships between the sexes as complex, as heterogeneous, and as rapidly changing and with as long-lived a population as ours, we could then consider how to have good and appropriate divorces. As things are, we insist that the most flimsy, ill-conceived, and unsuitable mating be treated as a sanctified, life-long choice. At the same time, we insist that every divorce, however much it is dictated by every consideration of the welfare of the children and parents, be regarded as a failure and be listed as an index of social disorder—along with suicide, homocide, narcotic addiction, alcoholism and crime. (p. 124)

Divorce trends   In 1976 divorce reached a record high level of 5.0 per 1000 population. The next two years showed no change; further, the number of divorces was about one-half the number of marriages. The proportion of marriages ending in divorce, on a life-time basis, is about 40 percent. These trends do not mean that Americans are abandoning the concept of marriage; in fact, of divorced males under 35 years of age, 50 percent remarry within a year, and of divorced women under 35 years of age, 50 percent remarry within a fourteen-month period. During a three year period, 75 percent of divorced people remarry (U.S. Department of Health, Education, and Welfare, 1973).

Divorce as crisis   Divorce is generally a stressful event. The role of husband or wife is lost, as is an object of love and attachment. Divorced people demonstrate lower self-esteem, suffer from feelings of loneliness, are less productive at work, and are anxious over social situations. New experiences—financial arrangements, living arrangements, child care problems, finding or maintaining a position, establishing a household, etc.—are also faced. The difficulty of the first year subsequent to a divorce should not be underestimated. This period is the time when sex differences in adjustment are most dramatic. Women generally report greater difficulty adjusting to the process of divorce (or separation), while men report greater difficulties following the event. Family members and children of divorced or separated couples also express distress as a reaction to divorce. Finally, although the degree of trauma experienced is related to numerous factors (e.g., to length of marriage, age of the people involved, number and ages of children, if any; who suggested the divorce; and how the course of action was carried out), few divorced people feel they made a mistake. In fact, feelings of having exercised the right course of action increase with the period of time following the divorce (e.g., Bernard, 1973; Stinnett & Walters, 1977).

Dissolving a relationship through the divorce process is disruptive for a couple and their children. (United Press International)

In a major study of divorce, Hetherington, Cox, and Cox (1979) studied family interaction among 144 divorced and married parents and their children. The mean ages of the four groups of parents ranged from 27 to 30. The investigators were primarily interested in the family relations and lifestyles of the divorced mothers and fathers as well as the coping strategies they used.

A key finding emerging from the interviews concerned practical problems. Divorced women felt overwhelmed by the quantity of tasks that faced them. They reported that there was not enough time or physical energy to deal with household maintenance, financial tasks, child care, and occupational and social demands. Compared to the married women, divorced women spent considerably more time on all these tasks. Women reporting the most extreme "chaotic life-style" were those whose sex roles had been rigid in their previous marriage. Both divorced men and women, however, reported family disorganization, involving such things as eating at irregular times and performing household tasks erratically. This feeling of disorganization peaked for women during the first year of their divorce; it lessened during the second year. For divorced fathers, family disorganization was at its highest point during the first two months after the divorce. Compared with mothers and fathers from intact homes, divorced parents' ratings of family disorganization were consistently higher two months, one year, and two years following divorce. When female friends helped divorced mothers with household tasks and when divorced fathers employed a cleaning person, some relief from the stress of disorganization was reported.

Many differences between parents in divorced and intact families were found in terms of self-concept and emotional adjustment. These differences drop extensively within one to two years following divorce. Parents feel the most anxious, depressed, angry, rejected, and incompetent one year after being divorced.

Divorced women reported feeling more depressed and incompetent than married women, and experienced more economic stress. They attributed these feelings to lack of experience, to discrimination encountered in financial dealings, and to sex-role ideology that encouraged incompetence in financial matters. Married women also stated that they were uninformed about economic matters, that their husbands "handled" them, and that they were not anxious about being incompetent. Surprisingly, feelings of competence were not strongly related to maternal employment.

Divorced fathers experience greater initial changes in self-concept than mothers, but the effects last longer in women. Feelings of unattractiveness and helplessness, and loss of identity associated with marital status, were reported by women. Men complained about not having structure in their lives. Parents who were older or married longer experienced the greatest changes in self-concept. Men seemed to cope with the problem of damaged self-concept by involving themselves in numerous social activities, altering their style of dress, and buying sports cars or motorcycles. Women showed greater weight gain, underwent cosmetic surgery, and altered their hairstyles. These activities appeared to be temporary adaptive strategies, however, because after a satisfying, intimate heterosexual relationship was developed, they no longer occurred. Moreover, the establishment of a new relationship was associated strongly with an improved self-concept.

Divorced parents had negative attitudes toward social activities. They felt that the social world is a world of couples, not singles. Women felt this even more so than men, stating that they were "locked into a child's world" (Hetherington, Cox, & Cox, 1979, p. 107). Although both parents reported a need for intimacy and were not satisfied with casual relationships, men were pleased with opportunities for sexual experiences immediately following divorce; women were not.

The parent-child relations of divorced parents and children were dramatically different from those of intact families. The differences were greatest during the first year. Father visitation was the source of biggest conflict. As time passed, fathers were increasingly late for visits, canceled visits, or did not appear when expected. Children reported distress, and mothers were infuriated. They coped by trying to console their children with presents they could not afford. Divorced parents in general demand less of their children, communicate less well, are less affectionate, and show inconsistent discipline and lack of control as compared with married parents.

The misuse of reinforcement appeared to be the major contributor to poor parent-child relations among divorced families. When children complied with parental requests, they received positive reinforcement less than half the time. Boys received significantly less than girls. Typical responses directed at boys were: "You didn't do that very fast" or "You'd better shape up if you know what's good for you" (p. 117). Over the two-year period, mothers' responses to compliance tended to become more appropriate, while fathers responses became less reinforcing. By the second year after divorce, therefore, disruptive behavior in girls had almost disappeared and was significantly reduced in boys. Children, especially sons however, still exhibited more negative behavior in the presence of mothers than in the presence of fathers.

The study concluded by saying divorce is not victimless. Among the families studied, at least one member showed distress and disrupted behavior. In some situations, however, divorce is a positive solution. Thus, divorce, although stressful, may represent a transition period, and can lead toward improved individual and family functioning.

COMPETENCE COMMITMENT

Commitment to competence in young adulthood often occurs in connection with entry into an occupation. Feelings of competency occur about one's work as interests deepen and a mastery of knowledge and skills is evident. As these feelings of competency increase, they produce a sense of self-satisfaction. Thus, job-connected social gains or attention, although perhaps initially important, have a diminishing role in job satisfaction over time (White, 1975).

White (1975) maintains that four changes during young adulthood are necessary for producing a commitment toward competency: (1) responding to people without anxiety, and with respect, warmth, and tolerance; (2) making decisions based upon one's own experiences, not on what others believe; (3) increasing one's awareness of the meaning of values and their relationship to social purposes; and (4) expanding a sense of caring to the community and others in general.

What types of occupational commitments do young adults make? Are these commitments similar for most young adults, or are they different? Four distinctly different types of occupational commitment emerged in a study of college students (Marcia, 1966): (1) those not committed to an occupation, with no concern, (2) those not committed to an occupation, with expressed concern, (3) those attempting to find occupational commitment, and (4) those who did not address the issue of commitment. Among female young adults, those who select more nonstereotyped majors, such as biology or prelaw, are more resolute about their occupational commitment. Male young adults, regardless of major, were distributed equally across the four types of groups. There appears to be evidence suggesting that there is a differentiation in occupational commit-

In Depth

BOX 9.4
LIFE-WORK PLANNING

The average adult worker will change careers three to five times in his or her lifetime. The reasons most often cited for this vacillation are changes in the changing economy or changes in technology (Bolles, 1978). As the number of Americans with college degrees, especially in liberal arts and education, continues to rise, degree holders are facing difficulty being absorbed into the labor market. In the past (pre-1960s), such difficulty affected individuals at the lower end of the educational ladder. In order to handle this situation, researchers (Bolles, 1978) are advocating a layered model of life-long learning, rather than a linear model of education during young adulthood, work during young adulthood and in the middle years, and leisure during old age. The life-work planning sequence developed by Crystal and Bolles (1974) is as follows:

1. Develop a "work-autobiography" by reviewing all that has been accomplished so far.
2. Identify demonstrated talents.
3. Group talents into clusters.
4. Rank the clusters from most to least preferred.
5. Identify the most important "thing" in your life (work, family, leisure, etc.).
6. Identify long-range goals and possible ways to implement them.
7. Create a broad timetable for reaching these long-range goals.
8. Set some immediate objectives.

Although life-work planning represents only one way to assist people of all ages in making career decisions, it meets a general need of people in our society today.

---

ment for young adults and that most young adults move toward establishing a commitment to an occupation.

Reality Shock

Coping with the difficulties caused by the discrepancy between idealistic training and the realities of the job is one of the key factors that postpones commitment toward competency. Just as playing house and babysitting, though they assist in the process of anticipatory socialization, are not adequate preparation for the role of parent, often the formal or informal training received during adolescence and young adulthood is not helpful in preparing an individual for an occupational role. If the shock caused by being unprepared is high and commitment does not begin, individuals may switch jobs. This is especially true of semiprofessionals. However, feelings of commitment develop as a consequence of an individual's investment in the job as well as the organization's investment (e.g., fringe benefits) in the individual. But many people are dissatisfied with their work, and are not challenged and excited by a paycheck. The attitude that one is not only entitled to a job, but to a job that is really liked, is pervasive in our society (Miernyk, 1975).

Holland (1973) assessed the vocational preferences of high school and college students in a variety of ways, and devised a personality-environment model for explaining career selection. Table 9.4 summarizes the six types of

TABLE 9.4
PERSONALITY-ENVIRONMENT MODEL FOR CAREER SELECTION

Personality-environment types	Characteristics	
	Environment	Personality
Realistic	Stimulates people to perform tasks Fosters technical competencies and achievement Encourages a world view in simple, tangible, and traditional ways Rewards people for showing conventional values	Conforming, frank, persistent, practical, stable, uninsightful
Investigative	Stimulates people's curiousity Encourages scientific competencies and achievements Encourages a world view in complex abstract, independent, and original ways Rewards people for displaying scientific values	Analytic, critical, curious, independent, intellectual, introspective, introverted, methodical, passive, pessimistic, precise, rational, reserved,
Artistic	Stimulates artistic activities Fosters artistic competencies and achievements Encourages a world view in complex, independent, unconventional, and flexible ways Rewards people for displaying artistic values	Unassuming, unpopular, complicated, disorderly, emotional, imaginative, impractical, impulsive, independent, introspective, intuitive, nonconforming, original
Social	Stimulates social activities Fosters social competencies Encourages a world view in flexibly cooperative social ways Rewards people for showing social values	Cooperative, friendly, generous, helpful, idealistic, insightful, kind, persuasive, responsible, sociable, tactful, understanding
Entertaining	Stimulates enterprising activities Fosters enterprising competencies and achievement Encourages a world view in terms of power, status, and sterotypical ways Rewards people for showing power, status, and money	Acquisitive, ambitious, argumentative, dependent, energetic, flirtatious, impulsive, pleasure-seeking, self-confident, social
Conventional	Stimulates conventional activities Fosters conventional competencies and achievements Encourages world view in simple, constricted ways Rewards people for showing conventional values of money, dependability, and conformity	Conforming, conscientious, defensive, efficient, inhibited, obedient, orderly, persistent, practical, self-controlled, unimaginative

Source: Based on Holland, 1973.

personality-environments he proposes and the specific characteristics of each. It seems that selection of a job is related to the degree of congruence between, or compatibility of, person and environment. Also, a person's vocational choice is likely to change when in a work environment that creates incongruence. Achievement and feelings of competency are thought to develop through a congruent match of person and work situation.

Mediating Variables

In general, occupational images are stable among adults and are perceived selectively depending upon one's social status, intelligence, and degree of involvement with the occupation in question (Holland, 1973). For example, several studies show that fifteen major occupations were perceived similarly by male and female high school students, college students, and faculty. However, bright high school students had more accurate perceptions of higher-level job stereotypes and less bright high school students had more accurate perceptions of lower-level jobs.

It appears that entry into a vocation and sense of commitment are related to one's perceptions of the world, which are influenced by various familial experiences. Mothers' and fathers' occupations and childrearing experiences influence career selection and feelings of competency. Conventional types (both male and female) have mothers who were most authoritarian. However, young adult males classified as realistic types were more likely to have both parents with authoritarian attitudes. When both parents expressed democratic childrearing attitudes, young adult males were classified as "investigative." Other associations between childrearing types and personality types were not significant (Holland, 1973). This suggests that familial experiences, e.g., parents as models, contribute to development of personality types. These, in turn, are thought to partially determine the way in which individuals select a work environment.

Again, it seems that cognitive abilities, personality factors, and socialization processes are all significant in selecting a career and in making a commitment toward competency. We will continue examining the world of work in the following two chapters. During middle age strivings toward mastery at work as well as coping with frustrations occur. Old age marks the time balancing fulfillment with one's work commitment and frustration with leaving the work world.

CONCLUSION

Young adulthood is a time of role transition. Hagestad (1979a) refers to such a period as a time of "ceasings" and "beginnings" or exits and entries. She proposes that during young adulthood entries are most typical, while during late adulthood exits are most typical. Roles entered into during this period, e.g., marriage and parenting, involve the development of intimate relationships with others. A strong sense of self seems to be required for making commitments during young adulthood, whether the commitment is to another person, to a job, or to a moral principle. Thus the "entries" of young adults involve making commitments, and are related to significant life events, as well as mediating influences such as the biological, social, and physical characteristics of the individual. Also crucial are the "interdependencies of lives." That is, the timing and patterning of one individual's life events may affect the opportunities and events of significant others. For example, the spacing of children is a timing pattern which varies from family to family. Such timing can influence and constrain the choices of family members, e.g., if several children are in college at the same time or are planning marriage simultaneously.

By the time young adulthood is completed, certain commitments have been made, and irreversible roles such as parenthood have been established. As the individual "exits" from young adulthood, the multiple roles and events of this stage have formed the context for entrance into middle age.

CHAPTER SUMMARY

Three major areas for adult commitment involve moral commitment, interpersonal commitment and competence. Specific life events associated with commitment are college, marriage, parenthood, and work.

Commitment can be to objects, or can refer to a more abstract, ongoing process. Cognitive abilities, personality, and socialization processes are all important in making commitments. Individuals more advanced in terms of Kohlberg's developmental scale of moral reasoning seem to be better able to handle cognitive conflict and to engage in role playing. Personality traits such as autonomy, coping with conflict, and tolerating differences are also associated with higher levels of moral reasoning. Aspects of socialization such as the family and college environment are related to advanced moral reasoning.

According to Erikson, love that enhances the other, a strong sense of self, and giving of oneself totally lead to interpersonal commitment and thus to establishing an intimate relationship. Data obtained from college students support Erikson's theory, and also suggest that the socialization which occurs in the college context may itself mediate the development of interpersonal commitment.

Although dating and courtship are processes leading to the event of marriage, they obviously serve as vehicles for establishing commitment. Again, cognitive, personality, and socialization mediating variables influence who marries whom. Premarital and marital sexual behavior are related to the development of interpersonal commitment.

Parenthood is a time of crisis for some young adults, and for others it represents a positive transition to a new role. In terms of parenting, investigators are turning from traditional ways of looking at mothering and fathering. Specifically, the idea of an innate "maternal instinct" is being questioned, as is the idea that fathering is limited to the role of provider.

Divorce appears to be a disruptive event in the lives of mothers, fathers, and children. Although individuals are affected differently, the first year is the most traumatic, and the mother and son relationship seems to involve the most problems. The greatest difficulty for divorced people is in reorganizing their lives. Practical tasks are especially difficult. Although divorce can be perceived positively, e.g., when it ends a conflict-ridden marriage, it takes a while (usually two years) for parent and child behavior and feelings to approach those of intact families.

White reported that young adults vary greatly in their degree of work commitment and their concern with it. "Reality shock," which involves the discrepancy between ideal training and the real work world, is one reason for delaying a career commitment. Again, besides personality, other mediating variables, such as intelligence and family experiences, influence vocational choice and the probability that an individual will develop a competence commitment.

Numerous new roles are assumed during young adulthood, which is also a time for establishing interdependencies among family members. (Young adulthood represents the stage on which the drama of the multiple responsibilities of middle age will be unfolded.)

10

MIDDLE AGE

CHAPTER
OVERVIEW

In this chapter, we will examine a major issue concerning middle age—is the midlife transition a time of crises or not? The rest of the chapter will extend our initial discussion by focusing on the achievements of generativity. Specifically, two major role areas—family and occupation—and their related events wil be considered.

Introduction
Views of Midlife
   Transition and crisis
   Transition, not crisis
   Transition or crisis?
Generativity: Intergenerational Relations
   Middle-aged parents and their adolescent children
   Middle-aged children and their elderly parents
Generativity: Occupational Roles
   A developmental perspective
   Career cycles: An emphasis on women
Conclusion

ISSUES
TO CONSIDER

What are the different positions regarding midlife, and what are the assumptions of each position?

What is meant by generativity and how can generativity be achieved?

In what ways can the relations between middle-aged parents and their adolescent children be described?

Is the empty-nest syndrome characterized by positive or negative effects?

How can the relations between middle-aged children and elderly parents be described?

Why do many middle-aged adults change careers, and what factors are associated with these changes?

What are the effects of multiple roles on working women, their children, and their husbands?

How can the career development of women who do not marry be characterized, and what factors influence this development?

What are some major work trends in the United States today?

In what ways does reentry into school and the work world influence women and their families?

INTRODUCTION

Until relatively recently, little research examined development during the middle years of adulthood. The bulk of developmental research has focused on children and adolescents, and more recently, the elderly. Of course, research on middle age is not totally lacking. In the 1930s, for example, Bühler (1935) incorporated ideas about changes in midlife into her personality theory. Further, many developmental studies have included middle-aged individuals as a comparison group against which to evaluate the performance of younger or older adults (Borland, 1978). Nevertheless, little attention was devoted to middle age as a developmental phenomenon in its own right until about fifteen years ago.

Thus, as one might expect, our understanding of midlife is limited. Conflicting images abound. Some views of middle age emphasize its stability. The middle-aged are seen as consistent, conservative, and responsible—the leaders of society and the parents of the next generation. Other views emphasize the changes which occur during this period. Midlife is seen as a time of crisis which evokes feelings of frustration and dissatisfaction and precipitates major life events such as divorce and career changes.

Middle age is a time when some of the roles assumed in young adulthood are "played out" and discarded (Hagestad, 1979a). Individuals are supposed to finish preparing children for the world and launch them into it. They are supposed to achieve career success and a better balance of energies and time among family, work, and community roles. But, the guidelines for how these midlife tasks are to be achieved are not as formalized as they are for the tasks of young adulthood. Informally, it seems that the responsibility for dealing with these areas rests with the individual (Hagestad, 1979b). Perhaps this is why researchers tend to focus on the crisis or transition aspects of this period of life. A similar focus is evident when the adolescent period of development is investigated. The adolescent is portrayed as struggling to find a sense of self or identity and a role in society. But, like middle-aged adults, adolescents are not given a prescription. The comparison of middle age with the adolescent period must be interpreted cautiously, however. We are not suggesting any similarities between these groups other than the emphasis on *Sturm und Drang* (storm and stress) and transition.

In any event, it is clear that interest in midlife is growing. Perhaps this is a logical outcome of demographic changes. There is a larger proportion of middle-aged adults in the population than ever before. In 1978, a full 25 percent of the population was between the ages of 40 and 64. In this chapter, we will examine some of the themes and life events which give shape and substance to the lives of these adults.

VIEWS OF MIDLIFE

Two major perspectives or models of midlife exist in the literature. One model views midlife as a period of transition and crisis. The major assumption is "that crisis is obligatory and a critical element of intrapsychic development in the life course of every individual" (Perun & Bielby, 1979, p. 278). Crises are thought to reoccur throughout development and are viewed as the mechanisms for changes within the individual. Thus, developmental crises are associated with each transition period—midlife being one.

The other model views midlife primarily as a period of transition and minimizes the role of crisis in adult development. Crisis is not viewed as normative or inevitable. Some researchers (e.g., Neugarten, 1964; Neugarten & Datan, 1974) feel that a crisis may occur, but only when developmental processes are interrupted. Others (e.g., Costa & McCrae, 1980) explain midlife crises as a continuation of early adjustment problems.

Transition and Crisis

Erikson is a major contributor to the perspective that midlife is a period of both transition and crisis. To Erikson, the crisis is the vehicle through which the transition is experienced. In his words:

It is this encounter, *together with the resulting crisis which is described in each stage. Each stage becomes a crisis because incipient growth and awareness in a significant part function together with a shift in instinctual energy. Each successive step, then, is a potential crisis because of a radical change in perspective. (1959, pp. 53–54)*

If the crisis is successfully resolved by the individual, it serves as the mechanism for completing the current stage and beginning its successor.

The concept of crisis seems to have lost theoretical specificity as it has gained popularity in the literature (Perun & Bielby, 1979). The term "crisis" is applied to any period of stress. This view is shared by Marmor (1968), who states: "The concept crisis has occupied an increasingly important position in psychiatric theory as a period in which an individual, subject to stress, reaches a crucial point of tension from which adaptive integration or maladaptive disorganization must eventuate" (p. 17).

Moreover, people appear to have conceptually entangled development and crisis so that the presence of one means the presence of the other (Perun & Bielby, 1979). For instance, Lidz (1974) states that "every life contains a series of developmental crises that arise from the need to meet the new challenges that are inherent in the life cycle. The individual gains new strength and self-sufficiency through surmounting these crises" (p. 243). Thus, because of this linking of crisis with development, midlife is viewed by many as a time of crisis. Gould (1978) states: "Mid-life, then, is every bit as turbulent as adolescence, except now we can use all this striving to blend a healthier, happier life. For unlike adolescents, in mid-life we know and can accept who we are" (p. 307).

Levinson (1978) and Vaillant (1977) have reached similar conclusions about the midlife period of development. Levinson's (1978) work (introduced in Chapter 8) is based on a study of forty men who were interviewed over a two-year period. The men were 35 to 45 years of age at the beginning of the study. Vaillant's observations are based on a follow-up of 94 men (of an original sample of 268) from Harvard University, originally interviewed as undergraduates and reinterviewed in their early thirties and late forties.

Levinson (1978) and Vaillant (1977) have in common the notion that midlife is characterized by a reevaluation of the commitments made in young adulthood. Vaillant (1977) makes the point clearly: "As adolescence is a period for acknowledging parental flaws and discovering the truth about childhood, so the forties are a time for reassessing and reordering the truth about adolescence and young adulthood" (pp. 219–220).

Levinson (1978), for instance, feels that the midlife transition spans a period of from four to six years, reaching its culmination when a person is in the early forties. Two fundamental tasks must be accomplished during this transition: (1) individuals must reappraise past life structures, and (2) individuals must begin to make choices which will modify earlier structures and provide a basis for living in middle adulthood.

These studies are open to criticism on a variety of points. The samples are small and, more importantly, are restricted to males. Moreover, Levinson's proposal of a universal sequence of periods, among which the midlife transition is only one, has been questioned (Brim, 1976; but see Box 10.1). Nevertheless, these studies provide the most dramatic view of midlife change to date and deal with other relevant constructs, such as Erikson's generativity, and specific life events such as divorce and career change. Accordingly, we shall review them in some detail.

Reappraising the past   On the one hand, Levinson (1978) says it becomes important to question what one has done with one's life—to examine one's talents, accomplishments, and relationships. This process does not reflect a simple evaluation of success versus failure, although this is an important element. Rather, it is more a matter of judging the "goodness of fit" between the life structure and the self (Levinson, 1978). During young adulthood certain choices are made as the life structure is developed. An individual may make commitments to certain values and goals and to a particular spouse and occupation. The choices reflect certain aspects of the self. Other aspects, however, are ignored, rejected, repressed, or remain undiscovered. Levinson suggests that in midlife these other aspects of the self must be dealt with, regardless of the degree of success the individual has had in attaining the goals of early adulthood.

Similarly, Levinson indicates that during midlife a person discovers how much of the young adult life structure is based on illusions. (For example, one illusion might be, "If I become Vice President of Ajax and have a home in Forest Acres I will be truly successful and happy.") An important part of the reappraisal process, then, is what Levinson labels "de-illusionment." This involves reducing or losing some of the illusions of young adulthood. Levinson notes that illusions can be both helpful and harmful and that it is probably neither desirable nor possible to discard all of one's illusions. For example, in adolescence and young adulthood our illusions often help us to sustain commitments in the face of

---

In Depth   **BOX 10.1** ◻

MIDLIFE AS CRISIS: RECENT OR ANCIENT HISTORY?

The crises associated with middle age are often portrayed as new phenomena. Researchers cite a number of social changes as reasons for the recent emergence of the view of middle age as a distinctive phase of the life cycle with its own special problems. These include the growing proportion of middle-aged adults in the population, the lengthening of the average life span, the decreasing number and earlier departure of children from the home, and the increasing diversity and flexibility of life-styles within the culture (Borland, 1978).

At least one author, however, believes the problems of middle age are quite ancient. Datan (1980, in press) has analyzed the myths and folktales of Western civilization and argues that these sources describe the developmental dilemmas of the life-cycle with great accuracy. For example, Datan suggests that the myth of Midas reflects the midlife crisis of achievement. Midas, you will recall, was granted his wish that all he touched would turn to gold. Datan observes that before long, however, he had touched his lunch and his daughter, depriving himself of both food and love. Datan notes;

The parallels between Midas and those whom we describe today as workoholics, whose dedication to work and its rewards at the expense of the inner self and its needs, are sufficiently close to persuade me that the mid-life crisis of affluence and achievement is not new. Current developmental and clinical portraits of the impoverished inner self in middle life are foreshadowed in the myth of Midas and others like him, who carry their

wishes just a little too far, and come to grief—a grief as old as human legends, and not a product of our times. (p. 14)

Datan also notes that many myths and fairy tales reflect developmental conflicts between parents and children. Hansel and Gretel, for instance, are sent into the woods by their father and stepmother because there is not enough food. Datan suggests that this fairy tale reflects the crisis of dependence associated with parenthood. She comments, "Faced with the boundless greediness of the very young child, what parent has not sometimes feared a scarcity—whether of money, time, energy, or in the cupboards of the heart?" (p. 18).

Similarly, according to Datan, the story of Snow White reflects a crisis associated with the growing maturity of the child. The maturing, vital adolescent is seen as a constant reminder of the aging parent's mortality. Datan comments: "Faced by her own vanishing youth in the person of her blossoming stepdaughter, Snow White's stepmother acts on the ambivalent rage that may stir in many mothers, and finally succeeds in halting her daughter's transition to adulthood with the long sleep of the poisoned apple." (p. 19)

Thus, Datan suggests that the crises of the human life-cycle, including those associated with midlife, are not historically determined. In this regard, she agrees with other organismically oriented theorists, such as Freud, Erikson, and Levinson, all of whom argue for universal sequences of development.

---

difficulty. In midlife however, effective reappraisal and change require an examination of these illusions.

Modifying to future According to Levinson (1978), a natural outcome of the reappraisal process is commitment to new choices or recommitment to old choices within a new framework. As the individual begins to make these commitments or recommitments, he leaves the transition phase and enters middle adulthood. For some men the modifications are extensive, for others they are limited. Levinson (1978) identifies several sequences during early adulthood and the midlife transition that reflect varying degrees of stability and success (some case examples are provided in Box 10.2).

Profile

BOX 10.2

PROFILES OF MIDLIFE AS TRANSITION AND CRISIS

In the following summaries, Levinson (1978) sketches the diverse development of several of his subjects through mid-life.

Perhaps the most stable, yet continually evolving life was that of Ralph Ochs. At 45, he is still working in the plumbing department of the factory where, at 18, he started as an apprentice to his father. A man of great integrity and modest aspirations, he enriched his life over the course of early adulthood by his active involvement in organizing and running a union, becoming a shop steward, and, as he passed 40, having increasingly mentorial relationships with other workers. His major investment is now in his family. He speaks with unusual perceptiveness and caring about his three adolescent children. He would like all three to go to college. His eldest son is graduating from high school and has no interest in college. Ochs recognizes that this is a source of tension between them, and he is trying with considerable tact and insight to be helpful but not overly controlling. He takes delight in the talents and projects of his youngest daughter, the brightest and most successful of the children. He enjoys and works at being an active father. (p. 280)

Larry Strode left a Black middle-class home in the South following military service in World War II. At 40, after fifteen years in the same factory, he was a skilled worker, shop steward and occasional foreman. He was oppressed by the realization that he could advance no further in industry and that his life was of little value. During his Mid-life Transition (age 40 to 45), he started his own barber shop, continued at the factory, completed high school, explored the work world for alternative occupations, and tried desperately to improve his failing marriage. The son of a minister, he had long wanted a career that would more directly benefit human minds and souls. At 45, Strode began to build a new life structure. He left the factory and became a mental health worker at a local hospital, while continuing to manage his barber shop. He separated from his wife, and divorced her a few years later. During the late forties he tried to develop a new occupation and family life (including the children of his former marriage, with whom he was strongly involved). At 49, when we last saw him, he was just beginning to succeed in making a life different from that of his early adulthood. (pp. 280–281)

At 39 Kevin Tyrone was a novelist and a professor of English. Although his novels were "difficult" for the average reader and not commercially successful, the critics considered him a writer of remarkable promise who might become one of the foremost novelists of his generation. Over the next six years, the struggles of Becoming One's Own Man and the Mid-life Transition led him into new explorations of self and world. Although he didn't complete a novel during this time, he wrote some unsuccessful plays, involved himself in the world of the theater, and participated in various educational projects. Several years were devoted to terminating the intense relationship with his long-term mentor. His marriage, which had been a vital support for his creative writing since his early twenties, came more deeply into question. During a severe midlife crisis in his early forties, he searched for new relationships, new occupational options, and new ways to deal with his own aging, destructiveness, femininity, and separateness.

At 45, Tyrone began to establish a life structure for Entering Middle Adulthood. Returning to his novels, he started on a major work in four volumes, which he completed over the next several years. He reaffirmed his commitment to the marriage, but on new terms and with a clearer understanding of its meaning and limitations. After the peregrinations of the early forties, his life after 45 was in many respects continuous with that of the thirties: he was a husband and father in the same family, still a novelist and professor. Yet there were significant changes in all aspects of living, and in the self that engaged in them. (pp. 291–292)

Almost from the start, Earl Northrop had a brilliant but flawed career. He became an assistant professor at 32, after doing some "very promising" research in a government agency. Over the next few years his research was solid but not outstanding. At 35 he was promoted to an intermediate rank largely on the grounds of his scholarly breadth, his success in teaching an important course, and his contributions to the administration of his department. At 40 came the crucial promotion: he was made professor with tenure, and thereby joined the senior ranks of his university and his scientific field. Again, however, the reward was blemished. He had continued to be an excellent teacher, and had written several comprehensive reviews of the work in his field, but it was becoming evident to him and others that he would probably never make a highly creative contribution through his own research. As he put it: "I became aware of the conflict in me, the strain of the intellectual side. . . . I lack what is needed to be really original in some imaginative sense. . . . It's an impediment to being in the very first rank."

During his Mid-life Transition, Northrop started coming to terms with what it meant to be a senior, semi-distinguished man in a university where the "second rank" is not good enough—and where most of the senior faculty are in this painful condition. He did better than most in facing these issues without illusions or hypocritical self-justification.

When I interviewed him at 44, Northrup was at the height of his tormenting reappraisal. His marriage, like his work, was adequate but unexciting. The marital difficulties were severe enough to cause him some anguish, but not so bad that he would seriously consider therapy or divorce. He was a devoted father and family man. An intensely pacifistic, nature-oriented, introverted person, he was deeply disturbed by our part in the Vietnam War, the violence of urban life and the pollution of the environment. He had not close collaborators or friends and, despite his many students acquaintances, felt utterly isolated at work: "If I retired or got sick, no one would come to see me—or even notice that I was gone." He would have loved to be a professor in another first-rank university, but the few offers came from lesser ones that his pride kept him from considering.

In our follow-up interview at age 46, the period of active questioning was over. For now he would stay put. He was finding small ways to enrich his family and work life, but there was little sense of reaffirmation in these choices. The structure was very provisional and open to change. Two years later Northrop took a chairmanship at a minor but growing English university—a further, but still tentative step toward building a satisfactory life structure in middle adulthood. (pp. 300–301)

David Jaffe was an engineer by education and early work experience. At 31 he embarked upon a managerial career. Although he worked hard to get ahead, his main involvement was in family and community. At 38, his ambitions heightened and he made a big effort for advancement to the position of purchasing manager. He also decided to get a bigger and better home. This was partly in response to the growth of his family, but it was also the fulfillment of a dream. His home was his castle, and having a lovely home of his own meant that he had arrived. Building a new home was his main project during the time of Becoming One's Own Man. Through his engineering and contracting skills, and his patience, he built a much more expensive home that he could have bought.

The twin culminating events of early adulthood came at 41: the Jaffe family moved into their new home, and he received his promotion. The home was a complete success. It gave them a more comfortable life and a more respected position in the community, where he was becoming a senior member. The promotion to purchasing manager was a total bust. The company had just been bought by a large corporation and purchasing policies were established from the top. He felt oppressed and humiliated. Despite the severe disappointment, he remained in this job for four years, refusing several attractive job offers in other states. He is one of the few men in our study who has lived his entire life, with the exception of a few years in military service, within an area no more than fifty miles across. If there is a traditional, tribal man—analogous to the traditional woman—he is it. The central elements of his life structure, in order of priority, were family, religio-ethnic community and occupation. He worked hard at his trade, but he left it behind at the end of the day and his most important satisfactions were elsewhere.

During the years from age 41 to 45, Jaffe stayed put and worked on various issues of the Mid-life Transition. At 45 he found his job unbearable. One day, in a fit of desperation, this cautious, deliberate man quit—impulsively, without knowing what he would do next. He still would not consider a big geographical move, but luckily found a job as purchasing manager at United Electronics, within commuting distance from home. I first interviewed him soon after he started this job at 45, and again two years later. The life structure he had begun at 45 was more secure and he was progressing well within it, but there were nagging questions. He was in top management, as Number 2 to the General Manager for Production. Though he had hopes of becoming a vice president, he knew about the instability of a "rapid growth" company and its leadership—and he counted on nothing. His familial nest was emptying, his aging mother-in-law was a heavy responsibility, and a new phase of life was in the offing. (pp. 302–303)

Roger Mohn, also an engineer by education, has spent his entire work life within a single company. Happily employed as head of the metals shop, he was unexpectedly promoted into middle management at 37, just in time for Becoming One's Own Man. The three years as purchasing manager were difficult but exciting. At 40 the culminating event was a promotion to head of manufacturing. This rapid advance in authority and income took him far beyond his youthful aspirations and managerial skills.

The promotion marked his entry into the Mid-life Transition. Within a year Mohn had developed an ulcer. He felt isolated and lonely. He thought a good deal about his college years and the friends who had meant so much to him; they were in another world that he had left behind and could no longer reach. A loving father and family man, he felt out of touch with his wife and children. At 42 he became ill with a cancer of uncertain prognosis. In the years from 42 to 44 he hit rock bottom. He was preoccupied with concerns about his own death, about the welfare of his family, and about giving his life some meaning when present and future were so bleak. His family life sustained him through this otherwise unbearable period.

When he was 44, a company reorganization eliminated most of his peers and gave him a "lateral shift" to a position of equal salary but less responsibility. He experienced the reorganization as a "blood bath," an "absolute slaughter" of the others and a humiliating demotion for himself. After several months, although he had offers from other companies, he decided to stay put: "I feel more secure in the surroundings I know than in a new environment."

The wish for security was only part of his reason for staying, I believe. At a deeper level, Mohn was ready to begin Entering Middle Adulthood and had made the basic choices for the next life structure. He had given up all pretense of interest in the competitive rivalries of the corporate world and in further advancement up the executive ladder. His strongest feeling at this time was relief—relief that he could remain in a well-paying, unchallenging job, and relief that his cancer now seemed under control. He lived more in the shadow of death than most of us, but he had reaffirmed his ties to life. He was content with the two central components of his life: his family and his leisure interests. He was learning to spend time with his loved and loving daughters, who were teaching him the pleasures of hiking, fishing, and nature. He was getting closer to his wife, and at the same time supporting her expansion from the home to new occupational and community involvements. As he acquired greater skill in the arts of intimacy and solitude, he was emerging into middle adulthood with a life fuller than ever before. (pp. 303–304)

Advancement within a stable life structure: The men in this group had established a stable life structure by the end of young adulthood. In addition, they had received moderate to notable success in their careers and other enterprises. The question then became, "Where do I go from here?" Fifty-five percent of the men were classified in this group. *55%*

Serious failure or decline within a stable life structure: These men also established a stable life structure in young adulthood. However, before the end of this period, it became clear that they were doing badly in certain critical areas. *20%* They were unable to advance in their occupations; their marriages were failing; they became physically ill. These failures had to be faced during the midlife transition. About 20 percent of the sample fit this pattern.

Breaking out: Men in this group had established a stable life structure early in young adulthood. By the end of that period, however, the choices had become unbearable and the individual had "broken out." This usually involved a major life event such as a divorce or job change. New commitments were made, *13%* which often quickly came under review as the individual entered the midlife transition. This sequence, often quite stressful, was shown by 13 percent of the subjects.

Advancement which produces a change in life structure: Some men experienced such a major advancement during young adulthood that it resulted in a significant change in their life structure. This usually involved a promotion or a drastic increase in income. Often this proved to be a mixed blessing, and the changes had to be dealt with during the midlife transition. Three men experienced this sequence.

Unstable life structure: Finally, three men were unable to form a stable life structure during young adulthood. None of them had sought that condition, and none of them found it a fulfilling state of affairs. They experienced frequent changes (e.g., jobs, residences, lovers, spouses) during their thirties, which is a time at which most men establish a relatively stable life. They were uniformly unable to cope with the tasks of the midlife transition.

80% moderate/severe crisis

Levinson estimates that for 80 percent of his subjects, the midlife transition was a time of moderate or severe crisis. He comments:

Every aspect of their lives comes into question, and they are horrified by much that is revealed. They are full of recriminations against themselves and others. They cannot go on as before, but need time to choose a new path or modify the old one. . . . A profound reappraisal of this kind cannot be a cool, intellectual process. It must involve emotional turmoil, despair, the sense of not knowing where to turn or of being stagnant and unable to move at all. . . . Every genuine reappraisal must be agonizing, because it challenges the illusions and vested interests on which the existing structure is based. (p. 199)

Vaillant (1977), however, is more conservative. He suggests that while change characterizes midlife, crisis is the exception rather than the rule:

Just as pop psychologists have reveled in the not-so-common high drama of adolescent turmoil, just so the popular press, sensing good copy, had made all too much of the mid-life crisis. The term mid-life crisis brings to mind some variation of the renegade minister who leaves behind four children and the congregation that loved him in order to drive off in a magenta Porsche with a twenty-five-year-old striptease artiste. Like all tabloid fables, there is much to be learned from such stories, but such aberrations are rare, albeit memorable, caricatures of more mundane issues of development. As with adolescent turmoil, mid-life crises are much rarer in community samples than in clinical samples. The high drama in Gail Sheehy's best-selling Passages was rarely observed in the lives of the Grant Study men. (pp. 222–223)

Transition, Not Crisis

Those suggesting that midlife is a transition but not a crisis emphasize an individual's perception of the life cycle as an integrated whole rather than as a series of crises. For example, Butler and Lewis (1977) comment:

[T]he development of an individual inner sense of the life cycle . . . is neither the same as the average expectable life cycle nor the same as a personal sense of identity, although it is related to both. It is a subjective feel for the life cycle as a whole, its rhythm, its variability, and the relation of this to the individual's sense of himself. This inner sense seems to be a necessary personal achievement in order for the individual to orient himself wherever he happens to be on the life cycle. (p. 138)

The concept of an individual's sense of the life cycle and the notion of the average expectable life cycle are illustrated by the work of Neugarten. She feels that a primary task of adulthood is to develop a sense of timing of events in the life course. Although periods of crisis may occur, these do not dramatically alter an individual's sense of self or sense of the life course. Neugarten (1970) feels that periods of crisis ". . . call forth changes in self-concept and in sense of identity . . . mark the incorporation of new social roles and accordingly . . . are the precipitants of new adaptations" (p. 79). She continues by saying that "a psychology of the life cycle is not a psychology of crisis so much as it is a psychology of timing" (p. 87). Thus, only a minority experience midlife as a crisis, and when it is experienced as such it is because of unanticipated interruptions in the rhythm of the life course.

Other research tends to support this view. For example, there appears to be little evidence that primary (e.g., anxiety, depression, physical complaints) or secondary (e.g., alcoholism, psychosis, suicide) crises peak in the middle years (Brim, 1976). Similarly, in a recent study of a large sample of men 33 to 79 years old, Costa and McCrae (1980) developed a Mid-Life Crisis Scale designed to reflect the stresses of this portion of the life cycle as described by others. However, no age differences were found on this scale. The scale did correlate significantly with Costa and McCrae's personality variables, particularly neuroticism. Further, there were positive correlations between scores on the crisis scale and measures of neuroticism obtained *ten years previously*. These findings led Costa and McCrae (1980) to suggest that men who seem to be crisis-prone at midlife may have exhibited problems of adjustment for a long time. Thus, Costa and McCrae feel that midlife crises may be the result of the fact that unadjusted adolescents and young adults grow up to be unadjusted middle-aged adults rather than the result of a universal crisis confined to midlife.

Riegel (1975) also rejects the concept of normative life crises. Moreover, Riegel (1975) emphasizes that normative events are experienced within the context of physical and cognitive boundaries, which may be different for different people. In order to understand Riegel's position, we will illustrate two normative physical and cognitive boundaries that serve as frameworks in which life events are experienced. This discussion will also illustrate how mediating variables can influence the impact of life events and the ways in which individuals cope with these events.

Physical decline The peak of human biological functioning tends to be reached between the late teens and the late twenties, depending on the system involved. By the forties most individuals have experienced a noticeable decline in muscle strength, lung capacity, cardiac output, and other physiological capacities. These changes are accompanied by other alterations which affect our appearance, baldness, wrinkles, and weight gain being the most prominent.

These biological reminders of middle age occur gradually. Further, they do not interfere with the everyday lives of most individuals. The exceptions are those persons whose activities require exceptional strength, endurance, or skill, such as professional athletes. In such cases, a career adjustment is often required. But for most adults, the physical changes associated with middle age do not in themselves significantly alter their life structure. Nevertheless, they do have psychological significance. For example, particularly in the case of men, physical changes appear to serve as a marker of middle age itself. In an interview study of 100 middle-aged men and women, Neugarten (1968) found that men commented more frequently on decreased physical efficiency and other health-related concerns than women. Even menopause and other changes associated with the reproductive system did not appear to be critical for women (Neugarten, Wood, Kraines, & Loomis, 1963). Women were, on the

With biological aspects of aging making their mark early, professional athletes like Frank Gifford often are forced into a career change. (United Press International)

rehearsal for widowhood

other hand, concerned with the physical health of their husbands. Neugarten (1968) has labeled this behavior pattern "rehearsal for widowhood."

Awareness of death   The physical decline that occurs in midlife and other cues which draw attention to the aging process may have an impact on the individual's time perspective. A number of studies have found that middle-aged individuals begin to restructure time so that life is thought of in terms of time left to live rather than time since birth (Jaques, 1965; Levinson, 1978; Neugarten, 1968). They realize that the time remaining to them is finite; they will die, and things will remain undone. Of course, we all realize that we will die. However, at midlife this realization appears to be qualitatively different. For the first time the inevitability of death becomes a psychological reality. One of Jaques's (1965) interviewees put it this way:

"Up till now," he said, "life has seemed an endless upward slope, with nothing but the distant horizon in view. Now suddenly I seem to have reached the crest of the hill, and there stretching ahead is the downward slope with the end of the road in sight—far enough away, it's true—but there is death observably present at the end." (p. 506)

Jaques argues that it is the realization of the inevitability of one's own personal death that precipitates the midlife crisis. Others (Riegel, 1975), reject this view. They feel that middle-aged adults should be ready to handle the boundaries of physical and cognitive development and to face the inevitability of death. Nevertheless, there seems to be substantial evidence pointing to a psychological shift in time perspective in midlife.

Transition or Crisis?

Perhaps the most valid conclusion that can be drawn about midlife is that this period, like other periods of the life cycle, is characterized by changes and transition. For some individuals this transition appears to precipitate a crisis; for others it does not. Thus, perhaps the question "Is midlife a crisis or not?" is not the right one to ask. Perhaps attention should be focused on how various events which tend to occur in the middle years affect the individual and on what role mediating variables play. To the extent that midlife is a transition with or without crisis, it is these events which are likely to trigger, mediate, or terminate it.

GENERATIVITY: INTERGENERATIONAL RELATIONS

Concept of Generativity

According to Erikson (1959, 1963), middle age is a time when social norms require that a person be a productive, contributing member of society. If a middle-aged individual has a sense of producing and contributing what is expected, that individual will have a sense of generativity. However, if output is perceived as being below expectations, or individuals feel they have not fulfilled role requirements, a sense of stagnation can result.

The key task associated with establishing a sense of generativity is being able to assume responsibility for new generations of adults. That is, middle-aged adults, married or not, are to become "parental" in new ways. Younger adults can no longer be treated as children, to be controlled. Ways to combine shared responsibility and authority must be achieved. Young adults should be taken seriously, and middle-aged adults should foster their independence, authority, and participation. Although stagnation may occur at this time, the experience is not totally negative. Stagnation can make people aware of their own weaknesses, defeats, and destructiveness. This allows people to understand the suffering of others and to be compassionate toward them. If a person during the middle years does not move toward generativity, then the experience of stagnation will lead to a sense of not growing, of being bogged down in a life full of obligation and devoid of self-fulfillment. In essence, it can lead to a sense of living in the shadow of death—of dying.

Generativity goals can be attained in a variety of ways. For example, one can achieve generativity by feeling successful in producing and rearing children, in occupational achievements, or in community involvement. Not all middle-aged people reach these goals. Some adults focus more on one area than others. For instance, midlife is often a time when one is concerned with properly sequencing events so children can be launched into a world with appropriate skills. This concern is accompanied by the realization that the past cannot be undone. Parental mistakes cannot be corrected. Thus, a parent may feel vulnerable in the parental role, which is about to undergo major changes.

While struggling toward generativity, middle-aged adults, who for the most part are in good health and well established financially, often feel unduly pressured by relationship obligations to both their children and their parents (Franzblau, 1971; Miller, 1969). As a consequence, they may feel frustrated and depressed—"caught" between demands of aged parents and adolescent children, which may reduce opportunities for pursuit of self-interests. Also, unlike their children and parents, they are supposed to be strong, to cope, and to solve problems. According to Chilman (1968), midlife is a time when the burdens of others become heavy on one's shoulders:

From the viewpoint of the middle-aged parent, one does, indeed, seem to be caught in the middle of three generational cycles; between the increasingly complex, costly and disturbing needs of adolescents . . . who are bursting with desire for entrance into the adult world and the increasing problems and needs of the grandparents who, generally, are bursting with desire not to leave their full status in the adult world. The middle-aged adult, who may feel that her own status is threatened somewhat by her own development stage is apt to feel further threatened by the competing, but somewhat similar claims of both the older and younger generations. (p. 307)

This period in the life cycle may also have its positive aspects. As the Group for the Advancement of Psychiatry (1973) states: "The grueling race to find a mate and establish a career—has been run; children no longer demand around-the-clock care; and social life is no longer dictated by the caprices of babysitters or the unpredictability of childhood diseases. . . . There is now time for enjoyment" (p. 121).

Parent-child relationships must be examined from more than one perspective. At the core of the relationships between middle-aged parents and their adolescent children and their elderly parents are people experiencing their own middle years while relating to children and parents who are making their own transitions to adulthood and to old age.

Middle-Aged Parents and Their Adolescent Children

Parents are usually anywhere from 30 to 55 years old when their first child reaches adolescence. Many factors, such as age at marriage and whether the marriage is a first or subsequent one, influence what the exact age will be. Also, this period can last a long time depending on how many children there are and how they are spaced.

Data on parent-adolescent relations tend to center on parents as role models (e.g., democratic, equalitarian, or autocratic; see Douvan & Adelson, 1966) and as exercisers of social control (e.g., ways in which friends are screened and behavioral limits are set; Brannen, 1975). Research portrays parental concern with sexuality, especially for daughters. With boys, however, parental anxieties deal with the company they keep, whether they will get into trouble or have accidents, and their hopes and aspirations about an occupation (Maizels, 1970; Thomas & Wetherell, 1974).

Socioeconomic status has an effect on parental expectations concerning their adolescents' behavior. Middle-class parents who experienced the value of education for employment opportunities tend to encourage their children to continue their education. Lower-class parents who either finished high school or other training and could not get a job, or who did not complete any form of specific training, are less likely to encourage their children to continue in school (Simpson, 1962). It appears that the extent to which lower-class parents feel they do not control their destiny is related to the lack of encouragement they give to their adolescents about a "worthwhile" career (Colemon & Associates, 1966).

Handling conflict   A central issue in the relationship between middle-aged parents and their children deals with handling conflict surrounding children's thinking and behavior (Byng-Hall & Miller,1975). Parents vary in the ways they interact with children. For instance, parents seem to respond to conflicts concerning idealism in one of two ways. Some parents are pedantic, telling children what are realistic goals (Conger, 1972). Other parents relate to their child's idealism and try to question the child and change some of their own standards and behaviors. This seems particularly true among parents who perceive their children as an important source of emotional support (Hagestad, 1980).

Evidence reveals that for satisfactory results of parent-child confrontations the elements of love and discipline must both be present (Glueck & Glueck, 1950; West, 1967). In order for these two elements to be present, each person must communicate and participate in the discussion. Also, parents need to respect their child's concerns, interests, goals, and perspectives (Rapoport & Rapoport, 1976).

Social change has been suggested as a major source of middle-aged parent-adolescent conflict. Although it may appear that young adults are rebelling against parental values, data indicate that they may be actualizing them. For instance, Troll (1970) selected fifty college students who were highly politically involved and compared them with a matched group who were not involved politically in order to determine the degree of similarity between student values and parental values. She found that parent and child values were similar whether or not students were activists. Kalish and Johnson (1972) conducted a related study in which the similarities and differences in values held by three generations of women were assessed. The subjects were fifty-three women, whose average age was 20, and the mothers and maternal grandmoth-

The elements of love and discipline should be present for parent-child confrontations to produce satisfactory results. (Christy Park/Monkmeyer)

ers of each young woman. Although the strength of value similarity varied with generational comparisons and the specific values involved, there was a trend for family members to hold similar values. Therefore, parents may be confusing "rebellion in manners" for a rebellion in morals (Group for the Advancement of Psychiatry, 1973, p. 43), or they may be overpersonalizing insofar as they regard their children's attacks on standards and authority as attacks directed at them as individual parents and people.

According to Elkind (1979), potential areas of conflict between parents and children reflect the social conditions of the culture. He suggests that parents and children form "contracts" to govern their behavior. To the extent to which contractual terms are violated, parent-child conflict and generational conflict result.

Elkind proposes that three basic contracts between parents and children exist. The first type of contract involves freedom and responsibility. Parents generally grant children freedom insofar as the children demonstrate that they can handle the responsibilities involved. During adolescence, certain freedoms can be taken without parental consent. However, parents can still set limits: for example, the use of the family car can be withdrawn until grades in school improve. The second type of parental contract involves loyalty and commitment. During adolescence, parents no longer expect the loyal affection that was received when their children were younger because friendships with peers are increasingly important. Yet parents still expect their children to remain loyal to the values and beliefs that they, the parents, support. In turn, before they will support their parents' values, adolescents require that parents express a dislike for hypocrisy and that parents be visibly committed to the ideals in question. The third type of contract involves achievement and support. Expected achievements, especially for middle-class parents, are academic, extracurricular (e.g., sports and music), and social (e.g., the children having friends the parents approve of). In return for this behavior, parents show approval for outstanding performances, extend material support by purchasing uniforms, lessons and the like, and provide transportation so that children can interact with friends.

Elkind argues that the exact way in which and to what extent responsibility, loyalty, and achievement demands are made of children depends upon social conditions. He points out that the relative emphasis on these different types of contracts has changed over time. During the Depression years of the 1930s parents were concerned with responsibility and freedom because, in most families, each member had to contribute to the family's welfare. Personal interests had to be ignored, with older children often forfeiting their education so younger children could go to school. Freedom and responsibility also were the focus of generational conflicts. Socialism and communism became attractive to adolescents who found their responsibilities too great compared with their freedom. These ideologies required less individual responsibility for such things as education and health care. The loyalty-commitment contract became a dominant theme in the late forties and fifties and continued to persist in the sixties. During this time a new nationalism came to the fore, an extreme example of which was McCarthyism. This spread like an infection to parents who were concerned about the influence of adults on their children. They did not want their children to be exposed to "leftist" teachers.

In the sixties, loyalty to parents and society was not reciprocated by society's commitment to the welfare of people. Adolescents saw minority groups mistreated, and viewed the Vietnam war as "morally unjust and dishonestly promulgated" (Elkind, 1979, p. 42). For them, these were symbols of societal hypocrisy, and led them to question commitment to American ideals in general. Because they felt their loyalty had been unrewarded, the youth revolted by becoming withdrawn. They felt cheated, believing that society had violated its commitment to them.

Elkind suggests that during the seventies the achievement-support contract appeared to youth to be violated. People who had worked hard in school for years, gone to college, and even completed graduate work had difficulty finding employment. Young adults felt personally violated because they had been told that education is the royal road to success, although in fact it is not. Reactions to this feeling of being not supported for achievement can be seen in the self-centeredness of our contemporary generations.

What about the future? Elkind suggests that parent-child contracts should return to themes of freedom and responsibility. In reaction to their own experience of achievement pressure, parents may be giving too much freedom to children in return for too little acceptance of responsibility. (It seems, therefore, that relationships between middle-aged parents and adolescent children are complex as parents and children move toward a relationship characterized by equality.)

Empty-nest syndrome   Many researchers feel that the process of launching children represents a sequence of significant life events for women. They refer to this experience as the *empty-nest syndrome* (Hagestad, 1980). Interestingly, however, strong positive—not negative—affective responses are associated with this event. Women report feeling a new freedom and looking forward to being able to utilize their talents in the future because now they have the time. In fact, during the empty-nest period (which varies in length depending upon the number of children in the family) females having a variety of life-styles report high levels of life satisfaction (Glenn, 1975). Moreover, the majority of women actually look forward to the time when their youngest child will leave home (Lowenthal & Chiriboga, 1973).

According to Hagestad (1980), one of the major problems in studying the empty-nest syndrome is the lack of conceptual and theoretical interpretations of the positive effects of children leaving home. She suggests that we should no longer view the event as role loss, but rather as a normal transition. That is, the mother-child dyad exists as long as its members are living, but the role relationship is renegotiated as conditions change. As a result of these changes, Hagestad suggests that children increasingly become resource persons for their mothers.

Using questionnaire data gathered on undergraduate students enrolled in four Midwestern colleges and universities, and a subgroup of middle-aged mothers, Hagestad (1980) tested her theoretical notions. The majority of mothers painted a rather positive picture of themselves. They identified many things in which they were interested in exploring and enjoying—more than health, time, or energy would permit. They also were realistic in seeing their lives as approaching old age, and said they noticed their children's growing independence. When mothers were asked what impact their college-aged child had on them, the majority discussed the child as "an interpersonal resource." Daughters were perceived as resources slightly more often than were sons. Very few mothers felt that their children negatively influenced their sense of self or well-being. Hagestad (1980) proposes that children are "cohort bridges" for their parents.

Middle-Aged Children and Elderly Parents

We have very little information about how parents influence their middle-aged children at this stage as compared with the earlier stages of the life span. It is not surprising that due to the increasing concern over the care of the elderly in our society, we know much more about how adult children influence their parents. Fortunately, however, the assumption that the socialization process ends with the attainment of adulthood is being challenged (Brim & Wheeler, 1965), and the attempts to study adult socialization have resulted in some research. The gap in our understanding of parental influences upon adult offspring is beginning to be bridged.

Maintaining social and emotional ties Adult children maintain their significant roles in parents' lives. For example, Riley, Johnson, and Foner (1972) found that 80 to 90 percent of parents have children who live within one hour's driving distance. Of these parents, 80 percent said they had seen one of their children in the past week and 60 percent said they had visited one of them either that day or the day before. Adult children also visit elderly parents, spending their leisure time with the parents and upholding family traditions (Sussman & Burchinal, 1962).

Changing norms The norms for how adult children and their elderly parents should interact are different from those for middle-aged parents and adolescent children. On the one hand, elderly parents are not supposed to intrude into the affairs of their children and are not expected to place demands on children's resources. In fact, if there is little dependence between parent and child, and attempts are not made by either parents or children to impose their values, then an optimal relationship develops. This is achieved more easily when individuals are financially secure (Clark & Anderson, 1967). On the other hand, a middle-aged adult child is expected to have achieved filial maturity (Blenker, 1965), to see parents as people, and to understand that the parents' life

Adult children usually have frequent contact with their parents. The view that older adults are abondoned by their families is largely a myth. (Bob Combs/ Photo Researchers)

histories have socialized them to be what they are. Adult children should be developing in a way that allows their parents to depend on them but also permits parents to maintain their sense of self and retain personal dignity.

✗ (Evidence indicates that parents want to be assured that their adult child can be depended upon in case they need help, although they value independence and do not want to be dependent.) This expressed need characterizes the type of relationship—one of <u>interdependence</u>—that comes with <u>filial</u> maturity (Blenker, 1965).   *due from offspring*

Children have demonstrated their sensitivity to parental needs. Some provide services such as escorting parents, running errands, shopping for them, or performing household tasks (Sussman & Burchinal, 1962). Others provide physical care, and still others take their parents into their homes (Spark & Brody, 1970; Sussman & Burchinal, 1962).

Conflicting norms   Our culture maintains a strong conviction that older parents should not be a burden to children, but should allow the children to live their own lives. But <u>often this is not the case.</u> Many children experience conflict about deciding upon the proper care for their parents. A 52-year-old unmarried son reported:

My 84-year-old mother lives with me in my four-room apartment. Her senility has become worse and she is totally confused, unable to sit still, care for herself, or even remain continent. Three years ago I had to quit my job in order to stay home with her, as she used to wander the streets and get lost. . . . Three weeks ago I placed her in an expensive, beautiful nursing home but she became more confused, totally dependent, and over-medicated. She lost 7 pounds, her bowels became impacted, and, in desperation I took her back home. I'm at my wit's end. What should I do? I love the poor woman. But I cannot enjoy life at all. What is the best thing for her? And me? (Butler & Lewis, 1977, p. 123)

Lowenthal and Robinson (1976) suggest that current norms do not allow older people to demand either attention or intimacy from their children. In fact, responses of older people to their adult children could be characterized as a mixture of "sterility, formality, and ritualism" (p. 438). They suggest that because personal needs are not expressed, older people express superficially assimilated norms when they report they are as close to their children as they hoped to be. These researchers also suggest that older people might benefit from more intimacy and less independence from adult children.

Sussman (1976) feels that the care of elderly parents is a major issue in parent–adult child relationships and that research on family care of the aged should be conducted. He also suggests that norms "treating people as commodities rather than human beings" (p. 238) need to be challenged. One way to provide material support would be to give money to individual families so that intimacy, nurturance, and privacy of older people can be maintained while providing health care. Communities could establish mobile services, which would reduce direct hospital costs, and paraprofessionals indigenous to communities could be utilized.

GENERATIVITY: OCCUPATIONAL ROLES

An occupational role can serve as a vehicle for establishing generativity during midlife. Middle-aged adults increasingly seem to be looking for occupational roles to meet personal goals and assist them in broadening their perspectives. The major evidence for this assertion is that an increasing number of middle-aged men and women are changing careers. Women are entering into the labor force or returning to school or work, and men are altering jobs. Also, as many middle-aged workers are completing retraining programs as are younger workers (Siegler & Edelman, 1977).

This apparent pattern does not occur in a vacuum. As work roles change, family roles and community roles are affected, too. Havighurst (1973) states:

It has become clear that there is likely to be a growing amount of movement from one job to another in the age period forty-five to seventy. The most desirable situation is one that maximizes freedom of choice for the individual so that he can change jobs if he wants to, retire early or late, take a part-time job, and combine a changing work role with developing leisure and community member roles. (p. 616)

A Developmental Perspective

The view that occupational choice, and subsequent work role, is made during young adulthood as a "one-time" decision is giving way to a perspective that views occupational development as a process that occurs throughout much of adult life. For most men and many women, occupational activity varies throughout middle age and influences family roles and relationships. This viewpoint is persuading people to study work in terms of occupational life cycle. The critical personality dimensions influencing shifts in career cycles are risk taking, willingness to assume new roles, and feeling a sense of control over one's destiny (e.g., Heath, 1976).

Since people today are engaging in second and even third careers, researchers have been trying to understand patterns of occupational stability and change as an explanation for why certain decisions make careers more satisfying, productive, and orderly (e.g., Murray, Powers, & Havighurst, 1971). Other researchers (e.g., Schein, 1975) have approached the problem from a societal perspective. They have been involved in studying what work patterns are chaotic as a result of overall loss of productivity. A general finding from these efforts is that a higher proportion of white-collar than blue-collar occupations are orderly and sequential.

In a major study, Murray, Powers, and Havighurst (1971) identified certain personality factors and situational pressures as instrumental in determining whether or not an individual changes or remains in an occupation. Table 10.1 presents four occupational patterns (routine career, flexible career, disjointed career, and orderly, sequential career), with their related personality and situational factors. It should be noted that these data were gathered on men.

Clopton (1973) supports the work of Havighurst and his associates with the findings from a study comparing two groups of men in their thirties and forties. One group made a midlife career shift, while the other group did not. He reported that adult life circumstances (situational factors) and personality accounted for differences between "shifters" and "persisters." The two groups were matched on family-background variables (e.g., birth order) and adolescent experiences (e.g., college). They also were similar on present family responsibilities and the degree of success achieved in their original careers. The "shifters" stated three major reasons for changing careers: (1) a gradual disenchantment with their first career as a result of not realizing their potential more fully; (2) discovery of a new career that promised more personal satisfaction; and (3) the reformulation of goals as a consequence of a series of events experienced over time or a set of events experienced simultaneously. Events cited were things such as divorce, sudden unemployment, death of a family member, and religious conversion.

TABLE 10.1
OCCUPATIONAL PATTERNS AS A FUNCTION OF PERSONALITY AND
SITUATIONAL FACTORS

Personality Factors	Situational Pressures	Stability or Change in Occupation
Low self-direction	Little pressure to change	Routine career; advancement follows seniority
High self-direction	Little pressure to change	Flexible career; initiative for change and type of work assumed by person
Low self-direction	Much pressure to change	Disjointed career; technologically oriented reasons for unemployment (e.g., blue-collar workers), no skill or experience (e.g., widow)
High self-direction	Much pressure to change	Orderly, sequential career; well-planned effort in making changes assumed by person

Source: From Murray, Powers, and Havighurst, 1971.

What are indexes of success in one's career? A person's performance in an occupation in terms of meeting personal goals and the goals of others is one index of success which is supposed to occur during middle age. Much more data, however, have been gathered identifying the variables that are related to unsatisfactory performance, and determining whether these relationships diminish with the age of workers, than on identifying variables related to satisfactory performance. For white-collar workers, unsatisfactory performance may be the result of an individual's not initially establishing commitment to the job or of an inability to internalize the norms and practices required for success in the position. This usually results in a "disjointed career" that starts during middle age because lengthy preparation is often required for career changes (e.g., Featherstone & Cunningham, 1963).

Although the possibility exists that prevailing feelings of stagnation contribute to the unsatisfactory performance of some middle-aged workers, data do not support this contention. Reasons for unsatisfactory occupational performance are difficult to uncover primarily because they often result in unemployment, and so poor performance and unemployment indexes are confounded. Thus, it is difficult to isolate individual mediating variables, such as personality, and societal mediating factors, such as the economic system.

The research that has been done on occupational success suggests that there are age-related differences in different career fields (e.g., Lehman, 1953). For fields which depend extensively on physical capacities, peak performance occurs in the early twenties and thirties. For the fields of arts and sciences, which rely upon intellectual capacities, peak performance occurs in the thirties or early forties. But in fields requiring social capacities, peak performance tends to occur even later in life (e.g., Lehman, 1953). Timing of and rate of decline from peak performance represent another way of analyzing successful performance. Although scientific performance peaks a few years later than athletic performance, for instance, its decline is far more gradual. Thus, the decline in peak performance occurs at about age 45 for athletic activities and at about age 70 for scientific activity. Box 10.3 addresses the issue of whether job success is related to life satisfaction.

Career Cycles:
An Emphasis on Women

Applying a developmental perspective to the examination of occupational roles is difficult because much of the literature, as illustrated above, suggests that numerous variables contribute to feelings of success or failure. Moreover, the majority of these studies are cross-sectional and represent the male in the work world. These problems exist, and cannot be swept under the rug. Having acknowledged them, however, we will try to tease them apart while we explore career cycles with an emphasis on women.

In Depth

BOX 10.3
CAREER SUCCESS AND LIFE SATISFACTION

Most of the writers who postulate a midlife transition as crisis suggest that the reappraisal associated with it occurs whether or not the individual has had career success or not. A recent report by Bray and Howard (1980) lends support to this notion. These investigators summarized the findings of a twenty-year longitudinal study of eighty middle-level managers of the Bell Telephone System.

Bray and Howard's analyses showed that career success was not related to overall life satisfaction. Furthermore, although more-successful men felt more satisfied with their careers and specific jobs than less-successful men, there were no differences between these groups on measures of marital satisfaction, marital stability, familial worries, avocational interests, cynicism, feelings of crisis, and adjustment. Success on the job, then, does not automatically bring success elsewhere.

What is the successful manager like? As one might expect, the more-successful managers had higher scores on measures of intelligence, achievement motivation, dominance, and aggression than the less-successful managers. Over the twenty years of the study, work increased in importance for the most-successful managers and decreased in importance for the less-successful managers. The former worked longer hours and showed greater identification with the professed values of the Bell System than the latter. In contrast, over the twenty years of the study, the more-successful managers showed almost no change in their involvement with their wives and families and only a small decline in their involvement in recreational activities, while the less-successful managers showed significant increases in their commitment in those areas. These data do not support the notion that career success must be purchased at the expense of other aspects of life. Rather they suggest that different individuals evolve different life structures over time. No single path appears to guarantee happiness.

Multiple roles   There are numerous differences in the career cycles of men and women. Most of these differences have little to do with biological or cognitive processes. It is unclear, however, to what extent these differences are mediated by socialization or by restriction of alternatives (Veroff & Feld, 1970; Kreps, 1976).

There have been an increasing number of certain types of women entering the work force during the past generations. Those with strong career interests and special talents tend to enter the work force, while those who marry young and are dependent do not. This type of selectivity consistently affects the demographic age trends for women in the work force. Employment rates for women peak during early adulthood, before they leave to raise children. (Currently, there is a trend toward leaving the work world for shorter periods of time)

When working women are studied, we must consider several different groups:

Those who are committed to an occupation and do not occupy a spousal or maternal role.

Those who occupy a work role and a family role.

Those who assume all three roles—worker, wife, and mother.

Those who reenter the work force after children are reared.

Earlier studies reporting the negative consequences of the mother's working on children did not consider social-class differences, maternal satisfaction or dissatisfaction, and provisions for child care. When these factors are

Although employment rates for women peak during early adulthood, there is still a trend for women to leave the work world to have and rear young children. (United Nations)

considered, maternal employment does not affect children adversely (e.g., Hoffman & Nye, 1974). For instance, role satisfaction is related to children's positive adjustment and success in school. "Better mothers," whether working or nonworking, were those who were satisfied with their roles. Also, adolescent daughters of working mothers were more likely to express the opinion that women are competent and more likely to value the accomplishments of women than daughters of nonworking mothers (Kreps, 1976).

Although many married women simply add the work role to their other ones, some have difficulty with employers who do not understand their need for "flex time," with family members who do not want to alter tasks, and with obtaining adequate child-care arrangements (Wilensky, 1968). In a study of middle-aged and older women, these females felt attention to their spousal role was not reduced because of work. But their role as mother and homemaker, especially the latter, received less attention when they were devoting energies to high work performance. Employed women reported spending half the amount of time doing housework as unemployed women did (Kreps, 1976). Consistently, women report career success and satisfaction when husbands are supportive of their careers (e.g., Kreps, 1976; Rapoport & Rapoport, 1971). Box 10.4 illustrates the meaning of work for women having multiple roles.

The career development of women who do not marry is markedly different from that of those who do marry. Hennig and Jardim (1976) studied twenty-five middle-aged women executives. They found that several aspects of family socialization were associated with these women, who had remained with the same company in order to achieve the highest management position. These females tended to be firstborn children. Their fathers were successful in their careers, encouraged them to use their abilities, and rewarded them for non-gender-stereotyped role behavior. Their mothers were full-time homemakers. They were academically excellent in college, and when they graduated, fathers gave them extensive emotional and financial support while they began careers. On the job, these women received assistance and encouragement from older male executives, but by the time they occupied middle-management roles the mentor-mentee relationship that had been established earlier was discontinued.

Work trends   In 1974 women constituted two-fifths of the labor force. This represents an increase from 25 percent in 1940 (U.S. Department of Labor, 1973). The working rates for single and no-longer-married women have remained constant, and are higher than the rates for married women with husbands present. However, the number of women in the labor force has doubled since 1950, with the greatest increase in work participation being among younger married women (Kievit, 1972; U.S. Department of Labor, 1975). Many factors influence the increase in labor-force participation by married women: (1) desire for increased family income, (2) needs for independence, social contact, and actualization, (3) interest in occupational achievement, status, and recognition, (4) more tolerant societal attitudes toward working

Controversy

BOX 10.4

ARE WORKING WOMEN MORE SATISFIED?

Interesting enough, there appears to be a sharp discrepancy in the literature examining the meaning of work for men and that examining the meaning of work for women (Wright, 1978). When the focus is on working men, work is generally pictured as degrading, alienating, and unsatisfying. In contrast, when the focus is on working women, work is generally pictured as enriching, liberating, and satisfying, in spite of the fact that women are more likely to be found in less desirable occupations. The positive aspects of work for women are often contrasted with views of the role of the full-time housewife, a role which is generally seen as lonely, boring, and demeaning.

Who does lead the more satisfying life—women with jobs outside the home or full-time housewives? Many studies find little difference in overall satisfaction between the two roles (Blood & Wolfe, 1960; Wright, 1978). For example, in an analysis of national survey data collected between 1971 and 1976, Wright (1978) found no significant differences between working women and housewives in satisfaction with their lives in general or components thereof—e.g., their work, marriages, or families. Similarly, in a study of 142 middle-class women, Baruch and Barnett (1980) found no differences between working women and women at home in their role satisfaction or

self-esteem. Thus, in spite of the fact that some studies have found working women to be happier than nonworking women (Ferree, 1976), the bulk of the studies suggest that involvement in the multiple roles of wife, mother, and worker neither enhances nor diminishes general satisfaction with life.

Yet perhaps this is not the most important issue. For example, Baruch and Barnett (1980) found that the sources of satisfaction and self-esteem varied for employed and nonemployed women. Specifically, the well-being of nonemployed women was highly dependent on their husbands' approval of their activities. In contrast, the well-being of employed women was significantly affected by their satisfaction with their jobs and careers as well as their interactions with their husbands. As Baruch and Barnett point out, these work-related variables are likely to constitute a more stable base for well-being since they are more directly under the woman's own control. Given the high rate of divorce in our contemporary society, building one's life on the approval of one's spouse can be a risky strategy. Baruch and Barnett conclude that the positive self-development of women is likely to be facilitated by the acquisition of occupational competence and the capacity for economic independence.

wives, (5) later age at first marriage, (6) decline in birth rate, (7) increased availability of child-care services, and (8) reduced sex discrimination (Hoffman & Nye, 1974; Kreps, 1976). Figure 10.1 shows rates of working by age category for single, married, and other women.

The distributions of type of occupational employment for men and women have not altered very much. Working women mainly occupy clerical, service, operative, professional, or sales positions, while men hold operative, management, professional, and service positions. When analyzed by educational level these differences are magnified (see Table 10.2).

Women in the same occupations with comparable qualifications and years of service as men receive 75 to 80 percent of men's earnings. This still reflects

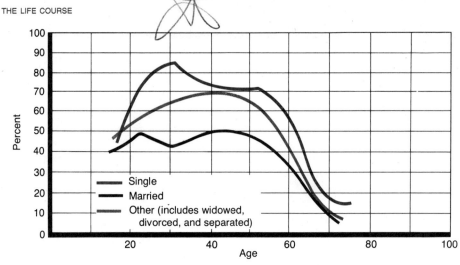

Figure 10.1 Rates of working as a function of age for single, married, and other women. (From U. S. Department of Labor, 1975.)

discrimination. However, single women who do not disrupt their career pattern earn slightly more than single men. Also, the rate of improvement of earnings for women in different occupations varies. Women in clerical and operative occupations have benefited from a lesser increase in rate of earnings than those in professional occupations (Sommers, 1974; U.S. Department of Labor, 1975).

One reason that rate of earnings may be lower for women is discontinuity in the work force. Often women stop work when the first child is expected and start again when the last child enters school. Thus, the career cycle for many women reflects two entry points, with a period in between of not using skills or abilities. When they reenter the work world, they often are unskilled or need retraining. As a consequence, an increasing number of women are resuming the role of student during their forties. They tend to use the vehicle of continuing-education programs, but some have enrolled as full-time graduate students.

Evidence shows that middle-aged women entering graduate school are interested in their field and consider the graduate work necessary for entering a profession. This is very different from what men in the same age group report. Men go to graduate school to increase the possibility of a change from one field to another or within a diverse field, or to increase their financial status (e.g., Hiestand, 1971).

These women tend to complete their degrees in about the same time as other graduate students, after which they become full-time professionals. The event of graduate school for these middle-aged women, however, serves as an arena for changes in self-concept and changes in roles. Upon entrance into graduate school, they see themselves as energetic and confident. Although they are apprehensive about success, they have positive attitudes toward their family roles as well as their student role. At the close of the first year of study,

TABLE 10.2

OCCUPATIONAL DISTRIBUTION OF EMPLOYED PERSONS BY EDUCATION AND SEX, 1970 (IN PERCENT)

| | High School | | | | College Graduates | |
| | 1–3 Years | | 4 Years | | | |
Occupational Groups	Men	Women	Men	Women	Men	Women
Total employed*	100.0	100.0	100.0	100.0	100.0	100.0
Professional, technical, and kindred workers	2.8	3.6	7.6	7.1	58.9	77.4
Managers and proprietors	6.9	2.9	11.4	3.8	20.1	4.8
Salesworkers	5.6	10.2	7.5	8.1	8.6	2.3
Clerical and kindred workers	6.8	25.3	10.0	50.4	4.9	12.1
Craftsmen	25.6	2.4	26.4	1.8	3.3	0.4
Operatives	27.3	22.5	20.6	11.4	1.4	0.6
Nonfarm laborers	9.9	1.6	5.3	0.8	0.5	0.1
Farm laborers and foremen	1.9	0.6	0.9	0.3	0.2	0.1
Service workers excluding private household	10.8	25.4	7.5	14.5	1.4	1.9
Private household service workers	.2	5.2	†	1.7	†	0.3

*Individual figures may not add to 100 because of rounding.

†Less than one-tenth of 1 percent.

Source: From U.S. Department of Labor, 1973.

they still report that they are satisfied, but also state that the multiple-role experience is strenuous. About half the women reported mixed reactions from children and said their husbands were basically supportive. Very few felt guilty about indulging themselves in an activity they personally desired. The low point for these middle- aged women tends to occur midway through a program. They express a general loss of self-confidence in being able to complete the task. Children's attitudes become increasingly negative, and the women are concerned over time spent with their spouse. However, with progress and accomplishment, this period of stress diminishes and an increase in self-esteem and assertiveness results. These women never return to the role of homemaker in the same way as they filled the role before, and family roles are perceived of as better than they were before they went back to school. Also, they express a different interest in community participation, often wanting to occupy leadership roles (e.g., Lefevre, 1972).

CONCLUSION

Many role changes occur during middle age, as in young adulthood, but the role changes during the middle years are marked by exits and dyadic renegotiations, rather than entrances (Hagestad, 1979a, b). Some researchers see this transition period primarily as a time of crisis, while others emphasize its transitional nature. Rossi (1972) states: "The time is now ripe to drop the concept of 'normal crisis.' . . . There is an uncomfortable incongruity in speaking of any crisis as normal. If the transition is achieved and if a successful reintegration of personality or social roles occurs, then crisis is a misnomer" (p. 295). Brim (1976) also cautions us about being too obsessed with identifying age-linked stages in adulthood. The evidence gathered thus far makes him ask:

Does this bring reminiscences of the 1920's in developmental psychology? It may be that the field of adult development is similar to child development some fifty years ago in its exploration of age-linked developmental sequences. And, like child development then, it is in real danger from pop culture renderings of "life stages," from the public seizing on the ideal of age-linked stages of development, such as "male mid-life crisis," just as it seizes on astrology and tea-leaf reading. Certainly, the evidence does not justify linkage of crises either to stages, or to specific ages, during the mid-life period. (p. 7)

CHAPTER SUMMARY

Can the midlife transition be characterized as a time of crisis? The work of Levinson and Vaillant stresses that for midlife transition to occur the individual must reappraise the past and make choices that can modify the future. Neugarten suggests that an individual's sense of the life cycle and understanding of the average expectable life cycle are important in determining how the individual will approach the midlife period. Crisis only occurs for those who experience unanticipated interruptions in the rhythm of their life course. Costa and McCrae regard midlife crisis as a continuation of an individual's overall inability to cope. Riegel places the experience of normative events within physical and cognitive boundaries. Research suggests that the impact of these boundaries is felt by middle-aged people, who are generally aware of their physical decline and inevitable death, but that biological reminders of middle age and approaching old age need not produce a crisis.

Erikson describes the main task during middle age as one involving generativity versus stagnation. Two arenas for establishing generativity are intergenerational relations and occupational roles.

Although many variables influence intergenerational relations, a central issue between middle-aged parents and children concerns handling conflict. The empty-nest syndrome may be a misnomer, for evidence indicates that women react positively to their children leaving home, not negatively, and that children can be an interpersonal resource for mothers. They actually serve as cohort bridges for their parents, and help them move their concerns outward.

The relations between middle-aged children and their parents are characterized by continuity, with emotional ties being maintained. However, changing and conflicting norms make a precise portrayal of the nature of this relationship difficult.

Middle-aged adults are faced with a double and perhaps triple bind. They are working on their own individual strivings at the same time they are balancing two relationships—with their children and with their parents.

Evidence of career changes throughout the life span, especially during middle age, is evidence that midlife can be a period of achieving generativity in occupational roles. Patterns of occupational stability and change indicate that personality and situational factors influence the type of occupational roles one has over the life span. Many age-related and social differences exist. White-collar workers have more orderly or sequential careers, even though they may change careers more than blue-collar workers. Often, these differences are accounted for by societal factors, such as economic conditions.

Working women reflect various types of roles—from the single-career role to the multiple roles of mother, wife, and worker. Groups of working women vary in terms of what mediating variables influence their career roles. For instance, unmarried career women were influenced greatly by supportive fathers who reinforced their non-gender-stereotyped behavior. Many women successfully handle multiple roles. The husband's support is critical in this regard. No negative effects of work on children was reported among women satisfied with their roles.

The number of working women has increased dramatically over the last few decades. However, the distributions of type of occupational employment for men and women have not altered very much over the same period. Many discriminatory practices still persist, and perhaps help explain why more and more married women are resuming the role of student during their forties. They reenter or enter the work force with an increased sense of self and assertiveness, and they often occupy leadership community roles.

It appears that middle age is a transitional time of successfully reintegrating one's personality and social roles. This often requires renegotiation between and among dyads. Thus, the evidence to date does not warrant our speaking of midlife transition as crisis or talking about inevitable age-linked stages that occur during the middle years.

11
OLD AGE

ISSUES
TO CONSIDER

What can be said about integrity and disengagement in old age?

How do life-time experiences, retiring early, and cohort differences influence attitudes toward retirement?

In what ways do different people successfully adjust to retirement in terms of their sense of self and their marital relations?

What does the grandparent role involve?

In what ways and to what extent do mediating variables influence the grandparent role?

What impact do grandparents have on their grandchildren?

How do widows and widowers differ?

What variables mediate the impact of widowhood?

How do people adapt to widowhood and in what ways can they be assisted?

Why and how can relocation be stressful for older adults?

What variables influence adjustment to relocation?

INTRODUCTION

I am writing this essay in my office overlooking the Mississippi River. While I am not exactly Old Man River, I do identify with that stream below me . . . on which now a barge comes around the bend and gently moves downriver. Downriver it is. I am getting older all the time.

I am getting older all the time. But that actually began when I was conceived. How old I am is measured by the amount of time from that beginning of my life until today. That amount is getting bigger and bigger . . . and bigger. This ever-increasing span of time taxes my memory, teases it, and perhaps, distorts it now and then without my consciously knowing it.

So, to get older is to get further and further away from my beginnings. Is it redundant to say that, or does it have real meaning? My children are at an age that I was 30 years ago and the grandson will soon be of the age his father was when I was 31.

Is there any use to think in numbers? They are real but as numbers they don't mean much. When our eldest son turned 30 my wife said, "Oh, he is catching up with us." Yes, that's what it feels like, and feelings are where it is.

But it is an oversimplification to go with the old adage, "you are as old as you feel." What does feeling mean in this connection? Feelings about myself or reflections about myself? I suppose it is the latter. A student of 20 came in the other day and she said she really felt old when she became 20. I asked her what that felt like. She couldn't really explain it at first. It was a strange feeling she said, but then it came to her; "What bothers me," she went on, "is the number 20, going into the third decade." I think she hit on something there. Those round numbers seem to symbolize a new venture, a turning point far beyond its significance. Few of us bother with becoming 23 or 47 and even fewer will get upset over those odd numbers; we are hooked on the decimal system and our anxieties are engendered by those zeroes that materialize every ten years. Yet we also make a big to-do over those occasions and celebrate them. What a fuss we make over those birthdays with the 0 in them!

We were all infants once and part of that remains in us. Nietzsche said that in every man (his term) there is a child that wants to play. Before long we are adolescents and about that we have another saying: Adolescence starts about 13 and ends . . . sometime. Infanthood, childhood and adolescence. Then the adult. About adulthood we are more definite. Once an adult, we go on being adult, though some researchers separate certain stages from each other and identify 20–40 as early adulthood and 40–60 as the middle years. To be followed by old age. About that we become somewhat cagey again, showing our ambivalence. We need euphemisms: Senior citizens, Golden Age. No, we are not charitable about old age. It is never in fashion, it is never desirable— political and economic movements such as the Gray Panthers not withstanding—at best it is tolerated. Mostly I believe it is so because, after all, it is the final stage before we die. A prelude to death . . . and who wants that!

So as we pile up the decades the zeroes become milestones on the road to the cemetery and our discomfort with, if not fear of, death explains that vague anxiety about becoming 40 or 50, 60 or 70. It's the other side of the coin that celebrates these occasions. The celebrations are reflections of the pride to have made it all the way up here; the wisdom accumulated, achievements visible, the body in good shape.

Yes, but . . . What about the body . . . my body. My skin is wrinkling, though my hair is plentiful. My hair's color is salt and pepper which is probably a euphemism for gray. Graying is a synonym for aging. Euphemisms are defenses against unpleasantness. Funny that balding is not equated very strongly to getting older. Well, I am not bald. My energy leaves little to be desired. My memory has lapses and I expect it to deteriorate. Perhaps it was never very good anyway but I anticipate that short term memory will be a handicap in my sixties/seventies but that, hopefully, the long term memory will remain good. My virility shouldn't be measured by the firmness of my erections or how often I get horny but it is inevitable in these days of sexual awareness not to be concerned with what my body—of course governed to a distinct degree by my head—can or cannot do in the way of sex.

For better or for worse my wife and I can no longer make babies. With someone younger than Ruth maybe a spurious sperm of mine might find its way into an available ovum . . . I'll never know. But my interest in having pleasurable sexual relations is undiminished, though I am aware that before very long that may begin to wane slowly. While I do not wish for that, I do anticipate it, which is saying simply that it is a reality . . . sad as it is. And occasionally now my body doesn't want to cooperate with my wishes and I wonder why the automatic reactions of my system are no longer so automatic. Fortunately the next time around I shape up again. Wonder upon wonder, we make love forever.

Isn't it strange that our society apologizes for being sexual after youth. We don't chide young people for being horny, there is no such expression as a "dirty young man." But the dirty old man (not yet dirty old woman, but that will come soon) concept is an accusation: At the non-youth time of life one has no business of being sexual. It is unwarranted, bizarre if not obscene. Children as a rule deny their parents' sexuality. How could they believe that grandpa and grandma still can get it on! My students, most of them members of the youth oriented culture must wonder when they first see me there up in front in charge of a course in Human Sexual Behavior about this old fogy: What does he know about sex, etc. . . . .

There is a special area about the elderly that interests me. All my life I have had a curious habit. When I look at a woman, I project her 20 years ahead into her life and imagine her in the flesh two decades older. Usually that is not a more attractive sight than the person I see at that moment, and that brings me to the point. What is this attraction between older men and younger women? Most of my life it was the other way around. True to the European tradition in my youth I was smitten by older women. For whatever reason—go and analyze me—I have since that time felt an appeal to what I perceived the more mature woman. Until recently, that is. The more mature woman is now too mature, aged that is. Though when I look at Ruth I feel there is the mature woman I always wanted. And attraction went out the window, victim that I am myself of the "60 is over the hill" prejudice. I am not displeased with this change of attitude nor am I planning to go in the opposite direction: The younger woman doesn't do anything for me particularly just because she is younger and interested in me, à la George Burns. But I am puzzled by the phenomenon of the age difference attraction. Perhaps, this will be my next research project.

And getting older is becoming a grandfather. My son's son. What, my son has a son (with a little help from his wife of course)! Yes, my son who is 36 has a son who is 6. But my son is 36. Yes, that is true. Yes, this kid of mine has a kid who calls me "Grandpa Gerry" in contrast to his other grandfather, who is "Grandpa Goo," named after the dog his other grandparents had. David—that is the name of my grandson—however, considers me more of an adjunct to his Grandmother Ruth. In fact, a sign on our front door which David made reads "David's grandmother lives here." I don't mind that a lot. David does use me to play ball and we go sledding, with him on top of me, and I believe he understands that I am his father's father. We are lucky that his parents live in the Twin Cities so we see a lot of each other. To see him grow up is a joy, but as grandparent, I am not responsible for the day by day caretaking which means I can escape from the demands of constant attention and having to say "no" a lot. I can say "yes" a lot and step backstage. Grandmother and David are a good match. He recently asked her, "Grandma, what are you going to be when you grow up?" Writing about grandma reminds me that David's birth made me a grandfather and Ruth a grandmother—that led to the line, "I always wanted to sleep with a grandmother." It was meant to be funny. It does not, however, obscure the feeling that somehow I had to justify the fact that I was now in the third generation.

All these wise comments and gentle observations notwithstanding, in spite of smart insights and sophisticated second guessing, the truth is that, for me, getting older is a burdensome beast. Relentlessly the aging proceeds. I can make it more bearable, make the proverbial best of it . . . but I cannot modify it. My existence is running out of time, I am running out . . . period. I will stop being in the not too distant future. Even the last part of that sentence is a euphemism. I hate death for that reason, the brutality of having no control over prolonging my love for living. Death, I hate you.

Yet this same love for living permits me to enjoy this final phase of my life. The idosyncracies of this current way of life are precious. My heart beats excitingly, my brain operates on both hemispheres and my loins still lie in lust. I am. That is why I could write this piece.

I look up and out the window. There is Old Man River flowing downstream. There are three barges on it now. (Neubeck, 1978, pp. 445–447)

Neubeck's (1978) commentary on growing older illustrates some of the richness and complexity of moving toward the transition to old age. The transition to old age is complex because *rites de passage* are "vague, amorphous, and unregulated" (Rosow, 1974, p. 27). The entries and exits of late adulthood are not under the control of the individual. In this chapter, we will examine several life events common to late life. Within our discussions, we will consider the impact of mediating variables on these life events. First, we will focus on retirement because the majority of older adults experience this exit from the occupational world. Then we will explore the impact of grandparenting and widowhood, which not only influence the individual but also affect the family. Finally, new living arrangements will be discussed, since as a consequence of widowhood and other events relocation is sometimes necessary. Throughout our examinations, we will focus on how older adults adjust to these events.

TOWARD INTEGRITY

Erikson (1959, 1963) proposes that the transition to old age is characterized by the crisis of integrity versus despair. As commitment to integrity develops, the *ego strength* of *wisdom* emerges. The concept of wisdom with integrity implies that the individual is able to accept that life is coming to a conclusion. Erikson (1968) states: "It is the acceptance of one's one and only life cycle as something that had to be and that, by necessity, permitted no substitutions" (p. 87).

Integrity provides the individual with the wisdom to understand his or her own life. According to Erikson, this understanding both balances the decreases of potency and performance in aging and allows the individual to serve as an example to the upcoming generation. Despair, on the other hand, represents a rejection rather than an acceptance of the past life, and involves a fear of death resulting from the realization that there is insufficient time to make up for past mistakes. Finally, the individual may deny or fail to deal with the crisis at all.

There does seem to be evidence to suggest that the attempt to achieve a sense of completion is important during old age. In particular, reminiscence (see Box 11.1) is thought to be an activity that facilitates the feeling that life is complete. Nevertheless, there are a number of questions that may be raised concerning the adequacy of integrity as an organizing concept for development in later adulthood. Clayton (1975), for example, suggests that relatively few individuals ever achieve a commitment to integrity and, therefore, wisdom in old age. In part, this failure reflects the tendency of individuals to become fixated at earlier stages of development—particularly at the adolescent stage involving crisis of identity. In part, it also reflects the lack of an appropriate social context for the emergence of integrity. Clayton (1975) comments: "We are living in an era that cannot provide the elderly person with a feeling of continuity. . . . Tradition is the one meaningful channel which might allow for the emergence of wisdom and instill a sense of continuity to the aging individual. Unfortunately, our present culture, being rootless in nature, seems to have lost all sense of tradition" (p. 122). Erikson's theory, then, like many other organismic theories (e.g., Kohlberg, 1969), is an elitist theory, suggesting that only a few individuals achieve the higher stages. Such a perspective does not provide a general description or explanation of adult development.

It also has been noted that Erikson's last stage is the most intrapersonal of his stages (Glenwick & Whitbourne, 1978). The previous stages are rooted in the context of ongoing interpersonal interactions. The final stage is rooted in the context of the person's past activities and future death. The research on

In Depth

BOX 11.1 □
THE LIFE REVIEW

It is commonly observed that older individuals spend a significant amount of time reminiscing about the past. What is the significance of this activity? Butler (1963) proposed that the *reminiscence* of the aged reflects, in part, a universal process of *life review* which may have both positive and negative outcomes.

Butler (1963) noted that reminiscence often is viewed as a nonpurposive activity, which, while filling the void of later life, reduces the individual's contact with reality. In contrast, Butler suggests that the life review is a necessary examination of past experiences, particularly unresolved conflicts.

In many respects, the life review appears to be a culmination of a life-long evaluative process that occurs prominently at various points in the life cycle, such as midlife. According to Butler (1963), the life review is brought about by the realization of impending death. As a result, it is commonly observed in the aged, although it also occurs in younger individuals who expect to die (e.g., the terminally ill).

The life review is accompanied by multiple affective manifestations and adaptive outcomes. Butler notes: "In its mild form, the life review is reflected in increased reminiscence, mild nostalgia, mild regret; in severe form, in anxiety, guilt, despair, and depression. In the extreme, it may involve the obsessive preoccupation of the older person with his past, and may proceed to a state approximating terror and result in suicide" (p. 489).

Thus, the life review can lead to maladaptive outcomes. Butler indicates that three groups appear to be particularly susceptible to such despair: those who always placed great emphasis on the future but disliked the present; those who are afflicted by real guilt because of purposive attempts to injure others; and the highly narcissistic, for whom death is the ultimate threat.

The life review also may lead to the reorganization of past experience, to expanded understanding, and to personality growth. Butler suggests that such positive manifestations of the life review may help to account for the serenity and wisdom of some older adults. Several studies provide support for this assertion. Boylin, Gordon, and Nehrke (1976) observed a correlation of .41 between frequency of reminiscing and scores on a measure of ego adjustment based on Erikson's theory in a group of institutionalized men. The investigators also found that negative affects (e.g., anxiety, depression) associated with reminiscing correlated moderately with ego integrity, confirming Butler's observation that the life-review process is sometimes painful.

reminiscence (cf. Butler, 1968) suggests that this linkage of past and future is important. However, as a result of this intrapersonal focus, Erikson's theory tends to ignore the ongoing events in the individual's life and does not consider how these are embedded within the changing social context.

Another major theoretical framework uses the concept of disengagement to explain how older adults exit from society. In its early formulation (Cumming & Henry, 1961), this view emphasized the adaptive consequences of the mutual disengagement occurring between the individual and society. As we noted in Chapter 7, this assertion produced considerable controversy, particularly with regard to the presumed mutuality of the process and its adaptive consequences (Havighurst, Neugarten, & Tobin, 1968; Maddox, 1964, 1966). Generally, it now has been concluded that while some individuals do disengage, the linkage of this behavior to successful aging is not useful. Neugarten (1973) says, "In short, disengagement proceeds at different rates and different patterns in different people in different places and has different outcomes with regard to psychological well-being" (p. 33). Accordingly, while the concept of disengagement emphasizes the linkage of the individual with society, it focuses on a very narrow definition of social influence.

Past views of the transition to old age, then, are partially useful but fail on a number of crucial points. More recently, several writers have agreed that what is required is a systematic conceptualization which would emphasize the points of articulation between the individual and society (Lowenthal, 1977; Glenwick & Whitbourne, 1978). This brings us back to our emphasis on life events and cultural change. As is the case with other transitions in the life course, an integrated perspective of the transition to old age has yet to be developed.

A large array of events occur in later adulthood. Some of these events are positive and some are negative. Some events, such as retirement, originally perceived to be negative, have more recently been viewed as positive. Regardless of whether particular events are negative or positive, adjustment to role changes must occur if individuals are to arrive at a level of life satisfaction at any point in the life span. Many individuals are satisfied with their lives during old age and view their lives as extensions of their past. The research conducted with people who have remained single illustrate this point (see Box 11.2). In the remainder of this chapter we will consider some of the significant events associated with the transition to old age.

In Depth

BOX 11.2
IS REMAINING SINGLE A PREMIUM?

People over 65 years of age who have remained single are the exception, for they represent only about 8 percent of the population (Gubrium, 1975). Elderly singles are not only special cases demographically and sociologically, but also psychologically. They are people who experience less change during old age. They do not experience the disruption of losing a spouse, for instance, or the adjustment to the grandparent role.

In a classic study, Townsend (1957) reported that unmarried or childless elderly said they were isolated, but not lonely. Those saying they were most lonely had been recently bereaved (Townsend, 1957). Isolation consistently has not been found to relate to loneliness in old age. In fact, single and married individuals were found to be similar in their reports of feelings of loneliness. However, the recently bereaved reported feelings of loneliness more than twice as often as other groups (Gubrium, 1974). Gubrium (1974) reported that single elders: (1) tend to be lifelong isolates; (2) are not especially lonely in old age; (3) evaluate everyday life similarly to married elders in that both groups are more positive than divorced or widowed older adults; and (4) have avoided the dislocating effects of bereavement following the death of a spouse. Thus, he concludes that the state of singleness in old age is a premium.

RETIREMENT

In life-span development, retirement is an ending and a beginning. It ends years of commitment, but it can represent new opportunities for using time and energy. It is a process that involves adjustments at both an individual level and a family level. Included in this process is preparation, decision, adjustment to the event, and assumption of a role. Some researchers argue that the attitude toward the process leading to retirement begins before adulthood is reached (Atchley, 1977). With the increasing proportion of the population that lives until retirement age and beyond, a major focus in social gerontology concerns retirement.

Retirement is difficult to define because people may retire at a specific age or after completing a certain number of years of service. Individuals may also switch jobs or move from full-time to part-time employment. Consequently, retirement may be experienced by the same person on a number of occasions. Individuals who leave the labor force during young or middle adulthood as a result of ill health are referred to as disabled rather than retired. But an older adult who leaves the work-force for health reasons is considered retired. Finally, retirement may be voluntary or involuntary. There is a great deal of variability in how people decide to retire and how they prepare for and adjust to retirement. Some individuals retire suddenly, and are not prepared. Others progressively reduce their commitments in a systematic and gradual way. In general, when the retirement process is normal (not confounded with other events, e.g., death of spouse or surrogate care of grandchild, or problems, e.g., poor health or financial difficulties), people adjust rather well, expressing little or no change in morale, contentment, or life satisfaction.

The literature focuses on three areas of retirement research: (1) plans or preparation for retirement; (2) adjustment to retirement; and (3) satisfaction with retirement. In all these areas, different factors such as age, sex, cohort, family variables (e.g., number of dependent children), and level of general health are considered. As a result of the different variables studied, it is difficult to draw substantive conclusions about the three aspects of the process mentioned above. Much information is still needed before the relationships among retirement preparation, adjustment, and satisfaction is understood. Moreover, the samples studied are extremely diverse. Some groups studied represent professors, some automobile workers, some rubber tire workers, some white-collar professionals, and so forth. Thus, it is difficult to generalize from existing findings.

Attitudes toward Retirement

Regardless of how difficult it is to synthesize the retirement literature, we can raise a basic question: "Which people, under what circumstances, anticipate retirement positively and which people anticipate retirement negatively?"

Lifetime experiences The accumulated impact of lifetime experiences affects retirement plans. A recent study (McPherson & Guppy, 1979) of men 55 to 64 years of age who represented a wide range of occupations, incomes, and levels of educational attainment found that most of the men were looking forward to retirement. However, men with higher socioeconomic status gave more thought to and made more specific retirement plans. Perceived health status was another factor associated with retirement plans. Men who perceived their health as good or excellent had more elaborate retirement plans. Also, those high in general life satisfaction (both in terms of leisure and of work) thought more about postretirement years with definite plans. Finally, men who were planning for early retirement were those who had leisure-time interests and wanted to increase the time spent in these activities, had financial means, and were in good to excellent health. McPherson and Guppy (1979) suggest that certain life-styles characterize those who are most likely to plan for and look forward to retirement.

Positive expectations of retirement were held by working men who felt they had the finances necessary for maintaining their standard of living, would be able to continue established friendships, and would maintain a level of social activity comparable to that held while working. Also, those men with a positive anticipation of retirement considered preparation plans to be critical. Major areas of preparation included income, social contacts, and use of leisure time. Lastly, a positive attitude toward retirement was not associated with a strong work commitment (Glamser, 1976).

What variables seem to predict a positive attitude toward retirement? Attitudes are influenced by a variety of factors, such as the type of work a person does, how much is earned, and educational level. People who find their jobs boring and unrewarding hold extremely favorable attitudes about retirement—so much so that researchers (e.g., Barfield & Morgan, 1978) suggest that this positive attitude reflects a desire to escape dissatisfying circumstances.

For white-collar male workers (e.g., clerks and salespeople), income is the best predictor of positive attitudes toward retirement (Shanas, 1972). However, women receiving higher incomes have been reported as wanting to continue working longer (Streib & Schneider, 1971). Although income appears to be a factor associated with favorable opinions about retirement, it is difficult to separate the effects of sex and even educational level on attitudes toward retirement. Sheppard (1976), for instance, reports that highly educated men are negative about retirement. Highly educated women, however, not only are positive about retirement, but also leave the work force at younger ages. Even studies dealing with one sex report controversial findings. For example, women with higher incomes, better education, and higher-status occupations wanted and continued to work longer (Streib & Schneider, 1971).

Cohort differences Historical events also alter the relative position of different cohorts' positive anticipation of retirement. Barfield and Morgan (1978) found that older cohorts hold more favorable prospects about retirement than younger cohorts who have not become well-established financially as a result of increased unemployment and inflation. Older adults, therefore, seem more willing to enter into retirement than younger adults primarily because of financial

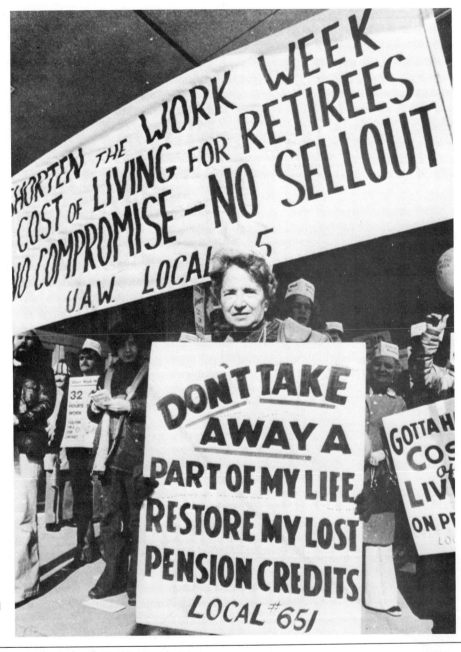

Money and health are two important factors that determine successful adaptations to retirement. (United Press International)

security. These new data contradict earlier findings that suggest that attitudes about retirement become increasingly negative with increasing age. The older literature is based on the notion that retirement is a crisis—it is "a major disruption of an adult's role and would tend to have deleterious consequences for the individual" (Streib & Schneider, 1971, p. 5). We will return to this issue when we examine adjusting to retirement and life satisfaction after retirement.

Early retirement   Retirements before age 65 have become more prevalent in our society. In several non-health-related industries, early retirement has even replaced mandatory retirement (Barfield & Morgan, 1974). In a study of fifty-two academics from four universities, it was found that individuals opted for early retirement because of increased annuities or substantial lump-sum severance payments. Thus, it seems that if individuals can retire early and still be financially secure, they will exercise the option (Kell & Patton, 1978).

It is a mistake, however, to believe that people who retire early necessarily have a favorable attitude toward retirement. More often than not, these people do not have a choice. The decision to retire early primarily occurs because people believe they are unable to work. Failing health is the reason most often expressed for leaving the work force voluntarily (Haynes, McMichael, & Tyroler, 1978). Another reason deals with attitudes of family and friends. It seems that if significant others sanction early retirement, then it is acceptable (Chown, 1977).

Adjusting to Retirement

If disengagement theory is correct, retirement should be perceived merely as a transitional process. Individuals should not experience significant stress or loss during what represents a mutual withdrawal from society. But evidence (e.g., Lowenthal, 1972) suggests that adjusting to retirement requires shifting from being instrumentally to emotionally goal-oriented. Also, successful adjustment to retirement requires a supportive and understanding spouse who also becomes more emotionally oriented than previously.

Work styles and marital roles   Lowenthal (1972) suggests that the way people have behaved throughout their work lives and the attitudes they hold will influence their adjustments to retirement. A person who has been work-oriented throughout life will consider retirement traumatic. Substitutions need to be planned by such a person; otherwise depression and fear of dependence may result. One such substitution is another job. Of those who said work was a major source of satisfaction, 73 percent returned to work after retirement from their other job (Streib & Schneider, 1971). These people were healthier, more educated, and held positions of higher status compared with those not returning to work. Others—who feel work is not an end in itself but a means to an end, i.e., social acceptance and approval—appear able to adjust to retirement more easily than the work-oriented type.

Lowenthal (1972) describes three additional types of people—self-protective, autonomous, and receptive-nurturant. If life has been viewed as a struggle, retirement for the self-protective person is a time when feelings of detachment and no responsibility for or dependency on others are maintained. This person disengages, and retirement presents no particular problem unless it is experienced with other interacting events. The autonomous individual is one who has selected a career that allows the individual to decide when to retire. If the person can exercise his or her option of when to retire, the transition will be smooth. On the other hand, if retirement is mandatory, depression is a likely consequence and reorientation is required. The autonomous person tends to be creative, has varied goals, and is self-generating. Finally, the receptive-nurturant individual is usually female and has devoted her life to affect and intimacy. Her positive adjustment to retirement is contingent on her perceived quality of the marital relationship. To the extent that the marriage is "good," she adjusts easily to retirement and may even feel relieved that she can devote more time to her marital role.

Wives can assist their husbands during their adjustment to retirement by finding tasks in the home that give them a sense of participation and usefulness. An excess of time is the problem for many male retirees. They have more time to spend around the house than ever before, save for times of prolonged illness. Wives have commented that their husbands often are unprepared to fill the time formerly devoted to work with other activities. They feel as if they have an additional dependent to teach and supervise (Kerckhoff, 1964). The assistance of wives is more successful in white-collar families than blue-collar ones because white-collar husbands are more apt to accept home-related tasks. White-collar men are also more likely to have had a history of shared leisure and recreational interests with their wives (Kent, 1966).

Successful adjustment to the impact of retirement on couples requires role changes—moving toward more expressive roles—for both husbands and wives. Troll (1971) states:

The husband adjusts from the instrumental role of "good provider" to a more expressive role: "helping in the house," and his wife also adjusts by moving from a relatively more instrumental "good homemaker" to even more expressive "loving and understanding." The retired husband ends up sharing in household tasks, but whether or not he feels good about it seems to depend on his value system. If, as is true of many working-class husbands, "women's work" is considered demeaning, the man sharing it feels devalued. This does not seem to be as true for middle-class men. (p. 274)

Troll therefore suggests that adjusting to retirement for blue-collar men can be more problematic than for white-collar men. However, blue-collar men also demonstrate adjustment to retirement. This occurs when a couple has a history of mutual satisfaction, because with such a situation the increase in time a husband spends at home furthers the couple's perceived happiness (Peterson & Payne, 1975). But in relationships that have a history of conflict, the increase in a husband's time at home contributes to the already established unhappiness and adds to the difficulty of adjusting to retirement (Lopata, 1966).

A theme cutting across Lowenthal's (1972) proposed retirement types is that a redistribution of energy is needed in order to accommodate to retirement and that this accommodation reflects the adaptation processes used by the person throughout life. Other data that we discussed earlier, such as that of

Maas & Kuypers (1974) (see Chapter 6), also support the idea that aspects of personality and life-style are good predictors of adjustment and subsequent life satisfaction.

Life satisfaction How satisfied are people with retirement? A major research question deals with the relationship between level of activity or use of leisure time and life satisfaction. In a classic longitudinal study by Streib & Schneider (1971) of more than 4000 people who held a variety of jobs, ranging from unskilled labor to professional positions, assessments of health status, economic status, and different psychosocial areas (e.g., satisfaction with life, feelings of usefulness, and adjustment to retirement) were gathered. The data indicate that most people were adjusted to retirement and satisfied with life. These individuals were healthy, and stated that their incomes were adequate. In fact, one-third of the sample said retirement was better than they thought it would be, and only 4 to 5 percent felt it was worse than they expected. However, 10 percent did return to work—again adding support to Lowenthal's and Atchley's conceptions (e.g., Barfield & Morgan, 1974; Fox, 1977).

Many cross-sectional and survey studies show that as long as income and health are maintained during retirement, life satisfaction and adjustment to retirement are positive. The only index differentiating men from women is that retired women express concern over loss of social contacts (Fox, 1977).

Oftentimes people who are retired engage in leisure activities. But data suggest that people who are work-oriented do not value leisure (Pfeiffer & Davis, 1974) and that money is an important variable influencing how leisure activities are viewed (Cottrell & Atchley, 1969). Perhaps attitudes toward leisure are related to being able to pay for activities. And how one views leisure activities may be related to the type of job held. If, for example, a person writes or paints for a living—activities often related to leisure—what activities would be considered a use of leisure? More research is needed in order to understand the use of leisure across the life span and especially after retirement. However, having a positive attitude toward leisure and being satisfied with life after retirement seem to be associated with both income and health status.

One event that often occurs in close proximity to retirement is becoming a grandparent. The grandparent role not only can contribute to one's feelings of completing life with satisfaction, but also can fill the excess of time which contributes to problems of adjustment to retirement.

GRANDPARENTING

The role of grandparent is a prevalent one in our society. In spite of this, it is one of the least-understood familial roles. During the last century, however, we have observed a quickening of the family life cycle (Neugarten & Moore, 1968). Marriage, the birth and departure of children, and grandparenthood all tend to occur earlier today than at the turn of the century. But what is the meaning of grandparenthood for various generations? How does the grandparent role vary for different individuals? How do grandparents influence their grandchildren? A developing literature is beginning to focus on these questions.

The Grandparent Role

There is relatively general agreement that the grandparent role is not clearly defined in today's society (Clavan, 1978; Kahana & Kahana, 1971; Robertson, 1977). Clavan (1978) suggests that, particularly for the middle class, it is a "roleless role." That is, there is a kinship status connected with the role of grandparent, but few normative rights and responsibilities are associated with that role. As a result, grandparents, parents, and grandchildren must construct the role. For instance, Troll (1971) notes that being a *valued* grandparent is not automatic, but must be earned. In this regard, grandparents often voluntarily engage in giving and helping behaviors with their children and grandchildren in return for attention and affection (Robertson, 1977).

Given the diffuse nature of the expectations associated with grandparenthood, we would expect multiple styles of playing out the grandparent role. Several studies have examined these different patterns. In one study, Neugarten and Weinstein (1964) interviewed seventy pairs of grandparents about their relationship with their grandchildren. Three dimensions were examined: the degree of comfort with the role as expressed by the grandparent; the significance of the role to the grandparent; and the style with which the role was enacted by the grandparent. The vast majority of grandparents expressed satisfaction with the role. However, a significant minority (approximately one-third) were experiencing difficulty in the role and said they felt discomfort or disappointment. These difficulties were often related to feeling uncomfortable in thinking of themselves as grandparents or to conflict with the parents over rearing or interacting with the grandchild.

Within this context, Neugarten and Weinstein found that grandparenthood had different meanings for different people. Five themes were predominant. For some, grandparenthood was a source of *biological renewal and/or continuity*. It evoked feelings of youth (renewal) or extensions of the self and family into the future (continuity). For others, grandparenthood was a source of *emotional self-fulfillment*. It evoked feelings of companionship and satisfaction from the development of a relationship between adult and child often missing in earlier parent-child interactions. As shown in Table 11.1, these themes were prominent for relatively large percentages of the respondents. Two other themes were suggested by relatively few grandparents. These were *resource person* and *vicarious achievement*. In the former case, satisfaction was derived from contributing to the development of the grandchild—for example, through financial aid, life experiences, and so on. In the latter case, grandparenthood was seen as providing an extension of the self in that the grandchild was seen as able to accomplish what neither the grandparent nor the parent were able to. Finally, 27 percent of the grandmothers and 29 percent of the grandfathers felt *remote* from their grandchildren. These respondents said that the role of grandparent had relatively little effect on their lives.

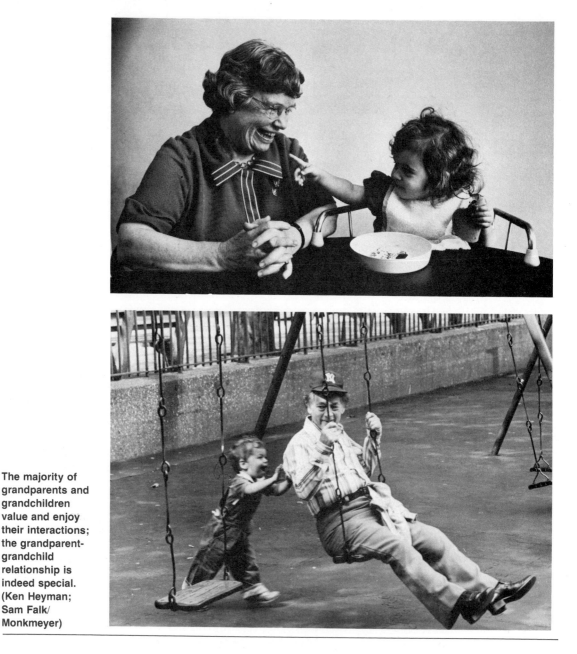

The majority of grandparents and grandchildren value and enjoy their interactions; the grandparent-grandchild relationship is indeed special. (Ken Heyman; Sam Falk/ Monkmeyer)

Neugarten and Weinstein (1964) also identified five styles of interaction which were somewhat independent of the meaning dimensions. As indicated in Table 11.1, a *formal* style was relatively frequent for both grandmothers and grandfathers. This style involved performing what was regarded as a proper

TABLE 11.1
MEANING AND STYLE OF GRANDPARENTING
(In percent)*

	Grandmothers	Grandfathers
Meaning of Grandparent Role		
Biological renewal/continuity	42	23
Emotional self-fulfillment	19	27
Resource person	4	11
Vicarious achievement	4	4
Remote	27	29
Style of Grandparenting		
Formal	31	33
Fun-seeking	29	24
Parent surrogate	14	0
Reservoir of family wisdom	1	6
Distant figure	19	29

*The difference between the total for each column and 100 percent reflects insufficient data.
Source: Based on Neugarten and Weinstein, 1964.

and prescribed role. While they maintained continued interest in the grandchild and sometimes provided him or her with special treats, formal grandparents left parenting to the parents. They were careful not to offer advice on childrearing or otherwise interfere with the parental role. The *fun-seeker* style was characterized by informality and playfulness. Grandchildren were viewed as a source of leisure activity, and the emphasis was on mutual satisfaction. Authority was seen as irrelevant. The *surrogate-parent* style was found only for grandmothers. In this case, the grandmother assumed actual care-taking responsibility for the grandchild while the mother worked. The *reservoir of family wisdom* occurred rarely and usually involved the grandfather. In this style, the grandparent was a dispenser of special skills or resources. Both parents and grandchildren were usually subordinate to an authoritarian grandparent. Finally, a substantial minority of both grandmothers and grandfathers were relatively *distant figures*. This style is benevolent, but contact is fleeting and infrequent. Of these styles, Neugarten and Weinstein found that the traditional style was more prevalent among the older grandparents (over 65), while the fun-seeker style was more prevalent among the younger (under 65) grandparents. This difference may reflect either differences between cohorts of grandparents or changes with increasing age in the grandparent role.

More recently, Robertson (1977) examined the significance of the grandparent role in a sample of women. Overall, 80 percent of the respondents indicated that they were excited, proud, and happy when they learned they were going to be a grandmother. Further, the majority indicated that their feelings had not changed over the years. However, like Neugarten and Weinstein (1964), Robertson found that this role has different meanings for different individuals. She drew a distinction between a social and a personal orientation. Those grandparents emphasizing a social orientation focused on normative expectations (they should set a good example, encourage grandchildren to work hard and be honest, etc.). Those emphasizing a personal orientation focused on the joys and pleasures of grandparenthood (grandchildren make me feel young, less lonely, etc.). About 26 percent of Robertson's (1977) sample emphasized the social orientation, 17 percent emphasized the personal orientation, and 29 percent emphasized both aspects of the role. An additional 28 percent of the grandmothers were remote from their grandchildren, having little expectation for or involvement in the role. These orientations tended to be predicted by the life-styles of the family in general and the grandmothers in particular. For example, younger grandmothers tended to emphasize the social orientation, while older grandmothers tended to emphasize the personal orientation. This appears to be related to the fact that most of the younger grandmothers were married and working. As a result, they were more involved with their own lives and placed less emphasis on grandparenting. In contrast, most of the older grandmothers were widowed and unemployed. As a result, grandparenting was a significant role. Indeed, these women had the greatest amount of interaction with their grandchildren.

Mediating Variables

Historical factors Several factors probably influence these diverse patterns of grandparenting. For example, the socioeconomic status of the family is a significant factor. Both the Neugarten and Weinstein (1964) and Robertson (1977) studies focused on middle-class individuals. Other studies indicate that grandparents from lower-class families more frequently function in the role of parent surrogates (e.g., Staples, 1971). Clavan (1978) notes, however, that current social and historical trends may reduce these class differences. For example, trends such as increased divorce and the movement of young mothers into the labor force may increase the number of middle-class grandparents who become familial resources.

Familial factors Others have noted that the kinship system is important in shaping grandparent roles. Kahana and Kahana (1971) indicate that maternal grandmothers and paternal grandfathers tend to express feelings of warmth toward their grandchildren, to view them as similar to their own children, and to approve of their upbringing. In contrast, maternal grandfathers and paternal grandmothers tend to express more negative attitudes toward their grandchildren. In this regard, Robertson (1975) has postulated that the grandparent role is mediated by the parent generation. She suggests that the grandparent-grandchild relationship is affected by the extent to which parents encourage, facilitate, and reward certain behaviors.

The Impact of Grandparents

What impact do grandparents have on their grandchildren? Very few studies have been directed toward this question. The little data that are available, however, suggest that grandparents are significant to their grandchildren, although the meaning of the relationship changes with the age of the children.

Kahana and Kahana (1970), for instance, examined the meaning of grandparents for middle-class children aged 4 to 5, 8 to 9, and 11 to 12 years. The youngest children (4 to 5) valued grandparents primarily for egocentric reasons, that is, for what the grandparent gave to the child in terms of love, food, and gifts. In contrast, in addition to egocentric responses, the older children (8 to 9 and 11 to 12) mentioned perceived positive characteristics of the grandparents (e.g., "He is a good man") and mutual activities (e.g., "We go to the ball game together") as reasons for valuing grandparents. These changes probably reflect the increasing cognitive and emotional development of the child.

However, a study by Robertson (1976) suggests that grandparents maintain their significance in the lives of their young adult grandchildren. Robertson used a questionnaire to assess attitudes toward grandparents, perceptions of appropriate or expected grandparent behavior, grandchildren's responsibility toward grandparents, and conceptions of the ideal grandparent. She found that young adult grandchildren held very favorable attitudes toward grandparents. For example, 92 percent agreed that children would miss much if there were no grandparents when they were growing up; 90 percent agreed that grandparents were not too old-fashioned or out of touch to be able to help their grandchildren; and 70 percent indicated that teenagers do not feel their grandparents are a bore.

Robertson's data suggest that adult grandchildren expect relatively little from grandparents other than gift giving (59 percent) and informing them of family history (56 percent). The majority did not expect them to provide financial aid (8 percent did) or serve as a role model (23 percent), advisor (31 percent), or liaison between child and parent (29 percent). Young adult grandchildren, in turn, feel definite responsibilities toward their grandparents. About two-thirds of those in the study felt grandchildren should help their grandparents, and 62 percent felt they should not expect money for such assistance. Over 50 percent said they visited with grandparents because they loved them or enjoyed being with them. In contrast, 20 percent visited with their grandparents because their parents did, and only 11 percent did so because it was expected of them. Robertson's (1976) data also show the importance of parents: almost two-thirds of the respondents agreed that parents set the pace of the grandparent-grandchild relationship. Finally, the ideal grandparent was seen as someone who loves and enjoys grandchildren, visits with them, and shows an interest in them. Characteristics receiving the highest ranking were "loving", "gentle", "helpful", "understanding", "industrious", "smart", "a friend", "talkative", and "funny". Characteristics receiving the lowest ranking were "lazy", "childish", "dependent", "mediator", "companion", and "teacher".

The studies reviewed above suggest that the grandparent-grandchild relationship can be significant for both parties. There are multiple patterns of interaction, however, and the significance of the relationship appears to depend to a great extent on how much the various generations work at it. Further, there is evidence to suggest that the grandparent role may be undergoing change as individuals become grandparents at earlier ages and as changes in family functioning place new demands on it. Finally, it is possible that this role may become particularly significant for older adults. Grandparenthood is one of the few social roles potentially available to many older adults. Participation in it either as a biological or foster grandparent could be highly positive in terms of the social function of older adults. As is evident from the account of the widow who became a foster grandmother (see Box 11.3), the role of grandparent can serve to fill a need in an aging person's life, especially when the individual is adjusting to widowhood.

Profile

BOX 11.3
FOSTER GRANDPARENTING

I felt like I was dead, but alive. I wasn't doing much. My husband died years ago. My children left years ago, too. They write once in awhile and call, but . . . most of my friends are sick or too old to do anything.

On the radio, I heard the hospital wanted people to be grandparents for some backward children. I never was close to a backward child before so I wasn't sure I'd be good enough for what they wanted. It took me weeks of thinking, but finally I decided to call. I told them I was interested in being helpful, but could not get there myself. I stopped driving when I was 75 'cause I could no longer see real well. They said they'd pick me up—some sort of pool.

I was afraid. I didn't sleep well that night. Maybe I couldn't see what the child needed. The man came on time, not like the other people who never fix the plumbing like they say.

The hospital was big. Everyone moved fast. I sat and waited. Then, two men came over. One had a cane and an attractive white beard. They took me to see the little boy. He was so darling.

They call him a mongoloid, but I couldn't tell. The first thing he did was hug me. He squeezed my legs so tight, I thought I'd fall over. I knew it would be okay. We didn't talk much that day. We just sat and hugged. I felt warm all over.

I came back the next week and the next. I made him cookies. He loves chocolate chip. I knitted him a scarf. I don't have to look to knit. We had a beautiful Christmas with all the children and foster grandparents.

I now have five children I buy and do things for and they are growing-up real well. I feel so good now . . . I'm not empty inside.

One of my friends goes with me, too. She has two children, but she has her grandchildren at home, too, so I don't know why she should have more. I go to sleep thinking of my children and how I can do for them. They've done so much for me.

(*Source*: Authors' files)

WIDOWHOOD

In 1970, there were 2.11 million widowers and 9.64 million widows in the United States; that is, there was a 5:1 ratio of widows to widowers (*Statistical Abstracts of the United States*, 1971). Of all women, 12.5 percent are widows, although the probability of remarriage is high for individuals (especially those aged 35 or younger). Men remarry faster than women. On an average, remarriage occurs 1.7 years after the death of a spouse for men and 3.5 years after the death of a spouse for women.

Widows versus Widowers

It appears that women who are widowed do not experience that life event in the same way that men do. For example, in a study of 403 community residents aged 62 and over, six major areas of life functioning were assessed: psychosocial needs, household roles, nutrition, health care, transportation, and education (Barrett, 1978). Widowers were found to experience lower morale, to feel lonelier and more dissatisfied with life, to consider community services more inadequate, to need more help with household chores, to have greater difficulty getting medical appointments, to eat more poorly, and to possess stronger negative attitudes about continued learning than widows. Moreover, widowers were more reluctant to talk about widowhood or death than widows were, and stated that they did not want a confidant.

Update

BOX 11.4

RETYING THE KNOT IN OLD AGE

To what extent does remarriage constitute a viable alternative for older widows and widowers? In terms of sheer numbers, remarriage among older adults has more than doubled in the last ten years. We know much less about these remarriages than we do about marriages and remarriages between younger couples. Recently, however, Vinick (1978) interviewed remarried couples aged 60 to 84 in order to determine how these individuals experienced the event of remarriage.

She found that most people had originally chosen to live alone after the death of their spouse. Men remarried more quickly than women. Over half the men remarried within a year or less after becoming widowed, while only three women were remarried within two years after losing their previous spouse. Most of the couples

had been introduced by a mutual friend or relative, or had known one another when one or both of them had been married to their previous spouses. Usually it was the men who took the initiative after the initial meeting. Often the relationship just seemed to grow gradually.

The most significant factor in the decision to remarry was the desire for companionship. Men also mentioned a desire for care, while women mentioned the personal qualities of the prospective spouse.

Vinick's data suggest that these remarriages were very successful: 87 percent of the men and 80 percent of the women described themselves as "satisfied" or "very satisfied" with the relationship. The exceptions were those who married for "external" reasons. For example, one woman had remarried in order to attain financial security

Increasing numbers of adults are remarrying late in life. (United Press International)

and then found that her husband was autocratic and miserly. While the majority of the respondents indicated that adjustments had been required, the marriages were characterized by a serenity usually not found among young marrieds. Vinick (1978) comments: "Most people had a 'live and let live' attitude toward the spouse. Time and again I heard that 'it doesn't pay to get angry,' 'it takes two to make an argument' and that one should contain his or her feelings. Old age marriage is free from the strains of early

marriage—child rearing, ambition for higher status, conflict with in-laws" (p. 362).

Vinick concludes that remarriage is a viable alternative for older adults. Many external conditions, of course, influence the practicality of this alternative. For example, the shorter average life span of men effectively limits the number of potential male partners. However, one obstacle has recently been removed. Since January 1979, widows retain their full Social Security benefits upon remarriage.

In our society, however, women outlive men. It is reported that half of all married women have been widowed by their early seventies and 80 percent have been widowed by their early eighties. However, only half of all married men are widowed in their early eighties (Atchley, 1977). Also, since there are more unmarried older women, widowers may be more likely to remarry. Further, one could argue that the loss of a husband would be more devastating than the loss of a wife because the male role is more prestigious in our society. Finally, most widows appear to be more strongly affected by the death of a spouse who is likely to be the sole breadwinner.

All life events are experienced differently by people at different points in their life spans, and the same is true of widowhood. However, although we are examining widowhood in this chapter because it tends to occur more often during the latter part of the life span, we will include data dealing with age-related differences in widowhood whenever possible.

Mediating Variables

What variables interact with the event of widowhood and what are the effects of these variables?

Age It appears that the social participation of widowers but not widows increases with age (Blau, 1975). However, Berardo (1967) reported that aged widowers are the most isolated, and he cited poor health as a contributing factor. When widowed individuals were compared with married persons of the same age and sex, widows and widowers were found to exhibit higher rates of mortality, mental disorder, and suicide than married people (Berardo, 1968).

Economic status Using a large national sample, Harvey and Bahr (1974) reported that economic status often accounts for the negative impact of widowhood on life satisfaction. Data indicate that widows with low incomes have lower social participation and greater loneliness (Atchley, 1975). There is also a greater likelihood for widows to have inadequate incomes compared with widowers. Atchley (1975) suggests that negative attitudes toward, and social isolation of, widows are influenced greatly by economic factors. Data collected by Lopata (1971) support the idea that poverty causes reduced social participation of widows. The question remains: "Does the event of widowhood account for the economic differential that is reported between married and widowed women?"

Morgan (1978) looked at the question of what economic change occurs with widowhood. The data used were drawn from the National Longitudinal Surveys Cohort of Mature Women (1967–1974). The 8000 women nationally sampled in 1967 were 30 to 44 years of age. The first question asked was whether there are cross-sectional differences in family income for particular years as a result of marital status. Table 11.2 compares married and currently widowed women by race in a year-to-year income comparison. Various sources of family income across all family members were used to index family income. The table shows that total family income is lower (between 48 and 53 percent) for widows compared with married women for all years, although both groups reflect an increase in mean income over time which is an inflationary response. For black widows, the mean income is lower in all years, but the ratios between widowed and married women are similar for blacks and nonblacks. Thus, it appears that both groups were relatively equal over this period of time, suggesting that the economic cycles are similar, with widows having substantially lower mean incomes than their married counterparts.

Reduced income is often a major source of difficulty for women in adjusting to widowhood. (Ann Chwatsky/Editorial Photocolor Archives)

When family income is considered for the year of the husband's death, one year later, and after the second year of widowhood, the following emerges. For 30- to 34-year-olds, there is a drop in family income after death of husband, but a recovery is noted in the next two years. For 35- to 39-years-olds a monotonic increase is experienced, while 40- to 44-year-olds demonstrate a monotonic

TABLE 11.2

MEANS AND RATIOS OF TOTAL FAMILY INCOME BY MARITAL STATUS AND RACE FOR FIVE INCOME YEARS

		Income Year				
		1966	1968	1970	1971	1973
		Total				
Married	Mean	$9474.43	$10,852.17	$12,825.92	$13,831.84	$15,973.37
	Standard deviation	5637.71	6,385.47	8,078.22	8,166.85	10,095.99
Widows	Mean	4916.00	5,373.47	6,462.21	6,588.14	7,637.30
	Standard deviation	3184.07	4,707.73	3,986.44	4,594.30	5,596.87
Ratio		.519	.495	.504	.476	.481
		Nonblack				
Married	Mean	$9783.63	$11,201.09	$13,241.84	$14,233.37	$16,505.75
	Standard deviation	5672.18	6,337.43	8,146.15	8,162.95	10,138.82
Widows	Mean	5562.54	5,919.47	7,404.79	7,361.79	8,450.03
	Standard deviation	3153.99	4,476.46	4,000.85	4,865.62	5,069.04
Ratio		.569	.528	.559	.518	.512
		Black				
Married	Mean	$6198.25	7,118.68	$ 8,365.90	$ 9,494.23	$10,166.57
	Standard deviation	3968.72	5,675.13	5,627.50	7,117.93	7,457.49
Widows	Mean	3111.79	4,078.71	4,482.56	4,408.85	5,388.09
	Standard deviation	2499.71	2,639.26	3,122.72	3,029.45	3,480.99
Ratio		.502	.572	.536	.464	.530

Notes: Income figures quoted are for the complete income year prior to data collection. Widowed in each year are only those respondents who were currently widowed. The dichotomous race breakdown includes the "other" ethnic identifiers with white respondents.

Source: From Morgan, 1978.

decline. Moreover, in the latter group there is a greater disadvantage for black widows. Perhaps the increase noted for the two age groups immediately after widowhood is a result of short-term death benefits. Also, of those women in the older group, fewer were working during this time period. It appears that one should be cautious about equating widowhood with economic disadvantage because other factors, such as age of widow and working versus nonworking status, contribute to the economic changes caused by the alteration in marital status.

Education In *Widowhood in an American City,* Lopata (1973c) concluded that widowhood is more disorganizing for more highly educated women than for those with less education. She found that, in general, widows feel incompetent in many areas (e.g., financial matters and social decisions), and these problems are magnified by the more highly educated women who report a stronger identification with the world of their husbands.

Adapting to Widowhood

The death of a spouse is disruptive not only to the dyadic relationship, but also to other relations that are organized around the marital role (Znaniecki, 1965; Lopata, 1971). The presence of a widow or widower in a social unit may have reactive consequences, such as husbands becoming concerned about their wives' loyalty, or wives about their husbands', because of the presence of the unattached person.

Grief work Researchers have been concerned with events that occur immediately after the loss of a spouse and during the subsequent year. The bereavement process is referred to by some as *grief work* (Parkes & Brown, 1972). The major grief reaction cited is the loss of the person's "working model of the world and working model of the self" (Rux, 1976, p. 14). A person's working model of the world is disrupted because of loss of the strong attachment that has developed, while the working model of the self is disrupted because of differences in the acceptance one feels from people deemed important (Bowlby, 1973; Parkes & Brown, 1972).

Grief work has been identified as a process leading to a new identity. The process can consist of healthy or unhealthy development. The stages involved are: (1) numbness, (2) pining for the lost person, (3) depression, and (4) recovery. This process is thought to be essential after the loss of a spouse regardless of sex, age at widowhood, economic situation, or expectations of one's own death (Rux, 1976). The next chapter examines the area of death and dying and discusses at length various ways in which family members cope with the death of a loved one.

Changing social roles With a large urban sample of 301 widows of all ages Lopata (1973a, b, c) reported that reactions to widowhood reflected women's social role backgrounds. Depending on the type of wife role held and other social roles assumed prior to the death of the husband, the type and intensity of the life-span disruption experienced after the death and following the death vary. For example, more highly educated middle-class women who were strongly involved in the role of wife reported "strong life disruption after the death of the husband" (Lopata, 1975, p. 229). Other women, living in more of a sex-segregated world, in which they were relatively independent of their husbands (e.g., engaging in neighboring or having a job), stated that they were lonely after the death but that their life-styles did not change much.

Lopata (1975) proposes five types of widows:

The *liberated widow,* who is able to lead a multidimensional life

The *merry widow,* who is socially active—dating and interacting with friends

The *working-widow,* who operates on the job in a committed and individualistic way (a subtype exists—the returning-to-work widow who takes any job, expecting minimal economic return)

The *widow's widow,* who remains in that role unwilling to relinquish it through remarriage, devotion to grandparenting, or other roles

The *traditional widow,* who devotes time to children, grandchildren, and siblings

Adapting to new social roles also seems important for widowers. In a recent study of 107 widowers and widows between the ages of 40 and 70, Rux (1976) found that life-satisfaction ratings correlated significantly with current instrumental skills. Thus, adjustment to widowhood seems to entail more than emotionally responding to the loss of a spouse. It also involves being able to adapt to new roles and responsibilities. Perhaps the maintenance of friendships can facilitate this adaptation (see Box 11.5).

Interventions Evidence indicates that widowed persons experience impaired mental and physical health compared with married persons of the same age (Barrett, 1977). Also, during the experience of this life event psychiatric symptoms are heightened (Clayton, 1974), mental illness increases (Bellin & Hardt, 1958), and suicides increase (Bock & Weber, 1972) compared with married individuals. As a consequence, a variety of interventions have been developed by mental health professionals (e.g., Miles & Hayes, 1975) and lay organizations (e.g., THEOS—They Help Each Other Spiritually), but few evaluations have been conducted.

Barrett (1978), however, recently assessed three different therapeutic group interventions dealing with consciousness raising for seventy urban widowed women. The effects of the intervention were evaluated, and the women were compared to a waiting-list control group. Treatments were designed to meet the needs of widows of all ages, because research suggests that stresses may be greater for younger widows (Kraus & Lilienfeld, 1959), even though the frequency of widowhood is higher among older women. Eighteen personality, attitude, and behavioral measures were obtained by written report on three occasions—pretest, posttest, and follow-up fourteen weeks later. At posttest and follow-up, higher self-esteem, increased intensity of grief feelings, and increased negative attitudes toward remarriage were reported by all groups. Intervention groups showed improvements in their ratings of their future health and became less other-oriented in their attitudes toward women relative to the controls.

One intervention approach, called Widow-to-Widow, uses lay widows and widowers who have experienced the event. A helper is matched for certain characteristics, such as age, education, and economic status, with the bereaved person. This person assists in the transition period and helps the widow acquire a new role. The approach appears to be generally successful (Silverman, 1977).

In Depth

BOX 11.5
FRIENDSHIPS

What types of people are selected as friends and how do friendships change over time? The selection of friends is affected by numerous variables, and so only some rather influential ones will be considered here. Propinquity, or physical proximity, is a strong determinant of friendship bonding. Obviously, two people need contacts to establish a friendship, which, once established, can be maintained at a distance. Proximity also may be a key variable because it reflects attitudinal similarity. For instance, many neighborhoods are quite homogeneous in terms of age, race, ethnicity, and socioeconomic status (Byrne, 1961). Also, people who have certain characteristics, such as being attractive, warm, and friendly, form friendships more easily than those who do not demonstrate such characteristics (Schneider, 1974). Self-disclosure, moreover, is a critical factor in forming friendships. Since women are more self-disclosing than men, some researchers (Troll, 1975) feel they develop closer relationships with friends than do men. Therefore, proximity, personality, and self-disclosure are key factors influencing the development of friendship. On an average, three or four close friendships are developed during young adulthood (Haan & Day, 1974).

Cross-sectional evidence suggests that sex differences in friendship patterns across the life span occur. Married middle-aged men spend more time with friends than with family and rely upon the advice of friends more than they rely on the advice of a spouse. Throughout their lifetimes, however, women maintain their friendships more than men (Maas & Kuypers, 1974; Riley, Johnson, & Foner, 1968).

The way adults perceive friendships also changes over the life span. Young adults feel that the sharing of experience creates intimacy between friends. Older adults mention this, too, but also feel that the emotional, interpersonal aspects and length of the friendships are important (Lowenthal, Thurnher, & Chiriboga, 1975; Troll, 1975).

After retirement, older adults do not conceal the negative aspects of their personalities as much with their friends as they did in the past. Perhaps this is because they are no longer competing. With their future becoming their past, older adults seem to glory in being open and reminiscing.

Friends also help with role adjustments and give social support for infirmities, problems, and concerns over death. Oftentimes friendships among the elderly serve as buffers against a stressful environment. Even superficial friends can assist in getting one through the day. Thus, friendship represents a form of human bonding that is different from marriage or parent-child relations. It is one of the freest forms of relating because it is unregulated by laws.

RELOCATION

With the death of a mate, many people are faced with having to move. In recent years considerable attention has been paid to the impact of this event in later life. Some of the studies have suggested that relocation has negative effects, such as increased mortality and decreased morale (Aldrich & Mendkoff, 1963; Killian, 1970; Lieberman, 1975). Relocation has been found to be a major life event that potentially affects individuals of all ages. For example, Lowenthal, Thurnher, and Chiriboga (1975) found that it was the second most frequent stress (after school) mentioned by female adolescents. Is relocation particularly stressful for older adults? In order to examine this question let us first consider some general factors involved in adaptation to the environment.

Adapting to the Environment

In examining the adaptation process it is important to consider both individual and environmental factors. This point is emphasized in the model developed by Lawton (Lawton & Nahemow, 1973; Lawton, 1975, 1977), which is shown in Figure 11.1. Lawton views adaptive behavior as a joint function of the individual's *competence* (capacity to function in physiological, sensory, motor, and cognitive areas) and *environmental press* (demand and potential of a given environmental quality that activates behavior). The impact of these variables on affective and adaptive behavior is mediated by other factors such as personality style.

Lawton's model can help to explain the impact of life events such as relocation. A change in competence (e.g., becoming ill), a change in environmental press (e.g., moving to a new neighborhood), or both will result in a shift in adaptation level. In Figure 11.1 the line labeled "adaptation level" defines the point at which positive outcomes occur with little awareness of environmental press. The most positive outcomes occur when environmental demands slightly exceed the adaptation level, yielding a "stimulating" environment. Environmental press which exceeds the individual's competencies, however, produces negative outcomes. Note that as competence decreases, environmental demands have an increasing effect (i.e., for the least competent there is a wide range of maladaptive outcomes related to environmental press. Note also that

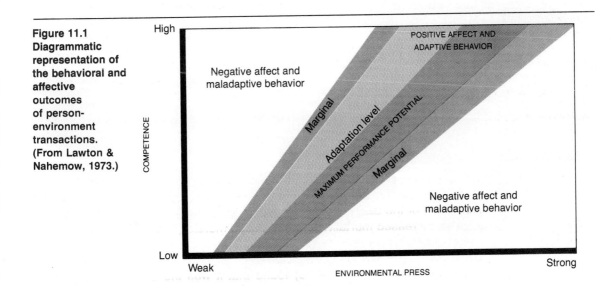

Figure 11.1 Diagrammatic representation of the behavioral and affective outcomes of person-environment transactions. (From Lawton & Nahemow, 1973.)

too little environmental press in relation to competence (e.g., sensory deprivation) produces maladaptive outcomes as well.

Within the general context of this model, other aspects of a particular event may also be significant. Basing their conclusions on a review of the stress literature, Schulz and Brenner (1977), for example, argue that choice and predictability are important. This suggests (1) that individuals who relocate voluntarily should adapt better than those who relocate involuntarily, and (2) that new environments which are predictable either because of their similarity to the old environment or because of preparatory learning should be easier to adapt to than those which are less predictable. These factors, however, are presumed to be subordinate to competence and environmental press. That is, if the demands of the environment significantly exceed the individual's competence, one would expect negative outcomes regardless of the individual's subjective perception of the situation. Given this general framework, let us now examine several types of relocation.

One of the difficulties of being forced to relocate is to leave old friends; but when environments can be maintained, adaptations are orderly. (Daniel Brody/Editorial Photocolor Archives)

Community Relocation

The bulk of the research on relocation within the community has focused on planned housing for the elderly. One of the most extensive projects was conducted by Carp (1966), who studied 352 individuals who applied for public housing. Of these, 204 were ultimately relocated in Victoria Plaza, while 148 were not. Self-report measures were obtained at the time of application and twelve to fifteen months following relocation. The overwhelming majority of the relocatees were highly satisfied with their new housing. This finding is perhaps not surprising considering that the tenant's previous accommodations were very inadequate, typically consisting of a small room on the second or third floor of an old house with communal bathroom facilities. The positive impact of relocation was seen in other measures as well, including increases in social relationships and activities and self-reported health and morale and decreases in the number of services needed.

Other studies generally have supported the conclusion that voluntary relocation within the community is not associated with significant negative effects (Lawton & Cohen, 1974; Storandt & Wittles, 1975; Wittles & Botwinick, 1974). For example, Lawton and Cohen (1974) found that several indexes of well-being (housing satisfaction, satisfaction with status quo) were higher among older adults who had moved into housing projects than among those who had remained in the community. Wittles and Botwinick (1974) did not observe a relocation mortality effect in their study of voluntary relocation of the elderly to new apartment complexes. Similarly, in a follow-up study, Storandt and Wittles (1975) found no decrements on measures of cognition (e.g., psychomotor speed, memory, intelligence), personality (e.g., neuroticism, depression, life satisfaction), self-rated health, and social activities.

There are exceptions to these largely positive findings. For example, the anticipation and experience of actually moving often result in a temporary decline in morale and other indicators of well-being (Schooler, 1975). Further, relocations which are involuntary or which involve moving to a less-desirable environment appear to have a negative impact (Brand & Smith, 1974; Kasteler, Grey, & Carruth, 1968).

Institutional Relocation

Contrary to popular belief the number of older adults living in institutions at any one time is relatively small—about 5 percent of the population over age 65. However, the total chance of being institutionalized at some time prior to death is greater than this. Palmore (1976) attempted to estimate this chance by analyzing the experience of individuals from the Duke First Longitudinal Study who were followed until their deaths. All 207 participants were community residents at the beginning of the study in 1955. Of these, 54 (26 percent) were institutionalized one or more times prior to death, suggesting a total chance of institutionalization of about one in four, at least for this sample. Table 11.3 shows a number of variables which influence the chance of institutionalization. It can be seen that women, those who live alone, those who never married or are

TABLE 11.3
PERCENTAGE INSTITUTIONALIZED IN SELECTED CATEGORIES

Variable	N	% Institutionalized	% Not	p*
Living arrangement				
Alone	42	33	67	.10
With spouse	119	24	76	
With others	46	24	76	
Marital status				
Never married	13	54	46	.001
Separated	10	40	60	
Spouse present	119	24	76	
Widowed	66	20	80	
Children living				
None	38	34	66	.05
1 or 2	74	27	73	
3+	95	22	78	
Sex				
Women	97	33	67	.01
Men	110	20	80	
Finances				
Enough or better	180	28	72	.10
Cannot make ends meet	23	13	87	
Education				
7 years +	123	30	70	.05
0–6 years	84	20	80	
Race				
White	139	32	68	.001
Black	68	15	85	
All persons	207	26	74	

*Probability of occurring by chance using Kendall's Tau C.
Source: From Palmore, 1976.

separated, and those who never had children have higher rates of institutionalization. These factors appear to be related to the availability of care outside of the institutional setting. Other factors appear to be related to the accessibility of institutional care. These include finances, education, and race.

What is the impact of institutionalization on older adults? Institutional relocation studies have focused both on the move from home to institution and from one institution to another. A major emphasis in this literature has been the impact of relocation on mortality. The results of this research have been mixed. Some studies have shown institutionalization or institutional relocation to be associated with increased mortality rates (Aldrich & Mendkoff, 1963; Killian, 1970; Lieberman, 1975), while others have not (Gutman & Herbert, 1976; Borup, Gallego, & Heffernan, 1979). Despite such conflicting evidence, Lawton (1977) concludes that the relocation mortality effect has been generally upheld.

In spite of the significance of the relocation mortality issue, it may be argued that too much attention has been devoted to it. Of more significance for both theory and intervention are efforts to specifically isolate the variables associated with adaptive and maladaptive outcomes to institutional relocations.

Several variables consistent with Lawton's (1977) model appear to be factors in adapting to institutionalization or institutional relocation. One of the most important of these is the degree of environmental change. For example, Lieberman (1975) reports the results of four major studies involving four different types of relocation: (1) healthy older women forced to move from a small institution to a large institution; (2) community dwelling older adults voluntarily relocated to homes for the aged; (3) highly selected older patients discharged from a mental hospital to community-based institutional and semi-institutional settings; and (4) elderly patients relocated from a state hospital to other institutional settings. In all instances, individuals were examined up to a year prior to the move and again a year after the move. In two studies, relocatees were compared with matched controls. Lieberman (1975) found significant declines in physical (including death) and behavioral functioning in roughly half (48 to 56 percent) of those experiencing relocation. The rate of change was considerably higher for those who moved than for those who did not. For example, in the study examining the transfer of mental patients, the death rate for relocatees was three times that of the controls.

Lieberman concludes that the most important predictor of adjustment to relocation was the degree of change involved. The frequency of breakdown roughly paralleled the degree of environmental change involved in the relocation. Further, within any one study the most important predictor of adjustment was the degree of similarity between the individual's two environments. Other research has supported this finding. For example, Schulz and Aderman (1973) found that the length of survival of terminal cancer patients depended significantly on the degree of disparity between their previous living arrangements and the institution. Patients who came from a similar institutional environment survived an average of almost one month longer than patients who came from a dissimilar home environment. Lieberman (1975) concludes: "People whose adaptive pattern fits or matches a new environment are less likely to make new adaptations and hence less likely to be stressed; conversely, when the person's adaptive pattern or style in the prior environment is ill matched to the new environment, high stress and frequent failures in adaptation may be expected" (p. 153). Within this context, there is evidence to suggest that preparatory programs, including visits to the institution and group or personal counseling, can reduce the stress of relocation (Pastalan, 1976; Zweig & Csank, 1975).

Consistent with Lawton's (1977) model, the characteristics of the individual have also been found to be important. As we mentioned in Chapter 8, Lieberman (1975) found that physical and cognitive resources set a lower limit on adaptation. That is, those who were physically or cognitively incompetent were unable to adapt. On the other hand, competence in these areas did not guarantee adaptation. Rather, other factors appeared to mediate the adaptation process. For example, Lieberman (1975) found certain personality characteristics to be significant resources for coping with the institutional environment. In particular, those individuals who were aggressive, irritating, narcissistic, and demanding were most able to cope with the demand characteristics of the institution. Hope and the ability to engage in introspection were also predictors of successful adaptation. Thus, the research on institutionalization and institutional relocation suggests that this event may be a stressful experience particularly when it produces a mismatch between the individual's competence and the demands of the environment.

In concluding this section, it should be noted that many of the studies of relocation suffer from a number of methodological problems. Generally, two types of quasi-experimental designs have been used. On the one hand, base-line designs contrast scores on various indexes prior to and following the relocation event (e.g., mortality rate following change contrasted with that of the institution prior to change). The major concerns in this instance are the adequacy of the base-line and the possibility that change is related to history or maturation effects rather than relocation. On the other hand, case-control studies compare individuals who are relocated with individuals who are not relocated. Generally, the groups are matched either a priori or statistically on a variety of characteristics. The major concern in this instance is sample equivalance. In both designs, the follow-up period is often relatively short. Examining these problems, Borup, Gallego, and Heffernan (1979) point out that studies using the more adequate case-control design are less likely to show relocation mortality effects than those using the base-line design. Similarly, Lawton (1977) points out that a complete longitudinal control-group study of institutionalization has yet to be done. Additional refinement in our research on this critical event is required.

CONCLUSION

We have considered old age from two perspectives—sociological and psychological—while we applied a life-event perspective. Our primary interest was to show the impact of events on the lives of the elderly and to analyze how they cope with and adjust to these events. There appears to be a major problem for the elderly in our society. At a time when they have earned a right to do what they want, they are often unable to exercise this right in formal ways. The majority of their role exits and entries are not regulated by them, but rather by others—their families and society.

The situation of the elderly is not all negative, however. We considered the role of grandparenting as one which produces many positive outcomes. Also, life is viewed with much satisfaction by single elderly people. This small proportion of people are not depressed or lonely. They selected their life-style and are content.

CHAPTER SUMMARY

Although achieving a sense of completion in old age is important, it is questionable whether this is done by moving toward integrity. Moreover, focusing only on the intrapersonal resolution of the crisis of integrity versus despair does not illuminate how life events affect individuals within a social context. Similarly, there are restrictions to using the concept of disengagement for exploring the transition to old age.

Role-change areas in old age are retirement, grandparenting, widowhood, and relocation, or adaptation to a new context for living. Life-time experiences (e.g., being work-oriented or leisure-oriented, and having a good marital relationship or not) are related to attitudes toward and adjustment to retirement. Wives can assist husbands to adjust to retirement by letting them perform meaningful tasks and being supportive and understanding. In general, people are pleased with retirement as long as they have health, money, and ways to occupy their time meaningfully.

Grandparenthood is an event being experienced by people for a longer period of their life spans. It appears to be a "roleless role" in that members of the dyad determine the role relationship. Older adults react differently to the role. Some see it as biological renewal or continuity, while others view it as a source of emotional satisfaction. They can have fun without childbearing responsibilities. Historical factors such as social class and familial factors mediate attitudes toward grandparenting. Finally, grandchildren regard grandparents differently, depending upon the children's age. Most children, however, feel they would have missed much if they had not interacted with their grandparents. It therefore seems that the grandparent-grandchild relationship is significant for both parties.

Men experience the event of widowhood differently than women do. Also, different mediating variables (e.g., age, economic status, and education) have an effect on how the event is experienced. Ways in which people adapt to widowhood are important to consider because the death of a spouse is disruptive not only to the dyadic relationship but also to other relations organized around the marital role. Adjustment to widowhood entails more than an emotional response and working through one's grief. It also involves adapting to new roles and responsibilities. Various types of intervention strategies exist designed to assist a person in adjusting to widowhood.

With the death of a mate many individuals have to move. Lawton suggests that change in competence or environmental press will produce a shift in level of adaptation to relocation. Most relocated people are satisfied with their new housing as long as the move is voluntary. Involuntary relocations, however, can have a negative impact.

A relatively small proportion of the population over age 65 live in institutions, and studies of the effects of institutionalization have produced mixed results. In general, mortality rates increase when people live in institutional settings.

However, since people are often institutionalized because of physical problems to begin with, even this finding needs a cautious interpretation. Basically, to the extent that there is a mismatch between the person's competence and demands of the institutional environment, a stressful experience results.

A paradox exists for the elderly in our society. They have made their major societal contributions, have honored their commitments, have coped with life's frustrations, and have continued to live. It would seem that they have earned the right to do what they want to do. But, on the contrary, they are in a position of not being able to regulate their role exits and entries any more than they could at other periods in their life span.

This fact does not mean that their situation is all negative. Many of those with grandchildren enjoy the role. For those without grandchildren, other roles (e.g., foster grandparenting) can be assumed. Even those who do not assume surrogate grandparenting roles report contentment and satisfaction.

28 pp.

12

DEATH AND DYING

ISSUES TO CONSIDER

What is meant by death and how can it be defined?

In what ways do people's perceptions and attitudes about death vary according to age?

What antecedents account for age differences in perceptions of death?

What are the stages of dying based upon Kübler-Ross's theory?

What is meant by the phase theory of dying, and how are dying trajectories related to this theory?

Where do most people die and where do they want to die?

Why do some physicians and health care providers have difficulty telling a patient of impending death?

Should a patient be told that he or she is dying?

In what ways can a dying patient's needs be met?

What are the goals and characteristics of hospices for treating the terminally ill?

What stages are experienced when grief is anticipated?

What happens during normal grieving?

What rituals and practices are associated with grief and bereavement?

In what ways can we help ourselves and others live?

INTRODUCTION

An old man lived alone in the forest. He was the last of his family and he was so sick and feeble that he could hardly cook his gruel. Well, one cold day he had no more firewood and he went out to gather some. He was stooped and old and he carried a rope. In the woods he spread the rope on the snow and he laid his fuel on it and tied a knot but he was too weak to lift the bundle. This was too much for him. He lifted his eyes and called to Heaven. "Gott meiner. Send me Death." At once he saw the Angel of Death coming toward him. And the Angel said to him, "You sent for me, what do you want?" And the old man thought quickly and said, "Yes, as a matter of fact I did. I can't get these sticks up on my back and wonder if you'd mind giving me a hand." . . . So, you see, when it comes to dying . . . nobody is really ready. (Bellow, 1963, p. 11)

In this chapter, we will examine death and dying first by discussing what is meant by death. We will see how death has many meanings to the person confronting impending death and to those who experience the death of others. Then we will explore the dying process. Does dying occur in universal stages or not? Are there certain phases of the dying process? What perceptions and attitudes about death do people of various ages hold? We also will consider the social milieu surrounding those involved in the dying process.

THE MEANING OF DEATH

What does death mean? For Kalish (1976), "Death means different things to the same person at different times; and it means different things to the same person at the same time" (p. 483). This apparent double-talk is not meant to be elusive, but rather to point out that the death of an individual is deeply personal and happens in various social contexts. How one faces the death of oneself and of others is one of the most difficult confrontations in life. Let us begin our analysis of death and dying by examining what is meant by death.

Definitions of Death

What do you think of when you think about death? Do you visualize a cemetery or a funeral home? Do you see a person very ill in a hospital or a person badly hurt in an accident? Do you feel that death occurs primarily among people who are older? Does death make you think about the many cultural processes it triggers? Is death a state? Do you portray death by using an analogy—by comparing it to a dead battery or a dead letter office? Is death a mystery for you such that you believe it can never be understood.

Each of these questions reflects one of the ways of looking at death proposed by Kastenbaum (1975)—a prominent researcher of death and the dying process. Kastenbaum conceptualizes death in six different ways. Death can be defined as a variable, a statistic, an event, a state, an analogy, or a mystery.

Death as a variable Certain images serve as death stimuli or responses. A corpse, a funeral home, or a cemetery can represent death. The stimulus "black," whether around a card or on a person, suggests one aspect of death. Individuals may retreat from such stimuli in order to avoid the "presence of death." Oftentimes people experience this presence as silence, emptiness, and immobility. Death can also be a response to certain circumstances or situations. Being ill for an extended period, experiencing a severe accident, or having cancer all may connote death.

Death as a statistic Who will die? People of what sex, age, and socioeconomic status will die? When will these people die and of what? Over the years, the statistical characteristics of death have been compiled. Politicians, insurance companies, and community planners, just to name a few people, use such information (Forrester, 1971; Preston, Keyfite, & Schoen, 1972).

Death as an event Our culture marks death as an event. A certificate marking the time and cause of death is issued. Depending upon the situation surrounding death, death takes on different social significance. Death may be natural or not. Death may occur violently or not. Death may happen to an important person. For example, the death of Jesus Christ still has an impact upon people. Or death may occur to someone who does not have a major influence on society.

Within a family, the death of one of its members has various implications for the remaining members. "The death event can fall like an iron gate, trapping some of the survivors in the past and liberating others to go forth to a new life style" (Kastenbaum, 1975, p. 25).

As an event, death can challenge our value system, especially when it occurs off-phase, under the wrong set of circumstances. Parents do not expect to bury children, and people do not expect someone who is physically healthy and at the peak of life to die.

Certain rituals have come to be associated with death, for example, specifying time and cause of death. Other rituals seem to mediate the immediate impact of death. For instance, people honor "the last words" of the person, and need to do something (e.g., send flowers or make a donation to an organization) for the individual when death strikes. After the immediate impact of the death event, certain sequenced sets of activities take place, such as contacting the funeral home and disposing of the estate and personal effects.

Death as a state Defining death as a state of being differs from focusing on it as a process. Belief in death as a state varies tremendously from person to person and is contingent on accumulated life experiences. Death can be viewed as a state which allows for more of the same, as an opportunity for perpetual development, as less of what was experienced on earth, as a period of restful waiting, as a time of recyling because "the core of one's being cannot be destroyed" (Kastenbaum, 1975, p. 31), as the end point in a biological process, as an abstract state of "nothingness," or as an abstract state of "nonliving." Regardless of one's positon, a person's view of death as a state is greatly determined by religious beliefs. Kastenbaum (1975) suggests that "the death state is to life as aging is to development. Both involve decrement that cannot be escaped" (p. 29).

Death as an analogy   A person who no longer is thought of as important may be considered dead by family or friends. A parent, for instance, may so totally disapprove of a child's behavior that the child is considered dead. Social "death," however, is usually a temporary state. It is reversed, for example, when a disapproved-of child becomes a part of the family fold once again.

People also can play dead, that is, engage in thanatomimetic behavior. Such behavior can be purposeful (e.g., feigning death to avoid a fatal blow, such as in combat), unintentional (e.g., the diabetic coma or postseizure state), or artful (e.g., learning anxiety control, such as with yoga).

When a role or function of an individual no longer exists, a person may feel dead. For instance, a pitcher's career may end because of an injury to the throwing arm. To speak of death on a continuum of deadness-aliveness is to view death phenomenologically. According to Kastenbaum (1975), "Difficulties in conceptualizing and studying phenomenological states need not be deterrents to acknowledgment of the fact that we are sometimes more alive than at other times, and perhaps owe this phenomenon more attention than it has yet received" (p. 36).

Controversy

BOX 12.1
IS THERE LIFE AFTER DEATH?

Moody (1975) collected interview data from people who had had close calls with death. Although individual differences existed, the six experiences listed below were the ones most often described by the people interviewed:

1. Hearing the news that one has died
2. Having the feeling of moving quickly through a dark tunnel, funnel, cave, etc., toward a brilliant light
3. Feeling the presence of or seeing dead relatives or ancestors who are there to help in the transition from life to death
4. Sensing the brilliant light as a power that required one to review his or her own life; the power is sometimes experienced as love

5. Seeing their lives pass before them—a panoramic view of actions and thoughts
6. Being aware that their time for death was not yet here and they must return to complete their lives

Moody makes no claim that there is life after death, but feels there is great significance in the data he collected. Of course, scientists can question whether these people "returned from the dead" or even had "close brushes with death" because none of the people interviewed fits in the categories of brain death or cerebral death.

Death as a mystery   Although death is an inevitable, universal event that occurs daily, our own death occurs only once. Death is a mysterious paradox, therefore, because it affects our developmental course even though we only experience it at the end of life. In fact, it is often a primary reason for living. If we did not have to face death, our lives would probably be transformed. We would have different views of life events and of the relevance of their timing.

Age Differences in Death Perceptions and Attitudes

Back (1965) asked residents of Western rural communities what they would do if they knew they were going to die in one month. The older respondents' comments reflected that they would be less likely than the younger respondents to alter their activities. This finding gains support from results of a more recent study of 434 Greater Los Angeles Area respondents, representing three age groups (20 to 39, 40 to 59, and 60+), who were asked, "If you were told that you had a terminal disease and six months to live, how would you want to spend your time?" The results, shown in Table 12.1, indicate that more people in the oldest group would not change their life-styles. Moreover, three times as many older people compared with younger people said they would spend time in prayer, reading, contemplation, or other activities that reflect inner life, spiritual needs, or withdrawal (Kalish & Reynolds, 1976).

With a separate sample of 434 people, Kalish and Reynolds (1976) asked people what major losses would occur as a result of death. Again, age differences were found. Older respondents were less concerned with caring for dependents and causing grief to relatives and friends. Perhaps older people, compared with younger people, are more aware that they are likely to have a reduced impact on others if only for the reason that they have fewer dependents.

TABLE 12.1

RESPONSES ON HOW TIME WAS SPENT BEFORE DEATH
(In percent)

	Age		
	20–39	40–59	60+
Marked change in life-style, self-related (travel, sex, experiences, etc.)	24	15	9
Inner-life-centered (read, contemplate, pray)	14	14	37
Focus concern on other, be with loved ones	29	25	12
Attempt to complete projects, tie up loose ends	11	10	3
No change in life-style	17	29	31
Other	5	6	8

Source: Kalish and Reynolds, 1976.

What antecedents account for these age differences in perceptions of death? To date, few data have been generated in attempts to answer this question. In light of what we know about adult development and aging, we could speculate that pressures for disengagement, a preference for an inward-directed personality, and physical changes, health-related changes, or both are possible explanations.

In a number of studies comparing death attitudes of the elderly and other age groups, data revealed that older people thought more and talked more about death, regardless of whether the index used was if they had thought about death in the last five minutes or how many times they had previously contemplated death (Kalish & Reynolds, 1976; Riley, 1970). Although the elderly seem preoccupied with death, consistent findings suggest that they are also less frightened by it (e.g., Feifel & Branscomb, 1973; Kalish & Johnson, 1972; Kalish & Reynolds, 1976; Kogan & Wallach, 1961; Martin & Wrightsman, 1965).

It might appear to be a contradiction that the elderly are less afraid of death than younger people at the same time that they are more consumed by it or find it more salient. Kalish (1976) proposes three reasons for this attitude. First, the elderly recognize the limitations affecting their futures, e.g., health problems, role loss, and economic restrictions. Moreover, our system of social values stresses the importance of "producers of tomorrow rather than those of yesterday" (p. 490).

Second, the fact that people in industrial nations are provided with data that estimate life expectancies for various cohort groups may affect their attitude about death. For instance, those who live longer than they might have been expected to live may feel that they "have received their entitlement" (p. 490) and those who face death ahead of schedule may feel they have been "cheated."

Third, older people, more than younger people, have been socialized in such a way that they have become accustomed to death. They have experienced death in various ways, e.g., through the loss of peers and family members. Thus, death may bring relief from a state of constant bereavement. Although experiencing death does not mean that one will develop a positive attitude about it, it does offer opportunity to rehearse feelings about one's own death.

Many variables other than age mediate how death is perceived and what attitudes are held. For example, people who are more religious have less anxiety about death than those who are less religious (Martin & Wrightsman, 1965; Templar, 1972). More specifically, there appears to be a curvilinear relationship between fear of death and being religious. That is, the very religious have the least fear of death, the very nonreligious have a moderate fear of death, and the irregular religious worshippers have the greatest fear of death (Kalish, 1963; Nelson & Nelson, 1973).

It seems that a strong attitude about a belief system outside of self, or a perception of one's ego as transcending reality-oriented states, may help explain why the very religious have the least fear of death. One study (Garfield, 1974) examined the reaction of four groups (graduate students of psychology, graduate students of religion, Zen meditators, and psychodelic drug users) to death-related stimuli. The two altered-state groups displayed significantly less negative reactions to death stimuli than the two student groups, as assessed by physiological measures. Also, these groups showed less anxiety toward death as measured by a standardized death anxiety scale. Perhaps those people who have had transcendent experiences perceive death as another such experience. The elderly may *also* be viewing death in this fashion. Peck (1968) has proposed that developmental tasks during this time include body and ego transcendence. An appreciation for or experience with transcendence, therefore, may explain why the elderly are less afraid of death than younger people but are preoccupied with it at the same time.

THE DYING PROCESS

Stage Theory of Dying

Kübler-Ross (1969) conducted clinical interviews with terminally ill people while she was working at the University of Chicago teaching and research hospital. From these clinical experiences, psychiatrist Kübler-Ross developed a theory that is designed "to summarize what we have learned from our dying patients in terms of coping mechanisms at the time of terminal illness" (p. 33). The coping mechanisms deal with feelings and behaviors of those patients who made the best adjustments in confronting and finally accepting their own deaths. From these comments she constructed a five-stage theory based on the concept of hope. Kübler-Ross points out

> . . . that even the most accepting, the most realistic patients left the possibility open for some cure, for the discovery of a new drug, of the last-minute success in a research project. . . . It is this glimpse of hope which maintains them through days, weeks, or months of suffering. (p. 123)

The five stages are (1) denial, (2) anger, (3) bargaining, (4) depression, and (5) acceptance.

Denial is the first stage. The person resists the reality of impending death. In essence, the person says "No!" to death. Whether medical authorities have told the person of his or her terminal status, or the person senses it, denial is displayed in various ways. For instance, some people sought other professional opinions and continued their search until they found a more favorable diagnosis. Others sought forms of religious assurance, and still others tried "miracle cures." Once they accepted that they were going to die, then anger and distress were expressed.

Anger is the second stage. During this time the person is saying, "Why me?" or "Why am I to die?" Their feelings are manifested in hostility, resentment, and even envy. They hate the fact that they are to die, resent their situation, and envy all of those who are not in such a predicament. These feelings may be directed at one or more targets such as family, friends, the medical staff, aspects of the environment (e.g., a pen that won't work), or even God. It seems that the anger flourishes because the person feels frustrated by all that will remain unfinished. When it is realized that the question-"Why me?"-cannot be answered satisfactorily, the person begins to make deals with fate.

Bargaining is the third and middle stage. Here the person decides to change strategies. That is, rather than saying "No!" and "Why me?" favors are asked that will extend life or postpone death. Although such bargaining is often conducted between the individual and God in a covert fashion, sometimes it is conducted overtly in interactions with others. For example, an individual might say: "If I rewrite my will and leave money to more people and charities rather than for a lavish funeral, then please let me live longer. I am a good person." Or "I will be a better person if I can have just a little more time." Typically, these bargains are not kept, and when the person outlives the first bargain another one is usually made.

Depression occurs "when the terminally ill patient can no longer deny his illness, when he is forced to undergo more surgery or hospitalization, when he begins to have more symptoms or becomes weaker and thinner. . . . His numbness or stoicism, his anger and rage will soon be replaced with a sense of great loss" (Kübler-Ross, 1969, p. 75). The person may feel guilty or afraid for different reasons, e.g., the individual may worry about letting family members down or not being able to accept impending death.

Acceptance is the final stage. Actually the person is resolute about death, although not happy. Tired and weak physically, the person "is almost void of feelings. It is as if the pain had gone, the struggle is over, and there comes a time for 'the final rest before the long journey' as one patient phrased it" (Kübler-Ross, 1969, p. 100).

Kübler-Ross (1974) cautions that not all people go through this stage sequence and that we could potentially harm dying patients by viewing this series of feelings as invariant and universal. Unfortunately, her stages have become a prescription for dealing with dying patients—a kind of "pop death." In fact, Kübler-Ross has recently emphasized individual differences in the death and dying process and the importance of identifying and accepting a patient's response pattern. She stresses that the defenses of dying people should not be challenged or broken down by family, friends, or medical staff. Denying death throughout the dying process may be exercised by some individuals, and it is not productive to attempt to push them through the stages. In fact, she feels it may even be cruel to try to disregard or undermine the type of hope a dying person expresses. Also, what might appear to be denial may be an attempt to protect others.

An important modification to Kübler-Ross's stage theory involves the fact that emotional responses constantly wax and wane throughout the dying process (Shneidman, 1973). Since each person is so different, people who deal with those who are dying should help them achieve an *appropriate death*. That is, a death that fulfills the patient's ideals and expectations within societal expectations of "dying well" versus not accepting death (Weisman, 1972).

Phase Theory of Dying

Since emotional responses to death and dying vary for many individuals, some researchers (Pattison, 1977b; Weisman, 1972) feel that talking about the dying process as consisting of three phases—an acute phase, a chronic living-dying interval, and a terminal phase—is appropriate. As illustrated in Figure 12.1, the acute phase is a crisis event. The individual becomes aware of impending death, manifests high levels of anxiety, denies, is very angry, and may even bargain. The chronic living-dying phase begins with a reduction in anxiety. During this phase, the person experiences various feelings, e.g., fear of the unknown, fear of loneliness, and anticipatory grief over the loss of friends, of body, of self-control, and of identity (Pattison, 1977b). Levels of anxiety and sorrow may occur alternating or simultaneously with levels of hope, determination, and acceptance (Shneidman, 1973). The terminal phase is marked by the person's withdrawing from the world. This phase is the shortest, and is ended by death.

In order to understand these three phases of the dying process, the concept of dying trajectories must be considered. A *dying trajectory* deals with the length and form of the dying process. For example, does the dying process have periods of stability, and if so how long are these periods?

Four dying trajectories, dealing with two types of certain and two types of uncertain death, have been proposed (Glaser & Strauss, 1968; Strauss & Glaser, 1970):

1. *Certain death:* Death is anticipated at a particular time (e.g., the individual has six months to live).

2. *Certain death:* Death is expected during a longer time frame (e.g., the individual has six months to a year to live).

3. *Uncertain death:* It is not known whether death will occur, but there is a time period in which the question will be resolved (e.g., surgery is scheduled and there is an anticipated time for recovery).

4. *Uncertain death:* The time of death is unknown and the question cannot be resolved in a time frame. (For instance, a person with a chronic heart problem or someone having had successful cancer surgery lives with this type of uncertain death.)

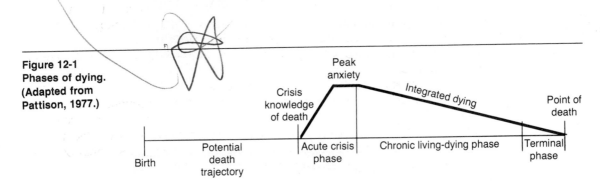

**Figure 12-1
Phases of dying.
(Adapted from
Pattison, 1977.)**

BOX 12.2

A COLLEGE STUDENT FACES DEATH

During the fall asthma flare-up a doctor at the Health Services put me on a drug. After exams I proceeded to take myself off it abruptly, precipitating a severe attack. I was hospitalized and put back on the drug.

By March, however, I developed another and more serious symptom: severe pain in my left arm. I was admitted to the hospital infirmary and finally, by the end of the six-week incarceration, there was for the first time serious talk that I would need surgery, an amputation for a malignant tumor.

These medical and social problems had a subtle depersonalizing effect on me. In preparation for the surgery I was withdrawing a little from my body. I began to think of myself almost completely as a creature of thought, a poet.

These are the defenses of a sick person, and I used them in personal relationships as well. By the end of the term I was reasonably convinced that life was little more than a passive game, an endurance test, if you will, a constant bid for attention counteracted by resentment over being treated either as a patient or a tool.

At any rate, my freshman year drew to a close. The surgery was set up in Boston. As far as the operation was concerned both parents, now remarried, were frightened and communicated this fright to me. There was also, of course, some relief that the disease would be arrested, for as my mother complained, "You just don't know what it's like to have a sick kid." She was, in her usual way, speaking to me.

Following the surgery I seemed to have little trauma over the body image. I used the defense of intellectualization: the routine of learning to use the prosthesis was imperative to learn, etc. The hate, the rage, the fear, and the grief didn't come to the surface until a suicide attempt at school that fall.

Finally one evening I was invited to smoke some marijuana with some casual acquaintances, and since I thought the pot might take my mind

off death, I complied. What happened, however, was the opposite of my expectations: death suddenly seemed to be an immediate certainty, and I went over the brink into pure terror.

I, the object, began to take walks. I tried desperately to focus my attention on something beyond me in the real world. The more I looked at the people around me, the more it seemed that they were just rubbery dolls with no personalities, no inner vitality or strength; just a body which they drove around in to go to classes, eat, sleep, make small talk. It was horrifying.

I had by this time almost completely separated what I called me from the everyday world, feeling that it, and my body, were responsible for my mortality. The horror of this depersonalization lasted for weeks. I was certain I was mad.

The thesis done, I moved into another room

For a young adult confronting death is a nonnormative event that is wrought with the emotion of feeling cheated. (Stan Levy/Photo Researchers)

with two other seniors unknown to me (the mechanics of the rooming situations for this year are complex and probably irrelevant), and I began to apply a little reason to the problem. I began to realize that first of all I had been living two lives. One self had been for the outside world, the doctors, and peers; and the other had been self as experienced by me. I had been encouraged to pay more attention to the objective self, and had

started to feel that all there was to me was what other people saw. In other words, the environment had urged me to commit a kind of psychological suicide. With the terror of that pot-revealing evening I was even consciously trying to destroy the ego so that I would not feel death when it struck. Yes, definitely weird.

Source: From Shneidman, 1972, pp. 139–142.

When death is uncertain, the time of the acute phase is extended. It is suggested that not knowing whether one will die and not being able to have the question resolved causes severe psychological difficulty because enormous ambiguity exists. Dysfunctional behavior such as hypochrondriacal reactions may result. If a condition is manageable by physicians or can be arrested for lengthy periods, individuals seem to make adjustments (Pattison, 1977a).

CONTEXTS FOR DYING

Where do most people die? Most people die in health care institutions, with the largest group dying in general hospitals (Lerner, 1970). Where do most people want to die? The majority of people say they want to die at home, although this is not as important for people between the ages of 40 and 59 (Kalish & Reynolds, 1976). What context do caregivers prefer for those who are dying? Most family members reported being glad that their family member died at home. These caregivers, however, said the burden of care was often excessive, and one-third of them wondered retrospectively about the wisdom of their decision—that is, perhaps the hospital would have provided a better environment (Cartwright, Hockey, & Anderson, 1973).

At the present time the leading causes of death are chronic diseases such as cardiovascular disease and cancer. As a result, patients, family members, and health care practitioners must often cope with a prolonged terminal phase of an individual's life. In this section, therefore, we will explore the patient and practitioner roles and discuss the needs of the dying patient to see how different contexts can be supportive.

Dying in a Hospital

For physicians and health care providers, death often represents failure and defeat. In fact, considerable evidence indicates that the majority of physicians avoid patients once they begin to die (e.g., Kastenbaum & Aisenberg, 1972; Livingston & Zimet, 1965). This avoidance may be the result of several factors. For example, several investigators (e.g., Feifel, 1965; Feifel, Hanson, Jones, &

Edwards, 1967) have suggested that the basic personality structure of physicians is responsible for their response to dying. That is, becoming a physician represents an attempt to overcome death. Although the hypothesis that such a personality structure exists has been advanced, obviously the attitude is reinforced by training. Moreover, physicians are not excluded from the negative associations with death. They are challenged to heal, but are made aware of the temporal limits on their own lives. Lief and Fox (1963) propose that the physician-patient relationship is one of "detached concern." Imagine the difficulty of facing death personally with each patient. Also, there is the problem of allocating time (e.g., saving the 80-year-old versus the 40-year-old heart patient). Therefore physicians, like others in society, are influenced by the fear and anxieties surrounding death and decisions regarding use of time.

To tell or not to tell the patient   Until recently, common medical practice was not to tell a patient that he or she was dying. A survey published in 1965 found that 70 to 90 percent of various groups of physicians refused to disclose information about a terminal condition even though 75 to 90 percent of those patients who were terminally ill wanted to be informed of their prognosis (Feifel, 1965; Nettler, 1971). Many researchers, however, feel that the physician can be an important catalyst for a patient achieving a "good death." Physicians should inform the patient of his or her condition, as well as let family members know.

The question "Should a patient be told that he or she is dying?" oversimplifies the situation. Such a question assumes that the physician really knows whether or not the individual is dying, but often this is not the case. The issue of dying is complicated by the uncertainty of medical knowledge and the uncertainty connected with the physical and mental state of the patient (Hinton, 1976).

It seems that the patient must take the initiative in requesting information from the physician. Thus, any questions the patient asks should be answered as honestly and completely as possible, with the patient controlling the quantity and quality of informational flow (Hinton, 1976). A recent study suggests that there is a trend toward informing patients within a framework of sensitivity. The results of a survey of physicians, nurses, chaplains, and college students (Carey & Posavac, 1978) suggest that patients have a right to know the truth about their situation but that physicians should exercise judgment on the timing of disseminating this information and not take the initiative in revealing information. Table 12.2 summarizes some of the data from this survey.

Meeting the patient's needs   The three major needs of terminally ill people are probably the needs to control pain, to maintain dignity or feelings of self-worth, and to receive love and affection. Although the use of addicting drugs such as morphine loses its social consequence for people who are dying, medical practitioners still must decide who determines dosage. It has been argued that the patient should have input in this decision because only the patient is aware of fluctuations of internal states. The best solution is for the

TABLE 12.2

PERCENT RESPONDING "YES" TO QUESTIONS ON DISCLOSING
INFORMATION TO AND MAINTAINING LIFE FOR TERMINALLY ILL PATIENTS

Question	Group			
	Physicians	Nurses	Chaplains	Students
If terminally ill patients request information, do they have an unqualified right to know the truth about their conditions?	87	86	79	81
As a general rule, the physician should:				
Give complete information without waiting for the patient to ask	29	45	25	47
Take the initiative in revealing the terminal condition, but then only answer specific questions	42	43	50	26
Answer specific questions, but not take the initiative	27	11	21	18
Answer patients' questions only to the extent the physician feels is appropriate	2	2	4	9
Should a doctor allow a patient to take pain medication even if it hastens death?	93	98	93	88
Do you support "passive euthanasia," that is, using ordinary means of maintaining life but otherwise allowing nature to run its course?	100	100	96	87

Source: Adapted from Carey and Posavac, 1978.

patient and medical staff to arrive at a situation in which pain is prevented rather simply alleviated (Neale, 1971).

Helping a patient feel a level of dignity or self-worth is often accomplished by letting a patient participate in decisions that affect treatment or outcomes. Control over one's life is thought to be as important during the terminal phase as it is during any other phase. Seligman (1975) reports that when individuals are not allowed to participate in such decisions, they experience feelings of helplessness, exhibit withdrawal, and show evidence of depression. Also, when institutionalized aged individuals were presented with an opportunity to control an aspect of their environment, they showed significant improvement in their physical and psychological status compared with others who were not afforded opportunities for self-control. Thus, it seems essential to allow terminal patients opportunities for exercising some control over their own destinies, especially when their fate is basically out of their control.

Love and affection for terminally ill patients often means holding, touching, or stroking. The medical staff usually has many opportunities to physically touch patients when caring for them. How the patient is handled can communicate a genuine concern. Also, by listening to the patient and supporting the patient's way of handling the situation people, especially family, can reassure the patient that he or she will not be abandoned (Schulz, 1978).

Dying in a Hospice

Cecily Saunders (1976), the director of St. Christopher's Hospice in London and a prominent figure in the hospice movement, maintains that the environment can be designed to facilitate achieving freedom from pain, regaining a sense of self-worth or dignity, and experiencing a loving atmosphere. Hospices provide more than sympathetic attentive care for the dying. Medical procedures, such as ways to ease pain, are explored and extensive psychological counseling for patients and families is provided. The primary goal of most hospices in the United States, therefore, is to help people live as individuals during the weeks and months left to them, and to help them die with as little discomfort and as much serenity as possible.

Specifically, staff members seek to alleviate pain and allay fear. In

The hospice environment permits family members to perform services, such as preparing special meals for their terminally ill relative. (Peter Southwick)

hospitals, terminal patients are often heavily drugged and have little control over their medication. The hospice staff does not follow the hospital model; rather they administer a mixture called "Brompton's cocktail," which consists of dirmorphine (heroin) or morphine (this is used in the United States), cocaine, gin, sugar syrup, and chlorpromazine syrup in small doses around the clock before severe pain begins. It is felt that this approach allows patients to trust that they will not be in pain and consequently reduces their fears. Moreover, that drug mixture allows the patient to maintain a clear mind.

Another characteristic of the hospice is to treat the patient and family together. Thus, visiting hours are not restricted, and family members are encouraged to perform practical services such as preparing special meals for their in-resident family member. Allowing family members to participate in the care of the patient is thought to minimize guilt during bereavement. Finally, the staff's involvement with the family does not end upon the patient's death. Family members are encouraged to contact hospice personnel if they experience problems during bereavement.

How successful will hospices be? The success of the hospice movement in the United States depends on whether they meet their stated goals and on the cost of treatment. At St. Christopher's Hospice in London, for instance, the cost per patient is 80 percent of what it would be in a general hospital. Frank Kryza, director of the first United States hospice, which was established in New Haven, Connecticut, in 1971, claims that the treatment fee for those involved in their home-care program is less than hospital fees would be.

Some people are concerned that the hospice movement will add to the overspecialization and fragmentation of American medicine. They feel that medical services should be integrated so that existing institutions such as hospitals are used and efforts are made to educate hospital staff in meeting the needs of the dying. Regardless of this reservation, it is clear that hospices are helping the dying and their families, and until we can improve our other contexts of care, much of the criticism of hospices is counterproductive.

Ethical Issues

Sustained by extraordinary means of mechanical life support, Karen Ann Quinlan lay comatose while her case was considered by the New Jersey courts. This case helped bring the American public face to face with issues surrounding *bioethics*. That is, what are the moral, ethical, and legal implications of contemporary life science technology? Specific issues can range from esoteric laboratory procedures to personal situations full of human pathos. Bioethics for Karen Ann involved her parents' taking legal action to allow her to live or die naturally, without a respirator, and the courts upheld their second request. The court instructed that the respirator could be turned off if "there [was] no reasonable possibility" that she would return to a "cognitive sapient state" (Seligmann, 1976). The court also added that these standards be applied to all patients whose condition is progressive and incurable. But the decision to turn off the respirator does not end the story because at the time of this writing Karen Ann Quinlan still lives in a coma, breathing unaided.

Euthanasia

Should the life of a human being be ended, and if so, under what circumstances? The desire to alleviate discomfort caused by irreversible damage by ending life ultimately leads to the euthanasia question. With advances in medical technology allowing machines to maintain all vital systems save for the brain, the medical profession and the public are wrestling with the moral, ethical, and legal issues surrounding the concept of euthanasia—the act or practice of killing for reasons of mercy (*eu*, derived from the Greek word meaning "good," and *thanasia,* from the Greek *thanatos,* "death").

Types of euthanasia   There are two types of euthanasia—active and passive. *Active euthanasia* refers to deliberate actions (e.g. injecting air bubbles) to shorten an individual's life. Supposedly, these acts are done to save a person from a protracted period of pain and suffering. *Passive euthanasia* refers to allowing a person to die because available preventive measures are not used. This means that a treatment might be withdrawn or withheld which permits a person to die earlier than if treatment were received. This was the situation for Karen Ann Quinlan, but, as you may recall, death has not yet occurred as a result. Moreover, oftentimes implementing passive euthanasia is more complex than in the example of Karen Ann Quinlan. Let us say, for instance, that a cancer patient is experiencing intense pain which requires morphine. This patient now contracts pneumonia. The physician must decide which to treat because both cannot be treated simultaneously. Therefore, if the morphine treatment is maintained, the pneumonia may kill the patient. But the reverse also is a possibility. That is, if the pneumonia is treated and morphine withheld, unbearable pain will result, although it will not necessarily cause death.

Attitudes toward Euthanasia   Fletcher (1974) proposes a range of possible attitudes toward euthanasia.

1. ____Absolute no
2. ____Qualified no
3. ____Decline to start treatment
4. ____Terminate treatment with consent
5. ____Terminate treatment without consent
6. ____Help patient end his/her own life
7. ____End life with prior consent or proxy consent of next of kin
8. ____End life without consent

Basically there are three possible positions: people who directly advocate euthanasia (steps 6 to 8), individuals who condone passive euthanasia (steps 3 to 5), and those who disagree totally or in a qualified way with the practice (steps 1 and 2).

Attitudes held by the public have changed in the past two decades. For example, in 1950, responding to a Gallup poll, 36 percent of the population said "yes" to the following question: "When a person has a disease that cannot be cured, do you think doctors should be allowed by law to end the patient's life by some painless means if the patient and his family request it?" By 1973, 53 percent of the population said "yes" to this question. At the American Medical Association convention in 1973 physicians supported a "death with dignity proposition" and the use of "living wills" that allow people to choose their fate in conditions where death is imminent. (See Figure 12.2)

Who decides on life or death? A major difficulty in arriving at a decision about euthanasia concerns two critical questions: "Who decides on life or death?" and "What constitutes death?"

According to the physician Dr. Christian Barnard, neither the patient nor his or her family should decide the fate of a terminally ill person. Barnard maintains that a person cannot discuss his or her own death. Moreover, families should not have to experience the pathos of such a decision. The position Barnard assumes is that ending a life is a technical (medical) decision and not a personal one. Other physicians, however, argue that death is a deeply personal matter and that the person and his or her family always must and should be consulted.

Regardless of one's personal view of who should decide on the life or death of a patient, the law still does not recognize the "mercy" aspect of euthanasia. In fact, the majority of euthanasia cases are brought before the court as murder cases. Some individuals (e.g., Maguire, 1974b) argue that euthanasia cannot be considered murder or even manslaughter. Murder refers to "express malice" in the first degree and "implied malice" in the second degree, and manslaughter refers to sudden, unintentional killing without malice. Euthanasia does not fit into any of these categories. It is never performed with malice either direct or indirect, and it is carried out with intent.

When physicians have been tried in euthanasia cases, juries have been reluctant to convict and have even showed sensitivity to "honorable motives" (Maguire, 1974a). Trials of family members are more common than trials for physicians. In these cases verdicts have ranged from first degree murder to outright acquittal or acquittal due to temporary insanity induced by sympathetic understanding associated with the suffering family member's pain or request to be killed. In the majority of the family euthanasia cases, the accused are acquitted.

For many people, religion determines what attitude is held about who should decide on life or death of a person. In 1957 Pope Pius XII issued a Catholic dictum on euthanasia which has not been revoked. He recognized that life-sustaining technology imposes moral problems involving questions of life or death and decreed that Catholics are not obligated morally to use "extraordinary measures" to keep hopelessly ill patients alive. What specifically is meant by "extraordinary measures" is unresolved (Maguire, 1974a).

To My Family, My Physician, My Lawyer and All Others Whom It May Concern

Death is as much a reality as birth, growth, maturity and old age—it is the one certainty of life. If the time comes when I can no longer take part in decisions for my own future, let this statement stand as an expression of my wishes and directions, while I am still of sound mind.

If at such a time the situation should arise in which there is no reasonable expectation of my recovery from extreme physical or mental disability, I direct that I be allowed to die and not be kept alive by medications, artificial means or "heroic measures". I do, however, ask that medication be mercifully administered to me to alleviate suffering even though this may shorten my remaining life.

This statement is made after careful consideration and is in accordance with my strong convictions and beliefs. I want the wishes and directions here expressed carried out to the extent permitted by law. Insofar as they are not legally enforceable, I hope that those to whom this Will is addressed will regard themselves as morally bound by these provisions.

Signed_____

Date _____

Witness_____

Witness_____

Copies of this request have been given to _____

_____

_____

_____

Figure 12.2 A living will. (From Euthanasia Education Council, 1980)

The Quinlans finally won their court battle to remove their daughter Karen from the respirator, but she is still living today. (United Press International)

Ancient Jewish law states that life is "intrinsically sacred" and should be preserved, even at great cost. Any active effort to hasten death is considered wrong, but removing artificial means of maintaining life or keeping a dying person alive is permissible (passive euthanasia).

For Protestants, there is no one set religious standard that determines who has the right to decide the life or death of an ill person. The emphasis is placed on discretion and personal choice, however. "Love thy neighbor" and "Thou shalt not kill" coexist (Shideler, 1966).

What constitutes death?   Since body cells die continuously, death should be considered a process rather than a moment. The two key bodily processes often used as barometers for deciding about death are spontaneous respiration and heartbeat. But with technology providing incredibly sensitive devices to detect pulse or breath and making various vital support systems available, it is difficult to define what constitutes being physically dead!

In 1968, the Ad Hoc Committee of the Harvard Medical School proposed the following criteria to be applied in combination to determine whether death has occurred: unreceptivity and unresponsivity, no movements or breathing, no reflexes, and a flat electroencephalogram (EEG) reading that remains so for twenty-four hours (Veatch, 1976). This state is referred to as an irreversible coma and describes what is called *brain death*.

For many people the concept of brain death, and the criteria advanced by the committee, are unsupported. These people prefer talking about *cerebral death,* or the cessation of activity in the higher brain center—the cortex. Thus, the person with vegetative functions in fact may be able to breathe unassisted, but will remain unconscious forever. The supporters of the cerebral-death criterion feel that an individual *is* the cortex, which houses the capacity for thought, voluntary action, and memory. So, by definition, when consciousness is gone the individual is no longer a person.

The position taken about what constitutes death is controversial. For instance, if the standards for cerebral death were applied to Karen Ann Quinlan, then she should be considered dead. However, in terms of the standards for brain death, she is living.

Conclusions   The issue of euthanasia lives on because it affects all of us. How do we want a loved one who is dying treated? How do we want to be treated when we are dying? And perhaps more importantly than "How?" is "By whom?"

Although the ethical and moral problems associated with euthanasia may never be resolved, it seems that as the delicate subject of death becomes more a part of life, we may be able to formulate some rules for facing the profound social problem of euthanasia.

GRIEF AND BEREAVEMENT

Grief, an emotional response to loss, is usually anticipated rather than unanticipated, follows a typical progression, and can manifest itself in atypical ways.

If death occurs unexpectedly and suddenly, such as in an accident or suicide, the family often has difficulty understanding why it occurred. The survivors may live in fear that such an event may be repeated. Usually the death of someone young produces unanticipated grief because the young are not "supposed" to die.

If death is expected, then, according to Fulton (1970), family members experience four stages in the process of anticipating grief: (1) depression, (2) heightened concern for the ill person, (3) rehearsals of the death, and (4) an attempt to adjust to the consequences of death. The issue surrounding anticipatory grief is whether or not it facilitates moving through the grief process after the family member's death.

Depression, the first stage of anticipatory grief, is well documented, but such feelings prior to death are not related to decreased grief after the death (Bornstein, Clayton, Halikas, Maurice, & Robins, 1973). For instance, in one study of Cambridge widows, data revealed that those who were upset the most during their husband's illness were those most upset by the death (Glick, Weiss, & Parkes, 1974).

Experiencing *a heightened concern for the ill person,* stage two, seems to obviate the guilt a person could feel when the person dies (Kübler-Ross, 1969). During this time an individual can do "those things" that after death become "those things she could have done but didn't."

The next two stages, *death rehearsal and contemplation of consequences,* serve to reduce the stressful impact of death. Although one is never really prepared for a person's death, certain aspects of an individual's life can be placed in order so the person will have more control over self at the time of death.

Normal Grief Process

What happens during normal grieving? Many researchers (e.g., Glick, Weiss, & Parkes, 1974; Parkes, 1972) feel that individuals move through distinct phases of grief. When the death occurs, there is the first phase, that of *initial response.* This is marked by shock or disbelief that lasts for a while after the funeral. People have stated that they felt empty, cold, numb, dazed, and confused. After this feeling leaves, an all-encompassing sorrow is experienced for an extended period. This manifests itself in crying and weeping. The difficulty during this time is deciding whether and how long one can be consumed with such emotion rather than being composed and controlled for others. With the passage of time, the ability to control emotions becomes associated with "doing well." Thus, the bereaved person is encouraged to inhibit emotional responses. Such encouragement is considered fine as long as the bereaved person does not feel that demands are unreasonable.

Coping with anxiety and fear is the next phase for the bereaved. Many bereaved respondents stated a fear of breaking down and not making it through this stage. For instance, one widow said:

Some days I'm worried about having a nervous breakdown. Sometimes I get more nervous than others, and I just feel like I'm ready to scream, especially if I'm alone. Like sometimes at night I'm sitting here and I just feel like I'm ready to scream. I'll put the music on to listen to that, or I'll sing to the records, just something to do, so that you're not talking to yourself. I think it helps. It helps me. I don't know if it would anybody else, but I'll just put the records on and I'll sing along with the records. Some people think I'm soft but it really helps me. (Glick, Weiss, & Parkes, 1974, p. 66)

During this period of time, bereaved people may turn to tranquilizers, sleeping pills, or alcohol, or they may report a variety of psychological and physiological symptoms (e.g., shortness of breath, tightness in the throat, loss of appetite, irritability, muscular aches and pains, and headaches). Typically, these symptoms are reduced during the first month of bereavement, although they may reoccur for short periods during the first year of bereavement.

The *intermediate phase of normal* grief usually occupies the balance of the first year. Behavior in this phase consists of obsessional review, searching for an understanding of death, and searching for the presence of the deceased. The obsessional review is highlighted by dwelling on specific events associated with the death and with berating one self for not doing enough (e.g., "If I had only called the ambulance sooner" or "If only I had been with him in the hospital"). Searching for answers to understand death often ends with: "It's God's will." Finally, searching for the deceased occurs in various ways. Many activities remind the bereaved of the person, which conjures up thoughts of or conversations with the person and leads to lengthy commentaries to others about what was shared. These three behaviors decrease during the first year. Glick, Weiss, and Parkes (1974) reported, for example, that 60 percent of the widows in their study were beginning to feel more like their old selves after a few months and felt they had done quite well by the end of the year.

The *second year* of bereavement is referred to as the *recovery phase* because the bereaved evidence a positive attitude toward life. They are alive and have a life to live. Most state that they have pride in having coped with and survived a traumatic, potentially devastating event.

Although professional treatment is available for those who are bereaved, the majority who experience bereavement do so with the support of family and friends. Typically, people who are more detached attend the funeral or acknowledge the death in some socially sanctioned way. An obvious source of support is the American funeral industry, which provides events that allow the ritualistic and emotional expressions of the bereaved and give others the opportunity to participate in the family's sorrow.

Society's Reactions

Specific rituals and practices have long been associated with death—from the use of cosmetics and the practice of embalming to the elaborate funerals held by the ancient Egyptians. What functions do such mourning rituals and funerals serve? Some people say that funerals provide a social vehicle for providing support for the bereaved family. To the extent that rituals are elaborate and extensive, the probability of maladaptive responses diminishes (Gorer, 1965).

Others (e.g., Mitford, 1963) feel that such culturally condoned behavior is self-serving and exploits negative attitudes and feelings about death and dying.

I always knew at an early age that any living thing dies. My turtle died when I was a child and I buried him in the backyard. Relatives died, but they were not the ones I saw often and they were old. Old people are supposed to die. My head told me that, but my heart rebelled. Those we love should be there forever. Obviously, untrue.

When I was in middle-childhood my uncle died. In retrospect, it is scary to think he died at the age I presently am. The tears, turmoil, and times flash vividly across my mind for he was my grandparents' third-born and children are not supposed to be buried by parents. It's to work the other way around. But, even then, realizing someone is no more was very difficult.

My grandfather buried his son with dignity. He behaved as men who are middle-aged are supposed to in our society. He exuded strength, understanding of others, and caring in perspective. That experience only briefly captures the type of man my grandfather was. His death has left me void. There is a part of me that will always be his and will always think about him, respect what he was, and love him, not neurotically, but in a way a granddaughter should love a grandfather who was so supportive.

His death was and is difficult. My grandparents lived with us for a good portion of my childhood and my parents always managed to save to send my brothers and me to them (wherever) for summer visits when they no longer shared our household. During one of these times, as I recall I was 16, I realized the fear of loss. The phone rang and my grandmother said he suffered a severe heart attack. Since such things are never planned, it happened to be a time when my parents were not home. We (my brother and I) drove hours to get to the hospital. To do what?

Comfort our grandmother and wait. He survived that attack and several others during his life, many of which were touchy. Then came a series of major health problems such as controlling for diabetes, kidney failure and subsequent removal of one kidney, pancreatitis and resultant treatment. Oh! The list is lengthy. But, he always managed to survive and I began to believe he was indestructable. His stamina and fortitude seemed to pull him through.

This is not always the case obviously and we knew that he was "living on borrowed time" for my family was so supportive as caretakers and especially my grandmother whose day evolved around my grandfather's health care.

My work called me abroad and I received a call from my parents telling me of his death and suffering through the dying process. I was shocked in disbelief that he could be dead—not Popop. I tried to return home, but it was impossible. I was so far away, unable to be supportive, unable to pay respects, unable to say goodbye . . . unable to even show my parents I cared.

I'm told by my brothers, parents, other family and friends that his "send off" was splashing and difficult. But, I was not there. Guilt is a terrible thing and even more terrible during a time of death. Rationalization sets in. He outlived his life expectancy. True. But, he was important to so many people. Death is a robber of the living and all the research that attempts to counteract or mask this truth is unfortunate. We need to feel the impact of another's life.

I am now so grateful that I was fortunate to know my grandfather so well. He will always be 10 feet tall in my mind's eye and my heart. And, I will always feel the loss. This book, for me, is especially for him—Mr. Irving (Popop) Deutsch.

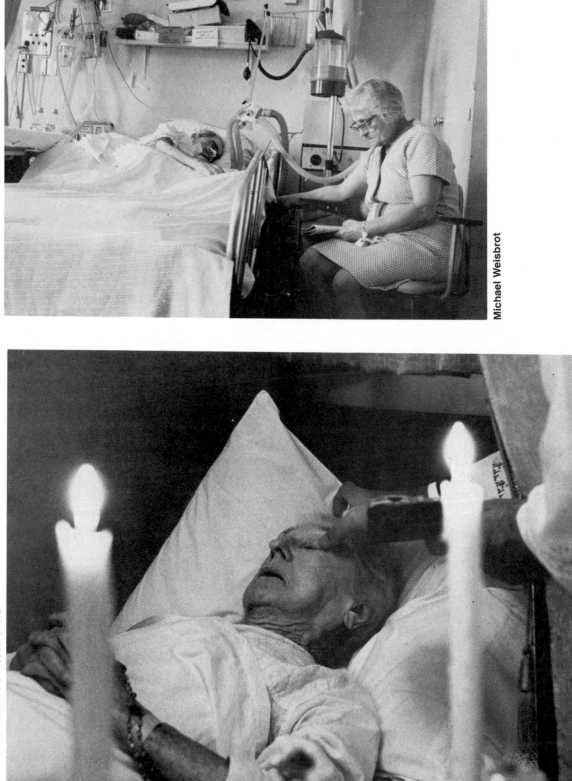

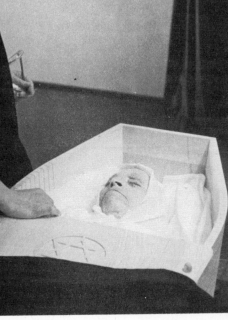

Michael Weisbrot

Pierre Wolff/Photo Researchers)

This occurs, supposedly, because the physical features of death rather than the spiritual are emphasized. Thus, for Mitford (1963), as a profit enterprise, the funeral industry thrives on our inability to face death and cope with our personal grief. But since it is true that many people are comforted in their grief by relying upon traditional customs, the issue of whether these customs make sense is irrelevant.

HELPING LIFE WORK OR PUTTING OFF DEATH

We may have opportunities throughout our lives to deal with death and try to forestall its occurrence. For many of us confronting death is not just unconfortable, but extremely difficult. We want to find ways to extend our lives and the lives of our loved ones.

Social Support

The effect of social support appears to interact with the timing of death. Phillips and Feldman (1973), for instance, found that deaths are reduced in the six months preceding birthdays and are increased in the succeeding six months (see Figure 12.3). Moreover, they demonstrated that this effect was most dramatic for distinguished people, and they interpreted their findings as evidence that social support does have an effect on the timing of death.

In another study (Berkman, 1977), support was offered for the notion that a good social network is associated with reduced mortality. The data were obtained from the California Human Population Laboratory study of 7000 residents of Alameda County over a ten-year period. Network support was

---

Up Date

BOX 12.4
DEATH EDUCATION

Schulz (1978) contends that death education serves two purposes: "It can make the final phase of life more predictable and controllable and it can give the individual the opportunity to understand and express his emotions about death and dying" (p. 169). He challenges us to teach people of all ages about death and dying in ways that do not produce anxiety or confusion. For example, Schulz (1978) questions why children are told a grandmother has gone on a long trip rather than letting them experience death and grief at their developmental level. Koocher (1975) reports that when discussions of death and dying

were implemented in classrooms at kindergarten and elementary school levels, the children knew the difference between living and nonliving things, could share their thoughts and fears, and could discuss the facts about how death is handled in different cultures. Teachers of those children said that the level of participation was high; children enjoyed the material while gaining insight. Perhaps these cohorts will be able to handle grief better than older cohorts and be able to make coping successfully with death become a part of life.

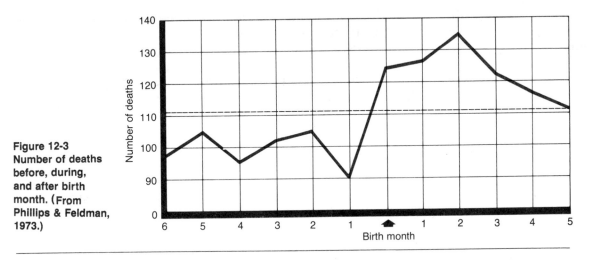

Figure 12-3
Number of deaths
before, during,
and after birth
month. (From
Phillips & Feldman,
1973.)

measured by: (1) marriage, (2) contact with close friends and relatives, (3) church membership, and (4) informal and formal group associations. For each of these levels of social support for men and women, successive decreases in age-adjusted mortality rates were reported. Also, for each level of social support this effect was independent of positive health practices, which supports the earlier work of Belloc (1973).

Increasing or decreasing the amount of social support directed toward a person also has an impact on the possibility of living or dying. On the one hand, the lack of social support is related to the onset of specific illnesses or even death. In an article called "The Broken Heart," Parkes (1972) found that men who recently lost their wives experienced excessive coronary deaths. On the other hand, high levels of social support facilitate recovery from illness such as cardiac failure (Chambers & Reiser, 1953) and surgical operations (Egbert, Battit, Welch, & Bartlett, 1964).

Personal Longevity

Given the general importance of social support for extending life, consider what factors would be more likely to increase or decrease your longevity. As a means of making a rough calculation of your personal longevity, consider the questions presented in Table 12.3. What factors are contributing to increasing or decreasing your life span? There is still time to register more pluses than minuses. As was noted in the short story at the beginning of the chapter, "When it comes to dying . . . nobody is really ready" (Bellow, 1963, p. 11).

CONCLUSION

In all likelihood, the figure you computed based on Table 12.3 is a substantial one. As we have seen, the phenomenon of adult development and aging is a

---

TABLE 12.3
HOW LONG WILL YOU LIVE?

This is a rough guide for calculating your personal longevity. The basic life expectancy for males is age 67 and for females it is age 75. Write down your basic life expectancy. If you are in your 50s or 60s, you should add ten years to the basic figure because you have already proven yourself to be quite durable. If you are over age 60 and active, add another two years.

Basic Life Expectancy _____

Decide how each item below applies to you and add or subtract the appropriate number of years from your basic life expectancy.

1. **Family history**

   Add 5 years if 2 or more of your grandparents lived to 80 or beyond. _____

   Subtract 4 years if any parent, grandparent, sister, or brother died of heart attack or stroke before 50. Subtract 2 years if anyone died from these diseases before 60. _____

   Subtract 3 years for each case of diabetes, thyroid disorders, breast cancer, cancer of the digestive system, asthma, or chronic bronchitis among parents or grandparents. _____

2. **Marital status**

   If you are married, add 4 years. _____

   If you are over 25 and not married, subtract 1 year for every unwedded decade. _____

2. **Economic status**

   Subtract 2 years if your family income is over $40,000 per year. _____

   Subtract 3 years if you have been poor for greater part of life. _____

4. **Physique**

   Subtract one year for every 10 pounds you are overweight. _____

   For each inch your girth measurement exceeds your chest measurement deduct two years. _____

   Add 3 years if you are over 40 and not overweight. _____

5. **Exercise**

   Regular and moderate (jogging 3 times a week), add 3 years. _____

   Regular and vigorous (long distance running 3 times a week), add 5 years. _____

   Subtract 3 years if your job is sedentary. _____

   Add 3 years if it is active. _____

6. **Alcohol**

   Add 2 years if you are a light drinker (1-3 drinks a day). _____

   Subtract 5 to 10 years if you are a heavy drinker (more than 4 drinks per day). _____

   Subtract 1 year if you are a teetotaler. _____

7. **Smoking**

   Two or more packs of cigarettes per day, subtract 8 years. _____

   One to two packs per day, subtract 4 years. _____

   Less than one pack, subtract 2 years. _____

   Subtract 2 years if you regularly smoke a pipe or cigars. _____

8. **Disposition**

   Add 2 years if you are a reasoned, practical person. _____

   Subtract 2 years if you are aggressive, intense, and competitive. _____

   Add 1-5 years if you are basically happy and content with life. _____

   Subtract 1-5 years if you are often unhappy, worried, and often feel guilty. _____

TABLE 12.3 *(Continued)*

9. **Education**
   Less than high school, subtract 2 years.   ———
   Four years of school beyond high school, add 1 year.   ———
   Five or more years beyond high school, add 3 years.   ———

10. **Environment**
   If you have lived most of your life in a rural environment, add 4 years.   ———
   Subtract 2 years if you have lived most of your life in an urban environment.   ———

11. **Sleep**
   More than 9 hours a day, subtract 5 years.   ———

12. **Temperature**
   Add 2 years if your home's thermostat is set at no more than 68°F.   ———

13. **Health care**
   Regular medical checkups and regular dental care, add 3 years.   ———
   Frequently ill, subtract 2 years.   ———

Source: Schulz, 1978

complex and changing one. You will experience the life events and transitions of adult life in ways both similar to and different from your parents and grandparents. It's bound to be an exciting journey. Let's get on with it.

CHAPTER SUMMARY

The death of an individual is probably one of the most deeply personal events that occurs in one's life. But confronting how one feels about the death of others and self is very difficult for most people. Kastenbaum conceptualizes death in six ways: (1) death as a variable, (2) death as a statistic, (3) death as an event, (4) death as a state, (5) death as an analogy, and (6) death as a mystery. Death is a mysterious paradox to many people because it affects the developmental course even though it is experienced only at the end of life. In fact, our lives probably would be transformed if we did not have to face death.

Age differences in death perceptions and attitudes exist. On the one hand, older respondents said that if they knew they were going to die, they would not be likely to alter their activities or life-styles, would increase inner-life activities, and would be less concerned with caring for dependents or causing grief to others compared with younger people. On the other hand, older people think more and talk more about death than younger people. Thus, the elderly are less afraid of death at the same time they are more consumed by it than younger people. Kalish proposes three reasons for their attitude. The elderly realize that their future is limited and that their life expectancy has almost been reached. Also, they have been socialized to become accustomed to the idea of death.

The dying process can be thought of in terms of stages or phases. Kübler-Ross proposes that dying people go through five stages: (1) denial, (2) anger, (3) bargaining, (4) depression, and (5) acceptance. She stresses strongly that the defenses of dying people should not be challenged or broken down by anyone. Thus, some people may stay at any of the stages when death arrives, and they should not be pushed through remaining stages. People who deal with those who are dying should help them achieve an appropriate death. Proponents of a phase theory of dying suggest three phases: acute phase, a chronic living-dying phase, and a terminal phase. Depending upon whether the time of death is relatively certain or not, the first and second periods will vary in length. Since denying and accepting death are complex features of the dying process, a person may experience more than one sequence of phases. Strauss and Glaser (1970) propose that there are four dying trajectories, or indexes, dealing with the length and form of the dying process: death is anticipated within a relatively short time; death is anticipated, but within a longer time frame; it is not known if death will occur, but the question will be resolved within a given time frame; the question cannot be resolved within a time frame.

There are different contexts for dying. Although most people die in general hospitals, they say they would rather die at home. Moreover, family members would be glad to have them die at home as long as the families could be sure they were able to provide the best care. Since the majority of people dying in hospitals are dying because of prolonged chronic disease, an often-asked question is: "Should a patient be told that he or she is dying?" Data show a trend toward informing patients with sensitivity. Thus, the questions a patient asks should be answered as honestly and completely as possible, allowing the patient to control the amount and degree of information shared. Moreover, health professionals need to meet the needs of terminally ill patients by controlling pain, helping the patient retain dignity or feelings of self-worth, and providing affection and love.

An alternative to dying in a hospital is to die at a hospice. The staff of a hospice do not follow a hospital model in their treatment. They supply patients with a mixture to drink in regular doses that will relieve their pain. They believe that pain and fear of death are strongly related. Thus, if the absence or reduction of pain is assured, the fear of death will be reduced. The patient's family also plays an important role in the program of hospices. Family members can participate by living in. This seems to help the dying person and minimizes guilt during bereavement.

Grief is an emotional response to loss which can be anticipated or not. Phases of the normal grieving process are: (1) initial response of shock or disbelief, (2) intermediate phase of reviewing the factors associated with death, and (3) the recovery phase of realizing one has coped with and survived a devastating event—death.

Social support can put off death, and the lack of social support can cause it to occur ahead of schedule. Many of us are fortunate enough to have the time to contribute to increasing our own life spans.

BIBLIOGRAPHY

Adams, G. M., & **de Vries, H. A.** Physiological effects of an exercise training regimen upon women aged 52 to 79. *Journal of Gerontology,* 1973, *28,* 50–55.

Adams, J. E., & **Lindemann, E.** Coping with long-term disability. In G. V. Coelho, D. A. Hamburg, & J. E. Adams (Eds.), *Coping and adaptation.* New York: Basic Books, 1974.

Agruso, V. M., Jr. *Learning in the later years: Principles of educational gerontology.* New York: Academic Press, 1978.

Albrecht, G. L., & **Gift, H. C.** Adult socialization: Ambiguity and adult life crises. In N. Datan & L. H. Ginsburg (Eds.), *Life-span developmental psychology: Normative life crises.* New York: Academic Press, 1975.

Aldrich, C., & **Mendkoff, E.** Relocation of the aged and disabled: A mortality study. *Journal of American Geriatrics Society,* 1963, *11,* 185–194.

American Psychological Association, Ad hoc Committee on Ethical Standards in Psychological Research. *Ethical principles in the conduct of research with human participants.* Washington, D.C.: American Psychological Association, 1973.

Anders, T. R., Fozard, J. L., & **Lillyquist, T. P.** Effects of age upon retrieval from short-term memory. *Developmental Psychology,* 1972, *6,* 214–217.

Anderson, B., Jr., & **Palmore, E.** Longitudinal evaluation of ocular function. In E. Palmore (Ed.), *Normal aging II: Reports from the Duke longitudinal studies, 1970–1973.* Durham, N.C.: Duke University Press, 1974.

Ansello, E. F. Age and ageism in children's first literature. *Educational Gerontology,* 1977, *2,* 255–274. (a)

Ansello, E. F. Old age and literature: An overview. *Educational Gerontology,* 1977, *2,* 211–218. (b)

Arbuthnot, J. Modification of moral judgement through role playing. *Developmental Psychology,* 1975, *11,* 319–324.

Arenberg, D. Anticipation interval and age differences in verbal learning. *Journal of Abnormal Psychology,* 1965, *70,* 419–425.

Arenberg, D. Age differences in retroaction. *Journal of Gerontology,* 1967, *22,* 88–91. (a)

Arenberg, D. Regression analyses of verbal learning on adult age at two anticipation intervals. *Journal of Gerontology,* 1967, *22,* 411–414. (b)

Arenberg, D. *Memory and learning do decline late in life.* Paper presented at Conference on Aging and Social Policy, Vichy, France, 1977.

Arenberg, D., & **Robertson-Tchabo, E. A.** Learning and aging. In J. E. Birren & K. W. Schaie (Eds.), *Handbook of the psychology of aging.* New York: Van Nostrand Reinhold, 1977.

Arlin, P. K. Cognitive development in adulthood: A fifth stage? *Developmental Psychology,* 1975, *11,* 602–606.

Atchley, R. C. Dimensions of widowhood in later life. *The Gerontologist,* 1975, *11,* 176–178.

Atchley, R. C. *The social forces in later life* (2d ed.). Belmont, Calif.: Wadsworth, 1977.

Back, K. W. Meaning of time in later life. *Journal of Genetic Psychology,* 1965, *109,* 9–25.

Bahrick, H. P., Bahrick, P. O., & **Wittlinger, R. P.**

Fifty years of memory for names and faces: A cross-sectional approach. *Journal of Experimental Psychology: General,* 1975, *104,* 54–75.

Baltes, P. B. Longitudinal and cross-sectional sequences in the study of age and generation effects. *Human Development,* 1968, *11,* 145–171.

Baltes, P. B. Prototypical paradigms and questions in life-span research on development and aging. *The Gerontologist,* 1973, *13,* 458–467.

Baltes, P. B. Life-span developmental psychology: Some converging observations on history and theory. In P. B. Baltes & O. G. Brim, Jr. (Eds.), *Life-span development and behavior* (Vol. 2). New York: Academic Press, 1979.

Baltes, P. B., Cornelius, S. W., & Nesselroade, J. R. Cohort effects in developmental psychology. In J. R. Nesselroade & P. B. Baltes (Eds.), *Longitudinal research in the study of behavior and development.* New York: Academic Press, 1979.

Baltes, P. B., & Danish, S. J. Intervention in life-span development and aging: Issues and concepts. In R. R. Turner & H. W. Reese (Eds.), *Life-span developmental psychology: Interventions.* New York: Academic Press, 1980.

Baltes, P. B., & Goulet, L. R. Exploration of developmental variables by manipulation and simulation of age differences in behavior. *Human Development,* 1971, *14,* 149–170.

Baltes, P. B., & Labouvie, G. V. Adult development of intellectual performance: Description, explanation, and modification. In C. Eisdorfer & M. P. Lawton (Eds.), *The psychology of adult development and aging.* Washington, D.C.: American Psychological Association, 1973.

Baltes, P. B., Nesselroade, J. R., Schaie, K. W., & Labouvie, E. W. On the dilemma of regression effects in examining ability-level-related differentials in ontogenetic patterns of intelligence. *Developmental Psychology,* 1972, *6,* 78–84.

Baltes, P. B., Reese, H. W., & Lipsitt, L. P. Life-span developmental psychology. *Annual Review of Psychology,* 1980, *31,* 65–110.

Baltes, P. B., Reese, H. W., & Nesselroade, J. R. *Life-span developmental psychology: Introduction to research methods.* Monterey, Calif.: Brooks/Cole, 1977.

Baltes, P. B., & Schaie, K. W. (Eds.). *Life-span developmental psychology: Personality and socialization.* New York: Academic Press, 1973.

Baltes, P. B., & Schaie, K. W. The myth of the twilight years. *Psychology Today,* March, 1974, 35–38, 40.

Baltes, P. B., & Schaie, K. W. On the plasticity of intelligence in adulthood and old age: Where Horn and Donaldson fail. *American Psychologist,* 1976, *31,* 720–725.

Baltes, P. B., Schaie, K. W., & Nardi, A. N. Age and experimental mortality in a seven-year longitudinal study

of cognitive behavior. *Developmental Psychology,* 1971, *5,* 18–26.

Baltes, P. B., & Willis, S. L. Toward psychological theories of aging and development. In J. E. Birren & K. W. Schaie (Eds.), *Handbook of the psychology of aging.* New York: Van Nostrand Reinhold, 1977.

Bandura, A., & Walters, R. W. *Social learning and personality development.* New York: Holt, Rinehart & Winston, 1963.

Barfield, R. E., & Morgan, J. N. *Early retirement: The discussion and the experience and a second look.* Ann Arbor, Mich.: Institute For Social Research, 1974.

Barfield, R. E., & Morgan, J. N. Trends in satisfaction with retirement. *The Gerontologist,* 1978, *18,* 19–23.

Barrett, C. J. Women in widowhood: Review essay. *Signs: Journal of Women in Culture and Society,* 1977, *2,* 856–868.

Barrett, C. J. Effectiveness of widows' groups in facilitating change. *Journal of Consulting and Clinical Psychology,* 1978, *46,* 20–31.

Bart, P. Depression in middle-aged women. In V. Gormick & B. K. Moran (Eds.), *Women in sexist society.* New York: New American Library, 1972.

Bartlett, F. C. *Remembering.* Cambridge, Eng.: University Press, 1932.

Barton, E. M., Plemons, J. K., Willis, S. L., & Baltes, P. B. Recent findings on adult and gerontological intelligence: Changing a stereotype of decline. *American Behavioral Scientist,* 1975, *19,* 224–236.

Baruch, G. K., & Barnett, R. C. On the well-being of adult women. In L. A. Bond & J. C. Rosen (Eds.), *Competence and coping during adulthood.* Hanover, N. H.: University Press of New England, 1980.

Bates, A. Parental roles in courtship. *Social Forces,* 1942, *20,* 433–486.

Bayley, N., & Oden, M. H. The maintenance of intellectual ability in gifted adults. *Journal of Gerontology,* 1955, *10,* 91–107.

Bearison, D. J. The construct of regression: A Piagetian approach. *Merrill-Palmer Quarterly,* 1974, *20,* 21–30.

Bell, A. B. Role models of young adulthood: Their relationship to occupational behaviors. *Vocational Guidance Quarterly,* 1970, *18,* 280–284.

Bell, R. Q. Convergence: An accelerated longitudinal approach. *Child Development,* 1953, *24,* 145–152.

Bell, R. Q. An experimental test of the accelerated longitudinal approach. *Child Development,* 1954, *25,* 281–286.

Bellin, S. S., & Hardt, R. H. Marital status and mental disorders among the aged. *American Sociological Review,* 1958, *28,* 155–162.

Belloc, N. Relationship of health practices in mortality. *Preventive Medicine,* 1973, *2,* 67–81.

Bellow, S. (Ed.). *Great Jewish short stories.* New York: Dell, 1963.

Benedek, T. Climacterium: A developmental phase. *Psychoanalytic Quarterly,* 1950, *19,* 1–27.

Benedek, T. Parenthood during the life cycle. In E. J. Anthony & T. Benedek (Eds.), *Parenthood.* Boston: Little Brown, 1970.

Bengtson, V. L. The generation gap: A review and typology of social-psychological perspectives. *Youth and Society,* 1970, *2,* 7–31.

Bengtson, V. L. *The social psychology of aging.* New York: Bobbs-Merrill, 1973.

Bengtson, V. L., & Black, K. D. Intergenerational relations and continuities in socialization. In P. B. Baltes and K. W. Schaie (Eds.), *Life-span developmental psychology: Personality and socialization.* New York: Academic Press, 1973.

Bengtson, V. L., & Cutler, N. E. Generations and intergenerational relations. In R. H. Binstock and E. Shanas, (Eds.), *Handbook of aging and the social sciences.* New York: Van Nostrand Reinhold, 1976.

Bengtson, V. L., Dowd, J. J., Smith, D. H., & Inkeles, A. Modernization, modernity, and perceptions of aging: A cross-cultural study. *Journal of Gerontology,* 1975, *30,* 688–695.

Berardo, F. M. Widowhood status in the United States: Perspectives on a neglected aspect of the family cycle. *Family Coordinator,* 1968, *17,* 191–203.

Berkman, L. F. *Psychosocial resources health behavior and mortality: A nine year follow-up study.* Paper presented at the meeting of the American Public Health Association, October 1977.

Bernard, J. *Sex-role learning in children and adolescents.* Paper presented at the meeting of the American Association for the Advancement of Science, Washington, D.C., December 1972.

Bernard, J. *The future of marriage.* New York: Bantam, 1973.

Bernard, J. Notes on changing life styles: 1970–1974. *Journal of Marriage and the Family,* 1975, *37,* 582–593.

Bijou, S. W., & Baer, D. M. *Child development: A systematic and empirical theory* (Vol. 1). New York: Appleton-Century-Crofts, 1961.

Birren, J. E. Psychophysiological relations. In J. E. Birren, R. N. Butler, S. W. Greenhouse, L. Sokoloff, & M. R. Yarrow (Eds.), *Human aging: A biological and behavioral study.* Washington, D.C.: U.S. Government Printing Office, 1963.

Birren, J. E. Translations in gerontology—from lab to life: Psychophysiology and speed of response. *American Psychologist,* 1974, *29,* 808–815.

Birren, J. E., & Botwinick, J. Age differences in finger, jaw, and foot reaction time to auditory stimuli. *Journal of Gerontology,* 1955, *10,* 429–432.

Birren, J. E., Butler, R. N., Greenhouse, S. W., Sokoloff, L., & Yarrow, M. R. (Eds.). *Human aging: A biological and behavioral study.* Washington, D.C.: U.S. Government Printing Office, 1963.

Birren, J. E., Riegel, K. F., & Morrison, D. F. Age differences in response speed as a function of controlled variations of stimulus conditions: Evidence of a general speed factor. *Gerontologia,* 1962, *6,* 1–18.

Birren, J. E., & Spieth, W. Age, response speed, and cardiovascular functions. *Journal of Gerontology,* 1962, *17,* 390–391.

Birren, J. E., & Woodruff, D. S. Human development over the lifespan through education. In P. B. Baltes & K. W. Schaie (Eds.), *Life-span developmental psychology: Personality and socialization.* New York: Academic Press, 1973.

Bjorksten, J. The cross linkage theory of aging. *Journal of the American Geriatrics Society,* 1968, *16,* 408–427.

Blau, F. D. Women in the labor force: An overview. In J. Freeman (Ed.), *Women: A feminist perspective.* Palo Alto, Calif.: Mayfield, 1975.

Blenkner, M. Social work and family relationships in later life with some thoughts on filial maturity. In E. Shanas & G. Streib (Eds.), *Social structure and the family.* Englewood Cliffs, N.J.: Prentice-Hall, 1965.

Block, J. *Lives through time.* Berkeley, Calif.: Bancroft, 1971.

Blood, M. R., & Hulin, C. L. Alienation, environmental characteristics, and worker responses. *Journal of Applied Psychology,* 1967, *51,* 284–290.

Blood, R. O., & Wolfe, D. M. *Husbands and wives.* New York: Free Press, 1960.

Blum, J. E., & Jarvik, L. F. Intellectual performance of octogenarians as a function of education and initial ability. *Human Development,* 1974, *17,* 364–375.

Bock, E. W., & Weber, I. L. Suicide among the elderly: Isolating widowhood and mitigating alternatives. *Journal of Marriage and the Family,* 1972, *34,* 24–31.

Bolles, R. N. *What color is your parachute?* San Francisco: Ten Speed Press, 1978.

Borland, D. C. Research on middle age: An assessment. *The Gerontologist,* 1978, *18,* 379–386.

Bornstein, P. E., Clayton, P. J., Halikas, J. A., Maurice, W. L., & Robins, E. The depression of widowhood after thirteen months. *British Journal of Psychiatry,* 1973, *122,* 561–566.

Borup, J. H., Gallego, D. T., & Heffernan, P. G. Relocation and its effect on mortality. *The Gerontologist,* 1979, *19,* 135–140.

Botwinick, J. Cautiousness in advanced age. *Journal of Gerontology,* 1966, *21,* 347–353.

Botwinick, J. *Cognitive processes in maturity and old age.* New York: Springer, 1967.

Botwinick, J. Sensory-set factors in age difference in

reaction time. *Journal of Genetic Psychology,* 1971, *119,* 241–249.

Botwinick, J. Intellectual abilities. In J. E. Birren & K. W. Schaie (Eds.), *Handbook of the psychology of aging.* New York: Van Nostrand Reinhold, 1977.

Botwinick, J., Robbin, J. S., & **Brinley, J. F.** Age differences in card-sorting performance in relation to task difficulty, task set, and practice. *Journal of Experimental Psychology,* 1960, *59,* 10–18.

Botwinick, J., & **Storandt, M.** *Memory, related functions and age.* Springfield, Ill.: Charles C Thomas, 1974.

Botwinick, J., & **Storandt, M.** Recall and recognition of old information in relation to age and sex. *Journal of Gerontology,* 1980, *35,* 70–76.

Botwinick, J., & **Thompson, L. W.** Components of reaction time in relation to age and sex. *Journal of Genetic Psychology,* 1966, *108,* 175–183.

Bourque, L. B., & **Back, K. W.** Life graphs and life events. *Journal of Gerontology,* 1977, *32,* 669–674.

Bousfield, A. K., & **Bousfield, W. A.** Measurement of clustering and of sequential constancies in repeated free recall. *Psychological Reports,* 1966, *19,* 935–942.

Bowerman, C. E., & **Day, B. R.** A test of the theory of complimentary needs as applied to couples during courtship. *American Sociological Review,* 1956, *31,* 602–605.

Bowlby, J. *Attachment and loss* (Vol. 1). London: Hogarth Press and Institute of Psychoanalysis, 1969.

Bowlby, J. *Child care and the growth of love.* Hamondsworth, Eng.: Penguin, 1972.

Bowlby, J. *Attachment and loss* (Vol. 2). New York: Basic Books, 1973.

Boylin, W., Gordon, S. K., & **Nehrke, M. F.** Reminiscing and ego integrity in institutionalized elderly males. *The Gerontologist,* 1976, *16,* 118–124.

Brand, F. N., & **Smith, R. T.,** Life adjustment and relocation of the elderly. *Journal of Gerontology,* 1974, *29,* 336–340.

Brannen, P. (Ed.). *Entering the world of work: Some sociological perspectives.* London: HMSO, 1975.

Bransford, J. D., & **Franks, J. J.** The abstraction of linguistic ideas. *Cognitive Psychology,* 1971, *2,* 331–350.

Bransford, J. D., McCarrell, N. S., Franks, J. J., & **Nitsch, K. E.** Toward unexplaining memory. In R. Shaw & J. D. Bransford (Eds.), *Perceiving, acting, and knowing: Toward an ecological psychology.* Hillsdale, N.J.: Erlbaum, 1977.

Bray, D. W., & **Howard, A.** Career success and life satisfaction of middle-aged managers. In L. A. Bond & J. C. Rosen (Eds.), *Competence and coping during adulthood.* Hanover, N.H.: University Press of New England, 1980.

Brim, O. G., Jr. Adult socialization. In J. A. Clausen (Ed.), *Socialization and society.* Boston: Little Brown, 1968.

Brim, O. G., Jr. Theories of the male mid-life crisis. *Counseling Psychologist,* 1976, *6,* 2–9.

Brim, O. G., Jr., & **Wheeler, S.** *Socialization after childhood: Two essays.* New York: Wiley, 1965.

Britton, J. H., & **Britton, J. O.** *Personality changes in aging.* New York: Springer, 1972.

Broadbent, D. E. *Perception and communication.* New York: Pergamon Press, 1958.

Bronfenbrenner, U. Toward an experimental ecology of human development. *American Psychologist,* 1977, *32,* 513–531.

Brückner, R. Longitudinal research on the eye. *Clinical Gerontology,* 1967, *9,* 87–95.

Bühler, C. *Der menschliche Lebenslauf als psychologisches Problem.* Leipzig: Hirzel, 1933.

Bühler, C. The curve of life as studied in biographies. *Journal of Applied Psychology,* 1935, *19,* 405–409.

Bühler, C. Theoretical observations about life's basic tendencies. *American Journal of Psychotherapy,* 1959, *13,* 561–581.

Bühler, C. Genetic aspects of the self. *Annals of the New York Academy of Sciences,* 1962, *96,* 730–764.

Buss, A. R. An extension of developmental models that separate ontogenetic changes and cohort differences. *Psychological Bulletin,* 1973, *80,* 466–479.

Busse, E. W., & **Obrist, W. D.** Significance of focal electroencephalographic changes in the elderly. *Postgraduate Medicine,* 1963, *34,* 179–182.

Butler, R. N. The life review: An interpretation of reminiscence in the aged. *Psychiatry,* 1963, *26,* 65–76.

Butler, R. N. The life review: An interpretation of reminiscence in the aged. In B. L. Neugarten (Ed.), *Middle age and aging.* Chicago: University of Chicago Press, 1968.

Butler, R. N. The creative life and old age. In E. Pfeiffer (Ed.), *Successful aging.* Durham, N.C.: Duke University Center for the Study of Aging and Human Development, 1974.

Butler, R. N., & **Lewis, M. I.** *Aging and mental health* (2d Ed.). St. Louis: C. V. Mosby, 1977.

Byng-Hall, J., & **Miller, M. J.** Adolescence and the family. In S. Meyerson (Ed.), *Adolescence.* London: Allen & Unwin, 1975.

Byrne, D. Interpersonal attraction and attitude similarity. *Journal of Abnormal and Social Psychology,* 1961, *62,* 713–715.

Caldwell, B. M., Wright, C. M., Honig, A., & **Tannenbaum, J.** Infant day care and attachment. *American Journal of Orthopsychiatry,* 1970, *40,* 397–412.

Cameron, D. E. Impairment at the retention phase of remembering. *Psychiatric Quarterly,* 1943, *17,* 395–404.

Campbell, A. The American way of mating: Marriage or children, only maybe. *Psychology Today,* May 1975, 39–42.

Campbell, D. T., & **Stanley, J. C.** Experimental and quasi-experimental designs for research on teaching. In

N. L. Gage (Ed.), *Handbook of research on teaching*. Chicago: Rand McNally, 1963.

Canestrari, R. E. Paced and self-paced learning in young and elderly adults. *Journal of Gerontology*, 1963, *18*, 165–168.

Canestrari, R. E. Age changes in acquisition. In G. A. Talland (Ed.), *Human aging and behavior*. New York: Academic Press, 1968.

Capon, N., & **Kuhn, D.** Logical reasoning in the supermarket: Adult females' use of a proportional reasoning strategy in an everyday context. *Developmental Psychology*, 1979, *15*, 450–452.

Carey, R. G., & **Posavac, E. J.** Attitudes of physicians on disclosing information to and maintaining life for terminally ill patients. *Omega: Journal of Death and Dying*, 1978, *9*, 67–77.

Carp, F. M. *A future for the aged: The residents of Victoria Plaza*. Austin: University of Texas Press, 1966.

Carpenter, D. G. Diffusion theory of aging. *Journal of Gerontology*, 1965, *20*, 191–195.

Cartwright, A., Hockey, L., & **Anderson, J. L.** *Life before death*. London: Routledge & Kegan Paul, 1973.

Carus, F. A. *Psychologie Zweiter Theil: Specialpsychologie*. Leizpig: Barth & Kummer, 1808.

Catteli, R. B. Theory of fluid and crystallized intelligence: A critical experiment. *Journal of Educational Psychology*, 1963, *54*, 1–22.

Cattell, R. B. *Abilities: Their structure, growth and action*. Boston: Houghton-Mifflin, 1971.

Chambers, W. N., & **Reiser, M. F.** Emotional stress in the precipitation of congestive heart failure. *Psychosomatic Medicine*, 1953, *15*, 38–60.

Chilman, C. S. Families in development at mid-stage of the family life cycle. *Family Coordinator*, 1968, *17*, 297–312.

Chinoy, E. *Sociological perspective* (2d ed.). New York: Random House, 1967.

Chiriboga, D. *Marital separation: A study of stress*. Paper presented at the Meeting of the Western Psychological Association, Seattle, 1977.

Chiriboga, D. *Life events and metamodels: A life span study*. Paper presented at the Meeting of the Gerontological Society, Dallas, November 1978.

Chown, S. M. Morale, careers, and personal potentials. In J. E. Birren & K. W. Schaie (Eds.), *Handbook of the psychology of aging*. New York: Van Nostrand Reinhold, 1977.

Christensen, H. T., & **Gregg, C. F.** Changing sex norms in America and Scandinavia. *Journal of Marriage and the Family*, 1970, *32*, 616–627.

Clark, M., & **Anderson, B.** *Culture and aging*. Springfield, Ill.: Charles C. Thomas, 1967.

Clavan, S. The impact of social class and social trends on the role of grandparent. *The Family Coordinator*, 1978, *27*, 351–358.

Clayton, P. J., Mortality and morbidity in the first year of widowhood. *Archives of General Psychiatry*, 1974, *30*, 747–750.

Clayton, V. Erikson's theory of human development as it applies to the aged: Wisdom as contradictive cognition. *Human Development*, 1975, *18*, 119–128.

Clayton, V., & **Overton, W. F.** Concrete and formal operational thought processes in young adulthood and old age. *International Journal of Aging and Human Development*, 1976, *7*, 237–245.

Clopton, W. Personality and career change. *Industrial Gerontology*, 1973, *17*, 9–17.

Colby, A. Evolution of a moral-developmental theory. *New Directions for Child Development*, 1978, *2*, 89–104.

Colby, A., Kohlberg, L., & **Gibbs, J.** *A longitudinal study of moral judgment*. Unpublished manuscript. Harvard University, 1980.

Coleman, J. S., & **Associates.** *Equality of educational opportunity*. Washington, D.C.: U.S. Government Printing Office, 1966.

Collette-Pratt, C. Attitudinal predictors of devaluation of old age in a multi-generational sample. *Journal of Gerontology*, 1976, *31*, 193–197.

Collins, G. The good news about 1984. *Psychology Today*, January 1979, 34–48.

Comfort, A. *Aging: The biology of senescence*. New York: Holt, Rinehart and Winston, 1964.

Conger, J. J. A world they never knew: The family and social change. In J. Kagan & R. Coles (Eds.), *Twelve to sixteen: Early adolescence*. New York: Norton, 1972.

Constantinople, A. An Eriksonian measure of personality development in college students. *Developmental Psychology*, 1969, *1*, 357–372.

Cook, T. C., & **Campbell, D. T.** The design and conduct of quasi-experiments and true experiments in field settings. In M. D. Dunnette (Ed.), *Handbook of industrial and organizational research*. Chicago: Rand McNally, 1975.

Cooper, K. H. *Aerobics*. New York: Bantam Books, 1968.

Costa, P. T., Jr., & **McCrae, R. R.** Age differences in personality structure: A cluster analytic approach. *Journal of Gerontology*, 1976, *31*, 564–570.

Costa, P. T., Jr., & **McCrae, R. R.** Age differences in personality structure revisited: Studies in validity, stability, and change. *International Journal of Aging and Human Development*, 1977, *8*, 261–275.

Costa, P. T., Jr., & **McCrae, R. R.** Objective personality assessment. In M. Storandt, I. C. Siegler, & M. F. Elias (Eds.), *The clinical psychology of aging*. New York: Plenum Press, 1978.

Costa, P. T., Jr., & **McCrae, R. R.** Still stable after all these years: Personality as a key to some issues in aging. In P. B. Baltes & O. G. Brim, Jr. (Eds.), *Life-span development and behavior* (Vol. 3). New York: Academic Press, 1980.

Cottrell, F., & **Atchley, R. C.** *Women in retirement: A* *preliminary report.* Oxford, Ohio: Scripps Foundation, 1969.

Craik, F. I. M. Short term memory and the aging process. In G. A. Talland (Ed.), *Human aging and behavior.* New York: Academic Press, 1968. (a)

Craik, F. I. M. Two components in free recall. *Journal of Verbal Learning and Verbal Behavior,* 1968, *7,* 996–1004. (b)

Craik, F. I. M. Age differences in recognition memory. *Quarterly Journal of Experimental Psychology,* 1971, *23,* 316–319.

Craik, F. I. M. Age differences in human memory. In J. E. Birren & K. W. Schaie (Eds.), *Handbook of the psychology of aging.* New York: Van Nostrand Reinhold, 1977.

Craik, F. I. M., & **Lockhart, R. S.** Levels of processing: A framework for memory research. *Journal of Verbal Learning and Verbal Behavior,* 1972, *11,* 671–684.

Craik, F. I. M., & **Tulving, E.** Depth of processing and the retention of words in episodic memory. *Journal of Experimental Psychology,* 1975, *104,* 268–294.

Cronbach, L. J. Beyond the two disciplines of scientific psychology. American Psychologist, 1975, *30,* 116–134.

Crystal, J. C., & **Bolles, R. N.** *Where do I go from here with my life.* New York: Seabury Press, 1974.

Cuber, J. F., & **Harroff, P. B.** *Sex and the significant Americans.* Baltimore: Penguin, 1965.

Cumming, E., & **Henry, W. E.** *Growing old: The process of disengagement.* New York: Basic Books, 1961.

Curtis, H. S. *Biological mechanisms of aging.* Springfield, Ill.: Charles C. Thomas, 1966.

Cutler, N. E., & **Bengtson, V. L.** Age and political alienation: Maturation, generation, and period effects. *Annals of the American Academy of Politics and Social Sciences,* 1974, *415,* 160–175.

Danish, S. J., & **D'Augelli, A. R.** Promoting competence and enhancing development through life development intervention. In L. A. Bond & J. C. Rosen (Eds.), *Competence and coping during adulthood.* Hanover N.H.: University Press of New England, 1980.

Dastur, D. K., Lane, M. H., Hansen, D. B., Kety, S. S., Butler, R. N., Perlin, S., & **Sokoloff, L.** Effects of aging on cerebral circulation and metabolism in man. In J. E. Birren, R. N. Butler, S. W. Greenhouse, L. Sokoloff, & M. R. Yarrow (Eds.), *Human aging: A biological and behavioral study.* Washington, D.C.: U.S. Government Printing Office, 1963.

Datan, N. Midas and other mid-life crises. In W. H. Norman & T. J. Scaramella (Eds.), *Mid-life: Developmental and clinical issues.* New York: Brunner/Mazel, 1980.

Datan, N., & **Ginsberg, L. H. (Eds.).** *Life-span developmental psychology: Normative life crises.* New York: Academic Press, 1975.

Datan, N., & **Reese, H. W. (Eds.).** *Life-span developmental psychology: Dialectical perspectives on experimental research.* New York: Academic Press, 1977.

DeLora, J. R. Social systems of dating on a college campus. *Marriage and Family Living,* 1963, *25,* 81–84.

Denney, D. R., & **Denney, N. W.** The use of classification for problem solving: A comparison of middle and old age. *Developmental Psychology,* 1973, *9,* 275–278.

Denney, N. W. Classification abilities in the elderly. *Journal of Gerontology,* 1974, *29,* 309–314. (a)

Denney, N. W. Classification criteria in middle and old age. *Developmental Psychology,* 1974, *10,* 901–906. (b)

Denney, N. W. Evidence for developmental changes in categorization criteria for children and adults. *Human Development,* 1974, *17,* 41–53. (c)

Denney, N. W. Problem solving in later adulthood: Intervention research. In P. B. Baltes & O. G. Brim, Jr. (Eds.), *Life-span development and behavior* (Vol. 2). New York: Academic Press, 1979.

Denney, N. W., & **Denney, D. R.** Modeling effects on the questioning strategies of the elderly. *Developmental Psychology,* 1974, *10,* 458.

Denney, N. W., & **Lennon, M. L.** Classification: A comparison of middle and old age. *Developmental Psychology,* 1972, *7,* 210–213.

Deutsch, F. *Child services: On behalf of children.* Monterey Calif.: Brooks/Cole, in press.

Deutsch, F., & **Goldberg, S. R.** Perspectives on love: Interviews. In F. Deutsch & S. R. Goldberg (Eds.), *Variations of individual development: Stage of the life span, concepts of love, adjustments, and expectations* (60-minute color video cassette). University Park, Pa.: Pennsylvania State University, 1974.

de Vries, H. A. Physiological effects of an exercise training regimen upon men aged 52 to 88. *Journal of Gerontology,* 1970, *25,* 325–336.

de Vries, H. A. Prescription of exercise for older men from telemetered exercise heart rate data. *Geriatrics,* 1971, *26,* 102–111.

de Vries, H. A. Physiology of exercise and aging. In D. S. Woodruff & J. E. Birren (Eds.), *Aging: Scientific perspectives and social issues.* New York: Van Nostrand, 1975.

Dixon, R. A., Simon, E. W., Nowak, C. A., & **Hultsch, D. F.** *Memory for text in adulthood as a function of input modality and delay interval.* Unpublished manuscript. Pennsylvania State University, 1980.

Dohrenwend, B. S., Krasnoff, L., Askenasy, A. R., & **Dohrenwend, B. P.** Exemplification of a method for scaling life events: The PERI life events scale. *Journal of Health and Social Behavior,* 1978, *19,* 205–229.

Domey, R. G., McFarland, R. A., & **Chadwick, E.** Threshold and rate of dark adaptation as functions of age and time. *Human Factors,* 1960, *2,* 109–119.

Donahue, W., Orbach, H. L., & **Pollak, O.** Retirement: The emerging social pattern. In C. Tibbets (Ed.), *Hand-*

book of social gerontology. Chicago: University of Chicago Press, 1960.

Douglas, K., & **Arenberg, D.** Age changes, cohort differences, and cultural change on the Guilford-Zimmerman Temperament Survey. *Journal of Gerontology,* 1978, *33,* 737–747.

Douvan, E., & **Adelson, J.** *The adolescent experience.* New York: Wiley, 1966.

Dowd, J. J., & **Bengtson, V. L.** Aging in minority populations: An examination of the double jeopardy hypothesis. *Journal of Gerontology,* 1978, *33,* 427–436.

Drachman, D. A., & **Leavitt, J.** Memory impairment in the aged: Storage versus retrieval deficit. *Journal of Experimental Psychology,* 1972, *93,* 302–308.

Duvall, E. M. *Family development.* Philadelphia: Lippincott, 1971.

Dyer, E. D. Parenthood as crisis: A restudy. *Marriage and Family Living,* 1963, *25,* 196–201.

Earhard, M. Retrieval failure in the presence of retrieval cues: A comparison of three age groups. *Canadian Journal of Psychology,* 1977, *31,* 139–150.

Egbert, L. D., Battit, G. E., Welch, C. E., Bartlett, M. K. Reduction of post-operative pain by encouragement and instruction of patients. *New England Journal of Medicine,* 1964, *270,* 825–827.

Eichorn, D. The Institute of Human Development Studies: Berkeley and Oakland. In L. F. Jarvik, C. Eisdorfer, & J. E. Blum (Eds.), *Intellectual functioning in adults: Psychological and biological influences.* New York: Springer, 1973.

Eisdorfer, C. Changes in cognitive functioning in relation to intellectual level in senescence. In C. Tibbits & W. Donahue (Eds.), *Social and psychological aspects of aging.* New York: Columbia University Press, 1962.

Eisdorfer, C. Verbal learning and response time in the aged. *Journal of Genetic Psychology,* 1965, *107,* 15–22.

Eisdorfer, C. Arousal and performance: Experiments in verbal learning and a tentative theory. In G. A. Talland (Ed.), *Human aging and behavior.* New York: Academic Press, 1968.

Eisdorfer, C., Axelrod, S., & **Wilkie, F. L.** Stimulus exposure time as a factor in serial learning in an aged sample. *Journal of Abnormal and Social Psychology,* 1963, *67,* 594–600.

Eisdorfer, C., Nowlin, J., & **Wilkie, F.** Improvement in learning in the aged by modification of autonomic nervous system activity. *Science,* 1970, *170,* 1327–1329.

Eisdorfer, C., & **Wilkie, F.** Stress, disease, aging and behavior. In J. E. Birren & K. W. Schaie (Eds.), *Handbook of the psychology of aging.* New York: Van Nostrand Reinhold, 1977.

Eisenstadt, S. N. *From generations to generations.* New York: Free Press, 1956.

Ekstrom, R. B., French, J. W., Harman, H. H., & **Dermen, D.** *Manual for kit of factor-referenced cognitive tests.* Princeton, N.J.: Educational Testing Service, 1976.

Elder, G. H., Jr. Appearance and education in marriage mobility. *American Sociological Review,* 1969, *34,* 519–533.

Elder, G. H., Jr. *Children of the Great Depression.* Chicago: University of Chicago Press, 1974.

Elder, G. H., Jr. Age differentiation and the life course. *Annual Review of Sociology,* 1975, *1,* 165–190.

Elder, G. H., Jr. Family history and the life course. *Journal of Family History,* 1977, *2,* 279–304. (a)

Elder, G. H., Jr. *Social structure and personality: A life course perspective.* Paper presented at Conference on Quantitative History and Prehistory, Mathematics Social Science Board and The National Science Foundation, University of Texas at Dallas, April 1977. (b)

Elias, M. F., & **Elias, P. K.** Motivation and activity. In J. E. Birren & K. W. Schaie (Eds.), *Handbook of the psychology of aging.* New York: Van Nostrand Reinhold, 1977.

Elkind, D. Growing up faster. *Psychology Today,* February 1979, 38–45.

Erber, J. T. Age differences in learning and memory on a digit-symbol substitution task. *Experimental Aging Research,* 1976, *2,* 45–53.

Erikson, E. H. Identity and the life cycle: Selected papers. *Psychological Issues,* 1959, *1,* 50–100.

Erikson, E. H. *Childhood and society.* New York: Norton, 1963.

Erikson, E. H. Generativity and ego integrity. In B. L. Neugarten (Ed.), *Middle age and aging.* Chicago: University of Chicago Press, 1968.

Erikson, E. H. *Dimensions of a new identity.* New York: Norton, 1974.

Eysenck, M. W. Age differences in incidental learning. *Developmental Psychology,* 1974, *10,* 936–941.

Falk, L. L. Occupational satisfaction of female college graduates. *Journal of Marriage and the Family,* 1966, *28,* 177–185.

Farrell, W. *Beyond masculinity.* New York: Random House, 1974.

Fasteau, M. *The male machine.* New York: McGraw-Hill, 1974.

Faust, D., & **Arbuthnot, J.** Relationship between moral and Piagetian reasoning and the effectiveness of moral education. *Developmental Psychology,* 1978, *14,* 435–436.

Featherstone, M. S., & **Cunningham, C. M.** Age of manual workers in relation to conditions and demands of work. *Occupational Psychology,* 1963, *37,* 197–208.

Feifel, H. The function of attitudes toward death. In Group for the Advancement of Psychiatry (Eds.), *Death and dying: Attitudes of patient and doctor.* New York: Mental Health Materials Center, 1965.

Feifel, H., & **Branscomb, A. B.** Who's afraid of death? *Journal of Abnormal Psychology,* 1973, *81,* 282–288.

Feifel, H., Hanson, S., Jones, R., & **Edwards, L.** Physicians consider death. *Proceedings of the 75th Annual Convention of the American Psychological Association,* 1967, *2,* 201–202.

Ferree, M. Working class jobs: Housework and paid work as sources of satisfaction. *Social Problems,* 1976, *23,* 431–441.

Festinger, L. A. *A theory of cognitive dissonance.* Stanford: Stanford University Press, 1957.

Finch, C. E. The regulation of physiological changes during mammalian aging. *The Quarterly Review of Biology,* 1976, *51,* 49–83.

Flavell, J. H. *The developmental psychology of Jean Piaget.* Princeton, N.J.: Van Nostrand, 1963.

Flavell, J. H. Cognitive changes in adulthood. In L. R. Goulet & P. B. Baltes (Eds.), *Life-span developmental psychology: Research and theory.* New York: Academic Press, 1970.

Fletcher, J. *Attitudes toward euthanasia.* Paper presented at the Seventh Annual Euthanasia Conference, New York, December 1974.

Forrester, J. W. *World dynamics.* Cambridge, Mass.: Wright-Allen Press, 1971.

Fox, J. H. Effects of retirement and former work life on women's adaptation in old age. *Journal of Gerontology,* 1977, *32,* 196–202.

Fozard, J. L., & **Popkin, S. J.** Optimizing adult development: Ends and means of an applied psychology of aging. *American Psychologist,* 1978, *33,* 975–989.

Fozard, J. L., Wolf, E., Bell, B., McFarland, R. A., & **Podolsky, S.** Visual perception and communication. In J. E. Birren & K. W. Schaie (Eds.), *Handbook of the psychology of aging.* New York: Van Nostrand Reinhold, 1977.

Franzblau, R. N. *The middle generation.* New York: Holt, Rinehart & Winston, 1971.

French, J. W., Ekstrom, R. B., & **Price, L. A.** *Kit of reference tests for cognitive factors.* Princeton, N.J.: Educational Testing Service, 1963.

Freud, S. *An outline of psychoanalysis.* New York: Norton, 1949.

Friedenberg, E. Current patterns of a generation conflict. *Journal of Social Issues,* 1969, *25,* 21–38.

Friedman, M., & **Rosenman, R. H.** *Type A behavior and your heart.* New York: Knopf, 1974.

Friedmann, E., & **Havighurst, R. J.** *The meaning of work and retirement.* Chicago: University of Chicago Press, 1954.

Fulton, R. Death, grief, and social recuperation. *Omega: Journal of Death and Dying,* 1970, *1,* 23–28.

Garfield, C. A. *Psychothanatological concomitants of altered state experience: An investigation of the relationship between consciousness alteration and fear of death.* Unpublished doctoral dissertation, University of California at Berkeley, 1974.

Gergen, K. L. Social psychology as history. *Journal of Personality and Social Psychology,* 1973, *26,* 309–320.

Gilbert, J. G. Age changes in color matching. *Journal of Gerontology,* 1957, *12,* 210–215.

Gladis, M. Age differences in repeated learning tasks in schizophrenic subjects. *Journal of Abnormal and Social Psychology,* 1964, *68,* 437–441.

Gladis, M., & **Braun, H. W.** Age differences in transfer and retroaction as a function of intertask response similarity. *Journal of Experimental Psychology,* 1958, *55,* 25–30.

Glamser, F. D. Determinants of a positive attitude toward retirement. *Journal of Gerontology,* 1976, *31,* 104–107.

Glaser, B. G., & **Strauss, A.** *Time for dying.* New York: Macmillan, 1968.

Glenn, N. D. Psychological well-being in the post-parental stage: Some evidence from national surveys. *Journal of Marriage and the Family,* 1975, *37,* 105–110.

Glenwick, D. S., & **Whitbourne, S. K.** Beyond despair and disengagement: A transactional model of personality and development in late life. *International Journal of Aging and Human Development,* 1978, *6,* 261–267.

Glick, I. O., Weiss, R. S., & **Parkes, C. M.** *The first year of bereavement.* New York: Wiley, 1974.

Glick, P. C. Updating the life cycle of the family. *Journal of Marriage and the Family,* 1977, *39,* 5–15.

Glick, P. C., & **Norton, A. J.** *Number, timing, and duration of marriages and divorces in the United States: June 1975* (U.S. Bureau of the Census Population Reports, No. 297). Washington, D.C.: U.S. Government Printing Office, 1976.

Glueck, S., & **Glueck, E.** *Unravelling juvenile delinquency.* New York: Commonwealth, 1950.

Goldberg, S. R., & **Deutsch, F.** *Life-span individual and family development.* Monterey, Calif.: Brooks/Cole, 1977.

Gorer, G. *The American people: A study of national character.* New York: Norton, 1964.

Gorer, G. *Death, grief, and mourning.* Garden City, N.Y.: Doubleday, 1965.

Gould, R. L. *Transformations: Growth and change in adult life.* New York: Simon & Schuster, 1978.

Goulet, L. R. New directions for research on aging and retention. *Journal of Gerontology,* 1972, *27,* 52–60.

Goulet, L. R., & **Baltes, P. B. (Eds.).** *Life-span developmental psychology: Research and theory:* New York: Academic Press, 1970.

Greenberg, M., & **Morris, N.** Engrossment: The newborn's impact upon the father. *American Journal of Orthopsychiatry,* 1974, *44,* 520–531.

Griew, S. Uncertainty as a determinant of performance in relation to age. *Gerontologia,* 1958, *2,* 284–289.

Group for the Advancement of Psychiatry. *Joys and sorrows of parenthood,* New York: Scribner, 1973.

Gruber, H. E., & **Vonéche, J. J.** *The essential Piaget.* New York: Basic Books, 1977.

Gubrium, J. F. Marital desolation and the valuation of everyday life in old age. *Journal of Marriage and the Family,* 1974, *35,* 107–113.

Gubrium, J. F. Being single in old age. *International Journal of Aging and Human Development,* 1975, *6,* 29–41.

Guerney, B. G., Jr. *Relationship enhancement: Skill training programs for therapy, problem prevention and enrichment.* San Francisco: Jossey-Bass, 1977.

Guilford, J. P. *The nature of human intelligence.* New York: McGraw-Hill, 1967.

Gutman, G. M., & **Herbert, C. P.** Mortality rates among relocated extended-care patients. *Journal of Gerontology,* 1976, *31,* 352–357.

Gutmann, D. L. An exploration of ego configurations in middle and later life. In B. L. Neugarten and Associates (Eds.), *Personality in middle and later life.* New York: Atherton Press, 1964.

Gutmann, D. L. The cross-cultural perspective: Notes toward a comparative psychology of aging. In J. E. Birren & K. W. Schaie (Eds.), *Handbook of the psychology of aging.* New York: Van Nostrand Reinhold, 1977.

Guttmann, D. Life events and decision making by older adults. *The Gerontologist,* 1978, *18,* 462–467.

Haan, N. ". . . Change and sameness . . ." reconsidered. *International Journal of Aging and Human Development,* 1976, *7,* 59–65.

Haan, N. Two moralities in action contexts: Relationship to thought, ego regulation, and development. *Journal of Personality and Social Psychology,* 1978, *36,* 286–305.

Haan, N., & **Day, D.** A longitudinal study of change and sameness in personality development: Adolescence to later adulthood. *International Journal of Aging and Human Development,* 1974, *5,* 11–39.

Haan, N., Smith, M. B., & **Block, J.** Moral reasoning of young adults: Political-social behavior, family background, and personality correlates. *Journal of Personality and Social Psychology,* 1968, *10,* 183–201.

Hackman, J. R. Work design. In J. R. Hackman & J. L. Suttle (Eds.), *Improving life at work.* Santa Monica, Calif.: Goodyear, 1977.

Hagestad, G. O. Life transitions and adult family roles. *Generations,* 1979, *4,* 16–17. (a)

Hagestad, G. O. Personal Communication. November, 1979. (b)

Hagestad, G. O. *Role change and socialization in adulthood: The transition to the empty nest.* Unpublished manuscript. The Pennsylvania State University, 1980.

Hahn, H. P. The regulation of protein synthesis in the aging cell. *Experimental Gerontology,* 1970, *5,* 323.

Hall, G. S. *Senescence: The last half of life.* New York: Appleton, 1922.

Harman, D. Free radical theory of aging: Effect of free radical reaction inhibitors on the mortality rate of male LAF$_1$ mice. *Journal of Gerontology,* 1968, *23,* 476–482.

Harris, D. B. Problems in formulating a scientific concept of development. In D. B. Harris (Ed.), *The concept of development.* Minneapolis: University of Minnesota Press, 1957.

Harvey, C. D., & **Bahr, H. M.** Widowhood, morale, and affiliation. *Journal of Marriage and the Family,* 1974, *36,* 97–106.

Havighurst, R. J. The leisure activities of the middle-aged. *American Journal of Sociology,* 1957, *63,* 152–162.

Havighurst, R. J. Research and development in social gerontology: A report of a special committee of the Gerontological Society. *The Gerontologist,* 1969, *9,* 1–90.

Havighurst, R. J. Social roles, work, leisure, and education. In C. Eisdorfer & M. P. Lawton (Eds.), *The psychology of adult development and aging.* Washington, D.C.: American Psychological Association, 1973.

Havighurst, R. J., Neugarten, B. L., & **Tobin, S. S.** Disengagement and patterns of aging. In B. L. Neugarten (Ed.), *Middle age and aging.* Chicago: University of Chicago Press, 1968.

Hayflick, L. The limited *in vitro* lifetime of human diploid cell strains. *Experimental Cell Research,* 1965, *37,* 614–636.

Haynes, S. G., McMichael, A. J., & **Tyroler, H. A.** Survival after early and normal retirement. *Journal of Gerontology,* 1978, *33,* 269–278.

Healy, C. C. The relation of esteem and social class to self-occupational congruence. *Journal of Vocational Behavior,* 1973, *3,* 43–51.

Heath, D. H. Adolescent and adult predictors of vocational adaptation. *Journal of Vocational Behavior,* 1976, *9,* 1–19.

Heglin, H. J. Problem solving set in different age groups. *Journal of Gerontology,* 1956, *11,* 310–317.

Henning, M., & **Jardim, A.** *The managerial woman.* New York: Doubleday, 1976.

Henry, W. E., Sims, J., & **Spray, L.** *The fifth profession: Becoming a psychotherapist.* San Francisco: Jossey-Bass, 1971.

Herzberg, F. *Work and the nature of man.* Cleveland, Ohio: World, 1966.

Hetherington, E. M., Cox, M., & **Cox, R.** Stress and coping in divorce: A focus on women. In J. E. Gullahorn (Ed.), *Psychology and women in transition.* Washington, D.C.: V. H. Winston & Sons, 1979.

Hickey, T., & **Kalish, R. A.** Young people's perceptions of adults. *Journal of Gerontology,* 1968, *23,* 215–219.

Hicks, M. W. An empirical evaluation about textbook

assumptions about engagement. *Family Life Coordinator,* 1970, *19,* 57–63.

Hiestand, D. L. *Changing careers after thirty-five.* New York: Columbia University Press, 1971.

Hinton, J. Speaking of death with the dying. In E. Shneidman (Ed.), *Death: Current perspectives.* Palo Alto, Calif.: Mayfield, 1976.

Hobbs, D. F., Jr., & **Cole, S. P.** Transition to parenthood: A decade of replication. *Journal of Marriage and the Family,* 1976, *38,* 723–731.

Hodgkins, J. Influence of age on the speed of reaction and movement in females. *Journal of Gerontology,* 1962, *17,* 385–389.

Hoffman, L. W. The effects of maternal employment on the child—a review of research. *Developmental Psychology,* 1974, *10,* 204–228.

Hoffman, L. W., & **Nye, F. I.** *Working mothers.* San Francisco: Jossey-Bass, 1974.

Hofland, B., Willis, S. L., & **Baltes, P. B.** *Retesting and intraindividual variability in fluid intelligence in the elderly.* Paper presented at the Meeting of the Gerontological Society, Dallas, November 1978.

Hogan, D. P. The variable order of events in the life course. *American Sociological Review,* 1978, *43,* 573–586.

Holland, J. I. *Making vocational choices: A theory of careers.* Englewood Cliffs, N.J.: Prentice-Hall, Inc., 1973.

Hollingworth, H. L. *Mental growth and decline: A survey of developmental psychology.* New York: Appleton, 1927.

Holmes, T. H., & **Masuda, M.** Life change and illness susceptibility. In B. S. Dohrenwend & B. P. Dohrenwend (Eds.), *Stressful life events: Their nature and effects.* New York: Wiley, 1974.

Holmes, T. H., & **Rahe, R. H.** The social readjustment rating scale. *Journal of Psychosomatic Research,* 1967, *11,* 213–218.

Honigmann, J. J. *The world of man.* New York: Harper & Row, 1959.

Hooper, F. H., & **Sheehan, N.** Logical concept attainment during the aging years: Issues in the neo-Piagetian research literature. In W. F. Overton & J. M. Gallagher (Eds.), *Knowledge and development: Advances in theory and research* (Vol. 1). New York: Plenum Press, 1977.

Hooper, F. H., Fitzgerald, J., & **Papalia, D.** Piagetian theory and the aging process: Extensions and speculations. *Aging and Human Development,* 1971, *2,* 3–20.

Horn, J. L. Organization of data on life-span development of human abilities. In L. R. Goulet & P. B. Baltes (Eds.), *Life-span developmental psychology: Research and theory.* New York: Academic Press, 1970.

Horn, J. L. Human ability systems. In P. B. Baltes (Ed.), *Life-span development and behavior* (Vol. 1). New York: Academic Press, 1978.

Horn, J. L., & **Cattell, R. B.** Age differences in primary mental ability factors. *Journal of Gerontology,* 1966, *21,* 210–220.

Horn, J. L., & **Cattell, R. B.** Age differences in fluid and crystallized intelligence. *Acta Psychologica,* 1967, *26,* 107–129.

Horn, J. L., & **Donaldson, G.** On the myth of intellectual decline in adulthood. *American Psychologist,* 1976, *31,* 701–719.

Horn, J. L., & **Donaldson, G.** Faith is not enough: A response to the Baltes-Schaie claim that intelligence does not wane. *American Psychologist,* 1977, *32,* 369–373.

Horn, J. L., & **Donaldson, G.** Cognitive development II: Adulthood development of human abilities. In O. G. Brim, Jr. & J. Kagan (Eds.), *Constancy and change in human development: A volume of review essays.* Cambridge: Harvard University Press, 1980.

Hornblum, J. N., & **Overton, W. F.** Area and volume conservation among the elderly: Assessment and training. *Developmental Psychology,* 1976, *12,* 68–74.

House, J. S., & **Mason, W. M.** Political alienation in America, 1952–1968. *American Sociological Review,* 1975, *40,* 123–147.

Hoyer, W. J., Labouvie, G. V., & **Baltes, P. B.** Modification of response speed deficits and intellectual performance in the elderly. *Human Development,* 1973, *16,* 233–242.

Hudgens, R. W. Personal catastrophe and depression: A consideration of the subject with respect to medically ill adolescents, and a requiem for retrospective life-event studies. In B. S. Dohrenwend & B. P. Dohrenwend (Eds.), *Stressful life events: Their nature and effects.* New York: Wiley, 1974.

Hulicka, I. M., & **Grossman, J. L.** Age-group comparisons for the use of mediators in paired-associate learning. *Journal of Gerontology,* 1967, *22,* 46–51.

Hulicka, I. M., Sterns, H., & **Grossman, J.** Age-group comparisons of paired associate learning as a function of paced and self-paced association and response times. *Journal of Gerontology,* 1967, *22,* 274–280.

Hultsch, D. F. Adult age differences in the organization of free recall. *Developmental Psychology,* 1969, *1,* 673–678.

Hultsch, D. F. Adult age differences in free classification and free recall. *Developmental Psychology,* 1971, *4,* 338–342.

Hultsch, D. F. Learning to learn in adulthood. *Journal of Gerontology,* 1974, *29,* 302–308.

Hultsch, D. F. Adult age differences in retrieval: Trace dependent and cue dependent forgetting. *Developmental Psychology,* 1975, *11,* 197–201.

Hultsch, D. F., & **Craig, E. R.** Adult age differences in the inhibition of recall as a function of retrieval cues. *Developmental Psychology,* 1976, *12,* 83–84.

Hultsch, D. F., & **Hickey, T.** External validity in the study of human development: Theoretical and methodological issues. *Human Development,* 1978, *21,* 76–91.

Hultsch, D. F., & **Pentz, C. A.** Encoding, storage, and retrieval in adult memory: The role of model assumptions. In L. W. Poon, J. L. Fozard, L. S. Cermak, D. Arenberg, & L. W. Thompson (Eds.), *New directions in memory and aging: Proceedings of the George A. Talland memorial conference.* Hillsdale, N.J.: Erlbaum, 1980.

Hultsch, D. F., & **Plemons, J. K.** Life events and life span development. In P. B. Baltes & O. G. Brim, Jr. (Eds.), *Life-span development and behavior* (Vol. 2). New York: Academic Press, 1979.

Hunt, M. *Sexual behavior in the 1970's.* Chicago: Playboy Press, 1974.

Huston-Stein, A., & **Baltes, P. B.** Theory and method in life-span developmental psychology: Implications for child development. In H. W. Reese (Ed.), *Advances in Child Development and Behavior* (Vol. 11). New York: Academic Press, 1976.

Hyde, J. S. *Understanding human sexuality.* New York: McGraw-Hill, 1979.

Jaques, E. Death and the mid-life crisis. *International Journal of Psychoanalysis,* 1965, *46,* 502–514.

Jarvik, L. F., & **Cohen, D.** A biobehavioral approach to intellectual changes with aging. In C. Eisdorfer & M. P. Lawton (Eds.), *The psychology of adult development and aging.* Washington, D.C.: American Psychological Association, 1973.

Jarvik, L. F., & **Falek, A.** Intellectual stability and survival in the aged. *Journal of Gerontology,* 1963, *18,* 173–176.

Jenkins, J. J. Remember that old theory of memory: Well forget it. *American Psychologist,* 1974, *29,* 785–795.

Jerome, E. A. Age and learning-experimental studies. In J. E. Birren (Ed.), *Handbook of aging and the individual.* Chicago: University of Chicago Press, 1959.

Jöreskog, K. G. Statistical estimation of structural models in longitudinal-developmental investigations. In J. R. Nesselroade and P. B. Baltes (Eds.), *Longitudinal research in the study of behavior and development.* New York: Academic Press, 1979.

Kaats, G. R., & **Davis, K. E.** The dynamics of sexual behavior in college students. *Journal of Marriage and the Family,* 1970, *32,* 390–399.

Kagan, J., & **Moss, H. A.** *Birth to maturity: A study in psychological development.* New York: Wiley, 1962.

Kahana, B., & **Kahana, E.** Grandparenthood from the perspective of the developing grandchild. *Developmental Psychology,* 1970, *3,* 98–105.

Kahana, B. & **Kahana, E.** Theoretical and research perspectives on grandparenthood. *Aging and Human Development,* 1971, *2,* 261–268.

Kahn, R. L., Zarit, S. H., Hilbert, N. M., & **Niederehe, G.** Memory complaint and impairment in the aged. *Archives of General Psychiatry,* 1975, *32,* 1569–1573.

Kalish, R. A. An approach to the study of death attitudes. *American Behavioral Scientist,* 1963, *6,* 68–80.

Kalish, R. A. *Late adulthood: Perspectives on human development.* Monterey, Calif.: Brooks/Cole, 1975.

Kalish, R. A. Death and dying in a social context. In R. H. Binstock and E. Shanas (Eds.), *Handbook of aging and the social sciences.* New York: Van Nostrand Reinhold, 1976.

Kalish, R. A., & **Johnson, A.** Value similarities and differences in three generations of women. *Journal of Marriage and the Family,* 1972, *34,* 49–54.

Kalish, R. A., & **Reynolds, D. K.** *Death and ethnicity: A psychocultural study.* Los Angeles: University of Southern California Press, 1976.

Kanter, R. M. *The changing shape of work: Psychological trends in America.* Address presented at the Plenary Session of the National Conference on Higher Education, Chicago, Ill., 1978.

Kasteler, J. M., Gray, R. M., & **Carruth, M. L.** Involuntary relocation of the elderly. *The Gerontologist,* 1968, *8,* 276–279.

Kastenbaum, R. Is death a life crisis? On the confrontation with death in theory and practice. In N. Datan and L. H. Ginsberg (Eds.), *Life-span developmental psychology: Normative life crises.* New York: Academic Press, 1975.

Kastenbaum, R., & **Aisenberg, R.** *The psychology of death.* New York: Springer, 1972.

Kausler, D. H., Kleim, D. M., & **Overcast, T. D.** Item recognition following a multiple-item study trial for young and middle-aged adults. *Experimental Aging Research,* 1975, *2,* 243–250.

Kausler, D. H., & **Lair, C. V.** Associative strength and paired-associate learning in elderly subjects. *Journal of Gerontology,* 1966, *21,* 278–280.

Kay, H. The effects of position in a display upon problem solving. *Quarterly Journal of Experimental Psychology,* 1954, *6,* 155–169.

Kay, H. Theories of learning and aging. In J. E. Birren (Ed.), *Handbook of aging and the individual.* Chicago: University of Chicago Press, 1959.

Kearsley, R. B., Zelazo, P. R., Kagan, J., & **Hartmann, R.** Separation protest in day care and home reared infants. In P. A. Mussen, J. J. Confer, & J. Kagan (Eds.), *Basic and contemporary issues in child developmental psychology.* New York: Harper and Row, 1975.

Kell, D., & **Patton, C. V.** Reaction to induced early retirement. *The Gerontologist,* 1978, *18,* 173–179.

Kelly, E. L. Consistency of the adult personality. *American Psychologist,* 1955, *10,* 659–681.

Keniston, K. *Young radicals.* New York: Harcourt, Brace & World, 1968.

Keniston, K. Youth as a stage of life. *American Scholarship,* 1970, *39,* 631–654.

Kent, D. P. Social and cultural factors affecting the mental health of the aged. *American Journal of Orthopsychiatry,* 1966, *36,* 680–685.

Kerckhoff, A. C. Husband-wife expectations and reactions to retirement. *Journal of Gerontology,* 1964, *19,* 510–516.

Kerlinger, F. N. *Foundations of behavioral research* (2d ed.). New York: Holt, Rinehart, & Winston, 1973.

Kievit, M. *Review and synthesis of research on women in the world of work.* Washington, D.C.: U.S. Government Printing Office, 1972.

Killian, E. Effects of geriatric transfers on mortality rates. *Social Work,* 1970, *15,* 19–26.

Kinsbourne, M., & **Berryhill, J. L.** The nature of the interaction between pacing and the age decrement in learning. *Journal of Gerontology,* 1972, *27,* 471–477.

Kinsey, A. C., Pomeroy, W. B., & **Martin, C.** *Sexual behavior in the human male.* Philadelphia: Saunders, 1948.

Kinsey, A. C., Pomeroy, W. B., & **Martin, C.** *Sexual behavior in the human female.* Philadelphia: Saunders, 1953.

Kintsch, W., & **van Dijk, T. A.** Toward a model of text comprehension and production. *Psychological Review,* 1978, *85,* 363–394.

Kleemeier, R. W. Intellectual change in the senium. *Proceedings of the Social Statistics Section of the American Statistical Association,* 1962, *1,* 290–295.

Klemer, R. H. Self-esteem and college dating experience as factors in mate selection and marital happiness: A longitudinal study. *Journal of Marriage and the Family,* 1971, *33,* 183–187.

Kogan, N. Creativity and cognitive styles: A life-span perspective. In P. B. Baltes & K. W. Schaie (Eds.), *Life-span developmental psychology: Personality and socialization.* New York: Academic Press, 1973.

Kogan, N., & **Wallach, M.** Age changes in values and attitudes. *Journal of Gerontology,* 1961, *16,* 272–280.

Kohlberg, L. The development of children's orientations toward a moral order: I. Sequence in the development of moral thought. *Vita Humana,* 1963, *6,* 11–33.

Kohlberg, L. Stage and sequence: The cognitive developmental approach to socialization. In D. A. Goslin (Ed.), *Handbook of socialization theory and research.* Chicago: Rand McNally, 1969.

Kohlberg, L. Continuities in childhood and adult moral development revisited. In P. B. Baltes & K. W. Schaie (Eds.), *Life-span developmental psychology: Personality and socialization.* New York: Academic Press, 1973.

Kohlberg, L. Moral stages and moralization: The cognitive-developmental approach. In T. Lickona (Ed.), *Moral development and behavior: Theory, research and social issues.* New York: Holt, Rinehart & Winston, 1976.

Kohlberg, L. Revisions in the theory and practice of moral development. *New Directions for Child Development,* 1978, *2,* 83–88.

Kohn, R. R. The heart and cardiovascular system. In C. E. Finch & L. Hayflick (Eds.), *Handbook of the biology of aging.* New York: Van Nostrand Reinhold, 1977.

Koocher, G. P. Why isn't the gerbil moving anymore? *Children Today,* 1975, *4,* 18–21, 36.

Kraus, A. S., & **Lilienfeld, A. M.** Some epidemiologic aspects of the high mortality rate in the young widowed group. *Journal of Chronic Diseases,* 1959, *10,* 207–217.

Kreps, J. M. (Ed.). *Women and the American economy.* New York: Prentice-Hall, 1976.

Krishnan, P. & **Kayani, A. F.** Estimates of age-specific divorce rates for females in the United States, 1960–1969. *Journal of Marriage and the Family,* 1974, *36,* 72–76.

Kübler-Ross, E. *On death and dying.* New York: Macmillan, 1969.

Kübler-Ross, E. *Questions and answers on death and dying.* Englewood Cliffs, N.J.: Macmillan, 1974.

Kuhlen, R. G. Social change: A neglected factor in psychological studies of the life span. *School and Society,* 1940, *52,* 14–16.

Kuhlen, R. G. Age and intelligence: The significance of cultural change in longitudinal vs. cross-sectional findings. *Vita Humana,* 1963, *6,* 113–124.

Kuypers, J. A., & **Bengtson, V. L.** Social breakdown and competence: A model of normal aging. *Human Development,* 1973, *16,* 181–201.

Labouvie-Vief, G. Adult cognitive development: In search of alternative interpretations. *Merrill-Palmer Quarterly,* 1977, *23,* 227–263.

Labouvie-Vief, G., & **Gonda, J. N.** Cognitive strategy training and intellectual performance in the elderly. *Journal of Gerontology,* 1976, *31,* 327–332.

Lachman, J. L., & **Lachman, R.** Age and the actualization of world knowledge. In L. W. Poon, J. L. Fozard, L. S. Cermak, D. Arenberg, & L. W. Thompson (Eds.), *New directions in memory and aging: Proceedings of the George A. Talland memorial conference.* Hillsdale, N.J.: Erlbaum, 1980.

Lachman, J. L., Lachman, R., & **Thronesbery, C.** Metamemory through the adult life span. *Developmental Psychology,* 1979, *15,* 543–551.

Lachman, R. The model in theory construction. *Psychological Review,* 1960, *67,* 113–129.

Lair, C. V., & **Moon, W. H.** The effects of praise and reproof on the performance of middle-aged and older subjects. *Aging and Human Development*, 1972, *3*, 279–284.

Lair, C. V., Moon, W. H., & **Kausler, D. H.** Associative interference in the paired-associate learning of middle-aged and old subjects. *Developmental Psychology*, 1969, *1*, 548–552.

Laurence, M. W. Memory loss with age: A test of two strategies for its retardation. *Psychonomic Science*, 1967, *9*, 209–210.

Laurence, M. W., & **Trotter, M.** Effect of acoustic factors and list organization in multitrial free recall learning of college age and elderly adults. *Developmental Psychology*, 1971, *5*, 202–210.

Lawton, M. P. Competence, environmental press, and the adaptation of older people. In P. G. Windley & G. Ernst (Eds.), *Theory development in environment and aging*. Washington, D.C.: Gerontological Society, 1975.

Lawton, M. P. The impact of the environment on aging and behavior. In J. E. Birren & K. W. Schaie (Eds.), *Handbook of the psychology of aging*. New York: Van Nostrand Reinhold, 1977.

Lawton, M. P., & **Cohen, J.** The generality of housing impact on the well-being of older people. *Journal of Gerontology*, 1974, *29*, 194–204.

Lawton, M. P., & **Nahemow, L.** Ecology and the aging process. In C. Eisdorfer & M. P. Lawton (Eds.), *The psychology of adult development and aging*. Washington, D.C.: American Psychological Association, 1973.

Lazarowitz, R., Stephen, W. G., & **Friedman, S. T.** Effects of moral justifications and moral reasoning on altruism. *Developmental Psychology*, 1976, *12*, 353–354.

Lazarus, R. S. *Psychological stress and the coping process*. New York: McGraw-Hill, 1966.

Lefevre, C. The mature woman as graduate student. *School Review*, 1972, *80*, 281–297.

Lehman, H. *Age and achievement*. Princeton, N.J.: Princeton University Press, 1953.

Leifer, M. Psychological changes accompanying pregnancy and motherhood. *Genetic Psychology Monographs*, 1977, *95*, 55–96.

Le Masters, E. E. Parenthood as crisis. *Marriage and Family Living*, 1957, *19*, 352–355.

Lerner, M. When, why, and where people die. In O. G. Brim, Jr., H. E. Freeman, S. Levine, & N. A. Scotch (Eds.), *The dying patient*. New York: Russell Sage Foundation, 1970.

Lerner, R. M. Nature, nurture and dynamic interactionism. *Human Development*, 1978, *21*, 1–20.

Lerner, R. M., & **Ryff, C. D.** Implementation of the life-span view of human development: The sample case of attachment. In P. B. Baltes (Ed.), *Life-span development and behavior* (Vol. 1). New York: Academic Press, 1978.

Lerner, R. M., & **Spanier, G. B.** A dynamic interactional view of child and family development. In R. M. Lerner &

G. B. Spanier (Eds.), *Child influences on marital and family interaction: A life-span perspective*. New York: Academic Press, 1978.

Lerner, R. M., & **Spanier, G.** *Adolescent development: A life-span perspective*. New York: McGraw-Hill, 1980.

Levine, J. A. *Who will raise the children? New options for fathers (and mothers)*. Philadelphia: Lippincott, 1976.

Levinson, D. J. *The seasons of a man's life*. New York: Knopf, 1978.

Lidz, T. The life cycle: Introduction. In S. Arieti (Ed.), *American Handbook of Psychiatry* (Vol. 2). New York: Basic Books, 1974.

Lieberman, M. A. Psychological correlates of impending death: Some preliminary observations. *Journal of Gerontology*, 1965, *20*, 181–190.

Lieberman, M. A. Adaptive processes in late life. In N. Datan & L. H. Ginsberg (Eds.), *Lifespan developmental psychology: Normative life crises*. New York: Academic Press, 1975.

Lief, H. I., & **Fox, R. C.** Training for detached concern in medical students. In H. I. Lief & N. R. Lief (Eds.), *The psychological basis of medical practice*. New York: Harper and Row, 1963.

Livingston, P. B., & **Zimet, C. N.** Death anxiety, authoritarianism, and choice of specialty in medical students. *Journal of Nervous and Mental Disease*, 1965, *140*, 222–230.

Livson, F. B. Evolution of self: Personality development in middle-aged women. Unpublished doctoral dissertation, Wright Institute, 1974.

Livson, F. B. Coming out of the closet: Marriage and other crises of middle age. In L. E. Troll, J. Israel, & K. Israel (Eds.), *Looking ahead: A woman's guide to the problems and ways of growing old*. Englewood Cliffs, N.J.: Prentice Hall, 1977.

Loevinger, J. The meaning and measurement of ego development. *American Psychologist*, 1966, *21*, 195–206.

Loevinger, J., & **Wessler, R.** *Measuring ego development* (Vol. 1). San Francisco: Jossey-Bass, 1970.

Looft, W. R. Egocentrism and social interaction across the life span. *Psychological Bulletin*, 1972, *78*, 73–92.

Lopata, H. Z. The life cycle of the social role of housewife. *Sociological and Social Research*, 1966, *51*, 5–22.

Lopata, H. Z. Widows as a minority group. *The Gerontologist*, 1971, *2*, 67–77.

Lopata, H. Z. Self identity in marriage and widowhood. *Sociological Quarterly*, 1973, *14*, 407–418. (a)

Lopata, H. Z. Social relations of Black and White widowed women in a northern metropolis. *American Journal of Sociology*, 1973, *74*, 1003–1010. (b)

Lopata, H. Z. *Widowhood in an American city*. Cambridge, Mass.: Schenkman, 1973. (c)

Lopata, H. Z. Widowhood: Societal factors in life-span disruptions and alternatives. In N. Datan & L. H. Ginsberg

(Eds.), *Lifespan developmental psychology: Normative life crises.* New York: Academic Press, 1975.

Lowenthal, M. F. Some potentialities of a life-cycle approach to the study of retirement. In F. M. Carp (Ed.), *Retirement.* New York: Behavioral Publications, 1972.

Lowenthal, M. F. Toward a sociopsychological theory of change in adulthood and old age. In J. E. Birren & K. W. Schaie (Eds.), *Handbook of the psychology of aging.* New York: Van Nostrand Reinhold, 1977.

Lowenthal, M. F., & **Chiriboga, D.** Social stress and adaptation: Toward a life-course perspective. In C. Eisdorfer & M. P. Lawton (Eds.), *The psychology of adult development and aging.* Washington, D.C.: American Psychological Association, 1973.

Lowenthal, M. F., & **Robinson, B.** Social networks and isolation. In R. H. Binstock & E. Shanas (Eds.), *Handbook of aging and the social sciences.* New York: Van Nostrand Reinhold, 1977.

Lowenthal, M. F., Thurnher, M., & **Chiriboga, D.** *Four stages of life: A comparative study of women and men facing transitions.* San Francisco: Jossey-Bass, 1975.

Lynn, D. B. *The father: His role in child development.* Monterey, Calif.: Brooks/Cole, 1974.

Maas, H. S., & **Kuypers, J. A.** *From thirty to seventy.* San Francisco: Jossey-Bass, 1974.

Maddox, G. L. Disengagement theory: A critical evaluation. *The Gerontologist,* 1964, *4,* 80–83.

Maddox, G. L. Retirement as a social event in the United States. In T. C. McKinney & F. T. deVyver (Eds.), *Aging and social policy.* New York: Appleton-Century-Crofts, 1966.

Maguire, D. C. Death by chance, death by choice. *Atlantic,* 1974, *233,* 57–65. (a)

Maguire, D. C. Death, legal, illegal. *Atlantic,* 1974, *233,* 72–85. (b)

Maizels, J. *Adolescent needs and the transition from school to work.* London: Athlove Press, 1970.

Mandler, G. Organization and memory. In D. W. Spence & J. T. Spence (Eds.), *The psychology of learning and motivation* (Vol. 1). New York: Academic Press, 1967.

Marcia, J. E. Development and validations of ego-identity states. *Journal of Personality and Social Psychology,* 1966, *5,* 551–558.

Marmor, J. The crisis of middle age. *Psychiatric Digest,* 1968, *18,* 17–21.

Marsh, G. R. & **Thompson, L. W.** Psychophysiology of aging. In J. E. Birren & K. W. Schaie (Eds.), *Handbook of the psychology of aging.* New York: Van Nostrand Reinhold, 1977.

Martin, D. S., & **Wrightsman, L.** The relationship between religious behavior and concern about death. *Journal of Social Psychology,* 1965, *65,* 317–323.

Martin, W., Bengtson, V. L., & **Acock, A.** Alienation and age: A context-specific approach. *Social Forces,* 1973, *54,* 67–84.

Mason, S. E. Effects of orienting tasks on the recall and recognition performance of subjects differing in age. *Developmental Psychology,* 1979, *15,* 467–469.

Masters, W. H., & **Johnson, V. E.** *Human sexual response.* Boston: Little Brown, 1966.

Masters, W. H., & **Johnson, V. E.** *Human Sexual Inadequacy.* Boston: Little Brown, 1970.

McCrae, R. R., Bartone, P. T., & **Costa, P. T., Jr.** Age, anxiety and self-reported health. *Aging and Human Development,* 1976, *7,* 49–58.

McKinlay, S. M., & **Jeffreys, M.** The menopausal syndrome. *British Journal of Preventive and Social Medicine,* 1974, *28,* 108.

McPherson, B., & **Guppy, N.** Pre-retirement life-style and the degree of planning for retirement. *Journal of Gerontology,* 1979, *34,* 254–263.

Meacham, J. A. A transactional model of remembering. In N. Datan & H. W. Reese (Eds.), *Life-span developmental psychology: Dialectical perspectives of experimental research.* New York: Academic Press, 1977.

Mead, M. Anomalies in American post-divorce relationships. In P. Bohannan (Ed.), *Divorce and after.* New York: Anchor, 1971.

Medvedev. Z. A. The nucleic acids in development and aging. In B. L. Strehler (Ed.), *Advances in gerontological research* (Vol. 1). New York: Academic Press, 1964.

Medvedev. Z. A. Caucasus and Altay longevity: A biological or social problem? *The Gerontologist,* 1974, *14,* 381–387.

Medvedev. Z. A. Aging and longevity: New approaches and new perspectives. *The Gerontologist,* 1975, *15,* 196–201.

Meichenbaum, D. Self-instructional strategy training: A cognitive prothesis for the aged. *Human Development,* 1974, *17,* 273–280.

Meltzer, H. Attitudes of workers before and after age 40. *Geriatrics,* 1965, *20,* 425–432.

Melville, L. *Marriage and family today.* New York: Random House, 1977.

Miernyk, W. H. The changing life cycles of work. In N. Datan & L. H. Ginsberg (Eds.), *Life-span developmental psychology: Normative life crises.* New York: Academic Press, 1975.

Miles, H. W., & **Hays, D. R.** Widowhood. *American Journal of Nursing,* 1975, *75,* 280–282.

Miller, A. H., Brown, T. A., & **Raine, A. S.** *Social conflict and political estrangement, 1958–1972.* Paper presented at the Convention of the Midwest Political Science Association, Chicago, August 1973.

Miller, B. C. A multivariate developmental model of marital satisfaction. *Journal of Marriage and the Family,* 1976, *38,* 643–657.

Miller, G. A. The magical number seven, plus or minus two: Some limits on our capacity for processing information. *Psychological Review,* 1956, *63,* 81–97.

Miller, W. B. White gangs. *Transaction,* 1969, *13,* 16.

Mischel, W. Toward a cognitive social learning reconceptualization of personality. *Psychological Review,* 1973, *80,* 252–283.

Mitford, J. *The American way of death.* New York: Simon & Schuster, 1963.

Monge, R. H., & **Hultsch, D. F.** Paired-associate learning as a function of adult age and the length of the anticipation and inspection intervals. *Journal of Gerontology,* 1971, *26,* 157–162.

Moody, R. A. *Life after life.* New York: Bantam, 1975.

Morgan, L. A. *Economic impact of widowhood in a panel of middle-aged women.* Unpublished doctoral dissertation, University of Southern California, 1978.

Morris, W. (Ed.). *The American heritage dictionary of the English language.* New York: Houghton Mifflin, 1975.

Moss, G. E. *Illness, immunity, and social interaction.* New York: Wiley, 1973.

Murdock, G. P. The common denominator of cultures. In R. Linton (Ed.), *The science man in the world crisis.* New York: Columbia University Press, 1945.

Murray, J. R., Powers, E. A., & **Havighurst, R. J.** Personal and situational factors producing flexible careers. *The Gerontologist,* 1971, *11,* 4–12.

Muus, R. E. *Theories of adolescence* (3rd ed.). New York: Random House, 1975.

National Society for the Prevention of Blindness. *Estimated statistics on blindness and vision problems.* New York: National Society for the Prevention of Blindness, 1966.

Neale, R. E. Between the nipple and the everlasting arms. *Archives of the Foundation of Thanatology,* 1971, *3,* 21–30.

Nelson, L. P., & **Nelson, V.** *Religion and death anxiety.* Paper presented at Society for the Scientific Study of Religion and Religious Research Association, San Francisco, 1973.

Nesselroade, J. R., & **Baltes, P. B.** Adolescent personality development and historical changes: 1970–72. *Monographs of the Society for Research in Child Development* 1974, *39* (Whole No. 154).

Nesselroade, J. R., & **Reese, H. W. (Eds.).** *Life-span developmental psychology: Methodological issues.* New York: Academic Press, 1973.

Nesselroade, J. R., Schaie, K. W., & **Baltes, P. B.** Ontogenetic and generational components of structural and quantitative change in adult behavior. *Journal of Gerontology,* 1972, *27,* 222–228.

Nettler, G. Review essay: On death and dying. In F. G. Scott & R. M. Brewer (Eds.), *Confrontations of death.*

Corvallis, Oreg.: Oregon Center for Gerontology, 1971.

Neubeck, G. Getting older in my family: A personal reflection. *The Family Coordinator,* 1978, *27,* 445–447.

Neugarten, B. L. *Personality in middle and late life.* New York: Atherton Press, 1964.

Neugarten, B. L. The awareness of middle age. In B. L. Neugarten (Ed.), *Middle age and aging.* Chicago: University of Chicago Press, 1968.

Neugarten, B. L. Continuities and discontinuities of psychological issues into adult life. *Human Development,* 1969, *12,* 121–130.

Neugarten, B. L. Dynamics of transition of middle age to old age. *Journal of Geriatric Psychiatry,* 1970, *4,* 71–87.

Neugarten, B. L. Personality change in later life: A developmental perspective. In C. Eisdorfer & M. P. Lawton (Eds.), *The psychology of adult development and aging.* Washington, D.C.: American Psychological Association, 1973.

Neugarten, B. L. Personality and aging. In J. E. Birren & K. W. Schaie (Eds.), *Handbook of the psychology of aging.* New York: Van Nostrand Reinhold, 1977.

Neugarten, B. L., & **Datan, N.** Sociological perspectives on the life cycle. In P. B. Baltes & K. W. Schaie (Eds.), *Life-span developmental psychology: Personality and socialization.* New York: Academic Press, 1973.

Neugarten, B. L., & **Datan, N.** The middle years. In S. Arieti (Ed.), *American handbook of psychiatry* (Vol. 1). New York: Basic Books, 1974.

Neugarten, B. L., & **Gutmann, D. L.** Age-sex roles and personality in middle age: A thematic apperception study. *Psychological Monographs,* 1958, *72* (Whole No. 470).

Neugarten, B. L., & **Hagestad, G. O.** Age and the life course. In R. H. Binstock & E. Shanas (Eds.), *Handbook of aging and the social sciences.* New York: Van Nostrand Reinhold, 1976.

Neugarten, B. L., Havighurst, R. J., & **Tobin, S. S.** Personality and patterns of aging. In B. L. Neugarten (Ed.), *Middle age and aging.* Chicago: University of Chicago Press, 1968.

Neugarten, B. L., & **Moore, J. W.** The changing age-status system. In B. L. Neugarten (Ed.), *Middle age and aging.* Chicago: University of Chicago Press, 1968.

Neugarten, B. L., Moore, J. W., & **Lowe, J. C.** Age norms, age constraints, and adult socialization. In B. L. Neugarten (Ed.), *Middle age and aging.* Chicago: University of Chicago Press, 1968.

Neugarten, B. L., & **Weinstein, K. K.** The changing American grandparent. *Journal of Marriage and the Family,* 1964, *26,* 199–204.

Neugarten, B. L., Wood, V., Kraines, R., & **Loomis, B.** Women's attitudes toward the menopause. *Human Development,* 1963, *6,* 140–151.

Norton, A. J. The family life cycle updated: Components and uses. In R. F. Winch & G. B. Spanier (Eds.), *Selected* *studies in marriage and the family.* New York: Holt, Reinhart & Winston, 1974.

Nuttall, R. L., & **Costa, P. T., Jr.** *Drinking patterns as affected by age and by personality type.* Paper presented at the Scientific meeting of the Gerontological Society, Louisville, October 1975.

Nydegger, C. N. *Late and early fathers.* Paper presented at the meeting of the Gerontological Society, Miami Beach, November 1973.

Obrist, W. D. The electroencephalogram of healthy aged males. In J. E. Birren, R. N. Butler, S. W. Greenhouse, L. Sokoloff, & M. R. Yarrow (Eds.), *Human aging: A biological and behavioral study.* Washington, D.C.: U.S. Government Printing Office, 1963.

Obrist, W. D. Cerebral physiology of the aged: Influence of circulatory disorder. In C. M. Gaitz (Ed.), *Aging and the brain.* New York: Plenum Press, 1972.

Obrist, W. D., & **Bissell, L. F.** The electroencephalogram of aged patients with cardiac and cerebral vascular disease. *Journal of Gerontology,* 1955, *10,* 315–330.

Obrist, W. D., Busse, E. W., Eisdorfer, C., & **Kleemeier, R. W.** Relation of the electroencephalogram to intellectual function in senescence. *Journal of Gerontology,* 1962, *17,* 197–206.

Obrist, W. D., Henry, C. E., & **Justiss, W. A.** Longitudinal study of EEG in old age. *Excerpta Medica International Congress Series,* 1961 (No. 37), 180–181.

Okun, M. A. Adult age and cautiousness in decision: A review of the literature. *Human Development,* 1976, *19,* 220–223.

Okun, M. A., Seigler, I. C., & **George, L. K.** Cautiousness and verbal learning in adulthood. *Journal of Gerontology,* 1978, *33,* 94–97.

Olsen, K. M. *Social class and age-group differences in the timing of family status changes: A study of age norms in American society.* Unpublished doctoral dissertation, University of Chicago, 1969.

Orgel, L. E. The maintenance of the accuracy of protein synthesis and its relevance to aging. *Biochemistry,* 1963, *49,* 517–521.

Overton, W. F. On the assumptive base of the nature-nurture controversy: Additive versus interactive conceptions. *Human Development,* 1973, *16,* 74–89.

Owens, W. A. Is age kinder to the initially more able? *Journal of Gerontology,* 1959, *14,* 334–337.

Palmore, E. *The honorable elders: A cross-cultural analysis of aging in Japan.* Durham, N.C.: Duke University Press, 1975.

Palmore, E. Total chance of institutionalization among the aged. *Gerontologist,* 1976, *16,* 504–507.

Palmore, E., Cleveland, W. P., Nowlin, J. G.,

Ramm, D., & **Siegler, I. C.** Stress and adaptation in late life. *Journal of Gerontology,* 1979, *34,* 841–851.

Palmore, E., & **Luikart, C.** Health and social factors related to life satisfaction. In E. Palmore (Ed.), *Normal aging II: Reports from the Duke longitudinal studies 1970–1973.* Durham, N.C.: Duke University Press, 1974.

Palmore, E., & **Whittington, F.** Differential trends toward equality between whites and non-whites. *Social Forces,* 1970, *49,* 108–117.

Papalia, D. E. The status of several conservation abilities across the life-span. *Human Development,* 1972, *15,* 229–243.

Papalia, D. E., & **Bielby, D. D. V.** Cognitive functioning in middle and old age adults: A review of research based on Piaget's theory. *Human Development,* 1974, *17,* 424–443.

Papailia, D. E., Kennedy, E., & **Sheehan, N.** Conservation of space in noninstitutionalized old people. *Journal of Psychology,* 1973, *84,* 75–79.

Papalia, D. E., Salverson, S. M., & **True, M.** An evaluation of quantity conservation performance during old age. *Aging and Human Development,* 1973, *4,* 103–110.

Parke, R., & **O'Leary, S.** Father-mother-infant interaction in the newborn period: Some findings, some observations, some unresolved issues. In K. Reigel & J. Meacham (Eds.), *The developing individual in a changing world: Social and environmental issues* (Vol. 2). The Hague: Mouton, 1975.

Parkes, C. M. *Bereavement: Studies of grief in adult life.* New York: International Universities Press, 1972.

Parkes, C. M., & **Brown, R.** Health after bereavement: A controlled study of young Boston widows and widowers. *Psychosomatic Medicine,* 1972, *34,* 449–461.

Pastalan, L. A. *Report on Pennsylvania nursing home relocation programs: Interim research findings.* Ann Arbor: Institute of Gerontology, University of Michigan, 1976.

Pastalan, L. A., Mautz, R. K., & **Merrill, J.** The simulation of age-related losses: A new approach to the study of environment barriers. In W. F. E. Preiser (Ed.), *Environmental design research* (Vol. 1). Stroudsberg, Pa.: Powden, Hutchinson, and Ross, 1973.

Pattison, E. M. Attitudes toward death. In E. M. Pattison (Ed.), *The experience of dying.* Englewood Cliffs, N.J.: Prentice-Hall, 1977. (a)

Pattison, E. M. The dying experience—retrospective analysis. In E. M. Pattison (Ed.), *The experience of dying.* Englewood Cliffs, N.J.: Prentice-Hall, 1977. (b)

Peck, R. C. Psychological developments in the second half of life. In B. L. Neugarten (Ed.), *Middle age and aging.* Chicago: University of Chicago Press, 1968.

Peck, R. F., & **Havighurst, R. J.** *The psychology of character development.* New York: Wiley, 1960.

Pepper, S. C. *World hypotheses.* Berkeley: University of California Press, 1942.

Perlmutter, M. What is memory aging the aging of? *Developmental Psychology,* 1978, *14,* 330–345.

Perlmutter, M. An apparent paradox about memory aging. In L. W. Poon, J. L. Fozard, L. S. Cermak, D. Arenberg & L. W. Thompson (Eds.), *New directions in memory and aging: Proceedings of the George A. Talland memorial conference.* Hillsdale, N.J.: Erlbaum, 1980.

Perry, W. G., Jr. *Forms of intellectual and ethical development in the college years.* New York: Holt, Rinehart, and Winston, 1970.

Perun, P. J., & **Bielby, D. D. V.** Mid life: A discussion of competing models. *Research on Aging,* 1979, *1,* 275–300.

Peterson, J. A., & **Payne, B.** *Love in the later years.* New York: Associated Press, 1975.

Pfeiffer, E., & **Davis, G. C.** Determinants of sexual behavior in middle and old age. In E. Palmore (Ed.), *Normal aging II; Reports from the Duke longitudinal studies, 1970–1973.* Durham, N.C.: Duke University Press, 1974.

Pfeiffer, E., Verwoerdt, A., & **Davis, G. C.** Sexual behavior in middle life. In E. Palmore (Ed.), *Normal aging II: Reports from the Duke longitudinal studies, 1970–1973.* Durham, N.C.: Duke University Press, 1974.

Pfeiffer, E., Verwoerdt, A., & **Wang, H. S.** Sexual behavior in aged men and women, I: Observations on 254 community volunteers. *Archives of General Psychiatry,* 1968, *19,* 753–758.

Phillips, D. P., & **Feldman, K. A.** A dip in deaths before ceremonial occasions: Some new relationships between social integration and mortality. *American Sociological Review,* 1973, *38,* 678–696.

Piaget, J. *The psychology of intelligence.* New York: Harcourt Brace, 1950.

Piaget, J. *Judgment and reasoning in the child.* London: Routledge and Kegan Paul, 1951.

Piaget, J. *The origins of intelligence in children.* New York: International Universities Press, 1952.

Piaget, J. *Six psychological studies.* New York: Random House, 1968.

Piaget, J. Intellectual evolution from adolescence to adulthood. *Human Development,* 1972, *15,* 1–12.

Piaget, J., & **Inhelder, B.** *The psychology of the child.* New York: Basic Books, 1969.

Pineo, P. C. Disenchantment in the later years of marriage. *Marriage and Family Living,* 1961, *23,* 3–11.

Pleck, J. H. *Men's roles in the family: A new look.* Paper presented at Sex Roles in Sociology Conference, Merrill-Palmer Institute, Detroit, 1975.

Plemons, J. K., Willis, S. L., & **Baltes, P. B.** Modifiability of intelligence in aging: A short-term longitudinal training approach. *Journal of Gerontology,* 1978, *33,* 224–231.

Powell, A. H., Eisdorfer, C., & **Bogdonoff, M. D.** Physiological response patterns observed in a learning task. *Archives of General Psychiatry,* 1964, *10,* 192–195.

Pressey, S. L., Janney, J. E., & **Kuhlen, R. G.** *Life: A psychological survey.* New York: Harper, 1939.

Preston, S. H., Keyfite, N., & **Schoen, R.** *Causes of death.* New York: Seminar Press, 1972.

Prins, A. H. J. *East African class systems.* Groninger, Djakarta: J. B. Wolters, 1953.

Quetelet, A. *Sur l'homme et le développement de ses facultés* (2 vols.). Paris: Bachelier, 1835.

Quinn, R., Staines, G., & **McCullough, M.** *Job satisfaction: Is there a trend?* (U.S. Department of Labor, Manpower Research Monograph No. 30). Washington, D.C.: U.S. Government Printing Office, 1974.

Rabbitt, P., & **Birren, J. E.** Age and responses to sequences of repetitive and interruptive signals. *Journal of Gerontology,* 1967, *22,* 143–150.

Rapoport, R., & **Rapoport, R. N.** *Dual career families.* Baltimore: Penguin, 1971.

Rapoport, R., Rapoport, R. N., & **Strelitz, Z.** *Fathers, mothers, and society.* New York: Basic Books, 1977.

Rauner, I. M. Occupational information and occupational choice. *Personnel and Guidance Journal,* 1962, *41,* 311–317.

Raymond, B. Free recall among the aged. *Psychological Reports,* 1971, *29,* 1179–1182.

Read, S. Living without children. *Sunday Times,* November 10, 1974, pp. 18; 30.

Reese, H. W. Models of memory and models of development. *Human Development,* 1973, *16,* 397–416.

Reese, H. W. The development of memory: Life-span perspectives. In H. W. Reese (Ed.), *Advances in child development and behavior* (Vol. 11). New York: Academic Press, 1976.

Reese, H. W., & **Overton, W. F.** Models of development and theories of development. In L. R. Goulet & P. B. Baltes (Eds.), *Life-span developmental psychology: Research and theory.* New York: Academic Press, 1970.

Reich, W. T. Ethical issues related to research involving elderly subjects. *The Gerontologist,* 1978, *18,* 326–337.

Rest, J. R. Longitudinal study of the defining issues test of moral judgement: A strategy for analyzing developmental change. *Developmental Psychology,* 1975, *11,* 738–748.

Richards, O. W. Vision at levels of night road illumination: XII: Changes of acuity and contrast sensitivity with age. *American Journal of Optometry,* 1966, *43,* 313–319.

Richman, J. The foolishness and wisdom of age: Attitudes toward the elderly as reflected in jokes. *The Gerontologist,* 1977, *17,* 210–219.

Riegel, K. F. Dialectic operations: The final period of cognitive development. *Human Development,* 1973, *16,* 346–370.

Riegel, K. F. Adult life crises: A dialectic interpretation of development. In N. Datan & L. H. Ginsberg (Eds.), *Life-span developmental psychology: Normative life crises.* New York: Academic Press, 1975.

Riegel, K. F. The dialectics of human development. *American Psychologist,* 1976, *31,* 689–700.

Riegel, K. F., & **Riegel, R. M.** Development, drop, and death. *Developmental Psychology,* 1972, *6,* 306–319.

Riegel, K. F., Riegel, R. M., & **Meyer, G.** Sociopsychological factors of aging: A cohort sequential analysis. *Human Development,* 1967, *10,* 27–56.

Riley, J. W., Jr. What people think about death. In O. G. Brim, Jr., H. E. Freeman, S. Levine & N. A. Scotch (Eds.), *The dying patient.* New York: Russell Sage Foundation, 1970.

Riley, M. W. Age strata in social systems. In R. H. Binstock, & E. Shanas (Eds.), *Handbook of aging and the social sciences.* New York: Van Nostrand Reinhold, 1976.

Riley, M. W. (Ed.). *Aging from birth to death: Interdisciplinary perspectives.* Boulder, Colo.: Westview Press, 1979.

Riley, M. W., Johnson, M. E., & **Foner, A. (Eds.).** *Aging and society: A sociology of age stratification.* New York: Russell Sage Foundation, 1972.

Ritzer, G. *Working: Conflict and change* (2d ed.). Englewood Cliffs, N.J.: Prentice-Hall, 1977.

Robertson, J. F. Interaction in three generation families, parents as mediators: Toward a theoretical perspective. *International Journal of Aging and Human Development* 1975, *6,* 103–109.

Robertson, J. F. Significance of grandparents: Perceptions of young adult grandchildren. *The Gerontologist,* 1976, *16,* 137–140.

Robertson, J. F. Grandmotherhood: A study of role conceptions. *Journal of Marriage and the Family,* 1977, *39,* 165–174.

Rollins, B. C., & **Feldman, H.** Marital satisfaction over the life cycle. *Journal of Marriage and the Family,* 1970, *32,* 20–28.

Rosen, J. L., & **Neugarten, B. L.** Ego functions in the middle and later years: a thematic appercetion study. In B. L. Neugarten (Ed.), *Personality in middle and late life.* New York: Atherton Press, 1964.

Rosenman, R. H. The role of behavior patterns and neurogenic factors in the pathogenesis of coronary heart disease. In R. S. Eliot (Ed.), *Stress and the heart.* New York: Futura, 1974.

Rosenman, R. H., & **Friedman, M.** Observations on the pathogeneis of coronary heart disease. *Nutrition News,* 1971, *34,* 9–14.

Rosenman, R. H., Friedman, M., Straus, R., Jenkins, C. D., Zyzanski, S., Jr., Wurm, M., & **Kositchek, R.** Coronary heart disease in the western collaborative group study: A follow-up experience of 4½ years. *Journal of Chronic Diseases,* 1970, *23,* 173–190.

Rosenman, R. H., Friedman, M., Straus, R., Wurm, M., Jenkins, C. D., Messinger, H. B., Kositchek, R., Hahn, W., & **Werthessen, N. T.** Coronary heart disease in the Western collaborative group study: A follow-up experience of two years. *Journal of the American Medical Association,* 1966, *195,* 86–92.

Rosenman, R. H., Friedman, M., Straus, R., Wurm, M., Kositchek, R., Hahn, W., & **Werthessen, N. T.** A predictive study of coronary heart disease: The Western collaborative group study. *Journal of the American Medical Association,* 1964, *189,* 15–22.

Rosow, I. The social context of the aging self. *The Gerontologist,* 1973, *13,* 82–87.

Rosow, I. *Socialization to old age.* Berkeley, Calif.: University of California Press, 1974.

Rosow, I. Status and role change through the life span. In R. H. Binstock & E. Shanas (Eds.), *Handbook of aging and the social sciences.* New York: Van Nostrand Reinhold, 1976.

Rosow, I. What is a cohort and why? *Human Development,* 1978, *21,* 65–75.

Rossi, A. S. Transition to parenthood. *Journal of Marriage and the Family,* 1968, *30,* 26–39.

Rossi, A. S. Transition to parenthood. In I. Reiss (Ed.), *Readings on the family system.* New York: Holt, Rinehart, & Winston, 1972.

Rowe, E. J., & **Schnore, M. M.** Item concreteness and reported strategies in paired-associate learning as a function of age. *Journal of Gerontology,* 1971, *26,* 470–475.

Rubin, I. Sex after forty—and after seventy. In R. Brecher & E. Brecher (Eds.), *An analysis of human sexual response.* New York: Signet Books, 1966.

Rubin, K. H., Attewell, P. W., Tierney, M. C., & **Tumolo, P.** Development of spatial egocentrism and conservation across the life span. *Developmental Psychology,* 1973, *9,* 432.

Russell, C. S. Transition to parenthood: Problems and gratifications. *Journal of Marriage and the Family,* 1974, *36,* 294–302.

Rust, L. D. *The performance of arteriosclerotic and non-arteriosclerotic subjects on a mediation-interference task.* Unpublished doctoral dissertation, State University of New York at Buffalo, 1965.

Rutter, M. Dimensions of parenthood: Some myths and some suggestions. In the *Family and Society: Dimen-*

sions of Parenthood. Seminar held by the Department of Health and Social Security, London, HMSO, 1974.

Rux, J. M. *Widows and widowers: Instrumental skills, socioeconomic status, and life satisfaction.* Unpublished doctoral dissertation, Pennsylvania State University, 1976.

Ryder, N. B. The cohort as a concept in the study of social change. *American Sociological Review,* 1965, *30,* 843–861.

Sanders, J. C., Sterns, H. L., Smith, M., & **Sanders, R. E.** Modification of concept identification performance in older adults. *Developmental Psychology,* 1975, *11,* 824–829.

Sanders, R. E., Sanders, J. C., Mayes, G. J., & **Sielski, K. A.** Enhancement of conjunctive concept attainment in older adults. *Developmental Psychology,* 1976, *12,* 485–486.

Sanford, E. C. Mental growth and decay. *American Journal of Psychology,* 1902, *13,* 426–449.

Saunders, C. St. Christopher's hospice. In E. Shneidman (Ed.), *Death: Contemporary perspectives.* Palo Alto, Calif: Mayfield, 1976.

Schaie, K. W. A general model for the study of developmental problems. *Psychological Bulletin,* 1965, *64,* 92–107.

Schaie, K. W. A reinterpretation of age-related changes in cognitive structure and functioning. In L. R. Goulet & P. B. Baltes (Eds.), *Life-span developmental psychology: Research and theory.* New York: Academic Press, 1970.

Schaie, K. W. Methodological problems in descriptive developmental research on adulthood and aging. In J. R. Nesselroade & H. W. Reese (Eds.), *Life-span developmental psychology: Methodological issues.* New York: Academic Press, 1973.

Schaie, K. W. Translations in gerontology from lab to life: Intellectual functioning. *American Psychologist,* 1974, *29,* 802–807.

Schaie, K. W. Toward a stage theory of adult cognitive development. *International Journal of Aging and Human Development,* 1977, *8,* 129–138.

Schaie, K. W. The primary mental abilities in adulthood: An exploration in the development of psychometric intelligence. In P. B. Baltes & O. G. Brim, Jr. (Eds.), *Life-span development and behavior* (Vol. 2). New York: Academic Press, 1979.

Schaie, K. W., & **Baltes, P. B.** On sequential strategies in developmental research: Description or explanation? *Human Development,* 1975, *18,* 384–390.

Schaie, K. W., & **Baltes, P. B.** Some faith helps to see the forest: A final comment on the Horn and Donaldson myth of the Baltes-Schaie position on adult intelligence. *American Psychologist,* 1977, *32,* 1118–1120.

Schaie, K. W., & **Labouvie-Vief, G.** Generational and cohort-specific differences in adult cognitive behavior: A fourteen-year cross-sequential study. *Developmental Psychology,* 1974, *10,* 305–320.

Schaie, K. W., Labouvie, G. V., & **Buech, B. V.** Generational and cohort-specific differences in adult cognitive functioning: A fourteen-year study of independent samples. *Developmental Psychology,* 1973, *9,* 151–166.

Schaie, K. W., & **Parham, I. A.** Stability of adult personality: Fact or fable? *Journal of Personality and Social Psychology,* 1976, *34,* 146–158.

Schaie, K. W., & **Parham, I. A.** Cohort-sequential analyses of adult intellectual development. *Developmental Psychology,* 1977, *13,* 649–653.

Schaie, K. W., & **Strother, C. R.** A cross-sequential study of age changes in cognitive behavior. *Psychological Bulletin,* 1968, *70,* 671–680.

Schein, E. H. How "career anchors" hold executives to their career paths. *Personnel,* 1975, *52,* 11–24.

Schneider, D. J. *Social psychology.* Reading, Mass.: Addison-Wesley, 1976.

Schonfield, D., & **Robertson, B. A.** Memory storage and aging. *Canadian Journal of Psychology,* 1966, *20,* 228–236.

Schonfield, D., & **Wenger, L.** Age limitation of perceptual span. *Nature,* 1975, *253,* 377–378.

Schooler, K. K. Response of the elderly to environment: A stress-theoretic perspective. In P. G. Windley & G. Ernst (Eds.), *Theory development in environment and aging.* Washington, D.C.: Gerontological Society, 1975.

Schultz, N. R., Jr., & **Hoyer, W. J.** Feedback effects on spatial egocentrism in old age. *Journal of Gerontology,* 1976, *31,* 72–75.

Schulz, R. *The psychology of death, dying, and bereavement.* Reading, Mass.: Addison-Wesley, 1978.

Schulz, R., & **Aderman, D.** Effect of residential change on the temporal distance to death of terminal cancer patients. *Omega: Journal of Death and Dying,* 1973, *4,* 157–162.

Schulz, R., & **Brenner, G.** Relocation of the aged: A review and theoretical analysis. *Journal of Gerontology,* 1977, *32,* 323–333.

Seeman, M. On the meaning of alienation. *American Sociological Review,* 1959, *24,* 783–791.

Seligman, M. E. P. *Helplessness.* San Francisco: Freeman, 1975.

Seligmann, J. A right to die. *Newsweek,* 1976, *88,* 52.

Shanas, E. Adjustment to retirement. In F. M. Carp (Ed.), *Retirement.* New York: Behavioral Publications, 1972.

Sheppard, H. Work and retirement. In R. H. Binstock, & E. Shanas (Eds.), *Handbook of aging and the social sciences.* New York: Van Nostrand Reinhold, 1976.

Shideler, M. M. Coup de grace. *Christian Century,* 1966, *83,* 1503–1506.

Shneidman, E. S. Psychological death and resurrection. In E. S. Shneidman (Ed.), *Death and the college student.* New York: Behavioral Publications, 1972.

Shneidman, E. S. *Deaths of man.* New York: New York Times Book Co., 1973.

Shock, N. W. Energy metabolism, caloric intake and physical activity of the aging. In L. A. Carlson (Ed.), *Nutrition in old age (x symposium of the Swedish Nutrition Foundation).* Uppsala, Sweden: Almqvist & Wiksell, 1972.

Shock, N. W. Biological theories of aging. In J. E. Birren & K. W. Schaie (Eds.), *Handbook of the psychology of aging.* New York: Van Nostrand Reinhold, 1977. (a)

Shock, N. W. System integration. In C. E. Finch & L. Hayflick (Eds.), *Handbook of the biology of aging.* New York: Van Nostrand Reinhold, 1977. (b)

Sidney, K. H., & **Shephard, R. J.** Frequency and intensity of exercise training for elderly subjects. *Medicine and Science in Sports,* 1978, *10,* 125–131.

Siegler, I. C., & **Edelman, C. D.** *Age discrimination in employment: The implications for psychologists.* Paper presented at the meeting of the Western Psychological Association, San Francisco, April 1977.

Siegler, I. C., George, L. K., & **Okun, M. A.** Cross-sequential analysis of adult personality. *Developmental Psychology,* 1979, *15,* 350–351.

Silverman, P. R. Widowhood and preventive intervention. In S. H. Zarit (Ed.), *Readings in aging and death: Contemporary perspectives.* New York: Harper & Row, 1977.

Simpson, R. L. Parental influence, anticipatory socialization, and social mobility. *American Sociological Review,* 1962, *27,* 517–522.

Sinex, F. M. The mutation theory of aging. In M. Rockstein (Ed.), *Theoretical aspects of aging.* New York: Academic Press, 1974.

Sinnott, J. D. Everyday thinking and Piagetian operativity in adults. *Human Development,* 1975, *18,* 430–443.

Sinnott, J. D., & **Guttmann, D.** Piagetian logical abilities and older adults' abilities to solve everyday problems. *Human Development,* 1978, *21,* 327–333.

Skolnick, A. Stability and interrelations of thematic test imagery over 20 years. *Child Development,* 1966, *37,* 389–396.

Skolnick, A. *The intimate environment: Exploring marriage and the family.* Boston: Little Brown, 1973.

Slater, P. *The pursuit of loneliness.* Boston: Beacon Press, 1970.

Smith, A. D. Response interference with organized recall in the aged. *Developmental Psychology,* 1974, *10,* 867–870.

Smith, A. D. Aging and interference with memory. *Journal of Gerontology,* 1975, *30,* 319–325.

Smith, A. D. Adult age differences in cued recall. *Developmental Psychology,* 1977, *13,* 326–331.

Smith, A. D. Age differences in encoding, storage, and retrieval. In L. W. Poon, J. L. Fozard, L. S. Cermak, D. Arenberg & L. W. Thompson (Eds.), *New directions in memory and aging: Proceedings of the George A. Talland memorial conference.* Hillsdale, N.J.: Erlbaum, 1980.

Sommers, D. Occupational rankings for men and women by earnings. *Monthly Labor Review,* 1974, *97,* 34–51.

Sorokin, P. A. Social differentiation. In D. L. Sills (Ed.), *International encyclopedia of the social sciences* (Vol. 14). New York: Macmillan, 1968.

Spanier, G. B., & **Casto, R. F.** Adjustment to separation and divorce: A qualitative analysis. In G. Levinger & O. Moles (Eds.), *Divorce and separation: Context, causes, and consequences.* New York: Basic Books, 1979.

Spark, G. M., & **Brody, E. M.** The aged are family members. *Family Process,* 1970, *9,* 195–210.

Spearman, C. *The abilities of man.* New York: Macmillan, 1927.

Spieth, W. Slowness of task performance and cardiovascular diseases. In A. T. Welford & J. E. Birren (Eds.), *Behavior, aging, and the nervous system.* Springfield, Ill.: Charles C. Thomas, 1965.

Stafford, R., Backman, E., & **Dibona, P.** The division of labor among cohabiting and married couples. *Journal of Marriage and the Family,* 1977, *39,* 43–58.

Stamford, B. A. Physiological effects of training upon institutionalized geriatric men. *Journal of Gerontology,* 1972, *27,* 451–455.

Staples, R. Toward a sociology of the black family: A theoretical and methodological assessment. *Journal of Marriage and the Family,* 1971, *33,* 119–138.

Sternberg, S. High-speed scanning in human memory. *Science,* 1966, *153,* 652–654.

Stinnett, N., Carter, L. M., & **Montgomery, J. E.** Older persons' perceptions of their marriages. *Journal of Marriage and the Family,* 1972, *34,* 665–670.

Stinnett, N., & **Walters, J.** *Relationships in marriage and family.* New York: Macmillan, 1977.

Storandt, M., & **Wittles, I.** Maintenance of function in relocation of community-dwelling older adults. *Journal of Gerontology,* 1975, *30,* 608–612.

Strauss, A. L., & **Glaser, B. G.** Anguish: A case history of a dying trajectory. Mill Valley, Calif.: Sociology Press, 1970.

Strehler, B. L. *Time, cells, and aging.* New York: Academic Press, 1962.

Strehler, B. L. The mechanisms of aging. *The Body Forum,* 1978, *3,* 44–45.

Streib, G. F., & **Schneider, C. J.** *Retirement in American society: Impact and process.* Ithaca, N.Y.: Cornell University Press, 1971.

Surwillo, W. W. The relation of simple response time to brain wave frequency and the effects of age. *Electroencephalography and clinical neurophysiology,* 1963, *15,* 105–114.

Surwillo, W. W. Timing of behavior in senescence and

the role of the central nervous system. In G. A. Talland (Ed.), *Human aging and behavior.* New York: Academic Press, 1968.

Sussman, M. B. Parental participation in mate selection and its effect upon family continuity. *Social Forces,* 1953, *32,* 76–81.

Sussman, M. B. Family life of old people. In R. H. Binstock & E. Shanas (Eds.), *Handbook of aging and the social sciences.* New York: Van Nostrand Reinhold, 1976.

Sussman, M. B., & **Burchinal, L.** Kin family network: Unheralded structure in current conceptualizations of family functioning. *Marriage and Family Living,* 1962, *24,* 231–240.

Svoboda, C. P. Senescence in Western philosophy. *Educational Gerontology,* 1977, *2,* 219–235.

Talland, G. A. Age and the immediate memory span. In G. A. Talland (Ed.), *Human aging and behavior.* New York: Academic Press, 1968.

Taub, H. A. Paired associate learning as a function of age, rate, and instructions. *Journal of Genetic Psychology,* 1967, *111,* 41–46.

Templar, D. I. Death anxiety in religiously very involved persons. *Psychological Reports,* 1972, *31,* 361–362.

Terkel, S. *Working: People talk about what they do all day and how they feel about what they do.* New York: Pantheon Books, 1972.

Tetens, J. N. *Philosophische Versuche über die menschliche Natur und ihre Entwicklung.* Leipzig: Weidmanns Erben und Reich, 1777.

Thomas, R., & **Wetherell, D.** *Looking forward to work.* London: HMSO, 1974.

Thurstone, L. L., & **Thurstone, T. G.** *Factorial studies of intelligence* (Psychometric Monograph No. 2). Chicago: University of Chicago Press, 1941.

Tomlinson-Keasey, C. Formal operations in females from eleven to fifty-four years of age. *Developmental Psychology,* 1972, *6,* 364.

Townsend, P. *The family of old people.* London: Routledge & Kegan Paul, 1957.

Treat, N. J., & **Reese, H. W.** Age, pacing, and imagery in paired-associate learning. *Developmental Psychology,* 1976, *12,* 119–124.

Troll, L. E. Issues in the study of generations. *Aging and Human Development,* 1970, *1,* 199–218.

Troll, L. E. The family of later life: A decade review. *Journal of Marriage and the Family,* 1971, *33,* 263–290.

Troll, L. E. *Early and middle adulthood.* Monterey, Calif.: Brooks/Cole, 1975.

Troyer, W. G., Eisdorfer, C., Bogdonoff, M. D., & **Wilkie, F.** Experimental stress and learning in the aged. *Journal of Abnormal Psychology,* 1967, *1,* 65–70.

Tulving, E. Subjective organization in free recall of unrelated words. *Psychological Review,* 1962, *69,* 344–354.

Tulving, E. The effects of presentation and recall of material in free recall learning. *Journal of Verbal Learning and Verbal Behavior,* 1967, *6,* 175–184.

Tulving, E., & **Pearlstone, Z.** Availability versus accessibility of information in memory for words. *Journal of Verbal Learning and Verbal Behavior,* 1966, *5,* 381–391.

Tulving, E., & **Thompson, D. M.** Encoding specificity and retrieval processes in episodic memory. *Psychological Review,* 1973, *80,* 352–373.

Turiel, E. Developmental processes in the child's moral thinking. In P. H. Mussen, J. Langer, & M. Covington (Eds.), *Trends and issues in developmental psychology.* New York: Holt, Rinehart & Winston, 1969.

Turner, R. R., & **Reese, H. W. (Eds.).** *Life-span developmental psychology: Intervention.* New York: Academic Press, 1980.

Uhlenberg, P. Demographic change and problems of the aged. In M. W. Riley (Ed.), *Aging from birth to death: Interdisciplinary perspectives.* Boulder, Colo.: Westview Press, 1979.

Underwood, B. J., & **Schulz, R. W.** *Meaningfulness and verbal learning.* Philadelphia, Pa.: Lippincott, 1960.

U.S. Department of Health, Education, and Welfare. *Marital status and living arrangements* (Current Population Reports, Series P-20, No. 255). Washington, D.C.: U.S. Government Printing Office, 1973.

U.S. Department of Health, Education, and Welfare. *The condition of education: A statistical report on the condition of education in the United States.* Washington, D.C.: U.S. Government Printing Office, 1976.

U.S. Department of Health, Education, and Welfare. *Vital statistics of the United States, 1976.* Hyattsville, Md.: National Center for Health Statistics, 1978.

U.S. Department of Health, Education, and Welfare. *Monthly vital statistics report: Advance report, final mortality statistics, 1977.* Hyattsville, Md.: National Center for Health Statistics, 1979.

U.S. Department of Labor, Women's Bureau, Employment Standards Administration. *The economic role of women* (reprinted from Economic Report to the President, 1973). Washington, D.C.: U.S. Department of Labor, 1973.

U.S. Department of Labor. *U.S. working women: A chartbook* (Bureau of Labor Statistics Bulletin 1880). Washington, D.C.: U.S. Department of Labor, 1975.

U.S. National Health Survey. *Monocular-binocular visual acuity of adults: U.S. 1960–1962.* Washington, D.C.: U.S. Department of Health Education and Welfare, 1968.

Vaillant, G. E. *Adaptation to life.* Boston: Little Brown, 1977.

van den Daele, L. D. Ego development and preferential judgment in life-span perspective. In N. Datan & L. H. Ginsberg (Eds.), *Life-span developmental psychology: Normative life crises.* New York: Academic Press, 1975.

Veatch, R. M. Brain death. In E. Shneidman (Ed.), *Death: Current perspectives.* Palo Alto, Calif.: Mayfield, 1976.

Vernon, P. E. *The structure of human abilities.* London: Methuen, 1961.

Veroff, J., Atkinson, J. W., Feld, S. C., & **Gurin, G.** The use of thematic apperception to assess motivation in a nationwide interview study. *Psychological Monographs, 1960, 74* (Whole No. 499).

Veroff, J., & **Feld, S. C.** *Marriage and work in America: A study of motives and roles.* New York: Van Nostrand Reinhold, 1970.

Verwoerdt, A., Pfeiffer, E., & **Wang, H. S.** Sexual behavior in senescence—changes in sexual activity and interest of aging men and women. *Journal of Geriatric Psychiatry, 1969, 2,* 163–180.

Vinick, B. H. Remarriage in old age. *The Family Coordinator, 1978, 27,* 359–364.

Vondracek, F. W., & **Urban, H. B.** Intervention within individual and family development: When? what kind? and how? In S. R. Goldberg & F. Deutsch (Eds.), *Life-span individual and family development.* Monterey, Calif.: Brooks/Cole, 1977.

Walford, R. L. *The immunologic theory of aging.* Baltimore: Williams & Wilkins, 1969.

Walker, L. J., & **Richards, B. S.** Stimulating transitions in moral reasoning as a function of stage of cognitive development. *Developmental Psychology, 1979, 15,* 95–103.

Waller, W. The rating and dating complex. *American Sociological Review, 1937, 2,* 727–734.

Waller, W. *The family: A dynamic interpretation.* New York: Gordon, 1938.

Waller, W. *The family: A dynamic interpretation* (Revised by R. Hill). New York: Dryden Press, 1951.

Walsh, D. A. Age differences in learning and memory. In D. S. Woodruff & J. E. Birren (Eds.), *Aging: Scientific perspectives and social issues.* New York: Van Nostrand, 1975.

Walsh, D. A., & **Baldwin, M.** Age differences in integrated semantic memory. *Developmental Psychology, 1977, 13,* 509–514.

Wang, H. S. Cerebral correlates of intellectual function in senescense. In L. F. Jarvik, C. Eisdorfer, & J. E. Blum (Eds.), *Intellectual functioning in adults: Psychological and biological influences.* New York: Springer, 1973.

Wang, H. S., & **Busse, E. W.** EEG of healthy old persons—A longitudinal study. I: Dominant background activity and occipital rhythm. *Journal of Gerontology, 1969, 24,* 419–426.

Wang, H. S., Obrist, W. D., & **Busse, E. W.** Neurophysiological correlates of the intellectual function of elderly persons living in the community. *American Journal of Psychiatry, 1970, 126,* 1205–1212.

Waring, J. M. Social replenishment and social change: The problem of disordered cohort flow. *American Behavioral Scientist, 1975, 19,* 237–256.

Waugh, N. C., & **Norman, D. A.** Primary memory. *Psychological Review, 1965, 72,* 89–104.

Wechsler, D. *The measurement and appraisal of adult intelligence* (4th ed.). Baltimore: Williams & Wilkins, 1958.

Weisman, A. D. *On dying and denying: A psychiatric study of terminality.* New York: Behavioral Publications, 1972.

Welford, A. T. *Ageing and human skill.* London: Oxford University Press, 1958.

Welford, A. T. Motor performance. In J. E. Birren & K. W. Schaie (Eds.), *Handbook of the psychology of aging.* New York: Van Nostrand Reinhold, 1977.

West, D. *The young offender.* Harmondsworth: Penguin, 1967.

Westhoff, L. A. Two-time winners. *New York Times Magazine,* August 10, 1975, 10–15.

Whitbourne, S. K. Test anxiety in elderly and young adults. *International Journal of Aging & Human Development, 1976, 7,* 201–210.

White, R. W. *Lives in progress.* New York: Holt, Rinehart, & Winston, 1961.

White, R. W. *Lives in progress: A study of the national growth of personality* (3d ed.), New York: Holt, Rinehart, & Winston, 1975.

Wickelgren, W. A. Age and storage dynamics in continuous recognition memory. *Developmental Psychology, 1975, 11,* 165–169.

Wilensky, H. L. *Women's work: Economic growth, ideology and structure.* Berkeley: Institute of Industrial Relations, University of California, 1968.

Wilkie, F., & **Eisdorfer, C.** Intelligence and blood pressure in the aged. *Science, 1971, 172,* 959–962.

Willems, E. P. Behavioral ecology and experimental analysis: Courtship is not enough. In J. R. Nesselroade & H. W. Reese (Eds.), *Life-span developmental psychology: Methodological issues.* New York: Academic Press, 1973.

Wimer, R. E., & **Wigdor, B. T.** Age differences in retention of learning. *Journal of Gerontology, 1958, 13,* 291–295.

Winch, R. F. *The modern family* (3d ed.). New York: Holt, Rinehart, & Winston, 1971.

Winsborough, H. H. Changes in the transition to adulthood. In M. W. Riley (Ed.), *Aging from birth to death: Interdisciplinary perspectives.* Boulder, Colo.: Westview Press, 1979.

Witte, K. L. Paired-associate learning in young and

elderly adults as related to presentation rate. *Psychological Bulletin,* 1975, *82,* 975–985.

Witte, K. L., & **Freund, J. S.** Paired-associate learning in young and old adults as related to stimulus concreteness and presentation method. *Journal of Gerontology,* 1976, *31,* 186–192.

Wittles, I., & **Botwinick, J.** Survival in relocation. *Journal of Gerontology,* 1974, *29,* 440–443.

Wohlwill, J. F. The age variable in psychological research. *Psychological Review,* 1970, *77,* 49–64.

Wolf, E. Glare and age. *Archives of Opthalmology,* 1960, *64,* 502–514.

Woodruff, D. S. Relationships among EEG alpha frequency, reaction time, and age: A biofeedback study. *Psychophysiology,* 1975, *12,* 673–681.

Woodruff, D. S. *Can you live to be 100?* New York: Chatham Square Press, 1977.

Woodruff, D. S. Brian electrical activity and behavior relationships over the life span. In P. B. Baltes (Ed.), *Life-span development and behavior* (Vol. 1). New York: Academic Press, 1979.

Woodruff, D. S., & **Birren, J. E.** Age changes and cohort differences in personality. *Developmental Psychology,* 1972, *6,* 252–259.

Wright, J. D. Are working women *really* more satisfied? Evidence from several national surveys. *Journal of Marriage and the Family,* 1978, *40,* 301–313.

Young, M. L. Problem solving performance in two age groups. *Journal of Gerontology,* 1966, *21,* 505–510.

Zablocki, B. *The joyful community: An account of the Bruderhof, a communal movement now in its third generation.* Baltimore: Penguin, 1971.

Znaniecki, F. *Social relations and social roles.* San Francisco, Calif.: Chandler, 1965.

Zweig, J., & **Csank, J.** Effects of relocation on chronically ill geriatric patients of a medical unit: Mortality rates. *Journal of American Geriatrics Society,* 1975, *23,* 133–136.

GLOSSARY

Accommodation In Piaget's theory, the alteration of an existing cognitive structure to fit new external stimulus objects.

Accommodative power The ability to focus and maintain an image on the retina.

Active euthanasia Deliberate, premeditated actions taken to shorten an individual's life, usually to prevent undue suffering.

Active mastery Being in charge of one's environment, viewing the self as a source of energy.

Active organism paradigm A developmental model, rooted in the organismic world view, in which the individual is inherently dynamic and development is explained by the individual's action on the environment.

Acute brain syndrome An organic brain syndrome which is reversible.

Adaptation In Piaget's theory, the functional principle involving the processes of assimilation and accommodation.

Adaptation process The process of adjusting to or coping with a life event.

Aerobic exercise Exercises which demand oxygen, such as jogging, swimming, and bicycling.

Age-change function Specification of the relationship between chronological age and a behavioral change process.

Age changes Age-related within-person changes and between-person differences in such changes.

Age differences Age-related between-person differences.

Age grades Age classes, for example, children, adults, the aged.

Ageism Inequality between age groups based on discrimination against the aging.

Age norms Expected and acceptable behaviors for a person of a given age.

Age-status system System of positions or locations in reference to others in a social network which is based on chronological age.

Age strata The demographic structure of a population's age and birth cohorts.

Alpha abundance Measure of the amount of time alpha rhythms are produced.

Alpha frequency Measure of the frequency of alpha rhythm in cycles per second.

Alpha rhythm Dominant brain wave patterns with a frequency of 8 to 13 cycles per second, associated with a relaxed, awake state.

Androgen A male sex hormone secreted by the testes; testosterone is the principal androgen.

Angina pectoris Agonizing pain in the area of the heart, left shoulder, and arm; a symptom accompanying any interference with blood supply or oxygenation of the heart muscle.

Anticipatory socialization The process of learning attitudes, values, and activities that will be adaptive in a future situation.

Anticipation interval In a paired-associate learning task, the time span of the test phase in the anticipation method of presentation.

Anticipation method Method of presenting paired-associate task in which the stimulus is presented followed by the stimulus-response pair.

Anxiety Fear or worry as measured by self-reports.

Appropriate death   A death that fulfills the dying person's ideals and expectations within societal death norms.

Arousal   Autonomic nervous system activity in response to stress.

Arteriosclerosis   A group of processes involving thickening and loss of elasticity of the arterial walls.

Assimilation   In Piaget's theory, the process whereby an object or event, external to the person, is altered to fit the person's existing cognitive structure.

Associative stage   Stage in the learning process of a paired-associate task during which the stimuli and responses are linked and recalled together.

Atherosclerosis   The development of arterial lesions accompanied by the accumulation of fat, cholesterol, and collagen at the lesion site.

Autoimmunity   The ability of the immune system to identify foreign material.

Behavior-change processes   A series of changes which form the bases of development.

Beta rhythm   Brain wave patterns with a frequency of 18 to 30 cycles per second, associated with an attentive, alert state.

Between-cohort differences in intraindividual change   Differences in intraindividual change from one cohort to another.

Between-cohort differences in interindividual differences   Differences in interindividual differences from one cohort to another.

Bioethics   That branch of ethics concerned with the moral, ethical, and legal implications of contemporary life science technology.

Birth cohort   That cohort consisting of persons born in a given year.

Brain death   A particular definition of biological death involving measurement of neocortex and brainstem activity.

Career   An organized path undertaken by an individual that traverses time and space; consistent involvement in a particular occupational role over time.

Cataracts   Opacities of the lens that obstruct light waves.

Causal modeling techniques   Statistical techniques which permit causal inference within the framework of nonexperimental designs.

Causal relationship   The situation where one set of events produces or causes another set.

Central nervous system   That part of the nervous system within the bony protection of the vertebral column and skull.

Cerebral death   The cessation of activity in the cortex.

Chronic brain syndrome   An organic brain disorder which is irreversible.

Chronological age   One's age in years.

Climacteric   The period of declining reproductive capacity in men and women; includes menopause in women.

Cognitive structure   A way of organizing knowledge that is constructed through interaction with the environment.

Cohort   A group of persons experiencing some common event, e.g., being born in the same year.

Cohort flow   The modification of different cohorts over their life course.

Cohort life table   A life table summarizing mortality rates which provides a longitudinal perspective, following the mortality experience of a single cohort.

Commitment   An affirmation or pledge established toward an object, person, or course of action over time.

Competence   Capacity to function in physiological, sensory, motor, and cognitive areas.

Competence (Piaget)   In Piaget's theory, the formal, logical representation of cognitive structures.

Concrete operations, stage of   In Piaget's theory, the third stage of cognitive development; characterized by operations such as conservation, classification, and seriation.

Congruence   Compatibility of person and environment.

Conservation   In Piaget's theory, the ability to know that certain aspects of a stimulus, e.g., number or volume, remain unchanged even when other aspects, e.g., shape or pattern, have changed.

Contextual world view   A world view which stresses that constant and completely interrelated changes characterize humans and their contexts.

Control operations   Means by which information is retrieved from one memory storage structure and entered into the next.

Coping strategy   The specific method used by an individual to adapt or adjust to a life event.

Correlation   The degree of relationship between variables or measurements in a research study.

Cross-linkages   Bonds between components of the same molecule or between molecules which develop with the passage of time.

Cross-sectional sequences   Successions of two or more cross-sectional studies completed at different times of measurement involving independent measures on different individuals.

Crystallized intelligence   General cognitive capacity reflecting the degree to which the individual has incorporated the knowledge and skills of the culture into thinking and actions; postulated to increase with age.

Cued recall Response mode in which the participant is given cues to aid recall.

Culture A legacy or heritage comprising knowledge, beliefs, values, assumptions, and patterns of behavior.

Current life table A life table summarizing mortality rates which provides a cross-sectional perspective, specifying the age-specific mortality rates for a population at a given time.

Dark adaptation The ability to adjust vision when moving from high to low levels of illumination.

Decay Loss of information from memory as a result of the erosion of the memory trace.

Delta rhythm Brain wave patterns with a frequency of 0.5 to 4 cycles per second; associated with sleep.

Dependent variable An outcome variable.

Description A task of the life-span developmentalist which involves the specification of the identity and timing of behavioral change.

Descriptive continuity When behaviors at a later point in time may be described as increases or combinations of elements present at an earlier point in time.

Descriptive discontinuity When behaviors at a later point in time may be described as qualitatively different from behaviors at an earlier point in time.

Descriptive methods Methods for the identification and dimensionalization of within-person change and between-person differences in such change.

Deoxyribonucleic acid (DNA) Complex molecule, arranged in a double helix, bearing coded genetic information.

Despair In Erikson's theory, the negative pole of the crisis of old age; characterized by a rejection of one's life as meaningless and wasted.

Dialectical paradigm A developmental model, rooted in the contextual world view, in which the individual is continually changing and development is the result of reciprocal interactions between the changing individual and the changing context.

Discontinuity hypothesis The hypothesis that behavioral functions are affected only when biological functions reach a critical or limiting level.

Disengagement The reduction of interaction between the individual and the environment considered by some theorists to be one component of successful aging.

Disjunctive reaction time The length of time before an individual makes a response to a task involving multiple signals and/or responses.

Double-jeopardy hypothesis The idea that the minority aged suffer from the impact of both age and race discrimination.

Dying trajectory The length and form of the dying process.

Ecological validity A consideration of external validity in terms of the generalization of the findings of simulation studies to the individual's ecology or natural habitat.

Ego In psychoanalytic theory, the personality structure whose sole function is to adapt to reality.

Egocentrism Embeddedness in one's own point of view; failure to differentiate between subject and object.

Ego strength The degree of capability of the ego to perform its function (to meet the demands of reality).

Ego theory Any one of a number of personality theories rooted in the orthodox psychoanalytic perspective of Sigmund Freud which emphasize the role of the ego in personality development.

Elaboration A control operation for retrieval from primary memory and entry into secondary memory which involves the processing of information at deeper, semantic levels.

Electroencephalogram (EEG) A record of the electrical activity of the brain.

Empiricism An approach to knowledge in which conclusions are formulated on the basis of careful, scientifically controlled observation.

Empty-nest syndrome A sequence of significant life events associated with the process of launching children from the home.

Encoding Formation of a code at the time of input into secondary memory.

Enrichment An intervention strategy which attempts to optimize individuals' knowledge, skills, and development.

Environment The context or system in which an individual develops; "nurture" in the nature-nurture controversy.

Environmental press Demand and potential of a given environmental quality for activating behavior.

Error catastrophe An accumulation of RNA transcription errors resulting in cell death.

Error of commission Providing an incorrect response (in paired-associate and serial learning tasks).

Error of omission Failure to give a response (in paired-associate and serial learning tasks).

Estrogen A female sex hormone produced by the ovaries.

Experiment Set of procedures designed to assess the consequences of an experimenter-controlled or naturally occurring event (treatment) which intervenes in the lives of the participants.

Experimental mortality The loss of individuals from a sample during the course of research which may threaten internal or external validity.

Experimental strategies Simulation strategies in which the independent causal variable is manipulated or controlled during the study.

Explanation A task of the life-span developmentalist which involves the specification of the antecedents, or causes, and the conditions of behavioral change.

Explanatory continuity When the same explanations are used to account for behavior across a person's life.

Explanatory discontinuity When different explanations are used to account for behavior across a person's life.

Explanatory methods Methods for the identification of the causes of within-person change and between-person differences in such change.

External validity The degree to which a relationship among variables observed in one data set can also be observed in other data sets.

Factor-analytic techniques Statistical techniques for determining the number and nature of underlying variables among larger numbers of measures.

Fluid intelligence General cognitive capacity reflecting the degree to which the individual has developed unique qualities of thinking independent of culturally based content; postulated to peak in early adulthood.

Free-classification task Task in which individuals are to group stimuli that are alike or that go together in some way.

Free radicals Unstable chemical compounds which react with nearby molecules.

Free-recall task Task in which a series of items is presented to an individual who is then asked to recall as many of the items as possible in any order.

Formal operations, stage of In Piaget's theory, the fourth and final stage of cognitive development; characterized by abstract, logical, and hypothetical reasoning and thought.

Functional invariants Abilities which serve the same or similar purpose throughout development.

General developmental model Schaie's system for incorporating assessment of all sources of developmental change (age, cohort, and time) into one of several research designs.

General intelligence A broad ability domain postulated to permeate all cognitive tasks.

Generativity In Erikson's theory, the positive pole of the crisis of middle age; a deep concern for and contribution to the maintenance and perpetuation of society.

Genes Chromosomal units of heredity.

Grief An emotional response to loss characterized by somatic distress and feelings of sadness, guilt, anger, and depression.

Grief work The process or task of shaping a new identity accompanying bereavement and mourning.

Heredity That which is genetically transmitted in one's genotype; the complement of genes received at conception.

Heterogamy Mate selection in which the partners are different on a wide array of social and psychological dimensions.

High associative strength One word frequently elicits another in a free-association task.

History effects A class of threats to internal validity consisting of events external to the individual which are confounded with the presumed causal variable under scrutiny.

Homogomy Marriage or mate selection in which the partners are similar on one or several social and psychological dimensions.

Hospice A medical facility specifically designed for the dying patient; emotional as well as medical care is provided.

Hypertension High blood pressure.

Hypothetical thought Abstract and systematic thought about complex problems and propositions.

Id In psychoanalytic theory, an innate personality structure which is the center of the libido.

Identity A sense of self-definition.

Immediate memory-span task Task involving both primary and secondary memory components which assesses the longest string of items that can be immediately reproduced in the order of presentation.

Interactive relation A relation between two or more elements wherein the function of any one element requires the full presence of the other elements in the relation.

Independent measures When different individuals are observed at different times.

Independent variable A causal variable.

Inspection interval In a paired-associate learning task, the time span of the study phase in the anticipation method of presentation.

Integrity In Erikson's theory, the positive pole of the crisis of old age; an inner sense of peace and order which allows one to view one's personal life as meaningful and worthwhile.

Interference Loss of information from memory as a result of information acquired prior to or following input.

Interindividual differences Between-person differences.

Interindividual differences in intraindividual change Between-person differences in within-person change.

Interiority Tendency to respond to inner rather than outer stimuli.

Internal validity The degree to which an observed relationship among variables is accurately identified and interpreted.

Intervention Helping to enhance an individual's personal, social, and physical development; attempting to help persons to change.

Intimacy In Erikson's theory, the positive pole of the crisis of young adulthood; the quality of affection and rapport found in deep, personal relationships.

Intraindividual change Within-person change.

Intrapsychic process Inner personality process, for example, active versus passive mastery, inner versus outer orientation.

Introversion Preoccupation with one's own feelings, thoughts, and inner processes.

In vitro In an artificial environment.

In vivo Within living tissue.

Isolation In Erikson's theory, the negative pole of the crisis of young adulthood; characterized by the inability to achieve a close personal relationship with another person.

Knowledge actualization Involving memory for world knowledge acquired through real-life experience.

Law A regular, predictable relationship among variables.

Legal blindness Corrected distance vision of 20/200 or worse in the better eye, or a visual field limited to 20° in its greatest diameter.

Libido In psychoanalytic theory, a psychic energy which governs life.

Life-course analysis An approach to the study of personality which focuses on the examination of age- and sex-differentiated life patterns within particular historical contexts.

Life event Any one of a wide array of events whose advent indicates or requires substantial change in the individual's life.

Life expectancy The average length of life.

Life review The process of reviewing one's life as the result of a realization of impending death.

Life-span developmental approach An orientation to the study of human development, from conception to death, which is concerned with the description, explanation, and optimization of within-person changes in behavior and between-person differences in such changes in behavior.

Life transition Change in pattern of behavior defined by major normative life events such as marriage, birth of children, and retirement.

Lipofuscin Dark-colored, waste pigment in old cells.

Longitudinal sequences Successions of two or more longitudinal studies begun at different times of measurement involving repeated measures of the same individuals.

Low associative strength One word infrequently elicits another in a free-association task.

Maturation effects A class of threats to internal validity consisting of events internal to the individual which are confounded with the presumed causal variable under scrutiny.

Maturity In a physiological sense, when an organism is capable of reproductive functioning.

Maximum life span The extreme upper limit of length of life.

Mechanistic world view A world view which stresses continuity and reductionism; a machine model of human functioning.

Mediation The formation of a covert response which forms a link between stimulus and response.

Menopause The cessation of menstruation, typically occurring during a two-year period at an average age of 47.

Metamemory Knowledge of one's own memory processes.

Model A metaphysical representation of a system which is judged on the basis of its usefulness.

Multidirectional Involving many directions or patterns of change.

Multivariate Involving the simultaneous examination of two or more dependent variables.

Myocardial infarction An area of dead tissue in the heart muscle resulting from excessive oxygen deprivation.

Nature-nurture controversy Controversy over whether the primary determinent of human behavior and development is genetic or environmental.

Noncued recall Response mode in which the participant is not given cues to aid recall.

Nonexperimental strategies A simulation strategy in which the independent causal variable has occurred prior to the study.

Nonnormative, life-event influences Person-specific determinants of behavior such as illness, divorce, promotion, death of spouse.

Nonspecific transfer Transfer-of-training effects which are the result of general factors such as warm-up or learning to learn.

Normative, age-graded influences Biological and

environmental determinants of behavior that are correlated with chronological age.

Normative, history-graded influences Biological and environmental determinants of behavior that are correlated with historical time.

Off time Age-inappropriate timing of life events.

On time Age-appropriate timing of life events.

Operation In Piaget's theory, an internalized action that is reversible.

Optimization A task of the life-span developmentalist which involves the modification and enhancement of behavioral change through intervention.

Organic brain disorders Chronic diseases involving mental conditions associated with impairment of brain functioning.

Organismic world view A world view which stresses emergence, qualitative discontinuity, nonreduction, and holism.

Organization (Piaget) In Piaget's theory, the ability to arrange cognitive activity into a system of interrelated elements.

Organization (strategy) A control operation for retrieval from primary memory and entry into secondary memory involving the coding of items into higher-order units.

Paired-associate learning task Task in which the individual learns to associate pairs of items so that the second item of the pair is given as a response upon presentation of the first item of the pair.

Paradigm of science A broad type of model intended to represent a large domain of knowledge, e.g., the discipline of psychology.

Passive euthanasia Withdrawing or withholding treatment which permits a person to die earlier than if treatment were received.

Passive mastery Perception of the environment as threatening and dangerous, and the self as passive and accommodating.

Performance The process by which available competence is assessed and applied in real situations.

Peripheral nervous system That part of the nervous system which primarily lies outside the bony protective area of the vertebral column and skull.

Placebo A substance having no physiological effect but given to a research participant who supposes it to be a pharmacologic agent.

Plasticity Capacity for change and variability.

Pluralism The use of many perspectives, assumptions, models, or world views.

Presbyopia A defect of vision characterized by recession of the near point of vision so that objects very near the eyes cannot be seen clearly.

Prevention An intervention strategy which attempts to reduce the likelihood that behavioral dysfunctions or problems will occur.

Primary memory A temporary maintenance system for conscious processing of information.

Primary mental ability A dimension of intelligence that describes what is common to various intellectual tests and accounts for individual differences in performance on the tests.

Progestogen A female sex hormone produced by the ovaries.

Psychoanalytic theory A personality theory based on psychoanalysis and the ideas of Sigmund Freud.

Psychometric approach A correlational approach to intelligence which focuses on specifying the interrelationships among different measures thought to characterize intelligence.

Psychosis associated with cerebral arteriosclerosis A chronic brain syndrome associated with vascular damage caused by arteriosclerotic diseases.

Quasi experiment Design in which the participants are assigned to treatments in a nonrandom fashion.

Randomization The assignment of a group of individuals to subgroups in such a way that each individual has an equal probability of being assigned to each subgroup.

Reactive-organism paradigm A developmental model, rooted in the mechanistic world view, in which the individual is inherently passive and behavior is the result of external forces.

Reaction time (RT) The length of time between the appearance of a signal and the beginning of a responding movement.

Recall Response mode in which the participant must produce the called-for response from memory.

Recency effect Phenomenon in the free-recall procedure in which the last few items of a list are recalled first.

Recognition Response mode in which the participant must choose the correct response from among several alternatives.

Rehabilitation An intervention strategy which attempts to reduce the intensity or duration of a behavioral dysfunction which has already appeared.

Remediation An intervention strategy which attempts to correct or remove a behavioral dysfunction which has already appeared.

Reminiscence Review and reconstruction of one's past life, particularly in old age.

Repeated measures When the same individuals are observed repeatedly at different times.

Research methods The set of specific procedures by which a scientist makes observations and collects data in order to examine relationships among variables.

Response learning stage Stage in the learning process of a paired-associate task during which the responses are identified and made available for recall.

Retrieval Utilization of a secondary memory input code at the time of output.

Ribonucleic acid (RNA) A complex molecule having the function of transcribing and transferring the information about protein synthesis contained in DNA.

Rigidity Inflexibility in unlearning previous habits in order to gain new ones.

Rites de passage Socially sanctioned ceremonies or events marking the transition of an individual from one status or age class to another.

Role Pattern of activity intrinsic to a status position.

Scale model The most specific type of model in which the elements of a system and their interrelationships can be depicted.

Scheme In Piaget's theory, a cognitive structure underlying organized patterns of behavior.

Scientific method A set of empirically based techniques used by researchers to study the phenomena of the world.

Secondary memory A permanent maintenance system for information processing characterized by semantic content.

Second-order abilities A set of higher-level dimensions of intelligence generated through factor analysis of first-order or primary abilities; describe what is common to the primary abilities.

Selection effects A class of threats to internal validity consisting of bias resulting from the differential selection of individuals in comparison groups.

Selective survival effects Changes in the mortality curve from one cohort to another which may jeopardize internal or external validity.

Senile psychosis A chronic brain syndrome sometimes called senile dementia or senile brain disease; associated with the degeneration of the brain cells.

Sensory memory Modality-specific (e.g., visual, auditory) peripheral memory system involving a literal copy of information.

Sequential strategies Complex descriptive research designs which permit the separation of within- and between-cohort changes and differences.

Serial-learning task Task in which the individual is to learn a list of items so that on presentation of an item, the succeeding item is given as a response.

Simple cross-sectional method Data-collection method in which individuals of different ages are observed on a single occasion at the same point in time.

Simple longitudinal method Data-collection method in which the same individuals of different ages are observed on at two or more points in time, thus yielding a comparison of the same individuals at different ages.

Simple reaction time The length of time required by an individual to make a single response to a single signaling stimulus.

Simulation strategies The construction of a controlled, time-compressed, artificial situation designed to represent or model a real situation in order to permit the specification of causes.

Social-breakdown model Hypothesized negative spiral of breakdown created by interaction of the social environment with the diminished self-concept and competence of the individual.

Socialization Process by which members of one generation shape the behaviors and personalities of members of another generation; acquisition of the knowledge, skills, and values which make individuals able members of society.

Social-learning theory A type of mechanistic theory emphasizing the role of external (learning) factors in personality development.

Socioadaptation When the individual adjusts to the demands and conditions of society.

Specific transfer Transfer-of-training effects which are dependent on the similarity between tasks.

Speeded task Simple assessment task in which the object is to complete the task as rapidly as possible.

Stagnation In Erikson's theory, the negative pole of the crisis of middle age; characterized by self-indulgence and a sense of impoverishment.

Status Position or location in a social system in reference to others.

Stimulus-response (S-R) bonds The association or linkage of a response to a stimulus event.

Storage Retention of a secondary memory input code until the time of output.

Storage structures Theoretical memory constructs modeled after computer processing units, including a sensory store, a short-term store, and a long-term store.

Strong interaction position A stance on the nature-nurture controversy, rooted in the contextual world view, in which nature and nurture are viewed as completely interdependent.

Superego In psychoanalytic theory, the personality structure composed of the conscience and the ego ideal.

Terminal drop Phenomenon in which an individual's

intellectual performance shows a marked decline up to several years prior to death.

Testing effects A threat to internal validity consisting of the effects of taking a test more than once.

Theoretical model A type of model which helps one to interpret, apply, and extend a theory by suggesting appropriate and useful research questions.

Theory A set of statements consisting of defined and interrelated concepts which integrate given laws.

Theta rhythm Brain wave patterns with a frequency of 5 to 7 cycles per second; associated with drowsiness.

Thrombis A blood clot.

Time-lag method Data-collection method in which same-aged individuals are observed at different points in historical time.

Trait A relatively stable characteristic or quality.

Transaction Reciprocal interaction and exchange between or among elements.

Transfer of training The effect of learning one task on the learning or retention of another task.

Transmissiveness The amount of light reaching the eye.

True experiment Designs in which the participants are assigned to treatments in a random fashion.

Type A behavior pattern In Rosenman and Friedman's typology, characterized by excessive competiveness, hostility, and accelerated pace of life, and feelings of struggling against time and the environment.

Type B behavior pattern In Rosenman and Friedman's typology, characterized by the relative absence of Type A behavioral tendencies, the ability to relax freely, and adaptive competiveness.

Universal sequence Fixed, invariant ordering of biologically based developmental stages.

Variable Characteristic of persons, objects, or events which is of interest in a research study.

Visual acuity The accurate perception of small details in one's visual field.

Weak-interaction position A stance on the nature-nurture controversy, rooted in the organismic world view, in which nature is viewed as the basic influence of development, with nurture determining the development rate or end point.

Wisdom The accumulation and integration of life knowledge.

Within-cohort interindividual differences in change Differences in change between individuals in a given cohort.

Within-cohort intraindividual change Change within individuals in a given cohort.

World view The most general type of model, one in which all phenomena in the universe are represented.

ACKNOWLEDGMENTS

Chapter 1

Figure 1.2 Adapted from Baltes, P. B. Life-span developmental psychology: Some converging observations on history and theory. In P. B. Baltes & O. G. Brim, Jr., (Eds.), *Life-span development and behavior* (Vol. 2). New York: Academic Press, 1979. Reprinted with permission from Academic Press.

Quotaton (pg. 20) From Butler, R. N. The life review: An interpretation of reminiscence in the aged. *Psychiatry, Journal for the Study of Interpersonal Processes*, 1963, *26*, 65-76. Copyright 1963 by The William Alanson White Psychiatric Foundation, Inc. Reprinted with permission.

Quotation (p. 27) From Baltes, P. B., & Danish, S. J. Intervention in life-span development and aging: Issues and concepts. In R. R. Turner & H. W. Reese (Eds.), *Life-span developmental psychology: Interventions.* New York: Academic Press, 1980. Reprinted with permission from Academic Press.

Chapter 2

Figure 2.1 From *Life-span developmental psychology: Introduction to research methods* by P. B. Baltes, H. W. Reese, and J. R. Nesselroade. Copyright © 1977 by Wadsworth, Inc. Reprinted by permission of the publisher, Brooks/Cole Publishing Company, Monterey, California.

Figure 2.2 From *Life-span developmental psychology: Introduction to research methods* by P. B. Baltes, H. W. Reese, and J. R. Nesselroade. Copyright © 1977 by Wadsworth, Inc. Reprinted by permission of the publisher, Brooks/Cole Publishing Company, Monterey, California.

Figure 2.3 Adapted from Baltes, P. B., & Labouvie, G. V. Adult development of intellectual performance: Description, explanation, and modification. In C. Eisdorfer & M. P. Lawton (Eds.), *The psychology of adult development and aging.* Washington, D.C.: American Psychological Association, 1973. Copyright 1963 by the American Psychological Association. Reprinted by permission.

Figure 2.4 From Hofland, B., Willis, S. L., & Baltes, P. B. *Retesting and intraindividual variability in fluid intelligence in the elderly.* Paper presented at the Meeting of the Gerontological Society, Dallas, November 1978. Reprinted with permission.

Box 2.3, Figure 2. From Nesselroade, J. R., Schaie, K. W., & Baltes, P. B. Ontogenetic and generational components of structural and quantitative change in adult behavior. *Journal of Gerontology*, 1972, *27*, 222-228. Reprinted with permission.

Box 2.4 American Psychological Association Ad Hoc Committee on Ethical Standards in Psychological Research. *Ethical principles in the conduct of research with human participants.* Washington, D.C.: American Psychological Association, 1973. Copyright 1973 by the American Psychological Association. Reprinted by permission.

Quotation (p. 55) From Sinnott, J. D. Everyday thinking and Piagetian operativity in adults. *Human Development*, 1975, *18*, 430-443. Reprinted by permission of S. Karger AG, Basel.

Chapter 3

Figure 3.2 From Shock, N. W. Energy metabolism, caloric intake, and physical activity of the aging. In L. A. Carlson (Ed.), *Nutrition in old age* (X Symposium of the Swedish Nutrition Foundation). Uppsala: Almqvist & Wiksell, 1972. Reprinted with permission.

Figure 3.5 From Fozard, J. L., Wolf, E., Bell B., McFarland, R. A. & Podolsky, S. Visual perception and communication. In J. E. Birren & K. W. Schaie (Eds.), *Handbook of the psychology of aging.* New York: Van Nostrand Reinhold, 1977. Reprinted with permission of authors and Leon Pastalan.

Figure 3.6 From deVries, H. A. Physiological effects of an exercise training regimen upon men aged 52 to 88. *Journal of Gerontology,* 1970, *25,* 325-336. Reprinted with permission.

Table 3.1 Copyright © 1975, The Society for Psychological Research. Reprinted with permission of the publisher from "Relationships among EEG alpha frequency, reaction time, and age: A biofeedback study," by D. S. Woodruff, *Psychophysiology,* 1975, *12,* 673-681.

Table 3.2 From Rosenman, R. H., Friedman, M., Straus, R., Jenkins, C. D., Zyzanski, S., Jr., Wurm, M., & Kositchek, R. Coronary heart disease in the western collaborative group study. A follow-up experience of 4½ years. *Journal of Chronic Diseases,* 1970, *23,* 173-190. Copyright 1970, Pergamon Press, Ltd. Reprinted with permission.

Table 3.3 and Table 3.4 From Pfeiffer, E., Verwoerdt, A., & Davis, G. C. Sexual behavior in middle life. In E. Palmore (Ed.), *Normal aging II: Reports from the Duke longitudinal studies, 1970-1973.* Durham, N.C.: Duke University Press, 1974. Copyright 1974 by Duke University Press. Reprinted with permission.

Quotation (p. 67) From Medvedev, Z. A. Caucasus and Altay longevity: A biological or social problem. *The Gerontologist,* 1974, *14,* 381-387. Reprinted with permission.

Quotation (p. 74) From Fozard, J. L., & Popkin, S. J. Optimizing adult development: Ends and means of an applied psychology of aging. *American Psychologist,* 1978, *33,* 975-989. Copyright 1978 by the American Psychological Association. Reprinted by permission.

Chapter 4

Figure 4.1 From Horn, J. L., & Donaldson, G. Cognitive development II: Adulthood development of human abilities. In O. G. Brim, Jr., & J. Kagan (Eds.), *Constancy and change in human development: A volume of review essays.* Cambridge: Harvard University Press, 1980. Reprinted by permission.

Figure 4.2 From Horn, J. L. Organization of data on life-span development of human abilities. In L. R. Goulet & P. B. Baltes (Eds.), *Life-span developmental psychology: Research and theory.* New York: Academic Press, 1970. Reprinted with permission from Academic Press.

Figure 4.4 and Figure 4.5 From Schaie, K. W., & Labouvie-Vief, G. Generational and cohort-specific differences in adult cognitive behavior: A fourteen-year cross-sequential study. *Developmental Psychology,* 1974, *10,* 305-320. Copyright 1974 by the American Psychological Association. Reprinted by permission.

Figure 4.6 From Plemons, J. K., Willis, S. L., & Baltes, P. B. Modifiability of intelligence in aging: A short-term longitudinal training approach. *Journal of Gerontology,* 1978, *33,* 224-231. Reprinted with permission.

Table 4.1 From Ekstrom, R. B., French, J. W., Harman, H. H., & Dermen, D. *Manual for kit of factor-referenced cognitive tests.* Princeton, N.J.: Educational Testing Service, 1976. And from French, J. W., Ekstrom, R. B., & Price, L. A. *Kit of reference tests for cognitive factors.* Princeton, N.J.: Educational Testing Service, 1963. Test questions reprinted by permission of Educational Testing Service, Copyright © 1962, 1976.

Table 4.3 From Papalia, D. E. The status of several conservation abilities across the life-span. *Human Development,* 1972, *15,* 229-243. Reprinted with permission of S. Karger AG, Basel.

Table 4.4 From Schaie, K. W., & Parham, I. A. Cohort-sequential analyses of adult intellectual development. *Developmental Psychology,* 1977, *13,* 649-653. Copyright 1977 by the American Psychological Association. Reprinted by permission.

Quotation (p. 113) The original version of this article appeared under the title "Recent Findings on Adult and Gerontological Intelligence: Changing a Stereotype of Decline," by Elizabeth M. Barton, Judy K. Plemons, Sherry L. Willis, and Paul B. Baltes, published in *American Behavioral Scientist,* vol. 19, no. 2 (Nov./Dec. 1975) pp. 224-236 and is reprinted herewith by permission of the publisher, Sage Publications, Inc.

Quotation (p. 113) From Labouvie-Vief, G. Adult cognitive development: In search of alternative interpretations. *Merrill-Palmer Quarterly,* 1977, *23,* 227-263. Reprinted with permission.

Chapter 5

Figure 5.3 From Hultsch, D. F. Adult age differences in free classification and free recall. *Developmental Psychology,* 1971, *4,* 338-342. Copyright 1971 by the American Psychological Association. Reprinted by permission.

Quotation (p. 129) From Richman, J. The foolishness and wisdom of age: Attitudes toward the elderly as reflected in jokes. *The Gerontologist,* 1977, *17,* 210-219. Reprinted with permission.

Chapter 6

Table 6.1 From Haan, N. ". . . Change and sameness. . ." reconsidered. *International Journal of Aging and Human Development,* 1976, *7*(2), 59-65. Copyright © 1976, Baywood Publishing Co., Inc. Reprinted with permission.

Table 6.2 Based on Maas, H. S., & Kuypers, J. A. *From thirty to seventy.* San Francisco: Jossey-Bass, 1974. Reprinted with permission.

Table 6.3 From Maas, H. S., & Kuypers, J. A. *From thirty to seventy.* San Francisco: Jossey-Bass, 1974. Reprinted with permission.

Box 6.2, quotations From Maas, H. S., & Kuypers, J. A. *From thirty to seventy.* San Francisco: Jossey-Bass, 1974. Reprinted with permission.

Quotation (p. 161) From van den Daele, L. D. Ego development and preferential judgment in life-span perspective. In N. Datan & L. H. Ginsberg (Eds.), *Life-span development psychology: Normative life crises.* New York: Academic Press, 1975. Reprinted with permission from Academic Press.

Quotations (pp. 161, 181, and 182) From Neugarten, B. L. Personality and aging. In J. E. Birren & K. W. Schaie (Eds.), *Handbook of the psychology of aging.* New York: Van Nostrand Reinhold, 1977. Reprinted with permission.

Quotation (p. 167) From Neugarten, B. L. *Personality in middle and late life.* New York: Atherton Press, 1964. Reprinted with permission.

Quotations (pp. 171, 175, and 178) From Maas, H. S. & Kuypers, J. A. *From thirty to seventy.* San Francisco: Jossey-Bass, 1974. Reprinted with permission.

Quotation (p. 181) From Costa, P. T., Jr., & McCrae, R. R. Still stable after all these years: Personality as a key to some issues in aging. In P. B. Baltes & O. G. Brim, Jr. (Eds.), *Life-span development and behavior* (Vol. 3). New York: Academic Press, 1980. Reprinted with permission from Academic Press.

Chapter 7

Figure 7.1 From Rosow, I. Status and role change through the life span. From *Handbook of aging and the social sciences,* Robert H. Binstock and Ethel Shanas, Editors, © 1976 by Litton Educational Publishing, Inc. Reprinted by permission of Van Nostrand Reinhold Company.

Figure 7.2 From Olsen, K. M. Social class and age-group differences in the timing of family status changes: A study of age norms in American society. Ph.D. dissertation, University of Chicago, 1969. Reprinted with permission of the author.

Figure 7.3 and Figure 7.4 From Kuypers, J. A., & Bengtson, V. L. Social breakdown and competence: A model of normal aging. *Human Development*, 1973, *16*, 181-201. Reprinted by permission of S. Karger AG, Basel.

Table 7.1 From Norton, A. J. The family life cycle updated: Components and uses. In *Selected studies in marriage and the family*, fourth edition, edited by Robert F. Winch and Graham B. Spanier. Copyright 1953, © 1962, 1968, 1974 by Holt, Rinehart and Winston, Inc. Reprinted by permission of Holt, Rinehart and Winston.

Table 7.2 From Stinnett, Nick, Linda Mittelstet Carter, and James E. Montgomery, "Older Persons' Perceptions of Their Marriages," *Journal of Marriage and the Family*, November 1972, part of Table 1 on page 667. Copyright © 1972 by the National Council on Family Relations. Reprinted by permission.

Table 7.3 Based on Table 1, page 174 of Neugarten, B. L., Havighurst, R. J., & Tobin, S. S. Personality and patterns of aging. In B. L. Neugarten (Ed.), *Middle-age and aging*. Chicago: University of Chicago Press, 1968. Reprinted with permission.

Quotations (pp. 190 and 191) From Neugarten, B. L., & Hagestad, G. O. Age and the life course. In R. H. Binstock & E. Shanas (Eds.), *Handbook of aging and the social sciences*. New York: Van Nostrand Reinhold, 1976. Reprinted with permission of the authors.

Quotations (pp. 192 and 193) From Bengtson, V. L., & Cutler, N. E. Generations and intergenerational relations. From *Handbook of aging and the social sciences*, Robert H. Binstock and Ethel Shanas, Editors. Copyright © 1976 by Litton Educational Publishing, Inc. Reprinted by permission of Van Nostrand Reinhold Company.

Quotations (pp. 194, 195, and 196) From Rosow, I. Status and role change through the life span. From *Handbook of aging and the social sciences*, Robert H. Binstock and Ethel Shanas, Editors, © 1976 by Litton Educational Publishing, Inc. Reprinted by permission of Van Nostrand Reinhold Company.

Quotations (p. 201) From Donahue, W., Orbach, J. L., & Pollak, O. Retirement: The emerging social pattern. In C. Tibbets (Ed.), *Handbook of social gerontology*. Chicago: University of Chicago Press, 1960. Reprinted with permission.

Chapter 8

Figure 8.1 Adapted from Hultsch, D. F. & Plemons, J. K. Life events and life span development. In P. B. Baltes & O. G. Brim, Jr. (Eds.), *Life-span development and behavior* (Vol. 2). New York: Academic Press, 1979. Reprinted with permission from Academic Press.

Figure 8.2 From Levinson, D. J. *The seasons of a man's life*. New York: Alfred A. Knopf, 1978. Copyright © 1978, Alfred A. Knopf, Inc. Reprinted with permission.

Figure 8.3 From Winsborough, H. H. Changes in the transition to adulthood. In M. W. Riley (Ed.), *Aging from birth to death: Interdisciplinary perspectives*. Boulder, Colo.: Westview Press, 1979. Reprinted with permission.

Table 8.1 From Riegel, K. F. Adult life crises: A dialectic interpretation of development. In N. Datan & L. H. Ginsberg (Eds.), *Life-span developmental psychology: Normative life crises*. New York: Academic Press, 1975. Reprinted with permission.

Table 8.2 From Holmes, T. H., & Masuda, M. Life change and illness susceptibility. In B. S. Dohrenwend & P. B. Dohrenwend (Eds.), *Stressful life events: Their nature and effects*. New York: Wiley, 1974. Reprinted by permission of John Wiley & Sons, Inc.

Table 8.3 and Table 8.5 From Lowenthal, M. F., Thurnher, M., & Chiriboga, D. *Four stages of life: A comparative study of women and men facing transitions*. San Francisco: Jossey-Bass, 1975. Reprinted with permission.

Table 8.6 From Uhlenberg, P. Demographic change and problems of the aged. In M. W. Riley (Ed.), *Aging from birth to death: Interdisciplinary perspectives*. Boulder, Colo.: Westview Press, 1960. Reprinted with permission.

Box 8.1, Social Readjustment Rating Scale From Holmes, T. H., & Rahe, R. H. The social readjustment rating scale. *Journal of Psychosomatic Research*, 1967, *11*, 213-218. Copyright © 1967, Pergamon Press, Ltd. Reprinted with permission.

Quotations (pp. 227, 228, 229, and 230) From Levinson, D. J. *The seasons of a man's life.* New York: Alfred A. Knopf, 1978. Copyright © 1978, Alfred A. Knopf, Inc. Reprinted with permission.

Quotations (pp. 242 and 243) From Spanier, G. B., & Casto, R. F. Adjustment to separation and divorce: A qualitative analysis. In G. Levinger & O. Moles (Eds.), *Divorce and separation: Context, causes, and consequences.* New York: Basic Books, 1979. Reprinted with permission.

Chapter 9

Figure 9.1 and Figure 9.2 From Colby, A., Kohlberg, L., & Gibbs, J. *A longitudinal study of moral judgment.* Unpublished manuscript. Harvard University, 1980. Reprinted with permission of the author.

Table 9.3 Adapted from DeLora, J. R. Social systems of dating on a college campus. *Marriage and Family Living*, 1963, *25*, 81-84. Copyrighted 1963 by the National Council on Family Relations. Reprinted by permission.

Box 9.1 From Deutsch, F., & Goldberg, S. R. Perspectives on love: Interviews. In F. Deutsch & S. R. Goldberg (Eds.), *Variations of individual development: Stage of the life span, concepts of love, adjustments, and expectations.* (60-minute color video cassette). University Park, Penn.: The Pennsylvania State University, 1974. Reprinted with permission.

Box 9.2 From *Life-Span Individual and Family Development* by S. R. Goldberg and F. Deutsch. Copyright © 1977 by Wadsworth, Inc. Reprinted by permission of the publisher, Brooks/Cole Publishing Company, Monterey, California.

Quotation (pp. 249 and 250) From Kohlberg, L. The development of children's orientations toward a moral order: I. Sequence in the development of moral thought. *Vita Humana*, 1963, *6*, 11-33. Reprinted by permission of S. Karger AG, Basel.

Quotations (pp. 256 and 257) From *Forms of Intellectual and Ethical Development in the College Years: A scheme* by William G. Perry, Jr. Copyright © 1968, 1970 by Holt, Rinehart and Winston, Inc. Reprinted by permission of Holt, Rinehart and Winston.

Quotations (p. 261) From *The family: A dynamic interpretation* by Willard Waller and Reuben Hill. Copyright 1938 by Holt, Rinehart and Winston, Inc. Revised edition copyright 1951 by Holt, Rinehart and Winston, Inc. Reprinted by permission of Holt, Rinehart and Winston.

Quotation (p. 272) From Mead, M. Anomalies in American post-divorce relationships. Excerpts from *Divorce and after* by Paul Bohannan. Copyright © 1970 by Paul Bohannan. Reprinted by permission of Doubleday & Company, Inc.

Chapter 10

Table 10.1 From Murray, J. R., Powers, E. A., & Havighurst, R. J. Personal and situational factors producing flexible careers. *The Gerontologist*, 1971, *11*, 4-12. Reprinted with permission.

Box 10.1, quotations From Datan, N. Midas and other mid-life crises. In W. H. Norman & T. J. Scaramella (Eds.), *Mid-life: Developmental and clinical issues.* New York: Brunner/Mazel, Inc., 1980. Reprinted with permission.

Box 10.2 and quotations (p. 290) From Levinson, D. J. *The seasons of a man's life.* New York: Copyright © 1978, Alfred A. Knopf, Inc. Reprinted with permission.

Quotation (p. 283) From Erikson, E. H. Identity and the life cycle: Selected papers. *Psychological Issues Monograph Series*, Series I, (No. 1). New York: International Universities Press, 1959; W. W. Norton & Company, Inc., New York, 1980.

Quotations (pp. 284 and 290) From Vaillant, G. *Adaptation to life.* Boston: Little, Brown and Company, 1977. Reprinted with permission.

Quotations (pp. 290 and 301)   From Butler, R. N. & Lewis, M. I. *Aging and mental health* (2nd Ed.), 1977, St. Louis, The C. V. Mosby Co. Reprinted with permission.

Quotation (p. 293)   From Jaques, E. Death and the mid-life crisis. *International Journal of Psychoanalysis*, 1965, *46*, 502-514. Reprinted with permission.

Quotation (p. 294)   From Chilman, C. S. Families in development at mid-stage of the family life cycle. *The Family Coordinator*, 1968, *17*, 307. Copyrighted 1968 by the National Council on Family Relations. Reprinted by permission.

Quotation (pp. 301 and 302)   From Havighurst, R. J. Social roles, work, leisure, and education. In C. Eisdorfer & M. P. Lawton (Eds.), *The psychology of adult development and aging*. Washington, D.C.: American Psychological Association, 1973. Reprinted with permission.

Quotation (p. 310)   From Brim, O., Jr. Theories of the male mid-life crisis. *Counseling Psychologist,* 1976, *6* (1), p. 7. Reprinted with permission.

Chapter 11

Figure 11.1   From Lawton, M. P., & Nahemow, L. Ecology and the aging process. In C. Eisdorfer & M. P. Lawton (Eds.), *The psychology of adult development and aging*. Washington, D.C.: American Psychological Association, 1973. Copyright 1973 by the American Psychological Association. Reprinted by permission.

Table 11.1   Based on Neugarten, Bernice L. and Karol K. Weinstein, "The Changing American Grandparent," *Journal of Marriage and the Family*, May 1964, part of Table 1 on page 201. Copyrighted 1964 by the National Council on Family Relations. Reprinted by permission.

Table 11.2   From Morgan, L. A. *Economic impact of widowhood in a panel of middle-aged women*. Unpublished Ph.D. dissertation, University of Southern California, 1978. Reprinted with permission.

Table 11.3   From Palmore, E. Total chance of institutionalization among the aged. *The Gerontologist*, 1976, *16*, 504-507. Copyrighted 1976 by the Gerontological Society. All rights reserved. Reprinted with permission.

Box 11.1, quotation   From Butler, R. N. The life review: An interpretation of reminiscence in the aged. *Psychiatry, Journal for the Study of Interpersonal Processes*, 1963, *26*, 65-76. Copyright 1963 by The William Alanson White Psychiatric Foundation, Inc. Reprinted with permission.

Box 11.4, quotation   From Vinick, Barbara H., "Remarriage in Old Age," *The Family Coordinator*, October 1978, partial paragraph on page 362. Copyrighted 1978 by the National Council on Family Relations. Reprinted by permission.

Quotation (pp. 313, 314, and 315)   From Neubeck, Gerhard, "Getting Older in My Family: A Personal Reflection," *The family coordinator*, October 1978, pp. 445-447. Copyrighted 1978 by the National Council on Family Relations. Reprinted by permission.

Quotation (p. 316)   From Clayton, V. Erikson's theory of human development as it applies to the aged: Wisdom as contradictive cognition. *Human Development*, 1975, *18*, 119-128. Reprinted by permission of S. Karger AG, Basel.

Quotation (p. 323)   From Troll, Lillian E., "The Family of Later Life: A Decade Review," *Journal of marriage and the family*, May 1971, partial paragraph on page 274. Copyrighted 1971 by the National Council on Family Relations. Reprinted by permission.

Quotation (p. 343)   From Lieberman, M. A. Adaptive processes in late life: In N. Datan & L. H. Ginsberg (Eds.), *Lifespan developmental psychology: Normative life crises*. New York: Academic Press, 1975. Reprinted with permission of Academic Press.

Chapter 12

Figure 12.1   Adapted from E. Mansell Pattison, *The experience of dying*, © 1977, p. 44. Reprinted by permission of Prentice-Hall, Inc., Englewood Cliffs, New Jersey.

Figure 12.2   From David P. Phillips and Kenneth A. Feldman, "A Dip in Deaths before Ceremonial Occasions: Some New Relationships between Social Integration and Mortality," *American Sociological Review*, vol. 38, 1973, Figure 1 on p. 683. Reprinted with permission by the American Sociological Association.

Table 12.1 From *Death and ethnicity: A psychocultural study* by R. A. Kalish and K. K. Reynolds. Copyright, 1976 by University of Southern California Press. Reprinted by permission.

Table 12.2 From Carey, R. G. & Posavac, E. J. Attitudes of physicians on disclosing information to and maintaining life for terminally ill patients. *Omega*, 1978, *9*, 67-77, © 1978, Baywood Publishing Co., Inc. Reprinted with permission.

Table 12.3 From the *Revised living will*. Reprinted with the permission of the Concern For Dying, 250 West 57th Street, New York, New York 10019.

Table 12.4 From Schulz, R., *The psychology of death, dying, and bereavement*, © 1978, Addison-Wesley Publishing Company, Inc., pages 97 & 98. Reprinted with permission.

Box 12.2, quotation From Shneidman, E. S. (Ed.), Psychological death and resurrection. In E. S. Shneidman, *Death and the college student*. New York: Behavioral Publications, 1972, pages 139-142. Copyright © 1972 Human Sciences Press.

Quotation (p. 348) From the Introduction to *Great Jewish Short Stories* by Saul Bellow (Ed.). New York: Dell Publishing Co., 1963. Copyright © 1963 by Saul Bellow. Reprinted by permission of Dell Publishing Company and the author.

Quotations (pp. 349 and 350) From Kastenbaum, R. Is death a life crisis? On the confrontation with death in theory and practice. In N. Datan & L. H. Ginsberg (Eds.), *Life-span developmental psychology: Normative life crises*. New York: Academic Press, 1975. Reprinted with permission.

Quotation (pp. 367 and 368) From Glick, I. O., Weiss, R. S., & Parkes, C. M. *The first year of bereavement*. New York: Wiley, 1974. Reprinted by permission of John Wiley & Sons, Inc.

NAME INDEX

SUBJECT INDEX

423